National-Level Adoption of International Standards on Expropriation, Compensation and Resettlement

National-Level Adoption of International Standards on Expropriation, Compensation and Resettlement

A Comparative Analysis of National Laws Enacted in 50 Countries Across Asia, Africa and Latin America

Nicholas Tagliarino

eleven
international publishing

Published, sold and distributed by Eleven International Publishing
P.O. Box 85576
2508 CG The Hague
The Netherlands
Tel.: +31 70 33 070 33
Fax: +31 70 33 070 30
email: sales@elevenpub.nl
www.elevenpub.com

Sold and distributed in USA and Canada
Independent Publishers Group
814 N. Franklin Street
Chicago, IL 60610, USA
Order Placement: +1 800 888 4741
Fax: +1 312 337 5985
orders@ipgbook.com
www.ipgbook.com

Eleven International Publishing is an imprint of Boom uitgevers Den Haag.

ISBN 978-94-6236-940-5
ISBN 978-94-6274-418-9 (e-book)

Table of Contents

Preface

This book is the result of several years of research on the topics of expropriation, compensation, and resettlement. After graduating law school in the United States in May 2014, I decided to work for the Land and Resource Rights Initiative (LRR), which is part of the Governance Center of Excellence at World Resources Institute (WRI). Starting as a Legal Intern in September 2014, I worked on a range of issues related to land, natural resource, and environmental rights. A key focus area was the land and resource tenure of Indigenous Peoples and local communities in Asia, Africa, and Latin America. After I began work at WRI, Peter Veit (Director of LRR at WRI) asked me to write a report summarizing the findings from a comparative analysis of expropriation laws conducted as a pilot study by WRI and the Harvard Law and International Development Society (LIDS). While I felt (and still feel) incredibly grateful that Peter Veit handed me this expropriation project, I did not envision the project lasting more than a few months. At the time, I never imagined I would have the opportunity to expand this study into a full-length Ph.D. dissertation.

In March 2015, I presented my initial findings from the study at the annual World Bank Land and Poverty Conference. After my presentation, Prof. Dr. Leon Verstappen, whom I did not know at the time, approached me and congratulated me on what he called a fascinating speech. Little did I know, I was in fact meeting one of the world's most passionate, dedicated, knowledgeable, hardworking, and friendly law professors. Prof. Dr. Verstappen is a highly reputable scholar with innovative ideas. He cares deeply about his students and makes big things happen.

Following our initial meeting at the Conference, Prof. Dr. Verstappen invited me to visit his University in Groningen, the Netherlands and attend the Rethinking Expropriation Law Conference in The Hague in June 2016. It was there that Prof. Dr. Leon Verstappen brought up the Land Portal Foundation, an organization for which he was and still is Chairman of the Board. Prof. Dr. Leon Verstappen talked about the potential of the Land Portal platform (www.landportal.org) as an effective tool for linking together legal information about land. He said that by linking together information on land laws in a variety of countries, Land Portal could enable users to understand how land laws operate and distill similarities and differences between legal systems applicable to land governance across the globe.

Prof. Dr. Verstappen had the idea of turning my WRI comparative study on expropriation laws into a full-length Ph.D. dissertation and have me publish open access legal indicator data on the Land Portal platform. I am forever grateful that Prof. Dr. Verstappen decided to take a chance on me. His helpful guidance and feedback throughout my three years as a Ph.D. student have enabled me to grow as a writer, thinker, scholar, and human being. Without his support, I would not have met or had the privilege of working with any of the remarkable individuals listed below.

In addition to Prof. Dr. Verstappen, there are two other individuals who were essential to making this Ph.D. project happen: Peter Veit (Director of LRR at WRI) and Laura Meggiolaro (Coordinator of Land Portal Foundation). These two individuals agreed to have their respective organizations sponsor my Ph.D. study and co-fund my salary as a Ph.D. student at the University of Groningen Faculty of Law. In exchange, I agreed to work part-time for WRI and Land Portal during my three years as a Ph.D. student. Working for Land Portal Foundation and WRI were truly unforgettable experiences that provided me with exciting opportunities to meet new people from around the world and gain more experience in the land governance sector.

I am also deeply thankful for the guidance and support I have received from my two other Ph.D. supervisors: Prof. Dr. Jacques Sluysmans and Dr. Björn Hoops. I had the pleasure of meeting Prof. Dr. Sluysmans when he was kind enough to host the 2015 Rethinking Expropriation Law Conference in The Hague. Since then, we have had several fascinating conversations related to expropriation and comparative legal research. Dr. Hoops was also very instrumental to my development as an academic scholar and provided me with helpful guidance and feedback throughout the process of publishing my Ph.D. articles. As his 800-page Ph.D. dissertation indicates, Dr. Hoops is not afraid to get his hands dirty in the weeds of in-depth comparative legal research on expropriation. Dr. Hoops is a great role model for me, especially since in 2017, he published his Ph.D. dissertation on expropriation law in four jurisdictions (South Africa, Netherlands, Germany, and New York) and his dissertation was awarded the distinction of *cum laude*. Furthermore, his friendship and willingness to help me adjust to Dutch life made the experience of living as an expat in Groningen very enjoyable.

I would like to thank the Faculty of Law of the University of Groningen and the Department of Private Law and Notarial Law for providing me with a paid position and an office at the University. I am also very grateful for the Faculty of Law providing me with two outstanding research assistants, Myat Noe and Daniel Babare. For academic credit, these assistants provided preliminary indicator research for several of the countries assessed. I also would like to thank Rachel Davakis for helping me proofread the text and my two other student assistants, Mark van der Meijs and Marjolein Anne van Eerde, who supported with the citations and bibliography.

I am very grateful to Prof. Dr. Michael Cernea for his continued interest in my Ph.D. study. Prof. Dr. Cernea and I met after he awarded me the Michael Cernea Involuntary Resettlement Travel Award in 2017. This award enabled me to attend the annual meeting of International Network on Displacement and Resettlement, which took place as a side event to the Society for Applied Anthropology Conference in Sante Fe, New Mexico in April 2017. After we met, Prof. Dr. Michael Cernea gave me the much-appreciated opportunity to publish a chapter in his latest book entitled *Challenging the Prevailing Paradigm on Displacement and Resettlement.* Through our lengthy phone conversations and lunch meetings, Prof. Dr. Michael Cernea has provided me with thorough and valuable comments to each of my published articles (cited below). Since he is one of the world's most highly regarded scholar on development-induced displacement and resettlement, it is quite an honor to have him engaged and interested in my Ph.D. project. As someone who is profoundly and tirelessly passionate about his field of study, Prof. Dr. Cernea is a great role model for aspiring academic researchers around the world.

Prof. Dr. Yakubu Bununu deserves particular recognition for his tireless support and guidance during our case study of the Lekki Free Trade Zone expropriation case in Lagos, Nigeria (see Chapter 6). The study was conducted in August 2017. Without Prof. Dr. Bununu, it would not have been possible to survey 140 households affected by expropriation or conduct interviews with government and private sector officials in Lagos (see Chapter 6). Along the same lines, I am also very lucky to have met and worked with Magbagbeola O. Michael, Marcello De Maria and Akintobi Olusanmi on our project on land expropriation in Nigeria. Their strong dedication to our research project on land expropriation in Nigeria made the experience of conducting the in-depth case study unforgettable.

I would also like to express my sincere gratitude to the following scholars/practitioners, who provided valuable feedback on my Ph.D. articles (listed below): Dr. Liz Alden Wily, Dr. Maartje Van Eerd, Prof. Dr. Julie Maldonado, Prof. Dr. Hanri Mostert, Prof. Dr. Ernst Marais, Prof. Susanna Price, and Louie Van Schalkwyk. Chapter 4 on compensation valuation procedures and Chapter 6 on the Nigeria case study contain information from articles that I published in the peer-reviewed journal entitled *Land (MDPI).* I am grateful for the peer reviewer's time and energy they dedicated in providing valuable feedback on my *Land* journal articles. Chapter 3 contains information from an article I published in a peer-reviewed book entitled *Rethinking Expropriation Law III: Fair Compensation.* Chapter 5 contains information from an article I published in a book edited by Prof. Dr. Michael Cernea and Prof. Dr. Julie Maldonado entitled *Challenging the Prevailing Paradigm on Displacement and Resettlement.*

Some of the information included in all 7 chapters comes for a WRI Working Paper entitled "Encroaching on Land and Livelihoods," which I published in June 2016. WRI has a lengthy peer review process that entails review by internal experts employed at WRI and external experts with relevant expertise. I want to thank my former colleagues at WRI who provided a peer review of my 2016 WRI Working Paper. These individuals are Peter Veit, Mark Robinson, Gaia Larsen, Lalanath De Silva, Niranjali Manel Amerasinghe, Daryl Ditz, and Celine Salcedo- La Vina. In addition, I would like to thank the external peer reviewers of the WRI Working Paper. These individuals are: Karol Boudreaux (Landesa), Caleb Stevens (USAID), Jon Lindsay (World Bank), and Darryl Vhugen (Independent Land Expert).

I am also very grateful to the Land Portal Team for their support during my time as a Ph.D. student: Laura Meggiolaro, Neil Sorensen, Lisette Mey, Marcello De Maria, Carlos Tejo, Jules Clemente, and Stacey Zammit. It was really a pleasure working with all of them on a variety of projects related to land governance data and information dissemination.

Last but certainly not least, I would like to thank my family: Scott, Donna, and Leah Tagliarino. I am also grateful for the support of my girlfriend, Shannon Hill. Without these important people in my life, whom I love very much, I would not have had the strength, courage, or confidence to complete a Ph.D. dissertation.

While a Ph.D. student, I had the opportunity to present my research findings on the 50 countries at the following conferences:

- The Conference on Expropriation 2015 (The Hague, Netherlands)
- The Conference on Fair Compensation for Expropriation 2016 (Cape Town, South Africa)
- The Annual World Bank Land and Poverty Conferences 2015, 2016, 2017, 2018 (Washington, DC)
- The Annual Meeting of the International Network on Displacement and Resettlement 2017 (Sante Fe, New Mexico)
- The LandAc Conference at Utrecht University (2017) (Utrecht, Netherlands)
- The UN Economic Commission for Africa Conference on Land Policy in Africa (2017) (Addis Ababa, Ethiopia)
- The India Land and Development Conference 2017 (Delhi, India)
- University of Reading Land Symposium 2017 (Reading, United Kingdom)
- The Young Property Lawyers Forum (YPLF) Conference at Maastricht University 2018 (Maastricht, Netherlands)
- The Association for Law, Property and Society Conference 2018 (ALPS) (Maastricht, Netherlands)

This book incorporates research and analysis from the following articles that I published:

- Tagliarino, N.K. 'The need for national-level legal protection of populations displaced by expropriation: land acquisition in 50 countries', *in* Cernea, M. and Maldonado, J. (Eds.) *Challenging the Prevailing Paradigm of Displacement and Resettlement: Risks, Impoverishment, Legacies and Solutions*. Routledge, NY, 2018.
- Tagliarino, N.K., 'Legal Limits on Government Authority to Expropriate Land: An Assessment of Expropriation Procedures in 50 Countries Across Asia, Africa, and Latin America', *In Proceedings of the Annual World Bank Conference on Land and Poverty*, Washington, DC, USA, 19-23 March 2018.
- Tagliarino, N.K., 'The status of national legal frameworks for valuing compensation for expropriated land: An analysis of whether national laws in 50 countries/regions across Asia, Africa, and Latin America comply with international standards on compensation valuation', *Land*, Vol. 37, No. 6, 2017.
- Tagliarino, N.K., Bununu, Y.A., Michael, M.O., De Maria, M. & Olusanmi, A., 'Compensation for Expropriated Community Farmland in Nigeria: An In-Depth Analysis of the Laws and Practices Related to Land Expropriation for the Lekki Free Trade Zone in Lagos', *Land*, Vol. 7, No. 1, 2018.
- Tagliarino, N. K. 2018, 'Avoiding the Worst-Case Scenario: An Assessment of Compensation Eligibility Requirements Applicable to Indigenous Peoples and Local Communities in 30 Countries', *in* B. Hoops, E.J. Marais, L.V. Schalkwyk, N.K. Tagliarino *Rethinking Expropriation Law III: Fair Compensation*, Eleven International Publishing, Juta, Johannesburg, South Africa, 2018.
- Tagliarino, N.K., *Encroaching on Land and Livelihoods: How National Expropriation Laws Measure Up Against International Standards*, World Resources Institute, Washington, DC, 2016.

The legal analysis and indicator scores presented in this book are available online at: https://landportal.org/book/dataset/nkt-vggt16. The legal research presented in this book was completed by March 1, 2018. Any developments that have taken place since then are not taken into account. Any remaining errors are unintentional and solely mine.

Nicholas K. Tagliarino

List of Acronyms

Table 1

- Asian Development Bank (ADB)
- Environmental Impact Assessment (EIA)
- Food and Agricultural Organization of the United Nations (FAO)
- FAO Land Tenure Studies 10: Compulsory Acquisition of Land and Compensation (FAO Handbook)
- Fair Market Value (FMV)
- Federal Capital Development Authority (FCDA)
- Free Prior and Informed Consent (FPIC)
- Harvard Law and International Development Society (LIDS)
- India's Right to Fair Compensation and Transparency in Land Acquisition, Rehabilitation, and Resettlement Act, 2013 (LARR Act)
- International Covenant on Economic Social and Cultural Rights (ICESCR)
- International Finance Corporation (IFC)
- International Labour Organization (ILO)
- Indigenous Peoples and local communities (IPLCs)
- Memorandum of Understanding (MOU)
- Nigeria's Land Use Act (LUA)
- Lagos State Government (LSG)
- Lekki Free Zone Development Company (LFZDC)
- Lekki Worldwide Investment Limited (LWI)
- Lekki Free Trade Zone (LFTZ)
- Land and Resource Rights Initiative (LRR)
- Millennium Challenge Corporation (MCC)
- Multilateral Development Banks (MDBs)
- Non-governmental organization (NGO)
- Rights and Resources Initiative (RRI)
- Social Impact Assessment (SIA)
- United States Agency for International Development (USAID)
- United Nations (UN)
- Voluntary Guidelines on the Responsible Governance of Tenure (VGGTs)
- World Bank Environmental and Social Framework (ESF)
- World Bank Environmental and Social Standards (ESS)
- World Bank Land Governance Assessment Framework (LGAF)
- World Resources Institute (WRI)

1 Introduction

1.1 What Is the Objective of the Study?

The overall objective of this study is to establish a benchmark that can influence the reformation of national laws so that they comply with international standards aimed at promoting responsible land governance and respecting land tenure rights, particularly the tenure rights of poor and marginalized groups. To fulfill this objective, this study examines the national-level laws applicable to expropriation, compensation, and resettlement in 50 countries. The main research question is whether these laws comply with international standards on expropriation, compensation, and resettlement as established in Section 16 of the *Voluntary Guidelines on the Responsible Governance of Tenure of Land, Fisheries, and Forests in the Context of National Food Security* (hereinafter "VGGTs"). The national laws of these 50 countries are assessed against a set of indicators designed to measure compliance with the international standards (see Appendix for all indicators scores). By highlighting gaps and pinpointing which legal provisions should be reformed, this benchmark can assist lawmakers, civil society, and other stakeholders in measuring progress toward the adoption of international standards on expropriation, compensation, and resettlement in domestic laws. More broadly, this study can inform law and policy debates related to expropriation, compensation, and resettlement.

The study focuses on the VGGTs because of the influence they have had (and may continue to have) on land governance reform efforts occurring throughout world. The VGGTs are the first comprehensive global instrument on governance of tenure. They establish best practices that "are backed by international consensus of governments, international NGOs, civil society, and the private sector."[1] The VGGTs were prepared through extensive intergovernmental negotiations launched in 2009 by the Food and Agriculture Organization of the United Nations (FAO).[2] Ten regional consultations with stakeholders brought together nearly 700 people from the public and private sectors, civil society, and academia, representing 133 countries, to ascertain and address tenure governance concerns.[3] In 2012,

---

1 M. Kropiwnicka, *A Brief Introduction to the Voluntary Guidelines on the Responsible Governance of Tenure of Land, Fisheries and Forests in the Context of National Food Security*; Actionaid, Johannesburg, South Africa, 2012, p. 1.

2 P. Munro-Faure & D. Palmer, 'An overview of the voluntary guidelines on the governance of tenure', *Land Tenure Journal*, Vol. 1, 2012, pp. 5-18.

3 Munro-Faure & Palmer 2012.

the United Nations Committee on World Food Security, a body with 193 member countries, endorsed the VGGTs.

While the VGGTs are not legally binding, they work in conjunction with other international human rights instruments, such as International Labour Organization Convention 169 and the UN Declaration on the Rights of Indigenous Peoples, to ensure that tenure rights are respected when state and non-state actors engage in activities that affect land. The VGGTs also reflect inalienable international human rights, such as the right to property,[4] the rights to housing,[5] and the right to an adequate standard of living.[6] As discussed in more detail in Section 1.7 of this Chapter, the VGGTs have become the most widely recognized standards on land governance among international institutions (e.g., UN agencies), governments, private companies, NGOs, academics, civil societies, activists, and other stakeholders.[7] Given the broad interest and engagement in ensuring the VGGTs are implemented at country-level, it seemed worthwhile to focus the study on whether national laws are adopting the standards on expropriation, compensation, and resettlement established in the VGGTs. Even though these standards are not legally binding, they reflect international human rights (e.g. the right to property); also, private companies, governments, NGOs, and other stakeholders are increasingly accepting the VGGTs as the new international standard on land tenure (see Section 1.7 below for more detail).[8] At the time this study was conducted, they were also the most comprehensive standards on expropriation, compensation, and resettlement available.

1.2 Definition of Terms

This Section provides definitions of key terms used in this study:

'Acquiring bodies' refers to the government and private entities that acquire rights to expropriated land and carry out the expropriation, compensation, and resettlement processes. In some cases of expropriation, there may be more than one acquiring body. Acquiring bodies can include government departments, ministries, and agencies or, in some cases, private entities, such as companies or donors investing in land.

4 United Nations. 1948. Universal Declaration of Human Rights. G.A. Res. 217 A (III): Art. 17.

5 International Covenant on Economic, Social and Cultural Rights. 1966, A/RES/2200: Art. 11.

6 Ibid.

7 Munro-Faure & Palmer 2012.

8 A. Arial, D. Palmer, M. Vidar, J.C.G. Cebola, F. Romano, L. Shamsaifar. Governance of Tenure: Making it happen. *Land Tenure Journal*, FAO, Rome, Italy, 2012; The Interlaken Group and RRI, *Respecting Land and Forest Rights: A Guide for Companies*, Washington, DC, The Interlaken Group and RRI, 2015.

'Affected landholders' are the individuals or groups whose tenure rights are affected by expropriations.

'Communities' or 'Indigenous Peoples and Local communities' (**'IPLCS'**) refer to groupings of individuals and families that share interests in a definable local land area within which they normally reside. IPLCS usually have strong connections to particular areas or territories and consider these domains to be customarily under their ownership and/or control. They themselves determine and apply the rules and mechanisms through which rights to land are distributed and governed. Usually, all or part of the community land is owned in common by members of the community.[9] As discussed in Chapter 3, some countries have laws that apply only to indigenous communities, while other countries have laws that apply to both indigenous and non-indigenous communities. It is important to recognize that not all communities are classified as 'indigenous.' Indigenous Peoples are also commonly characterized by (1) self-identification as indigenous peoples and acceptance of that identification by neighbors; (2) distinct social, economic, or political systems; (3) non-dominant groups of society; and (4) resolve to maintain and reproduce their ancestral environments and systems as distinctive peoples and communities.[10]

'Customary tenure' is a set of rules and norms that govern community allocation, use, access, and transfer of land and other natural resources. The term 'customary tenure' invokes the idea of 'traditional' rights to land and other natural resources; it is usually associated with indigenous communities and administered in accordance with their customs, as opposed to statutory tenure usually introduced during the colonial period.[11] Customary tenure is based upon continuous practice by communities as opposed to statutory law.

'Community Lands' are all lands that fall under the customary governance of communities, whether or not this is recognized in national law. Community land is variously described in different countries as the community domain, community land areas, collectively held land, community territory, common property, and/or other terms (e.g., Tanzania refers to village lands, Ghana to customary lands, China to collectives, Cambodia refers to indigenous lands). This study adopts LandMark's definition of IPLCs/communities and community lands) because the findings presented in Chapter 3 focus on compensation

9 L.A. Wily, P. Veit, R. Smith, F. Dubertret, K. Reytar, and N. Tagliarino. 'Guidelines for Researching, Scoring and Documenting Findings on 'What National Laws Say about Indigenous & Community Land Rights', Methodology document from LandMark: The Global Platform of Indigenous and Community Lands. Available at landmarkmap.org.

10 J. Alcorn, 'USAID Issue Brief: Tenure and Indigenous Peoples', USAID, Washington, DC, 2013, p. 1.

11 FAO, '*Land Tenure Series 3: Land Tenure and Rural Development*', FAO, Rome, Italy, 2002, p. 8.

eligibility requirements applicable to IPLCs and incorporate an analysis of LandMark's indicators of legal security of indigenous and community tenure (see Chapter 3 and landmarkmap.org for more detail).

'Compensation' is the payment, in cash or in kind, made by governments or acquiring bodies to affected populations for expropriation of their tenure rights.[12]

'Displaced persons' are the affected landholders who are forced to involuntary resettle as a result of expropriation. As discussed in Chapter 5 and in the relevant international standards (e.g. World Bank ESF, IFC Performance Standards), expropriation can cause physical displacement (relocation or loss of shelter) and economic displacement (loss of assets or access to assets that leads to loss of income or means of livelihood) (see Chapter 5 for more detail).

'Expropriation' is the process by which governments acquire privately held tenure rights, without the willing consent of the landholder, in order to serve a public purpose or public interest.[13] The definition of public purpose and public interest varies from country to country. In this study, 'expropriation' refers to eminent domain, takings, compulsory purchase, compulsory acquisition, and other names given to this government power around the world.

'Expropriation process' is defined as the process of implementing projects involving expropriation, compensation, and resettlement. This term refers to the entire project cycle (i.e. the processes carried out during the pre-expropriation planning stage as well as the expropriation, compensation, and resettlement stages) because it is included in Section 16.2 of the VGGTs.

'Forced eviction' is the permanent or temporary removal against the will of individuals, families and/or communities from the homes and/or the land that they occupy, without the provision of, and access to, appropriate forms of legal or other protection.[14] The key difference between 'expropriation' and 'forced eviction' is that expropriation usually requires the government to show land was acquired for a 'public purpose' and it usually requires some form of compensation for legally recognized tenure rights. 'Forced eviction,'

12 N. Tagliarino, *Encroaching on Land and Livelihoods: How National Expropriation Laws Measure up against International Standards*, World Resources Institute, Washington, DC, 2016.

13 S. Keith, P. McAuslan, R. Knight, J. Lindsay, P. Munro-Faure, D. Palmer, *Food and Agriculture Organization of the United Nations. Land Tenure Studies 10: Compulsory Acquisition of Land and Compensation*, FAO, Rome, Italy, 2008.

14 United Nations. *Forced Evictions Fact Sheet No. 25/Rev.1*, United Nations, New York, NY, USA; Geneva, Switzerland, 2014.

on the other hand, is broader because it can occur whenever people are removed from their land against their will, without legal and other protection. Although international human rights law dictates that people must be consulted before they can be forcibly evicted,[15] national laws sometimes permit governments to forcibly evict so-classed 'informal occupants' from government-owned land without satisfying the 'public purpose' or providing compensation. Governments sometimes justify forced evictions on the grounds that the rights of landholders to state-owned land are not formally recognized and therefore not compensable.[16]

'International instruments' refer to sources that establish international law and policy standards, including the VGGTs, the UN Declaration on the Rights of Indigenous Peoples (2007), ILO International Labour Organization Convention 169, the World Bank Environmental and Social Framework, the IFC Performance Standards, and other sources discussed in this book.

'Improvements' refer to the attached and unattached assets on the land (e.g. crops, buildings). As discussed in Chapter 4, some but not all of the compensation valuation procedures established in the 50 countries require that compensation must reflect the value of the improvements on the land. In some countries (e.g. Nigeria), compensation is limited to the value of the improvements on the land, but does not cover the value of the land itself. Such valuation procedures make landholders vulnerable to receiving insufficient payment.

'International standards' for purposes of this study primarily refer to the provisions established in Section 16 of the VGGTs.[17] However, other international instruments and guidance documents inform the development of the indicators (see Section 1.8 on Methodology), including the FAO Land Tenure Studies 8 on Compulsory Acquisition of Land and Compensation (hereinafter "FAO Handbook").[18] The indicators are also informed by other international policy documents, including World Bank ESS5 on Land Acquisition and Involuntary Resettlement, IFC Performance Standard 5.[19]

'Land tenure' is the statutory or customarily defined relationship among people—as individuals or groups—with respect to land. It includes the full range of relationships

15 United Nations 2014.

16 Amnesty International, 'At the Mercy of the Government: Violation of the Right to an Effective Remedy in Badia East, Lagos State, Nigeria', Amnesty International, London, 2013, p. 15.

17 Food and Agriculture Organization (FAO), *The Voluntary Guidelines on the Responsible Governance of Tenure of Land, Fisheries, and Forests in the Context of National Food Security*, FAO, Rome, 2012, Sec. 16.6

18 Keith *et al.* 2008.

19 World Bank, *Environmental and Social Framework*, World Bank Group, Washington, DC, 2017.

between people and communities with regard to accessing, possessing, and controlling land and natural resources.[20]

'Land tenure security' is the certainty that the rights to land held by an individual or community will be recognized by others and protected in case of challenges.[21] This term is further defined as (a) the degree of confidence that land users will not be arbitrarily deprived of the rights they enjoy over land and the economic benefits that flow from it and (b) the right of individuals and groups to effective government protection against forced evictions.[22]

'Land governance' is the system of rules, processes, and structures through which decisions are made about access to land and its use.[23] While land can be governed under statutory, customary, religious, and other systems, this study is only concerned with the laws, rules, and procedures established under statutory law.

'Landholders' are the individuals or communities that hold tenure rights.

'Laws' for purposes of this study are defined as national-level constitutional, legislative, and regulatory provisions that apply in cases of expropriation, compensation, and resettlement. Although I reviewed several court cases (see References in Appendix) to gain a better understanding of the rules pertaining to expropriation, case law is not included in the indicator analysis. Instead, the indicator analysis is based solely on legal provisions codified in national-level constitutions, statutes, and regulations.

'Lawmakers' are the government officials charged with drafting constitutions, legislation and regulations, including legislative and administrative bodies.

'Legality Principle' refers to that principle calling for government actions to be limited by enacted laws that are clearly written, ascertainable, and non-retrospective.[24] A key element of the 'legality principle' is that state action must be authorized by legislation.

---

20 FAO 2002, p. 7; International Finance Corporation (IFC), *Performance Standards on Environmental and Social Sustainability, Performance Standard 5: Land Acquisition and Involuntary Resettlement,* IFC, Washington, DC, USA, 2012, p. 5

21 FAO 2002, p. 18.

22 United Nations Human Settlements Program (UN-Habitat). Secure Land Rights for All, UN-Habitat, Nairobi, Kenya, 2008, p. 5.

23 D. Palmer, S. Fricska, B. Wehrmann, 'Land Tenure Working Paper 11: Toward Improved Land Governance', *FAO*, Rome, Italy, 2009, p. 1.

24 J. Raz, *The Rule of Law and Its Virtues in The Authority of Law: Essays on Law and Morality*; Clarendon Press, Oxford, UK, 1979; pp. 210, 213, 218.

'Resettlement' for purposes of this study refers to circumstances in which displaced populations must involuntarily relocate and resettle on alternative land as a result of expropriation. Resettlement is not defined in the VGGTs, but it is widely referenced in the policy standards of institutions that invest in projects involving the expropriation of land, such as the World Bank, IFC, and other institutions (see Chapter 5 for more detail).

'Rule of law' is defined as "authority of law in society, especially when viewed as a constraint on individual and institutional behavior; the principle whereby all members of society (including those in the government) are equally subject to publicly disclosed legal codes and processes."[25]

'Tenure rights' are the rights of individuals or communities over land and resources.[26] Tenure rights include ownership, possession, use rights, and rent, as well as customary and collective tenure arrangements. The bundle of tenure rights can include the rights of access, withdrawal, management, exclusion, and alienation.[27] In this study, I use 'tenure rights' to cover a broad range of land rights that are both statutorily recognized by the laws of countries as well as rights that are not always statutorily recognized, such as customary and informal tenure rights. As discussed below, the protection and recognition of 'legitimate tenure rights' is the primary focus of the VGGT; however, the VGGTs gives states discretion to interpret what constitutes 'legitimate' tenure. In this study, I do not use the term 'legitimate tenure' because I aim to stay objective and thus do not wish to make a judgment regarding which particular set of rights in a given country should be considered as 'legitimate' tenure. Such a judgment depends on the country and context, and, in my opinion, should be made on a case-by-case basis. However, this study uses 'tenure rights' to cover the broad range of rights attached to land that can be affected by expropriation, including customary and informal tenure rights that are broadly granted some level of protection by international standards and national laws.

'Valuers' are the government and non-government entities charged with valuing compensation for expropriation. For purposes of this study, I decided not to make a judgment regarding which types of valuers have adequate capacity and should be charged with carrying out the valuation. UN agencies, NGOs, and Academia have developed guidance on valuation (see discussion in Chapter 4).

25 'Rule of Law', World Encyclopedia of Law, 2018; The Oxford English Dictionary. 2nd ed. 1989. OED Online.
26 FAO 2002, p. 11.
27 E. Schlager and E. Ostrom, 'Property-Rights Regimes and Natural Resources: A Conceptual Analysis', *Land Economics*, Vol. 68, No. 3, 1992, pp. 249-262.

1.3 Why Does This Study Focus on the Law?

There are at least three reasons why this study focuses on the law as a means of establishing a benchmark that can be used to measure progress toward the realization of international standards. First, since laws impose a set of legally binding obligations on private actors and the government, this study indicates whether (or not) laws compel actions and behavior that complies with international standards.

Second, laws provide landholders and the public with a set of rights and protections in cases where the government expropriates land. Landholders can use laws as a point of reference when they wish to challenge government and private actor decisions that infringe on tenure rights recognized by law. For example, if laws provide adequate consultation, compensation, and resettlement assistance to affected landholders, then affected landholders can exercise their legal rights and seek redress in court if such rights are violated.

Third, laws provide courts with guidance when ruling on whether expropriation, compensation, and resettlement decisions were conducted in violation of the law. Courts have the authority to enforce legal requirements and hold government and private actors accountable for expropriation decisions that violate the law.

The justification of this study is predicated on the assumption that the rule of law is essential to implementation of land governance standards established in the VGGTs. By imposing legally binding obligations on governments and acquiring bodies that carry out expropriation, compensation, and resettlement processes, the rule of law can affect the ways in which land is governed, managed, and utilized. This study focuses on codified law. Assuming the rule of law is respected (and, admittedly, in many of the 50 countries assessed, this may be a problematic assumption), examining the law on the books is a useful starting point for determining whether international land governance standards are being adopted in practice. Once it is determined what is the current status of laws in each of these countries, it then becomes clearer what legal reforms should be made in order for laws to comply with international standards.

According to the legality principle, government actions should be limited by enacted laws that are written with adequate precision, clarity, and unambiguity; such laws should prevent governments from making arbitrary decisions that violate the law.[28] In many democracies, legislators enact general laws, and executive and judicial branches administer and apply

---

28 P. Robinson, 'Fair Notice and Fair Adjudication: Two Kinds of Legality'. *Univ. Penn. L. Rev.* Vol. 154, 2005, pp. 335-398.

those laws in specific cases. If the legality principle is adopted, and laws are written with clarity and specificity, these laws can be viewed as more democratic, stable, and predictable by the general public.[29] This is because the public plays an indirect role in shaping those laws through voting for legislative representatives charged with enacting laws. Such laws also provide the government and the public with clear, effective guidance so they can form expectations and plan accordingly.[30]

On the other hand, when laws are unclear, imprecise, or vaguely worded, they may be viewed as undemocratic or contrary to the rule of law, since vague terminology can ostensibly grant too much discretion to executive and administrative branches of government that are not as representative as the legislature.[31] If vague laws enable decisions to be made in an arbitrary, ad-hoc manner, the rule of law may be contravened.[32] Adopting the legality principle, this study examines gaps and vagueness in expropriation laws in order to identify ways of improving laws to ensure compliance with international standards.

It is worth noting that, even if laws do not adopt international standards, governments and acquiring bodies may decide to follow international standards when expropriating land, regardless of a legal obligation to do so. For example, governments and acquiring bodies may pay sufficient compensation following international standards in order to avoid reputational and financial risks associated with lawsuits and conflicts over land. Or they may adhere to the land acquisition and resettlement policies of the World Bank and other donor agencies that fund development projects involving the expropriation of land. However, in the absence of legal obligations, compliance with international standards is not guaranteed. Assuming that the rule of law is a necessary precondition for the implementation of good governance standards, it makes sense to identify whether compliance with international standards is required by law and, if not yet required, then how laws can be improved to provide clear guidance and procedures for adopting international standards.

1.4 What Is Covered by This Study?

When considering the concept of the rule of law, the question arises: rule of *what* law? This study addresses this question in 50 jurisdictions because it identifies what national

29 Robinson pp. 335-398; H. Dagan, 'Expropriatory Compensation, Distributive Justice, and the Rule of Law'. In *Rethinking Expropriation Law I: Public Interest in Expropriation*; Hoops, B., Marais, E.J., Mostert, H., Sluysman, J.A.M.A., Verstappen, L.C.A., Eds.; Eleven International Publishing: Den Haag, The Netherlands, 2015; pp. 349-365.

30 Raz 1979, pp. 210, 213, 218; Dagan 2015, pp. 349-365.

31 A. Scalia, 'The Rule of Law as a Law of Rules'. *U. Chi. L. Rev.*, Vol. 56, No. 4, 1989, pp. 1175-1188.

32 Robinson pp. 335-398.

laws and international standards apply in cases of expropriation. It provides clarity regarding the extent to which government expropriation authority is limited and the tenure rights of affected landholders are protected in cases of expropriation. To conduct this study, I reviewed a broad range of legal instruments reviewed (see Appendix and Bibliography for full list of laws reviewed). These instruments included national constitutions, land acquisition acts, land acts, communal land acts, agricultural land acts, land use acts, regulations, and some court decisions (though the indicator scores do not account for court decisions: see discussion of methodology below). The 50 countries assessed in this book are listed in Table 2.

Table 2 List of Countries Assessed in This Study

Asia	Africa	Latin America
1. Afghanistan	22 Angola	42 Argentina
2. Bangladesh	23 Burkina Faso	43 Belize
3. Bhutan	24 Botswana	44 Brazil
4. Cambodia	25 Eritrea	45 Ecuador
5. China	26 Ethiopia	46 Honduras
6. Hong Kong	27 Ghana	47 Mexico
7. India	28 Kenya	48 Nicaragua
8. Indonesia	29 Lesotho	49 Peru
9. Laos	30 Liberia	50 Trinidad and Tobago
10. Kazakhstan	31 Namibia	
11. Sri Lanka	32 Nigeria	
12. Malaysia	33 Rwanda	
13. Mongolia	34 South Africa	
14. Myanmar	35 South Sudan	
15. Nepal	36 Sierra Leone	
16. Papua New Guinea	37 Swaziland	
17. Pakistan	38 Tanzania	
18. Philippines	39 Uganda	
19. Taiwan	40 Zambia	
20. Thailand	41 Zimbabwe	
21. Vietnam		

1.5 How Were the 50 Countries Chosen?

There are several reasons why these 50 countries were chosen. I began this project in 2014 at the World Resources Institute (WRI) Land and Resource Rights Initiative (LRR) with initial research support from students at the Harvard Law and International Development Society (LIDS). In 2014, 30 countries in Asia and Africa were chosen randomly for the initial stage of this legal indicator study. This initial list of countries was altered slightly so that the study would cover a broad geographical area in Africa, Asia, and Latin America. WRI's LRR focuses on securing land rights for the rural poor, including indigenous and local communities with customary tenure, and thus the primary focus of the initial study was on the expropriation of land held by informal and customary landholders. For this reason, the list of 30 countries was altered slightly to include countries with large populations of informal and customary landholders. The list of countries was also altered slightly because accessing information about laws was not possible for some of the initial countries chosen. Once a list of thirty countries was formulated, students at the LIDS conducted a preliminary legal analysis of these countries. I then conducted an independent review and quality control of the LIDS students' legal research. After I comprehensively reviewed and edited their analyses, I was produced a more in-depth legal analysis and published a WRI Working Paper entitled *Encroaching on Land and Livelihoods* in June 2016.[33]

Following the publication of the WRI Working Paper, I chose an additional 20 countries (nine Latin American countries, five additional African countries, and six additional Asian countries) in order to increase the number of countries or regions assessed to 50 and to ensure the study covers Latin American countries. In Chapters 2, 4, and 5, the indicator analysis covers 50 countries; however, Chapter 3 of this book shows indicator findings for only 30 countries on compensation eligibility requirements for IPLCs with customary tenure rights (See Appendix). The reason this chapter only covers 30 countries is because I chose to combine and compare my research on compensation procedures with the LandMark indicators on the legal security of indigenous and community tenure (for more details, see Chapter 3). At the time this part of the study was conducted, LandMark did not have reliable data for 20 of the 50 countries assessed in this study, so there are only 30 countries covered in the analysis presented in Chapter 3.

1.6 Why Does This Study Include a Case Study of Nigeria?

To shed more light on how the legal indicator analysis was conducted and examine how expropriation, compensation, and resettlement processes have been carried out in one of the 50 countries, Chapter 6 examines the Lekki Free Trade Zone (LFTZ) expropriation case in Nigeria.[34] There were two main reasons why I chose Nigeria as a case study. First, I chose to focus on Nigeria was because Nigeria scored relatively poorly against the legal indicators on expropriation, compensation, and resettlement (discussed in Chapters 2-5). I wanted to understand what types of impacts Nigeria weak legal framework has on affected landholders in Nigeria. Prior to conducting the Nigeria study, I had read a fair amount of

33 N.K. Tagliarino, *Encroaching on Land and Livelihoods: How National Expropriation Laws Measure Up Against International Standards*, World Resources Institute, Washington, DC, 2016.

34 This chapters presents the findings that from N.K. Tagliarino, Y. A. Bununu, M. O. Micheal, M. De Maria, A. Olusanmi, 'Compensation for Expropriated Community Farmland in Nigeria: An In-Depth Analysis of the Laws and Practices Related to Land Expropriation for the Lekki Free Trade Zone in Lagos', *Land*, Vol. 7, No. 23. 2018.

background literature on expropriation and forced eviction in rural and urban areas throughout Nigeria, and thought the legal analysis and survey research provided in Chapter 6 would be particularly useful for informing the law reform process in Nigeria.

Second, Nigeria was chosen, in part, because the Global Land Tool Network (part of UN Habitat) had an interest in funding academic research in this country given Nigeria's history of expropriations, forced evictions, and displacement that have triggered negative impacts for affected landholders. In 2017, my research team and I were awarded a small grant to cover the cost of carrying out a legal analysis, field visit, and survey of affected community members. The aim of the research project was to examine whether the government complied, both in law and in practice, with internationally recognized standards on expropriation, compensation, and resettlement. In August 2017, my research team and I surveyed 140 affected households from 10 different communities affected by land expropriation. The reason we developed a methodology that combines both legal and survey research is that we aimed to assess the law on the books as well how the law operates on the ground in Nigeria. As discussed in Chapter 6, the responses to survey indicate, to some extent, whether the government has effectively enforced the law when expropriating land for the LFTZ. Chapter 6's case study on Nigeria fits within the framework of this book because it discusses the indicator findings (initially presented for 50 countries including Nigeria in Chapters 2-5) for Nigeria in more detail and then dives into how Nigeria's legal framework translated into practice in LFTZ expropriation case. In doing so, Chapter 6 provides the reader with a deeper understanding of the negative impacts associated with poor legal frameworks on expropriation, compensation, and resettlement.

1.7 Why Does This Study Focus on the VGGTs?

This study describes the standards established in the VGGTs and additional international instruments that shed light and meaning of the VGGTs. While the legal indicators used in this study are primarily based on the VGGT, it is important to recognize that there are a variety of related international instruments that address land and property rights. The land and resource rights of Indigenous Peoples International treaties and declarations are recognized in International Labour Organization Convention 169 (1989) and the UN Declaration on the Rights of Indigenous Peoples (2007). More broadly, the right to property is recognized in international human rights treaties, including in Article 17 of the UN Declaration on Human Rights, Article 1 of the European Convention on Human Rights, Article 14 of the African Charter on Human and People's Rights, Article 21 of the American

Convention on Human Rights, and other international instruments.[35] The right to property and the right to be compensated for expropriated property are recognized by other international instruments, including:

- Article 5 of the International Convention on the Elimination of All Forms of Racial Discrimination;[36]
- Article 15 of the International Convention on the Protection of the Rights of All Migrant Workers and Members of Their Families;[37]
- Article 31 of the Arab Charter on Human Rights;[38]
- Article 13 of the Convention relating to the Status of Refugees identifies immovable property as well as moveable property;[39]
- The Universal Declaration on the Eradication of Hunger and Malnutrition, 1974.[40]

While these other international treaties, declarations, and guidance documents are noteworthy, they do not present a comprehensive set of consensus-based standards for governing land tenure systems responsibly. I chose to base the legal indicators on the VGGTs, instead of these other international instruments because, in my opinion, the VGGTs were the most comprehensive, widely supported, and influential standards on expropriation available at the time this study was conducted.[41] These standards can be used to guide governments, companies, civil society organizations, communities, and other stakeholders on the responsible governance of land tenure systems.

Between 2009 and 2012, the VGGTs were developed through an extensive negotiation process involving input and support from governments, NGOs, civil society, and the private sector.[42] Over the course of two and a half years, ten regional consultations with stakeholders

35 M. Monteagudo, 'The Right to Property in Human Rights and Investment Law: A Latin American Perspective of an Unavoidable Connection', *SECO / WTI Academic Cooperation Project Working Paper Series 2013/06*, 2013. L. Verstappen, 'Multilevel governance of property titles in land: The voluntary guidelines on the responsible governance of tenure of land, fisheries, and forests in the context of national food security', *in* C. Godt Ed., *Regulatory Property Rights: The Transforming Notion of Property in Transnational Business Regulation*, Brill/Nijhoff, Leiden, Netherlands, 2016, p. 105.

36 United Nations, *International Convention on the Elimination of All Forms of Racial Discrimination*, United Nations, New York, NY, 1969.

37 United Nations, *International Convention on the Protection of the Rights of All Migrant Works and the Members of Their Families*, United Nations, New York, New York, 1990.

38 League of Arab States, *Arab Charter on Human Rights*, Cairo, Egypt, 1997.

39 L. Verstappen, 'Multilevel governance of property titles in land: The voluntary guidelines on the responsible governance of tenure of land, fisheries, and forests in the context of national food security', *in* C. Godt Ed., *Regulatory Property Rights: The Transforming Notion of Property in Transnational Business Regulation*, Brill/Nijhoff, Leiden, Netherlands, 2016, p. 103.

40 United Nations, *The Universal Declaration on the Eradication of Hunger and Malnutrition*, United Nations, New York, New York, 1974.

41 Munro-Faure & Palmer, 2012; Arial *et al.* 2012.

42 Kropiwnicka 2012, p. 1.

took place that brought together nearly 700 people from the public and private sectors, civil society, and academia, representing 133 countries, to ascertain and address tenure governance concerns.[43] The consultation process facilitated a dialogue between various actors at the national, regional, and global levels. Regional consultations were held in Brazil, Burkina Faso, Ethiopia, Jordan, Namibia, Panama, Romania, the Russian Federation, Samoa, and Vietnam.[44] Consultations were held with hundreds of people from civil societies in Africa, Asia, Europe, and Latin America. Additional private sector consultation attracted over 70 people from 21 countries. As a result of this far-reaching, inclusive consultation process, the VGGTs enjoy a large consensus among private companies, governments, civil societies, NGOs, and other stakeholders who are increasingly accepting the VGGTs as a new international standard on land tenure.[45]

The VGGTs contain a set of standards that aim to protect the tenure rights of all people, but have a particular focus on poor and marginalized groups, such as Indigenous Peoples and women landholders. They provide a framework that states can use when developing their own strategies, policies, legislation, programs and activities.[46] The VGGTs cover a range of issues relating to land tenure governance, such as legal recognition and allocation of tenure rights, customary tenure systems, land redistribution, administration of tenure (i.e., recording and valuation of tenure), and other topics. The VGGTs respect all forms of land tenure, including public, private, communal, indigenous, customary, and informal tenure.[47] Section 16 of the VGGTs provides a comprehensive set of standards on expropriation, compensation, and resettlement (see Table 3).

Table 3 Highlights for Section 16 of the VGGT

- **Section 16.1:** "States should expropriate only where rights to land ... are required for a public purpose. States should clearly define the concept of public purpose in law, in order to allow for judicial review."
- **Section 16.1:** "[States should acquire only] the minimum resources necessary."
- **Section 16.1:** "[States] should respect all legitimate tenure rights holders, especially vulnerable and marginalized groups, by ... providing just compensation in accordance with national law."
- **Section 16.2:** "States should be sensitive where proposed expropriations involve areas of particular cultural, religious or environmental significance, or where the land ... [is] particularly important to the livelihoods of the poor or vulnerable."
- **Section 16.2:** "States should ensure that the planning and process for expropriation are transparent and participatory. Anyone likely to be affected should be identified, and properly informed and consulted at all stages."

43 Munro-Faure & Palmer 2012, pp. 5-18.

44 Verstappen 2016, p. 105.

45 The Interlaken Group and RRI 2015.

46 Munro-Faure & Palmer 2012, p. 10.

47 Munro-Faure & Palmer 2012.

- **Section 16.3:** "States should ensure a fair valuation and prompt compensation ... Among other forms, the compensation may be, for example, in cash, rights to alternative areas, or a combination."
- **Section 16.5:** "Where the land ... [is] not needed due to changes of plans, States should give the original rights holders the first opportunity to re-acquire these resources."
- **Section 16.6:** "All parties should endeavor to prevent corruption, particularly through use of objectively assessed values, transparent and decentralized processes and services, and a right to appeal."
- **Section 16.8:** "States should, prior to eviction or shift in land use which could result in depriving individuals and communities from access to their productive resources, explore feasible alternatives in consultation with the affected parties ... with a view of avoiding, or at least minimizing, the need to resort to evictions."
- **Sec. 16.9:** "States should, to the extent that resources permit, take appropriate measures to provide adequate alternative housing, resettlement or access to productive land."

Section 16 of the VGGTs aims to reduce commonly identified risks associated with expropriation, compensation, and resettlement by ensuring legitimate tenure rights are respected and protected by state and non-state actors. Empirical research conducted in many countries shows that expropriation, compensation, and resettlement can impose significant risks on affected landholders, including landlessness, homelessness, hunger, poverty, and other socioeconomic risks.[48] As discussed in Chapters 2-6 of this book, additional risks include arbitrary expropriation/compensation decision-making, limited opportunities for participation in decision-making and redress in case of tenure rights violations, as well as insufficient compensation and resettlement assistance in cases where expropriation causes displacement. Chapter 6 of this book highlights issues that occur in practice when it comes to land expropriation in Nigeria by examining the case of the LFTZ expropriation. Given these risks, it may be in the best interest of governments to comply with these international standards if they wish to ensure that affected populations avoid land and resource conflicts as well as the adverse socioeconomic impacts of expropriations, such as poverty and hunger that are commonly cited in the literature.[49]

While the VGGTs are comprehensive and widely supported, they have several limitations. First, they are international soft law, meaning they are not legally binding on state or non-state actors. Soft law cannot compel government action and does not provide affected landholders with justiciable legal rights that can be used to seek redress in court. International soft law is also limited because there is no executive, legislative, or judicial body charged with implementation, administration, interpretation, or enforcement.

Second, the VGGTs contain open-ended terminology that is intentionally left undefined to provide flexibility to states when interpreting its provisions. For example, the VGGTs

48 M.M. Cernea, 'The risks and construction model for resettling displaced populations', *World Dev.* Vol. 25, 1997, pp. 1569-1587.

49 Cernea 1997.

call for states to respect all "legitimate tenure rights holders," but do not define the term "legitimate tenure."[50] While it is widely agreed among scholars that the term "legitimate" includes both legal legitimacy (rights recognized by law) and social legitimacy (rights that have broad acceptance among society),[51] states have discretion to impose limits when it comes to developing procedures for legally recognizing tenure rights, since the term is left undefined in the VGGTs. Additionally, the terms "public purpose" and "fair [and prompt] valuation of compensation" are not defined in the VGGTs, meaning states have discretion to interpret these terms in various ways.

Third, there is no designated international body or court charged with interpreting the meaning of the VGGTs. As a result, the terms will likely have various meanings that differ depending on the country and context. For this reason, I drew on the FAO Handbook and other international guidance when interpreting the VGGTs to develop the legal indicators (see discussion of methodology in Section 1.8 below).[52] The FAO Handbook was written by highly reputable land tenure experts and reflects what FAO and its many international collaborators consider to be good practices for ensuring equitable access to land and land tenure security.

Although there are limitations to the VGGTs, I still decided that they were the best available standards on which to base the legal indicator analysis. Even though they are unenforceable without implementing domestic legislation, the VGGTs can have a meaningful and influential impact on the governance of tenure, as seen by the fact that private companies, governments, NGOs, and other stakeholders are increasingly accepting the VGGTs as a new international standard on land tenure.[53] Additionally, the VGGTs reflect and work in conjunction with binding international human rights instruments, such as ILO Convention 169,[54] and non-binding yet influential instruments, such as the UN Declaration on the Rights of Indigenous Peoples. The VGGTs also reflect international human rights, such as the right to property,[55] the rights to housing,[56] and the right to an adequate standard of living.[57] The VGGTs are also the first international standard with widespread support that comprehensively deals with issues related to expropriation, compensation, and resettlement.

---

50 FAO 2012.
51 Palmer *et al.* 2009, p. 8.
52 Keith *et al.* 2008.
53 Arial *et al.* 2012.
54 ILO, *Convention No. 169, Indigenous and Tribal Peoples Convention*, 1989; ILO, Geneva Switzerland, 1989.
55 United Nations. 1948. Universal Declaration of Human Rights. G.A. Res. 217 A (III): Art. 17.
56 International Covenant on Economic, Social and Cultural Rights. 1966, A/RES/2200: Art. 11.
57 Ibid.

1.8 What Is the Methodology Used to Assess National Laws in This Study?

The functional approach to comparative law methodologically guides the comparative examination of the laws applicable to expropriation, compensation, and resettlement in the 50 different jurisdictions (see Appendix).[58] This approach first requires identifying the societal issues that the comparative analysis aims to address. In this case, the societal issues are expropriation, compensation, and resettlement. Next, this approach entails identifying the laws in each jurisdiction that have an effect on how a jurisdiction treats this issue. Finally, once such laws are identified, this approach entails comparing those laws with international standards as established in the VGGTs.

This study presents an innovative method for conducting comparative legal research. By reviewing legal provisions in 50 countries against a set of indicators (i.e., questions pertaining to the law) that are designed to align with Section 16 of the VGGTs, and categorizing the answers to these indicators into color-coded charts (see Chapters 2-6), this analysis allows the reader to see how the laws in various countries measure up against each other and against international standards. Scholars can adopt this approach and develop legal indicator analyses of other research areas.

For this study, I conducted an in-depth desk review of legal provisions enacted in constitutions, statutes, and regulations in the 50 countries to answer a list of indicator questions. I carefully read through all legally binding provisions applicable to expropriations to determine whether the law provides guidance in a manner that complies with international standards. Answering the questions posed by these indicators entailed analyzing a broad range of national-level laws, including national constitutions, land acquisition acts (i.e. expropriation acts), land acts, community land acts, agricultural land acts, land use regulations (See Bibliography and Appendix). Laws were found online using the FAOLEX, UrbanLex and other databases containing laws and regulations.[59] I sent indicator scores for 20 of the 50 countries to peer reviewers with relevant expertise, but was unable to find experts to review scores for all 50 countries. Thus, due to time and resource constraints, not all indicator scores for the 50 countries were peer reviewed by experts (see Appendix for list of peer reviewers). The indicator data is publicly available on the Land Portal platform (landportal.org) in case additional reviewers would like to review and provide feed-

---

58 R. Michaels, 'The Functional Method of Comparative Law' *in* M. Reimman & R. Zimmerman (Eds.), *Oxford Handbook on Comparative Law*, 2006, pp. 340-382; M.V. Hoecke, 'Methodology of Comparative Legal Research', *Law and Method*, 2015.

59 See FAOLEX database at http://www.fao.org/faolex/en/; see also Urbanlex database at http://urbanlex.unhabitat.org/

back. To understand how the law functions in the countries assessed, I also analyzed a limited number of secondary sources, including the World Bank's Land Governance Assessment Framework reports, academic books, journal articles, and other literature (See Bibliography in Appendix).

I designed the indicators into relevant yes or no questions so that they can be used to measure whether national laws comply with Section 16 of the VGGTs. Table 4 provides an example of how the VGGTs were translated into indicators:

Table 4 Examples of How VGGTs Were Translated into Indicators

Relevant Principle in the VGGTs	Indicators
– Sec. 16.1 of the VGGTs: "States should clearly define the concept of public purpose in law, in order to allow for judicial review."	– Do the national laws provide a clear definition of public purpose to allow for judicial review?
– Sec. 16.1 of the VGGTs: "States should respect all legitimate tenure right holders, especially vulnerable and marginalized groups, by acquiring the minimum resources necessary and promptly providing just compensation in accordance with national law."	– Do the national laws require the government to minimize the amount of land acquired to an amount that is necessary to achieve a public purpose? – Do the national laws require that compensation must be paid prior to the taking of possession of the land and within a specified timeframe thereafter?

As demonstrated in Table 4, the indicators in each chapter ask yes or no questions about legal provisions established in expropriation laws. In some cases, a 'partial' answer was given to the indicators where laws only partially satisfy the question asked by the indicators. For example, if the legal provisions are not clear or applicable to all cases of expropriation, this warrants a score of 'partial.' Two examples are presented as follows:

- When assessing the indicator that asks whether laws require assessors to account for improvements made on the land, a 'partial' score was given where the law only requires the assessor to account for some (but not all) improvements made on the land.
- Regarding the procedural requirements (e.g., a right to be consulted prior to expropriation), if laws only grant a right under certain circumstances, a score of 'partial' is given in some cases. For example, when addressing the indicator that asks 'do the national laws require the government to consult affected landholders prior to expropriation?' South Sudan receives a 'partial' score because Section 74(2) of South Sudan's 2009 Land Act provides that "a public hearing *may* be carried out before expropriation for public purposes *for large scale development*" (emphasis added).[60] Since the provision contains the word "may" and public hearings are only required in cases where land is expropri-

60 Government of South Sudan, Land Act, 2009, Article 74(2).

ated for the purpose large-scale development, South Sudan's score for this indicator is 'partial.'

Additionally, if a law only applies to certain land areas (e.g., urban areas) or to certain types of landholders (e.g., Indigenous Peoples), then a score of 'partial' is given. In the absence.of explicit or implicit indication from the law that questions asked by the indicators can be answered with a 'yes' or 'partial', the indicator scores received a 'no' score, meaning the question posed by the indicators were answered in the negative. Additional explanations are provided in Chapters 2-6. All indicator scores and explanations for the 50 countries are included in the Appendix.

1.9 What Are the Caveats and Research Limitations?

While every attempt was made to ensure that only accurate, reliable, and current information was used to answer the indicator questions, there are several important caveats regarding the analysis presented in this book.

1. It focuses on legally binding national-level statutory and regulatory laws relating to expropriation, compensation, and resettlement; it does not assess non-binding policies. This analysis does not comprehensively examine case law in the 50 countries. For a fascinating in-depth examination of case law related to expropriation processes in four countries, readers should refer to Hoops (2017).[61]
2. The analysis does not assess whether expropriation, compensation, and resettlement procedures are implemented or enforced on the ground. In some of the countries assessed, the government and private actors may not respect the rule of law or otherwise enforce legal procedures related to expropriation, compensation, and resettlement. While an in-depth, multi-disciplinary study of whether the law is respected and enforced on the ground is necessary to obtain a comprehensive analysis of expropriation and compensation practices, I did not have the financial and other resources needed to do so. I did, however, conduct a case study of land expropriation in Nigeria using mixed methods, including a survey of affected landholders, interviews with government officials, and a review of primary and secondary sources to determine whether the government complied with international standards in the LFTZ expropriation case (see Chapter 6). However, aside from the Nigeria case study in Chapter, this book's analysis is primarily based on a desk review of national-level expropriation laws, land laws, and secondary sources available online, including the World Bank's Land Governance Assessment Framework (LGAF) assessments.

61 B. Hoops, *The Legitimate Justification of Expropriation: A Comparative Law and Governance Analysis*, Juta Law Publishers, Cape Town, 2017.

3. The analysis focuses on expropriation and does not address other types of land transfers (e.g., voluntary land transfers).
4. The analysis focuses on compensation for land, and does not assess whether compensation is granted for natural resources (e.g., trees, minerals).
5. The analysis focuses on national-level laws and does not include an assessment of subnational laws (e.g., state and district-level laws). Expropriation laws at national and state levels may differ from one another, but it was only viable to assess national-level laws when conducting this study. Given the broad range of subnational laws in the 50 countries, it was not feasible to conduct a comparative assessment of subnational laws using this book's methodological approach.
6. Some of the laws assessed, particularly the Latin American countries' laws, were unofficial, English-translated versions of laws originally written in non-English languages. For laws written in Spanish, I translated the laws myself with some guidance from fluent speakers and Google Translate.
7. The findings are based on my legal interpretations of the laws assessed. For 20 of the 50 countries, I was able to contact country-level experts to peer review the findings (see Appendix for list of peer reviewers). However, I was unable to find country-level experts to peer review indicator scores for all 50 countries.
8. The research was conducted up until March 1, 2018 so any laws passed after this date are not accounted for in the analysis.

It is worth highlighting that this study does not examine situations in which governments wrongfully interpret and outright violate expropriation laws. On state or public land, tenure rights are often recognized as compensable, especially when registered (see Chapter 3), but governments may wrongfully interpret laws as granting them discretion to evict landholders and without paying compensation. If it is unclear whether expropriation procedures apply, governments may try to avoid compensation obligations by invoking the justification that these landholders are informally occupying state-owned land. In several documented cases, governments decided to forcibly evict or otherwise infringe on the rights of landholders in rural and urban areas without paying compensation by invoking the justification that these landholders did not have compensable tenure rights since they were informally occupying state-owned land.[62]

This study does not examine particular cases of expropriation (with the exception of the LFTZ case in Nigeria discussed in Chapter 6), and make a judgment regarding whether expropriation procedures should or should not apply. The legal question of whether expropriation procedures apply to a given case is sometimes complex and must be answered

62 Amnesty International 2013, p. 15.

depending on the facts at hand.[63] Laws sometimes allow governments to designate, convert, lease, allocate, grant concessions to, or otherwise alienate state-owned land without following expropriation or compensation procedures.

Since this study focuses exclusively on expropriation, it does not examine other powers granted to governments to regulate property. Governments are often permitted to regulate, interfere with, or deprive people of their property rights using regulatory powers (i.e., 'police powers')[64] without actually expropriating property and paying compensation.[65] An examination of these issues would serve as useful complimentary research, but are beyond the scope of this study.

Since the analysis only examines national-level constitutional, statutory, and regulatory provisions, the analysis is limited. While the underlying assumption that clear constitutional, statutory, and regulatory requirements can help foster domestic compliance with the VGGTs, explicit legal provisions are not always necessary for countries to adopt international standards. Especially in common law countries, courts may step in and fill gaps in expropriation laws. However, research indicates that this rarely happens; courts often defer to the executive and legislative branches regarding expropriation decision-making.[66]

Even if courts decide to thoroughly scrutinize expropriation decisions and fill in legislative gaps, it is arguably still worthwhile to investigate the status of national-level constitutional, legislative, and regulatory provisions in relation to international standards. Such an exercise provides an indication of whether courts are given adequate guidance when ruling on expropriation cases. Furthermore, clearly prescribed expropriation, compensation, and resettlement provisions may help protect affected landholders before it is too late. Even if affected landholders have the resources, time, and capacity to challenge decisions in court, they may lose their property and experience a significant loss in income and livelihood by the time they receive a judgment. Imposing legal obligations, clearly written in statutes and regulations, on governments and acquiring bodies may increase the likelihood of compliance with international standards and reduce the risks to tenure rights and livelihoods.

---

63 E.J. Marais,'When does state interference with property (now) amount to expropriation? An analysis of the Agri SA court's state acquisition requirement (part I), *Potchefstroom Electronic Law Journal*', Vol. 18, 2015, pp. 2983-3031.

64 "Police powers" as used here refers to the state's inherent right to regulate an individual's conduct or property to protect the health, safety, welfare, and morals of the community. Examples of exercises of police power include zoning and land use regulations that set certain restrictions for landholders but do not actually amount to an expropriation of their land.

65 Marais 2015.

66 *See, generally* Hoops 2017.

An analysis of the actions of governments in countries with non-existent or weak rule of law is beyond the scope of the book. In such countries, if governments and private actors fail to respect the law, land may be confiscated due to conflict or other reasons, even when such confiscation does not serve a genuine public purpose. Without enforceable legal rights, affected populations in countries with weak rule of law may be unable to seek redress in court and before tribunals when governments and private actors acquire their land. On the other hand, in countries where governments and private actors respect the rule of law, the existence of robust legislation and regulations that comply with international standards may provide a greater degree of certainty that expropriation will be conducted in accordance with international standards in practice. For instance, strong legal rights to compensation and resettlement assistance ensure that affected populations may be afforded redress in court in the event of a violation by government or private actors. These rights can serve as a point of reference when the public or affected landholders wish to challenge expropriation, compensation, and resettlement decisions in court.

1.10 Who Can Benefit from This Research?

This study has academic value because it presents an innovative methodology for conducting broad comparative research. The indicator method applied in this study can be used to track the status and development of laws over time. Not only can this study be applied to other areas of the law besides expropriation, but it can also be repeated in the future to show trends over time (e.g., whether additional countries have enacted laws that adopted international standards).

This analysis and the citations to various legal instruments can be used as tools for lawmakers to draft new legislation and regulations related to expropriation, compensation, and resettlement. Lawmakers can use this study to track progress toward the realization of the VGGTs and compare laws across a variety of countries and continents. Law and policy makers can use this book as a reference when deciding which provisions to include in revised versions of expropriation laws.[67]

Affected landholders and land rights advocacy groups can use this analysis to better understand tenure rights and whether such rights are vulnerable to expropriation without adequate compensation. With increased knowledge on domestic expropriation laws and the VGGTs, landholders can also use this analysis to measure government performance

67 See https://landportal.org/book/dataset/nkt-vggt16 for detailed explanation of indicator scores for each country.

and hold governments and private actors accountable for decisions and actions affecting their tenure rights.

This study can support companies in aligning their operations with Section 16 of the VGGTs. NGOs, civil society, and companies have worked together recently to develop operational guidelines that help private companies address land tenure risks by aligning their operations with the VGGTs, but these guidelines do not focus specifically on Section 16 of the VGGTs.[68] In conjunction with those guidelines, this study can also support companies engaging in activities that involve expropriation, compensation, and resettlement. Companies can use this study to understand the domestic legal frameworks of the countries in which they make land investments and implement activities that require access to land, so they can make sound business decisions. For this reason, this study may incentivize companies to push for reforms to expropriation laws. This study may also help companies meet corporate social responsibility objectives and industry-specific commitments, such as commitments to transparency, responsible investment, and compliance with applicable laws.

This study can also inform investment decisions of multilateral development banks (MDBs), including the World Bank, IFC, and regional development banks (see discussion of the ESF). The new World Bank ESF comes into effect in 2018. ESS5 on Land Acquisition, Restrictions on Land Use and Involuntary Resettlement standards on land acquisition and resettlement rely on borrowers to implement resettlement programs for projects involving the acquisition of land following borrower frameworks, a term vaguely defined in the ESF as including aspects of domestic law, policy, and other frameworks. This requirement in the ESF means that borrowers of World Bank funds will likely implement expropriation projects following both national laws and ESF policy standards (see Chapter 5 for more detail). Since the standards established in Section 16 of the VGGTs are related to the ESF standards on land acquisition, this study is relevant to decision-making related to investments in development projects funded by the World Bank.

This study can also support the creation of new guidance on improving laws and practices related to expropriation, compensation, and resettlement. For instance, this book can support the creation of a new Protocol on Fair Compensation, an ongoing project involving University of Groningen and True Price.[69]

68 Interlaken Group and RRI 2015; Bledsoe *et al.* 2015.

69 True Price and University of Groningen, *Towards a Protocol on Fair Compensation in Case of Land Tenure Changes. Input Document to a Participatory Process*; True Price: Amsterdam, The Netherlands; University of Groningen: Groningen, The Netherlands, 2016.

More broadly, by highlighting gaps in the law and pinpointing which legal provisions must be amended to adopt international standards on expropriation, compensation, and resettlement, this study can inform law and policy debates among scholars, practitioners, policymakers, affected populations, and other actors. The benchmark established by this study can assist civil society organizations and activists in measuring government progress towards adopting the VGGTs on expropriation, compensation, and resettlement.

1.11 Roadmap

This book is organized as follows. Chapter 2 examines public purpose provisions in 50 countries, and whether laws impose limits on the expropriation decision-making in accordance with the VGGTs. More specifically, this Chapter examines the extent to which the government's authority to justify the use of expropriation is limited, and whether laws require a transparent and participatory expropriation process that enables affected landholders and the public to be informed and able to meaningfully participate in expropriation decision-making.

Chapter 3 discusses compensation eligibility requirements and whether these preclude Indigenous Populations and local communities with customary tenure (IPLCs) from obtaining compensation entitlements. Specifically, the indicators presented in this Chapter ask whether registration is required before customary tenure rights holders can obtain compensation, and whether compensation can be awarded to communities regardless of whether they develop, cultivate, or make improvements on the land. To assess whether IPLCs are granted a level of tenure security sufficient to obtain compensation, findings and analyses from LandMark's ten legal indicators on the legal security of indigenous and community land were also examined.[70] Since reliable data was not available on LandMark for all 50 countries, the findings presented in this chapter only contain 30 countries. Landmark is a global online platform of indigenous and community land (see www.landmarkmap.org). The LandMark legal indicators examine the tenure security of community land by focusing on the extent to which the law upholds the land rights of IPLCs, and whether these rights are protected through formalization and recognition of community-based governance. The LandMark legal indicators relate to the issue of compensation eligibility because, depending on the extent to which community land is formally recognized

70 L.A. Wily, N. Tagliarino, Harvard Law and International Development Society (LIDS), A. Vidal, C. Salcedo-La Vina, S. Ibrahim, B. Almeida, *Indicators of the Legal Security of Indigenous and Community Lands.* Data file from *The Global Platform of Indigenous and Community Lands,* Landmark, 2017. Available at: www.landmarkmap.org.

and protected, communities may be vulnerable to expropriation without compensation (e.g. if compensation can only be obtained by legally recognized tenure rights holders).

Chapter 4 examines compensation valuation procedures in the 50 countries using legal indicators that focus on the substantive and procedural requirements pertaining to the calculation of compensation. The indicators discussed in this Chapter ask whether laws require assessors to account for various land values when calculating compensation, and whether there are legal processes in place that allow affected persons to negotiate compensation amounts, receive prompt payments, and hold governments accountable by appealing compensation decisions in courts or before tribunals.

Chapter 5 examines the content of the countries' resettlement frameworks by comparing national laws with the standards established in the VGGTs, as well as other international standards, such as the World Bank ESS5 on Land Acquisition, Restrictions on Land Use and Involuntary Resettlement, and the International Finance Corporation (IFC) Performance Standard 5. The indicators in this chapter are used to determine whether these legal frameworks are consistent with existing international standards on resettlement and rehabilitation in cases of land expropriation for development projects.

Chapter 6 provides a detailed examination of one of the 50 countries to show in more detail how the legal indicator assessment was conducted—using Nigeria as an example. This Chapter also provides insight on the implementation of expropriation laws in Nigeria. It looks at Nigeria's legal framework and practices related to expropriation, compensation, and resettlement, and compares this framework to Section 16 of the VGGTs. This Chapter examines how expropriation laws function in practice in Nigeria by analyzing the expropriation practices followed in the LFTZ case. A major takeaway of this Chapter is that the lack of a strong legal framework on expropriation can result in insufficient compensation, resettlement assistance, and other entitlements. This Chapter concludes with a set of recommendations for reforming Nigeria's LUA.

Chapter 7 provides a summary of the findings and draws overall conclusions from the analysis of the 50 countries assessed. This Chapter also presents a full list of recommendations for reforming national laws so that they comply with the VGGTs and other international standards on expropriation, compensation, and resettlement. It also provides overall findings, concluding remarks, and suggested areas of future research.

2 Legal Limits on the Government's Authority to Expropriate Land

2.1 Summary and Roadmap

This Chapter examines whether the national laws in the 50 developing countries impose limitations on the government's authority to invoke a public purpose justification for the expropriation of land. Furthermore, this Chapter looks at whether the national laws require governments to follow a transparent and participatory expropriation process. The findings indicate that only a few of the 50 countries provide a clear legal definition of 'public purpose', impose limitations on the government's expropriation authority, and require that a transparent and participatory expropriation process be followed.

This Chapter is organized as follows. Section 2.2 provides some background and context that illustrates how expropriation decision-making has been a contentious issue in several countries. This Section also provides a discussion of common trends of expropriation decision-making. It highlights how expropriation decisions have in some cases led to social unrest and protest. Section 2.3 discusses the standards on expropriation as established in Section 16 of the VGGT. Section 2.4 looks at whether the 50 countries have laws that conform to the VGGTs on public purpose decision-making. Section 2.5 discusses whether national laws impose obligations on governments to be sensitive to certain types of land areas (e.g. indigenous land or areas of cultural, historical, and environmental significance) as called for by the VGGTs. Section 2.6 examines whether national laws contain provisions that ensure a transparent and participatory expropriation process is followed as called for by VGGTs. Section 2.7 provides concluding remarks and suggests recommendations for countries that scored 'no' on the indicators to improve their laws by adopting the VGGTs.

2.2 Background and Context Regarding Expropriation Decision-Making

In nearly all countries, governments retain some level of discretion to establish a public purpose justification for the expropriation of land. When used for purposes that actually serve the public interest, expropriation can be an effective mechanism for making land available for the development of public infrastructure such as roads, schools, airports, hospitals, railways, and other public goods. However, as demonstrated by the findings presented in this Chapter, few of the countries assessed have laws that effectively limit expropriation authority so that it is only used when necessary to achieve genuine public purposes. Many of the laws enacted in the 50 countries assessed have vague definitions of 'public purpose', and often open the door for governments to justify the use of expropriation for a broad range of purposes with limited oversight or scrutiny from the public or the judiciary.

In theory, the decision of whether to utilize expropriation power should entail effectively balancing the needs of the public against the interests of private landholders.[71] Yet when broad legal authority is granted to governments to expropriate property, and laws do not establish checks on this authority that ensure the public benefits, expropriations may fail to serve a public purpose while causing unjust infringements on the tenure rights of affected landholders.[72]

In some countries, governments transfer expropriated land to private companies, often for the purpose of 'economic development', including extracting natural resources for export.[73] These expropriations are usually justified as serving public needs by increasing public revenues, creating jobs, and otherwise stimulating local economic growth.[74] If 'economic development' expropriations are not subjected to oversight, companies that are granted expropriated land may focus entirely on generating profit to serve their own private interests as opposed to serving public needs, especially in cases where public and private interests are mutually exclusive.[75]

Expropriations for 'economic development' purposes have occurred frequently in many parts of the world. For example, empirical research conducted by the World Bank in Ethiopia, Tanzania and other countries demonstrates that a significant amount of expropriated land has been transferred to private investors or companies that do not always

71 Hoops 2017; Tagliarino 2016.

72 H. Mostert, 'The Poverty of Precedent on Public Purpose/Interest: An Analysis of Pre-Constitutional and Post-Apartheid Jurisprudence in South Africa', *in* B. Hoops, E.J. Marais, H. Mostert, J.A.M.A. Sluysmans & L.C.A. Verstappen (eds) *Rethinking Expropriation Law I: Public Interest in Expropriation*, Eleven International Publishing, Den Haag, The Netherlands, 2015.

73 Hoops 2017; J. Lindsay, K. Deininger & T. Hilhorst 'Compulsory Land Acquisition in Developing Countries: Shifting Paradigm or Entrenched Legacy?' *in* I. Kim, H. Lee, & I. Somin (Eds.), *Eminent Domain: A Comparative Perspective*, Cambridge, Cambridge University, 2017, pp. 118-155.

74 L. Verstappen, 'Rethinking Public Interest in Expropriation Law: Introductory Observations' *in* Hoops, B., Marais, E.J., Mostert, H., Sluysman, J.A.M.A. & Verstappen, L.C.A. (Eds.), *Rethinking Expropriation Law I: Public Interest in Expropriation*, Eleven International Publishing, Den Haag, The Netherlands, 2015, pp. 15-25

75 Verstappen 2015, p. 26; Hoops 2017.

generate local economic growth or otherwise serve public interests.[76] In China, over 3.15 million hectares of farmland (more than 2 percent of China's total arable land) were expropriated between 1990 and 2002, which caused roughly 36.4 million farmers to lose their land.[77] Much of this land was expropriated for commercial interests.[78] Outside of China, an increasing number of expropriations have occurred in Asia and elsewhere. According to Ingalls *et al.* (2018), "... land expropriation[s] appear to be on the rise across the Mekong, principal among which are Special Economic Zones (SEZs) and Cross-Border Economic Zones (CBEZs)."[79]

If government expropriation decisions are not subjected to sufficient oversight, land may be taken from citizens under the pretext of serving the public interest by claiming the expropriation will boost the economy by increasing agricultural production, job creation, and public revenues.[80] Meanwhile, the ulterior motive behind the government's decision to expropriate property may be to line its own pockets or collude with private companies through secret deals made behind closed doors without public input or judicial scrutiny.[81] Without proper checks in place to ensure the proposed expropriation will actually serve the public interest by boosting the economy and creating jobs for local populations, expropriation may become a tool used exclusively for the benefit of private companies.[82]

Since the cost of paying compensation for expropriated property may be relatively lower in blighted areas, expropriations may be used to target the poor, especially when the proposed project aims at economic revitalization.[83] As stated by Stern, "blight condemnations, urban renewal programs, and redevelopment projects—which often serve the public use justification for eminent domain—all affect, not coincidentally, assets belonging to poor property owners."[84] In many urban areas, for example, expropriation has often been used

76 K. Deininger, H. Selod, A. Burns, *The Land Governance Assessment Framework: Identifying and Monitoring Good Practice in the Land Sector*, World Bank, Washington, DC, USA, 2012, p. 86.

77 ADB. *Compensation and Valuation in Resettlement: Cambodia, People's Republic of China, and India*, Rural Development Institute, Seattle, DC, USA, 2007.

78 ADB 2007; Z. Keliang, R. Prosterman, Y. Jianping, L. Ping, J. Riedinger, O. Yiwen, 'The Rural Land Question in China: Analysis and recommendations based on a seventeen-province survey', *JILP*, Vol. 38, 2006.

79 M.L. Ingalls, J.C. Diepart, N. Truong, D. Hayward, D. Neil, T. Sem, M. Phomphakdy, R. Bernhard, S. Fogarizzu, M. Epprecht, V. Nanthavong, D.H. Vo, , D. Nguyen, P.A. Nguyen, T. Saphanthong, C. Inthavong, C. Hett, N. Tagliarino, *The Mekong State of Land*, Centre for Development and Environment, University of Bern and Mekong Region Land Governance, Bern, Switzerland, Bern Open Publishing (BOP), 2018, p. 56.

80 Hoops 2015.

81 N.S. Garnett, 'The Public Use Question as a Takings Problem', *Geo Wash L. Rev.*, Vol. 71, 2003, p. 934.

82 Hoops 2017.

83 S. Stern, 'Expropriation Effects on Residential Communities', *in* B. Hoops, E.J. Marais, H. Mostert, J.A.M.A. Sluysman, L.C.A. Verstappen (Eds.), *Rethinking Expropriation Law II: Context, Criteria, and Consequences of Expropriation*, Den Haag, The Netherlands, Eleven International Publishing, 2015, pp. 359-391.

84 Stern 2015, p. 377.

to stimulate economic growth by pushing the urban poor of their land to make way for large-scale development projects, including for real estate development, factories, and other projects.[85] Bell and Parchomovsky persuasively argue that expropriations pose a concern for the distribution of societal burdens since economic development takings may disproportionately harm the poor.[86] I agree with these scholars and found extensive evidence from the literature suggesting the poor are often targets of expropriation in many of the 50 countries assessed in this study.[87] For example, in rural areas with fertile agricultural land, government authorities seeking to increase the productivity of land may decide the expropriation of smallholder farms is justified for the purpose of increasing agricultural production and economic growth.[88] Especially if laws do not establish limits on decision-making power, these government authorities may easily transfer land from smallholders to large-scale agricultural producers.[89]

When land in developing countries is expropriated and transferred to foreign companies, there is a risk that those foreign companies may hire foreign workers instead of local workers, and take profits from expropriation projects back to their home countries.[90] Under such circumstances, expropriations may unjustly burden expropriated landholders without actually generating jobs or otherwise benefitting local populations. After the expropriation occurs, affected landholders may become landless, homeless, and otherwise unable to grow crops to maintain income and food supplies.[91] The public may also fail to reap economic benefits from the project, especially if the project involves natural resource extraction for export or other activities that generate revenues for foreign companies that end up avoiding paying local taxes or investing in the local economy.[92]

The literature indicates that expropriation has often been used for private gain with limited economic development benefits reaching the public and harmful impacts endured by affected landholders. In Ethiopia, for example, the government expropriated 100,000 hectares of Gambella farmland for a large-scale agricultural producer.[93] This expropriation

85 Keliang *et al.* 2006.

86 A. Bell, G. Parchomovsky, 'Takings Reassessed', *Va. Law Rev.* Vol. 87, 2001, p. 378.

87 Deininger *et al.* 2012; Lindsay *et al.* 2017; Asian Development Bank, *Compensation and Valuation in Resettlement: Cambodia, People's Republic of China, and India*, Rural Development Institute, Seattle, 2007.

88 L. Cotula, S. Vermeulen, R. Leonard & J. Keeley, *Land Grab or Development Opportunity? Agricultural Investments and International Land Deals in Africa*, FAO, International Institute for Environment and Development, International Fund for Agricultural Development, Rome, Italy, 2009.

89 Cotula 2009; N.K. Tagliarino *et al.* 2018.

90 Tagliarino *et al.* 2018.

91 M.M. Cernea, 'The Risks and Reconstruction Model for Resettling Displaced Populations', *World Development*, Vol. 25, No. 10, 1997, pp. 1569-1587.

92 Tagliarino *et al.* 2018.

93 D. Vhughen & A. Gebru, 'Large-Scale Acquisitions of Land in Ethiopia', *Focus on Land in Africa*, 2013.

was justified as promoting a "better development project"—a vaguely defined "public purpose" included in Ethiopia's expropriation law.[94] Ultimately, the company did not fulfill its promises to create jobs, provide water to villages, and build public infrastructure.[95] Likewise, in Nigeria, the government expropriated 16,000 hectares of rural farmland, which was historically held and used by indigenous communities, in order to build the LFTZ.[96] Research indicates that the LFTZ has not led to significant job or economic growth and the government has not fulfilled many its promises to provide compensation, alternative land, equity shares, jobs and other entitlements to affected landholders (see Chapter 6).[97]

'Economic development' expropriations are a prevalent issue in the United States as well. One source documented 10,000 cases from 1998 to 2002 in which the government threatened to condemn or actually condemned property for private interests.[98] A notable case was *Kelo vs. City of New London*, which was decided by the United States Supreme Court in 2005.[99] While the United States Supreme Court ruled that the City of New London's expropriation authority was not misused in the *Kelo* case, the outcome of this case suggests that expropriation for economic development purposes, if not planned properly, can cause poor citizens to lose their land, and also fail to stimulate growth, create jobs, and otherwise benefit the public.[100]

The case arose after the City of New London, Connecticut condemned an area of privately owned real property in order to implement a comprehensive redevelopment plan. The City's plan was to transfer the expropriated land to Pfizer Corporation and other businesses for the purpose of stimulating economic growth. *Kelo* held that land can be expropriated from private landowners and given to private companies for economic development. It further held that the potential benefits the community would enjoy from economic growth qualified private redevelopment plans as a permissible public use under the Takings Clause of the Fifth Amendment of the U.S Constitution. The Court granted deference to the City to determine whether areas are sufficiently economically distressed to justify a program of economic rejuvenation. Citing the previous *Midkiff* Supreme Court case,[101] the Court in *Kelo* stated that, while the City could not expropriate land simply to confer a benefit on

94 Government of Ethiopia, Proclamation No. 455/2005, Expropriation of Landholdings for Public Purposes and Payment of Compensation Proclamation, Section 3(1), 2005.

95 Vhughen & Gebru 2013, p. 5.

96 Tagliarino *et al.* 2018.

97 Tagliarino *et al.* 2018.

98 D. Berliner, *Public Power, Private Gain: A Five-Year, State-By-State Report Examining the Abuse of Eminent Domain*, Institute for Justice, Arlington, Virginia, 2003.

99 Supreme Court of the United States, Kelo *et al. v.* City of New London *et al.*, 545 U.S. 469, 2005.

100 Supreme Court of the United States 2005.

101 Supreme Court of the United States, Housing Authority *v.* Midkiff 467 U.S. 229, 1984.

a private party, the Takings Clause was executed following a carefully considered development plan, which was not adopted "to benefit a particular class of identifiable individuals."[102]

Overall, the *Kelo* decision defined the concept of public purpose broadly and gave deference to the government to determine what public needs justify the use of expropriation. The Court refused to inquire whether there is reasonable certainty that the proposed expropriation would actually serve a public benefit. Justice O'Connor wrote a noteworthy dissenting opinion stating,

> Any property may now be taken for the benefit of another private party, but the fallout from this decision will not be random. The beneficiaries are likely to be those citizens with disproportionate influence and power in the political process, including large corporations and development firms... Under the banner of economic development, all private property is now vulnerable to being taken and transferred to another private owner, so long as it might be upgraded.[103]

O'Connor's dissenting opinion should be kept in mind as one reads the remainder of this book. Her opinion stimulates at least two questions that may arise in cases of expropriation: who decides what counts as 'upgraded,' and what is meant by this term. In many countries, vague terms like 'economic development' may enable governments to transfer property from one owner to another whenever the government is of the opinion that the latter owner might put the land to use in a more productive or beneficial way. Such legal precedence poses a significant risk to the land rights and livelihoods of smallholder farmers or other poor and vulnerable landholders who rely on land for subsistence purposes.

It is worth noting that the redevelopment project at issue in *Kelo* ultimately failed to achieve economic benefits for the City of New London.[104] After the *Kelo* case was decided, the private developer responsible for implementing the redevelopment plan eventually gave up on the project, and the expropriated land subsequently remained empty and unutilized.[105] The *Kelo* case serves as useful background to the issues discussed in this book because it illustrates some of the negative outcomes that can occur when courts give deference to legislative and administrative entities to decide what constitutes a public purpose.

---

102 Supreme Court of the United States 2005.

103 Supreme Court of the United States 2005.

104 I. Somin, 'The story behind Kelo *v.* City of New London- how an obscure takings case got to the Supreme Court and shocked the nation', *Washington Post*, 29 May 2015.

105 Somin 2015.

Similar to United States jurisprudence, South African courts have often been lenient when ruling on whether expropriations are needed for public purposes.[106] In South Africa, courts will often take this reason at face value and not investigate whether the proposed expropriation is actually likely to serve public interests.[107] In the *Bartsch* case, for example, the Free State High Court had to rule on whether the construction of a private shopping complex constituted a legitimate public purpose.[108] The Court held that if the private shopping complex "could be brought within the realms of an act performed in the public interest," the expropriation would be legitimately justified.[109] In response to the case, Van der Walt argued that the expropriation for the shopping complex might only have been valid because it was merged with the primary purpose of construction of the road.[110]

In *Soораram Pratap Reddy v. District Collector* (2008), the Supreme Court of India interpreted public purpose as including "any purpose wherein even a fraction of the community may be interested or by which it may be benefitted."[111] As stated by Downing, based on Court's interpretation, there does not seem to be a conceivable limit as to what purposes will be deemed in the best interest of the public.[112] While the Indian Supreme Court historically would often defer to the executive branch's authority to determine what constitutes a public purpose, the Court has more recently begun to actively scrutinize public purpose decision-making. In *Radhey Shyam v. The State of Uttar Pradash*, the Court stated

> It must be accepted that in construing public purpose, a broad and overall view has to be taken and the focus must be on ensuring maximum benefit to the largest number of people. Any attempt by the State to acquire land by promoting a public purpose to benefit a particular group of people or to serve any particular interest at the cost of the interest of a large Section of people especially of the common people defeats the very concept of public purpose.[113]

---

106 H. Mostert, 'Trends in the South African Constitutional Court's jurisprudence on property protection and regulation', *Amicus Curia*, Vol. 72, 2007.

107 Mostert 2007; Hoops 2017, p. 449; A.J. van der Walt, *Constitutional Property Law,* 3rd edn., Juta, Cape Town 2011.

108 South Africa Free State High Court, *Bartsch Consult (Pty) Limited v Mayoral Committee of the Maluti-A-Phofung Municipality [2010] ZAFSHC 11,* 2010; Hoops 2017, p. 429.

109 [2010] ZAFSHC 11, para 5.2.

110 van der Walt 2011, p. 503; A.J. van der Walt, 'Constitutional Property Law', *ASSAL*, 2010, 251-294, 284; Mostert 2015, p. 77.

111 Sooraram Pratap Reddy *v.* District Collector (2008) 9 S.C.C. 552.; C. Downing, 'Eminent Domain in 21 st Century India: What New Delhi Can Learn From New London?', *Journal of International Law and Politics*, vol. 46, 2013, pp. 207-289, 245.

112 Downing 2013, p. 245.

113 Supreme Court of India, Radhey Shyam *v.* The State of Uttar Pradash, 5 SCC 553, 2011.

With this ruling, the Court gave itself a more expansive role in determining whether the public purpose requirement is satisfied; it would check for abuse of power, violations of legal requirements, and "[whether] public purpose has been diverted for private use."[114]

New limitations on the discretion of the Indian government to define 'public purpose' were solidified with the passage of the Right to Fair Compensation and Transparency in Land Acquisition, Rehabilitation and Resettlement Act, 2013 (LARR Act).[115] In addition to comprehensive compensation and resettlement packages for affected families, the LARR Act provides a clearly defined list of public purposes and requires a review and approval by an Independent Expert Group. The LARR Act is also viewed as a milestone because of its requirement that 70-80% of affected families must consent to the decision to expropriation depending on the proposed project. The LARR Act replaces the colonial-era Land Acquisition Act 1894, a law that, according to the Minister of Rural Development, "was draconian and led to the impoverishment of livelihood losers."[116] According to Cernea, under the old law "the state distorted the eminent domain principle by expropriating land not only for projects of public interest but also for private-for-profit projects, thus acting against vital interests of its most vulnerable citizens."[117] Likewise, Lindsay *et al.* states,

> The LARR Act was adopted after many years of debate, against a backdrop of increasingly vociferous public protest about large land acquisitions on behalf of private industries [...] [that] were facilitated in part by expansive legal interpretations of the public use/purpose doctrine in the 1894 Land Acquisition Act.[118]

The long history of expropriation and forced displaced galvanized a large population of rural farmers and other marginalized groups to demand legal reform in India.[119] Large protests against expropriations after a long, bloody history of involuntary resettlement for large-scale development projects.[120] In response to an expropriation in 2011, farmers vehemently protested a government decision to expropriate village land in 2011, arguing the expropriation was unjustified because it did not serve a public benefit.[121] The Supreme

114 Supreme Court of India 2011.

115 Government of India, *The Right to Fair Compensation and Transparency in Land Acquisition, Rehabilitation, and Resettlement Act* (LARR Act), 2013.

116 M.M. Cernea, *Progress in India: New Legislation to Protect Persons Internally Displaced by Development Projects*, Brookings Institution, 2015.

117 Cernea 2015.

118 Lindsay *et al.* 2017

119 D. Sathe, *The Political Economy of Land Acquisition in India*, Springer Singapore, Singapore, 2017.

120 H.M. Mathur, 'Resettling People Displaced by Development Projects: Some Critical Management Issues', *Social Change*, Vol. 36, No.1, 2006.

121 IDE-Jetro, 'Land Acquisition Issues in Noida District: background to 'Land Wars' in India', *IDE-Jetro*, 2011.

Court of India ultimately ruled the expropriation illegal, on the grounds that in the name of the public interest, the government was serving private interests.[122]

Since expropriation is a severe infringement on individual rights—taking one's land and home can be equivalent to taking one's livelihood—failure to establish proper safeguards and mechanisms for keeping expropriating authority in check can result in significant social unrest.[123] Expropriations have often sparked heated protests and opposition from the public and affected landholders. In China, for example, affected landholders organized a protest in the early 2000s, which lasted for several years after government officials seized farmland that had been under village control since imperial times.[124] The government expropriated the landholders' farmland for the purpose of real estate development. In response to the sit-in, Chinese police reportedly sprayed tear gas and fired rubber bullets at the protesters.[125] According to the New York Times book about the protest,

> Women were attacked with cattle prods. Farmers sleeping nearby were beaten in their beds [...] like other land transactions in rural China, negotiations for land had been one-sided: government officials, citing an obscure legal clause, ordered farmers to leave and offered them $60 per parcel of land. The farmers screamed robbery.[126]

In Tanzania, land can be expropriated where the President is satisfied that a corporation requires any land for "agricultural, commercial, and industrial development" or for the purposes of construction of any work that in the President's opinion would be of public utility or in the public interest or in the interest of the national economy.[127] According to a World Bank study, expropriated rural land has routinely been transferred to private actors in Tanzania.[128] The government usually justifies these expropriations as serving the public purposes of 'rational town planning' or 'productive rural investment.' The study indicated that expropriations were often perceived by the public as aiming to push out poor and indigenous landowners to allow the rich or the state to derive major benefits.[129] Likewise, in Nigeria, empirical research suggests that local landholders commonly view

---

122 Supreme Court of India, Savitri Dev *v.* State of Uttar Pradesh, Civil Appeal No. 4506, 2015.
123 Berliner 2003.
124 J. Yardley, 'Farmers Being Moved Aside by China's Real Estate Boom', *New York Times,* 2004. Available at: www.nytimes.com/2004/12/08/world/asia/farmers-being-moved-aside-by-chinas-real-estate-boom.html?_r=0
125 Yardley 2004.
126 Yardley 2004.
127 Government of Tanzania, Land Acquisition Act, 1967, *Sec.* 3 and 4.
128 Deininger *et al.* 2012.
129 Deininger *et al.* 2012, p. 85.

expropriation as a tool for "dispossessing the poor to elevate the rich."[130] Similarly, in Rwanda, one study indicated that expropriations have been on the rise since 2012, and many affected households surveyed expressed dissatisfaction due to income loss and limited opportunities for meaning participation in expropriation decision-making.[131]

In response to the *Kelo* case discussed above, many Americans vehemently protested the City of New London's decision; this decision was also widely criticized by scholars and highlighted as a prime example of a poorly executed expropriation.[132] Protests against eminent domain have occurred in many other parts of the United States due to widespread expropriation of property.[133]

The studies highlighted above suggest that granting governments and broad authority, with limited oversight, to determine what constitutes a public purpose for the expropriation of land can be problematic, both for the affected landholder and the general public. Moreover, these studies also indicate that judicial scrutiny is often ineffective in keeping expropriation decisions in check, since courts usually give deference and refuse to second-guess the executive and legislative rationales for expropriations.[134] The widespread protest and conflict over expropriated land also suggests that governments do not always sufficiently account for public opinion in their expropriation decision-making.[135] To avoid these negative outcomes, lawmakers may need to rethink the ways in which they reach expropriation decisions and consider democratizing the decision-making process in compliance with the VGGTs. The VGGTs call for the reformation of national-level legal frameworks so they effectively keep expropriating power in check and ensure a transparent and participatory expropriation process is followed. These standards are outlined in the following Section.

2.3 VGGTs on Expropriation

The VGGTs that are relevant to the indicators are:

130 The World Bank, *Land Governance Assessment Framework Final Report: Nigeria*, World Bank, Washington, DC, USA, 2011, p. 256.

131 H. Rose, F. Mugisha, A. Kananga & D. Clay, *Implementation of Rwanda's Expropriation Law and Its Outcomes on the Population*. In Proceedings of the Annual World Bank Conference on Land and Poverty, Washington, DC, USA, 14-18 March 2016.

132 I. Somin, 'Controlling the Grasping Hand: Economic Development Takings After Kelo' *George Mason Law & Economics Research Paper*, No. 06-01, 2007.

133 Berliner 2003.

134 *See, generally*, Hoops 2017.

135 Rights and Resources Initiative (RRI) & TMP Systems, *Tenure and Investment in Africa: Comparative Analysis of Key Trends and Contextual Factors*, RRI, Washington, DC, USA, 2017.

Table 5 VGGTs on Expropriation

- Section 16.1: "States should expropriate only where rights to land [...] are required for a public purpose. States should clearly define the concept of public purpose in law, in order to allow for judicial review."
- Section 16.1: "[States should acquire only] the minimum resources necessary."
- Section 16.2: "States should be sensitive where proposed expropriations involve areas of particular cultural, religious or environmental significance, or where the land [...] [is] particularly important to the livelihoods of the poor or vulnerable."
- Section 16.2: "States should ensure that the planning and process for expropriation are transparent and participatory. Anyone likely to be affected should be identified, and properly informed and consulted at all stages."
- Section 16.5: "Where the land [...] [is] not needed due to changes of plans, States should give the original rights holders the first opportunity to re-acquire these resources."

Table 6 List of Expropriation Indicators

1. Do the national laws provide a clear conceptualization of public purpose to allow for judicial review?
2. Do the national laws require the government to minimize the amount of land acquired to the amount necessary to achieve a public purpose?
3. Do the national laws require the government to conduct a proportionality test prior to expropriation?
4. Do the national laws require the government to conduct a feasibility study prior to expropriation?
5. Do the national laws require an environmental impact assessment (EIA) prior to expropriation?
6. Do the national laws require a social impact assessment (SIA) prior to expropriation?
7. Do the national laws establish special protections from expropriation for areas held by poor and vulnerable groups?
8. Do the national laws grant affected landholders the right to reacquire the land in the event that the land is unutilized or no longer needed for the project?
9. Do the national laws obligate the government to identify all affected landholders prior to expropriating land?
10. Do the national laws require the government to provide information to affected landholders about the reasons for expropriation?
11. Do the national laws require the government to consult affected populations prior to expropriating land?

2.4 FINDINGS ON PUBLIC PURPOSE DECISION-MAKING

Section 16.1 of the VGGTs calls for states to provide a clear conceptualization of public purpose to allow for judicial review. According to the FAO Handbook, "an exercise in compulsory acquisition is more likely to be regarded as legitimate if land is taken for a purpose clearly identified in legislation."[136] Clearly defined lists of public purposes in legislation provide an established inventory of permissible purposes beyond which the government may not expropriate land. This inventory provides criteria that the public and affected landholders can use to challenge proposed justification decisions in court. Laws

136 S. Keith *et al.* 2008, p. 11.

with clear lists of public purposes (e.g., public infrastructure and national defense projects) provide courts with guidance when ruling on expropriation cases and diminish the potential for conflicting judicial interpretations of whether the public purpose standard was met. Moreover, specificity in the legal definition of public purpose takes away judges' incentives to practice deference when scrutinizing public purpose decisions by executive and legislative branches.[137]

The indicator analysis revealed that five of the 50 countries assessed (Afghanistan, India, Indonesia, Mongolia, Rwanda) have laws that provide a clear definition of public purpose to allow for judicial review. In these five countries, the national laws provide clearly defined lists of public purposes (e.g., public infrastructure projects). These laws also indicate that governments cannot expropriate land for a purpose not explicitly included in the list. These five countries have relatively newer expropriation laws compared to the other 46 countries assessed, which suggests that there may be a growing trend of clearly defining public purpose in some expropriation laws.[138] Afghanistan's Land Acquisition Act, 2017, for example, contains a clear list of purposes for which land must be expropriated, such as military centers, manufacturing factories, highways, airports, electricity dams, schools, mosques, and other public infrastructure.[139]

Seventeen of 50 countries[140] provide a partially clear definition of public purpose, but the public purpose provisions also include open-ended clauses (e.g., clauses that state 'or other public purposes'). The open-ended clause grants governments flexibility in interpreting what constitutes 'other public purposes.' For example, Papua New Guinea's Land Act, 1996 contains a long list of permissible public purposes (e.g., economic development, public infrastructure, national defense, industrial development), but also includes a clause "[or] any purpose declared by any law to be a public purpose [or] [...] ancillary to or necessary or convenient for the carrying out of a purpose [listed in the Act]."[141] This open-ended clause provides the government with some flexibility and suggests that the government can expropriate for additional public purposes not specified in the Land Act.

137 Hoops 2017, p. 101, 215, 216.

138 Afghanistan, India, and Indonesia enacted expropriation laws within the last decade, and Mongolia's law was enacted in 2002.

139 Government of Afghanistan, Land Acquisition Act, 2017, Article 5.

140 Brazil, Burkina Faso, Cambodia, China, Ecuador, Kazakhstan, Kenya, Lesotho, Mexico, Nigeria, Papua New Guinea, South Sudan, Swaziland, Taiwan, Tanzania, Thailand, Vietnam. For a full analysis and list of country indicator scores, see, N.K. Tagliarino Voluntary Guidelines Section 16 Indicators on Expropriation, Compensation, and Resettlement. University of Groningen: Groningen, Netherlands, 2018. Available at: <https://landportal.org/book/dataset/nkt-vggt16>.

141 Government of Papua New Guinea, Land Act, 1996, Sec. 2.

Of the 50 countries assessed, 28 have laws that either do not provide a definition of public purpose or grant government authorities broad discretion to determine on a case-by-case basis what constitutes a public purpose and thereafter expropriate land. For example, according to Myanmar's and Pakistan's Land Acquisition Act, 1894, a law that was passed during the British colonial era yet is still in effect today, land can be expropriated "whenever it appears to the President of the Union that land in any locality is needed or is likely to be needed for any public purpose."[142] Such broad authority potentially opens the door for abuse of power by executive authorities; for instance, these authorities may expropriate land under the pretext of a public purpose, when the actual purpose is not intended to serve public interests. As Hoops points out,

> Third-party transfers for economic development are prone to abuse by private actors and corrupt government bodies. If the private project developer and the municipality collude, for example, they may use 'economic development' as a pretext to disguise that projects for which the state seeks to expropriate property are actually intended solely to serve private interests [...][143]

I agree with Hoops' statement regarding the risks associated with third-party transfers for economic development. In reaction to the arbitrary decision-making by the government and abuse of expropriation power, citizens may be less likely to consider expropriation decisions as legitimate, and more likely to protest or challenge decisions in court. Protests and challenges that result from expropriation projects can cause significant delays, work stoppages, and increased costs for project developers.[144] For this reason, clarity around the concept of 'public purpose' may not only serve the interests of the public and affected landholders, but also private investors looking to avoid high risk investments. Clear limits on the government's authority establish a 'public purpose' justification can safeguard investor interests by reducing the risk of arbitrary expropriation of investment projects. As stated by Cotula *et al.*,

> Specific-enough wording for compliance requirements to be enforceable and transparency in their application is key to ensure fair implementation in the public interest - avoiding on the one hand creeping expropriation of the investment through arbitrary government application of these requirements,

142 Governments of Myanmar (and Pakistan), Land Acquisition Act, 1894, Sec. 5.

143 B. Hoops, *The Legitimate Justification of Expropriation: A Comparative Law and Governance Analysis,* Juta and Company, Ltd., Cape Town, South Africa, 2017, p. 211.

144 RRI & TMP Systems 2017.

and on the other collusion between government officials and investors to avoid sanctioning where investment plans are not complied with.[145]

As Cotula rightly asserts, clearly prescribed procedures the government must follow when making expropriation decisions can benefit private investors by decreasing the risk of expropriation, protecting their land rights, and incentivizing additional investments in land.

2.4.1 Requirements to Minimize Expropriated Land

According to Section 16.1 of the VGGTs, states should acquire only the minimum resources necessary. Yet the legal analysis reveals that only five of the 50 countries[146] establish explicit requirements that the government must minimize the amount of land acquired to the amount necessary to achieve a public purpose. In the remaining 45 countries, national laws do not require the government to minimize the amount of land it expropriates.

Such broad authority is problematic given that, in several countries, governments have reportedly acquired far more land than was needed to achieve a public purpose. In Ghana, for example, where the government is not legally obligated to minimize the amount of land expropriated, the government expropriated 167 hectares of land to build a school when only 20 hectares were needed.[147] Larbi *et al.* found that, in several other cases of expropriation, excess land subsequently remained unutilized.[148] Likewise, in Bangladesh, where the government has broad discretion to expropriate any amount of land when it is of the opinion that such land is needed for a public purpose, one study concluded that an excessive amount of land was expropriated for the Jamuna Multipurpose Bridge; a large amount of land this subsequently remained unutilized.[149]

145 Cotula *et al.* 2009, p. 83.

146 Afghanistan, India, Lesotho, Malaysia, and Taiwan.

147 The State Lands Act, 1962 does not explicitly require the government to minimize the amount of land acquired through expropriation; W.O. Larbi, A. Antwi & P. Olomolaiye, 'Compulsory land acquisition in Ghana: Policy and praxis', *Land Use Policy*, Vol. 21, 2004, pp. 115-127, 124.

148 Larbi *et al.* 2004, p. 124.

149 S. Atahar, 'Development Project, Land Acquisition and Resettlement in Bangladesh: A Quest for Well Formulated National Resettlement and Rehabilitation Policy', *International Journal of Humanities and Social Science*, 3(7), 2013.

2.4.2 Proportionality Test and Feasibility Study

In order to fully comprehend the costs and adverse impacts of expropriations vis-à-vis the benefits and determine whether the amount of resources expropriated is the minimum amount necessary (Section 16.1 of the VGGTs), it would be useful for governments and acquiring bodies to conduct a 'proportionality test.' A 'proportionality test' is defined here as a procedure by which governments and/or project developers must, prior to the expropriation, weigh its social costs (e.g., impact on tenure rights and livelihoods) and environmental costs (e.g., pollution) against the potential public benefit generated by the project. According to the FAO Handbook, for example:

> The planning phase of a major public investment project should include the identification of any lands to be acquired for the project. Options should be analysed and presented to the public for its understanding and consultation in order to choose the site that presents the fewest obstacles and the best outcomes, having regard to all impacts, including those on any owners and occupants.[150]

In Germany, for example, courts have required proposed expropriations to be proportional, meaning the extent to which the expropriated property contributes to the implementation of the project is not disproportionate to the burden that the expropriation imposes upon the holder of that property.[151] This proportionality test ensures that expropriation is only used when it is not disproportionately burdensome on tenure rights and livelihoods to do so.[152]

Four countries (Burkina Faso, India, Indonesia, and Taiwan) have national laws that require that the government conduct a proportionality test prior to expropriating land. These requirements explicitly oblige the government to weigh the costs of the expropriation (e.g., environmental and social costs) against its potential public benefits. For example, Indonesia's Law No. 2 of 2012 requires expropriating authorities to conduct a feasibility study of proposed expropriation; this study must incorporate a social-economic survey, location feasibility, analysis of cost and development benefit to the area and the community, the estimated land value, and an analysis of the environmental and social impacts.[153] It is worth noting that a statutory obligation that requires expropriating entities to conduct a

150 Keith *et al.* 2008, p. 19.

151 Hoops, 2017, p. 71; Bundesverfassungsgericht, Judgment of 17 December 2013, *ZUR* 2014, 160, 163.

152 Hoops, 2017, p. 71.

153 Government of Indonesia, Law No. 2 of 2012, Acquisition of Land for Development in the Public Interest, Article 15(2), 2012.

proportionality test does not necessarily guarantee that courts will actually scrutinize the result of the test.

Five countries (China, India, Indonesia, Malaysia, Taiwan) have national-level laws that require a feasibility study (i.e., an assessment of whether the proposed project is financially viable or otherwise likely to achieve its intended objectives) prior to expropriation. For example, among other requirements, Taiwan's Land Expropriation Act, 2000 states that the Central Competent Authority shall review the following:

1. Is the expropriation for public interest purpose, necessary, appropriate and reasonable?
2. Does the land use applicant have the ability to carry out the undertaking?
3. Is the financial assessment of the proposed undertaking reasonable and viable?[154]

Figure 1 Legal Limitations on Public Purpose Decision-Making Authority

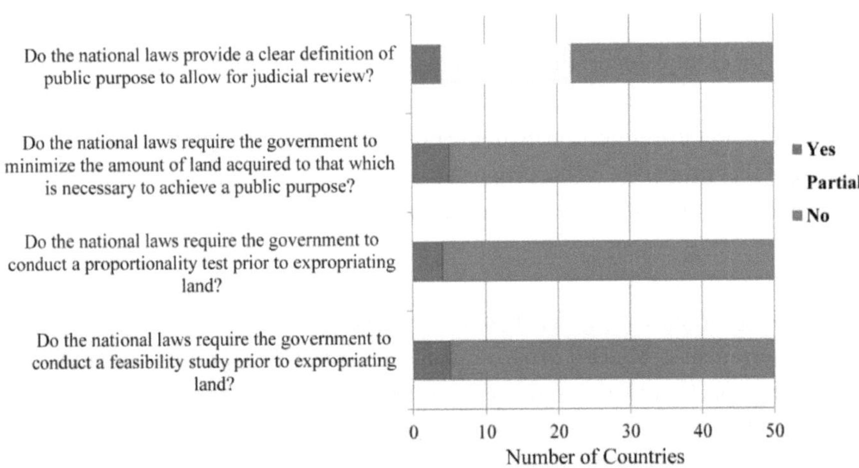

2.5 Limitations on the Type of Land That Can Be Expropriated

This Section examines whether the national legal frameworks of the 50 countries establish certain limitations on the government's authority to expropriate certain land areas, such as areas of cultural, religious, and environmental significance, or areas held by poor and vulnerable groups (e.g., Indigenous Peoples). Additionally, this Section investigates whether

154 Government of Taiwan, Expropriation Act, Art. 13, 2000.

reacquisition rights are granted to affected landholders in the event that a proposed project is abandoned and the land is no longer needed for a public purpose.

2.5.1 Social and Environmental Impact Assessments

Section 16.2 of the VGGTs provides that "States should be sensitive where proposed expropriations involve areas of particular cultural, religious or environmental significance." In order for expropriating authorities to determine whether they must be sensitive to particular land areas, they may need to first conduct an assessment of whether such areas have cultural, religious, and environmental significance. For this reason, the national laws of the 50 countries are examined in this Section to determine whether they require project developers to conduct social and environmental impact assessments prior to expropriation of land.

Of the 50 countries assessed, 49 have enacted national laws that impose obligations on project developers to conduct Environmental Impact Assessments (EIA). These requirements apply whenever proposed development projects involving the expropriation of land may impact the environment. Eritrea is the only country assessed that received a 'no' score for this indicator because the passage of an EIA requirement is still pending.[155]

However, the analysis revealed that only five countries (Afghanistan, India, Indonesia, Laos, and South Sudan) have national-level laws that require governments to conduct a social impact assessment (SIA) prior to expropriating land. For purposes of this indicator, an SIA is defined as a study of a proposed expropriation's social impact, including an assessment of the costs and benefits of a proposed project on the land tenure rights and livelihoods of affected populations. MDBs, such as the World Bank and Asian Development Bank, initially promoted SIAs and made them a requisite to funding for development projects. While some developing countries have adopted SIA requirements simply as window-dressing to receive aid from donors, many developing countries still have not established legally binding SIA requirements that apply when land is expropriated.[156] In 2015, Vanclay *et al.* developed widely cited guidelines on SIAs; these guidelines define SIAs as the process of identifying and managing the social issues of project development and include the effective engagement of affected communities in participatory processes

155 T.K. Zeremariam & N. Quinn, 'An evaluation of environmental impact assessment in Eritrea', *Impact Assessment and Project Appraisal*, Vol. 25, No.1, 2007, pp. 53-63.

156 J. Horberry,'International organization and EIA in developing countries'. *Environ. Impact Assess. Rev.* Vol. 5, 1985, pp. 207-222; B. Tang, S. Wong & M.C. Lau, 'Social impact assessment and public participation in China: A case study of land requisition in Guangzhou', *Environ. Impact Assess. Rev.* Vol. 28, 2008, pp. 57-72.

of identification, assessment, and management of social impacts.[157] For example, article 4(4) of India's LARR Act 2013 stipulates that SIAs, which are mandatory whenever land is expropriated, must include the following:

a. assessment as to whether the proposed acquisition serves a public purpose;
b. estimation of affected families and the number of families among them likely to be displaced;
c. the extent of lands, public and private, houses, settlement, and other common properties;
d. whether the extent of land proposed for acquisition is the absolute bare-minimum extent needed for the project;
e. whether the land acquisition at an alternate place has been considered and found not feasible;
f. study of social impacts of the project, and the nature and cost of addressing them and the impact of those costs on the overall cost of the project vis-a-vis the benefits of the project.[158]

While in some countries, SIAs are included as a part of EIAs, this article includes a separate indicator that focuses on whether national laws require that an SIA is conducted (in addition to an EIA) prior to expropriation. Vanclay provides useful insight on the distinction between EIAs and SIAs:

> SIA arose in the 1970s alongside environmental impact assessment (EIA) and originally attempted to emulate EIA as much as possible. Often SIA was done as part of EIA, usually badly. Over time, however, the practice of SIA has diverged from EIA because of the growing realisation that social issues fundamentally differ from biophysical issues [...] A key difference between SIA and EIA is the increasing focus in SIA on enhancing the benefits of projects to impacted communities. Although the need to ensure that the negative impacts are identified and effectively mitigated remains, also of value is revising projects and ancillary activities to ensure greater benefits to communities. This is necessary for the project to earn its 'social license to operate.[159]

I agree with Vanclay's claim that in order for development projects to obtain a social license to operate, SIAs are necessary. Without a SIA, it is unlikely project developers will be able to fully comprehend the magnitude of the losses borne by affected landholders and account

157 F. Vanclay, A.M. Esteves, I. Auchamp & D. Franks, *Social Impact Assessment: Guidance for Assessing and Managing the Social Impacts of Projects*, International Association for Impact Assessment, Fargo, ND, USA, 2015.

158 Government of India. LARR Act, Sec. 4(4), 2013.

159 Vanclay *et al.* 2015, p. iv.

for these losses and impacts in their project plans and compensation/resettlement schemes. This may be problematic given that the failure to fully understand the range of losses borne by affected landholders can lead to protest and conflict as well as impoverishment and other negative outcomes.[160]

2.5.2 *Special Protections for Poor and Vulnerable Groups, Such as Indigenous Peoples*

This Section examines whether governments must be sensitive to areas inhabited by poor and vulnerable groups, such as Indigenous Populations. Such requirements would comply with Section 16.2 of the VGGTs, which provides "states should be sensitive where proposed expropriations involve areas [...] where the land, fisheries, and forests in question are particularly important to the livelihoods of the poor and vulnerable." According to 16.2 and other Sections of the VGGTs (e.g., Section 9), state and non-state actors must respect and protect the tenure rights of poor and vulnerable groups, including Indigenous Peoples and local communities with customary tenure. For this reason, the analysis investigates whether national laws recognize the right to Free Prior and Informed Consent (FPIC).[161] Although not explicitly mentioned in Section 16 of the VGGTs, the indigenous right to FPIC is recognized in other Sections of the VGGTs (e.g., Sec. 9.9) and other international instruments, such as ILO Convention 169 on Indigenous and Tribal Peoples, 1989 and the UN Declaration on the Rights of Indigenous Peoples, 2007.[162]

Based on the wording of the relevant international standards, FPIC does not necessarily mean that indigenous land cannot be expropriated; however, it means that indigenous communities must be freely informed, fully consulted, and must give their consent before the government's permission to expropriate is granted to project proponents.[163] According to Goodland,

> [If FPIC rights are respected] eminent domain cannot be applied widely to [indigenous] villages or communities. Where consent has been obtained properly from all potentially impacted communities, one or two holdouts

160 *See, generally* RRI 2017; Cernea 1997.

161 United Nations, *Free Prior and Informed Consent of Indigenous Peoples*, United Nations Human Rights Office of the High Commissioner, Geneva, Switzerland, 2013.

162 ILO, *Convention No. 169, Indigenous and Tribal Peoples Convention*, 1989; ILO, Geneva Switzerland, 1989; United Nations, *Declaration on the Rights of Indigenous Peoples*; G.A. Res. 61/295, U.N. Doc. A/RES/61/295; United Nations: New York, NY, USA, 2007.

163 R. Goodland, 'Free, Prior, and Informed Consent and the World Bank Group', *Sustainable Development Law & Policy*, Vol. 4, Issue 2, Summer 2004, pp. 66-74.

> against the consent of the community could possibly be circumvented through eminent domain, but even then, compensation combined with development benefits for the affected families would have to be fair and just.[164]

In the mid-1990s, the World Bank interpreted the 'meaningful consultation' requirement embedded in the FPIC right as granting communities the right to say 'no' to development projects. However, scholars have argued FPIC "does not mean a single obdurate family can cancel a project; eminent domain should remain available for such cases, but resorted to only sparingly."[165] FPIC requires a careful balancing of public interests with indigenous rights, and if there are a few holdouts against a development project in the community, compulsory acquisition of the holdouts' property rights may be justified. As Goodland explains, "if an extraordinarily lucrative mine, for example, was held hostage by one absentee family [...] eminent domain could rightly be used."[166]

The legal analysis reveals that four of the countries (India, Peru, the Philippines, and Taiwan) have enacted national-level legislation that fully recognizes the international right of Indigenous Peoples to FPIC. In these countries, the national-level laws establish procedures for implementing FPIC. At the same time, further research is needed to investigate whether FPIC rights are being respected and enforced by governments and private actors in these countries.

Seven of the countries studied (Brazil, Ecuador, Honduras, Nepal, Nicaragua, South Sudan, and Tanzania) received a 'partial' score because they ratified ILO Convention 169 or otherwise enacted legislative or regulatory provisions that recognize the right of Indigenous Peoples and traditional communities to be consulted prior to expropriation.[167] For example, Section 41 of India's LARR Act, 2013 provides that "as far as possible, no acquisition of land shall be made in the Scheduled Areas. Where such acquisition does take place it shall be done as demonstrable last resort..." The government must develop comprehensive social impact assessment and acquisition plans, which are subject to appraisal by an Independent Expert Group and the courts.[168] This provision provides some protection to lands held by Scheduled Tribes and Castes recognized by law as historically vulnerable groups in India. Furthermore, the LARR Act is path-breaking because it requires 70-80%

164 Goodland 2004, p. 69.
165 Goodland 2004, p. 66.
166 Goodland 2004, p. 72.
167 Brazil, Ecuador, Honduras, Nepal, Nicaragua, South Sudan, Tanzania.
168 Government of India, *The Right to Fair Compensation and Transparency in Land Acquisition, Rehabilitation, and Resettlement Act* (LARR Act), 2013.

of affected families to consent to land acquisitions depending on the type of proposed project.[169]

On the other hand, 39 of the 50 countries have not enacted national-level legislation that recognizes the indigenous right to FPIC. In these countries, indigenous land may be more vulnerable to acquisition by governments and outsiders since there are no laws in place that recognize FPIC rights of Indigenous Peoples.[170]

2.5.3 *Reacquisition Rights*

If a proposed project is abandoned, and the expropriated land subsequently remains idle and unutilized, the identities of rightful landholders may become unclear, resulting in land disputes. By granting original landholders the right to reacquire the land in the event that a proposed expropriation project is abandoned, legal frameworks can enable land to remain utilized. Moreover, reacquisition rights ensure that affected landholders do not suffer from long-term impoverishment and other displacement outcomes as a result of losing their land, even though the land is not needed for a public purpose. Furthermore, as Hoops, Saville, and Mostert point out, if a project is not implemented or the expropriator wishes to change the purpose for which the land was expropriated, "the democratic legitimacy falls away" and tensions or protests of the expropriation may resume; therefore, reacquisition rights may serve as an incentive to implement the project.[171]

The legal review of the 50 countries reveals that only seven countries grant reacquisition rights whenever the expropriated land is no longer needed for a public purpose.[172] Five countries received 'partial' scores for this indicator because their national laws grant reacquisition rights that are subject to certain limitations; in other words, in these countries, a right to reacquire the land may only be provided in *some* cases of expropriation. For example, Section 101 of India's LARR Act 2013 provides that,

> When any land acquired under this Act remains unutilised for a period of five years from the date of taking over the possession, the same shall be returned

169 Government of India 2013, Section 2.

170 *See* Indicator 7 of the Indicators of the Legal Security of Indigenous and Community Land on LandMark map: <http://www.landmarkmap.org>.

171 B. Hoops, J. Saville & H. Mostert, 'Expropriation and the Endurance of Public Purpose', *European Property Law Journal*, 4(2), 2015, pp. 115-151.

172 Afghanistan, India, Indonesia, Laos, Rwanda, Taiwan, Vietnam.

> to the original owners or owners or their legal heirs, or, as the case may be, the Land Bank...[173]

Since the LARR Act suggests that the land may, in some cases, be submitted to the Land Bank instead of original owners, the score is 'partial' for this indicator. In the remaining 38 countries, reacquisition rights are not granted to affected landholders.

Figure 2 Limitation on the Type of Land that Can Be Expropriated

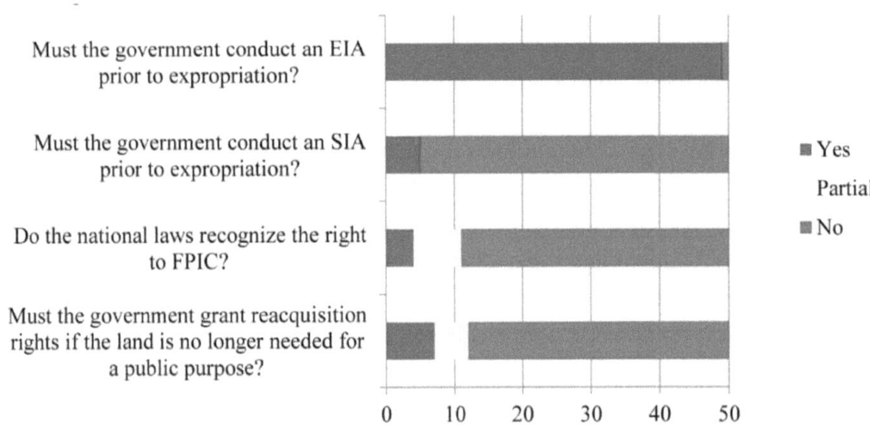

2.6 Legal Provisions That Help Ensure a Transparent and Participatory Expropriation Process

Section 16.2 of the VGGTs stipulates that "States should ensure that the planning and process for expropriation are transparent and participatory. Anyone likely to be affected should be identified, and properly informed and consulted at all stages." Identifying, informing, and consulting affected landholders prior to expropriating land can reduce the risk of land disputes, which delay and disrupt project implementation. Research conducted by Rose *et al.* in Rwanda indicated that over 70% of expropriated individuals who were involved in decision-making actually supported the final value given to their property, whereas less than 14% of individuals who reported being ignored during the valuation process were satisfied with the level of compensation they received.[174] In Tanzania, it was

173 Government of India, LARR Act, 2013, Section 101.

174 H. Rose, F. Mugisha, A. Kananga & D. Clay, *Implementation of Rwanda's Expropriation Law and Its Outcomes on the Population.* In Proceedings of the Annual World Bank Conference on Land and Poverty, Washington, DC, USA, 14-18 March 2016.

found that expropriation and compensation decisions were often made behind closed doors, causing the public to perceive expropriation and compensation decisions as arbitrary, and causing public mistrust of the government.[175]

In addition to the VGGTs, the World Bank Environmental and Social Framework, IFC Performance Standards, and other international policy standards stipulate that land acquisition should involve transparency on the part of project developers so that affected landholders can meaningfully participate in decision-making related to expropriation, compensation, and resettlement.

2.6.1 Identifying Affected Landholders

Seven of the 50 countries have national laws that require governments to identify all affected landholders prior to the expropriation.[176] For example, Article 7 of Laos' Decree on Compensation and Resettlement Management in Development Projects (2016) states that "before project implementation or before the signing of a concession project, the project owner must [...] collect information on people to be affected..."[177] Likewise, Articles 27(2) and 28 of Indonesia's Law No. 2 of 2012 states "the Land Acquisition implementation as intended [...] shall include [...] inventory and identification of possession, ownership, use, and utilization of land [...] [which] shall include [...] surveying and mapping on a parcel-by-parcel basis, and [...] gathering data on the Entitled Parties and the Objects of the Acquired Land."[178]

Four of the 50 countries (Cambodia, China, Peru, and Philippines) received 'partial scores' for these indicators because their national laws only require governments to identify *some* affected landholders. Pursuant to Cambodia's Law on Expropriation 2010, for example, the Expropriation Committee must publicly conduct a survey by recording a detailed description of all rights of the owners and/or rightful owners (see Art. 16). However, the law does not require the government to survey users, occupants, and other tenure rights holders (aside from owners) prior to expropriating land. National laws enacted in 39 of the 50 countries do not establish an identification requirement, which means that governments may be less likely to ascertain the total livelihood impact of the expropriations as well as the viewpoints and interests of all affected landholders prior to expropriation.

175 Deininger *et al.* 2012, p. 85

176 Afghanistan, India, Indonesia, Laos, Rwanda, Taiwan, Vietnam.

177 Government of Laos, Decree on Compensation and Resettlement Management in Development Projects 2016, Art. 7.

178 Government of Indonesia, Acquisition of Land for Development in the Public Interest, 2012, Article 27-28.

2.6.2 *Informing Affected Landholders of the Reasons for the Expropriation*

Information about the reasons for expropriating land and how it is intended to serve the public interest is crucial to ensure the public is able to monitor government action and hold governments and private actors accountable for decisions that violate expropriation laws. As stated by the FAO Handbook, "the information [provided to affected landholders] should explain the purpose of the acquisition, identify the land to be acquired, and provide a clear description of the procedures."[179] Yet the analysis reveals that 18 of the 50 countries have enacted national laws that explicitly require governments to proactively inform affected landholders of the reasons for expropriation prior to compulsorily expropriating land.[180] For example, Section 35.3 of Mongolia's Law on Allocation of Land to Mongolian Citizens for Ownership (2002) provides that "the decision to replace or take back Citizen's owned land for a fee shall clearly indicate the grounds of inevitable replacement or taking the land back."

Four of the 50 countries (China, Ecuador, Peru, and South Sudan) received a 'partial' score for this indicator because their national laws only require the government to proactively disclose the reasons for the expropriation in *some* cases of expropriation. For instance, China received a yellow 'partial' because information on the reasons for the expropriation must be provided only when buildings on state-owned land are expropriated, but not necessarily when rural land is expropriated. Peru's national laws require disclosure in cases where the expropriation affects indigenous peoples, but not for other types of expropriations.

In 28 of the 50 countries, the national laws do not require governments to proactively inform landholders or the public of the reasons for the expropriation. In these countries, affected landholders and the public may still have the option of obtaining information about expropriation by submitting information requests. However, since the governments are not required to proactively disclose the reasons for expropriating land, there may be an increased likelihood of the public being left in the dark and unable to effectively hold governments accountable or monitor whether expropriations are achieving their intended objectives. In Ethiopia, for example, where proactive disclosure is not required by law, research indicates "there is no tradition of consultation with rural communities [...]

179 Keith *et al.* 2008, p. 21.

180 Afghanistan, Belize, Burkina Faso, Cambodia, India, Indonesia, Laos, Malaysia, Mongolia, Nepal, Rwanda, South Africa, Taiwan, Tanzania, Thailand, Trinidad and Tobago, Vietnam, Zimbabwe.

Peasants are almost always the last to know [about proposed expropriations] [...] and they are informed only when implementation is to be undertaken."[181]

2.6.3 *Consulting Affected Landholders Prior to the Expropriation*

Eight of the 50 countries require the government to consult all affected landholders prior to expropriating land.[182] For example, Article 16 of Cambodia's Law on Expropriation 2010 states,

> The Expropriation Committee shall arrange a public consultation with authorities at capital, provincial, municipal, district, khan levels, and with the commune and Sangkat councils and village representatives or the communities affected by the expropriation in order to give them clear and specific information and to have opinions from all concerned parties about the proposal for a public physical infrastructure project.[183]

Thirteen of the 50 countries have laws that require the government to consult affected landholders in *some* cases; for instance, if the expropriation involves indigenous land.[184] Nicaragua's score on this indicator is 'partial' because the consultation requirement only applies when land is expropriated in the Autonomous Regions of the Atlantic Coast and Rivers of Bocay, Coco, Indio, and Maiz.[185] Likewise, Tanzania received a 'partial' score Section 4(6) of the Village Land Act, 1999 provides that village land transfers for public purposes must have community consent if the land acquired is less than 250 hectares.[186] The Minister must only consider the viewpoints of villagers but may approve the acquisition of village land when acquiring more than 250 hectares. There is no explicit consultation requirement established by law that applies in cases where non-village land is expropriated.

Twenty-nine of the 50 countries do not require the government to consult affected landholders prior to expropriating land. In these countries, acquiring bodies may be subject to higher financial, reputational, and other risks for project developers, since consultations

181 B. Alemu, *Expropriation, Valuation, and Compensation in Ethiopia* (Academic Dissertation for the Degree of Doctor of Technology), Royal institute of Technology, Stockholm, Sweden, 2013.

182 Afghanistan, Burkina Faso, Cambodia, India, Indonesia, Laos, Lesotho, Taiwan.

183 Government of Cambodia, Law on Expropriation, 2010, Article 16.

184 Brazil, China, Ecuador, Ethiopia, Honduras, Nicaragua, Peru, Philippines, Rwanda, South Sudan, Tanzania, Thailand, Zambia.

185 Government of Nicaragua, Law of Communal Property Regime of the Indigenous Peoples and Ethnic Communities of the Autonomous Regions of the Atlantic Coast of Nicaragua and of the Rivers Bocay, Coco, Indio and Maiz, 2003.

186 Government of Tanzania, Village Land Act, 1999, Section 4(6).

can reduce the chance of delays that may arise when affected landholders decide to protest or appeal expropriation decisions in court.[187] According to the FAO Handbook,

> Open discussion at public meetings should help the government to improve its understanding of the needs and concerns of affected communities, and to prepare responses that reduce the number of challenges to the compulsory acquisition. Ongoing, open communication about the project can be crucial to its success: when people are not given sufficient opportunity to express dissent as part of the normal process, they may engage in other forms of protest that block the project.[188]

In addition to increasing the risk of conflict and protest, failure to consult affected landholders may result in poorly planned projects since governments and acquiring bodies are not obliged to conduct due diligence and develop better expropriation plans by learning, ahead of time, the likely impacts on affected landholders, the costs of compensation, and how the expropriation may impact the environment.[189]

Figure 3 Transparent and Participatory Expropriation Process

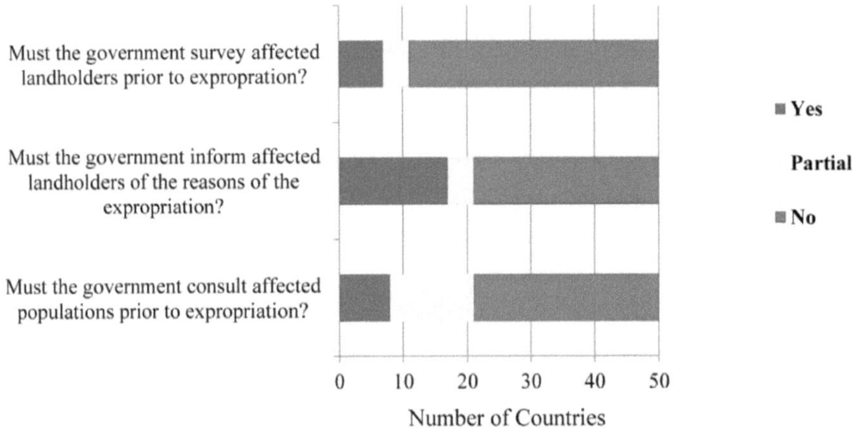

187 S. Keith *et al.* 2008, p. 21.
188 S. Keith *et al.* 2008, p. 21.
189 S. Keith *et al.* 2008, p. 19.

2.7 SUGGESTED AVENUES FOR LAWMAKERS TO PURSUE

The findings presented in this Chapter highlight how many of the national legal frameworks assessed should be reformed to ensure compliance with international standards on expropriation as established in Section 16 of the VGGTs. Lawmakers in countries that scored 'no' on these indicators should consider the following suggestions for reforming expropriation procedures:

1. Establish clear legal definitions of public purpose to provide courts with sufficient guidance when scrutinizing expropriation decisions. If a clearly defined list of permissible purposes is outlined in the law, expropriating authorities are given non-negotiable inventory beyond which they are not permitted to expropriate. Using this list, judiciaries will be able to effectively monitor and rule on whether the proposed purpose violates the law. As the FAO Handbook indicates, the public may be more likely to accept expropriations as legitimate if land is only taken for purposes that are clearly identified in legislation.[190]

2. Require expropriating authorities to limit the amount of land acquired to that which is necessary to achieve a public purpose. To prevent the government from taking an excessive amount of land, laws should also impose obligations on expropriating authorities to conduct a proportionality test and feasibility study. These obligations will help prevent unjustified expropriation by requiring authorities to investigate whether (a) the proposed amount of land is necessary to serve a public purpose (there are no less intrusive alternatives), (b) the project is suitable (reasonably likely to achieve the intended public benefit), and (c) the benefits deriving from the expropriation are proportionate to costs borne by affected populations and the environment. Laws should allow for proportionality tests and feasibility studies to be scrutinized by independent and impartial bodies (e.g., judiciaries) to ensure proper checks and balances.

3. Compel expropriating authorities and project developers to conduct an EIA and SIA prior to expropriation of land, thereby ensuring expropriation decisions are sensitive to areas of cultural, historical, and environmental significance. Laws should ensure these areas are acquired only as a last resort, and, if expropriation is unavoidable, the risks to these impacted areas are adequately addressed. One option for ensuring states are sensitive to these areas is for laws to obligate governments to conduct and publish a cost-benefit analysis, whereby the government weighs the costs borne by the affected populations and environments against potential public benefits. In addition to thor-

190 S. Keith *et al.* 2008, p. 11.

oughly examining project plans (e.g., financial costs, schedules, and monitoring capacity), SIAs and EIAs should incorporate public consultations.

4. Respect the indigenous right to FPIC by ensuring indigenous populations are adequately consulted and given the opportunity to participate in expropriation decision-making. As stipulated in Section 9 of the VGGTs, effective participation of all members, men, women, and youth, in decisions regarding their tenure systems should be promoted in local or traditional institutions, including in the case of collective tenure systems. Governments should not forcibly evict Indigenous Peoples from their land without obtaining their FPIC. In the event that expropriation of indigenous land is absolutely necessary and a demonstrable last resort, governments should reach an agreement with Indigenous Peoples regarding fair compensation and should grant these populations suitable alternative land, rehabilitation assistance, and other measures aimed at reconstructing their livelihoods. Governments should provide Indigenous Peoples the first opportunity to return to their land upon completion of the project, if possible.[191]

5. Allow affected landholders to reacquire expropriated land in the event that the proposed project is abandoned or the land is no longer needed for a public purpose. Reacquisition rights may incentivize expropriating actors to implement projects as agreed and prevent expropriating land from becoming abandoned, unutilized, and wasted.

6. Establish transparent and participatory procedures for the expropriation of land. More specifically, to conform to Section 16.2 of the VGGTs, governments should be legally obligated to identify, inform, and consult affected populations in an open and participatory manner prior to taking possession of expropriated land. By surveying affected populations, governments can determine who is entitled to compensation and understand the impact of the expropriation on tenure rights and livelihoods. Providing information on expropriation plans to affected landholders and the general public can be an effective step toward ensuring meaningful participation in expropriation decision-making and other processes (e.g., compensation processes, resettlement processes). With adequate access to information on the proposed expropriation, affected populations and the general public will be better able to monitor expropriations and hold expropriating actors accountable for decisions that violate the law.

191 United Nations, *Declaration on the Rights of Indigenous Peoples*, Article 10, G.A. Res. 61/295, U.N. Doc. A/RES/61/295, United Nations, New York, NY, USA, 2007.

3 Compensation Eligibility Requirements

3.1 Summary and Roadmap

Now that the issues and analysis related to expropriation decision-making have been discussed, this book shifts focus to the subject of compensation, particularly compensation eligibility requirements (Chapter 3) and valuation procedures (see Chapter 4). Chapter 3 examines whether national expropriation and land laws in 30 countries across Asia and Africa put Indigenous Peoples and local communities with customary tenure (IPLCs) at risk of expropriation without payment of compensation. The reason this chapter only covers 30 countries is because to conduct the indicator analysis of compensation eligibility requirements for IPLCs with customary tenure, I chose to combine and cross-analyze my research on compensation procedures with the LandMark indicators on the legal security of indigenous and community tenure (www.landmarkmap.org). At the time this part of the study was conducted, LandMark did not have reliable data for 20 of the 50 countries assessed, so there are only 30 countries covered in the analysis presented in this Chapter.

The legal indicators in this Chapter examine whether compensation eligibility requirements effectively close the door on communities seeking compensation. The findings indicate that, in many of the countries assessed, there are limits on the extent to which IPLC tenure rights are statutorily recognized as compensable upon expropriation. Based on the findings from the analysis, this Chapter presents a set of recommendations for reforming laws to ensure IPLCs are granted compensation in a manner that conforms to the standards established in Section 16 of the VGGT.[192]

This Chapter is organized as follows. Section 3.2 provides a discussion of the background and context related to compensation eligibility for IPLCs. Section 3.3 examines the right of IPLCs to Compensation as established by the VGGTs and other international guidance. Section 3.4 explains the reasons why this Chapter incorporates findings from LandMark's legal indicators. Section 3.5 presents the research findings and analysis. Section 3.6 highlights additional limitations on IPLC rights to compensation that are not covered by the indicator analysis. Section 3.7 draws conclusions and recommends legal reforms for ensuring that IPLCs are entitled to compensation when their land is expropriated.

192 FAO 2012.

3.2 Background and Context Related to Compensation Eligibility Requirements

Once the decision to expropriate land is made, legal frameworks may dictate that compensation can only be granted to individual private property owners and others with statutorily recognized tenure rights. Without legal recognition, IPLCs may be precluded from submitting claims for compensation unless or until their tenure rights are registered or otherwise recognized by law.[193] As Wily points out,

> provisions for compensation at compulsory acquisition are meaningless for those who are not to be lawful owners or whose lesser interests are not due recompense [...] this most acutely affects untitled customary landholders and slum dwellers with longstanding occupancy.[194]

If expropriation and compensation procedures only grant compensation for registered tenure rights and unregistered communities with customary tenure are removed from their land without compensation, these communities may subsequently fall into poverty, endure a reduced standard of living, and potentially be subjected to landlessness, food insecurity, and other risks.[195] Legal barriers to recognition and entitlement to compensation are potentially very problematic given that, globally, up to 2.5 billon people hold land under customary tenure.[196] In Africa, for example, it is estimated that 625 million people are customary tenure holders and that 90% of rural Africa is undocumented and informally administered.[197] Due to the profound ramifications expropriation can have on IPLCs, scholars have argued the expropriation of community land may, in some cases, necessitate additional compensation for the loss of communality.[198]

---

193 L.A. Wily, 'Compulsory Acquisition as a Constitutional Matter: The Case in Africa.', *Journal of African Law*, Vol. 62, Issue 1, 2018, pp. 77-103.

194 Wily 2018.

195 M.M. Cernea 1997.

196 Oxfam, International Land Coalition & Rights and Resources Initiative, *Common Ground: Securing land rights and safeguarding the earth*, Oxfam, Oxford, 2016, p. 7.

197 Wily, 2018; F.F.K. Byamugisha, *Securing Africa's land for shared prosperity: a program to scale up reforms and investments (English)*. Africa Development Forum, World Bank Group, Washington, DC, 2013; RRI, 2015.

198 S. Stern, 'Expropriation Effects on Residential Communities', *in* B. Hoops, E.J. Marais, H. Mostert, J.A.M.A. Sluysman & L.C.A. Verstappen (Eds.), *Rethinking Expropriation Law II: Context, Criteria, and Consequences of Expropriation*, Den Haag, The Netherlands, Eleven International Publishing, 2015, pp. 359-391; M. Cernea, 'Compensation and benefit sharing: Why resettlement policies and practices must be reformed', *Water Science and Engineering*, Vo. 1, No. 1, 2008, pp. 89-120.

Historically, community land was commonly governed under customary tenure systems, which have long-standing origins in the norms and practices rooted in the community and often go back centuries.[199] Under customary systems, IPLCs historically held, used, and depended on land for food, shelter, income, traditional practices, and other basic needs.[200] However, beginning in the colonial period, governments often encroached on and claimed statutory rights to community land, including communal natural resources in forests, rangelands, wetlands, and other common properties; consequently, many community land areas were legally classified as vacant, idle, or state-owned property.[201] According to McAuslan,

> in all countries in Africa, there has been legislative intrusion into customary land law; in Tanzania this has been going on for several years, including several attempts to 'abolish' it altogether.[202]

While communities are estimated to hold and use as much 65 percent of the world's land, research shows that national-level statutes and regulations only grant communities legal rights to a fraction of this land.[203] The gap between formally recognized and customarily held land continues to be a significant source of underdevelopment, conflict, and environmental degradation.[204] As the analysis presented in this Chapter demonstrates, without secure tenure rights that are legal recognized and enforceable against government and private actors, IPLCs may be vulnerable to expropriation without compensation.

IPLCs' tenure rights may not be compensable if governments only consider IPLCs as permissive occupiers of state-owned land.[205] In many countries, there may be a broad range of possession, use, and other tenure rights attached to land that is classified by law as 'state-

199 L.A. Wily, 'Custom and commonage in Africa. Rethinking the orthodoxies', *Land Use Policy*, Vol. 25, Issue 1, 2008, pp. 43-52.

200 L.A. Wily, P. Veit, R. Smith, F. Dubertret, K. Reytar, and N. Tagliarino, 'Guidelines for Researching, Scoring and Documenting Findings on '*What National Laws Say About Indigenous & Community Land Rights.*' Methodology document from *LandMark: The Global Platform of Indigenous and Community Lands.* Available at: <www.landmarkmap.org> 2016; Wily 2008.

201 Wily 2008.

202 P. McAuslan, 'Making Law Work: Restructuring Land Relations in Africa', *Development and Change*, Vol. 29, 1998, pp. 525-552, 543.

203 F. Dubertret & L.A. Wily, 'Percent of Indigenous and Community Lands.' Data file from *LandMark: The Global Platform of Indigenous and Community Lands*; L. A. Wily, *The tragedy of public lands: The fate of the commons under global commercial pressure*, International Land Coalition, Rome, 2011; RRI, *Who Owns the World's Land? A Global Baseline of Formally Recognized Indigenous and Community Land Rights*, RRI, Washington, DC, 2015, p. 10.

204 Oxfam *et al.* 2016.

205 Lindsay *et al.* 2017

owned' or 'public property.'[206] According to Lindsay, Deininger, and Hilhorst, governments may not view customary tenure rights to public property as compensable even though such interests in land are widely considered legitimate in a social context.[207] Similarly, Terminiski states,

> An observed practice in countries of the global south is the lack of or very slight compensation received by people who have no legal right to the land they live on (such as tribals, adivasi people and several categories of illegal settlers) [...] [and] the lack of formalized rights to the land not only leads to lack of profit for local communities from its exploitation, but just as often makes it impossible to obtain compensation for loss of property.[208]

There are well-documented examples in the literature of government expropriation of IPLC tenure rights without fair compensation. For example, Banerjee and Van Eerd conducted a broad empirical study on expropriation, eviction, and resettlement practices in several countries and found that compensation was not provided to affected communities in Nigeria, Indonesia, Cambodia, China, and Sri Lanka because governments refused to recognize their tenure rights.[209] As a consequence of expropriation without compensation, many of these communities became homeless, experienced income loss, and suffered other negative impacts.[210] In Tanzania, the government evicted several thousand Maasai from the Mkomazi Game Reserve without compensation.[211] According to Wickama *et al.*,

> This eviction culminated into a prolonged legal battle between pastoralists (mostly Maasai and Pare) and the Government until 1990's when the Government prevailed. It is understood that the Government did allocate an alternative area in Handeni District (Tanga region) where the evicted pastoralists were advised to take their livestock. Very few went there.[212]

206 Lindsay *et al.* 2017; see www.landmarkmap.org.

207 Lindsay *et al.* 2017.

208 B. Termininski, 'Development-Induced Displacement and Resettlement: Theoretical Frameworks and Current Challenges', *Universtity of Geneva*, Research Paper 9/2013, Geneva, 2013, pp. 38, 86.

209 M. Van Eerd & B. Banerjee, 'Working Paper I: Evictions, Acquisition, Expropriation and Compensation: Practices and selected case studies', *United Nations Human Settlements Programme*, Nairobi, 2013, pp. 12-13.

210 Van Eerd & Banerjee 2013, pp. 12-13.

211 P.G. Veit, R. Nshala, M.O. Odhiambo & J. Manyindo, *Protected Areas and Property Rights: Democratizing Eminent Domain in East Africa*, World Resources Institute, Washington, DC, 2008, p. 14.

212 Wickama, J., Ngailo, J., Masuki, K. & Mkalimoto, D., 'Eviction of Pastoralists from Mkomazi Game Reserve in North Eastern Tanzania: Analysis of new conflicts and impact on the affected communities', *ARI-Mlingano*, Tanzania, 2005; A. Rwegasira, *Land As a Human Right: A history of Land Law and Practice in Tanzania*, Mkuki Na Nyota, Tanzania, 2012.

In Nigeria, the Lagos state government refused to grant compensation to affected communities because it considered the communities as "illegal occupiers" of the expropriated land.[213] The government stated in its project plan that it was "mindful of setting a precedent or communicating a policy whereby illegal occupiers of land without development permits have to be paid full compensation upon eviction."[214] Empirical research in Afghanistan also found that community lands are often not sufficiently protected by law. According to the World Bank's LGAF Assessment of Afghanistan,

> [A] major problem in the recognition of rural tenure rights in Afghanistan is that Afghan land laws do not protect collective ownership, very commonly used in Afghanistan [...] Particularly in the rural context, where due to the historical, tribal and ethnical linkages most of the lands are held collectively without any or only a customary documentation, according to the World Bank assessment [of relevant laws], there were weak or no real provisions to protect collectively owned lands.[215]

Furthermore, in Botswana, a report published by the World Bank found that "while the government has tended to pay handsomely for freehold land acquired by the state, the compensation offered by land boards for repossessed tribal land has been inadequate [...]"[216]

Although governments have often failed to adequately compensate IPLC when their tenure rights are expropriated, these rights are recognized by the VGGTs and international human rights instruments. These legal instruments are described in Section 3.3 of this Chapter.

3.3 The Right to Compensation as Established by the VGGTs and Other International Instruments

Section 16.1 of the VGGTs calls for states to "respect *all legitimate tenure rights*, especially vulnerable and marginalized groups, by [...] *providing just compensation in accordance with national law*" (emphasis added). The VGGTs do not explicitly define 'legitimate tenure,' but Section 5.3 of the VGGTs states that "legitimate tenure rights includ[e] legiti-

213 Amnesty International, 'At the Mercy of the Government: Violation of the Right to an Effective Remedy in Badia East, Lagos State, Nigeria', *Amnesty International*, London, 2014, p. 15.

214 Amnesty International 2014, p. 15.

215 World Bank, *Land Governance Assessment Framework Synthesis Report: Afghanistan*. World Bank Group, Washington, DC, 2016, p. 51.

216 Arid Environmental Consultancy (Pty) Ltd., *Resettlement policy framework*, World Bank Group, Washington, DC, 2008, p. 12

mate customary tenure rights that are not currently protected by law." The term 'legitimate' is commonly defined in other international instruments as including both legal legitimacy (rights recognized by law) and social legitimacy (rights that have a broad acceptance among society).[217] While states presumably have flexibility in defining in law which tenure rights are legally 'legitimate,' Sections 9 and 10 of the VGGTs call for states to respect and protect a broad range of customary and informal tenure rights. For instance, Sections 9.4-9.6 of the VGGTs states that,

> States should provide appropriate recognition and protection of indigenous peoples and other communities with customary tenure systems [...] Such recognition should take into account the land, fisheries and forests that are used exclusively by a community and those that are shared [...] where indigenous peoples and other communities with customary tenure systems have legitimate tenure rights to ancestral lands on which they live, States should recognize and protect these rights [...] States should consider adapting their policy, legal and organizational frameworks to recognize tenure systems of [IPLCs].

Based on Sections 5.3, 9, and 16.1 of the VGGTs, it can be argued that the VGGTs recognize IPLCs as a subset of 'legitimate tenure rights holders,' entitled to just compensation when their land is expropriated.

Aside from the VGGTs, several other international instruments recognize the rights of communities and other informal tenure rights holders to compensation upon compulsory acquisition. For instance, Articles 10 and 28 of the UN Declaration on the Rights of Indigenous Peoples (2007), Article 15 of ILO Convention 169 on Indigenous and Tribal Peoples (1989), and IFC Performance Standard 7 recognize the right of indigenous communities to receive compensation for the lands, territories, and resources they have traditionally owned or otherwise occupied or used.[218] Additionally, the draft World Bank Environmental and Social Framework and other policies, including IFC Performance Standard 5, require that compensation must be provided to displaced persons regardless of whether they have a legal right to the land or assets they occupy and use.[219] However,

217 Palmer *et al.* 2009, p. 8; United Nations, 'Report of the Special Rapporteur on adequate housing as a component of the right to an adequate standard of living, and on the right to non-discrimination in this context', 2013 *United Nations*, A/HRC/25/54.

218 United Nations, *Declaration on the Rights of Indigenous Peoples*, G.A. Res. 61/295, U.N. Doc. A/ RES/61/295, United Nations, 2007; ILO (International Labour Organization), *Convention No. 169, Indigenous and Tribal Peoples Convention*, ILO, 1989 ; IFC (International Finance Corporation) *Performance Standards on Environmental and Social Sustainability*, Performance Standard 7, IFC, Washington, DC, 2012.

219 World Bank 2017, pp. 54-55; IFC 2012, p. 5.

these policies only apply to finance by the World Bank, IFC, and other MDBs with compensation policies. For other types of projects financed without support from these MDBs, there is a risk that communities without legal rights will not be fairly compensated if there is no clear legal obligation to compensate community tenure rights under domestic laws.[220]

While community rights to compensation are clearly recognized by international human rights instruments, MDB policy documents, and international land governance standards, a systematic comparative analysis of country frameworks has not yet been conducted to determine whether national laws put IPLCs at risk of expropriation without compensation. This Chapter seeks to address this knowledge gap.

3.4 EXPLANATION OF WHY THIS CHAPTER INCORPORATES FINDINGS FROM LANDMARK'S LEGAL INDICATORS

To assess whether IPLCs are granted a level of tenure security sufficient to obtain compensation, findings and analyses from LandMark's ten legal indicators on the legal security of indigenous and community land were also examined.[221] At the time this part of the study was conducted, LandMark did not have reliable data for 20 of the 50 countries assessed, so there are only 30 countries covered in the analysis presented in this Chapter. The LandMark legal indicators examine the tenure security of community land by focusing on the extent to which the law upholds the land rights of IPLCs and whether these rights are protected through formalization and recognition of community-based governance. The LandMark legal indicators relate to the issue of compensation eligibility because depending on the extent to which community land is formally recognized and protected, communities may be vulnerable to expropriation without compensation (e.g., if compensation can only be obtained by formal tenure rights holders).

This Chapter examines national legal frameworks in the following 30 countries:

Table 7 List of Countries

Asia	Africa
1. Afghanistan	1. Burkina Faso
2. Bangladesh	2. Botswana

220 M.M. Cernea & H.M. Mathur, *Can Compensation Prevent Impoverishment? Reforming Resettlement through Investments and Benefit-Sharing*; Oxford University Press, New Delhi, India, 2008.

221 *LandMark* is a global online platform of indigenous and community land; L. Alden *et al.*, *Indicators of the Legal Security of Indigenous and Community Lands. Data file from LandMark: The Global Platform of Indigenous and Community Lands*, 2016. Available at: www.landmarkmap.org.

3. Cambodia
4. China
5. Hong Kong
6. India
7. Indonesia
8. Kazakhstan
9. Sri Lanka
10. Malaysia
11. Mongolia
12. Philippines
13. Taiwan
14. Thailand
15. Vietnam

3. Ethiopia
4. Ghana
5. Kenya
6. Liberia
7. Namibia
8. Nigeria
9. Rwanda
10. South Africa
11. South Sudan
12. Tanzania
13. Uganda
14. Zambia
15. Zimbabwe

This analysis focuses on compensation eligibility requirements, specifically whether customary tenure holders and users of undeveloped land are legally eligible for compensation. Furthermore, the analysis examines whether national laws preclude unregistered communities from obtaining compensation entitlements. The analysis uses a set of indicators (hereinafter "compensation eligibility indicators"). The indicators are based on the principles established in the VGGTs, particularly Sections 9 and 16 of the VGGTs as discussed above in Section 4.2.

Table 8 List of Compensation Eligibility Indicators

1. Is compensation provided for formally recognized IPLC tenure rights?
2. Is compensation provided for unregistered IPLC tenure rights?
3. Is compensation provided for formally recognized IPLC tenure rights regardless of whether the IPLCs developed or made improvements on the land?

Like in other chapters in this book, the scope of this Chapter's analysis is limited to the written law and does not cover situations in which compensation is provided to IPLCs without following national-level laws. An analysis of compensation following MDB policies (e.g., World Bank or IFC policies), compensation following voluntary land transfers (e.g., lease agreements), or compensation following other land-related processes aside from expropriation is not provided here.

It is worth emphasizing again that the law on the books does not necessarily translate to good practices by governments and acquiring bodies. Therefore, the scope of this analysis is limited. On state land in Africa and other regions, community rights are often recognized, especially when registered, but governments may wrongfully interpret laws as granting them discretion to remove unregistered communities without paying compensation.[222] If it is unclear or the government has broad discretion to determine whether expropriation

222 Wily 2018.

procedures apply, government and non-government expropriating entities may try to avoid compensation obligations by invoking the justification that these landholders are informally occupying state-owned land and are therefore not eligible for compensation.[223] In parts of Africa and other regions where all land is legally owned or 'held in trust for the people' by governments, these governments may wrongfully interpret laws as enabling them to evict informal occupants or unrecognized customary tenure holders living on state-owned land without paying compensation.[224] On the other hand, in some cases, governments may decide to grant compensation to communities even if the law does not formally recognize their rights. Governments may also regulate, restrict, or deprive people of their property rights using regulatory police powers without actually expropriating property and paying compensation.[225] Such government actions are beyond the scope of this analysis.

3.5 RESEARCH FINDINGS AND ANALYSIS

This Section explains the findings from the compensation eligibility indicator analysis. First, this Section discusses whether the 30 countries have national laws that grant compensation for formally recognized tenure rights. Second, this Section provides an explanation of whether registration is required for IPLCs to receive compensation in the 30 countries. Third, this Section discusses whether the national laws of these countries require communities to develop or make improvements on their land in order to be eligible for compensation.

3.5.1 Compensation for Formally Recognized Tenure Rights Held by IPLCs[226]

As discussed above, IPLC rights to compensation are recognized in Sections 9 and 16 of the VGGTs and other international instruments, such as the UN Declaration on the Rights of Indigenous Peoples. However, this Section's analysis focuses on whether national legal frameworks provide compensation for formally recognized community tenure rights when

223 Tagliarino *et al.* 2018; Tagliarino 2016.

224 Wily 2018.

225 Marais 2015, pp. 2983-3031.

226 This Section examines whether national statutory and regulatory laws recognize the rights of communities to obtain expropriation. This chapter does not address whether laws ensure that compensation is allocated to community members themselves as opposed to paramount chiefs or other intermediaries. Further research is needed on this issue of "elite capture" of compensation. See, for instance, the expropriation case of the Lekki Free Trade Zone in Lagos, Nigeria, where research suggests possible corruption and elite capture of community compensation by intermediaries. N.K., Tagliarino *et al.*, 'Compensation for Expropriated Community Farmland in Nigeria: An In-Depth Analysis of the Laws and Practices Related to Land Expropriation for the Lekki Free Trade Zone in Lagos', *Land*, Vol. 7, Issue 1, 2018, pp. 29-30.

community land is acquired in a compulsory manner. Since payment of compensation is usually conditional on showing a legally recognized right to land,[227] national-level legal frameworks were assessed, using the LandMark legal indicators, to determine whether laws recognize the land rights of IPLCs to such an extent that the IPLCs qualify for compensation. For instance, if national laws only grant communities rights to use land on a temporary basis, but the national expropriation laws establish that compensation is only payable to freeholders, such laws do not ensure that communities will be legally eligible to compensation upon expropriation.

By analyzing compensation provisions together with legal frameworks on community tenure, 22 of the 30 countries assessed[228] were found to have laws that grant compensation to communities with formally recognized tenure rights. In most of these 22 countries, national expropriation laws establish that any person with a recognized tenure right or interest in land is eligible to a submit claim for compensation. Therefore, the key question is whether IPLCs have tenure rights that are recognized by national laws. In these 22 countries, there is a broad range of formally recognized tenure rights held by IPLCs, ranging from ownership to temporary use rights. Green 'yes' scores were only designated if national land laws grant communities legally recognized rights to land, and those rights are legally eligible for compensation upon expropriation. In other countries, such as Vietnam, national expropriation laws stipulate that compensation may be provided for use rights, so green 'yes' scores were provided if land laws grant communities rights to use land. In countries for which World Bank Land Governance Assessment Framework (LGAF) data is available, findings from the indicators analysis were also cross-examined with LGAF data.

In five of these 22 countries (Malaysia, South Sudan, Taiwan, Philippines, and China), national laws explicitly provide that communities with customary tenure rights are entitled to compensation. For example, Article 42 of China's Property Rights Law (2007) provides "for expropriation of collectively-owned land, such fees shall be as compensations for the land expropriated."[229] Such explicit legal provisions provide communities with a degree of certainty that they will be eligible for compensation if the government decides to expropriate its property.

---

227 Lindsay *et al.* 2017.

228 Afghanistan, Botswana, Burkina Faso, China, Ethiopia, Ghana, India, Indonesia, Kenya, Liberia, Malaysia, Namibia, Nigeria, Philippines, South Africa, South Sudan, Taiwan, Tanzania, Uganda, Vietnam, Zambia, Zimbabwe.

229 Government of China 2007, Article 42.

Cambodia received a 'partial' score because the laws provide for payment of compensation to indigenous landholders. However, non-indigenous communities are not entitled to compensation because they are only granted legal rights to use traditional forests, and payment of compensation is conditional on proving ownership.[230]

Seven of the 30 countries assessed (Bangladesh, Hong Kong, Kazakhstan, Mongolia, Rwanda, Sri Lanka, and Thailand) have national laws that do not provide communities with a right to compensation upon expropriation. In Thailand and Mongolia, for example, communities are only granted rights to use state-owned property for limited periods of time, and the government retains broad discretion to revoke these use rights without compensation.[231] Likewise, Kazakhstan's national laws do not formally recognize the rights of local communities.[232] In practice, Kazakh communities sometimes manage municipal pastures, but communities are not granted explicit legal rights to these state-owned lands.[233] Hong Kong's Basic Law (1990) vaguely recognizes the "traditional rights and interests" of Indigenous inhabitants in the Northern Territory; however, the Land Resumption Ordinance (1998) only provides compensation to registered property owners of land and there is no clear legal process by which communities can obtain ownership rights to land.[234] In Bangladesh and Sri Lanka, national-level laws do not explicitly recognize the tenure rights of IPLCs, and expropriation laws do not grant communities a right to receive compensation upon expropriation.

230 Government of Cambodia, Law on Land, 2001, Art. 25; Government of Cambodia, Law on Forestry, 2002, Art. 42; Government of Cambodia, Law on Expropriation, 2012, Art. 16 and 22.

231 See legal indicator analyses of Thailand and Mongolia at: www.landmarkmap.org; Government of Mongolia, Law on Land (2002), Art. 54; Government of Thailand, Regulation of the Prime Minister's Office on the Issuance of Community Land Title Deeds (2011).

232 See Appendix.

233 RRI 2015.

234 Hong Kong's national laws do not provide a clear process by which Indigenous inhabitants can obtain formally recognized ownership rights to their land; Government of Hong Kong, Basic Law of the Hong Kong Special Administrative Region of the People's Republic of China Government of Hong Kong (1990); Land Resumption Ordinance (1998), Section 2 and 8.

Figure 4 Compensation for Formally Recognized Tenure Rights

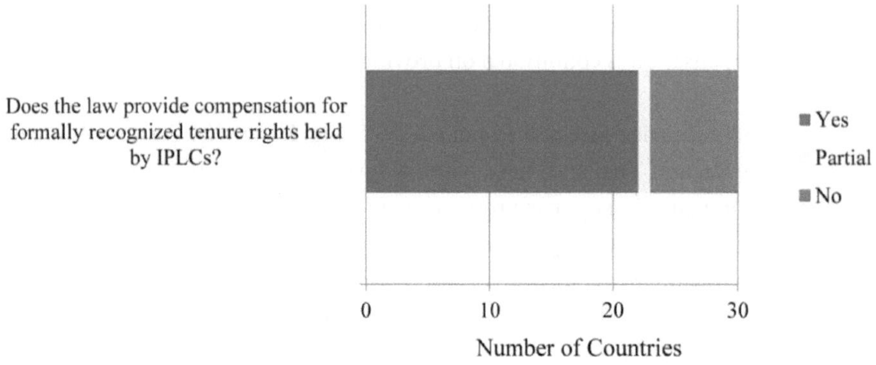

3.5.2 *Compensation for Unregistered IPLC Tenure Rights*

As discussed in Section 2, the VGGTs call for the recognition and protection of legitimate tenure rights, whether formally recorded or not.[235] Simply because an expropriation law grants compensation for recognized customary tenure rights does not necessarily mean all communities will be eligible for compensation upon expropriation. In documented cases of expropriation and eviction in Cambodia, for example, there are regulations in respect of compensation but, according to research published by Ingalls *et. al* in 2018,

> Smallholder farmers with ownership titles tend to receive better compensation than others who have possession certificates (soft titles) and a fortiori better than farmers who do not have any documentation covering the land they occupy.[236]

In some countries, there are registration requirements and other procedures that communities must satisfy in order to achieve formal recognition and obtain compensation.[237] To determine which countries have these requirements, this Section's analysis focuses on whether legal processes for registering community rights are mandatory or voluntary, and whether communities can still obtain compensation even when their land rights are not formally registered.

235 FAO, 2012, Sections 3.1 and 5.3.

236 Ingalls *et al.* 2018, p. 94.

237 Notess, L., Veit, P.G., Monterroso, I., Andiko, Sulle, E., Larson, A.M., Gindroz, A.S., Quaedvleig, J., Williams, A., *Scrambling for Land Rights: Reducing Inequity Between Communities and Companies*, World Resources Institute, Washington, DC, 2018.

Empirical research indicates that registration processes can often be difficult to access, time-consuming, and expensive for communities.[238] Registration requirements often stipulate that communities must demarcate clear boundaries around their land, establish clear governance structures, obtain approval from land surveyors and other officials, and fulfill other cumbersome tasks.[239] In Peru, for example, indigenous forest communities must clear 27 bureaucratic hurdles to achieve official recognition and formal land titles; this process can take more than a decade.[240] Registration may also inhibit effective governance of community land by causing the evaporation of customary tenure systems, if, for example, registration requirements impose an obligation on communities to establish new boundaries, decision-making processes, and governance structures that were not previously existent under the customary tenure system. Registering the boundaries of all lands held by the community, and allowing the community to define individual rights within its land boundary, can be much more cost-effective than registering individual rights within a community.[241]

If registration is required to obtain compensation, many of the world's communities are at risk of not receiving compensation upon expropriation. For example, in India, where registration is required to receive compensation for customary forest rights, the process for registering customary forestlands under the Forest Rights Act (2006) has been riddled with delays.[242] As of 2015, it was estimated that only a fraction of community forest land was formally registered in India.[243] Yet approximately 40 million hectares of forestland, an area in which approximately 150 million people (including 90 million tribal people) reside, remain eligible for registration under the Forest Rights Act.[244] According to the World Bank Land Governance Assessment (LGAF) study of India, "missing, inaccurate, and outdated records [...] make it difficult to provide compensation."[245]

---

238 Notess *et al.* 2018.
239 Notess *et al.* 2018.
240 Rainforest Foundation US, 'Getting a Land Title in Peru is Almost Impossible for Indigenous Communities', *Rainforest Foundation US*, 2015, Available at: www.rainforestfoundation.org/landtitlesperu/.
241 K. Deininger, *Land policies for growth and poverty reduction*, The World Bank, Washington, DC; Oxford University Press, Oxford, 2003.
242 Times of India, 'Explaining delay in implementing forest rights in Mahan: Tribals', *Times of India*, New Delhi, 2013. Available at: http://timesofindia.indiatimes.com/city/bhopal/Explain-delay-in-implementing-forests-rights-in-Mahan-Tribals/articleshow/21815227.cms.
243 RRI, Potential for Recognition of Community Forest Resource Rights Under India's Forest Rights Act, Washington, DC, RRI, 2015. Available at: http://rightsandresources.org/wp-content/uploads/Community-Forest_RR_A4Final_web1.pdf.
244 RRI 2015.
245 World Bank, *Land Governance Assessment National Synthesis Report: India*, World Bank, Washington, DC, 2016.

In Ethiopia, where formal registration is required to achieve legal recognition and compensation upon expropriation,[246] unrecorded rights, such as the rights to grazing, access, and gathering forest products are usually not compensated.[247] Estimates made by Dubertret and Wily in 2015 revealed that over 66 percent of community lands are not formally recognized.[248] This suggests that most of Ethiopia's community land remains vulnerable to expropriation without compensation. In 2010, expropriation of Ethiopia's Gambella farmland displaced affected communities without compensation because they lacked formal certificates to their land.[249] Likewise, in Ghana, where compensation is limited to registered or documented rights, the law has, in some cases, allowed for non-community members with formal, written land leases granted by traditional authorities, to become eligible for compensation, while undocumented community members who actually lived on expropriated land were ineligible for compensation.[250]

Figure 5 Compensation Provided for Unregistered IPLC Tenure Rights

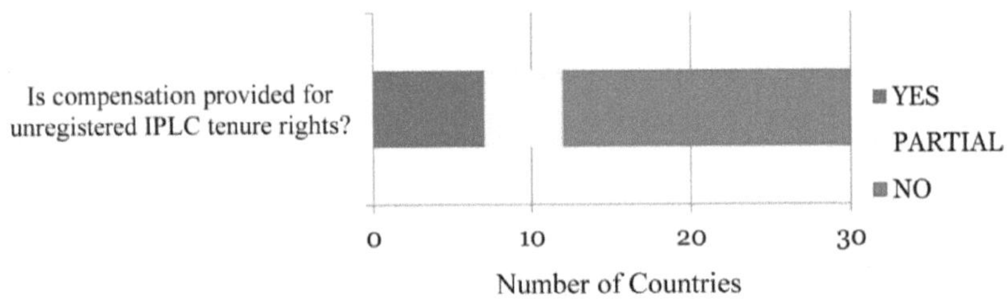

The legal analysis indicates that only seven of the 30 countries assessed (Kenya, Philippines, South Sudan, Tanzania, Uganda, South Africa, and Zambia) have laws that grant communities the right to obtain compensation regardless of whether their land rights are formally registered or not. Tanzania's Land Act (1999), for instance, pays "full, fair and prompt" compensation to any person whose right of occupancy or recognized long-standing

246 Ethiopian communities must show a "holding certificate" which is defined as a certificate of title issued by a competent authority as proof of rural land use right; Government of Ethiopia, *Rural Land Administration and Land Use Proclamation*, 2005, Sections 2(14) and 6(1).

247 World Bank, *Land Governance Assessment Synthesis Report: Ethiopia*, World Bank, Washington, DC, 2016, p. 82.

248 F. Dubertret and L. Alden Wily, 'Percent of Indigenous and Community Lands'. Data file from: *LandMark: The Global Platform of Indigenous and Community Lands*, 2015.

249 D. Vhughen & A. Gebru, 'Large-Scale Acquisitions of Land in Ethiopia', *Focus on Land in Africa* (Brief), 2013.

250 W.O. Larbi, A. Antwi & P. Olomolaiye, 'Compulsory land acquisition in Ghana: Policy and praxis', *Land Use Policy*, Vol. 21, 2004, pp. 115-127.

occupation or customary use of land is revoked.[251] It is not obligatory for customary landholders to register their village lands to receive compensation.[252]

In South Sudan, the right to compensation is granted regardless of registration; compensation is guaranteed for any person customarily occupying expropriated land.[253] Under South Sudan's Land Act (2009), "rights of ownership and derivative rights to land may be proven by any other practices recognized by communities in Southern Sudan in conformity to equity, ethics, and public order."[254] According to Kenya's Constitution and Community Land Act 2016, unregistered community lands are entitled to compensation.[255] The 2016 Community Land Act in Kenya recognizes the right to compensation for community land based on customary occupation.[256] However, the actual payment of compensation is withheld until the process of adjudication, survey, and registration of community land boundaries is complete.[257] When the process is complete, compensation is awarded to the appropriate community. In these seven countries, IPLC legal rights to compensation are clearly provided; however, further research is needed to investigate the extent to which these rights are enforced in practice.

Five of the 30 countries (Afghanistan, Burkina Faso, India, Liberia, and Vietnam) received a 'partial' score for this indicator because their national laws contain provisions indicating that *some* communities may be afforded compensation even without obtaining formally registered land rights. In Liberia, for example, the Community Forest Rights Law, 2009 provides that "to be registered as customary land, it is not necessary for the land to have been registered under statutory entitlements," but the law only recognizes customary rights to forest lands, and not pastures and other types of land customarily held by communities.[258] At the time this study was conducted, Liberia was in the process of passing a Land Rights Bill designed to protect customary land rights to some extent. However, based on the laws

251 Government of Tanzania, *Land Act*, 1999, Sec. 3(g)).

252 L.A. Wily, *Community-based land tenure management: Questions and answers about Tanzania's New Village Land Act, 1999*, International Institute for Environment and Development, 2003, Issue Paper no. 120. Available at: http://pubs.iied.org/pdfs/9295IIED.pdf.

253 Dubertret and Wily 2015; Government of South Sudan, *Land Act*, 2009, Section 75(3).

254 Government of South Sudan 2009, Section 39(3).

255 Government of Kenya, *Constitution of Kenya*, 2010, Articles 40, 63; L.A. Wily, 2016, 'The road to land titling: Kenya finally enacts new laws', *Thompson Reuters Foundation News*, 2016. Available at: http://news.trust.org/item/20160902102932-xsime/.

256 L.A. Wily, 'The Community Land Act in Kenya: Opportunities and Challenges for Communities', *Land*, Vol. 7, Issue 12, 2018, p. 19; Government of Kenya, *Community Land Act*, 2016, Section 6(2)-6(3).

257 Wily 2018, p. 19.

258 Government of Liberia, *An Act to Establish Community Rights Law of 2008 with Respect to Forest Lands*, 2008, Sec. 1.3.

in effect at the time of the study, it was unclear whether communities in pastures and other non-forest land areas are entitled to compensation without registration.[259]

Eighteen of the 30 countries assessed[260] do not have laws that provide compensation for formally recognized IPLC tenure rights regardless of whether those rights are registered. Unless and until their tenure rights are registered, communities in these 18 countries remain vulnerable to expropriation without compensation.

3.5.3 *Compensation for Formally Recognized IPLC Tenure Rights Regardless of Whether the Land Is Developed, Cultivated, or Has Improvements*

Section 9.7 of the VGGTs provides that,

> States should, in drafting tenure policies and laws, take into account the social, cultural, spiritual, economic and environmental values of land [...] held under tenure systems of indigenous peoples and other communities with customary tenure systems.

This provision suggests that, in order for states to adopt the VGGTs, they must not only base compensation on the fair market value of crops, buildings, and other improvements (i.e., attached and unattached assets on the land), but also compensate for undeveloped or uncultivated lands traditionally held by communities with customary tenure. Across Asia and Africa, there are millions of hectares of grasslands, woodlands, wetlands, deserts, pastures, and other undeveloped commons, which communities depend on and use for growing crops, grazing livestock, hunting animals, and other traditional practices (e.g., ancestral burial grounds).[261] Without statutorily recognized rights to compensation that can be granted regardless of whether the land is developed or cultivated, communities who customarily hold and use undeveloped land areas may be not eligible for compensation when these areas are expropriated.

---

259 Government of Liberia, *Draft Land Rights Act*, 2013 (pending); H. Karmo, 'Land Rights Act Suffers Setback at Liberian Legislature', *Font Page Africa*, 2017.

260 Bangladesh, Botswana, Cambodia, China, Ethiopia, Ghana, Hong Kong, Indonesia, Kazakhstan, Malaysia, Mongolia, Namibia, Nigeria, Rwanda, Sri Lanka, Taiwan, Thailand, & Zimbabwe.

261 Wily, 2011.

Figure 6 Compensation for IPLC Tenure Rights Regardless of Improvements

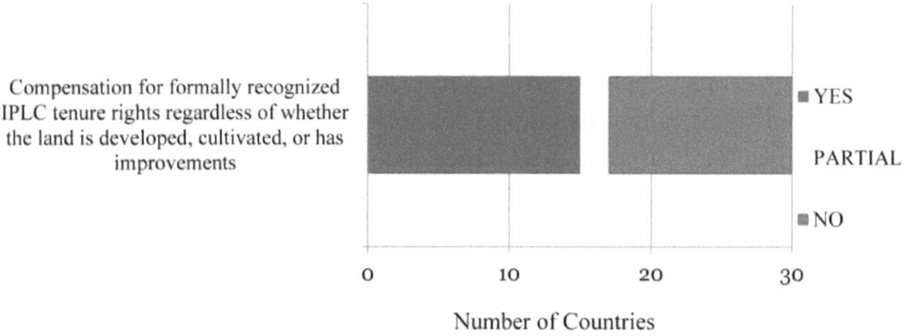

Fifteen of the 30 countries[262] grant compensation for community land regardless of whether that land is developed, cultivated, or has improvements. These countries have compensation provisions that broadly provide for compensation based on the value of the land itself, as opposed to the land's improvements (i.e., the land's attached and unattached assets, including crops and buildings).

Zimbabwe and Tanzania received 'partial' scores because their national laws suggest compensation may, at least in some cases, be limited to improved or developed land.[263] For example, the Tanzanian government is only required to pay compensation for land not classified as "vacant." Tanzania's law states, regardless whether such land is in an urban area or in a rural area, any compensation awarded shall be limited to the value of the unexhausted improvements of the land.[264] Agricultural and pastoral lands are not considered vacant, but must be in "good estate management" to be eligible for compensation.[265]

262 Afghanistan, Botswana, Burkina Faso, Ghana, India, Indonesia, Kenya, Liberia, Malaysia, Philippines, South Africa, South Sudan, Taiwan, Uganda & Vietnam.

263 Article 72 of the Constitution of Zimbabwe (2013) states: "where agricultural land…is required for a public purpose…no compensation is payable in respect of its acquisition, except for improvements." However, Section 12 of the Communal Land Act (1983) and Section 20 of the Land Acquisition Act (1992) indicate that compensation is not limited to the value of the improvements when non-agricultural community land is expropriated. Government of Zimbabwe, *Constitution of Zimbabwe*, 2013; Government of Zimbabwe, *Communal Land Act Ch. 20:04 (amended 2002)*, 1983; Government of Zimbabwe, *Land Acquisition Act, Ch. 20:10*, 1992.

264 Government of Tanzania, *Land Acquisition Act (Act No. 47 of 1967)*, 1967, Secs. 12(1)-(2); *see, generally* P. Veit *et al.* 2008.

265 Government of Tanzania 1967, Sec. 12(5)(b); P. Veit *et al.* 2008.

In contrast, 13 of the 30 countries assessed[266] have laws that do not provide compensation for IPLC tenure rights regardless of whether their land is developed, cultivated, or has improvement. For example, Cambodia, China, Ethiopia, Namibia, Nigeria, and Zimbabwe have laws that require communities to cultivate, develop, or improve the land to receive compensation.[267] For example, Nigeria's Land Use Act, 1978 (CAP 202) provides that customary land rights cannot be granted for areas of land in excess of 500 hectares if granted for agricultural purposes, or 5,000 hectares if granted for grazing purposes, except with the consent of the Governor.[268] Under this provision, communities must graze the land or conduct agricultural activities to qualify for a formal land right, and thus be entitled to compensation for expropriation. Likewise, in Namibia, recognized customary rights are only granted for farming and residential units, and compensation is limited to improvements made on the land.[269] In China, compensation is limited to agricultural outputs (yields) and land-attached assets.[270] A survey of Chinese farmers affected by expropriations found that farmers often did not receive sufficient compensation that was calculated in a consistent manner.[271]

3.6 Additional Limitations on IPLC Rights to Compensation

The review of national-level legal frameworks revealed additional insights regarding ILPC tenure rights that could not adequately be captured using the legal indicator method, but are nonetheless worth discussing. This Section first examines the legal definition of 'community land,' and then whether the national-level legal frameworks establish time requirements, which must be satisfied for communities to receive compensation.

3.6.1 *Legal Definition of 'Community Land'*

One issue that became apparent when examining the legal frameworks of the 30 countries is a lack of clear definitions of public, private, and communal land. Section 8.3 of the VGGTs states that,

266 Bangladesh, Cambodia, China, Ethiopia, Hong Kong, Kazakhstan, Mongolia, Namibia, Nigeria, Rwanda, Sri Lanka, Thailand, Zambia.

267 See Appendix.

268 Government of Nigeria, *Land Use Act*, Government of Nigeria, Abuja, 1990, Sec. 6(2).

269 Government of Namibia, *Communal Land Reform Act*, 2002, Sections 40 and 42.

270 Government of China. *Law on Land Administration*, 1986 (amended 2004), Art. 47.

271 Keliang, *et al.* 2006.

> Noting that there are publicly-owned land, fisheries and forests that are collectively used and managed (in some national contexts referred to as commons), States should, where applicable, recognize and protect such publicly-owned land, fisheries and forests and their related systems of collective use and management.[272]

However, the absence of a clear, definitional distinction between public and community land often means that, in many countries, the state can, at its own convenience, claim certain types of community land as state, public, and national property.[273] Therefore, how national laws define public, private, and communal properties directly affects whether communities will be entitled to compensation upon expropriation.

If governments claim ownership or control over all forest reserves or protected areas, communities living in these areas may be ineligible for compensation upon eviction. When laws only recognize community rights to certain land areas (e.g., forest lands), there is a risk that communities living outside these areas will not be compensated when their land is expropriated. For example, in India, national laws only recognize IPLC compensation rights to forest lands, which account for only around 23% of the country's land area.[274] Registration of common properties outside of forests remains weak, according to the World Bank's Land Governance Assessment study of India.[275] Even in parts of India where sub-national laws recognize community rights to non-forest commons, such rights are often not recorded.[276]

According to Almeida,

> Depending on how Indigenous Peoples and local communities are legally defined, the law may discriminate against particular groups by imposing requirements of time (the need to exist as a community prior to a particular date) or size (the need to have a particular number of members), among other arbitrary constraints.[277]

---

272 FAO 2012, Section 8.3.

273 L. Wily, *The Tragedy of Public Lands: The Fate of Commons Under Global Commercial Pressure*; CIRAD and International Land Coalition, Rome, Italy, 2011.

274 Government of India, National Ministry of Environment and Forests, State of the Environment Report, 2009.

275 World Bank, *Land Governance Assessment National Synthesis Report: India*, World Bank, Washington, DC, 2016.

276 World Bank, *Land Governance Assessment National Synthesis Report: India*, World Bank, Washington, DC, 2016.

277 Almeida, *Legislative Pathways for Securing Community-Based Property Rights*, Rights and Resources Initiative (RRI), Washington, DC, 2017, p. 3.

Communities living on land that is statutorily classified as 'public property' or 'state land' may not always be entitled to compensation if expropriation and compensation procedures only apply when privately held land is acquired for a public purpose. Wily highlights that, when the state claims ownership rights over lands and resources, even acknowledged derivative rights can be seriously undermined at compulsory acquisition on grounds that "the state owns all land or all resources anyway."[278] On land that is classified as 'stated-owned' or 'public,' there is a risk that governments may lease, designate, or otherwise repurpose such land for a range of private purposes without paying compensation to communities informally occupying and using such land. In South Sudan, for example, when state land is leased, the procedures applicable to compensation must be established in lease agreements; the compensation procedures established in the Land Act do not apply in such cases.[279] Under such circumstances, communities may be particularly vulnerable to losing their land without being fully compensated, since the Land Act does not establish what types of compensation benefits must be provided by these lease agreements.[280]

In three of the countries assessed (China, Philippines, and Taiwan), community land is defined more broadly. For example, China's Property Law (2007) broadly defines collectively owned property as "lands, forests, mountains, grasslands, unclaimed land and beaches owned collectively."[281] The Philippines and Taiwan also have laws that define community land broadly. Under Taiwan's Indigenous Peoples Basic Act (2005), "Indigenous Peoples Regions" is defined as "all areas within which Indigenous Peoples traditionally live."[282] The Philippines' Indigenous Peoples Rights Act, 1997 defines Indigenous Ancestral Domains as including "forests, pasture, residential, agricultural, and other lands individually owned whether alienable and disposable or otherwise, hunting grounds, burial grounds, worship areas, bodies of water."[283]

In the other countries assessed, the more restrictive legal definitions of 'community land' puts communities at risk of encroachment by governments that may interpret the law as granting them authority to designate or classify communal land areas as 'state-owned' or 'public' land. For example, in Botswana, South Sudan, Uganda, and Rwanda, among other countries, governments claim exclusive ownership over certain land areas (e.g., forests, wetlands) for conservation purposes, such as the establishment of protected areas.[284] The

278 Wily, 2018, p. 5.
279 Government of South Sudan, *Land Act*, 2009, Section 27(8).
280 Government of South Sudan, *Land Act*, 2009, Section 27(8).
281 Government of China, *Property Rights Law*, 2007, Article 58.
282 Government of Taiwan, *Indigenous People's Basic Law*, 2005, Article 2(3).
283 Government of the Philippines, *Indigenous Peoples' Rights Act*, 1997, Article 3.
284 *See* LandMark's indicators of the legal security of indigenous and community lands, indicators 8 and 10. Available at: www.landmarkmap.org.

laws in these countries seem to ignore the fact that many of these communities have customarily held and used land and natural resources in forests and protected areas for centuries. It has been demonstrated in sample studies that conservation objectives could be more effectively achieved if communities were granted secure rights to manage and protect forests and other conservation areas. A recent study of 80 forest areas in ten countries in South Asia, East Africa, and Latin America shows that community-owned and managed-forests for which legal rights were recognized tended to show lower carbon emissions and deforestation.[285] Robinson *et al.* conducted a meta-study of 118 cases of different forest rights, including for community forests, derived from 150 publications, and concluded that weak community rights are "tightly linked" to high deforestation while strong rights are linked to low deforestation.[286] Instead of classifying certain land areas as exclusively state or public land, states should adopt laws that recognize rights to all lands customarily held and used by communities, and require that communities conserve and manage protected areas in order to fulfill international conservation and climate change mitigation/adaptation objectives.

3.6.2 *Time Requirements*

In Afghanistan, India, and Namibia, communities must prove they have held and used the expropriated land for a specified period of time in order to qualify for compensation. Under India's Right to Fair Compensation and Transparency in Land Acquisition, Rehabilitation and Resettlement Act, 2013, affected families must prove their "primary source of livelihood for three years prior to the acquisition of the land is dependent on forests or water bodies [...] [and] affected due to acquisition of land."[287] Under India's Forest Rights Act, 2006, to qualify for formal recognized community forest rights and receive compensation for forest rights lost due to compulsory acquisition, forest communities must prove they "primarily resided in and [depended] on the forest or forest land for bona fide livelihoods needs" for at least three generations prior to December 13, 2005.[288]

Such legal procedures for proving how long community ancestors have held a particular tract of land may be ineffective since it is difficult to ascertain the moment of a community's

285 C. Stevens, R. Winterbottom, J. Springer & K. Reytar, *Securing Rights, Combating Climate Change*, World Resources Institute and Rights and Resources Initiative, Washington, DC, 2014, p. 3.

286 B.E. Robinson, M.B. Holland & L. Naughton-Treves, 'Does secure land tenure save forests? A meta-analysis of the relationship between land tenure and tropical deforestation', *Global Environmental Change*, Vol. 29, 2014, pp. 281-293.

287 Government of India, The Right to Fair Compensation and Transparency in Land Acquisition, Rehabilitation and Resettlement Act, 2013, Section 3(c)(iv).

288 Government of India, The Scheduled Tribes and Other Traditional Forest Dwellers (Recognition of Forest Rights) Act, 2006, Section 2(o).

origin. For instance, India's Forest Rights Act, 2006 provides that "other traditional forest dwellers" must prove they have resided in and depended on the land for at least three generations prior to December 13, 2005, but the Forest Rights Act and its implementing regulations do not clearly define or specify what constitutes a 'generation' or what counts as proof of "depend[ing]" on the land.[289] Setting arbitrary time requirements may effectively exclude communities with legitimate claims to land from obtaining compensation upon expropriation.

Instead, the determination of whether a particular community should be entitled to compensation should be based on whether that community has, in good faith, customarily occupied, used, or depended on the expropriated land. If the community submits a claim for compensation and has legitimately used and depended on the expropriated land for some time, then communities should not also have to prove they have used the land for a minimum period of time. An appropriate alternative to establishing a rigid time restriction is to oblige governments to survey affected land and consult affected persons to ascertain whether tenure rights are legitimate and eligible for compensation.

3.7 Suggested Avenues for Lawmakers to Pursue

This Chapter aims to establish a benchmark for progress to assist civil society organizations, NGOs, policymakers, advocates, affected populations, investors, and other stakeholders in measuring national progress toward adopting VGGTs on compensation for IPLC tenure rights. However, it is worth reiterating that the law on the books is often far from the full picture of what is happening on the ground. In South Sudan, Uganda, and other countries that recognize customary tenure without registration and requirements to cultivate or development land, communities remain vulnerable to encroachments by government and private actors who operate with impunity. Strong legal rights to compensation are necessary but insufficient to ensure communities are compensated. Governments must also respect and enforce IPLC rights to compensation.

When looking at the wording of the laws in these 30 countries, it is evident there are broad limitations on community rights to obtain compensation when their lands are expropriated in many of the countries assessed. These legal hurdles must be addressed if national laws are to adopt the VGGTs, which call for states to ensure that compensation for the legitimate tenure rights of IPLCs is provided.

289 Government of India, 2006, Section 2(o).

This Section provides several recommended approaches for countries that received 'no' scores for the indicators. These recommendations can help ensure compliance with the VGGTs and compensation for IPLCs in the event their lands are expropriated.

1. To conform to the VGGTs, states must protect and respect the legitimate tenure rights of IPLCs whether formally recorded or not.[290] Laws should be designed to grant compensation for unregistered IPLC tenure rights. Although the term 'legitimate' is left undefined in the VGGTs, this term is defined in other international instruments as including both *legal* legitimacy (rights recognized by law) and *social* legitimacy (rights that have a broad acceptance among society).[291] For this reason, states should initiate flexible systems that look beyond registered property rights when determining who is entitled to compensation.

2. In order for governments to adequately and effectively assess the 'social legitimacy' of tenure rights held by IPLCs, they should survey the affected land and conduct in-person consultations and negotiations with affected communities. Establishing legal requirements to identify and consult affected communities prior to expropriation would help bring states into conformity with Section 16.3 of the VGGTs, which calls for transparency and participation in expropriation processes. Based on the information gathered through these consultations and negotiations, compensation may be agreed upon on a case-by-case basis. This is an effective alternative to requiring that affected persons show titles, certificates, and other legal documents to prove they are entitled to compensation.

3. Governments should consider adopting the legal provisions established in the laws of the Philippines, South Sudan, Tanzania, Uganda, and Zambia, which formally recognize community land rights regardless of whether those rights are registered. Registration processes in many developing countries are often slow, costly, and ineffective at capturing the full range of legitimate tenure rights attached to land parcels.[292] Showing registered titles and other formal documents may be one way to prove an affected landholder is entitled to compensation, but it should not be the *only* way. In these countries, customary tenure rights are formally and automatically recognized through customary occupation and use of the land by the community.

290 FAO 2012, Sections 3.1 & 5.3.
291 Palmer *et al.* 2009.
292 Notess *et al.* 2018.

4. National laws should ensure compensation is provided for IPLC tenure rights regardless of whether their lands are developed, cultivated, or improved. As previously discussed, Sections 9 and 18 of the VGGTs call for the valuation of land to reflect spiritual, cultural, and other non-market values. In order to conserve and protect their environments and common properties, such as rangelands, forests, pastures, and wetlands, communities may decide to deliberately leave such areas undeveloped and uncultivated. Since these communities serve important conservation purposes, they should not be penalized (by being ineligible for compensation) just because they conserved their environments rather than developed them. In many parts of Asia and Africa, communities use and depend on undeveloped commons for grazing, hunting, burying ancestors, and traditional practices.[293] Community tenure rights to these areas should be considered legitimate, even in communal land areas that are not cultivated or developed. Instead of basing eligibility on whether the community developed or improved the land, the determination of whether a particular community should be entitled to compensation should be based on whether that community has, in good faith, customarily occupied and used the expropriated land and common property resources.

5. Lastly, states should recognize how restrictive community land definitions and time requirements may prevent communities with legitimate claims to land and resources from obtaining compensation upon expropriation. Again, good faith occupation and use by the community should be the benchmark on which eligibility for compensation is assessed. Compensation eligibility requirements should not shut the door on communities who have traditionally occupied and used land and resources in good faith, otherwise, these requirements may continue to put communities at significant risk of impoverishment, landlessness, food insecurity, and other negative outcomes commonly associated with expropriation without compensation.

293 Wily 2008.

4 Compensation Valuation Procedures

4.1 Summary and Roadmap

The challenges associated with determining what is 'fair' compensation for expropriated land have been extensively discussed and debated among scholars, practitioners, policymakers, and the public. However, to date, a comprehensive study considering whether national-level compensation procedures established by law comply with international standards on compensation valuation has not yet been conducted. This Chapter aims to bridge this gap by serving as a reference point and informing fair compensation debates among scholars, practitioners, and policymakers. It examines national-level legal provisions on compensation in the 50 countries against a set of legal indicators that are based on international standards on the valuation of compensation. The legal indicators focus on the substantive and procedural requirements pertaining to the valuation of compensation. The indicators ask whether laws require assessors to account for various land values when calculating compensation, and whether there are legal processes in place that allow affected persons to negotiate compensation amounts, receive prompt payments, and hold governments accountable by appealing compensation decisions in courts or before tribunals. Based on the findings from the legal indicator analysis, this Chapter presents a set of recommendations for reforming compensation procedures to bring them into conformity with international standards.

This Chapter is organized as follows. Section 4.2 provides some background and context related to compensation valuation procedures. Section 4.3 highlights the VGGTs on Compensation valuation and the indicators used to assess the national legal frameworks of the 50 countries. Section 4.4 discusses the findings from the review of the 50 countries' laws. Section 4.5 suggests various approaches to reforming compensation procedures so that they comply with international standards

4.2 Background and Context Related to Compensation Valuation Procedures

Even when expropriation is used for genuine public purposes, monetary compensation for expropriated land has consistently proven to be insufficient in ensuring the livelihood reconstruction and long-term socioeconomic stability of affected communities.[294] Empirical studies conducted in a broad range of countries indicate that insufficient compensation often subjects affected landholders to impoverishment following expropriation.[295] Banerjee and Van Eerd found that, in Cambodia, Indonesia, Nigeria, Sri Lanka, and the Philippines, the compensation and resettlement assistance provided to affected populations was not enough to cover their losses, allow them to purchase alternative land, and sustain an adequate standard of living after their land was expropriated.[296] In China, a survey of 476 expropriation cases conducted by Keliang and others revealed that 65.5 percent of affected farmers were dissatisfied with the amount of compensation allotted.[297] The World Bank's LGAF found that in many cases, the affected populations in countries such as Afghanistan, Brazil, Ethiopia, South Africa, South Sudan, Tanzania were not granted sufficient compensation for expropriated land.[298] In Nigeria, for example, the LGAF study found,

> A large number of acquisitions occurs without prompt and adequate compensation, thus leaving those losing land worse off, with no mechanism for independent appeal even though the land is often not utilized for a public purpose.[299]

The recurring problem of insufficient compensation begs the question of what can be done to diminish the impoverishment risks associated with expropriation and forced displacement, and to ensure that affected landholders are not poorer than before their land was compulsorily acquired.

As a response to the recurring issue of insufficient compensation, scholars and practitioners have advocated for project developers to start investing more financial resources into compensation resettlement processes and allowing affected populations to share in the project benefits while obtaining access to alternative land, education, healthcare, and other basic amenities.[300] According to Cernea, for example, resources for financing resettlement

294 M.M. Cernea, 'Reforming the foundations of involuntary resettlement: Introduction', *in* M.M. Cernea & H.M. Mathur (Eds.), *Can Compensation Prevent Impoverishment? Reforming Resettlement through Investments and Benefit-Sharing*, New Delhi, India, Oxford University Press, 2008, pp. 1-8.

295 Cernea 1997 ; S. Price, 'Is there a global safeguard for development displacement?', *in* I. Satiroglu &N. Choi (Eds.), *Development Induced Displacement and Resettlement: New Perspectives on Persisting Problems*, Oxford, UK, Routledge, 2015, pp. 127-141; Z. Keliang *et al.* 2006, pp. 761-839; F, F. Vanclay, 'Project induced displacement and resettlement: From impoverishment risks to an opportunity or development', *Impact Assess. Proj. Apprais*, No. 35, 2017, pp. 3-21.

296 M. Van Eerd & B. Banerjee, 2013.

297 Z. Keliang *et al.* 2006, pp. 761-839.

298 World Bank, *Land Governance Assessment Framework: Country Reports*, World Bank, Washington, DC, USA, 2016.

299 World Bank, *Land Governance Assessment Framework Final Report: Nigeria*, World Bank, Washington, DC, USA, 2011.

300 Cernea 2008, pp. 89-120

processes can come from economic rents (i.e., windfall profits) generated by development projects (e.g., natural resource extractive projects) Cernea also explains that benefit-sharing between affected populations and project developers is feasible, as shown in a number of documented cases, including development projects initiated in China, Brazil, Canada, Columbia, and Japan.[301] In addition to establishing benefit-sharing arrangements, it is important to consider whether national laws provide compensation valuation procedures that ensure various land values are accountable for when compensation is calculated. Moreover, it is useful to understand whether there are legal processes in place that allow affected persons to negotiate compensation amounts, receive prompt payments, and hold governments accountable by challenging compensation decisions in courts or before tribunals.

4.3 Standards on Compensation Valuation Established in the VGGTs

Section 16.3 of the VGGTs provides that,

> States should ensure a fair valuation and prompt compensation in accordance with national law. Among other forms, the compensation may be, for example, in cash, rights to alternative areas, or a combination.

The VGGTs do not define the term 'fair valuation,' which presumably means that states are permitted to develop their own definitions of 'fair valuation' in national laws. Section 16.5 of the VGGTs provides that "all parties should endeavor to prevent corruption, particularly through use of objectively assessed values, transparent and decentralized processes and services, and a right to appeal." Furthermore, Section 18.2 of the VGGTs establishes additional standards on land valuation and states "policies and laws related to valuation should strive to ensure that valuation systems take into account non-market values, such as social, cultural, religious, spiritual and environmental values where applicable."

While the VGGTs do not define the term 'fair valuation,' there are several other international guidance documents that shed light on the meaning of 'fair valuation.' The FAO Handbook, for example, provides guidance on determining compensation and recommends that compensation should be based on the principles of equity and equivalence. These principles mean that affected persons should receive "no more or no less than the loss resulting from the compulsory acquisition of their land."[302] The FAO Handbook is discussed in more detail in subsequent Sections of this Chapter.

301 Cernea 2008, pp. 89-120.
302 Keith *et al.* 2008, p. 23.

While the VGGTs and FAO Handbook collectively form the basis of the indicators analyzed in this Chapter, it is important to acknowledge other international instruments that establish standards on land valuation and compensation for expropriation. For example, the World Bank Environmental and Social Standard 5 on Land Acquisition, Restrictions on Land Use and Involuntary Resettlement (ESS5) establishes that compensation should reflect the 'replacement cost.' 'Replacement cost' is defined as a method of valuation yielding compensation sufficient to replace assets, plus necessary transaction costs associated with asset replacement.[303] Standards on the valuation of compensation are also established in the United Nations Basic Principles and Guidelines on Development-Based Evictions and Displacement, IFC Performance Standards 5 and 7, the Asian Development Bank Handbook on Resettlement, the Centre on Housing Rights and Evictions Pinheiro Principles; and the UN Human Rights Commission Principles and Guidelines on Development-Based Evictions and Displacement establish best practices. Several of the standards established in these instruments are similar to those established in the VGGTs.

Table 9 List of Compensation Valuation Indicators

1. Does the law allow for assessors to follow an alternative approach (e.g., 'replacement cost' approach) instead of a "'air market value approach' to calculating compensation in cases where land markets are weak or non-existent?
2. Does the law provide compensation for unregistered customary tenure rights held by Indigenous Peoples and local communities?
3. Does the law establish special protections for women landholders regarding compensation entitlements?
4. Does the law require assessors to take into account the loss of business and other economic activities?
5. Does the law require assessors to take into account the improvements (i.e., attached and unattached assets on the land (e.g., crops, buildings) made on the land?
6. Does the law require assessors to take into account intangible land values (e.g., cultural, social, and historical land values)?
7. Does the law provide affected populations with the right to opt for alternative land instead of compensation in cash?
8. Does the law provide affected populations with the right to negotiate the amount of compensation?
9. Does the law require that compensation must be paid prior to the taking of possession of the land or within a specified timeframe thereafter?
10. Are affected populations granted the right to appeal decisions on the amount of compensation in court or before a tribunal?

4.4 Research Findings and Analysis

This Section is divided into four Subsections that provide the findings from the compensation valuation analysis of the 50 countries. The Subsections focus on (1) whether national laws ensure fair compensation for poor and marginalized groups; (2) whether national

303 World Bank 2017, p. 54.

laws ensure a comprehensive valuation of compensation; (3) whether national laws establish compensation procedures that provide affected populations with a right to negotiate, receive prompt payment of compensation, and appeal compensation in courts or before tribunals; and (4) the overall conclusions from the ten compensation valuation indicators and findings by country.

4.4.1 Compensation for Poor and Marginalized Groups

There are at least three reasons why compensation procedures may disproportionately burden poor and marginalized groups, such as women and Indigenous Peoples and local communities who hold land under customary tenure. First, poor and marginalized groups may be disadvantaged by legal systems that base compensation on the 'fair market value' of their property and improvements made on the property. Second, compensation eligibility requirements may preclude communities with customary tenure rights from submitting claims for compensation. Third, women landholders may be disadvantaged by gender-neutral compensation procedures, which fail to provide special protections ensuring that women are able to obtain compensation. Each of these reasons is discussed in detail below.

4.4.1.1 The 'Fair Market Value' Approach

The legal analysis presented below shows that, in many countries, compensation must be calculated based on the 'fair market value' (hereinafter 'FMV') of land, which is commonly defined as the amount a willing seller would pay and a willing buyer would accept in an open market. However, as previously discussed, the VGGTs call for states that account for non-market values such as social, cultural, religious, spiritual, and environmental values. Additionally, the World Bank Environmental and Social Standards (ESS5) and IFC Performance Standard 5 establish that compensation should be based on the cost of replacing the expropriated property (i.e., replacement cost approach).[304] In countries with robust and functioning land markets, the replacement cost should be roughly equivalent to FMV, but this is not always the case. Where land markets are weak or non-existent, there may not be a market value for land, or the market value may be less than the replacement cost. In such cases, the 'replacement cost' approach, or a combination of the FMV and

304 ESS5 provides "Where functioning markets exist, replacement cost is the market value as established through independent and competent real estate valuation, plus transaction costs. Where functioning markets do not exist, replacement cost may be determined through alternative means, such as calculation of output value for land or productive assets, or the un-depreciated value of replacement material and labor for construction of structures or other fixed assets, plus transaction costs. In all instances where physical displacement results in loss of shelter, replacement cost must at least be sufficient to enable purchase or construction of housing that meets acceptable minimum community standards of quality and safety." World Bank 2017, p. 54.

replacement cost approach, may be preferable since it focuses more on the amount it would actually take to replace lost assets.[305] The FAO Handbook points to this issue, and states that:

> Assessing the market value of a land parcel is not always simple, particularly where land markets are weak. A variety of complex factors must often be considered [...] It may not always be possible to determine compensation based on market value. Alternative approaches vary depending on the political economy of a country, the qualities of the land acquired, and the nature of the land rights.[306]

I agree with these scholars given that in many contexts, particularly when the land in question is held and used by Indigenous Peoples; the market value approach is problematic providing such lands have probably never been sold. In such cases, alternative methods, such as the 'replacement cost' method, should be considered.

Empirical research shows that compensation based on FMV can be insufficient to cover the losses borne by affected landholders. In Peru, for example, the World Bank's LGAF study found the market value approach was not always successful in ensuring that affected populations maintain their economic status after expropriation.[307] FMV can provide sufficient compensation in areas where functioning land markets exist. With adequate access to information on the market price of nearby properties of similar size and quality, it may be possible for assessors to correctly determine FMV of expropriated properties. However, FMV is an ineffective basis on which to calculate compensation in areas where land markets are weak or non-existent. According to a study commissioned by the Asian Development Bank,

> [In] particularly remote, rural settings, markets are not sufficiently active to provide reliable information about prices. Even when markets do provide reliable information about the value of the expropriated land, it may not be possible to identify comparable land for purchase.[308]

305 J. Lindsay, *PPP Insights: Compulsory Acquisition of Land and Compensation in Infrastructure Projects*, World Bank, Washington, DC, USA, 2012.

306 Keith *et al.* 2008, p. 28.

307 World Bank, *Land Governance Assessment Framework Final Report: Peru*, World Bank, Washington, DC, USA, 2013, p. 37.

308 ADB, *Compensation and Valuation in Resettlement: Cambodia, People's Republic of China, and India*, Rural Development Institute, Seattle, DC, USA, 2007.

As Merill wrote, "the concept of fair market value is essentially a fiction in the context of takings of property" due to the lack of information available to accurately measure land values.[309] Even the United States Supreme Court observed that FMV may not always be the appropriate standard to apply, such as when "FMV has been too difficult to find, or when its application would result in manifest injustice to the owner or public."[310]

In many developing countries, rural communities, including indigenous and local communities with customary tenure, have never sold rights to their ancestral lands. Therefore, it is difficult, if not impossible, to ascertain the market value of these lands. In these countries, governments often impose restrictions or limitations on the ability of rural landholders to sell their land, which makes it difficult to ascertain the land's market value. In India, for example, tribal landholders cannot accurately assess the FMV of land because restrictions on alienation have prevented tribes from selling their land since the 1970s.[311]

Scholars have extensively discussed and debated the inherent pitfalls of the FMV approach. For example, they argue that the FMV approach incentivizes governments to target poor and marginalized landholders with lower valued properties rather than expropriate the properties of the rich and politically influential.[312] According to Stern,

> Blight condemnations, urban renewal programs, and redevelopment projects which often serve as the 'public use' justification for eminent domain- all affect, not coincidentally, assets belonging to poor property owners [...] Stronger communities are more likely to have the resources and influence to avoid the damaging effects of eminent domain without government assistance. Politically strong communities may use their political ties and influence to fend off expropriation, and economically strong communities may be safe because of the high costs that the state would incur by taking their land.[313]

In areas where the cost of expropriating land is relatively inexpensive, government may be incentivized to overuse its expropriation power, which, in turn, could threaten land tenure security. Landholders may be more likely to protest and appeal expropriation and

309 T. Merril, 'Incomplete Compensation for Takings', *N.Y.U. Envtl. L.J.*, Vol. 11, 2002, p. 116.

310 Supreme Court of the United States, United States *v.* Commodities Tradition Corp, 339 U.S. 121, 123, 1950.

311 R. Mahapatra, 'Acquisition Made Easy', *Down Earth*, 2011.

312 S. Stern, 'Expropriation Effects on Residential Communities', *in* B. Hoops, E.J. Marais, H. Mostert, J.A.M.A. Sluysman & L.C.A. Verstappen (Eds.), *Rethinking Expropriation Law II: Context, Criteria, and Consequences of Expropriation*, Den Haag, The Netherlands, Eleven International Publishing, 2015, pp. 359-391, 377, 378.

313 Stern 2015, p. 378.

compensation decisions, resulting in delays in implementation of development projects. As argued by Bell and Parchomovsky,

> Takings law permits undercompensation whenever the reserve value of the proper owner exceeds market price...partial compensation will lead the government to take too much land [...] by failing to pay full compensation for its taking, the government incentivizes property owners to oppose potentially society beneficial projects.[314]

Similarly, Dyrkolbotn and Freilich examine how benefit-sharing on the part of the affected landholder can rarely be achieved when compensation is set at pre-project 'market value' levels.[315]

The FMV approach to valuing compensation is also criticized by scholars as an inadequate approach because it fails to capture the affected landholders' personal, sentimental attachments to the land. Stern, for example, examines the ways in which expropriation leads to a 'loss of communality' and how compensation at market value fails to capture this loss of interpersonal ties. Cernea and Vanclay highlight the failure of FMV compensation to account for intangible or personal land values and the consequential emotional pain and harmful social impacts endured by affected populations.[316] Dagan argues that transaction costs and subjective preferences may cause affected landholders to "oppose the forced transfer of their proprietary rights against its fair market value, and shift the burden to other landholders resulting in unjust and inefficient outcomes." Krier and Serkin highlight the failure of FMV compensation to bridge the gap between market and subjective values.[317] Radin writes that "[FMV] seems quite wrong in cases where property interests are apprehended as personal and incommensurate with money", and rejects the use of FMV for family homes and other property with personal value.[318]

---

314 A. Bell & G. Parchomovsky, 'Taking Compensation Private', *Stanf. Law Rev.*, Vol. 59, 2007, pp. 871-906, 873-874; *see also*, A. Bell & G. Parchomovsky, 'Takings Reassessed', *Va. Law Rev.* Vol. 87, 2, 2001, pp. 277-318.

315 S. Dyrkolbotn, 'On Benefit Sharing and the Compensatory Approach to Economic Development Takings', *in* B. Hoops, E.J. Marias, H. Mosters, J.A.M.A. Sluysman & L.C.A. Verstappen (Eds.), *Rethinking Expropriation Law II: Context, Criteria, and Consequences of Expropriation*, Eleven International Publishing, Den Haag, The Netherlands, 2015, pp. 319-355; R.H. Freilich, 'Condemnation Blight: Analysis and Suggested Solutions', *in* A.T. Akerman & D.W. Dynkowski (Eds.), *Current Condemnation Law: Takings, Compensation and Benefits*, 2nd edn., American Bar Association Chicago, IL, USA, , 2006, p. 81.

316 M.M. Cernea, 'Compensation and benefit sharing: Why resettlement policies and practices must be reformed', *Water Sci. Eng.*, Vol. 1, 2008 pp. 89-120; F. Vanclay *et al.*, *Social Impact Assessment: Guidance for Assessing and Managing the Social Impacts of Projects*, International Association for Impact Assessment, Fargo, ND, USA, 2015; J. Krier & C. Serkin, 'Public Ruses', *Mich. St. Law Rev.* Vol. 2004, 2004, pp. 859-875.

317 J. Krier & C. Serkin, 'Public Ruses', *Mich. St. Law Rev.* Vol. 2004, 2004, pp. 859-875.

318 J. Radin, *Reinterpreting Property*, University of Chicago Press, Chicago, IL, USA; London, UK, 1993, p. 154.

Lee, on the other hand, disagrees with the argument that FMV does not account for sentimental value. He states that FMV is capable of capturing

> [...] sentimental values [...] [for example] willing sellers' reservation prices will include the value of their sentimental attachments and that value will be reflected in the resulting market price for their properties.[319]

After considering the viewpoints of these scholars, I agree with those who argue that the calculation of FMV cannot adequately reflect intangible land values and the personal attachments, especially if the land in question is held and used by Indigenous Peoples. In such cases, alternative methods (e.g., the 'replacement cost' method) should be considered, since such methods would reflect what it would actually cost to replace the expropriated property.

The first compensation valuation indicator examines whether national laws enacted in the 50 countries allow assessors to calculate compensation using alternative methods to FMV. It was found that seven of the 50 countries[320] establish alternative approaches to calculating compensation, which can be applied in cases where land markets are weak or non-existent. Tanzania's Village Land Regulations, 2001 provides,

> The market value of any land and unexhausted improvement shall be arrived at by use of a comparative method evidenced by actual recent, sales of similar properties or by the use of income approach or replacement cost method where the property is of a special nature and not saleable.[321]

Similarly, in Sierra Leone, the 'replacement cost' approach may be used to calculate compensation if the land is devoted to a purpose of such a nature that there is no general demand or market for land for that purpose.[322]

Six of 50 countries received a 'partial' score because their laws indicate that alternative approaches to FMV may be used in certain circumstances.[323] However, these countries' laws do not specifically state whether alternatives to FMV may be applied whenever land

319 B. Lee, 'Just Undercompensation: The Idiosyncratic Premium in Eminent Domain', *Columbia Law Rev.*, Vol. 113, 2013, p. 613.
320 Belize, Cambodia, Ethiopia, Ghana, Sierra Leone, South Africa, Tanzania.
321 Government of Tanzania. *Village Land Regulations*, 2001, Section 10.
322 Government of Sierra Leone, *Public Lands Ordinance*, Chapter 116, Section 18(1) (g).
323 Mongolia, Bhutan, India, Kenya, Laos, Lesotho.

markets are weak or non-existent. Section 26(3) of India's LARR Act, 2013, for example, provides that,

> Where the market value ... cannot be determined for the reason that [...] the land is situated in such area where the transactions in land are restricted ... the [s]tate [g]overnment [...] shall specify the floor price and minimum price per unit area of the said land based on the price calculated [...] in respect of similar types of land situated in the immediate adjoining areas.

The answer is 'partial' because it is unclear which approach the state government is required to adopt when establishing a floor price/minimum price of the land.

The remaining 37 countries received a 'no' score because their laws establish FMV as the required approach and do not provide alternatives to FMV in cases where land markets are weak or non-existent.[324] In these 37 countries, compensation is primarily based on the market value of the land at the time of the acquisition, meaning that poor and vulnerable landholders living in parts of these countries where land markets are weak or non-existent may be at risk of insufficient compensation.

4.4.1.2 Special Protections Ensuring Women Landholders Receive Fair Compensation

Section 3b of the VGGTs establishes that states should promote gender equality, which is defined as:

> Ensur[ing] the equal right of women and men to the enjoyment of all human rights, while acknowledging difference between women and men and taking specific measures aimed at accelerating de facto equality when necessary. States should ensure that women and girls have equal tenure rights.

In addition to Section 3b, other Sections of the VGGTs call for states to adopt gender-sensitive approaches to tenure governance, including Sections 4.4, 4.7, 5.3, 5.7, and 10.1. Additionally, Section 16.1 of the VGGTs calls for states to "respect all legitimate tenure rights holders by providing just compensation," and women landholders are a subset of 'legitimate tenure rights holders.' Similar to the VGGTs, the World Bank ESS5 provides

324 Afghanistan, Angola, Argentina, Bangladesh, Botswana, Brazil, Burkina Faso, China, Ecuador, Eritrea, Honduras, Hong Kong, Indonesia, Kazakhstan, Liberia, Malaysia, Mexico, Myanmar, Namibia, Nepal, Nicaragua, Nigeria, Pakistan, Papua New Guinea, Peru, Philippines, Rwanda, South Sudan, Sri Lanka, Swaziland, Taiwan, Thailand, Trinidad and Tobago, Uganda, Vietnam, Zambia, Zimbabwe.

that "particular attention will be paid to gender aspects and the needs of the poor and the vulnerable."

Compensation procedures may place a disproportionate burden on women landholders if procedures do not establish special protections ensuring women are appropriately compensated. Throughout the world, women play an important role in sustaining rural societies by caring for household members, attending to family vegetable gardens, feeding animals, collecting firewood, and supplementing income with jobs outside of the home.[325] However, compared with men, women only have rights and access to a small fraction of land.[326]

The effect of gender-neutral compensation procedures, particularly in patriarchal societies, may be especially burdensome for women landholders.[327] In societies where women are considered dependents of their husbands and have no direct right to land, compensation is usually paid to the male head of the household. As the FAO Handbook explains, if compensation is paid to the male head of household, the "needs of women and children may be ignored as the money vanishes, to the detriment of the family's health and welfare."[328] In such cases, women are put at risk of being disproportionately burdened by expropriations. The loss of access to farmland hits women harder than men in many communities, and women are often excluded from compensation and benefit schemes.[329] Where compensation comes in the form of employment opportunities, these opportunities usually favor men.[330]

The second compensation valuation indicator asks whether national laws establish special protections for women landholders ensuring they are entitled to fair compensation. This indicator investigates whether the compensation procedures assessed explicitly provided special protections for women landholders for the purposes of obtaining compensation upon expropriation.[331] In other words, if the compensation procedures were written in

325 Oxfam International, *Unearthed: Land, Power and Inequality in Latin America*, Oxfam, Oxford, UK, 2016.

326 Landesa, 'The Law of the Land: Women's Rights to Land', Landesa, Seattle, WA, USA, 2016. Available online: www.landesa.org/resources/property-not-poverty/ (accessed on 25 May 2017).

327 United Nations. *Realizing Women's Rights to Land and Other Productive Resources*, HR/PUB/13/04, United Nations, New York, NY, USA, Geneva, Switzerland, 2013

328 FAO 2008, p. 40.

329 C. Salcedo-La Viña, M. Morarji, *Making Women's Voices Count in Community Decision-making on Land Investments*, World Resources Institute, Washington, DC, USA, 2016.

330 J. Behrman, J., R. Meinzen-Dick & A. Quisumbing, *The Gender Implications of Large-Scale Land Deals. Discussion Paper 01056*, International Food Policy Research Institute (IFPRI), Washington, DC, USA, 2011.

331 I acknowledge that the topic of "women's land rights" is not sufficiently covered in this book. When assessing this indicator, I did not consider, beyond national expropriation and compensation procedures, the range of other constitutional, legislative, and regulatory provisions that address women's access and

gender-neutral terms, a score of 'no' was given. For this indicator, it was found that of the 50 countries assessed, only India has compensation procedures that partially protect women from expropriation without fair compensation. Under India's LARR Act 2013, for example, widows and divorcees are considered a separate category of affected persons entitled to compensation, meaning that women are at least partially protected as legally recognized class of persons entitled to compensation. India did not receive a 'yes' score because its laws do not ensure that all women will be protected (e.g., in cases that do not involve expropriation of land rights held by widows and divorcees). The findings from the three indicators discussed in this sub-Section are displayed in Figure 7.

Figure 7 Compensation for Poor and Marginalized Groups

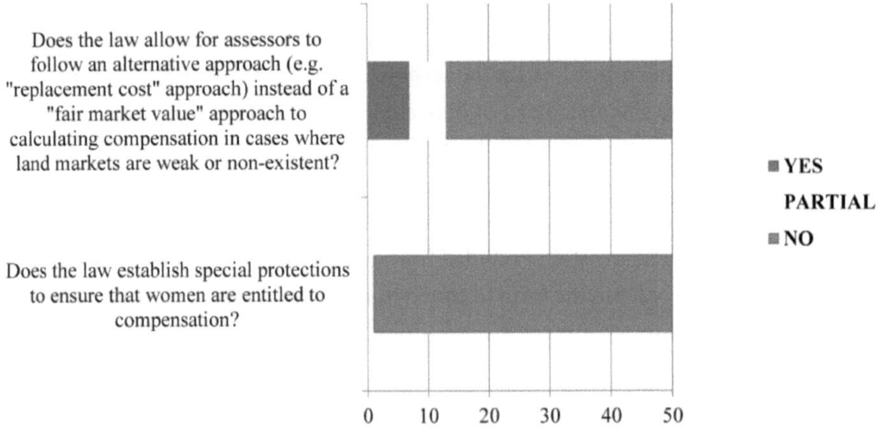

4.4.2 *Valuation of Compensation*

This Section discusses the findings from the analysis of compensation valuation procedures in 50 countries. Specifically, this Section addresses whether national laws provide compensation for loss of economic activities, improvements made on the land, and intangible land values. This Section also examines whether the laws provide alternative land instead of or in addition to cash payment.

---

rights to land. Such a legal analysis is beyond the scope of this study since the focus of this comparative study was on the national-level compensation procedures.

4.4.2.1 Compensation for Loss of Economic Activities and Improvements Made on the Land

As discussed in Section 4.3, the VGGTs call for a fair valuation of compensation but do not define the term 'fair.' However, additional insight on the meaning of 'fair' in the context of compensation for land can be derived from the FAO Handbook. It states the following:

> Compensation should be for buildings and other improvements to the land acquired; for the reduction in value of any land retained as a result of the acquisition; and for any disturbances or other losses to the livelihoods of the owner and occupants caused by the acquisition and dispossession. The disturbance accompanying compulsory acquisition often means that people lose access to the sources of their livelihoods. This can be due to a farmer losing agricultural fields, a business owner losing a shop, or a community losing its traditional lands.[332]

For rural farmers, grazers, hunters, and other landholders whose land is their primary source of income, accounting for the land's economic activities and improvements in the assessment of compensation is particularly crucial.[333] When rural farmers cultivate and sell crops from their lands, expropriation may leave them without a source of income. A recent USAID study in Rwanda found that 77 percent of expropriated households surveyed experienced income loss after their property was expropriated.[334] Moreover, if compensation procedures fail to account for the land's buildings, crops, and other improvements, affected populations who built, used, and maintained these improvements might be poorer than they were before their property was taken. For example, the World Bank LGAF study of Brazil found:

> Although compensation is generally paid for ownership and other rights (e.g., use rights, access rights, etc.), in the majority of cases the level is insufficient for the displaced households to either afford comparable assets or maintain their prior social and economic status.[335]

---

332 Keith *et al.* 2008, pp. 27, 29.

333 "Improvements" as used here refers to the land's attached and unattached assets (e.g., crops, buildings).

334 H. Rose *et al.*, *Implementation of Rwanda's Expropriation Law and Its Outcomes on the Population*, In Proceedings of the Annual World Bank Conference on Land and Poverty, Washington, DC, USA, 14-18 March 2016.

335 World Bank, *Land Governance Assessment Final Report: Brazil*, World Bank, Washington, DC, USA, 2016, p. 62.

The third compensation valuation indicator asks whether the law requires assessors to account for the loss of business or other economic activities when calculating compensation. It was found that 28 of 50 countries provide compensation for economic activities associated with the land.[336] For example, Indonesia's law provides compensation for other appraisable losses, such as loss of business or job, cost to change location, and cost to change profession.[337]

Ten of 50 countries received 'partial' scores because their laws suggest compensation may reflect *some* types of economic activities.[338] However, these countries' laws are not entirely clear regarding whether assessors must account for economic activities in every case. For instance, in South Sudan, while the law does not explicitly require that compensation reflect the economic activity attached to the land, Section 75 of the 2009 Land Act requires that compensation levels reflect "the purpose for which the land is being utilized." It can be inferred from this provision that economic activities may be accounted for in the valuation of compensation, at least in some cases.

Twelve countries have national laws that do not explicitly or implicitly provide compensation for economic activities associated with the land.[339] In these countries, compensation is based on FMV, without additional provisions indicating that business and other economic activities are compensable. In these countries, business owners and other landholders who use their land for economic purposes may be at risk of receiving insufficient compensation.

The fourth compensation valuation indicator asks whether assessors must account for the value of improvements made on the land when calculating compensation. It was found that 32 of 50 countries have laws that provide compensation for improvements made on the land.[340] According to Belize's law, the Land Acquisition (Public Purposes) Act, 2000 provides that "in assessing the compensation payable the Board shall assess separately the

336 Afghanistan, Bangladesh, Belize, Botswana, Brazil, Cambodia, China, Hong Kong, India, Indonesia, Kazakhstan, Kenya, Laos, Lesotho, Malaysia, Myanmar, Nepal, Pakistan, Peru, Rwanda, Sierra Leone, South Africa, Sri Lanka, Swaziland, Taiwan, Tanzania, Thailand, Vietnam.

337 Government of Indonesia, *Acquisition of Land for Development in the Public Interest, Law No. 2 of 2012*, Art. 33(f), Government of Indonesia, Jakarta, Indonesia, 2012.

338 Bhutan, Philippines, South Sudan, Burkina Faso, Ethiopia, Ghana, Mongolia, Namibia, Uganda, Zimbabwe.

339 Angola, Argentina, Ecuador, Eritrea, Honduras, Liberia, Mexico, Nicaragua, Nigeria, Papua New Guinea, Trinidad and Tobago, Zambia.

340 Afghanistan, Angola, Bangladesh, Belize, Botswana, Brazil, Burkina Faso, China Ethiopia, Honduras, India, Indonesia, Kenya, Laos, Mexico, Mongolia, Myanmar, Nepal, Nigeria, Pakistan, Peru, Philippines, Rwanda, Sierra Leone, South Africa, South Sudan, Taiwan, Tanzania, Trinidad and Tobago, Vietnam, Zambia, Zimbabwe.

compensation payable in respect of [...] developed land and any buildings standing on the land."[341]

Ten of 50 countries received 'partial' scores because their laws suggest that compensation may reflect *some* of the improvements made on the land.[342] Under Article 67 of Kazakhstan's Law on State-Owned Property, 2011 provides that, "the value of buildings and other real estate on the land is included in the compensation." However, since the law does not account for other types of improvements aside from buildings and other real estate (e.g., crops), the answer is 'partial.'[343]

Eight of 50 countries have laws that do not require assessors to take into account the value of improvements when calculating compensation.[344] In these countries, affected populations that built, used, and maintained improvements on their land may receive compensation that is insufficient to cover their losses.

4.4.2.2 Compensation for Intangible Land Values (e.g., Cultural, Spiritual, and Historical Values)

As mentioned above, Section 18.2 of the VGGTs calls for policies and laws related to valuation to take into account non-market values, including social, cultural, religious, and spiritual values. In addition to the VGGTs, Article 5 of International Labour Organization Convention 169 (the Indigenous and Tribal Peoples Convention) calls for recognition of intangible, non-market values and states, "the social, cultural, religious and spiritual values and practices of [Indigenous and tribal peoples] shall be recognized and protected." Moreover, the United Nations Declaration on the Rights of Indigenous Peoples and IFC Performance Standard 7 indicate that ancestral territories and other lands used for religious, cultural, and traditional practices must be protected and respected.[345]

Land has cultural, historical, religious, and sentimental value. This is especially true for Indigenous Peoples and local communities that have used their lands for traditional norms and practices for centuries. It may be difficult to assess the value of intangible losses; for instance, how can the government put a price tag on graveyards, historical places of worship, and other cultural heritage sites? There is a diversity of viewpoints among scholars

341 Government of Belize, *Land Acquisition (Public Purposes)*, Art. 20(b), Government of Belize, Belmopan, Belize, 2000.
342 Argentina, Cambodia, Ghana, Hong Kong, Kazakhstan, Malaysia, Namibia, Swaziland, Thailand, Uganda.
343 Government of Kazakhstan, *Law on State-Owned Property*, 2011, Art. 67.
344 Bhutan, Ecuador, Eritrea, Lesotho, Liberia, Nicaragua, Sri Lanka, Papua New Guinea.
345 IFC, *Performance Standards on Environmental and Social Sustainability, Performance Standard 7: Indigenous Peoples*, IFC, Washington, DC, USA, 2012.

regarding the conceptualization of compensation for intangible land values. Some scholars propose allowing affected populations to take a 'self-evaluation' to ascertain intangible land values. Bell and Parchomovsky, for example, propose basing compensation on the affected populations' self-assessed valuation in order to establish subjective valuation as the applied measure of compensation.[346] Likewise, Lunney also argues in favor of using the landholder's subjective preferences and proposes defining 'just compensation' as the amount of compensation "that made the landowners indifferent between accepting the payment and the loss they experienced."[347]

Wyman, on the other hand, argues against considering the subjective preferences of affected populations when calculating compensation because it would cause some subjective values to be prioritized more than others.[348] She proposes compensation rules would make affected populations objectively indifferent to expropriations. The measure would not be the:

> Takee's personal assessment of her losses [...] rather, it would be a considered judgment by outsiders about the amount of compensation required to allow a takee to enjoy the elements of a socially valuable life to the same extent that she enjoyed them before the taking.[349]

The fifth compensation valuation indicator examines whether assessors must account for intangible land values when calculating compensation. For this indicator, I investigated whether laws establish any procedures by which intangible land values, such as historical, cultural, or personal values, may be reflected in the calculation of compensation. It was found that only two of 50 countries (Bhutan and the Philippines) have laws that explicitly require acquiring bodies to consider the land's intangible land values (e.g., historical, cultural, and spiritual values) when assessing compensation. According to Bhutan's Land Act, 2007, for example, "the valuation of the land and property shall consider [...] other elements such as scenic beauty, cultural and historical factors, where applicable."[350] The Philippine's Indigenous People's Rights Act, 1997 helps ensure that compensation payments

346 According to Bell and Parchmovosky, "Under the proposed mechanism, property owners would get to set the price of the property designated for condemnation. The government could then either take the property at the designated price or abstain, leaving the property subject to two new proposed restrictions. First, for the life of the owner, the property could not be sold for less than the self-assessed price, adjusted on the basis of the local housing price index. Second, the self-assessed price—Discounted to take account of the peculiarities of property tax assessments—Would become the new benchmark for the owner's property tax liability." Bell & G. Parchomovsky, 'Taking Compensation Private', *Stanf. Law Rev.*, Vol. 59, 2006, p. 871.

347 G.S. Lunney, 'Takings, Efficiency, and Distributive Justice: A Response to Professor Dagan', *Mich. Law Rev.*, Vol. 99, 2000, p.168.

348 K. Wyman, 'The Measure of Just Compensation', *UC Davis Law Rev.* Vol. 41, 2007, p. 239.

349 Wyman 2007, p. 239.

350 Government of Bhutan, *Land Act*, 2007, Section 151.

reflect the historical/cultural connections associated with land. In addition to establishing special protections for ancestral lands held by Indigenous Peoples, the Act establishes an Ancestral Domains Fund, which can be used to compensate Indigenous Peoples when their ancestral domains are expropriated.[351]

Seven of 50 countries received 'partial' scores because their laws require assessors to account for intangible land values to some extent.[352] However, these countries' legal provisions do not ensure that intangible land values will be accounted for in every case. Article 20(3) of the Ghana's Constitution, for example, requires that:

> Where compulsory acquisition or possession of any land affected by the State [...] involves displacement of any inhabitants, the State shall resettle the displaced inhabitants on suitable alternative land with due regard for their economic well-being and social and cultural values.

However, Ghana received a 'partial' score because Ghana has not passed legislation or regulations, which define the term 'due regard' or otherwise provide guidance on implementing this provision.

The remaining 41 countries assessed have laws that do not require intangible land values (e.g., cultural, spiritual, and historical values) to be reflected in the assessment of compensation.[353] In these countries, Indigenous Peoples and local communities may suffer irreparable damage and livelihood losses if their ancestral lands are expropriated.

4.4.2.3 The Right of Affected Populations to Opt for Alternative Land Instead of or in Addition to a Cash Payment of Compensation

Section 16.3 of the VGGTs provides that "among other forms, the compensation may be, for example, in cash, rights to alternative areas, or a combination." For farmers and rural landholders whose land is their primary source of income and livelihood needs, cash compensation payments may be insufficient to revitalize their livelihoods subsequent to expropriations. The World Bank Environmental and Social Standards and the IFC Perfor-

351 Government of Philippines, *Indigenous People's Rights Act*, 1997, Section 71.

352 Ghana, India, Laos, Nepal, Sri Lanka, Tanzania, Vietnam.

353 Afghanistan, Angola, Argentina, Bangladesh, Belize, Botswana, Brazil, Burkina Faso, Cambodia, China, Ecuador, Eritrea, Ethiopia, Honduras, Hong Kong, Indonesia, Kazakhstan, Kenya, Lesotho, Liberia, Malaysia, Mexico, Mongolia, Myanmar, Namibia, Nicaragua, Nigeria, Pakistan, Papua New Guinea, Peru, Rwanda, Sierra, Leone, South Africa, South Sudan, Swaziland, Taiwan, Thailand, Trinidad and Tobago, Uganda, Zambia, Zimbabwe.

mance Standards obligate borrowers to provide land-based compensation or in-kind compensation. Likewise, the FAO Handbook states:

> Providing suitable alternative land may be difficult in light of current population pressures on the land [...] [h]owever, many owners and occupants may prefer to receive land as compensation rather than money [...] resettlement of vulnerable people on alternative land is required when the loss of their land means a loss of their livelihoods.[354]

In Bangladesh, for example, where national laws do not provide alternative land as a compensation option, 77 percent of the affected households surveyed in one expropriation case stated that compensation payments did not sufficiently cover their losses, and 90 percent stated they were unable to use the cash to purchase land equivalent in area to the land they lost.[355] According to Lindsay *et al.*, "Some land rights that are critical to rural livelihoods [...] may simply not be susceptible to monetization - their loss may only be genuinely addressed by providing [alternative land]."[356] I agree with this viewpoint, especially if one considers circumstances in which rural farmers are expropriated with no alternative means of growing crops or sustaining livelihoods.

The sixth compensation valuation indicator asks whether affected landholders are granted the right to opt for alternative land as a compensation option, if such land is available. It was found that 18 of 50 countries have laws that provide affected populations with a right to opt for alternative land instead of or in addition to compensation.[357] For example, Article 31 of Afghanistan's Law on Land Acquisition, 2017 grants affected landholders the right to receive "equivalent land to the expropriated property in terms of type, location, grade and business value of related area" as compensation if it is available."[358]

Eight of 50 countries have laws that suggest alternative land may be provided in some cases; however, it was unclear, based on the wording of these countries' laws, whether alternative land may be provided as a compensation option in every case.[359] In some countries or regions, compensation may be provided in cash or 'in kind.' In this case, I

354 Keith *et al.* 2008, p. 38.

355 S. Atahar, 'Development Project, Land Acquisition and Resettlement in Bangladesh: A Quest for Well Formulated National Resettlement and Rehabilitation Policy', *Int. J. Hum. Soc. Sci. Res.* Vol. 3, No. 7, 2013, pp. 306-319.

356 Lindsay *et al.*, 2017

357 Afghanistan, Cambodia, Eritrea, Ghana, India, Indonesia, Kazakhstan, Kenya, Laos, Mongolia, Nepal, Nigeria, Philippines, South Sudan, Sri Lanka, Tanzania, Vietnam, Zambia.

358 Government of Afghanistan, *Law on Land Acquisition*, 2017. Art. 31.

359 Argentina, Bhutan, Botswana, Burkina Faso, Ethiopia, Rwanda, Taiwan, Zimbabwe.

interpreted the law as implicitly suggesting that alternative land may be a compensation option in some cases, though not necessarily guaranteed in *every* case. For example, Article 12 of Argentina's Ley No. 21.499, 1977 establishes that compensation must be paid in cash, except when the payment for the expropriated property is made in another kind of value.[360] This provision suggests that compensation may be payable in alternative land, although the provision is unclear.

Twenty-four of 50 countries have laws that do not explicitly or implicitly provide alternative land as a compensation option.[361] In these countries, compensation must be paid in cash, which can provide a number of problems, especially if the affected landholders are not accustomed to managing large sums of money. If the expropriation causes farmers to lose land that is especially fertile, they may be at particular risk of impoverishment if the money provided is not enough to allow them to purchase productive alternative land. The findings from the indicators discussed in this sub-Section are displayed in Figure 8.

360 Government of Argentina, *Ley No. 21.499 Nacional de Expropriaciones*, 1977, Article 12.

361 Angola, Bangladesh, Belize, Brazil, China, Ecuador, Honduras, Hong Kong, Lesotho, Liberia, Malaysia, Mexico, Myanmar, Namibia, Nicaragua, Pakistan, Papua New Guinea, Peru, Sierra Leone, South Africa, Swaziland, Thailand Trinidad and Tobago, Uganda.

Figure 8 Valuation of Compensation

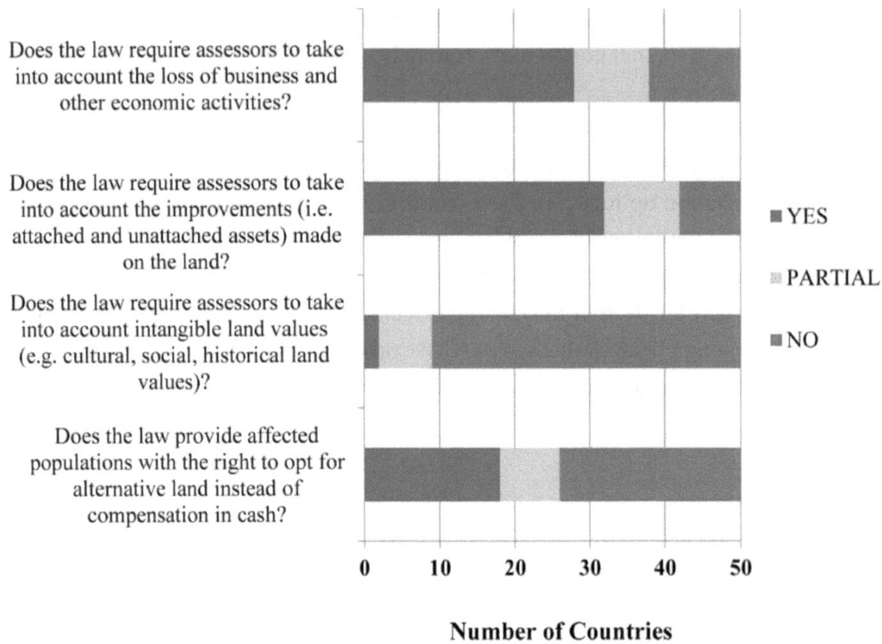

4.4.3 *Prompt Payment and Objective Assessment of Compensation*

This Section discusses whether national laws establish procedures that are aimed at ensuring compensation is objectively assessed and promptly paid. Specifically, the legal indicators discussed in this Section examine whether there are legal processes in place that allow affected populations to negotiate compensation amounts, receive prompt payments, and hold governments accountable by appealing compensation decisions in courts or before tribunals.

4.4.3.1 The Affected Populations' Right to Negotiate Compensation Amounts

In this context, the term 'negotiate' refers to the right to submit written or verbal claims for compensation, or, in some cases, 'reach an agreement' with the government, as stated by the law. It does not necessarily mean that affected populations have the final say regarding compensation amounts. In most cases, the government makes the final decision, but this decision is appealable in court or before a tribunal.

Although the VGGTs do not explicitly call for states to provide affected landholders with the right to negotiate compensation levels, negotiation proceedings may help countries adopt Section 16.6 of the VGGTs, which provides that states should "prevent corruption through the use of values that are objectively assessed using transparent and decentralized processes." The FAO Handbook states that:

> Fair and transparent negotiations [between governments and affected populations] help break down the barriers between the acquiring agency and the people whose land is being acquired, and can allow each party to have a better understanding of the needs of the others.[362]

Additionally, good faith negotiating between parties can reduce the chance of delays later in the expropriation process; for instance, delays may arise when affected populations are unsatisfied with their compensation amounts and decide to appeal to courts.

Fair negotiations may prevent outcomes, such as those witnessed in Tanzania, where compensation allotments were reportedly calculated behind closed doors, were perceived as arbitrary, and caused mistrust of the government.[363] After long delays, affected landholders in Tanzania were asked to either "take it or leave it" and were not given the chance to negotiate.

Scholars have examined and deliberated various approaches to negotiating fair compensation. Bell and Parchomovsky, for instance, argue that since the "subjective value [of property] is neither observable nor readily ascertainable by third parties; only the aggrieved property owners know the true value of their land," it may be useful to include a self-assessment apparatus by which landowners set the compensation rate.[364] The rate then must be either accepted or rejected by the government, but, if the government rejects the compensation rate, the landowners can keep their land but cannot sell their land for a price below the proposed compensation rate.[365] If they do sell their land for a price below the proposed rate, they must pay the difference to the government. Bell and Parchomovsky argue that this 'self-assessment apparatus' would ensure fair compensation and balance the interests of the government and affected populations. By imposing restrictions on alienation, this 'apparatus' is designed to discourage landholders from exaggerating the subject value of their property. In my view, the self-assessment apparatus presents a useful method of determining a level of fair compensation that accounts for the subjective value.

---

362 Keith *et al.* 2008, p. 28.
363 Deininger *et al.* 2012, p. 86.
364 Bell & Parchomovsky 2006, p. 871.
365 Bell & Parchomovsky 2006, p. 871.

Regardless, negotiation procedures are needed to ensure that when calculating compensation, governments and acquiring bodies account for the viewpoints of affected landholders.

The seventh legal indicator examines whether affected populations have the right to negotiate compensation amounts. It was found that 27 of 50 countries have laws that provide affected landholders the right to negotiate compensation levels.[366] In these countries, affected landholders do not necessarily have the 'final say' regarding compensation amounts, but are granted the right to submit claims for compensation and give input regarding what they consider to be fair levels of compensation. If they disagree with the government's final decision, affected landholders can often appeal the compensation decision in court or before a tribunal (see Section 5.3.3). Papua New Guinea's 1996 Land Act, for example, provides that affected persons and the Minister must reach an agreement on compensation.[367] Likewise, Article 37 of Indonesia's Law No. 2 of 2012 provides,

> The Land Administrator shall conduct a negotiation with the Entitled Parties within 30 working days of the submission of the results of appraisal of the Appraiser to the Land Administrator for determination of the form and/or the amount of Compensation under the results of appraisal of Compensation.

Seven of 50 countries have laws that provide affected populations with the right to negotiate compensation, but only under certain circumstances.[368] However, these country/regional laws impose certain limitations on the rights, which triggered a score of 'partial' for this indicator. For example, Article 6 of Rwanda's Law No. 18/2007 provides that "if necessary, the owner of the actives shall negotiate with the person to be expropriated and shall give him or her just compensation in accordance with relevant laws and in consultation with competent authorities." The answer is 'partial' because this legal provision indicates that a right to negotiate may only be granted "if necessary"; a right to negotiate is not guaranteed in every expropriation case.

Sixteen of 50 countries have laws that do not provide affected populations with the right to negotiate compensation amounts.[369] Without a right to negotiate compensation levels, affected populations may become dissatisfied and protest compensation decisions. In Ethiopia, for example, where Law No. 455/2005 does not grant affected populations the

366 Argentina, Belize, Botswana, Burkina Faso, Cambodia, China, Eritrea, Ghana, Hong Kong, India, Indonesia, Kazakhstan, Kenya, Laos, Malaysia, Mongolia, Papua New Guinea, Philippines, Sierra Leone, South Africa, South Sudan, Sri Lanka, Swaziland, Tanzania, Uganda, Vietnam, Zambia.

367 Government of Papua New Guinea, *Land Act*, 1996, Section 21, 25, 26.

368 Bhutan, Ecuador, Honduras, Namibia, Nicaragua, Rwanda, Taiwan.

369 Afghanistan, Angola, Bangladesh, Brazil, Ethiopia, Lesotho, Liberia, Mexico, Myanmar, Nepal, Nigeria, Pakistan, Peru, Thailand, Trinidad and Tobago, Zimbabwe.

right to negotiate compensation levels, scholars underscore the little participation of community in compensation decision-making and benefit packages.[370] Many Ethiopians are dissatisfied on the limited involvement of affected communities in the compensation computation process and on the level of compensation payment.[371]

4.4.3.2 Delays in Compensation Payments

Section 16.3 of the VGGTs calls for states to provide 'prompt' payments of compensation. However, there is no specified deadline established by the VGGTs. The FAO Handbook states that laws should ensure people receive full payment of the agreed-upon compensation sum in a timely manner, and that governments should be prohibited from taking possession of acquired land until after a substantial percentage of compensation has been paid.[372] Delays in payments could potentially cause affected landholders to become impoverished while continuing to wait for compensation payments.

Without a legally imposed deadline for compensation payment, acquiring bodies may be less likely to pay within a short timeframe. Empirical research shows that in many countries, compensation payment is often delayed. A recent USAID survey in Rwanda found that payments of compensation for expropriation were, on average, delayed 16 months past the legally imposed deadline for compensation payments. In Ghana, compensation was not paid for approximately 90 percent of all land expropriated between 1966 and 2001.[373] As of 2001, there were hundreds of pending cases in courts petitioning the government to either pay compensation or return lands to indigenous landholders. In China, the promise of cash compensation payments was unfulfilled in approximately one-third of the 476 land expropriations surveyed.[374] In Kenya, landowners are often not compensated promptly, according to the World Bank's LGAF study.[375] In Nigeria, the LGAF study found,

> The speed at which compensations are paid to property owners is also very slow. This may be attributed to the lack of planning on the part of the expropriating institution and the inadequate understanding of the need to pay compensation on the part of the government, which results in the poor budgetary

370 Government of Ethiopia, Proclamation No. 455/2005 Expropriation of Landholdings for Public Purposes and Payment of Compensation Proclamation, 2005; World Bank, *Land Governance Assessment Framework Final Report: Ethiopia*, World Bank, Washington, DC, USA, 2016, p. 72.

371 World Bank 2016, p. 72.

372 Keith *et al.* 2008, p. 55.

373 W.O. Larbi, A. Antwi, & P. Olomolaiye, 'Compulsory land acquisition in Ghana: Policy and praxis', *Land Use Policy*, Vol. 21, 2004, pp. 115-127.

374 Z. Keliang *et al.* 2006. 782.

375 World Bank, *Land Governance Assessment Framework Final Report: Kenya*, World Bank, Washington, DC, USA, 2016, p. 47.

allocation to the institutions saddled with the responsibility of land acquisition in the country.[376]

The eighth compensation valuation indicator asks whether laws mandate that affected populations receive payment prior to the taking of possession or within a specified timeframe thereafter. It was found that 20 of 50 countries have laws that require governments to pay compensation before acquiring land or within a specified timeframe thereafter.[377] For example, Article 93 of Vietnam's Law on Land, 2013 provides that "within 30 days after decision on the land recovery by the competent state agency takes effect, agencies and organizations in charge of compensation shall pay compensation and support to people whose land is recovered."[378]

Thirteen of 50 countries received 'partial' scores because their laws establish deadlines for compensation payments but also provide exceptions by which the deadline may be extended.[379] In Trinidad and Tobago, for example, claimants can petition for advance payment of compensation, made before possession of their land is taken; however, without a petition, advance payment is not required by law.[380]

Seventeen of 50 countries have laws that do not require prior payment of compensation or payment within a specified timeframe.[381] For example, according to Tanzania's Land Acquisition Act 1967, the Minister can pay compensation "at any time" after the publication of the acquisition notice in the *Gazette*.[382]

4.4.3.3 A Right to Challenge Compensation Decisions in Court or before a Tribunal

Section 16.3 of the VGGTs calls for states to provide a right to appeal compensation decisions. Avenues of redress may be needed when governments use incorrect or illegal procedures for calculating compensation and, consequently, affected populations are allotted insufficient compensation. Subjecting compensation decisions to judicial or tribunal review

---

376 World Bank, *Land Governance Assessment Framework Final Report: Nigeria*, World Bank, Washington, DC, USA, 2011.

377 Bangladesh, Bhutan, Botswana, Cambodia, Ecuador, Eritrea, Ethiopia, Indonesia, Kazakhstan, Laos, Lesotho, Mexico, Philippines, Rwanda, Swaziland, Taiwan, Thailand, Uganda, Vietnam, Zimbabwe.

378 Government of Vietnam, 2013, Art. 93

379 Argentina, Brazil, China, India, Malaysia, Mongolia, Namibia, Nepal, Papua New Guinea, South Africa, South Sudan, Sri Lanka Trinidad and Tobago.

380 Government of Trinidad and Tobago, *Land Acquisition Act Ch. 58:01*, 1994, Section 22.

381 Afghanistan, Angola, Belize, Burkina Faso, Ghana, Honduras, Hong Kong, Kenya, Liberia, Myanmar, Nicaragua, Nigeria, Pakistan, Peru, Sierra Leone, Tanzania, Zambia.

382 Government of Tanzania, *Land Acquisition Act*, 1967, Section 14(2), 15.

reduces the risk that compensation will be illegally or insufficiently assessed. According to Cotula,

> Effective judicial review processes [...] prevent and remedy abuse. This includes complaints [...] on the amount of compensation and/or on the quality of in-kind compensation; on who should be entitled to the compensation; on delays in the payment of compensation; and on other aspects.[383]

The tenth legal indicator examines whether national laws provide affected populations with a right to challenge compensation decisions in court or before a tribunal. It was found that 35 of 50 countries have laws that grant affected populations the right to challenge compensation decisions in court or before tribunals.[384] For example, under Brazil's Decree-Law No. 3.365, regulating land expropriation for public use (1941) indicates that affected persons have a right to appeal the decision that fixes the prices of compensation.[385]

Nine of 50 countries have laws that partially grant affected populations the right to challenge compensation decisions.[386] However, these laws impose certain limitations on the right to challenge compensation decisions in court or before a tribunal. For example, in Swaziland, Section 10 of the Acquisition of Property Act, 1961 (No. 10 of 1961) provides that the Board of Assessment shall rule on disputes regarding compensation claims, but there is not a clear provision that grants affected persons the right to challenge compensation decisions in court or before a tribunal.[387]

Six of 50 countries have laws that do not provide affected populations with the right to challenge compensation decisions in court or before a tribunal.[388] In these six countries, affected populations must either take or leave the amount of compensation granted to them, and have no means of legal redress if they are dissatisfied with compensation allotment. The findings from the indicators discussed in this sub-Section are displayed in Figure 9.

---

383 L. Cotula, *Legal Empowerment for Local Resource Control: Securing Local Rights Within Foreign Investment Projects*, International Institute for Environment and Development, London, UK, 2007.

384 Afghanistan, Argentina, Bangladesh, Belize, Brazil, Burkina Faso, Cambodia, China, Ecuador Eritrea, Ethiopia, Honduras, Hong Kong, India, Indonesia, Kazakhstan, Kenya, Laos, Liberia, Malaysia, Mongolia, Nigeria, Papua New Guinea, Peru, Philippines, Sierra Leone, South Africa, South Sudan, Sri Lanka, Taiwan, Tanzania, Thailand, Trinidad and Tobago, Uganda, Zambia.

385 Government of Brazil. *The Law of Expropriation for Public Utility, Decree-Law No. 3.365 of June 21, 1941*, Art. 28.

386 Botswana, Ghana, Lesotho, Myanmar, Namibia, Pakistan, Rwanda, Swaziland, Zimbabwe.

387 Government of Swaziland, *Acquisition of Property Act No. 10, 1961.*

388 Angola, Bhutan, Mexico, Nepal, Nicaragua, Vietnam.

Figure 9 Prompt Payment and Objective Assessment of Compensation

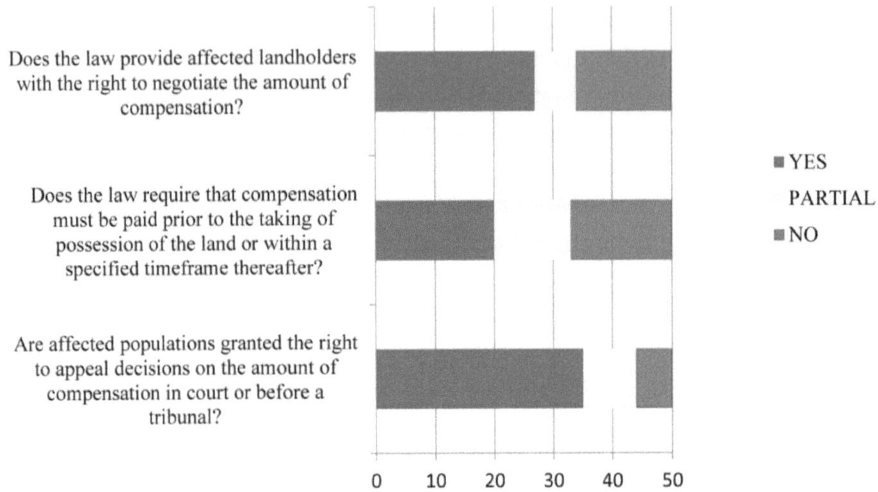

4.4.4 *Overall Conclusions from the Nine Compensation Valuation Indicators*

Figure 4 aggregates the findings from the nine compensation valuation indicators and shows the total 'yes,' 'partial,' and 'no' scores for each country. The chart shows that Laos, Philippines, Tanzania, Indonesia, and Cambodia have the laws that are closest to adopting the VGGTs. However, the chart shows that none of the 50 countries assessed scored a 'yes' for all ten indicators chosen for this study. This indicates that all national laws assessed must be reformed in order to fully comply with international standards on valuation of compensation. The chart also shows that Liberia, Angola, Namibia, and Nicaragua lag behind many of the other countries because their national laws mostly fail to adopt international standards on the valuation of compensation.

Figure 10 also shows that the Asian and African countries assessed achieved better scores on the indicators than the Latin American countries. While Belize received five 'yes' scores on the indicators, the remaining eight Latin American countries assessed (Argentina, Brazil, Ecuador, Honduras, Mexico, Nicaragua, Peru, and Trinidad and Tobago) received fewer than three 'yes' scores on the indicators.

Figure 10 Findings by Country

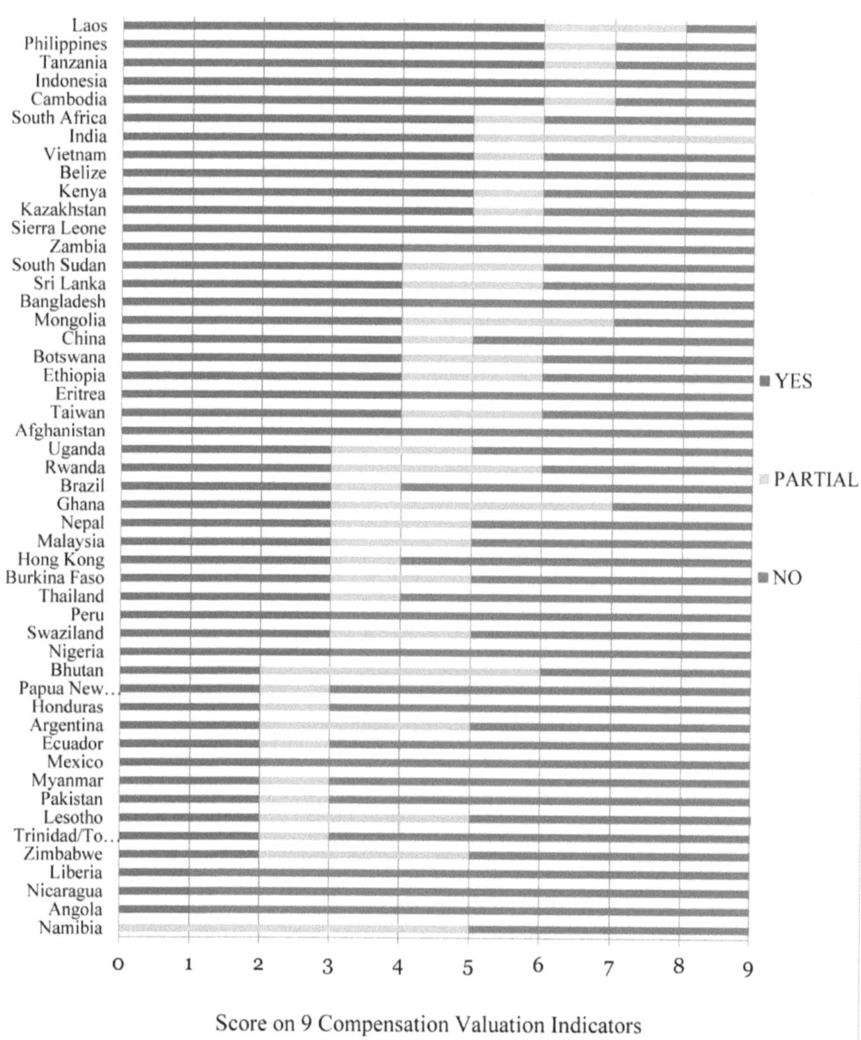

4.5 Suggested Avenues for Lawmakers to Pursue

This Chapter established a benchmark for measuring government progress toward adopting VGGTs on compensation valuation in domestic laws. Some countries, such as Laos, Philippines, Tanzania, Indonesia, and Cambodia, have enacted laws with relatively robust compensation procedures that largely adopt the VGGTs on compensation. However, there is ample room for progress. In most of the 50 countries or regions assessed, there are a number of gaps in national laws that put affected populations at risk of being insufficiently compensated upon expropriation. These legal gaps must be filled if national laws are to adopt the VGGTs on compensation. Robust compensation procedures are necessary but inadequate to ensure affected landholders are sufficiently compensated. Governments must also respect and enforce robust compensation procedures. Based on the findings from the research, I propose several recommendations for ensuring international standards on compensation valuation are adopted in countries that scored 'no' on the indicators.

1. Law should ensure that compensation procedures respect and protect the tenure rights of poor and marginalized groups. In cases where land markets are weak or non-existent, laws should be flexible and provide alternatives to the FMV approach to calculating compensation. As discussed in Section 5, the 'replacement cost' approach may be a suitable alternative to FMV since it requires an assessment of what it would actually require to replace lost assets in a given market. Section 10 of Tanzania's Village Land Regulation, 2001, is a good provision for countries or regions without robust land markets to adopt because it grants assessors flexibility to follow a variety of approaches when calculating compensation.[389] The law should provide clear and specific guidelines for valuing compensation; it must also be flexible enough to allow for the determination of full compensation in special cases where land markets are weak or non-existent.

2. To conform to the VGGTs, governments must protect and respect the legitimate tenure rights of communities with customary tenure rights. Although the term 'legitimate' is undefined in the VGGTs, this term is defined in other international instruments as including both *legal* legitimacy (rights recognized by law) and *social* legitimacy (rights that have a broad acceptance among society).[390] For this reason, states should initiate flexible systems that look beyond registered property rights when determining who is entitled to compensation. In order for governments to adequately and effectively assess the 'social legitimacy' of tenure rights held by IPLCs, they should survey the affected land and conduct in-person consultations and negotiations with affected landholders. Governments should consider adopting the legal provisions established in the laws of the Philippines, South Sudan, Tanzania, Uganda, and Zambia, which formally recognize community land rights, regardless of whether those rights are registered. In these

389 Section 10 of the Village Land Regulations states: "The market value of any land unexhausted improvement shall be arrived at by use of comparative method evidenced by actual recent, sales of similar properties or by use of income approach or replacement cost method where the property is of special nature and not saleable." Government of Tanzania 2001, Sec. 10.

390 D. Palmer, S. Fricska & B. Wehrmann, *Land Tenure Working Paper 11: Toward Improved Land Governance*, FAO, Rome, Italy, 2009.

countries, customary tenure rights are recognized automatically, once the community proves it has customarily occupied and used the land. As an alternative to registration, states could also adopt Rwanda's compensation provision, which allows for affected persons to claim compensation by submitting written testimony from their neighbors stating they own the expropriated land.[391]

3. The finding that only India has enacted a law that establishes special protections for women relating to compensation is particularly problematic given the risk that expropriations may disproportionately burden women landholders. More countries need to establish compensation procedures that require governments to respect women's' land rights and follow a gender-sensitive approach to providing compensation, which accounts for the varying ways in which women and men use land. As discussed in the FAO Handbook, compensation that is directly paid to the male head of household could be detrimental to the family's health and welfare "since the needs of women and children may be ignored as the money vanishes."[392]

4. Laws should establish procedures that ensure a comprehensive valuation of compensation, accounting for all losses borne by affected populations. For compensation to comprehensively reflect all of these losses, payments should reflect the land's historical and cultural value, in addition to economic activities and improvements associated with the land. Consultations with male and female landholders about the ways in which they use their land, and their land's historical/cultural value, can be an effective measure to ensure that compensation is sufficient. In order to ensure adequate compensation for farmers, herders, gatherers and other landholders who use land as a primary source of income and livelihood needs, laws should provide affected populations the right to opt for alternative land as a compensation payment instead of cash. Such land must be suitable for affected populations to maintain an adequate standard of living (e.g., through cultivating or grazing purposes). Moreover, laws should require valuers[393] to research relevant customary laws and practices to ensure the approach to assessing compensation is acceptable to members of the community.[394] The FAO Handbook

391 Government of Rwanda, Law No. 18/2007 Relating to Expropriation in the Public, 2007, Art. 18.

392 Keith *et al.*, 2008, p. 40.

393 The term "valuers" is defined in this study as the government or private entities charged with conducting the valuation of compensation. For purposes of this study, I chose not to make judgment call regarding which type valuer is best fit to conduct the valuation. Choosing a knowledgeable, independent valuer must be done on a case-by-case basis based on the country and context.

394 The Asian Development Bank's Summary of the Handbook on Resettlement: *A Guide to Good Practice* (1998) provides a broad range of losses which should be accounted for in the assessment of compensation, including agricultural land house plot (owned or occupied), business premises (owned or occupied), access to forest land, traditional use rights, community or pasture land, access to fishponds and fishing places, house or living quarters, other physical structures, structures used in commercial/industrial activity, income

further recommends "when there is a shared use of a resource such as forest land or pastures, the total value should take into account the value of each affected community member."[395]

5. Laws should establish measures that ensure compensation is promptly paid and objectively assessed. Governments and acquiring bodies should be legally obligated to compensate affected populations prior to taking possession of the expropriated property. Laws should ensure affected landholders are granted the right to negotiate compensation amounts and appeal compensation decisions to courts or tribunals. In addition to protecting the interests of affected populations, negotiating with affected landholders can benefit acquiring bodies by reducing costs from project delays that occur when landholders protest or appeal expropriation projects.[396] Laws should grant affected populations the right to challenge compensation decisions in court or before a tribunal. Legal avenues of redress enable affected population to hold governments and acquiring bodies accountable for poor compensation decisions; for instance, assessors may use incorrect methods of valuation, resulting in partial compensation to the affected landholder.

---

from standing crops, income from rent or sharecropping, income from wage earnings, income from affected business, income from forest products, income from fishponds and fishing places, income from grazing land, subsistence from other shrines, religious sites, places of worship and sacred grounds, cemeteries and other burial sites, and other factors.

395 Keith *et al.*, 2008, p. 35

396 In India and other countries where displaced persons are usually not consulted during the resettlement process, inability to participate and monitor the resettlement process can lead to protests and resistance among affected populations. These conflicts may delay projects and increase costs for governments and acquiring bodies. R. Hemadri, *Dams, Displacement, Policy and Law in India*, World Commission on Dams, Cape Town, South Africa, 1999.

5 Resettlement Procedures

5.1 Summary and Roadmap

Now that the issues and analysis related to compensation eligibility and valuation have been discussed, this Book shifts focus and examines resettlement procedures enacted in the 50 countries. Specifically, this Chapter examines whether the national-level expropriation laws require governments and expropriating actors to resettle and rehabilitate affected landholders who are displaced as a result of the expropriation.

This Chapter is organized as follows. Section 5.2 provides background and context related to resettlement issues that arise in cases of expropriation. Section 5.3 provides details on the international standards, guidance, and human rights instruments that are relevant to resettlement.

Section 5.4 summarizes several main takeaways from the literature on the gap between national-level resettlement procedures and international standards on resettlement. Section 5.5 presents the indicator analysis on whether national laws comply with the VGGTs on resettlement. Section 5.6 discusses several approaches to legal reform that lawmakers could adopt to bring national-level resettlement procedures into conformity with international standards.

5.2 Background and Context on Resettlement

Although the exact number of landholders displaced by expropriation is unknown, it is estimated that approximately 10-15 million people are displaced by development projects annually, and most of these people suffer from a reduced standard of living subsequent to displacement.[397] According to Shi Quoqing, approximately 80 million people in China were displaced between 1950 and 2015;[398] in India, 65 million people were displaced between 1950 and 2005.[399] Due to increased land and resource scarcity, pressure from population

397 A. Oliver-Smith, *Development and Dispossession: The Anthropology of Displacement and Resettlement*, School for Advanced Research Press, Santa Fe, NM, 2009.

398 M.M. Cernea, 'Foreword: State Legislation Facing Involuntary Resettlement: Comparing the Thinking in China and India on Development Displacement', *In* F. Padovani (Ed.), *Development-Induced Displacement in India and China*, Lanham Maryland, Lexington Books, 2016.

399 N. Walicki & M. Swain, *Pushed Aside: Displaced for 'Development' in India*, Norwegian Refugee Council (NRC) & Internal Displacement Monitoring Committee, Oslo, Norway, 2016.

growth, and the expansion of cities, the number of people displaced by development projects is likely to increase.[400] Customarily held rural land and informal settlements in urban areas may be the primary targets of expropriations, particularly expropriations justified on the grounds of 'economic development.'[401]

Although the exact number of landholders displaced by expropriation is unknown, it is estimated that approximately 10-15 million people are displaced by development projects annually, and most of these people suffer from a reduced standard of living subsequent to displacement.[402] According to Shi Quoqing, approximately 80 million people in China were displaced between 1950 and 2015;[403] in India, 65 million people were displaced between 1950 and 2005.[404] Due to increased land and resource scarcity, pressure from population growth, and the expansion of cities, the number of people displaced by development projects is likely to increase.[405] Customarily held rural land and informal settlements in urban areas may be the primary targets of expropriations, particularly expropriations justified on the grounds of 'economic development.'[406]

Empirical research conducted in a broad range of developing countries demonstrates the harmful impacts displacement has on the economic wellbeing of displaced populations. In Ethiopia, the income levels of displaced persons dropped significantly after they were evicted.[407] In Addis Ababa, Ethiopia, for example, 1,320 households were displaced from their lands for an urban development project.[408] Of the 66 displaced persons surveyed, 29 percent earned less than 500 Ethiopian Birr (ETB) (roughly $23) per month in their old villages. In the new resettlement sites, the number of households earning less than 500 ETB per month increased to 77 percent.[409] In Rwanda, 77 percent of expropriated house-

---

400 S. Price, 'Is there a Global Safeguard for Development Dislacement?', *in Irge Satiroglu and Narae Choi Development Induced Displacement and Resettlement: New Perspectives on Persisting Problems.* Oxford, Routledge, Oxford, 2015, pp. 127-141.

401 B. Terminski 2013.

402 A. Oliver-Smith, *Development and Dispossession: The Anthropology of Displacement and Resettlement*, School for Advanced Research Press, Santa Fe, NM, 2009.

403 M.M. Cernea, 'Foreword: State Legislation Facing Involuntary Resettlement: Comparing the Thinking in China and India on Development Displacement', *In* F. Padovani (Ed.), *Development-Induced Displacement in India and China*, Lanham Maryland, Lexington Books, 2016.

404 N. Walicki & M. Swain, *Pushed Aside: Displaced for 'Development' in India*, Norwegian Refugee Council (NRC) & Internal Displacement Monitoring Committee, Oslo, Norway, 2016.

405 S. Price, 'Is there a Global Safeguard for Development Dislacement?', *in Irge Satiroglu and Narae Choi Development Induced Displacement and Resettlement: New Perspectives on Persisting Problems.* Oxford, Routledge, Oxford, 2015, pp. 127-141.

406 B. Terminski 2013.

407 B. Alemu 2013

408 B. Alemu 2013, 130-132.

409 B. Alemu 2013, 130-132.

holds surveyed experienced income loss after their land was expropriated.[410] In Bangladesh, 103 of 133 households (77 percent) surveyed in Tangail district of Bangladesh said their economic status worsened after being resettled from land expropriation for the Jamuna Bridge.[411] In China, many affected farmers suffered a reduced standard of living after the government expropriated over 3.15 million hectares of farmland more than two percent of China's total arable land) between 1990 and 2002, which caused roughly 36.4 million farmers to lose their land.[412]

Studies of development-induced displacement often indicate that many displaced persons were not consulted or given adequate information to meaningfully participate in decision-making on the development and implementation of resettlement plans. For example, when land was acquired for the Pong Dom in India, affected landholders only became aware of the project's existence after the construction began.[413] A survey of 800 people evicted from development projects in eight countries found that 88% were not consulted during the planning phase of the development project.[414] Of those consulted, 85% stated in the survey that they "did not think their ideas or opinions were incorporated into project plans."[415] Survey research conducted by Anyuru *et al.* (2016) found that "out of the 257 surveyed people affected by a development project, the majority (64%) reported that they were not consulted. Only 35% said their views were sought."[416] In India, an estimated 200,000 people were evicted from 19 sites to pave the way for the 2010 Commonwealth Games in New Delhi, an event involving the development of sports arenas, roads, parking areas, and hotels.[417] There were no consultations or public hearings in any of the cases surveyed.[418]

---

410 H. Rose *et al., Implementation of Rwanda's Expropriation Law and Its Outcomes on the Population. In Proceedings of the Annual World Bank Conference on Land and Poverty*, Washington, DC, USA, 14-18 March 2016

411 S. Atahar, 'Development Project, Land Acquisition and Resettlement in Bangladesh: A Quest for Well Formulated National Resettlement and Rehabilitation Policy', *Int. J. Hum. Soc. Sci. Res*, Vol. 3, 2013, pp. 306-319.

412 ADB. *Compensation and Valuation in Resettlement: Cambodia, People's Republic of China, and India*, Rural Development Institute, Seattle, DC, USA, 2007.

413 Mathur 2006, pp. 36-86.

414 International Accountability Project (IAP), *Back to Development: A Call For What Development Could Be*, IAP, 2014.

415 IAP 2014.

416 M.A. Anyuru,, R. Rhoads, O. Mugyenyi, J. Ekwenyu, & T. Balemsa., *Balancing Development and Community Livelihoods: A Framework for Land Acquisition and Resettlement in Uganda*, ACODE Policy Research Series, No. 75, Advocates Coalition for Development and Environment, Kampala, Uganda, 2016.

417 N. Walicki & M. Swain, *Pushed Aside: Displaced for 'Development' in India*, Norwegian Refugee Council (NRC) & Internal Displacement Monitoring Committee, Oslo, Norway, 2016.

418 Ibid.

Displacement can be physical (e.g., physical relocation, loss of shelter), economic (e.g., loss of income-generating assets) or both.[419] There is no simple, 'one-size-fits-all' approach to revitalizing the livelihoods of displaced populations; however, there are several risks that should be addressed when development projects cause displacement. For example, the widely-cited Risks and Reconstruction Model, developed by Cernea, identifies eight primary risks that must be addressed following displacement: landlessness, joblessness, homelessness, marginalization, food insecurity, increased morbidity and mortality, loss of access to common property and services, and social disarticulation.[420] Scudder and Colson highlight additional problems associated with displacement, particularly how displaced persons can experience multidimensional stress, meaning stress of a physiological, psychological, social, or cultural nature.[421] According to Downing, displacement can dismantle social networks and life-support mechanisms, reducing the ability of displaced groups to self-manage.[422] The social disarticulation and fragmentation of displaced communities can lead to vulnerability and powerlessness.[423] The loss of livelihoods comprises not only of economic and physical displacement, but also social, cultural and spiritual displacement; in other words, displacement can cause a loss of a sense of place.[424]

Implementers of development projects that involve land expropriation and displacement must face the difficult question of how to reconstitute the livelihoods of the displaced. Beyond the economic wellbeing, how can the social and cultural fabrics of displaced communities be sufficiently revitalized? In some cases, fully addressing all of the risks associated with displacement may be unlikely since expropriation and loss of land may permanently alter the livelihoods beyond restoration. Nevertheless, legally mandated resettlement and rehabilitation assistance programs, coupled with sufficient financial and institutional capacity to implement such programs, may help mitigate some of the risks borne by landholders when they are displaced from their land. Robust legal frameworks provide a foundation on which displaced persons hold governments and private actors

---

419 International Finance Corporation (IFC), *Performance Standards on Environmental and Social Sustainability, Performance Standard 5: Land Acquisition and Involuntary Resettlement*; IFC, Washington, DC, USA, 2012

420 M.M. Cernea, 'The risks and construction model for resettling displaced populations', *World Dev.* Vol. 25, 1997, pp. 1569-1587.

421 T. Scudder & E. Colson, 'From welfare to development: a conceptual framework for the analysis of dislocated people', *In* A. Hansen & A. Oliver-Smith (Eds.), *Involuntary migration and resettlement: the problems and responses of dislocated people*, Boulder, NV, Westerview Press, 1982, pp. 267-287.

422 T. Downing, 'Mitigating social impoverishment when people are involuntarily displaced', *in* C. McDowell (Ed.), *understanding impoverishment: the consequences of development-induced displacement*, Providence, RI and Oxfod, England, Berghahn, 1996, pp. 33-48.

423 M.M. Cernea, 'Risks, safeguards, and reconstruction: A model for population displacement and resettlement', *in* M.M. Cernea & C. McDowell (Eds.), *Risks and Reconstruction: Experiences of Resettlers and refugees.* Washington, DC, The World Bank, 2000, pp. 11-55.

424 F. Vanclay, 'Conceptualising social impact', *Environmental Impact Assessment Review*, Vol. 22, 2002, pp. 183-211.

accountable for decisions that infringe on the land and human rights of the displaced. If the rule of law is respected, the adverse impacts of resettlement may be lessened even if these legal safeguards do not necessarily ensure positive outcomes for displaced persons in every case. Where large tracts of land are needed to serve genuine public purposes, resettlement may be unavoidable. The key question is how to minimize the social risks and reconstitute the livelihoods of displaced populations.[425] As stated by Cernea, "all forced displacements are prone to major socio-economic risks, but not fatally condemned to succumb them."[426]

Unless national legal frameworks ensure adequate legal protection, landholders may be at serious risk of displacement without sufficient resettlement assistance. A study conducted by the World Bank found that income restoration was lacking in countries that initiated displacing projects without first establishing country-wide policy or legal frameworks for resettlement and income restoration.[427] According to a World Bank study conducted in 1996, Bank-financed projects that resettled people on alternative land and in jobs, tended to restore incomes more effectively than projects for which only compensation was provided.[428] The study found that displaced persons who were able to immediately benefit from the project experienced full income restoration.[429] For example, income and livelihood restoration occurred when displaced persons were granted access to develop aquaculture and fisheries in the new reservoirs in Indonesia and new irrigation areas in China and India.[430]

If laws do not establish binding resettlement and consultation requirements, and consequently displaced populations are not consulted or provided adequate resettlement assistance, they may be more inclined to protest development projects. Protests and legal challenges against projects can cause delays and increase costs for project developers. For example, Ruggie found cases in which mining executives were spending 50-80% of their time resolving community protests that were delaying production, and their companies were losing $2 million per day as a consequence of delayed or suspended production.[431]

---

425 World Bank, *Resettlement and Development: The Bankwide Review of Projects Involving Resettlement 1986-1994 Paper 032*, World Bank, Washington, DC, USA, 1996.

426 M.M. Cernea, 'Impoverishment Risks, Risk Management, and Reconstruction: A Model of Population Displacement and Resettlement', *Proceedings of the UN Symposium on Hydropower and Sustainable Development*, Beijing, China, 27-29 October 2004.

427 World Bank, *Resettlement and Development: The Bankwide Review of Projects Involving Resettlement 1986-1994 Paper 032*, World Bank, Washington, DC, USA, 1996.

428 World Bank 1996.

429 World Bank 1996, p. 9.

430 World Bank 1996, p. 9.

431 Ruggie stated this in his keynote remarks at the Keynote Association of International Petroleum Negotiators Conference in Washington, DC; S. Price, 'Is there a global safeguard for development displacement?', *in*

In order to keep costs and financial risks low, it may be a worthwhile investment for developers to consult affected landholders before the project begins, allow these landholders to participate in resettlement decision-making, and provide adequate resettlement and rehabilitation assistance.

5.3 International Standards on Resettlement

This Section considers the various international standards on resettlement and rehabilitation of displaced populations. In addition to Sections 16.8 and 16.9 of the VGGTs, there are several important resettlement policies internationally adopted by MDBs such as the World Bank. These policies, which are discussed in detail in this Section, function as the governance tools for lending funds to projects involving land acquisition and involuntary resettlement. These policies include, but are not limited to, the World Bank ESF (2017) and IFC Performance Standard 5 (2012). The Asian Development Bank, African Development Bank, and the Inter-American Development Bank have also adopted resettlement policies. Since the focus of the legal analysis conducted for this book is on Asia, Africa, and Latin America, these MDB policies may apply to many of the ongoing development projects in the countries assessed in this book.

5.3.1 VGGTs on Resettlement

Section 16.8-16.9 of the VGGTs provides that,

> States should, prior to eviction or shift in land use which could result in depriving individuals and communities from access to their productive resources, explore feasible alternatives in consultation with the affected parties, consistent with the principles of these Guidelines, with a view to avoiding, or at least minimizing, the need to resort to evictions [...] Evictions and relocations should not result in individuals being rendered homeless or vulnerable to the violation of human rights. Where those affected are unable to provide for themselves, States should, to the extent that resources permit, take appropriate measures to provide adequate alternative housing, resettlement or access to productive land, fisheries and forests, as the case may be.[432]

I. Satiroglu & N. Choi (Eds.), *Development Induced Displacement and Resettlement: New Perspectives on Persisting Problems*, Routledge, Oxford, UK, 2015, pp. 127-141.

432 FAO 2009. Section 16.8-16.9.

The indicators used to assess national legal frameworks on resettlement are primarily based on these VGGTs. However, before presenting the research findings, it is important to first consider other international standards on resettlement. The reason why this Chapter highlights several of the policies adopted by MDBs (e.g. the World Bank, IFC) is that expropriation-inducing development projects financed by MDBs usually must adhere to MDB policy standards on land acquisition and resettlement as well as relevant domestic laws. For this reason, it is important to understand what types of requirements these MDB policy standards impose on borrowers.

5.3.2 World Bank Environmental and Social Framework (ESF)

The World Bank and other MDBs have funded projects that have caused millions of people to be displaced.[433] For this reason, it is worthwhile to discuss the various standards these institutions put in place to protect impoverishment and other displacement risks.

The World Bank has published four different resettlement policies since 1980. In 1980, the Bank issued its first resettlement policy entitled "Operational Manual 2.33 Social Issues Associated with Involuntary Resettlement in Bank-Financed Projects." This policy was the result of extensive in-house discussions and debates at the Bank about the adverse effects that some Bank-funded projects had on livelihoods.[434] While some Bank officials argued that a resettlement policy should not be the responsibility of the Bank but instead the borrowers, others argued that it would be too costly to implement.[435] Ultimately, the Bank decided to adopt the 1980 resettlement policy and not turn a blind eye to the social impacts deriving Bank-financed projects.[436]

The Bank revised and reissued this policy and published Operational Directive 4.30 on Involuntary Resettlement in 1990 (OD 4.30).[437] OD 4.30 was the first policy that adopted a development-oriented strategy, which allocated resources toward resettlement programs and focused on "improving [...] the economic basis for the relocated."[438] Throughout the 1990s, the Bank conducted several reviews of the OD 4.30's implementation.

433 S. Chavkin & M. Hudson, 'New investigation reveals 3.4m displaced by World Bank', *International Consortium of Investigative Journalists*, 2015.

434 M.M. Cernea, 'The 'Ripple Effect' in Social Policy and its Political Content: A Debate on Social Standards in Public and Private Development Projects', *in* M. Likosky (Ed.), *Privatizing Development: Trans-National Law, Infrastructure and Human Rights*, Leiden-Boston, Martinus Nijhoff, 2005, pp. 65-101.

435 M.M. Cernea 2005.

436 M.M. Cernea 2005.

437 World Bank, *Operational Directives 4.30: Involuntary Resettlement*, World Bank, Washington, DC, 1990.

438 M.M. Cernea 2005.

In 2001, after several attempts by Bank officials to scale back the resettlement policy in order to cut costs, the World Bank adopted Revised Operational Policy and Procedures: OP 4.12.[439] While some critics argued that certain aspects of OD 4.30 were diluted in OP 4.12, the Bank claimed that OP 4.12 contained more stringent requirements; for instance, OP 4.12 was the first policy to address the issue of 'impoverishment risks' of displaced persons.[440] OP 4.12 was later revised in 2013. OP 4.12 established three main policy objectives: (1) resettlement should be minimized or avoided; (2) alternatives to resettlement should be explored; and (3) displaced persons should be assisted in their efforts to improve their livelihoods and standards of living.[441]

In August 2016, the Bank adopted the new draft version of the Environmental and Social Framework (ESF).[442] This Framework is supposed to take effect in late 2018. The new ESF places more responsibility on borrowers of Bank funds to establish and implement resettlement programs through 'borrower frameworks' (e.g., domestic laws or policies).[443] The new ESF was the result of extensive debate between the World Bank, governments, civil society organizations, the private sector, and other stakeholders.[444] According to Larsen,

> While the bank wants to make sure its money supports activities approved by its directors and managers, countries want more control over how they use the money they borrow [...] Many borrower countries called for greater flexibility in the bank's requirements, while many members of a civil society groups wanted a more stringent way to avoid harming people or the environment.[445]

The debate resulted in a series of compromises, including the requirement that banks and borrowers must now agree and report on plans for implementing social and environmental protections, referred to as Environmental and Social Commitment Plans.[446] Under the new World Bank ESF, Borrowers now have greater flexibility in showing how they can

---

439 M.M. Cernea 2005.

440 M.M. Cernea 2005.

441 World Bank, *Operational Policy 4.12: Involuntary Resettlement*, World Bank, Washington, DC, 2001 (revised 2013).

442 World Bank 2017.

443 World Bank 2017, pp. 17-18.

444 *See* comments on proposed World Bank, *ESF: Bank on Human Rights Council. Key Human Rights Concerns and Recommendations Regarding the World Bank's Proposed Social and Environmental Safeguards*, 2015; Comments on *Overarching Human Rights Provisions in the World Bank's Environmental and Social Framework*, 2016; *Human Rights Watch Submission: World Bank's Draft Environmental and Social Framework*, among others.

445 G. Larsen, *The World Bank Just Overhauled its Safeguards for the First in 30 Years*, World Resources Institute, Washington, DC, 2016.

446 Larsen 2016.

implement social and environmental protections, and what documents they must provide in order to obtain approval.[447]

The new ESF includes Environmental and Social Standard (ESS) 5 on Land Acquisition, Restrictions on Land Use and Involuntary Resettlement.[448] ESS5 applies whenever a development project acquires or restricts land rights and causes the relocation of people with or without formal or recognized land rights.[449] Among other requirements outlined to borrowers under ESS5, borrowing agencies must develop a resettlement plan that includes the following activities and objectives:

- Avoid involuntary resettlement or, when unavoidable, minimize involuntary resettlement by exploring project design alternatives;
- Mitigate unavoidable social and economic impacts from land acquisitions;
- Improve living conditions of poor and vulnerable persons who are physically displaced through provision of adequate housing, access to services and facilities, and security of tenure;
- Provide displaced persons an option for replacement land (i.e., alternative land) unless it can be demonstrated to the Bank's satisfaction that equivalent replacement land is unavailable;
- Consult with affected communities and disclose relevant information that enables the communities to meaningfully participate in the resettlement process; and
- Provide relocation assistance, in lieu of compensation for land, sufficient for displaced populations to restore their standards of living at an adequate alternative site.[450]

Under certain circumstances, Bank-financed projects may follow the borrower's framework (e.g., domestic laws), the World Bank ESS, or a combination of both frameworks. The ESF states that,

> When a project is proposed for Bank support, the Borrower and the Bank will consider whether to use all, or part, of the Borrower's ES framework in the assessment, development and implementation of a project.[451]

The term 'Borrower ES frameworks' is too broadly and imprecisely defined as including "aspects of the country's policy, legal, and institutional framework."[452] The ESS states,

447 Larsen 2016.
448 World Bank 2017.
449 World Bank 2017, p. 53.
450 World Bank 2017, p. 56.
451 World Bank 2017, p. 17.
452 World Bank 2017, p. 18.

> The Borrower's ES Framework will include those aspects of the country's policy, legal and institutional framework, including its national, subnational, or sectoral implementing institutions and applicable laws, regulations, rules and procedures, and implementation capacity, which are relevant to the environmental and social risks and impacts of the project. The aspects that are relevant will vary from project to project, depending on such factors as the type, scale, location and potential environmental and social risks and impacts of the project and the role and authority of different institution.[453]

The Bank's ESS document lacks a clear definition of what it understands under the term 'borrower's framework' and, mainly, of whether a borrower's framework is or is not legally binding on state or non-state borrowers that carry out expropriations involving the involuntary resettlement of people. Such specification is needed because only legally-binding frameworks (e.g., statutes or regulations) provide justiciable legal rights that serve as a reference point when displace populations wish to challenge expropriation and resettlement decisions in court. "Policies", on the other hand, are merely declarative statements and not justiciable.

The ESF states that, if the Bank's assessment identifies gaps in the Borrower's ESS framework (e.g., gaps in national laws), the Borrower will work with the Bank to identify measures and actions to address such gaps."[454] While the World Bank certainly will strive to ensure that borrower's projects are adopting ESS5 standards, there is still the possibility that many borrowers will operate using domestic frameworks, which, as the analysis in this Chapter indicates, often lack national-level, binding laws on socially and economically sustainable resettlement.

For several reasons, the ESS puts populations that are displaced by Bank projects at significant risk of impoverishment, landlessness, and other socioeconomic risks. Compared with the Bank's 2001 Operational Policy (OP/BP 4.12) on Involuntary Resettlement, the new ESS Framework represents a systemic shift to a weaker paradigm. The ESS substitutes 'safeguard policies,' which were mandatory on all World Bank Projects and Staff and on the borrowing countries when implementing Bank-financed projects, with 'performance standards,' which are not mandatory on the Bank as an institution. According to the ESS, borrowers of World Bank funds must fulfill these performance standards through so-called 'Borrower ES Frameworks' or 'country systems.'

---

453 World Bank 2017, p. 18.
454 World Bank 2017, p. 18.

As the findings from this Chapter's analysis demonstrate, a borrower framework is only binding law in a small minority of countries assessed (five of the 50 countries reviewed). The vast majority of countries analyzed - 44 out of 50 - do not have legally binding 'frameworks.' The absence of laws that legally require the displacing agent (the state or a land acquiring party) to also provide resettlement and rehabilitation assistance jeopardizes the livelihoods of project-displaced populations because a 'framework' is not a recognized legal instrument with compelling power that can be invoked in court. Some countries have adopted non-binding policies. But since such policies are only non-justiciable statements (not laws), many populations forcibly removed from their lands will not have a legal basis to seek redress in court if their property or human rights are violated by a Bank project.

The ESS is also deeply problematic because it is not candidly transparent: it deliberately avoids recognizing and warning the governments and the affected populations about the impoverishment and other severe risks intrinsic to forced displacement and resettlement. In the past, the Bank was the world's leading agency in uncovering, warning about, and counteracting the impoverishment risks of displacement, but today the ESF/ESS avoids naming these risks.[455] As argued by Cernea, the omission of naming the displacement risks is a textbook case of self-defeating cognitive dissonance.[456] Without explicit, legally binding measures for overcoming displacement's chronic risks, the ESS leaves room for Borrowers to forcibly remove people from land taken for Bank-financed projects without ensuring the socio-economic restoration of these populations. The Bank has not provided statistical evidence that legally-binding 'ESS frameworks' exist in most developing countries. Furthermore, many developing countries do not have binding laws to prevent impoverishment by expropriation-cum-displacement and to ensure the restoration of resettlers' livelihoods. Therefore, the World Bank's reliance on Borrowers frameworks, combined with Borrowers' unwillingness to enact binding laws on resettlement, is immensely problematic for populations displaced by expropriations.

5.3.3 *IFC Performance Standard 5*

The IFC is a lending arm of the World Bank that is focused exclusively on the private sector in developing countries. In 2012, the IFC established a set of Performance Standards applicable to all borrowers of IFC funds. The 2012 version of the IFC Performance Standards applies to all investment and advisory clients whose projects go through IFC's initial credit review process. The IFC Performance Standards also apply to projects funded

455 Cernea 1997; World Bank 1996.

456 Cernea & Maldonado 2018.

by banks that have signed the Equator Principles.[457] Many consulting firms, private corporations, and industries consider the IFC Performance Standards as a mandatory benchmark to apply to development projects involving the acquisition of land. IFC Performance Standard 5 on land acquisition and involuntary resettlement must be adhered to whenever IFC borrowers initiate projects that result in involuntary resettlement.[458]

IFC Performance Standard 5 on land acquisition and involuntary resettlement must be adhered to whenever borrowers initiate projects that result in involuntary resettlement.[459] Performance Standard 5 is similar to the World Bank's ESS5 in many ways. For example, the IFC also establishes the objectives of: avoiding or minimizing forced displacement; improving and restoring the livelihoods and standards of living of displaced persons; consulting and negotiating with project-affected populations; and providing alternative housing with security of tenure at resettlement sites. Performance Standard 5 also states the following:

> To help avoid expropriation and eliminate the need to use governmental authority to enforce relocation, clients are encouraged to use negotiated settlements meeting the requirements of this Performance Standard, even if they have the legal means to acquire land without the seller's consent.[460]

One critique of the IFC Performance Standards is that they do not offer specific guidance regarding the timing of consultation and negotiation.[461] The IFC Performance Standards provide that,

> Decision-making processes related to resettlement and livelihood restoration should include options and alternatives, where applicable. Disclosure of relevant information and participation of Affected Communities and persons will continue during the planning, implementation, monitoring, and evaluation of compensation payments, livelihood restoration activities, and resettlement to

457 F. Vanclay, 'Project induced displacement and resettlement: From impoverishment risks to an opportunity or development', *Impact Assess. Proj. Apprais*, Vol. 35, 2017, pp. 3-21; The Equator Principles are a risk management framework based on adoption of the 10 safeguard policies by a number of large private sector investment banks, which is used to identify, counter act, and eliminate or mitigate environmental and social risks. Currently 89 financial institutions form 37 countries have signed the Equator Principles. See: http://www.equator-principles.com/.

458 IFC 2012.

459 IFC 2012.

460 IFC 2012, p. 1.

461 S. Flynn & L. Vergara, *Land access and resettlement planning at La Granja. CSRM Occasional Papers: Mining-induced Displacement and Resettlement.Centre for Social Responsibility in Mining*, The University of Queensland, Brisbane, 2015.

achieve outcomes that are consistent with the objectives of this Performance Standard.[462]

Despite the delineation of processes and goals, there is no explicit timeframe for consulting and negotiating with displaced persons established in the Standards. Without an explicit timeframe established by the Standards, there is a risk that consultations with affected communities may occur so late in the project cycle that the time for meaningful participation in decision-making will have passed.

IFC Performance Standard 5 differentiates between physical displacement and economic displacement and provides that clients (i.e. borrowers) must adequately address both types of displacement. In cases of physical displacement, clients must develop a Resettlement Action Plan that covers, at a minimum, the applicable requirements of this Performance Standard regardless of the number of people affected.[463] In the cases of economic displacement, clients must develop a Livelihood Restoration Plan to compensate affected persons and/or communities and offer other assistance that meets the objectives of this Performance Standard.[464] As discussed in detail below, the IFC Performance Standards and national legal frameworks differ in this respect.

5.3.4 *Regional Development Bank Policies*

The Asian Development Bank, the African Development Bank, and the Inter-American Development Bank adopted resettlement policies that are alike, in many respects, to the World Bank's Standards.[465] For example, similar to the World Bank Safeguards, the Asian Development Bank's resettlement framework states that borrowers cannot lower their policy standards if such standards differ from or are incomplete compared to ADB policy standards.[466]

---

462 IFC 2012, p. 3.

463 IFC 2012, p. 5.

464 IFC 2012, p. 5.

465 African Development Bank Group, *Involuntary Resettlement Policy. African Development Bank*, Tunis, 2003; ADB, *Involuntary Resettlement Policy. Asian Development Bank*, Bahasa, 1998; Inter-American Development Bank (IDAB), *Involuntary Resettlement. Inter-American Development Bank*, Washington, DC, 1998.

466 S. Price, 'National Standards on Involuntary Resettlement: Are They Achievable?', Paper at XI International Congress of Anthropological and Ethnographical Sciences, Florence, 2003.

5.3.5 *Bilateral Institutional Policies*

The United States Agency for International Development (USAID) recently enacted voluntary guidelines on compulsory displacement and resettlement.[467] The USAID Guidelines are a:

> Voluntary tool intended for use by USAID Operating Units and their partners at all stages of the program cycle, [ensuring that USAID-funded programming] minimizes and mitigates risks of impoverishment of affected legitimate landholders.[468]

The Australian Department of Foreign Affairs and Trade published a guidance document on displacement and resettlement. This policy applies to projects that are funded by direct Australian aid, co-financed by Australian and multilateral development banks, or delegated by the Australian government to an implementing organization.[469]

5.3.6 *Resettlement Guidance in International Human Rights Instruments*

Aside from the international policy standards established by the VGGT, World Bank, IFC, and regional development banks, there are several standards on resettlement embedded in international human rights instruments. For example, the International Covenant on Economic, Social and Cultural Rights (ICESCR) is a multilateral treaty adopted by the United Nations (UN) General Assembly, which came into effect in 1966.[470] Article 11 of the ICESCR establishes the right to housing and an adequate standard of living. Nations are not technically bound to comply with the ICESCR unless they ratify the treaty; 165 governments have ratified the ICESCR. However, the ICESCR is not considered legally binding in many countries. For example, the United States, Great Britain, and other Western powers have not ratified the ICESCR.

---

467 C. Stevens & C. Dear, *Guidelines on Compulsory Displacement and Resettlement in USAID Programing*, United States Agency for International Development, Washington, DC, 2016.

468 Stevens & Dear 2016, p. 2.

469 Australian Department of Foreign Affairs and Trade (DFAT), *Displacement and Resettlement of People in Development Activities*, DFAT, Canberra, 2015.

470 United Nations, *International Covenant on Economic, Social and Cultural Rights*, A/ RES/2200, New York, 1966.

In 1997, the UN Committee on Economic, Social and Cultural Rights issued a General Comment (No. 7) on the right to adequate housing and forced evictions.[471] The General Comment states the following:

> Whereas some evictions may be justifiable, such as in the case of persistent non-payment of rent or of damage to rented property without any reasonable cause, it is incumbent upon the relevant authorities to ensure that they are carried out in a manner warranted by a law which is compatible with the Covenant and that all the legal recourses and remedies are available to those affected.[472]

In 2007, the United Nations adopted the Basic Principles and Guidelines on Development-based Evictions and Displacement.[473] These Principles provide for a right to alternative land of better or equal equality and housing that must satisfy the following criteria for adequacy: accessibility, affordability, affordability, habitability, security of tenure, cultural adequacy, suitability of location, and access to essential public services, such as health an education.[474]

5.4 Literature on the Gap between National-Level Resettlement Procedures and International Standards

Most projects involving the acquisition of land are conducted without borrowing funds from the World Bank or other institutions with safeguard policies that may supplement national laws with weak resettlement procedures.[475] According to a 1994 World Bank report, World Bank-funded projects accounted for only three percent of dam-induced displacement worldwide and only one percent of urban development and transportation-related displacement.[476] For the majority of other projects are not funded by the World Bank, IFC, regional development banks, or other institutions with resettlement policies, domestic laws may be the only shield that provides displaced populations with legal protection and redress. The risk is that, in countries with weak or non-existent legal frameworks applicable to resettlement, companies and governments can potentially avoid establishing

471 UN Committee on Economic, Social and Cultural Rights (CESCR), *General Comment No. 7: The right to adequate housing (Art. 11.1): forced evictions*, E/1998/22, 1997.

472 CESCR 1997, para. 11.

473 UN, *Basic Principles and Guidelines on Development-Based Evictions and Displacement*, A/HRC/4/18, 2007.

474 UN 2007, p. 6.

475 S. Price, 2015, pp. 127-141.

476 World Bank Environment Department, *Resettlement and development: the Bankwide review of projects involving involuntary resettlement 1986-1993*, World Bank, Washington, DC, 1994.

and implementing resettlement and rehabilitation procedures by expropriating land and only paying market value compensation.

Previous studies have indicated that national laws only require governments to follow 'compensation only' approaches to land expropriation as opposed to establishing robust resettlement and rehabilitation procedures.[477] According to Cernea,

> In most developing countries, resettlement policies are absent (except land expropriation/compensation laws) or differ considerably from international standards. A big 'policy gap' or 'development gap' has emerged between [international agency] policies and 'country polices.[478]

Cernea further states that there has been little progress on national-level resettlement procedures; since resettlement became a visible and talked-about issue in the context of Bank-financed on other development projects, few countries have enacted laws or adopted policies that protect displaced persons.[479] Price conducted a study of country-level adoption of resettlement policies in seven Asian countries: Bangladesh, Indonesia, Nepal, Pakistan, the Philippines, China, and Vietnam.[480] The study concluded that none of these countries had enacted legal provisions requiring that resettlement effects be avoided or minimized. Additionally, none of the seven countries established comprehensive legal safeguards that:

> [...] identify fully all of the losses borne by displace populations; to use replacement cost compensation; to re-establish the full economic and social bases of those affected; to provide special assistance to improve the status of the poor and vulnerable; or to assist those people lacking land title.[481]

5.5 Findings on Resettlement Procedures in National Laws

While many scholars and practitioners are generally cognizant of the fact that national laws often fail to meet international standards, a broad comparative analysis of which

---

477 S. Price, 'Compensation, Restoration and Development Opportunities: National Standards on Involuntary Resettlement', *in* M.M. Cernea & H.M. Mathur, *The Resettlement Dilemma: Can Compensation Prevent Impoverishment?*, Oxford University Press, New Delhi, 2008, pp. 147-179; A. Rew, E. Fisher & B. Pandey, 'Policy Practices in Development-Induced Displacement and Resettlement', *Development-Induced Displacement: Problems, Policies and People*, Berghahn Books, Oxford, 2006, pp. 38-69.

478 Cernea 2005, p. 87.

479 Cernea 2005. p. 98.

480 Price 2008.

481 Price 2008.

countries are particularly in need of legal reforms relating to resettlement has not been undertaken. To fill this gap, this Section examines the laws enacted in 50 countries across Asia, Africa, and Latin America against a set of 'rehabilitation and resettlement indicators,' which measure whether national laws comply with international standards on resettlement.

Table 10 Resettlement and Rehabilitation Indicators

1. Is there a national-level resettlement policy that is legally binding on all projects involving the expropriation of land?
2. Do the national laws provide displaced populations with relocation allowance?
3. Do the national laws provide displaced populations with alternative land, housing, or resettlement?
4. Do the national laws provide displaced populations with productive or suitable alternative land?
5. Do the national laws require that displaced populations be consulted during the resettlement process?
6. Do the national laws require the government or acquiring bodies to minimize or avoid involuntary resettlement?
7. Do the national laws require the government or acquiring bodies to provide sufficient funding to implement resettlement programs?

5.5.1 *Legally Binding Resettlement and Rehabilitation Procedures*

According to the ESF, the World Bank supports the use of the Borrower's ES Framework "provided this is likely to address the risks and impacts on the projects, and enable the project to achieve objectives materially consistent with the ESSs."[482] The Framework further states "the use of all, or part, of the Borrower's ES Framework will be agreed between the Bank and the Borrower, following completion of the assessment."[483] The Borrower's ESS Framework is defined as including "aspects of the country's policy, legal, and institutional framework."[484] Since the World Bank and other international financial intermediaries are currently trying to shift more responsibility onto private and state actors to address resettlement risks through country systems, it is worthwhile to investigate whether national-level constitutions, statutes, and regulations in developing countries establish legally binding resettlement and rehabilitation procedures.

The first resettlement indicator asks whether the country has enacted a national-level laws containing resettlement and rehabilitation procedures that are legally binding on all projects involving the expropriation of land. 'Resettlement and rehabilitation procedures' in this Chapter refer to procedures that require governments and acquiring bodies to resettle and

482 World Bank, *The World Bank Environmental and Social Framework*, World Bank, Washington, DC, 2017, p. 18.
483 World Bank 2017, pp. 6-7.
484 World Bank 2017, p. 18.

otherwise accommodate affected landholders that must vacate their lands as a result of expropriation. These procedures should theoretically address issues of physical displacement (relocation or loss of shelter) and economic displacement (loss of assets or access to assets that leads to loss of income sources or means of livelihood). The World Bank ESS5 and IFC Performance Standard 5, for example, contain examples of resettlement procedures (e.g., they require borrowers to develop a 'resettle displacement action plan' or 'livelihood restoration plan' to accommodate displaced persons. Resettlement and rehabilitation procedures are crucial given the 'compensation only' approach to addressing landholder interests has often been found to be inadequate. First, not all displaced persons qualify for compensation. Under domestic legal frameworks, usually only displaced persons with registered or statutorily recognized land rights are eligible to receive compensation. Second, compensation payments usually do not provide enough resources to allow displaced persons to purchase alternative land or otherwise reconstruct their livelihoods post-displacement.[485]

While all of the 50 countries have laws that, at least to some extent, recognize the right to compensation for expropriation, none of these constitutions establish robust procedures for ensuring or measures for resettling and rehabilitating the livelihoods of displaced persons. As stated by Ibrahim Shihata (former Legal Counsel and Senior Vice- President of the World Bank),

> Compensation is what the owner of property, unilaterally acquired by the government, receives in lieu of that property [...] rehabilitation, on the other hand, constitutes a series of measures, including but not limited to monetary compensation, aimed at affording the affected populations the possibility to become re- established and economically self- sustaining in the shortest period. Compensation is usually only provided to land and property owners, while rehabilitation measures are to be provided to all those severally affected by development projects.[486]

Of the 50 countries assessed, only three (India, Laos, and Vietnam) have enacted resettlement procedures in statutes or regulations that are legally binding on all development projects involving the expropriation of land. For example, India's Right to Fair Compensation and Transparency in Land Acquisition, Rehabilitation and Resettlement Act, 2013 (LARR Act) provides robust rehabilitation and resettlement procedures for accommodating persons displaced by expropriations. Pursuant to the Act, the government must hold public consultations, conduct social impact assessments, and formulate comprehensive

485 Cernea 2008, pp. 89-120.
486 Shihata 1993.

rehabilitation and resettlement schemes including the provision of alternative land, housing, and other assistance to displaced populations. In Vietnam, the government passed the Decree Regulations on Compensation, Support and Resettlement Upon Land Expropriation by the State in 2014.[487] These Regulations provide specific procedures that apply in cases of involuntary resettlement, and include procedures for providing alternative land and financial resettlement assistance to displaced populations. In 2016, the Laos government passed a Decree on Compensation and Resettlement Management in Development Projects, which applies to all public and private sector development projects.[488]

China and the Philippines received a 'partial' score for this indicator because these countries enacted resettlement and rehabilitation procedures in laws that apply to some types of development projects involving the expropriation of land; however, these procedures do not apply to all expropriation projects and therefore do not provide all displaced persons with resettlement and rehabilitation assistance. For example, the Philippines' Executive Order 1035 of 1985 provides relocation and resettlement assistance to displaced tenants of agricultural lands, and the Indigenous Peoples Rights Act, 1997 provides resettlement assistance to Indigenous communities. However, the Philippines has not enacted a broadly applicable law with robust resettlement and rehabilitation procedures that protect all displaced populations whenever land is expropriated.

China has enacted several sector-specific regulations that establish provisions for resettling and rehabilitating displaced persons. However, China received a 'partial' score because it has not enacted an overarching law or regulation that applies to all types of development projects involving the expropriation of land (e.g., there is no resettlement procedure applicable to mining projects and other projects outside the water sector). According to Shi, there is still "broad scope for improvement, particularly outside the water sector" in China.[489]

Of the 50 countries considered, 44 have not enacted resettlement procedures that are legally binding on development projects involving the expropriation of land. Among these 44 countries, I found evidence of either draft or adopted resettlement policies in 12 countries (Afghanistan, Belize, Brazil, Cambodia, Kenya, Indonesia, Pakistan, Nepal, the Philippines, Sri Lanka, Tanzania, and Zambia). These 12 countries still received red 'no' scores because

487 Government of Vietnam, *Decree Regulations on Compensation, Support and Resettlement Upon Land Expropriation by the State*, 2014.

488 Government of Laos, *Decree on Compensation and Resettlement Management in Development Projects*, 2016.

489 S. Quoqing, 'Comparing China's and the World Bank's displacement policies over time: the ascent of the "Resettlement with Development', *in* M. Cernea and J. Maldonado (Eds.), *Challenging the Prevailing Paradigm of Displacement and Resettlement*, Routledge, NY, 2018.

these policies are not legally binding. In Sri Lanka, for example, the Cabinet approved the National Involuntary Resettlement Policy (NIRP) in 2001.[490] However, NIRP is not legally binding. Full compliance with NIRP requires the government to amend existing laws in order to bring them into line with NIRP principles. In 2013, the Brazilian Ministry of Cities passed a resettlement policy to protect the rights of urban residents who are involuntarily resettled from their homes.[491] However, this policy is also not legally binding.

Honduras received 'unclear' scores for all seven of the rehabilitation and resettlement content indicators examined in this Article. Although secondary sources indicate that national resettlement procedures exist in Honduras, I was unable to obtain a copy of the resettlement procedures.

Figure 11 National-Level Legally Binding Resettlement Procedures

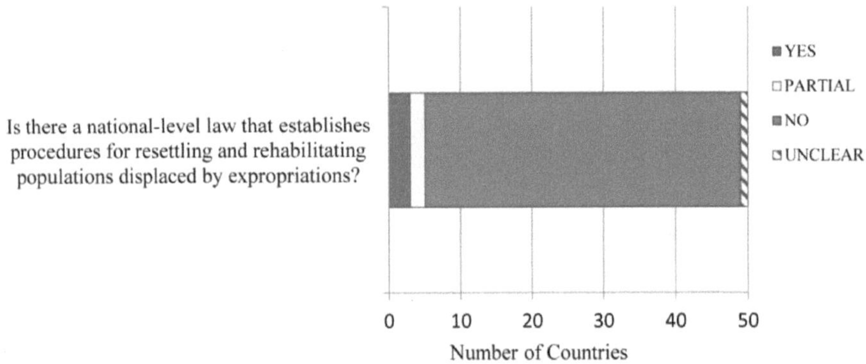

5.5.2 *Relocation Allowance*

The World Bank ESS5 provides financial and other forms of assistance to displaced populations to cover the cost of resettling on alternative land. Borrowers must also provide a "transitional allowance sufficient to meet temporary rental expenses and other costs until occupancy is available."[492] IFC Performance Standard 5 states that clients must offer displaced persons choices among feasible resettlement options, including adequate replacement housing or cash compensation where appropriate.[493] Clients must also provide relocation

490 V. Nathaniel, 'The National Involuntary Resettlement Policy: A case for implementation', *Daily FT*, 2015.
491 Cities Alliance, *Government of Brazil Passes Landmark Involuntary Resettlement Policy*, Cities Alliance, Brussels, 25 July 2013.
492 World Bank, *The World Bank Environmental and Social Framework*, World Bank, Washington, DC, 2017, p. 62.
493 IFC 2012, p. 5.

assistance suited to the needs of each group of displaced persons.[494] Performance Standard 5 states that "based on consultation with such displaced persons, the client will provide relocation assistance sufficient for them to restore their standard of living at an adequate alternative site."[495]

The second resettlement indicator asks whether national laws provide displaced populations with relocation allowances to cover the transportation costs associated with resettling on alternative land, regardless of whether these persons have a legally recognized right to land. Four of 50 countries (China, Laos, India, and Vietnam) received 'yes' scores on the indicator. For example, Article 16 of Lao's Decree on Compensation and Resettlement Management in Development Projects (2016) requires project owners to provide affected landholders with assistance throughout the transitional period for at least three years.

On this indicator, 17 of the 50 countries received a 'partial' score because their national laws provide a relocation allowance as part of the compensation package provided to landholders eligible for compensation.[496] However, these laws do not ensure that all displaced persons will receive a relocation allowance, regardless of legal status. In these countries, only displaced persons with registered or otherwise statutorily recognized land rights are entitled to relocation allowance as part of the compensation package. For example, Section 16.2 of Nepal's Land Acquisition Act, 1977 provides compensation for "the losses that the concerned person will suffer as a result of shifting his/ her residence, or the place of his/ her business, by reason of the acquisition of his/ her land." Since Nepal's Land Acquisition Act 1977 only provides compensation to landholders with legally recognized tenure rights, Nepal received a 'partial' score for this indicator.

A total of 28 of the 50 countries assessed received a 'no' score because the national-level laws do not provide displaced populations with relocation allowance to cover the costs of relocating from expropriated land.

494 IFC 2012, p. 5.
495 IFC 2012, p. 6.
496 Botswana, Ethiopia, Hong Kong, Indonesia, Kenya, Malaysia, Mongolia, Myanmar, Nepal, Pakistan, Philippines, Sierra Leone, South Africa, South Sudan, Sri Lanka, Taiwan and Tanzania.

Figure 12 Relocation Allowance

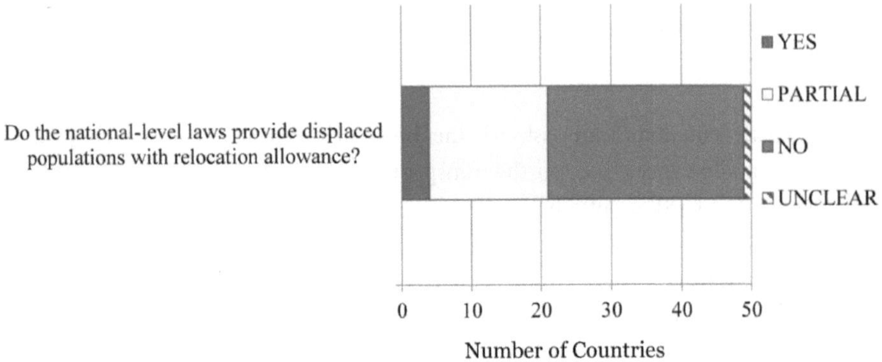

5.5.3 *A Right to Alternative Land and/or Housing That Is Suitable or Productive*

Section 16.9 of the VGGTs provides the following:

> Evictions and relocations should not result in individuals being rendered homeless or vulnerable to the violation of human rights. Where those affected are unable to provide for themselves, States should, to the extent that resources permit, take appropriate measures to provide adequate alternative housing, resettlement or access to productive land, fisheries and forests, as the case may be.[497]

Pursuant to ESS5, Borrowers must offer feasible resettlement opinions, including adequate replacement housing.[498] ESS5 also states that,

> New resettlement sites will offer living conditions at least equivalent to those previously enjoyed, or consistent with prevailing minimum codes or standards, whichever set of standards is higher [...] the Borrower will provide arrangements to allow them to obtain adequate housing with security of tenure.[499]

The IFC Performance Standard 5 also imposes these requirements.[500]

497 FAO 2012, sec. 16.9.
498 World Bank 2017, p. 58.
499 World Bank 2017, p. 62.
500 IFC 2012, pp. 5-6.

The third resettlement indicator revealed that only three of the 50 countries (India, Laos, the Philippines) have laws that provide all displaced persons with the right to alternative land, regardless of the legal status of the displaced person. For example, the Philippines has a national- level statute that requires the government to provide for "squatter relocation sites."[501]

'Partial' scores were awarded to 26 of the 50 countries because according to these countries' laws, alternative land may be provided as a compensation option. However, the provision of alternative land is granted at the discretion of the government, so there is no guarantee that all displaced persons will be granted alternative land. For example, Section 11(2) of Tanzania's Land Acquisition Act, 1967 provides that:

> The President may, with the consent of the person entitled to compensation [...] make to the person entitled to compensation a grant of public land not exceeding the value of the land acquired [...][502]

In 20 of the countries assessed, national laws do not provide displaced persons with a right to alternative land. In these countries, displaced populations may be particularly vulnerable to impoverishment, landlessness, and other risks associated with involuntary resettlement unless laws are reformed to ensure alternative land is provided. In Bangladesh, where the law does not provide affected landholders with a right to alternative land, a survey conducted by Atahar found that 77 percent of displaced persons surveyed said the compensation received was insufficient to cover all of their losses, and about 90 percent could not purchase the same amount of land with the compensation money provided.[503]

The fourth resettlement indicator shows that of the 50 countries, only Laos has a law requiring that displaced populations *must* be resettled in productive alternative land or suitable alternative housing. Articles 12 of the Decree on Compensation and Resettlement Management in Development Projects (2016) requires suitable housing, agricultural sites of "equivalent forms and size." Article 15 of Laos' 2016 Decree requires project owners to provide "agricultural land in appropriate ways including the creation of new livelihood options and income generation activities."

Four countries (Ghana, India, the Philippines, and Vietnam) received 'partial' scores because their laws may ensure, in some cases, that suitable or productive alternative land

501 Government of Philippines, *An Act to Facilitate The Acquisition of Right-of-Way, Site, or Location for National Government Infrastructure Projects and For other Purposes*, RA 8974, 2000, Section 9.
502 Government of Tanzania, 1967, Section 11(2).
503 Atahar 2013, p. 312.

is provided. However, the laws of these four countries do not guarantee that the alternative land or housing will be suitable or productive in every case. In the Philippines, for example, Section 7(c) of the RA 8974 (Indigenous People's Rights Act 1997) establishes that Indigenous communities must be provided

> In all possible cases with lands of quality and legal status at least equal to that of the land previously occupied by them, suitable to provide for their present needs and future development [...]

However, this provision only applies when Indigenous land is expropriated. Non-Indigenous landholders are not granted the right to suitable or productive alternative land in the Philippines.

In 44 of the 50 countries, displaced persons are not provided with the right to productive alternative land or suitable alternative housing subsequent to expropriation. In these countries, displaced populations may be at risk of suffering a reduced standard of living from having to relocate to degraded or lower-quality land.

Figure 13 Alternative Land or Housing

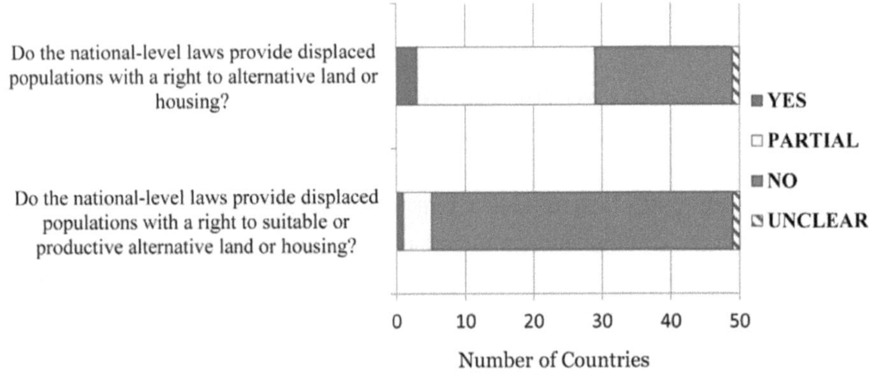

5.5.4 *Consulting Displaced Populations during the Resettlement Process*

Section 16.8 of the VGGTs provides that:

> States should, prior to eviction or shift in land use which could result in depriving individuals and communities from access to their productive

> resources, explore feasible alternatives in consultation with the affected parties [...]

ESS5 requires Borrowers to engage communities through a process of stakeholder engagement. ESS5 states,

> Decision- making processes related to resettlement and livelihood restoration will include options and alternatives from which affected persons may choose. Disclosure of relevant information and meaningful participation of affected communities and persons will take place during the consideration of alternative project design [...][504]

Furthermore, the ESS requires consultation regarding planning options, and access to resettlement plans.[505] The IFC Performance Standard 5 also requires that clients consult project-affected persons and allow them to participate "during the planning, implementation, monitoring, and evaluation of compensation payments, livelihood restoration activities, and resettlement."[506]

Section 16.8 of the VGGTs provides that,

> States should [...] explore feasible alternatives in consultation with the affected parties, consistent with the principles of these Guidelines, with a view to avoiding, or at least minimizing, the need to resort to evictions.

Section 16.2 of the VGGTs establishes that "States should ensure that the planning and process for expropriation are transparent and participatory."

The fifth resettlement indicator focuses only on whether consultation about the resettlement process must occur before displacement; the analysis does not address consultation requirements that may apply in other stages of the expropriation (e.g., consultations before or during the expropriation and compensation decision-making stages). Unless resettlement provisions indicate that consultation is specifically required during the resettlement process, countries were given a 'no' score for this indicator.

---

504 World Bank 2017, p. 56.
505 World Bank 2017, pp. 56, 61-62.
506 IFC 2012, p. 3.

Five of the 50 countries (China, India, Laos, South Sudan, and Vietnam) have laws that explicitly require the government to consult affected populations about the resettlement process before displacement. For example, Section 72(2) of South Sudan's Land Act, 2009 provides that "internally displaced persons shall be consulted and shall have opportunities to participate in planning and implementing resettlement programs."

The Philippines received 'partial' scores because its national laws require consultation during resettlement processes in *some* expropriation cases. The Philippines' laws require consultation before the resettlement process when Indigenous land is expropriated, but this requirement is not imposed when non-Indigenous land is expropriated.

In 43 of the 50 countries assessed, governments and acquiring bodies are not legally required to consult displaced populations before displacement about the resettlement process. If left in the dark or otherwise not adequately consulted, displaced populations in these countries may be more likely to protest resettlement decisions, which may delay projects and increase costs for project developers.[507]

Figure 14 Consultations with Displaced Populations

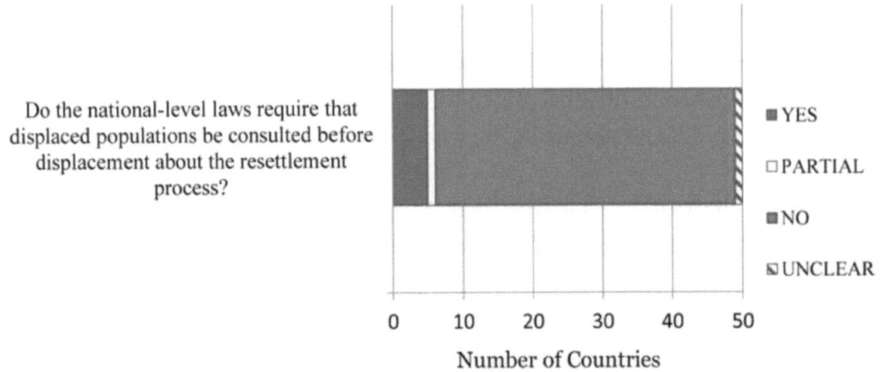

5.5.5 *Requirement to Minimize or Avoid Involuntary Resettlement*

The standards established by ESS5, IFC Performance Standard 5, and the Section 16.8 of the VGGTs state that involuntary resettlement should be minimized or avoided. These international standards call for project designers to consider feasible alternatives to implementing the project without resettling landholders. To answer the question posed

507 *See, generally* Hemadri *et al.* 1999.

by the sixth resettlement indicator, the analysis investigated whether national laws impose similar requirements. India is the only country assessed with a national law that requires the government to minimize or avoid involuntary resettlement in every expropriation case. According to India's LARR Act of 2013, an expert group must appraise the Social Impact Assessment and report on whether the land proposed to be acquired is the bare-minimum needed for the project, and whether there are other options available that involve less displacement.[508]

Two of the 50 countries (the Philippines and Taiwan) received 'partial' scores for this indicator. A 'partial' score means that in some cases the government may be required to minimize or avoid resettlement, although not necessarily in every case.

In 46 of the countries assessed, the government and acquiring bodies are not legally obligated to minimize or avoid involuntary resettlement. Without this obligation, there is an increased risk that an excessive number of landholders will be displaced by expropriations. In these countries, the law allows for displacement to occur even when it is not necessary for a legitimate public use. In Ghana and Bangladesh, for example, where there is no legal obligation of the government to minimize or avoid forced displacement, excessive amounts of land were expropriated for various development projects.[509] Much of this land subsequently remained unutilized. In other words, some landholders were displaced even though the development project did not require all of their land.

Figure 15 Minimize of Avoid Involuntary Resettlement

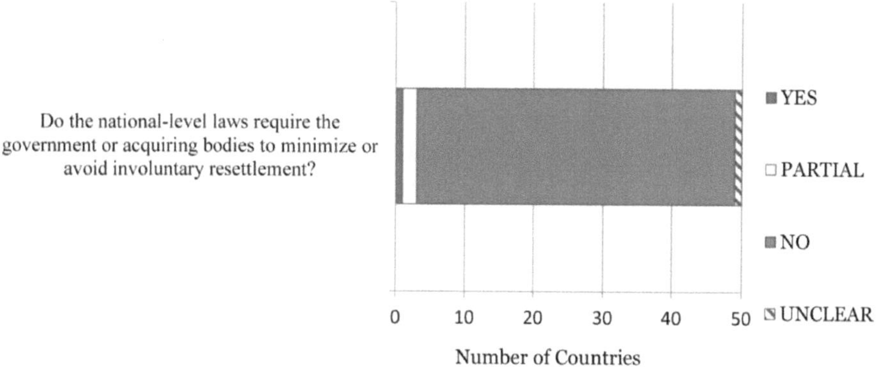

508 Government of India, 2013, sec. 7(5),

509 Larbi *et al.* 2004, pp. 115-127; Atahar 2013, pp. 306-319.

5.5.6 *Sufficient Funding to Implement Resettlement Programs*

Sufficient funding to implement resettlement programs ESS5 requires borrowers to establish roles and responsibilities relating to the financing and implementation of resettlement programs, including funding arrangements to meet unanticipated costs of resettlement.[510] ESS5 states "the full costs of resettlement activities necessary to achieve the objectives of the project are included in the total costs of the project."[511] The seventh resettlement indicator shows that only India, Laos, and Vietnam have enacted national-level laws that obligate the government or acquiring bodies to provide an amount of funding that is sufficient to cover the cost of implementing resettlement programs when land is expropriated. For example, Article 17(3) of Lao's Decree on Compensation and Resettlement Management in Development Projects (2016) requires project owners to prepare detailed budgets and cost estimates when preparing resettlement plans. Project owners must allocate funds to meet the needs of the resettlement program. India and Vietnam have similar provisions in their national- level laws on resettlement, which require that sufficient funding be allocated to cover the costs of implementing resettlement programs. Of the 50 countries surveyed, 46 have not enacted laws that require governments or acquiring bodies to provide sufficient funding for resettlement and reconstruction programs.

Figure 16 Sufficient Funding for Resettlement Plans

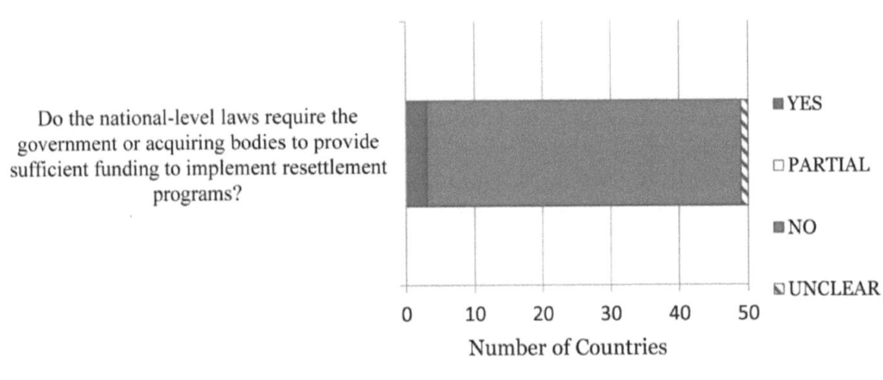

510 World Bank 2017, p. 57.
511 World Bank 2017, p. 57.

5.6 Suggested Avenues for Lawmakers to Pursue

The findings from the indicator analysis establish a benchmark that can inform debates on legal reforms related to resettlement and reconstruction among policymakers, practitioners, and scholars, including development agencies like the MDBs, which finance projects that cause millions of people to be displaced every year. This benchmark can be used to measure and promote national progress on adopting domestic laws and regulations and on strengthening laws to conform to international standards on resettlement and reconstruction. The findings from this Chapter can influence and help both donor agencies and lawmakers enact legally binding risk prevention measures and adequately financed resettlement and reconstruction obligations for owners and finance-providers.

In nearly all of the countries assessed, there are significant gaps in national-level legal frameworks that leave displaced persons without adequate legal protections to ensure not only physical relocation, but also socio-economic reconstruction. The finding that only three of the 50 countries (India, Laos, and Vietnam) have enacted laws or regulations that establish resettlement and rehabilitation procedures applicable to all expropriations suggests that many displaced populations around the world remain vulnerable to impoverishment and landlessness, among other risks. In 2016, after the World Bank published the ESF, it became evident that the legal analysis included in this Chapter has serious implications for many landholders displaced by Bank-financed development projects. As the World Bank itself has indicated, the ESF shifts responsibilities that used to be mandatory for World Bank staff onto country borrowers. These borrowers are now obligated to implement resettlement programs through "country systems" (which we can see are not yet defined with precision and clarity). The Bank's reliance on borrowers and on 'country systems' is particularly problematic given that many developing countries have not enacted laws for protecting or accommodating displaced persons against impoverishment.[512] Some countries have adopted nonbinding 'policies' on resettlement (e.g., Angola, Brazil, Namibia, and Sri Lanka), but these policies do not provide displaced persons with justiciable legal rights that can be exercised to seek redress in court. In this regard, country-level resettlement policies are different than the World Bank's previous 'safeguard' policies (now replaced by the ESS). World Bank safeguard policies were mandatory for all Bank staff; country-level resettlement policies, on the other hand, are voluntary and aspirational, and thus not legally binding for the states or Bank staff.

---

512 M. Cernea, 'The State and Involuntary Resettlement: Reflections on Comparing Legislation on Displacement in China and India', *in* F. Padovani ed., *Development- Induced Displacement in India and China: A Comparative Look*, Lexington Book, Lanham, 2016.

Based on the findings from the legal analysis, this study submits several recommendations for reforming laws to address resettlement and reconstruction:

1. Resettlement procedures should require the government and/or project developers to conduct a social impact assessment and develop a plan for resettling and rehabilitating displaced populations whenever land is acquired in a compulsory manner. India's LARR Act 2013 provides a model for other lawmakers to follow because it requires that a social impact assessment and comprehensive resettlement and rehabilitation scheme is developed whenever projects involve involuntary resettlement. While resettlement procedures should be binding on all development projects, they should be flexible enough to adapt to new and unanticipated circumstances that arise in cases of displacement. Resettlement plans may vary slightly from case to case in order to effectively respond to the needs of the displaced. In addition to establishing a robust resettlement procedure, countries must strengthen their institutional capacity to implement and enforce resettlement procedures. Governments and private actors should allocate sufficient funding, technical experts, and other resources to ensure there is sufficient capacity to effectively implement resettlement procedures.

2. Resettlement procedures should require the government and/or project developers to provide displaced populations with adequate relocation allowance to cover the transportation and other costs associated with resettling on alternative land. Countries should consider adopting the provision provided in Laos' 2016 Decree on Compensation and Resettlement in Development Projects, which provides allowance to cover transportation costs, and livelihood rehabilitation plans. It is important for developers to bear in mind that the burden on displaced populations does not end the moment the relocation site is reached. In some cases, fully revitalizing the economic and other losses borne by the displaced can take months or years. Financial and other assistance should be provided until income and livelihood restoration occurs, and proper monitoring mechanisms should be put in place to verify that no one is abusing or freeloading off assistance programs opportunistically. Determining the appropriate level of assistance is a balancing act that must be done on a case-by-case basis, but, in all cases, it must be done to some extent.

3. Resettlement procedures should require the government and/or project developers to provide productive alternative land and suitable alternative housing. For many displaced landholders, such as indigenous and local communities in rural areas, land is not a fungible commodity; the loss of land means the loss of the means to sustain their livelihood. Cash compensation payments may be insufficient to ensure livelihoods are reconstructed post-displacement. In cases where the expropriated land has been

inhabited by the same community for centuries, it may be difficult to find alternative land that is sufficiently suitable. Nevertheless, imposing a legal obligation on governments and developers to investigate options for alternative land in consultation with displaced populations will make it more likely that these populations will not be landless, homeless, or impoverished subsequent to displacement.

4. Resettlement procedures should require the government and/or project developers to consult displaced populations and allow these populations to participate in decision-making during all stages of the project cycle, including the resettlement stage. The World Bank ESS Framework, the IFC Performance Standards, and the VGGTs all require that affected landholders are adequately informed and allowed to meaningfully participate in the project design and implementation. In cases where development projects infringe on indigenous territories, project developers should not relocate indigenous communities without prior and informed consent, and after agreement on just and fair compensation. Consultations and negotiations with affected landholders before a project begins can reduce the costs and financial risks that may arise when displaced populations decide to protest projects or file for injunctions in courts. Allowing displaced populations to participate in the development of resettlement plans can help ensure that the assistance provided in resettlement plans adequately addresses the risks of impoverishment and other consequences.

5. Resettlement procedures should require the government and/or project developers to minimize or avoid involuntary resettlement wherever possible. In some cases, involuntary resettlement may be unavoidable, but in other cases, there may be feasible alternatives to implementing the project that do not also require landholders to be displaced. If national laws require the government or private developers to explore feasible alternatives, there may be less of a risk of excessive expropriations and involuntary resettlement. Land expropriation and involuntary resettlement should only occur where it is absolutely necessary to achieve a genuine public purpose and there are no less invasive means.

Overall, this Chapter demonstrates the urgent need to enact legally binding laws and regulations that establish robust resettlement and reconstruction procedures that ensure development projects do not harm or threaten the livelihoods of landholders who are forcibly displaced. India's LARR Act 2013 provides a model for lawmakers to follow because they provide robust resettlement and rehabilitation procedures that adopt international standards on resettlement. While resettlement legal procedures should be binding on all development projects, they should be flexible enough to adapt to unanticipated circumstances that arise in cases of displacement. Laws should enable resettlement programs to vary from case to case in order to effectively respond to the particular needs of displaced landholders.

6 The Laws and Practices Related to Land Expropriation in Nigeria: The Case of the Lekki Free Trade Zone (LFTZ) in Lagos[513]

6.1 Summary and Roadmap

This Chapter takes a closer look at one of the 50 countries. It examines whether the laws and practices related to land expropriation in Nigeria comply with international standards on expropriation, compensation, and resettlement. The main objectives of this Chapter are to provide (1) more detail as to how the legal indicator assessment was conducted using Nigeria as an example, and (2) insight on the implementation of expropriation laws in Nigeria. This Chapter first looks at Nigeria's legal framework and practices related to expropriation, compensation, and resettlement, and compares this framework to Section 16 of the VGGTs. Next, this Chapter examines how expropriation laws function in practice in Nigeria by analyzing the expropriation practices followed in the LFTZ case. A major takeaway of this Chapter is that the lack of strong legal framework on expropriation can result in insufficient compensation, resettlement assistance, and other entitlements. This Chapter concludes with a set of recommendations for reforming Nigeria's Land Use Act (LUA).

This Chapter includes a study of the LFTZ expropriation case as an illustrative example of how expropriation is conducted in Nigeria. It presents an interdisciplinary study that combines both an analysis of the laws applicable to expropriation and compensation in Nigeria, and a survey of affected landholders and other empirical research related to the LFTZ. In August 2017, I worked with a research team in Nigeria to survey 140 affected households from ten different communities affected by land expropriation for the LFTZ. We also interviewed government officials and representatives from private companies

513 This chapter contains analysis and discussion from the following publication: Tagliarino *et al*, 'Compensation for Expropriated Community Farmland in Nigeria: An In-Depth Analysis of the Laws and Practices Related to Land Expropriation for the Lekki Free Trade Zone in Lagos', *Land 2018*, Vol. 7, 2008, p. 23. I wrote the article and conducted the legal analysis with feedback and guidance from the other co-authors. Yakubu Bununu provided extensive feedback and comments on the article. Bununu also managed the field research and organized meetings and interviews with government and company representatives. In Nigeria in 2017, Nicholas Tagliarino, Yakubu Bununu, Akintobi Olusanmi and Magbagbeola O. Micheal conducted the surveys and interviews with government and company representatives involved in the LFTZ. Marcello De Maria provided extensive feedback on the article, analyzed the survey data, wrote the Section that discusses the survey findings, and created the figures and tables shown in Section 5 that present the survey results.

involved in the development of the LFTZ. As discussed below, the responses to survey indicate whether the government followed international standards when expropriating land for the LFTZ. The survey responses also provide some indication of landholder perceptions of government expropriation practices. The main research questions examined in this Chapter are as follows:

1. Do Nigeria's laws comply with internationally recognized standards on expropriation, compensation, and resettlement?
2. Did the government follow international standards on expropriation, compensation, and resettlement in the LFTZ expropriation case?
3. What are some recommendations for reforming Nigeria's legal framework related to expropriation, compensation, and resettlement so that it complies with international standards?

Section 6.2 discusses legal reform as a solution to arbitrary expropriation and insufficient compensation in Nigeria. Section 6.3 highlights empirical research on expropriation and forced eviction in Nigeria. Section 6.4 provides a comparative legal analysis of Nigeria's LUA with Section 16 of the VGGTs. Section 6.5 provides an in-depth examination of the LFTZ case, including a discussion of the survey methodology as well as the findings from the survey of 140 households. Section 6.6 provides a set of suggested recommendations for Nigerian lawmakers to pursue when reforming the LUA to comply with the VGGTs.

6.2 Legal Reform as a Solution to Arbitrary Expropriation and Insufficient Compensation in Nigeria

This Chapter argues that statutory reform of Nigeria's LUA is key to ensure that more investment in the reconstruction of landholder livelihoods occurs when land in Nigeria is expropriated. While there are a number of factors that contribute to affected landholder impoverishment, such as corruption, lack of financing, lack of political will, and limited capacity, the lack of a legal framework has been shown to be a significant factor contributing to affected landholder impoverishment. A study published by the World Bank in 1996 found that income restoration was lacking in countries that initiated displacing projects without first establishing country-wide policy or legal frameworks for resettlement and income restoration.[514] The same study found that projects with sufficient funding for resettlement, initiated in countries with policy and legal frameworks that protect the rights

514 World Bank, *Resettlement and Development: The Bankwide Review of Projects Involving Resettlement 1986-1994 Paper 032*, World Bank, Washington, DC, 1996.

of affected landholders, enabled successful income restoration of landholders post-expropriation.[515]

As discussed below, Nigeria's LUA contains several legal gaps and ambiguities, and grants broad discretion to State Governors to make expropriation and compensation decisions without informing or consulting affected landholders or the public. The LUA leaves affected populations vulnerable to expropriation without adequate compensation or remedies in the event that their tenure rights are violated. To ensure compensation covers the losses borne by affected landholders, the LUA should require the government to follow clear legal procedures that ensure transparent decision-making and landholder participation throughout the expropriation, compensation, and resettlement processes. If sufficiently clear and robust, such procedures can enable affected landholders the right to seek redress in court and allow for judges to effectively scrutinize expropriation and compensation decision-making. Following an in-depth comparative analysis of the LUA and the international standards established in Section 16 of the VGGT, specific recommendations for reforming the LUA are provided at the end of this Chapter.

6.3 Empirical Research on Expropriations and Forced Evictions in Nigeria

The World Bank Land Governance Assessment Framework found that local landholders in Nigeria commonly view expropriation as a tool for "dispossessing the poor to elevate the rich."[516] Regarding the Niger Delta, a region of Nigeria that for many years has been plagued by piracy, kidnappings, and violent conflict over oil, Nigerian scholars have argued that the lack of a strong and coherent legal framework for protecting the land and resource rights of local communities has been a root cause of the ongoing conflict.[517] According to Obi,

> The impact of the [LUA] on the Niger Delta was serious, as the people viewed it as an act of injustice [...] having lost ownership of their land to the government, the most the oil communities could claim from oil multinationals was compensation or surface rents [compensation for crops and other above-ground resources [...] Since the oil-producing communities had no legal claim to the

515 World Bank 1996.

516 World Bank, *Land Governance Assessment Framework Final Report: Nigeria*, World Bank, Washington, DC, 2011, p. 113.

517 C.I. Obi, 'Oil extraction, dispossession, resistance and conflict in Nigeria's oil-rich Niger Delta', *Can. J. Dev. Stud.*, No. 30, 2010, pp. 219-236.

> 'ownership' of oil produced from under their lands and waters, they had little or no leverage in making successful compensatory claims as a result of land expropriation.[518]

Lack of ownership rights to land, adequate compensation, benefit-sharing arrangements, and jobs from the oil industry reportedly led several community members in the Niger Delta to take up piracy and extract oil and money from companies operating in the region through illegal means such as kidnapping, theft, and violent attacks against refineries and ships.[519] A representative from Transparency International suggested that government officials might have colluded with pirates to extract money and oil from industries.[520]

Outside of the Niger Delta, the Nigerian government has been criticized several times by human rights organizations for its expropriations and forced evictions, particularly in urban areas where millions of Nigerians have been displaced for urban expansion and redevelopment purposes.[521] Large-scale development projects also caused many displacements in rural areas.[522] UN Habitat estimated that, between 2000 and 2007, the pattern of forced eviction in Nigeria left at least two million people displaced from their home in different parts of the country.[523] The following paragraphs highlight a few of the many cases of forced eviction and displacement in Nigeria.

6.3.1 *Forced Evictions in Abuja*

In the early 2000s, Abuja's Federal Capital Development Authority (FCDA) evicted an estimated 800,000 people to implement the Abuja Master Plan.[524] Research shows the FCDA did not adequately inform the public ahead of time about which settlements would be demolished.[525] Consequently, bulldozers suddenly arrived before affected landholders had the opportunity to find alternative land and housing. According to a UN Habitat

518 Obi 2010.

519 Al Jazeera, 'Report: Piracy in Nigeria- Power & People', November 2016. Available online: https://www.youtube.com/watch?v=866fXIAZsDk (accessed on 1 March 2018).

520 Al Jazeera 2016.

521 Global Land Tool Network, *Forced Evictions-Towards Solutions?*, UN Habitat, Nairobi, 2007; Amnesty International, *At the Mercy of the Government: Violation of the Right to an Effective Remedy in Badia East, Lagos State, Nigeria*, Amnesty International, London, 2013.

522 M. Van Eerd & B. Banerjee 2013; K. Idhoko, 'The process of Land Acquisition in Nigeria: A case study of Oyo state', *Int. J. Innov. Res. Stud*, No. 5, 2016, p. 1.

523 Global Land Tool Network 2007, p. 67.

524 Global Land Tool Network 2007.

525 The Centre on Housing and Evictions (COHRE) & Social and Economic Rights Action Center (SERAC), *The Myth of the Abuja Master Plan: Forced Evictions as Urban Planning in Abuja*, COHRE, Geneva, SERAC, Lagos, 2008.

report, "the FCDA demolished homes, schools, clinics, churches, mosques, and businesses without adequate consultation with communities, and without providing adequate notice, compensation, or adequate resettlement."[526] Likewise, another report by two local human rights organizations found that,

> The [Abuja] evictions have resulted in the massive displacement of hundreds of thousands of people from entire communities, with a spiraling effect on health, education employment, and family cohesion. Some of the demolitions were accompanied by violence perpetrated by heavily armed security operatives against residents and business owners.[527]

As a result of forced eviction in Abuja, homelessness became pervasive, families were torn apart, robbery and crime became rampant, and children lost access to healthcare and education.[528]

6.3.2 *Forced Evictions in Lagos*

Forced evictions for urban development have also been common in Lagos. In 1996, over 250,000 businesses and homes were demolished in Lagos as part of a three-week slum clearance operation; an estimated 750,000 people were affected by this operation.[529] More recently, the Lagos state government (LSG) came under international scrutiny for reportedly stripping communities of their homes and violating human rights. In 2013, Amnesty International published a report, which found that the LSG violated human rights when forcefully evicting people from their homes for urban redevelopment in Badia East, where over 200 homes and business structures were demolished.[530] According to the report, the government refused to grant compensation to affected communities on the grounds that it was "mindful of setting a precedent [...] whereby illegal occupiers of land without development permits have to be paid full compensation upon eviction."[531] At least 10,000 people were forcibly evicted in Badia East between 2013 and 2015.[532]

---

526 Global Land Tool Network 2007.

527 The Centre on Housing and Evictions (COHRE) & Social and Economic Rights Action Center (SERAC), *The Myth of the Abuja Master Plan: Forced Evictions as Urban Planning in Abuja*, COHRE, Geneva, SERAC, Lagos, 2008.

528 COHRE & SERAC 2008

529 Global Land Tool Network 2007.

530 Amnesty International 2013.

531 Amnesty International 2013.

532 E. Akinwotu, 'The forced Evictions of Badia East, Lagos: 'This is not right'', *The Guardian*. Available online: https://www.theguardian.com/cities/2015/oct/16/forced-evictions-badia-east-lagos-this-is-not-right (1 March 2018).

In November 2016, the LSG reportedly evicted over 30,000 residents of Otodo Gbame, Ilubirin, and Ebute Ikate waterfront communities in Lagos State; an additional 4000 residents were removed in March 2017.[533] Amnesty International reported that, since 2000, more than two million people were displaced from their homes in informal settlements and waterfront communities across Lagos state.[534] The government justified these evictions "as a security measure in the overall interest of all Lagosians," claiming these communities posed a security risk, but without giving further explanation.[535] The government reportedly did not provide notice and suddenly began bulldozing; further, after members of the Otodo Gbame community formed human chains around their houses, armed police reportedly fired bullets at them and sprayed them with tear gas.[536] This incident forced communities to flee in terror to nearby canoes while their homes were demolished.[537] At least one person was reportedly shot in the neck by police and died.[538] In June 2017, the Lagos High Court ruled that the government-ordered evictions of Lagos waterfront communities were "unconstitutional" and ordered that the government stop forced evictions—if respected and enforced by the government, this ruling could prevent an estimated 270,000 other residents of Lagos from losing their homes.[539]

Based on the aforementioned empirical research, it can be argued that tenure right in many parts of Nigeria are insecure, and that both rural and urban communities remain vulnerable to expropriation, forced eviction, and displacement. The following Sections highlight a key reason for this tenure insecurity by discussing the LUA's failure to comply with international standards on land expropriation and compensation, and protect affected communities in the LFTZ case.

6.4 Comparative Legal Analysis of Nigeria's LUA with the Section 16 VGGTs

This Section illustrates the significant gaps between Nigeria's legal framework and international standards on expropriation and compensation. The governing law on expropriation in Nigeria is the LUA, a law that has been highly criticized by NGOs, scholars, and the

533 Amnesty International, *Nigeria: Further Information: Forced Evictions in Lagos State Must Stop*, Amnesty International, London, 2017.

534 Amnesty International 2017.

535 Aljazeera, *Police Displace Thousands in Nigeria's Otodo-Gbame Slum*, Aljazeera, Doha, 2017.

536 Amnesty International, *Nigeria: Further Information: Forced Evictions in Lagos State Must Stop*, Amnesty International, London, 2017; Aljazeera, *Police Displace Thousands in Nigeria's Otodo-Gbame Slum*, Aljazeera, Doha, 2017.

537 Aljazeera, *Police Displace Thousands in Nigeria's Otodo-Gbame Slum*, Aljazeera, Doha, 2017.

538 Aljazeera 2017.

539 P. Totaro, *Nigerian Courts Rule Against Mass Eviction in Lagos: Activists*, Thomson Reuters, Toronto, 2017.

public.[540] As previously discussed in this Chapter, the Nigerian government has been condemned by human rights organizations for its forced evictions and poor expropriation practices. Since there is significant room for improvement in terms of law and practice in the country, we chose to focus on Nigeria. Moreover, given how much land was expropriated and the expansive nature of the LFTZ (as discussed below, the LFTZ may eventually become the largest free trade zone in Africa), we considered the LFTZ case to be particularly important and worthy of attention and analysis. In our view, the findings and recommendations presented in this Article can be used to reform laws and practices related to expropriation, not only in Nigeria, but also in other countries in which legal reforms to expropriation laws are desperately needed.

The Constitution of Nigeria (1999) states that no property can be acquired without "prompt payment of compensation" and a right to access courts of law or tribunals for the determination of "his interest in property and the amount of compensation."[541] This constitutional provision is implemented through Section 29 of the LUA, 1978 which permits State governors to acquire land for "overriding public interests."[542] The LUA applies to all land expropriations in the country. Initially passed as a Presidential Decree in 1978 during Nigeria's military era, this LUA eventually became an Act in 1990. Widely considered to be an inadequate and flawed law, the LUA has undergone several failed attempts at revision since its enactment in 1990.[543]

Section 1 of the LUA vests all land in State Governors in trust and administered "for the use and common benefit of all Nigerians." Based on this provision, individuals and communities are not legally permitted to own land in Nigeria. However, under Section 5, State Governors are authorized to grant statutory rights of occupancies to "any person" in rural and urban areas. State Governors can also grant customary rights of occupancy to "any person or organization" for agricultural, residential, grazing, and other purposes. The LUA does not define the terms 'person' or 'organization,' so it is unclear who qualifies as 'person' or 'organization' for purposes of the LUA; however, in practice, these terms have been interpreted to include individuals or communities. Corporations can also be granted rights to land under Section 51 of the LUA. Section 6(b)(2) of the LUA states that "no single right of occupancy shall be granted...in excess of 500 hectares if granted for agricultural purpose, or 5000 hectares if granted for grazing purposes." According to Sections 21 and 22 of the

540 A.K. Otubu, 'Private property rights and compulsory acquisition process in Nigeria: The past, present and future', *Acta Univ. Danub. Jurid*, No. 8, 2012, pp. 25-42.

541 Government of Nigeria, *Constitution of Nigeria*, Government of Nigeria, Abuja, 1999, Section 44.

542 Government of Nigeria, *Land Use Act*, Government of Nigeria, Abuja, 1990.

543 A.K. Otubu, 'Land reforms and the future of land use act in Nigeria', *Niger. Curr. Law Rev*, No. 4, 2008, pp. 126-143.

LUA, statutory and customary rights of occupancy cannot be alienated by assignment, mortgage, transfer of possession, or sublease without the government's consent.

Under Section 36 of the LUA, customary occupiers or holders who used land for agricultural purposes prior to passage of the LUA are considered lawful possessors of their agricultural land "as if a customary right of occupancy had been granted to the occupier and holder."[544] However, there are no transitional provisions concerning rural land that is not used for agricultural purposes; presumably all statutory rights to such land were extinguished upon the enactment of the LUA.[545] In many parts of Nigeria and other countries, groups of individuals and familiars share common interests in land areas, and govern, manage, and use land based on long-standing customs and traditions (i.e., customary tenure). Customary land tenure typically refers to community-based systems of land ownership and administration that have longstanding origins in the norms and practices of communities that often go back centuries. Customary land tenure exists in most countries, even though statutory law does not always recognize it. In Nigeria and other countries, legal rights to land (e.g., titles or deeds) can be granted rights to communities as well as individuals.

Importantly, the LUA does not explicitly recognize legal rights to unfarmed, undeveloped land.[546] The Local Government, if it is satisfied that an occupier or holder is entitled to possession, and upon the production of the occupier's sketch, diagram or sufficient description of land, may register the holder or occupier and grant a customary right of occupancy.[547] However, State Governors retain broad discretion to revoke rights of occupancy.[548] Moreover, the World Bank's LGAF report on Nigeria found that in practice,

> Enforcement of rights of the recognized tenure types is [...] a problem because most individual land rights (in rural and urban areas) are not mapped/registered...the mechanisms for rights recognition is poor because the absence of legislated procedures makes land management agencies develop administrative procedures for recognizing land rights which are often implemented arbitrarily. For instance, although non-documentary forms of evidence can be used to

544 Government of Nigeria 1990, Sec. 36.

545 P. Francis, 'For the use and common benefit of all Nigerians: Consequences of the 1978 land nationalization', *Afr. J. Int. Afr. Inst*, No. 54, 1984, pp. 5-28; L.A. Wily, *Legal Indicator Scores on the Tenure Security of Indigenous and Community Land in Nigeria, on* LandMark Map, 2016. Available online: www.landmarkmap.org (accessed on 8 February 2018).

546 Francis 1984; Wily 2016.

547 Government of Nigeria, *Land Use Act*, Government of Nigeria, Abuja, 1990, Sec. 36(3).

548 Government of Nigeria 1990, Sec. 38.

obtain claims to property, they have less strength than the documented evidences that are acceptable based on the judgment of the officer in charge.[549]

For the various reasons discussed in detail below, LUA fails to adopt internationally recognized standards on expropriation and compensation as established in the VGGTs.

6.4.1 *Definition of Public Purpose*

According to Section 16.1 of the VGGTs, "States should expropriate only where rights to land [...] are required for a public purpose. States should clearly define the concept of public purpose in law, in order to allow for judicial review." An international survey revealed that 'public purposes' commonly includes public buildings, public utilities, transportation, public parks, and defense purposes.[550] However, in many countries, governments retain broad authority to expropriate land for 'economic development' purposes, including natural resource extraction, agricultural production, and other revenue-generating activities.[551] In Peru, for example, the government issued a ministerial decree in 2000 declaring oil palm to be a crop that serves the "national interest."[552] This decree gave the government and expropriating companies broad discretion to extract oil palm from the Amazon rainforest without following environmental and land use planning requirements. Unless laws clearly define the concept of 'public purpose,' there is a risk that governments will abuse their expropriation power, which could result in public mistrust, tenure insecurity, displacement, and other negative outcomes.[553] For instance, land may be acquired under the pretext of a public purpose when the actual purpose is to transfer land to private companies that will use the land for purposes that do not support local economic growth or otherwise benefit the public.

Nigeria's LUA 1978 fails to comply with VGGTS principle 16.1 because it provides a vague, open-ended legal definition of 'public purpose,' ostensibly granting State Governors broad discretion to interpret what constitutes a 'public purpose.' The LUA does not adequately

549 World Bank, *Land Governance Assessment Framework Final Report: Nigeria*, World Bank, Washington, DC, 2011, p. 12.

550 Keith *et al*, *Food and Agriculture Organization of the United Nations. Land Tenure Studies 10: Compulsory Acquisition of Land and Compensation*, Food and Agriculture Organization (FAO), Rome, 2008.

551 J. Lindsay, K. Deininger, & T. Hilhorst, 'Compulsory land acquisition in developing countries: Shifting paradigm or entrenched legacy', *in* H. Lee, I. Kim, & I. Somin (eds.), *Eminent Domain: A Comparative Perspective*, Cambridge University Press, Cambridge, 2017.

552 M.L. Tarabochia, 'Peru's Climate Commitment threatened by advancing oil palm', *Mongabay*. 2016. Available online: https://news.mongabay.com/2016/04/perus-climate-commitments-threatened-advancing-oil-palm (accessed on 1 March 2018).

553 Tagliarino 2016.

limit the Governor's authority to expropriate land under the pretext of a public purpose and transfer such land to private companies that aim to use the land exclusively for profit-making activities that may not necessarily benefit the public. For instance, there is no explicit provision that subjects the Governor's expropriation decision to a review by an independent committee or judiciary. The LUA does not require the government to determine, prior to expropriating land, whether the proposed project is (1) necessary to serve a public purpose; (2) suitable (reasonably likely to achieve the intended public benefit), and (3) whether the benefits deriving from the expropriation are proportionate to the costs borne by affected populations.[554]

Section 28 of the LUA grants the Governor the right to revoke a right of occupancy for overriding public interest. Both statutory and customary rights of occupancy can be revoked. Statutory rights can be acquired when land is needed for "public purposes within the State," including when land is needed for mining or the construction of oil pipelines. Similarly, customary rights can be acquired for public purposes, mining purposes, the extraction of building materials, and a broad range of other purposes. As argued by Francis, the LUA,

> [...] empowers the local land allocation committees to expropriate almost any land within their areas of control and to allocate it for either public or private use [...] The tenure of rural land is allowed to remain undisturbed except where it conflicts, at any point, with the interests of capital holding developers, whether public or private.[555]

Section 51 of the LUA broadly defines 'public purpose' as including for "exclusive Government use or for public use," for "use by any body corporate," for mining, public works, or "economic, industrial, or agricultural development." The LUA does not subject State Governors' decisions on what constitutes a public purpose to oversight by the judiciary. Governors have broad discretion to establish a justification for compulsorily acquiring land. Since Section 51 states "public purpose *includes...*," the list of purposes is therefore not exhaustive, suggesting the State Governor can expropriate for other purposes not listed in the Act. The vaguely defined purposes in the LUA are problematic for a number of reasons. Since there are no checks in place to ensure corporations that are granted expropriated land continue to serve the public interest, this provision could allow expropriation to be used exclusively for private economic gain, without benefitting the public. Moreover, the LUA does not limit the State Governor's authority to acquire land under the pretext

554 B. Hoops, *The Legitimate Justification of Expropriation: A Comparative Law and Governance Analysis*, Juta and Company Ltd., Cape Town, 2017.

555 P. Francis, 'For the use and common benefit of all Nigerians: Consequences of the 1978 land nationalization', *Afr. J. Int. Afr. Inst*, No. 54, 1984, pp. 5-28.

of a public purpose and transfer such land to private companies, even when the actual purpose will not promote local economic development or otherwise serve a public purpose. The LUA's broad definition of 'public purpose' opens the door for misuse and abuse by the Governor. For instance, the Governor may acquire land under the pretext of a 'public purpose,' where the real motive is to transfer land to private companies for private gain, without ensuring these companies will create jobs or otherwise boost the local economy.

Even if a Nigerian court decides to review a State Governor's expropriation decision, the 'public purpose' provision is so broad that it remains unclear on what grounds courts can overrule public purpose justification decisions. In other words, the LUA does not provide guidance for courts to scrutinize 'public interest' decisions. For this reason, the LUA's vagueness opens the door for potential misuse and abuse of expropriation power. In practice, Nigerian courts rarely overrule expropriation decisions made by the State Governors. In our legal review of expropriation cases, we found only one instance in which the Lagos High Court ruled that the State Governor's decision to expropriate land for development purposes was ruled unconstitutional.[556] However, this High Court ruling did not focus on the 'public purpose' issue, but rather held the expropriation and forced eviction of communities were unconstitutional because there was no resettlement plan in place.[557]

6.4.2 *Limitations on the Amount or Type of Expropriated Land*

As discussed in Chapter 3, Section 16.1 of the VGGTs provides that "[States should acquire only] the minimum resources necessary." Moreover, Section 16.2 establishes that,

> States should be sensitive where proposed expropriations involve areas of particular cultural, religious, or environmental significance, or where the land is particularly important to the livelihoods of the poor and vulnerable.

Additionally, Article 9.9 of the VGGTs and Article 10 of the UN Declaration on the Rights of Indigenous Peoples and Article 16 of ILC Convention 169 provide that Indigenous Peoples shall not be forcibly removed from their land or territories without their FPIC.[558] The VGGTs also explain that,

556 P. Totaro, *Nigerian Courts Rule Against Mass Eviction in Lagos: Activists*, Thomson Reuters, Toronto, 2017.

557 BBC, 'Otodo-Gbame: Nigeria court rules eviction unconstitutional', *BBC News*, 2017. Available online: http://www.bbc.com/news/world-africa-40357103 (accessed on 15 October 2017).

558 ILO (International Labour Organization), *Convention No. 169, Indigenous and Tribal Peoples Convention, 1989*, ILO, Geneva, 1989; United Nations, *Declaration on the Rights of Indigenous Peoples*, G.A. Res. 61/295 U.N. Doc. A/RES/61/295, United Nations, NY, 2007; United Nations, *Free Prior and Informed Consent of Indigenous Peoples*, United Nations Human Rights Office of the High Commissioner, Geneva, 2013.

> States and other parties should hold good faith consultation with indigenous peoples before initiating any project or before adopting and implementing legislative or administrative measures affecting the resources for which communities hold rights.[559]

The LUA, on the other hand, does not require State Governors to minimize the amount of land acquired to the amount necessary to achieve a public purpose. Moreover, indigenous and other rural communities are not granted special protection from expropriation. Section 28 of the LUA merely states that it shall be "lawful for the Governor to revoke a right of occupancy for overriding public interest."[560] Yet, there are no restrictions on the type of land that the Governor is permitted to acquire. The LUA does not oblige the government to respect the indigenous right to Free Prior and Informed Consent prior to initiating development projects. The LUA does not require the government to be sensitive to when deciding to expropriate areas of cultural, religious, or environmental significance, or areas held by the poor and vulnerable groups, such as indigenous communities.

When land is expropriated for development projects, government and private sector bodies must conduct an Environmental Impact Assessment (EIA) before initiating development projects in Nigeria. Under Nigeria's Environmental Impact Assessment Decree of 1992, "the public or private sector of the economy shall not undertake or [...] authorise projects or activities without prior consideration, at an early stage, of their environmental effects."[561] The EIA must include a description of the potential affected environment including specific information necessary to identify and assess the environmental effects of the proposed activities.[562] Section 7 of the Decree states,

> Before the [Environmental Standards and Regulations Enforcement] Agency gives a decision on an activity to which an environmental assessment has been produced, the Agency shall give opportunity to government agencies, members of the public, experts in any relevant discipline and interested groups to comment on the environmental impact assessment of the activity.[563]

559 FAO, *The Voluntary Guidelines on the Responsible Governance of Tenure of Land, Fisheries, and Forests in the Context of National Food Security*, FAO, Rome, 2012, Sec. 9.9.

560 Government of Nigeria, *Land Use Act*, Government of Nigeria, Abuja, 1990, Sec. 28.

561 Government of Nigeria, *Environmental Impact Assessment Decree*, Government of Nigeria, Abuja, 1992, Section 2.

562 Government of Nigeria 1992, Section 4.

563 Government of Nigeria 1992, Section 7.

However, as Aldinger points out, public participation in the EIA process in Nigeria has been average at best due to low levels of public knowledge and awareness of projects and hearings regarding projects.[564]

6.4.3 *The Process of Expropriating Land*

Section 16.2 of the VGGTs calls for states to "ensure that the planning and process for expropriation is transparent and participatory. Anyone likely to be affected should be identified, and properly informed and consulted at all stages."[565] Similar requirements are established in the World Bank ESS5 and IFC Performance Standard 5; these requirements apply to projects funded by the World Bank and IFC. IFC Performance Standard 5 requires clients to engage with affected communities and disclose relevant information on projects to allow participation in the planning, monitoring, and implementation of projects. Moreover, IFC clients must conduct a census to collect appropriate socio-economic baseline data to identify the persons who will be displaced by project and determine who is eligible for compensation and resettlement assistance.

In contrast, the LUA does not require the government to survey affected landholders, provide information on the project, or consult landholders prior to expropriating land for development projects. Notices of acquisition do not necessarily have to be served prior to expropriating land. Section 28(7) of the LUA merely states that rights of occupancy shall be extinguished on receipt of a notice or on such later date, as may be stated in the notice.[566] As Otubu rightly states,

> The Act does not provide for pre-acquisition notices to be issued and or served on the affected citizens, thus engendering ambushing tactics, executive tyranny and surprise conducts on the part of the acquiring authority to the detriment of the populace.[567]

---

564 P. Aldinger, 'Addressing environmental justice concerns in developing countries: Mining in Nigeria, Uganda and Ghana', *Georget. Int. Environ. Law Rev.*, No. 26, 2014, pp. 345.

565 Food and Agriculture Organization (FAO), *The Voluntary Guidelines on the Responsible Governance of Tenure of Land, Fisheries, and Forests in the Context of National Food Security*, FAO, Rome, 2012, Sec. 16.2.

566 Government of Nigeria, *Land Use Act*, Government of Nigeria, Abuja, 1990, Sec. 28 (7).

567 A.K. Otubu, 'Private property rights and compulsory acquisition process in Nigeria: The past, present and future', *Acta Univ. Danub. Jurid.*, No. 8, 2012, pp. 25-42.

6.4.4 Compensation for Unregistered Landholders

Section 16.1 of the VGGTs call for states to "respect all legitimate tenure rights holders, especially vulnerable and marginalized groups, by [...] providing just compensation in accordance with national law." The VGGTs do not define the term 'legitimate tenure,' and allow states to define this term in national laws.[568] Section 3.1 of the VGGTs calls for states to "respect legitimate tenure holders and their rights, whether formally recorded or not."[569] The term 'legitimate' with regard to land tenure is commonly defined as including both legal legitimacy (rights recognized by law) and social legitimacy (rights that have broad acceptance among society).[570] In addition to the VGGTs, The UN Declaration on the Rights of Indigenous Peoples, ILO Convention 169 on Indigenous and Tribal Peoples, and IFC Performance Standard 7, establish that indigenous communities have a right to fair compensation when their lands, territories, and resources are expropriated.[571]

The LUA only grants compensation for statutory and customary rights of occupancy that are recognized by the State Governor.[572] Although the LUA indicates a customary right of occupancy can be recognized based on customary use and occupation, it can be inferred from the law that landholders must obtain a certificate of occupancy or otherwise register their land rights with the State Governor in order to be eligible for compensation upon expropriation. Section 36(4) of the LUA provides that Governors may register customary rights of occupancy "if satisfied," indicating the Governors have broad discretion to decide whether or not to recognize customary rights.[573] The World Bank LGAF report found that in Nigeria,

> Compensation [...] is paid for some unregistered rights (such as possession, occupation etc.) however those with other unregistered rights (which may

568 L. Verstappen, 'Multilevel governance of property titles in land: The voluntary guidelines on the responsible governance of tenure of land, fisheries, and forests in the context of national food security', *in* C. Godt Ed., *Regulatory Property Rights: The Transforming Notion of Property in Transnational Business Regulation*, Brill/Nijhoff, Leiden, 2016, pp. 98-118.

569 FAO 2012, Sec. 3.1.

570 D. Palmer, S. Fricska, & B. Wehrmann, *Land Tenure Working Paper 11: Toward Improved Land Governance*, FAO, Rome, 2009.

571 ILO (International Labour Organization), *Convention No. 169, Indigenous and Tribal Peoples Convention, 1989*, ILO, Geneva, 1989; United Nations, *Declaration on the Rights of Indigenous Peoples*, G.A. Res. 61/295, U.N. Doc. A/RES/61/295, NY, 2007; International Finance Corporation (IFC), *Performance Standards on Environmental and Social Sustainability, Performance Standard 7: Indigenous Peoples*, IFC, Washington, DC, 2012.

572 Government of Nigeria 1990, Sections 6, 29, 36(4).

573 Government of Nigeria 1990, Section 36(4).

include grazing, access, gathering forest products etc.) are usually not paid compensation.[574]

6.4.5 *Valuation of Compensation*

As stated above, the VGGTs call for the creation of land valuation systems that take into account non-market values, such as social, cultural, religious, spiritual and environmental values where applicable. In 37 of 50 countries analyzed, fair market value (FMV) is the legally required method expropriating authorities must use to value compensation for land; there are no allowable alternatives that can be used to value land in areas where land markets are weak or non-existent.[575] For a variety of reasons and in a range of locations, 'market value' may be an insufficient approach to value land, especially when indigenous and rural community land is expropriated because there is no FMV and no clear way to compensate for the social, cultural, spiritual values attached to such land.[576] In India, for example, several laws restrict community rights to sell their land; as a result, there is a lack of robust land markets in many community land areas.[577]

In terms of appropriate alternatives to valuing compensation, the 'replacement cost' approach (required by the World Bank Environmental and Social Framework), or a combination of the FMV and replacement cost approach, may be preferable since 'replacement cost' focuses more on the amount it would actually take to replace lost assets.[578] In countries with robust and functioning land markets, the replacement cost should be approximately equal to FMV, but this is not always the case.[579] In areas with weak or non-existent land markets, the FMV may be less than the replacement cost. The FAO Handbook further explains,

> Compensation should be for any disturbances or other losses to the livelihoods [...] The disturbance accompanying compulsory acquisition often means that people lose access to the sources of their livelihoods. This can be due to a farmer

574 World Bank, *Land Governance Assessment Framework Final Report: Nigeria*, World Bank, Washington, DC, 2011, p. 113.
575 B. Banerjee & M. Van Eerd, *Working Paper I: Evictions, Acquisition, Expropriation and Compensation: Practices and Selected Case Studies*, United Nations Human Settlements Programme, Nairobi, 2013.
576 Banerjee & Van Eerd 2013.
577 R. Mahapatra, *Acquisition Made Easy. Down To Earth*, 2011. Available online: http://www.downtoearth.org.in/blog/acquisition-made-easy-33633 (accessed on 1 March 2018).
578 J. Lindsay, *PPP Insights: Compulsory Acquisition of Land and Compensation in Infrastructure Projects*, World Bank, Washington, DC, 2012.
579 Tagliarino 2017, p. 37.

> losing agricultural fields, a business owner losing a shop, or a community losing its traditional lands.[580]

Under Section 29(1) of the LUA, when land is expropriated, holders and occupiers are entitled to compensation based only on the land's "unexhausted improvements."[581] "Unexhausted improvements" are defined in Section 51 of the LUA

> [...] as anything of any quality permanently attached to the land, directly resulting from the expenditure of capital or labour by an occupier [...] and increasing the productive capacity, the utility or the amenity thereof and includes buildings, plantations of long-lived crops or trees, fencing [...] but does not include the result of ordinary cultivation other than growing produce.[582]

In other words, compensation is limited to the improvements and crops on the land, but does not cover the value of the land itself. Presumably the government has discretion to determine which assets attached to the land have a level of "productive capacity" that is sufficient to justify compensation. Since the government has discretion to determine which improvements and crops are worthy of compensation, all landholders are at risk of receiving insufficient compensation. Yet indigenous communities who use land for subsistence purposes and for other unproductive purposes (e.g., ancestral burial grounds) are at risk of income loss and poverty since this provision precludes any holders of unfarmed and undeveloped land from obtaining any compensation when their land is expropriated.[583] As argued by Otubu,

> Not only is there no compensation for bare undeveloped land irrespective of whatever cost incurred at acquiring the land either from the state or the community...the Act does not recognize the need to pay compensation for severance...no compensation [is payable] for injurious affection and any other incidental and collateral losses...[584]

The LUA does not require that compensation reflect the loss of economic activities and intangible land values, such as spiritual or cultural values. While there is no clear formula

580 Keith *et al.* 2008, p. 29.

581 Government of Nigeria,1990, Section 29(1).

582 Government of Nigeria,1990, Section 51.

583 United Nations, *Declaration on the Rights of Indigenous Peoples*, G.A. Res. 61/295, U.N. Doc. A/RES/61/295, United Nations, NY, 2007.

584 A.K. Otubu, 'Private property rights and compulsory acquisition process in Nigeria: The past, present and future', *Acta Univ. Danub. Jurid.*, No. 8, 2012, pp. 25-42.

for calculating such values, good faith negotiations between developers and communities could be used to capture the viewpoints of affected landholders regarding these values. Since the LUA does not contain clear and robust legal provisions that ensure compensation addresses all of these losses, landholders are vulnerable to losing land without sufficient compensation.

According to a Nigerian lawyer at Lekki Free Zone Development Company (LFZDC) that we interviewed, the Lagos Lands Bureau has broad discretion to value compensation for crops and has often used arbitrary, outdated assessment methods, resulting in insufficient compensation rates. Since the LUA does not contain clear legal provisions that ensure compensation addresses all land values and livelihood losses, and ensure compensation is adjusted for inflation and reflects current market rates, landholders may have little recourse or ability to hold the Lands Bureau accountable if they are dissatisfied with compensation decisions. Even if affected landholders challenge compensation decisions in court, the LUA does not provide adequate guidance for judges to follow when determining whether compensation decisions violate the law. In essence, the LUA fails to prevent the Lands Bureau from engaging in arbitrary, ad-hoc, decision-making on compensation, and leaves Nigerian landholders uncertain about whether they have justiciable legal rights to full compensation.

6.4.6 *Prompt Payment of Compensation*

The VGGTs call for "prompt" payments of compensation, but the VGGTs do not establish an explicit deadline by which compensation must be paid. International standards established by the World Bank, IFC, and other bodies typically call for compensation to be paid to the landholder prior to the taking of possession of acquired land. For instance, IFC Performance Standard 5 states, "The client will take possession of acquired land and related assets only after compensation has been made available."[585] The FAO Handbook further explains "when an acquiring agency takes possession before full compensation is paid, there may be little incentive for it to make the final payment."[586]

Although Section 44 of the Constitution of Nigeria, 1999 requires "prompt" compensation, the LUA does not require compensation to be paid prior to the taking of possession of the acquired land.[587] The LUA does not even establish a deadline for payment of compensation.

585 International Finance Corporation (IFC), *Performance Standards on Environmental and Social Sustainability, Performance Standard 5: Land Acquisition and Involuntary Resettlement*, IFC, Washington, DC, 2012.
586 Keith *et al* 2008, p. 26.
587 Government of Nigeria, *Constitution of Nigeria*, Government of Nigeria, Abuja, 1999, Section 44.

Ostensibly, this means that compensation may be paid at any time after the acquisition of land. Landholders may have to wait years to receive compensation and thus may be prone to poverty, landlessness, homelessness, food insecurity, and other serious risks. According to the World Bank LGAF report on Nigeria, "the speed at which compensations are paid to property owners is also very slow [...] a large number of acquisitions occur without prompt and adequate compensation."[588]

6.4.7 *A Right to Negotiate Fair Compensation*

Although the VGGTs do not explicitly call for states to provide affected landholders with the right to negotiate compensation levels, Section 16.6 of the VGGTs establishes that "all parties should endeavor to prevent corruption, particularly through use of objectively assessed values, transparent and decentralized processes [...]"[589] It can be argued that compensation negotiations are necessary to obtain "objectively assessed values," since the alternative is compensation rates based solely on the government's opinion. The FAO Handbook explains that "fair and transparent negotiations help break down barriers between the acquiring agency and these land is being acquired, and permit each party to better understand the needs of the other."[590] Other international standards call for procedures by which affected landholders are granted the opportunity to negotiate fair compensation; for instance, IFC Performance Standard 5 requires project developers (i.e., clients) to a consult with and facilitate the informed participation of affected persons and communities following disclosure of all relevant information.[591] Under the IFC, affected landholders are permitted to reject offers of compensation and participate in compensation and resettlement decision-making.[592]

588 World Bank, *Land Governance Assessment Framework Final Report: Nigeria*, World Bank, Washington, DC, 2011, p. 113.

589 FAO 2012, Sec. 16.6.

590 Keith *et al* 2008, p. 26.

591 F. Vanclay, 'Project induced displacement and resettlement: From impoverishment risks to an opportunity or development', *Impact Assess. Proj. Apprais*, No. 35, 2017, pp. 3-21; IFC, Washington, DC, 2012, Sec. 9.

592 International Finance Corporation (IFC), *Performance Standards on Environmental and Social Sustainability, Performance Standard 5: Land Acquisition and Involuntary Resettlement*, IFC, Washington, DC, 2012, Sec. 13.

6.4.8 *The Right to Challenge Compensation Decisions in Court or before Tribunals*

Section 16.6 of the VGGTs also calls for states to provide a right to appeal compensation decisions. Such appeals may be needed if the government calculates compensation using illegal or incorrect methods and landholders are left with insufficient compensation.[593]

Nigerian law complies with this VGGTs principle because it grants affected landholders the right to seek redress in court. Section 44 of the Constitution of Nigeria, 1999 provides,

> Any person claiming such compensation [shall be given] a right of access, for determinations of his interest in the property and the amount of compensation, to the High Court having jurisdiction in that part of Nigeria.[594]

Also, Section 39(1)(b) of the LUA grants the High Court original jurisdiction over proceedings to determine any question as to the persons entitlement to compensation payable for improvements on the land."[595] However, further research is needed to determine whether landholders are usually afforded redress in court when they wish to challenge compensation decisions. As previously discussed, since the LUA does not provide clear procedures or guidance on valuing compensation, it is unclear whether courts will be able to effectively scrutinize compensation decisions. The World Bank LGAF report found that "in the instances where complaints about expropriation were lodged [in the three years prior to the LGAF study], a few were listened to but decisions on them were rarely reached on time."[596]

6.4.9 *Provision of Productive Alternative Land*

Section 16.9 of the VGGTs establishes that, when acquiring land in a compulsory manner, "States should, to the extent that resources permit, take appropriate measures to provide adequate access…to productive land."[597] The World Bank ESF and IFC Performance Standards also require options for alternative land.[598]

593 Tagliarino 2016, p. 22.
594 Government of Nigeria 1999, Section 44.
595 Government of Nigeria 1990, Section 39(1)(b).
596 World Bank, *Land Governance Assessment Framework Final Report: Nigeria*, World Bank, Washington, DC, 2011, p. 114.
597 FAO 2012, Sec. 16.9.
598 World Bank 2017, p. 56; IFC 2012, Sec. 18.

The LUA partially complies with this provision because it permits alternative land to be granted to affected landholders if their right of occupancy is revoked; the Governor has discretion to offer alternatives, but is not legally obligated to do so. The LUA grants affected landholders either monetary compensation or alternative land, but not both. Moreover, there is nothing in the LUA requiring alternative land be productive, suitable, or of the same status as the land acquired. Section 33 of the LUA provides that the

> Governor […] may in his or its discretion offer in lieu of compensation […] resettlement in any other place or area by way of reasonable alternative accommodation (if appropriate in the circumstances).[599]

Nonetheless, there is no language in this provision that guarantees suitable alternative land for affected landholders. More importantly, Nigerian law lacks a robust resettlement and rehabilitation procedure that protects landholders displaced by expropriation and ensures their livelihood reconstruction post-displacement. Without such a procedure, affected populations may be far more likely to suffer from displacement, homelessness, joblessness, increased morbidity, food insecurity, and other risks.[600] For a summary of the legal analysis provided in this Section, see Table 10.

6.4.10 *Summary of Legal Analysis*

Table 11 Summary of the Legal Analysis

International Standard	Origin of the Standard	Does Nigeria's LUA Comply with This Standard?	Comment
States should clearly define the concept of public purpose in law, in order to allow for judicial review.	FAO VGGTs Section 16.1	No	• Section 51 of the LUA vaguely defines "public purpose."
• States should acquire only the minimum resources necessary. • States should be sensitive where proposed expropriations involve areas of particular cultural, religious, or environmental significance, or where the land is particu-	FAO VGGTs 16.1-16.2	Mostly no with the exception of the EIA Decree 1992	• The LUA does not require State Governors to minimize the amount of land acquired to the amount necessary to achieve a public purpose. • Aside from the EIA requirement, Nigeria's laws do not require the government to be sensitive to areas of cultural,

599 Government of Nigeria, *Land Use Act*, Government of Nigeria, Abuja, 1990, Section 33.

600 M.M. Cernea 1997.

International Standard	Origin of the Standard	Does Nigeria's LUA Comply with This Standard?	Comment
larly important to the livelihoods of the poor and vulnerable.			religious, or environmental significance or areas held by the poor and vulnerable groups such as indigenous communities when deciding to expropriate.
States should ensure that the planning and process for expropriation is transparent and participatory. Anyone likely to be affected should be identified, and properly informed and consulted at all stages.	FAO VGGTs Section 16.2	No	• The LUA does not require the government to survey affected landholders, provide information on the project, or consult landholders prior to expropriating land for development projects.
• States should respect all legitimate tenure rights holders, especially vulnerable and marginalized groups, by providing prompt and just compensation • Land valuation systems should take into account non-market values, such as social, cultural, religious, spiritual and environmental values.	FAO VGGTs Sections 16.1 and 18.2	Partial	• The LUA only grants compensation for statutory and customary rights of occupancy that are recognized by the State Governor • Compensation is limited to the improvements and crops on the land, but does not cover the value of the land itself. • The LUA precludes holders of unfarmed, undeveloped land from obtaining any compensation when their land is expropriated • The LUA does not require compensation to be paid prior to the taking of possession of the acquired land. There is no established deadline for payment.
All parties should endeavor to prevent corruption, particularly through use of objectively assessed values, transparent and decentralized processes.	FAO VGGTs Section 16.6	No	• The LUA does not grant affected landholders the right to negotiate compensation. • The Lands Bureau is granted broad discretion to determine a rate of compensation. There is no guidance on valuing compensation to allow for judges to scrutinize compensation decisions.
States should provide a right to appeal compensation decisions.	FAO VGGTs Section 16.6	Yes	• Section 44 of the Constitution of Nigeria provides the

International Standard	Origin of the Standard	Does Nigeria's LUA Comply with This Standard?	Comment
			right to appeal compensation decisions in court.
States should, take appropriate measures to provide adequate access to productive land.	FAO VGGTs Section 16.9	Partial	• The LUA permits alternative land to be granted to affected landholders if their right of occupancy is revoked; however, the Governor has discretion to offer alternatives but is not legally obligated to do so: affected landholders can receive either monetary compensation or alternative land, but not both. • There is no established resettlement procedure, which ensures livelihood reconstruction for affected populations.

6.5 Examination of LFTZ Case

This Section provides an overview of the events that unfolded in Lekki since the inception of the LFTZ. It also reveals findings from in-person surveys of 140 affected households; these surveys were conducted with ten communities affected by the LFTZ. This Section also discusses findings on the LFTZ case gathered from interviews with government officials and company representatives as well as a desk review of relevant primary and secondary sources.

6.5.1 *Background on the Development of the LFTZ*

To address economic stagnation, the Nigerian government has sought to attract foreign investors to stimulate economic growth through public infrastructure investment.[601] Chinese investors have been among those most willing to finance development projects in Nigeria.[602] Trade between China and Nigeria increased from $2 billion in 2000 to $18 billion in 2010,

601 M. Egbula & Q. Zheng, *West African Challenges No. 5: China and Nigeria: A Powerful South-South Alliance*, Sahel and West Africa Club Secretariat (SWAC/OECD), Paris, 2011.

602 Egbula *et al.* 2011.

making Nigeria a top destination for Chinese Foreign Direct Investment.[603] In 2015 alone, $9.2 billion of Chinese goods were shipped from China to Nigeria.[604]

Nigeria became a target for Chinese investors following the end of Nigerian military rule and the democratic election of President Olusegun Obasanjo in 1999.[605] Throughout Obasanjo's presidency, China and Nigeria signed a series of agreements and MOUs establishing trade offices and investment centers. Obasanjo's main goals with China were to trade "oil for infrastructure," to improve the quality of Chinese manufactured goods entering the Nigerian market, and to establish tax-exempted export processing zones (i.e., free trade zones).[606] The Lekki Free Trade Zone is the first zone in Nigeria in which Chinese companies are majority shareholders.[607]

In 2006, the LFTZ was initiated through a joint venture between a state-owned company called Lekki Worldwide Investments (LWI), the Lagos State Government, and a Chinese consortium of companies, led by China Civil Engineering Construction Corporation (CCECC), which is now called China-Africa Lekki Investment Ltd. (CALI, Lagos, Nigeria).[608] This joint venture resulted in the establishment of the Lekki Free Zone Development Company (LFZDC). The China Railway Construction Company, China-Africa Development Fund, China Civil Engineering Construction Corporation, and Nanjing Jianging Economic and Technological Development Corporation established CALI as a joint venture in March of 2006.[609] CALI owns sixty percent of the LFZDC equity, and LWI owns 40 percent.[610] Following the Nigeria Export Processing Zones Act 63 of 1992, the Nigerian federal government and Lagos State government authorized LFZDC as the sole legal entity responsible for developing, operating, and managing the LFTZ.[611] The main investment sectors of the LFTZ are manufacturing, oil and gas (storage and distribution), real estate, tourism and infrastructure development. According to the LFZDC website, the stated objectives of the LFTZ are to stimulate the Nigerian economy, create a global economic haven, create and encourage integration with foreign partners, generate employment

603 Egbula *et al.* 2011.
604 Heinrich Bol Stiftung, *Urban Planning Processes in Lagos*, Heinrich Bol Stiftung, Lagos, 2016.
605 Egbula *et al.* 2011.
606 Business & Maritime West Africa, *Lekki Free Trade Zone: A Pathway to Economic Development in Nigeria*, Business & Maritime West Africa, 2012.
607 Business & Maritime West Africa 2012.
608 Lekki Free Zone Development Company, available online: http://lfzdc.org/about-us/ (accessed on 10 February 2018).
609 Lekki Free Zone Development Company, available online: http://lfzdc.org/about-us/ (accessed on 10 February 2018).
610 Lekki Free Zone Development Company, available online: http://lfzdc.org/about-us/ (accessed on 10 February 2018).
611 Heinrich Bol Stiftung 2016.

opportunities, attract foreign investment, diversify the Lagos revenue base, "ensure effective exploration" of Nigeria's resources, and create wealth for citizens.[612]

In October 2006, LFZDC began developing phase 1 of the LFTZ, which required 1200 hectares of land for the creation of China-Nigeria Economic and Trade Cooperation Zone.[613] The initial agreement stated that the Chinese consortium must provide $200 million for the LSG to allocate the land, and for Nigerian investors to invest $67 million in the LFTZ.[614] However, there was no stipulation in the agreement that the Consortium's money must be paid up front. Consequently, LSG had to spend $67 million of the state's budget in 2009 to fill this financial gap [9].

According to the LFTZ Master Plan, the LFTZ will serve as a multi-functional economic zone and a new modern city (see Figure 17). The construction of the LFTZ is divided into the following four phases:

- Phase 1 (Southwest Quadrant) will serve a mixed of industries, workers housing, and residences;
- Phase 2 (Southeast Quadrant) will serve petrochemical, oil, and gas industries;
- Phase 3 (Northwest Quadrant) will provide workers housing and space for a mix of industries; and
- Phase 4 (Northeast Quadrant) will serve commercial businesses, tourism, residential, and other purposes.

Thus far it appears that only Phase 1 has been completed.[615] However, progress on the other phases has been slow and riddled with delays resulting from financial planning and other issues.[616] Based on our tour of the LFTZ, it appears some factories employ Nigerians. We saw a few Nigerians working security at the front gate of the LFTZ and producing goods in one of the factories located inside the LFTZ. The LFTZ officials we interviewed did not provide us information about job creation, but it was apparent from our tour and research of the LFTZ that the goal of 300,000 direct jobs for Nigerians was far from reach.

---

612 Lekki Free Zone Development Company, available online: http://lfzdc.org/about-us/ (accessed on 10 February 2018).

613 Heinrich Bol Stiftung 2016.

614 G. Mthembu-Salter, *Chinese Investment in African Free Trade Zones: Lessons from Nigeria's Experience*, South Africa Institute of International Affairs, Johannesburg, 2009.

615 Heinrich Bol Stiftung 2016.; G. Mthembu-Salter 2009.

616 Heinrich Bol Stiftung 2016, pp. 208-216.

6.5.2 MOU between LWIL, LSG, and Affected Communities

After publishing a notice in an Official Gazette, the Government acquired 823 Sq. Kilometers of land through expropriation in 1993.[617] In 2004, 16,500 hectares of this land was set aside for the LFTZ. According to a lawyer we interviewed at Social and Environmental Rights Action Center (SERAC),[618] a Nigerian NGO consisting primarily of human rights lawyers, the LSG did not consider compensating affected communities or providing them with alternative land until SERAC began advocating on behalf of the communities in 2007. As shown from the survey findings, the LSG apparently left many community members in the dark about its plans to build the LFTZ and did not promise them compensation, either in 2007 or in subsequent years prior to our August 2017 survey. After SERAC decided to represent and defend communities affected by the LFTZ, a series of meetings led to the development of an MOU in 2007 between the LSG, the Ibeju-Lekki Local Government Council, nine affected communities, and Lekki Worldwide Investment Limited (LWIL).[619] It is unclear as to why exactly the LSG finally agreed to develop an MOU, but the lawyer we interviewed indicated that pressure from human rights advocates and affected communities contributed to compensation plans becoming part of the government's agenda. Accredited representatives of the affected communities signed the MOU, which obtained consent from the village chiefs. However, it is doubtful, based on our survey research, that all community members were consulted and informed about the MOU prior to the signing. Nine communities, which are parties to the MOU, reside along the Lekki coast. These communities are:

1. Idasho
2. Idotun
3. Illege
4. Imobido
5. Itoke
6. Okunraiye
7. Illekuru
8. Tiye
9. Imagbon-Segun

617 Lagos State Government (LSG), *Government Write Paper on the Report of the Tribunal of Inquiry into the Cause of Civil Disturbances at the Lekki Free Trade Zone on 12 October, 2015*, LSG, Lagos, 2016.

618 SERAC is a Nigerian human rights organization that represented nine affected communities when negotiating the 2007 MOU with the LSG and interested companies.

619 Lagos State Government (LSG), *Memorandum of Understanding Between the Lagos State Government, the Ibeju-Lekki Local Government Council, Lekki Worldwide Investment Limited, and the Accredited Representatives of Villages and Communities (Idasho, Idotun, Ielge, Imobido, Itoke, Okunraiye, Ilekuru, Tiye, and Imagbon-Segun) Affected by the Lekki Free Trade Zone Project*, LSG, Lagos, 2007.

Although SERAC represented nine communities in the MOU, there may be as many as 26 communities actually affected by the LFTZ, according to the SERAC representative. The MOU states that the LFTZ must comply with all applicable national and international legal standards. The MOU obliges the LSG to provide a number of compensation entitlements to affected communities, including the following:

- A 2.5% equity share capital in LWIL;
- Workforce development initiatives such as skills training, job creation, and capacity building;
- Access to educational opportunities at primary and secondary schools;
- Access to health care and recreational services;
- Prompt payment of compensation for all genuine claims made by members of affected villages;
- No less than 750 hectares of unencumbered land for the resettlement of communities displaced by the project; and
- Certificates of occupancy covering the 750 hectares of unencumbered land.

The MOU also states that the LSG shall not displace the three communities (Idotun, Itoke, and Okunraiye) whose land is identified for a proposed seaport and, if such seaport is developed, shall provide no less than 170 hectares of unencumbered alternative land. These communities have not yet been displaced; however, the seaport is currently under construction and communities in the area believe displacement is imminent. In their interviews, some communities alleged they had been threatened to vacate by company officials involved in the seaport's construction.

A close examination of the MOU reveals serious flaws. First, the MOU does not provide specifics regarding where the resettlement land must be located, how many jobs must be provided, how many schools and healthcare facilities must be built, and how much compensation must be paid.

Second, there is no deadline by which MOU entitlements must be honored, meaning they may be honored at any time. As discussed below, the lack of a deadline enabled the LSG and LWIL to proceed for the past ten years without honoring the provisions of the MOU.

Third, the MOU lumps all entitlements into one pot to be given to all nine communities, and thus ignores inter- and intra-community differences, such as different socio-economic and demographic profiles, endowments of land, crop yields, income levels, and more. According to the MOU, the 750 hectares promised as resettlement land are supposed to be shared by all nine communities. As discussed below, the implementation of this MOU provision led to a convoluted tenure arrangement in which overlapping claims and competing interests prevented affected communities from taking possession of resettlement land.

Fourth, the MOU designates a Resettlement Committee as the entity responsible for implementing the provisions of the MOU, but fails to establish specific obligations that the Committee must fulfill. There is no requirement in the MOU stipulating how often the Committee must meet and the MOU does not prescribe a timeframe for fulfilling the various provisions. The MOU further states that the Committee must ensure that "members of the affected villages and communities have free and effective access to information relevant to their understanding and participation in the LFTZ."[620] The MOU states, in the event of a dispute regarding the MOU, parties can appoint mediators and, if that fails, they can settle the dispute through arbitration. However, the lack of clear deadlines and other obligations imposed on the Resettlement Committee makes it difficult for affected communities to find grounds on which to challenge decisions taken by the Committee and otherwise hold the Committee accountable for ensuring compliance with the MOU.

For the reasons stated above, the wording of the MOU is problematic because it does not impose specific, concrete obligations on the LSG and LWI that ensure the reconstruction of community livelihoods post-expropriation. While the empirical research presented in the following Sections do not clarify why the MOU was worded in such a vague manner, the research presented in this Chapter does show what can happen when an MOU contains ambiguous language and why clearer MOU provisions are needed to ensure fair compensation and livelihood reconstruction.

6.5.3 *Background on the Survey of Affected Communities*

The research findings discussed below are based on surveys conducted in August 2017 with 140 households from ten different affected communities. The survey findings indicate, to some extent, whether the LSG abided by the MOU and the LUA as they are currently written. Specifically, the survey research provides an indication of whether compensation, alternative land, and other entitlements were paid to communities, and whether the LSG followed a transparent and participatory process when expropriating community farmland. For this reason, the survey findings serve the purpose of providing readers with a deeper understanding of the impact of Nigeria's weak expropriation laws on local populations, and what steps must be taken to ensure expropriation practices comply with international standards on expropriation, compensation, and resettlement in the future.

620 LSG 2007.

To support the information given by these communities, interviews were also conducted with Social and Environmental Rights Action Center (SERAC), the Lekki Free Zone Development Company (LFZDC), the Lands Bureau, Lagos Ministry of Commerce, Industry and Cooperatives, and Lekki Worldwide Investment Limited (LWIL). Public records, including the 2007 MOU and the 2016 "Government White Paper on the Report of the Tribunal of Inquiry into the Cause of Civil Disturbances at the Lekki Free Trade Zone on 12 October 2015" (hereinafter "Government White Paper")[621] were also reviewed.[622] The evidence provided here is also supported by secondary sources, including news articles.

We surveyed 140 households from ten affected communities (nine of which signed the MOU through their representatives) to determine whether they had received compensation, alternative land, or other entitlements promised by the MOU. We conducted the surveys during group meetings with community members and asked questions using a questionnaire. For the sake of clarity, the main survey questions are displayed in Table 12.

Table 12 List of Survey Questions

1. How many people live in your household?
2. What is the highest level of education you attained?
3. What is your age?
4. What is your primary occupation?
5. Can you read and write?
6. What types of crops did you grown on your land before the expropriation?
7. How many hectares was your farmland?
8. Approximately how many kilograms (kg) of crops did you grow annually?
9. Was access to your farmland limited as a result of the LFTZ?
10. How many crops have you grown annually since the expropriation?
11. Were you informed about the LFTZ before construction began?
12. Were you consulted about the implications of the project on your community?
13. Were you given an opportunity to given input in the expropriation?
14. Were you given the opportunity to negotiate compensation?
15. Were you made aware of an environmental impact assessment or social impact
16. assessment conducted for the project?
17. Were you told which factors were considered when calculating compensation?
18. What types of compensation were you promised? (e.g., money, alternative land,
19. jobs, or equity shares)
20. Did the amount of compensation provided cover all of your losses?

621 The White Paper was published in response to a clash between affected communities and police that ensued after communities barricaded the entrance to LFTZ in protest of the project. The incident resulted in the death of the Managing Director of the LFTZ, Tajudeen Disu. Disu reportedly died from a gunshot, but there were conflicting accounts of who fired the shot. The police subsequently arrested Okunraiye community members believed to be responsible for the death. Meanwhile, community members stated in a sworn affidavit that a stray bullet fired by police killed Disu.

622 Lagos State Government (LSG), *Government Write Paper on the Report of the Tribunal of Inquiry into the Cause of Civil Disturbances at the Lekki Free Trade Zone on 12 October, 2015*, LSG, Lagos, 2016.

In order to conduct the surveys, we had to first obtain permission from each community chief. Once the chiefs consented, they would ask members of the community to come and participate in the survey. Under customary norms and practices of the communities, the male heads of household have sole authority to speak on behalf of the household. A total of seven widows also participated in the survey. Due to customary rules imposed on us, we were not able to ensure a gender-sensitive survey was conducted. Respondents had to be selected for the survey based on whether they were willing and able to participate in the community meetings during which we were allowed to administer the questionnaire. For these reasons, randomization of the sample was not possible because we had to comply with communities' customary norms (i.e., if we refused to comply with the chief's rules, we would not be allowed to conduct the surveys). Before beginning the surveys, we gave community members an opportunity to discuss their opinions about the LFTZ in front of the whole group. Some information obtained at the community meetings was included in the analysis. We then began surveying respondents—one household at a time—using tablets and a program called Survey CTO, which enabled us to collect and analyze the survey results electronically.

For this survey, any sampling stratification would be highly speculative, since there is no official register or list of all those living within the affected communities, so the total population of affected communities and their socio-economic and demographic composition is unknown. Due to time and funding constraints, we were only able to spend a few hours in each community, so participant observation and ethnographic data was not collected to supplement the survey data. When asked how many households and individuals lived within each community, the chiefs and other community members were only able to give us a rough estimate of total households. Using this information provided by the chiefs, we estimate that our sample represents around 13 percent of the total number of households in the ten communities based on the estimated total number of households in each community, as shown in Table 13. For information on the gender, age, literacy levels, education, and employment status of affected communities, see Table 14.

Table 13 Sample Composition: Respondents by Community

Community	No. of Respondents (Household Heads) [a]	Share (%) of Resp. in the Sample [b]	Estimated Total No. of Households [c]	Respondents/Total No. of Households (%) [d]
Idasho	20	14.29	110	18.18
Idotun	23	16.42	80	28.75
Ilege	6	4.29	120	5.00
Imobido	6	4.29	100	6.00

Community	No. of Respondents (Household Heads) [a]	Share (%) of Resp. in the Sample [b]	Estimated Total No. of Households [c]	Respondents/Total No. of Households (%) [d]
Itoke	21	15.00	90	23.33
Okunraye	17	12.14	250	6.80
Ilekuru	11	7.86	50	22.00
Tiye	17	12.14	100	17.00
Imagbon-Segun	9	6.43	150	6.00
Oke-Segun	10	7.14	40	25.00
Total	**140**	**100.00**	**1090**	**12.84**

Table 14 Sample Composition: Main Socio-Economic and Demographic Features

GENDER		
Sex	N	%
Male	123	87.86
Female	17	12.14
Total	**140**	**100.00**
AGE		
Age group	N	%
25-34	34	24.29
35-44	42	30.00
45-54	27	19.28
55-64	3	2.14
65+	34	24.29
Total	**140**	**100.00**
LITERACY		
Literacy level	N	%
Cannot read and write	41	29.29
Can sign (write) only	3	2.14
Can read only	3	2.14
Can read and write	93	66.43
Total	**140**	**100.00**
EDUCATION		
Highest grade completed	N	%
None/never attended school	27	19.29

Pre-primary/Kindergarten	1	0.71
Primary	49	35
Secondary	50	35.71
Higher	13	9.29
Total	**140**	**100.00**
EMPLOYMENT STATUS		
Current employment status (last week)	N	%
Worked for pay (salary, wage, self-employed, ...)	51	36.42
Worked without pay (apprentice, family business, ...)	39	27.86
Did not work but have a job (sick, vacation, seasonal, ...)	3	2.14
Did not work but looked for a job	13	9.29
Did not work and didn't look for a job (unemployed, retired...)	34	24.29
Total	**140**	**100.00**

6.5.4 *Access to Information and Participation during the Expropriation Process*

Several survey questions focused on the extent to which households were given access to information about the LFTZ project, and whether communities were given an opportunity to provide input on project plans or otherwise participate in the decision-making expropriation process. Furthermore, since Nigerian law stipulates that an EIA must be conducted prior to initiating development projects that impact the environment, the survey also asked whether respondents were made aware of an EIA conducted for the project.

As shown in Table 15, our survey coupled with our interview with SERAC indicates that the LSG failed to adequately survey, inform, and consult many of the affected communities living in the vicinity of the LFTZ prior to the acquisition of 16,500 hectares of land in 2004. The vast majority of households interviewed responded that the government and private companies did not inform or consult them regarding the LFTZ prior to taking possession of the land (see Table 16). Overall, the results from the survey suggest that the level of participation of local communities during the land acquisition process was very low, and communities were granted little to no information on the LFTZ project as shown in Table 16.

Table 15 Participation and Information of Local Communities Affected by the LFTZ

Question	Yes		No	
	N	%	N	%
Were you informed about the LFTZ project before the project began?	34	24.29	106	75.71
Before the project began, were you consulted about the implications of the project on your community?	5	3.57	135	96.43
Were you informed about the expropriation before the project began?	21	15.00	119	85.00
Were you given an opportunity to give input in the expropriation plans?	4	2.86	136	97.14
Were you made aware of any environmental/social impact assessment conducted for the project?	3	2.14	137	97.86

Table 16 Level of Information Given to each Community

	Were you informed about the LFTZ Project before the Project Began?		Were you informed about the Expropriation before the Project Began?	
Community	**No**	**Yes**	**No**	**Yes**
Idasho	18	2	18	2
Idotun	22	1	22	1
Ilege	4	2	5	1
Imobido	1	5	1	5
Itoke	19	2	20	1
Okunraye	13	4	15	2
Ilekuru	5	6	6	5
Tiye	15	2	16	1
Imagbon-Segun	1	8	8	1
Oke-Segun	8	2	8	2
Total	**106**	**34**	**119**	**21**

6.5.5 *Compensation Paid for Crops*

From 2010-2013, the LSG paid some compensation for crops and buildings, but not for empty land, even though the MOU entitles affected communities to compensation for land.[623] Based on the evidence available, it is not clear exactly how much total compensation was paid or how the compensation was calculated. According to the Government White Paper,

> The scale used by LSG for compensation in 2010-2013 was drawn up in 2000, at least a 10 year gap. That scale has by reason of inflation and depreciation of the Naira become obsolete and should have been revised upwards.[624]

The LFZDC, LWIL, the Lands Bureau, and Ministry of Commerce were unable to provide us with records of compensation payments or details on the methods used to calculate compensation. The Lands Bureau stated in the interview that some compensation was paid to the local chiefs and heads of families and that the Bureau is still in the process of compensating communities. In 2016, a local newspaper reported that Lagos State Governor Ambode paid an initial 66 Million Naira to affected communities (approximately $183,000) and that Ambode approved an additional 740 Million Naira (approximately $2 million) in compensation for the affected communities.[625] Presumably all of the compensation was sent to the Resettlement Committee, which, under the MOU, is charged with allocating compensation and other entitlements among the affected communities. According to the Guardian article,

> Ambode said that an initial 66 million [Naira] had been paid to owners of Parcel A lands, which houses the Dangote Refinery and some other companies while the new compensation approved was for host communities of Parcel B, comprising Yegunda and Abomiti zones.[626]

Table 17 shows that 56 of 140 households (40%) surveyed were promised compensation, but only one household claimed it was given an opportunity to negotiate compensation. Only 4 of those 56 households (7%) were told how compensation was calculated. Only 38 respondents out of 140 (27%) stated they actually received any compensation. Figure 17 and the vast majority of them (97%) felt that this compensation did not cover all of their losses.

623 Heinrich Bol Stiftung 2016; Lagos State Government (LSG), *Government Write Paper on the Report of the Tribunal of Inquiry into the Cause of Civil Disturbances at the Lekki Free Trade Zone on 12 October, 2015*, LSG, Lagos, 2016.

624 LSG 2016.

625 The Guardian (Nigeria), 'Ambode Approves N740M for Lekki Free Zone Communities', *The Guardian*, Lagos, 2016.

626 The Guardian (Nigeria) 2016.

Figure 17 Actual Compensation and Level of Satisfaction (N = 140 Respondents)

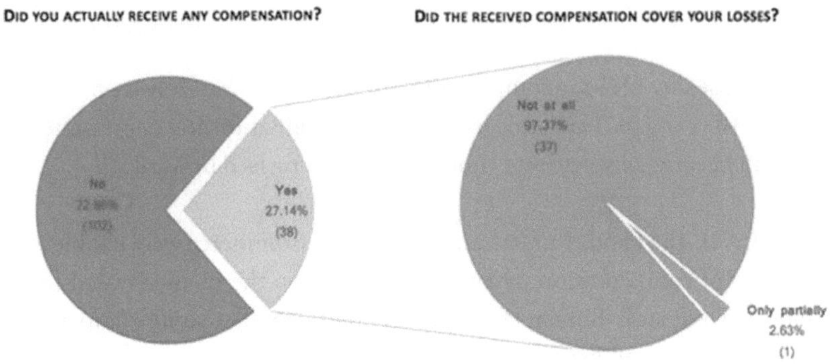

Table 17 Promised Compensation

QUESTION	YES		NO		DO NOT KNOW	
	N	%	N	%	N	%
Were you promised any compensation for the expropriation?	56	40.00	83	59.29	1	0.71
Were you given the opportunity to negotiate compensation? (Only if answered YES to previous question)	1	1.79	55	98.21	0	0.0
Were you told how compensation was calculated? (Only if answered YES to the first question)	4	7.14	52	92.86	0	0.0

In a few cases, only a lump sum payment for all crops was granted, but it was unclear to the households surveyed how exactly this payment was calculated. In other cases, the respondents were able to report the value of the compensation received for a specific crop, but again the method used to calculate this amount remained unclear. For instance, the reported compensation for cassava ranged from a minimum of 20,000 Naira to a maximum of 100,000 Naira, while the reported compensation for maize ranged between 10,000 and 20,000 Naira (see Table 18). Moreover, the survey findings suggest there is no clear proportionality between the reported compensation and the average number of hectares of farmland cultivated by households, or the average seasonal yield claimed by respondents before the expropriation.

Table 18 Reported Compensation for Selected Crops and Estimates of Compensation at Market Price

CASSAVA						
[1] Community	[2] Reported average ha of farmland cultivated before expropriation	[3] Reported average Cassava production before expropriation (Kg/season)	[4] Reported total value of the compensation received for cassava (NGN)	[5] Reported compensation (NGN/Kg)	[6] Value of compensation at market price (Assuming cassava @141.23 NGN/Kg)	[7] Difference between reported compensation vs. compensation at market price (simulation @141.23 NGN/Kg)
Imagbon-Segun	5	0	20,000	NA	0	20,000.00
Imagbon-Segun	10	5000	20,000	4.00	706,150	-686,150.00
Okunraye	2	600	20,000	33.33	84,738	-64,738.00
Okunraye	5	3500	40,000	11.43	494,305	-454,305.00
Okunraye	61	2000	60,000	30.00	282,460	-222,460.00
Okunraye	0.4	0	100,000	NA	0	100,000.00
Okunraye	6	5000	65,000	13.00	706,150	-641,150.00
Okunraye	5	0	65,000	NA	0	65000.00
Tiye	1.5	6400	20,000	3.13	903,872	-88,3872.00
Tiye	2	800	25,000	31.25	112,984	-87,984.00
Ilekuru	0.3	9600	42,000	4.38	1,355,808	-1,313,808.00
Idotun	120	8000	30,000	3.75	1,129,840	-1,099,840.00
Idotun	112	57,600	25,000	0.43	8,134,848	-8,109,848.00
Ilege	20	3000	20,000	6.67	423,690	-403,690.00
AVERAGE	**25.01**	**7250.00**	**39,428.57 ($109 USD)**	**12.85 ($0.03 per Kg)**	**1,023,917.50 ($2844)**	**-984,488.93 (-$2735)**

MAIZE						
Community	Reported average ha of farm-land cul-tivated before expropri-ation	Reported average pro-duction before expro-priation (Kg/season)	Reported total value of the compen-sation received for maize (NGN)	Reported compensa-tion (NGN/Kg)	Value of compensa-tion at mar-ket price (Assuming Maize @119.66 NGN/Kg **)	Difference between reported compensa-tion vs. com-pensation at market price (@119.66 NGN/Kg **)
Imagbon-Segun	7	0	0	NA	0	0
Imagbon-Segun	0	0	10,000	NA	0	10000
Okunraye	5	4500	10,000	2.22	53,8470	-52,8470
Okunraye	6	3000	65,000	21.67	358,980	-293,980
AVERAGE	**4.50**	**1875.00**	**21,250.00 ($59)**	**11.94 ($0.03 per Kg)**	**224,362.50 ($623)**	**-203,112.50 (-$565)**

Despite restrictions on the sample size and the risk of respondents overstating or misreporting the quantity of cassava or maize produced on an average season before the expropriation, we calculated the average price at which cassava was reportedly compensated at 12.85 Naira/kg and the average compensation price paid for maize (1.94 Naira/kg. Both values appear to be only a fraction of the retail market price we estimated for cassava (average 141.23 Naira/kg; Min = 60; Max = 412.96) and maize (average 119.66 Naira/kg; Min = 60; Max = 412.96) based on FEWS NET data.[627] Even including those who declared they were compensated for a crop that their household was not cultivating at the time of the expropriation, our simulations shows the reported compensation tended to be, on average, much lower in value when compared to a compensation calculated based on the market price of the crop.

We interviewed an official at the Lagos Lands Bureau who stated compensation was paid, but did not provide us with documentation or exact figures on compensation payments. This official also stated the Lands Bureau is in the process of providing more compensation to communities. Some community members we interviewed stated that compensation was, in some cases, as low as 10,000 Naira ($27) for all crops. Results from the survey suggest that the calculation of the amount of compensation to be paid for the loss of crops was often discretional. Indeed, respondents frequently reported different levels of compen-

627 Price estimates are obtained from the Famine Early Warning System Network (FEWS NET), a project funded by USAID. We used all of the historical data available for Cassava and Maize Retail Prices in the Mile 12 Market in Lagos. Staple Food Price Database, available online: http://www.fews.net/content/staple-food-price-data(accessed on 8 February 2018).

sation for the very same crop, even inside the same community. Alternatively, some community members reported they were compensated for a crop they did not grow before expropriation (see Table 18). In turn, the survey results suggest that compensation was often underestimated and paid discretionally, even within individuals belonging to the same community, in a context where there is no evidence of a clear and transparent calculation method. This is particularly important, especially considering that 140 respondents declared that they were cultivating land—both for income generation and household consumption—before the expropriation, while only five stated that they are still farming after the expropriation.

In Table 18, we attempted to verify whether the amount of the compensation received by respondents for selected crops—as they reported it in our survey—was consistent with market prices for crops in Nigeria. While the LUA does not specify whether compensation for crops must be set at market rates—instead section 29(4) of the LUA simply grants the "appropriate officer" discretion to calculate compensation rates—market value is generally used as a benchmark for valuing compensation in many other countries.[628] Column 7 of Table 18 shows significant discrepancies between the amount of compensation provided and the amount that would have been provided if a "market value" approach to valuing compensation was followed, and therefore supports our conclusion that insufficient compensation was provided to affected communities in the LFTZ case.

Each row in the Table represents a household in our sample that reported the total value of the compensation received for cassava (see Column 4, upper table) or maize (see Column 4, lower table). Table 18 also shows the community to which each respondent belongs (Column 1), the reported average size of farmland cultivated before the expropriation (Column 2), the reported average seasonal yield (Column 3) and the reported total value of compensation received for selected crops (Column 4). Column 5 shows the average compensation rate in terms of Nigerian Naira per kg. The numbers in Column 5 were obtained by dividing the total value of the compensation received (Column 4) by the average seasonal yield for a given crop (Column 3). We focused on two crops only, namely cassava and maize, due to the availability of information on market values. For these two crops, we were able to retrieve the average retail price per kilogram—in local currency—at which each crop was sold at the Mile 12 Market in Lagos. Once we estimated the average price per kg, we multiplied that price (stated for each crop in the header of Column 6) by the reported average seasonal yield (Column 3), thus obtaining an estimate for the value of compensation at market price (Column 6). The numbers in Column 7 represent the difference between the total value of the reported compensation for each crop (Column

628 Tagliarino 2017, p. 37.

4) and our best estimate of the total compensation calculated using average market prices (Column 6). Overall, this Table suggests that the compensation provided for some crops was far below market rates.

6.5.6 *Possible Corruption*

There is a noticeable difference between the amount that the LSG reportedly paid (66 million Naira) and the amount that surveyed communities claimed they received.[629] If compensation has not trickled down to the household level, then it is possible that intermediaries, including members of the Resettlement Committee, may have taken significant portions of the compensation payments. Intermediaries could have also included chiefs or other community "elites" involved in the negotiation around the MOU. Section 29(3) of the LUA provides that compensation may be paid to "the community, the chief, or leader of the community to be disposed of by him for the benefit of the community in accordance with…customary law", or into "some fund specified by the Governor." The Government White Paper does not thoroughly investigate crimes of theft or embezzlement, but states,

> The revelation at the Tribunal was that beneficiaries of compensation were paid in cash and sometimes through proxies in circumstances which facilitate diversion of money, theft, embezzlement, manipulation, and fraud…it is no wonder that some of the alleged beneficiaries denied receiving stated amounts of money shown against their names.

Due to the potential corruption in this case, it can be argued that the actions of chiefs and other community elites need to be more closely monitored and that these entities need to be held accountable. Consultation and negotiation with all community members, including women and youth, during the compensation process is needed to ensure that that payments are satisfactory, calculated in compliance with international standards, and made to every affected household.

6.5.7 *Environmental Impact Assessment (EIA)*

As previously discussed, when land is expropriated for development projects, government and private sector bodies are legally required to conduct an EIA before initiating develop-

629 The Guardian (Nigeria), 'Ambode Approves N740M for Lekki Free Zone Communities', *The Guardian*, Lagos, 2016.

ment projects in Nigeria. When interviewed, the Lagos Lands Bureau stated that an EIA was conducted pursuant to the EIA Decree 1992; however, the official we interviewed was unable to provide us with documentation that indicates an EIA was conducted. None of the community members we interviewed stated that they were able to view the EIA. Other research groups were also unable to access the EIA for the LFTZ; according to report by Heinrich Boll Stiftung, a Nigerian research NGO,

Even though the existence of an EIA report for the LFZ was claimed, it was not made available throughout the research of this report. Also, the community heads have not seen the EIA report. Upon asking the LFZDC to make it accessible, they were told to get a copy from the local government. Getting to the local government they were told that LFZDC has not submitted any EIA report to them.[630]

6.5.8 *Alternative Land*

According to our interview with the SERAC representative, a certificate of occupancy for 750 hectares of resettlement land was provided to the Resettlement Committee in 2009. This resettlement land was supposed to be shared by all affected communities. However, it encroached on land held by three other affected communities, so three more affected communities were added to the MOU.[631]

In 2014, a certificate of occupancy of 375 hectares was provided to the Lekki Coastal Development Association, which is a legal entity managed by the Resettlement Committee.[632] The Government White Paper found that this constituted a breach of the MOU since it is only half of what was promised by the MOU. Moreover, the alternative land was not clearly demarcated, making the boundaries unknown. According to our interview with the Ilekuru community, roughly 96 hectares were sold to a third party, and the remaining portion is largely uncultivable swampland. When interviewed, Ilekuru community members claimed they were unable to access the resettlement land for farming and other subsistence purposes because the land is far away from their homes and widely considered to be uncultivable swampland. Since the MOU is a legally binding document and the LUA provides a right to alternative, affected communities have a legal right to bring claims and seek redress in court. The MOU states,

630 Heinrich Bol Stiftung, *Urban Planning Processes in Lagos*, Heinrich Bol Stiftung, Lagos, 2016, pp. 206-208.
631 Stiftung 2016, pp. 210-211.
632 Lagos State Government (LSG), *Government Write Paper on the Report of the Tribunal of Inquiry into the Cause of Civil Disturbances at the Lekki Free Trade Zone on 12 October, 2015*, LSG, Lagos, 2016.

> In the event of any dispute, difference or claim arising out or in connection with this MOU, the parties may appoint mediators…if the parties fail to reach a settlement via mediation… The matter shall be settled by arbitration…this MOU is a legal document and nothing in this Section shall fetter the constitutional rights of the parties to seek judicial interpretation and, or enforcement of the terms of the MOU.[633]

6.5.9 *Jobs and Equity Shares*

While jobs are equity shares are not explicitly called for by the VGGTs, these entitlements were promised in the MOU. None of the affected households we surveyed stated that they were employed by LWIL, even though jobs were promised in the MOU. According the Government White Paper, "LWIL insists that members of the communities have been favoured with jobs," but affected communities disagree. Without records showing that jobs were allotted to communities, it is the word of one against another.[634] Additionally, none of the affected households we surveyed received equity shares in the LFTZ. Regarding the 2.5 percent equity share promised by the MOU, the Government White Paper found these "entitlements have been and are still being denied to the affected communities."[635]

6.5.10 *Displacement of the Illekuru Community*[636]

One of the ten communities we interviewed lost their homes as a consequence of the LFTZ. According to our interview with the community, the Ilekuru community lived and depended on the expropriated agricultural land since the 1700s. Historically, the primary occupations of community members were blacksmithing, farming, hunting and fishing. In the early 2000s, the government demanded land from the community and promised to resettle them to a new land with structure and other basic amenities, such as electricity and water. According to one community member, "the government made promises, but nothing was done." The government valued their land based on crops and other perennial trees. As farmers, the community primarily cultivated cassava and banana majorly, because they

633 Lagos State Government (LSG), *Memorandum of Understanding Between the Lagos State Government, the Ibeju-Lekki Local Government Council, Lekki Worldwide Investment Limited, and the Accredited Representatives of Villages and Communities (Idasho, Idotun, Ielge, Imobido, Itoke, Okunraiye, Ilekuru, Tiye, and Imagbon-Segun) Affected by the Lekki Free Trade Zone Project*, LSG, Lagos, 2007.

634 Lagos State Government (LSG), *Government Write Paper on the Report of the Tribunal of Inquiry into the Cause of Civil Disturbances at the Lekki Free Trade Zone on 12 October, 2015*, LSG, Lagos, 2016.

635 Lagos State Government 2016.

636 All of the information described in this Section comes from an interview we conducted in August 2017 with the Chiefs and other members of the community.

were all farmers. Ultimately, the ancestral land of Illekuru was granted to the Indomie Food Processing Company.

In 2002, the government brought in a bulldozer and heavy machinery and started grading and leveling the Ilekuru's land. People from the community protested the bulldozing of their land and demanded resettlement land. According to a community member we interviewed, "people from the community stood their ground and temporarily stopped the government Caterpillar from working, we demanded that the government grant us our new resettlement land." The Government temporarily suspended work until it could bring in more security personnels (i.e., mobile police). In 2003, the Baale's (i.e., community chief's) house was demolished by the development project. The Ilekuru community demanded resettlement land. The government promised to grant them 15 hectares of land but only ended up granting 6.3 hectares. The government promised to give the remaining land at a later point, but still had not done so as of August 2017. Consequently, many Illekuru community members have migrated and are living elsewhere. Structures made of brick and bamboo on the original Ilekuru land were demolished, but the government did not provide financing or alternative housing: the community was only given 6.3 hectares of bare land. The Ilkeuru community had to use the little income they had to build new dwellings. The community was given a fraction of the land previously held, and the resettlement area encroached on the Okunraiye community's land, so both communities were forced to share the little remaining land.

From our survey of the area, the apparent living condition of the present Ilekuru community was very poor: the community lacked essentials such as schools, healthcare, and security from theft. Many members had moved away to find homes elsewhere. Vibrations from dredging conducted by Dangote Company caused cracks to form in their dwellings. The same dredging also caused flooding in the nearby Okunraiye community. Some community members could not live with the vibration and noise and needed to relocate somewhere else. Land surveyors were consulted on the resettlement land and confirmed that the Ilekuru community could not possess the land because they did not have a Certificate of Occupancy. The Ilekuru community stated that their resettlement land had more recently been sold to someone who claimed to have bought the land from Okunraiye community. The said buyer, unnamed yet presumed by community members to be a powerful politician, told the Illekuru community to sell its land and collect a small lump sum amount of money or else forfeit their land. In 2016, the Ilekuru Community conceded and sold its land.

At least three other communities (Idotun, Itoke and Okunraiye) remain vulnerable to displacement since the LFTZ is currently building a seaport, the expansion of which may displace these communities in the near future. According to community members, several private contractors warned them to leave and told them that, if nothing else, the noise and vibrations from construction will force them to vacate their land.

6.6 Suggested Avenues for Nigerian Lawmakers to Pursue

The evidence put forth in this Chapter indicates that the government failed to adequately inform, consult, compensate and resettle communities whose livelihoods were affected by the development of the LFTZ. Our interviews and empirical research conducted indicates that the government did not follow a transparent and participatory process when acquiring land and compensating communities, and thus did not comply with international standards.

Since Chinese investors are the majority shareholders of the LFZDC, it is important to recognize potential influence these investors have over the LSG and the possible power dynamic between investors, the government, and the public. Investors typically have a primary interest in making profit, and may be incentivized to avoid the costs associated with investing in countries with extensive regulations, including obligations to compensation and resettle affected landholders. For this reason, investors may view Nigeria as attractive since there are only minimal compensation and resettlement requirements established in the LUA. As it stands, the LUA enables investors to acquire land from governments relatively easily without having to overcome too many legal hurdles. Investor influence over development projects may affect whether the LSG decides to reform the LUA to include more robust compensation and resettlement requirements that safeguard the rights of local landholders. Reforming the LUA may be unappealing to government and private investors that currently benefit from the status quo because the establishment of more robust compensation packages and resettlement and rehabilitation procedures may slow down the land acquisition process and increase costs for project backers. Nevertheless, even if it is more expensive for governments and investors in the short term, it may be in their best interests in the long term to fully compensate and otherwise accommodate affected landholders prior to initiating projects because research has shown that failure to do so could lead to significant project delays, work stoppages, and increased costs if local communities choose to protest or challenge projects in court.[637] Research that quantifies the tenure risks associated with land investments indicates that the failure to consult and compensate can lead to such protests or challenges.[638]

637 The Munden Project, 'The Financial Risks of Insecure Land Tenure: An Investment View', *Rights and Resources Initiative*, Washington, DC, 2012.

638 The Munden Project 2012.

Another issue to consider is that, even if the LUA is reformed so that it adopts international standards, the LSG may still decide to turn a blind eye to violations or only selectively enforce the law in a way that advantages investors as opposed to landholders and the public. For example, the LSG may promise the public that a proposed expropriation will create many jobs and use 'economic development' as pretext to disguise an expropriation that is actually intended solely to serve private interests. These potential issues warrant their own study since they are not sufficiently examined in this Chapter.

Since there are no clear deadlines or procedures for paying compensation, the LUA permits the governments and private companies to protect their reputation by arguing that they did not violate the law whenever compensation is delayed or insufficient. A major gap in the law is the lack of a clear, transparent process for calculating compensation that incorporates a negotiation process with affected landholders. Such gaps in the law pose the risk of impoverishing landholders displaced or affected by expropriation for development projects. In the LFTZ case, the LUA allowed the LSG to make arbitrary expropriation and compensation decisions behind closed doors using outdated methods. Overall, reforms to the LUA should include provisions that require governments and private actors to comply with international standards by ensuring inclusive, democratized decision-making regarding expropriation and compensation. Specifically, the LUA should

1. Provide a clear definition of public purpose to allow for judicial review of State Governor's expropriation decisions. State Governor's should thus be obliged to conduct a proportionality test, which entails examining a proposed expropriation project to determine whether (a) the expropriation project is necessary to serve a public purpose (there are no less intrusive alternatives), (b) the project is suitable (reasonably likely to achieve the intended public benefit), and (c) the benefits deriving from the expropriation are proportionate to costs borne by affected populations and the environment.[639] The State Governor's decision on whether a project satisfies the proportionality test should be subject to oversight by the courts.

2. Require government and entities and/or project developers to conduct both an environmental impact assessment and social impact assessment prior to expropriating so that environmental and social issues associated with proposed development projects, including the project's impact on local land rights, will be thoroughly identified and managed.

639 Hoops 2017.

3. Establish a consultation and negotiation process whereby affected landholders must be surveyed, informed, and consulted about proposed development projects and the potential impact on their land rights and livelihoods. The LUA should stipulate that all members of communities, not just the chiefs, must be consulted about proposed projects and compensation entitlements. Such a requirement may reduce the risk of expropriation and compensation decisions being made behind closed doors as well as the risk of elite capture of compensation.

4. Recognize the indigenous right to FPIC and require the government to be transparent and ensure meaningful community participation in expropriation, compensation, and resettlement decision-making.

5. Require that compensation must be granted directly to households and establish monitoring committees to ensure compliance with compensation plans and prevent elite capture by chiefs and other intermediaries. Require assessors of compensation to consider both the value of land as well as the value of improvements, crops, economic activities, disturbance to livelihood, and other incidental and collateral injuries suffered by landholders, even if the land in question is undeveloped.

6. Base the calculation of compensation on the 'replacement cost' where land is expropriated in areas where land markets are weak or non-existent and thus 'market value' is difficult to ascertain. In cases where compensation is based on market value, the LUA should adopt the International Valuations Standards definition of "market value."

7. Require that compensation must be paid prior to the moment at which the government or private companies take possession of the land. In cases where possession is taken before compensation is paid, require the government to pay interest based on the delay.

8. Require the government to provide affected communities with productive alternative land, where available.

9. Require investment and benefit-sharing arrangements whereby companies must allow affected landholders to own equity in development projects and invest in the education, healthcare facilities, and other basic amenities for affected landholders

10. Establish an independent valuation board with expert valuers charged with consulting and compensating affected landholders. The process for valuing land and crops should be well-documented and transparent, and valuers should reflect current market rates

for the average amounts of crops, livestock, and other improvements found on the land.

7 Conclusion and Recommendations

7.1 Summary and Roadmap

The findings from Chapters 2-6 of this book establish a benchmark for measuring national-level progress against the VGGTs on expropriation, compensation, and resettlement. By providing insight on the global legal landscape and highlighting which laws and provisions are in need of reform, this study can inform and influence law and policy discussions among lawmakers, scholars, civil society, and other stakeholders.

The findings indicate that many of the 50 countries assessed have legal frameworks that do not fully comply with international standards on expropriation, compensation, and resettlement established in the VGGTs. Failure to establish a strong legal framework may not only jeopardize the land tenure and livelihoods of affected landholders, but also trigger other negative outcomes such as landholder impoverishment, conflict, food insecurity, and landlessness.[640] Overall, there remains ample room for progress in achieving compliance with the VGGTs through national law reform.

This Chapter is organized as follows. Section 7.2 summarizes the findings and recommendations from Chapters 2-6. Section 7.3 provides a discussion of overarching findings and trends that were seen when viewing all of the legal indicators. Section 7.4 provides concluding remarks and suggested areas of future research.

7.2 Summary of the Findings

This Section provides a brief summarization of the research findings presented in Chapters 2-6 of this book. Each sub-section also summarizes each chapter's recommendations for reforming laws in the countries that scored poorly on the indicators.

7.2.1 Findings on Public Purpose Decision-Making (Chapter 2)

Chapter 2 of this book described common issues that arise when governments have broad discretion to justify the expropriation of land for 'economic development' and other public purposes often vaguely defined by law. The indicator analysis provided insight both on

640 Cernea 1997.

legal requirements applicable to public-purpose decision-making as well as an examination of whether expropriation processes are designed to be transparent and participatory. The expropriation indicators related to public purpose decision-making are based on Section 16.1 of the VGGTs:

- Section 16.1 of the VGGTs: "States should expropriate only where rights to land ... are required for a public purpose. States should clearly define the concept of public purpose in law, in order to allow for judicial review... [States should acquire only] the minimum resources necessary."

Based on this standard, the first expropriation indicator asked whether national laws provide a clear definition of public purpose to allow for judicial review. It was found that only five of the 50 countries assessed (Afghanistan, India, Indonesia, Mongolia, Rwanda) have laws that provide a clear definition of public purpose to allow for judicial review. In these five countries, the national laws provide clearly defined lists of public purposes (e.g, public infrastructure projects). These laws also indicate that governments cannot expropriate land for a purpose not explicitly included in the list. Seventeen of 50 countries[641] provide a partially clear definition of public purpose, but the public purpose provisions also include open-ended clauses (e.g., clauses that state "or other public purposes"). Of the 50 countries assessed, 28 of the countries assessed have laws that either do not provide a definition of public purpose or grant government authorities broad discretion to determine on a case-by-case basis what constitutes a "public purpose" and thereafter expropriate land.

7.2.1.1 Limits on the Type and Amount of Land That Can Be Expropriated

The indicators related to the legal limitations on the type and amount of land are based on Section 16.2 and 16.5 of the VGGTs:

- Section 16.2 of the VGGTs: "States should be sensitive where proposed expropriations involve areas of particular cultural, religious or environmental significance, or where the land [...] [is] particularly important to the livelihoods of the poor or vulnerable...
- Section 16.5 of the VGGTs: "Where the land [...] [is] not needed due to changes of plans, States should give the original rights holders the first opportunity to re-acquire these resources."

641 Brazil, Burkina Faso, Cambodia, China, Ecuador, Kazakhstan, Kenya, Lesotho, Mexico, Nigeria, Papua New Guinea, South Sudan, Swaziland, Taiwan, Tanzania, Thailand, Vietnam. For a full analysis and list of country indicator scores, see N.K Tagliarino. 'Voluntary Guidelines Section 16 Indicators on Expropriation, Compensation, and Resettlement', University of Groningen, Groningen, Netherlands, 2018. Available at: <https://landportal.org/book/dataset/nkt-vggt16>.

The second expropriation indicator examined whether laws require governments to minimize the amount of land they expropriate. It was found that only five of the 50 countries[642] establish explicit requirements that the government must minimize the amount of land acquired to the amount necessary to achieve a public purpose. In the remaining 45 countries, national laws do not require the government to minimize the amount of land it expropriates.

The third and fourth expropriation indicators asked whether national laws require governments or acquiring bodies to conduct a proportionality or feasibility study prior to expropriating land. It was found that four countries (Burkina Faso, India, Indonesia, and Taiwan) have national laws that require that government to conduct a proportionality test prior to expropriating land. These requirements explicitly oblige the government to weigh the costs of the expropriation (e.g. environmental and social costs) against its potential public benefits. Five counties (China, India, Indonesia, Malaysia, and Taiwan) have national-level laws that require a feasibility study prior to expropriation (i.e., an assessment of whether the proposed project is financially or otherwise likely to achieve its intended public purpose objective). Seven of 50 countries grant reacquisition rights whenever the expropriated land is no longer needed for a public purpose.[643]

The fifth and sixth expropriation indicators asked whether governments or acquiring bodies must conduct an EIA or an SIA prior to expropriating land. Of the 50 countries assessed, forty-nine have enacted national laws that impose obligations on project developers to conduct Environmental Impact Assessments (EIA). Five countries (Afghanistan, India, Indonesia, Laos, and South Sudan) have national-level laws that require governments to conduct an SIA prior to expropriating land.

The seventh expropriation indicator asks whether national laws establish special protections for poor and marginalized landholders, such as Indigenous Peoples, by respecting FPIC. It was found that four of the countries (India, Peru, the Philippines, Taiwan) have enacted national-level legislation that fully recognizes the international right of Indigenous Peoples to FPIC. Seven of the countries studied (Brazil, Ecuador, Honduras, Nepal, Nicaragua, South Sudan, Tanzania) received a 'partial' score because they either ratified ILO Convention 169 or otherwise enacted legislative or regulatory provisions that recognize the right of Indigenous Peoples and traditional communities to be consulted prior to expropriation.[644] Thirty-nine of 50 countries have not enacted national-level legislation that recognizes the indigenous right to right to FPIC.

---

642 Afghanistan, India, Lesotho, Malaysia, and Taiwan.

643 Afghanistan, India, Indonesia, Laos, Rwanda, Taiwan, Vietnam.

644 Brazil, Ecuador, Honduras, Nepal, Nicaragua, South Sudan, Tanzania.

The eighth expropriation indicator asks whether national laws grant affected landholders the right to reacquire the land in the event that the land is unutilized or no longer needed for the project. The analysis revealed that only seven countries grant reacquisition rights whenever the expropriated land is no longer needed for a public purpose.[645] Five countries received 'partial' scores for this indicator because their national laws grant reacquisition rights that are subject to certain limitations; in other words, in these countries, a right to reacquire the land may only be provided in some (but not all) cases of expropriation. In the remaining 38 countries, reacquisition rights are not granted to affected landholders.

7.2.1.2 Transparent and Participatory Expropriation Process

The indicators related to the legal limitations on the type and amount of land are based on Section 16.2 of the VGGTs:

- Section 16.2 of the VGGT: "States should ensure that the planning and process for expropriation are transparent and participatory. Anyone likely to be affected should be identified, and properly informed and consulted at all stages."

The ninth, tenth, and eleventh expropriation indicators asked whether governments or acquiring bodies must identify, inform, and consult affected landholders prior to expropriation.

Identification

Only seven of 50 countries have national laws that require governments to identify all affected landholders prior to the expropriation.[646] Four of 50 countries (Cambodia, China, Peru, and the Philippines) received partial scores for these indicators because their national laws only require governments to identify *some* affected landholders. However, 39 of 50 countries do not establish an identification requirement, which means that governments may be less likely to ascertain the total livelihood impact of the expropriations as well as the viewpoints and interests of all affected landholders prior to expropriation.

Proactive Disclosure of Information

Eighteen of 50 countries have enacted national laws that explicitly require governments to proactively inform affected landholders of the reasons for expropriation prior to compulsorily expropriating land.[647] Four of 50 countries (China, Ecuador, Peru, and South Sudan) received a partial score for this indicator because their national laws only require the government to proactively disclose the reasons for the expropriation in some (but not

645 Afghanistan, India, Indonesia, Laos, Rwanda, Taiwan, Vietnam.

646 Afghanistan, India, Indonesia, Laos, Rwanda, Taiwan, Vietnam.

647 Afghanistan, Belize, Burkina Faso, Cambodia, India, Indonesia, Laos, Malaysia, Mongolia, Nepal, Rwanda, South Africa, Taiwan, Tanzania, Thailand, Trinidad and Tobago, Vietnam, Zimbabwe.

all) cases of expropriation. In 28 of 50 countries, the national laws do not require governments to proactively inform landholders or the public of the reasons for the expropriation.

Consultation

Eight of 50 countries require the government to consult all affected landholders prior to expropriating land.[648] Thirteen of 50 countries have laws that require the government to consult affected landholders in some (but not all) cases; for instance, if the expropriation involves indigenous land.[649] Twenty-nine of 50 countries do not require the government to consult affected landholders prior to expropriating land.

7.2.1.3 Recommendations from Chapter 2

Based on these recommendations, Chapter 2 made the following recommendations for lawmakers in countries that scored 'no' on the expropriation indicators:

First, lawmakers should establish clear legal definitions of public purpose to provide courts with sufficient guidance when scrutinizing expropriation decisions. Laws should require expropriating authorities to limit the amount of land acquired to that which is necessary to achieve a public purpose. In order to prevent the government from taking an excessive amount of land, laws should also impose obligations on expropriating authorities to conduct a proportionality test and a feasibility study. These obligations will help prevent unjustified expropriation by requiring authorities to investigate whether (a) the proposed amount of land is necessary to serve a public purpose (there are no less intrusive alternatives), (b) the project is suitable (reasonably likely to achieve the intended public benefit), and (c) the benefits deriving from the expropriation are proportionate to costs borne by affected populations and the environment. Laws should require proportionality tests and feasibility studies to be scrutinized by independent and impartial bodies (e.g., judiciaries) to ensure proper checks and balances.

Second, laws should compel expropriating authorities and project developers to conduct an EIA and an SIA prior to expropriation land, thereby ensuring that expropriation decisions are sensitive to areas of cultural, historical and environmental significance. Laws should ensure that these areas are acquired only as a last resort, and, if expropriation of these areas is unavoidable, that the risks to these impacted areas are adequately addressed. In addition to thoroughly examining project plans (e.g., financial costs, schedules, and monitoring capacity), SIAs and EIAs should incorporate public consultations.

648 Afghanistan, Burkina Faso, Cambodia, India, Indonesia, Laos, Lesotho, Taiwan.

649 Brazil, China, Ecuador, Ethiopia, Honduras, Nicaragua, Peru, Philippines, Rwanda, South Sudan, Tanzania, Thailand, Zambia.

Third, laws should respect the indigenous right to FPIC by ensuring indigenous populations are adequately consulted and given the opportunity to participate in expropriation decision-making. As stipulated in Section 9 of the VGGT, effective participation of all members, men, women, and youth, in decisions regarding their tenure systems should be promoted through their local or traditional institutions, including in the case of collective tenure systems. Indigenous Peoples should not be forcibly evicted from their land without obtaining their FPIC. In the event that expropriation of indigenous land is absolutely necessary and a demonstrable last resort, indigenous populations should first agree to fair compensation and be granted suitable alternative land, rehabilitation assistance, and other measures aimed at reconstructing their livelihoods. Indigenous Populations should be provided the first opportunity to return to their land upon completion of the project, if possible.[650]

Fourth, laws should allow affected landholders to reacquire expropriated land in the event that the proposed project is abandoned or the land is no longer needed for a public purpose. Reacquisition rights may incentivize expropriating actors to implement projects as agreed and prevent expropriating land from becoming abandoned, unutilized, and wasted.

Fifth, laws should establish transparent and participatory procedures for the expropriation of land. To conform to Section 16.2 of the VGGTs, governments should be legally obligated to identify, inform, and consult affected populations in an open and participatory manner prior to taking possession of expropriated land. By surveying affected populations, governments can determine who is entitled to compensation and understand the impact of the expropriation on tenure rights and livelihoods. Providing information on expropriation plans to affected landholders and the general public can be an effective first step toward ensuring meaningful participation in expropriation decision-making and other processes (e.g., compensation processes, resettlement processes). With adequate access to information on the proposed expropriation, affected populations and the general public will be better able to monitor expropriations and hold expropriating actors accountable for decisions that violate the law.

7.2.2 Compensation Eligibility Indicator Findings (Chapter 3)

Chapter 3 examined compensation eligibility issues related to IPLCs with customary tenure, and investigated whether the national laws in 30 countries grant compensation for IPLCs when their lands are expropriated. As discussed in Chapter, the compensation eligibility analysis only covers 30 countries (as opposed to 50) because the analysis incorporates

650 United Nations 2007, Art. 10.

findings from LandMark's legal indicators on the tenure security of indigenous and community lands, and reliable LandMark indicator data was not available for 20 of the 50 countries at the time the study was conducted. The compensation eligibility indicators discussed in Chapter 3 are primarily based on Section 16.1. Since these indicators address the legal security of IPLCs with customary tenure, Sections 9.5 and 9.7 of the VGGTs also inform the indicators presented in this Chapter.

- Section 16.1 of the VGGTs: "[States] should respect all legitimate tenure rights holders, especially vulnerable and marginalized groups, by...providing just compensation in accordance with national law."
- Sections 9.4-9.6 of the VGGTs: "States should provide appropriate recognition and protection of indigenous peoples and other communities with customary tenure systems...Such recognition should take into account the land, fisheries and forests that are used exclusively by a community and those that are shared...where indigenous peoples and other communities with customary tenure systems have legitimate tenure rights to ancestral lands on which they live, States should recognize and protect these rights...States should consider adapting their policy, legal and organizational frameworks to recognize tenure systems of [IPLCs]."

As discussed in Chapter 3, the first compensation eligibility indicator asked whether national laws provide compensation for formally recognized IPLC tenure rights in the event of expropriation. The analysis revealed that 22 of the 30 countries assessed[651] have laws that grant compensation to communities with formally recognized tenure rights. In five of these 22 countries (Malaysia, South Sudan, Taiwan, Philippines, and China), national laws explicitly provide that communities with customary tenure rights are entitled to compensation. Cambodia received a 'partial' score because the laws provide for payment of compensation to indigenous landholders. Seven of the 30 countries assessed (Bangladesh, Hong Kong, Kazakhstan, Mongolia, Rwanda, Sri Lanka, Thailand) have national laws that do not provide communities with a right to compensation upon expropriation.

The second compensation eligibility indicator asked whether national laws provide compensation for unregistered IPLC tenure rights. It was found that seven of the 30 countries assessed (Kenya, Philippines, South Sudan, Tanzania, Uganda, South Africa and Zambia) have laws that grant communities the right to obtain compensation regardless of whether their land rights are formally registered or not. Five of the 30 countries (Afghanistan, Burkina Faso, India, Liberia, and Vietnam) received a 'partial' score for this indicator

---

651 Afghanistan, Botswana, Burkina Faso, China, Ethiopia, Ghana, India, Indonesia, Kenya, Liberia, Malaysia, Namibia, Nigeria, Philippines, South Africa, South Sudan, Taiwan, Tanzania, Uganda, Vietnam, Zambia, Zimbabwe.

because their national laws contain provisions indicating that some (but not all) communities may be afforded compensation even without obtaining formally registered land rights. Eighteen of the 30 countries assessed[652] do not have laws that provide compensation for formally recognized IPLC tenure rights regardless of whether those rights are registered.

The third compensation eligibility indicator examined whether national laws provide compensation for formally recognized IPLC tenure rights regardless of whether the IPLCs developed or made improvements on the land. The analysis revealed that 15 of the 30 countries[653] grant compensation for community land regardless of whether that land is developed, cultivated, or has improvements. Zimbabwe and Tanzania received partial scores because their national laws suggest compensation may, at least in some cases, be limited to improved or developed land.[654] Thirteen of the 30 countries assessed[655] have laws that do not provide compensation for IPLC tenure rights regardless of whether their land is developed, cultivated or has improvement.

Chapter 3 also highlighted additional limitations on IPLC rights to compensation. First, laws that narrowly define 'community land' impose limits on the ability of the communities to achieve legal recognition and compensation upon expropriation. Legal definitions of community land are important because the ways in which national laws define public, private, and communal properties directly affects whether communities will be entitled to compensation in the event that their lands are compulsorily acquired. For example, some national laws state that 'government land' includes all forest reserves (e.g. Kenya Forest Rights Act 2005), and therefore communities living in such reserves are precluded from obtaining legally recognized rights and compensation if they are evicted. Second, three of the countries assessed (e.g. Afghanistan, India, and Namibia) have laws that set arbitrary time requirements, which stipulate that communities must have lived or depended on the expropriated land prior to a particular date in order to be eligible for compensation. This requirement may not only be difficult to implement, since exact date on which IPLCs originated is often unknown, but it may effectively preclude certain communities with

---

652 Bangladesh, Botswana, Cambodia, China, Ethiopia, Ghana, Hong Kong, Indonesia, Kazakhstan, Malaysia, Mongolia, Namibia, Nigeria, Rwanda, Sri Lanka, Taiwan, Thailand, Zimbabwe.

653 Afghanistan, Botswana, Burkina Faso, Ghana, India, Indonesia, Kenya, Liberia, Malaysia, Philippines, South Africa, South Sudan, Taiwan, Uganda, Vietnam.

654 Article 72 of the Constitution of Zimbabwe (2013) states: "where agricultural land…is required for a public purpose…no compensation is payable in respect of its acquisition, except for improvements." However, Section 12 of the Communal Land Act (1983) and Section 20 of the Land Acquisition Act (2002) indicate that compensation is not limited to the value of the improvements when non-agricultural community land is expropriated. Government of Zimbabwe 2013.

655 Bangladesh, Cambodia, China, Ethiopia, Hong Kong, Kazakhstan, Mongolia, Namibia, Nigeria, Rwanda Sri Lanka, Thailand, Zambia.

otherwise justifiable claims to recognized tenure rights and compensation upon expropriation.

7.2.2.1 Recommendations from Chapter 3

Based on the findings, Chapter 3 proposed several recommendations for legal reform that can be adopted by lawmakers in countries that scored 'no' on the indicators:

To conform to the VGGTs, states must protect and respect the legitimate tenure rights of IPLCs whether formally recorded or not.[656] Laws should be designed to grant compensation for unregistered IPLC tenure rights. Although the term "legitimate" is left undefined in the VGGTs, this term is defined in other international instruments as including both legal legitimacy (rights recognized by law) and social legitimacy (rights that have a broad acceptance among society).[657] For this reason, states should initiate flexible systems that look beyond registered property rights when determining who is entitled to compensation.

In order for governments to adequately and effectively assess the 'social legitimacy' of tenure rights held by IPLCs, they should survey the affected land and conduct in-person consultations and negotiations with affected communities. Establishing legal requirements to identify and consult affected communities prior to expropriation would help bring states into conformity with Section 16.3 of the VGGTs, which calls for expropriation processes to be transparent and participatory. Based on the information gathered through these consultations and negotiations, compensation may be agreed upon on a case-by-case basis. This would be an effective alternative to requiring that affected landholders show titles, certificates, and other legal documents to prove they are entitled to compensation.

States should consider adopting the legal provisions established in the laws of the Philippines, South Sudan, Tanzania, Uganda, and Zambia. These countries have laws that formally recognize community land rights regardless of whether those rights are registered. Research has shown that registration processes in many developing countries are slow, costly, and ineffective at capturing the full range of legitimate tenure rights attached to land.[658] Showing registered titles and other formal documents may be one way to prove an affected landholder is entitled to compensation, but it should not be the only way. In these countries, customary tenure rights are formally recognized automatically through customary occupation and use of the land by the community.

656 FAO 2012, Sections 3.1 & 5.3.
657 Palmer *et al.* 2009.
658 L. Notess *et al.* 2018.

National laws should ensure compensation is provided for IPLC tenure rights regardless of whether their lands are developed, cultivated, or improved. As previously discussed, Sections 9 and 18 of the VGGTs call for the valuation of land to reflect spiritual, cultural, and other non-market values. In order to conserve and protect their environments and common properties, such as rangelands, forests, pastures, and wetlands, communities may decide to deliberately leave such areas undeveloped and uncultivated. Since these communities serve important conservation purposes, they should not be penalized for conserving their environments instead of developing them. In many parts of Asia and Africa, communities use and depend on undeveloped commons, for grazing, hunting, burying ancestors, and traditional practices.[659] Community tenure rights to these areas should be considered legitimate, even in communal land areas that are not cultivated or developed. Instead of basing eligibility on whether the community developed or improved the land, the determination of whether a particular community should be entitled to compensation should be based on whether that community has, in good faith, customarily occupied and used the expropriated land and common property resources.

States should recognize how restrictive community land definitions and time requirements may prevent communities with legitimate claims to land and resources from obtaining compensation upon expropriation. Again, good faith occupation and use by the community should be the benchmark by which eligibility for compensation is assessed. Compensation eligibility requirements should not shut the door on communities who have traditionally occupied and used land and resources in good faith, otherwise these requirements may continue to put communities at significant risk of impoverishment, landlessness, food insecurity, and other negative outcomes commonly associated with expropriation without compensation.

7.2.3 Compensation Valuation Indicator Findings (Chapter 4)

The compensation valuation indicators presented in Chapter 4 of this book are based on Section 16.3 and 18.2 of the VGGTs.

- Section 16.3 of the VGGTs: "States should ensure a fair valuation and prompt compensation in accordance with national law. Among other forms, the compensation may be, for example, in cash, rights to alternative areas, or a combination."
- Section 18.2 of the VGGTs: "Policies and laws related to valuation should strive to ensure that valuation systems take into account non-market values, such as social, cultural, religious, spiritual and environmental values where applicable."

659 Wily 2008.

The first compensation valuation indicator examines whether national laws enacted in the 50 countries assessed allow assessors to calculate compensation using alternative methods to FMV. It was found that seven of the 50 countries[660] establish alternative approaches to calculating compensation that can be applied in cases where land markets are weak or non-existent. Six of 50 countries received a 'partial' score because their laws indicate that alternative approaches to FMV may be used in certain circumstances.[661] However, these countries' laws do not specifically state whether alternatives to FMV may be applied whenever land markets are weak or non-existent. The remaining 37 countries received a 'no' score because their laws establish FMV as the required approach and do not provide alternatives to FMV in cases where land markets are weak or non-existent.[662]

The second compensation valuation indicator asks whether national laws establish special protections for women landholders ensuring they are entitled to fair compensation. This indicator investigates whether the compensation procedures assessed explicitly provided special protections for women landholders for the purposes of obtaining compensation upon expropriation. For this indicator, it was found that only one of the 50 countries assessed (India) has compensation procedures that partially protect women from expropriation without fair compensation. Under India's LARR Act 2013, for example, widows and divorcees are considered a separate category of affected persons entitled to compensation, meaning that women are at least partially protected as legally recognized class of persons entitled to compensation. At the same time, these two countries did not receive a 'yes' score because they do not ensure that women will be protected in every case (e.g., in cases that do not involve expropriation of land rights held by widows and divorcees)

The third compensation valuation indicator asks whether the law requires assessors to account for the loss of business or other economic activities when calculating compensation. It was found that 28 of 50 countries provide compensation for economic activities associated with the land.[663] Ten of 50 countries received 'partial' scores because their laws suggest that compensation may reflect some (but not all) types of economic activities.[664] Twelve

660 Belize, Cambodia, Ethiopia, Ghana, Sierra Leone, South Africa, Tanzania.

661 Mongolia, Bhutan, India, Kenya, Laos, Lesotho.

662 Afghanistan, Angola, Argentina, Bangladesh, Botswana, Brazil, Burkina Faso, China, Ecuador, Eritrea, Honduras, Hong Kong, Indonesia, Kazakhstan, Liberia, Malaysia, Mexico, Myanmar, Namibia, Nepal, Nicaragua, Nigeria, Pakistan, Papua New Guinea, Peru, Philippines, Rwanda, South Sudan, Sri Lanka, Swaziland, Taiwan, Thailand, Trinidad and Tobago, Uganda, Vietnam, Zambia, Zimbabwe.

663 Afghanistan, Bangladesh, Belize, Botswana, Brazil, Cambodia, China, Hong Kong, India, Indonesia, Kazakhstan, Kenya, Laos, Lesotho, Malaysia, Myanmar, Nepal, Pakistan, Peru, Rwanda, Sierra Leone, South Africa, Sri Lanka, Swaziland, Taiwan, Tanzania, Thailand, Vietnam.

664 Bhutan, Philippines, South Sudan, Burkina Faso, Ethiopia, Ghana, Mongolia, Namibia, Uganda, Zimbabwe.

countries have national laws that do not explicitly or implicitly provide compensation for economic activities associated with the land.[665]

The fourth compensation valuation indicator asks whether assessors must account for the value of improvements made on the land when calculating compensation. It was found that 32 of 50 countries have laws that provide compensation for improvements made on the land.[666] Ten of 50 countries received 'partial' scores because their laws suggest that compensation may reflect some (but not all) of the improvements made on the land.[667] Eight of 50 countries have laws that do not require assessors to take into account the value of improvements when calculating compensation.[668]

The fifth compensation valuation indicator examines whether assessors must account for intangible land values when calculating compensation. For this indicator, I investigated whether laws establish any procedures by which intangible land values, such as historical, cultural, or personal values, may be reflected in the calculation of compensation. It was found that only two of 50 countries (Bhutan and the Philippines) have laws that explicitly require acquiring bodies to consider the land's intangible land values (e.g., historical, cultural, and spiritual values) when assessing compensation. Seven of 50 countries received 'partial' scores because their laws require assessors to account for intangible land values to some extent.[669] The remaining 41 countries assessed have laws that do not require that intangible land values (e.g., cultural, spiritual, and historical values) will be reflected in the assessment of compensation.[670]

The sixth compensation valuation indicator asks whether affected landholders are granted the right to opt for alternative land as a compensation option, if such land is available. It was found that 18 of 50 countries have laws that provide affected populations with a right

665 Angola, Argentina, Ecuador, Eritrea, Honduras, Liberia, Mexico, Nicaragua, Nigeria, Papua New Guinea, Trinidad and Tobago, Zambia.

666 Afghanistan, Angola, Bangladesh, Belize, Botswana, Brazil, Burkina Faso, China, Ethiopia, Honduras, India, Indonesia, Kenya, Laos, Mexico, Mongolia, Myanmar, Nepal, Nigeria, Pakistan, Peru, Philippines, Rwanda, Sierra Leone, South Africa, South Sudan, Taiwan, Tanzania, Trinidad and Tobago, Vietnam, Zambia, Zimbabwe.

667 Argentina, Cambodia, Ghana, Hong Kong, Kazakhstan, Malaysia, Namibia, Swaziland, Thailand, Uganda.

668 Bhutan, Ecuador, Eritrea, Lesotho, Liberia, Nicaragua, Sri Lanka, Papua New Guinea.

669 Ghana, India, Laos, Nepal, Sri Lanka, Tanzania, Vietnam.

670 Afghanistan, Angola, Argentina, Bangladesh, Belize, Botswana, Brazil, Burkina Faso, Cambodia, China, Ecuador, Eritrea, Ethiopia, Honduras, Hong Kong, Indonesia, Kazakhstan, Kenya, Lesotho, Liberia, Malaysia, Mexico, Mongolia, Myanmar, Namibia, Nicaragua, Nigeria, Pakistan, Papua New Guinea, Peru, Rwanda, Sierra Leone, South Africa, South Sudan, Swaziland, Taiwan, Thailand, Trinidad and Tobago, Uganda, Zambia, Zimbabwe.

to opt for alternative land instead of or in addition to compensation.[671] Eight of 50 countries have laws that suggest alternative land may be provided in some cases; however, it was unclear, based on the wording of these countries' laws, whether alternative land may be provided as a compensation option in every case.[672] Twenty-four of 50 countries have laws that do not explicitly or implicitly provide alternative land as a compensation option.[673]

The seventh compensation valuation indicator asks whether national laws provide affected landholders with the right to negotiate compensation. It was found that 27 of 50 countries have laws that provide affected landholders the right to negotiate compensation levels.[674] Seven of 50 countries have laws that provide affected populations with the right to negotiate compensation under certain circumstances.[675] Sixteen of 50 countries have laws that do not provide affected populations with the right to negotiate compensation amounts.[676]

The eighth compensation valuation indicator asks whether laws mandate that affected populations receive payment prior to the taking of possession or within a specified time-frame thereafter. It was found that 20 of 50 countries have laws that require governments to pay compensation before acquiring land or within a specified timeframe thereafter.[677] Thirteen of 50 countries received 'partial' scores because their laws establish deadlines for compensation payments but also provide exceptions by which the deadline may be extended.[678] Seventeen of 50 countries have laws that do not require prior payment of compensation or payment within a specified timeframe.[679]

The ninth compensation valuation indicator examines whether national laws provide affected populations with a right to challenge compensation decisions in court or before a tribunal. It was found that 35 of 50 countries have laws that grant affected populations

671 Afghanistan, Cambodia, Eritrea, Ghana, India, Indonesia, Kazakhstan, Kenya, Laos, Mongolia, Nepal, Nigeria, Philippines, South Sudan, Sri Lanka, Tanzania, Vietnam, Zambia.

672 Argentina, Bhutan, Botswana, Burkina Faso, Ethiopia, Rwanda, Taiwan, Zimbabwe.

673 Angola, Bangladesh, Belize, Brazil, China, Ecuador, Honduras, Hong Kong, Lesotho, Liberia, Malaysia, Mexico, Myanmar, Namibia, Nicaragua, Pakistan, Papua New Guinea, Peru, Sierra Leone, South Africa, Swaziland, Thailand, Trinidad and Tobago, Uganda.

674 Argentina, Belize, Botswana, Burkina Faso, Cambodia, China, Eritrea, Ghana, Hong Kong, India, Indonesia, Kazakhstan, Kenya, Laos, Malaysia, Mongolia, Papua New Guinea, Philippines, Sierra Leone, South Africa, South Sudan, Sri Lanka, Swaziland, Tanzania, Uganda, Vietnam, Zambia.

675 Bhutan, Ecuador, Honduras, Namibia, Nicaragua, Rwanda, Taiwan.

676 Afghanistan, Angola, Bangladesh, Brazil, Ethiopia, Lesotho, Liberia, Mexico, Myanmar, Nepal, Nigeria, Pakistan, Peru, Thailand, Trinidad and Tobago, Zimbabwe.

677 Bangladesh, Bhutan, Botswana, Cambodia, Ecuador, Eritrea, Ethiopia, Indonesia, Kazakhstan, Laos, Lesotho, Mexico, Philippines, Rwanda, Swaziland, Taiwan, Thailand, Uganda, Vietnam, Zimbabwe.

678 Argentina, Brazil, China, India, Malaysia, Mongolia, Namibia, Nepal, Papua New Guinea, South Africa, South Sudan, Sri Lanka, Trinidad and Tobago.

679 Afghanistan, Angola, Belize, Burkina Faso, Ghana, Honduras, Hong Kong, Kenya, Liberia, Myanmar, Nicaragua, Nigeria, Pakistan, Peru, Sierra Leone, Tanzania, Zambia.

the right to challenge compensation decisions in court or before tribunals.[680] Nine of 50 countries have laws that partially grant affected populations the right to challenge compensation decisions.[681] Six of 50 countries have laws that do not provide affected populations with the right to challenge compensation decisions in court or before a tribunal.[682]

Chapter 4 also highlighted that Asian and African countries assessed achieved better scores on the compensation valuation indicators than the Latin American countries assessed. While Belize received five 'yes' scores on the indicators, the remaining eight Latin American countries assessed (Argentina, Brazil, Ecuador, Honduras, Mexico, Nicaragua, Peru, and Trinidad and Tobago) received fewer than three 'yes' scores on the indicators.

7.2.3.1 Recommendations from Chapter 4

Based on the findings from the research highlighted in Chapter 4, I proposed three recommendations for lawmakers to pursue in order to ensure the international standards on compensation valuation are adopted and sufficient compensation is provide:

First, laws should ensure that compensation procedures respect and protect the tenure rights of poor and marginalized groups. In cases where land markets are weak or non-existent, laws should be flexible and provide alternatives to the 'FMV' approach to calculating compensation. The 'replacement cost' approach may be a suitable alternative to fair market value since it requires an assessment of what it would really take in a given market to replace lost assets. Section 10 of Tanzania's Village Land Regulation, 2001, is a good provision for countries or regions without robust land markets to adopt because it grants assessors flexibility to follow a variety of approaches when calculating compensation.[683] The law should provide clear and specific guidelines for valuing compensation that are flexible enough to allow for the determination of full compensation in special cases where land markets are weak or non-existent. The finding that only one of the 50 countries (India) has enacted laws which establish special protections for women relating to compensation is particularly problematic given the risk that expropriations may disproportionately burden women landholders. More countries need to establish compensation procedures that

680 Afghanistan, Argentina, Bangladesh, Belize, Brazil, Burkina Faso, Cambodia, China, Ecuador Eritrea, Ethiopia, Honduras, Hong Kong, India, Indonesia, Kazakhstan, Kenya, Laos, Liberia, Malaysia, Mongolia, Nigeria, Papua New Guinea, Peru, Philippines, Sierra Leone, South Africa, South Sudan, Sri Lanka, Taiwan, Tanzania, Thailand, Trinidad and Tobago, Uganda, Zambia.

681 Botswana, Ghana, Lesotho, Myanmar, Namibia, Pakistan, Rwanda, Swaziland, Zimbabwe.

682 Angola, Bhutan, Mexico, Nepal, Nicaragua, Vietnam.

683 Section 10 of the Village Land Regulations states "The market value of any land unexhausted improvement shall be arrived at by use of comparative method evidenced by actual recent, sales of similar properties or by use of income approach or replacement cost method where the property is of special nature and not saleable."

require governments to respect women's land rights and follow a gender-sensitive approach to providing compensation, which accounts for the varying ways in which women and men use land.

Second, laws should establish procedures that ensure a comprehensive valuation of compensation, accounting for all of the losses borne by affected populations. For compensation to comprehensively reflect all of the losses borne by affected populations, compensation payments should reflect the land's historical and cultural value, in addition to economic activities and improvements associated with the land. Consultations with male and female landholders about the ways in which they use their land, and their land's historical/cultural value, can be an effective measure to ensure that compensation is sufficient. In order to ensure adequate compensation for farmers, herders, gatherers and other landholders who use land as a primary source of income and livelihood needs, laws should provide affected populations the right to opt for alternative land instead of cash as a compensation payment. Such land must be suitable for affected populations to maintain an adequate standard of living (e.g., through cultivating or grazing purposes). Moreover, laws should require valuers to research relevant customary laws and practices to ensure that its approach to assessing compensation is acceptable to members of the community.

Third, laws should establish measures that ensure compensation is promptly paid and objectively assessed. Governments and acquiring bodies should be legally obligated to pay compensation to affected populations prior to taking possession of the expropriated property. Laws should ensure that affected landholders can negotiate compensation amounts and appeal compensation decisions to courts or tribunals. In addition to protecting the interests of affected populations, negotiating with affected landholders can benefit acquiring bodies by reducing costs from project delays that occur when landholders or appeal acquisition projects. Laws should grant affected populations the right to challenge compensation decisions in court or before a tribunal. Legal avenues of redress enable affected population to hold governments and acquiring bodies accountable for poor compensation decisions; for instance, if assessors use incorrect methods of valuation resulting in partial compensation to the affected landholder.

7.2.4 Resettlement Indicator Findings (Chapter 4)

The resettlement indicators presented in Chapter 5 are based on Section 16.8-16.9 of the VGGTs.

- Section 16.8 of the VGGTs: "States should, prior to eviction or shift in land use which could result in depriving individuals and communities from access to their productive

resources, explore feasible alternatives in consultation with the affected parties, consistent with the principles of these Guidelines, with a view to avoiding, or at least minimizing, the need to resort to eviction."
- Section 16.9 of the VGGTs: "Evictions and relocations should not result in individuals being rendered homeless or vulnerable to the violation of human rights. Where those affected are unable to provide for themselves, States should, to the extent that resources permit, take appropriate measures to provide adequate alternative housing, resettlement or access to productive land, fisheries and forests, as the case may be."[684]

Chapter 5 present research findings and analysis on resettlement procedures established in the 50 countries. The first resettlement indicator asks whether the country has enacted a national-level law containing resettlement and rehabilitation procedures that is legally binding on all projects involving the expropriation of land. While all of the constitutions of the 50 countries assessed establish the right to compensation for citizens whose land is expropriated, none of these constitutions establish robust procedures for ensuring correct compensation or measures for resettling and rehabilitating the livelihoods of displaced persons. Of the 50 countries assessed, only three (India, Laos, and Vietnam) have enacted resettlement procedures in statutes or regulations that are legally binding on all development projects involving the expropriation of land. China and the Philippines received a 'partial' score for this indicator because these countries enacted resettlement and rehabilitation procedures in laws that apply to some types of development projects involving the expropriation of land; however, these procedures do not apply to all expropriation projects and do not provide all displaced persons with resettlement and rehabilitation procedures. China has enacted several sector-specific regulations that establish provisions for resettling and rehabilitating displaced persons. Of the 50 countries considered, 44 have not enacted resettlement procedures that are legally binding on all development projects involving the expropriation of land. Among these 44 countries, I found evidence of either draft or adopted resettlement policies in 12 countries (Afghanistan, Belize, Brazil, Cambodia, Kenya, Indonesia, Pakistan, Nepal, the Philippines, Sri Lanka, Tanzania, and Zambia). These 12 countries still received red 'no' scores because these policies are not legally binding, and are also often short- lived. Honduras received 'unclear' scores for all seven of the rehabilitation and resettlement content indicators examined in this article.

The second resettlement indicator asks whether national laws provide displaced populations with relocation allowances to cover the transportation costs associated with resettling on alternative land, regardless of whether these persons have a legally recognized right to land. On this indicator 17 of the 50 countries received a 'partial' score because their national

684 FAO 2009, Section 16.8-16.9.

laws provide a relocation allowance as part of the compensation package provided to landholders eligible for compensation.[685] A total of 28 of the 50 countries assessed received a 'no' score because the national- level laws do not explicitly or implicitly provide displaced populations with relocation allowance to cover the costs of relocating from expropriated land.

The third resettlement indicator asks whether national laws provide displaced persons with a right to alternative land. It was found that three of the 50 countries (India, Laos, the Philippines) have laws that provide all displaced persons with the right to alternative land, regardless of the legal status of the displaced person. 'Partial' scores were awarded to 26 of the 50 countries because, according to these countries' laws, alternative land may be provided as a compensation option. However, the provision of alternative land is granted at the discretion of the government, so there is no guarantee that all displaced persons will be granted alternative land. In 20 of the countries assessed, national laws fail to provide displaced persons with a right to alternative land.

The fourth resettlement indicator asks whether national laws provide displaced persons with productive or suitable alternative land. Of the 50 countries, Laos was the only country assessed which requires that displaced people must be resettled in productive alternative land or suitable alternative housing. Four countries (Ghana, India, the Philippines, and Vietnam) received 'partial' scores because their laws may ensure, in some cases, that suitable or productive alternative land is provided. However, the laws of these four countries do not guarantee that the alternative land or housing will be suitable or productive in every case. In 44 of the 50 countries displaced persons are not provided with the right to productive alternative land or suitable alternative housing subsequent to expropriation.

The fifth resettlement indicator asks whether displaced persons are granted to a right to be consulted during the resettlement process. This indicator focuses only on whether consultation about the resettlement process must occur before displacement; the analysis does not address consultation requirements that may apply in other stages of the expropriation (e.g., consultations before or during the expropriation and compensation decision-making stages). Five of the 50 countries (China, India, Laos, South Sudan, and Vietnam) have laws that explicitly require the government to consult affected populations about the resettlement process before displacement. The Philippines received 'partial' scores because its national laws require consultation during resettlement processes in some (but not all) expropriation cases. In 43 of the 50 countries assessed, governments and acquiring bodies

685 Botswana, Ethiopia, Hong Kong, Indonesia, Kenya, Malaysia, Mongolia, Myanmar, Nepal, Pakistan, Philippines, Sierra Leone, South Africa, South Sudan, Sri Lanka, Taiwan, Tanzania.

are not legally required to consult displaced populations before displacement about the resettlement process

The sixth resettlement indicator asks whether national laws require governments to minimize or avoid involuntary resettlement of displaced persons when making expropriation decisions. India is the only country assessed with a national law that requires the government to minimize or avoid involuntary resettlement in every expropriation case. Two of the 50 countries (the Philippines and Taiwan) received 'partial' scores for this indicator, meaning that in some cases the government may be required to minimize or avoid resettlement, although not necessarily in every case. In 46 of the countries assessed, the government and acquiring bodies are not legally obligated to minimize or avoid involuntary resettlement. Of the 50 countries surveyed, 46 have not enacted laws that require governments or acquiring bodies to provide sufficient funding for resettlement and reconstruction programs.

The seventh resettlement indicator asks whether national laws require the government or acquiring bodies to provide sufficient funding to implement resettlement programs. It was found that India, Laos, and Vietnam have enacted national-level laws that obligate the government or acquiring bodies to provide an amount of funding that is sufficient to cover the cost of implementing resettlement programs when land is expropriated. Of the 50 countries surveyed, 46 have not enacted laws that require governments or acquiring bodies to provide sufficient funding for resettlement and reconstruction programs.

7.2.4.1 Recommendations from Chapter 5

Based on the findings from the legal analysis, Chapter 5 submitted several recommendations for reforming laws so that they comply with international standards on address resettlement:

Resettlement procedures should require the government and/or project developers to conduct a social impact assessment and develop a plan for resettling and rehabilitating displaced populations whenever is acquired in a compulsory manner. India's LARR Act 2013 provides a model for other lawmakers to follow because it requires that a social impact assessment and comprehensive resettlement and rehabilitation scheme be developed whenever projects involve involuntary resettlement. While resettlement procedures should be binding on all development projects, they should be flexible enough to adapt to new and unanticipated circumstances that arise in cases of displacement. Resettlement plans may vary slightly from case to case in order to effectively respond to the needs of the displaced. In addition to establishing a robust resettlement procedure, countries must strengthen their institutional capacity to implement and enforce resettlement procedures. Governments and private actors should allocate adequate funding, technical experts, and other resources to ensure there is sufficient capacity to effectively implement resettlement procedures.

Resettlement procedures should require the government and/or project developers to provide displaced populations with adequate relocation allowance to cover the transportation and other costs associated with resettling on alternative land. Countries should consider adopting the provision provided in Laos' 2016 Decree on Compensation and Resettlement in Development Projects which provides allowance to cover transportation costs and livelihood rehabilitation plans. It is important for developers to bear in mind that the burden on displaced populations does not end the moment the relocation site is reached. In some cases, fully revitalizing the economic and other losses borne by the displaced can take months or years. Financial and other assistance should be provided until income and livelihood restoration occurs, and proper monitoring mechanisms should be put in place to make sure no one is abusing or freeloading off assistance programs opportunistically. Determining the appropriate level of assistance is a balancing act that must be done on a case-by-case basis.

Resettlement procedures should require the government and/or project developers to provide productive alternative land and suitable alternative housing. For many displaced landholders, such as indigenous and local communities in rural areas, land is not a fungible commodity; the loss of their land means the loss of the means of sustaining their livelihood. Cash compensation payments may be insufficient to ensure livelihoods are reconstructed post-displacement. In cases where the expropriated land has been lived on and used by the same community for centuries, it may be difficult to find alternative land that is sufficiently suitable. Nevertheless, imposing a legal obligation on governments and developers to investigate options for alternative land in consultation with displaced populations will make it more likely that these populations will not be landless, homeless, or impoverished subsequent to displacement

Resettlement procedures should require the government and/or project developers to consult displaced populations and allow these populations to participate in decision-making during all stages of the project cycle, including the resettlement stage. The World Bank ESS Framework, the IFC Performance Standards, and the VGGTs all require that affected landholders are adequately informed and allowed to meaningfully participate in the project design and implementation. In cases where development projects infringe on indigenous territories, project developers should not relocate indigenous communities without their FPIC and after agreement on just and fair compensation. Consultations and negotiations with affected landholders before a project begins can reduce the costs and financial risks that may arise when displaced populations decide to protest projects or file for injunctions in courts. Allowing displaced populations to participate in the development of resettlement plans can help ensure that the assistance provided in resettlement plans adequately addresses the risks of impoverishment and other consequences.

Resettlement procedures should require the government and/or project developers to minimize or avoid involuntary resettlement wherever possible. In some cases, involuntary resettlement may be unavoidable, but in other cases there may be feasible alternatives to implementing the project that do not also require landholders to be displaced. If national laws require the government or private developers to explore feasible alternatives, there may be less of a risk of excessive expropriations and involuntary resettlement. Land expropriation and involuntary resettlement should only occur where it is absolutely necessary to achieve a genuine public purpose and there are no less invasive means.

7.2.5 Examination of the Laws and Practices Related to Expropriation in Nigeria (Chapter 6)

Chapter 6 provided an in-depth examination of the laws and practices related to land expropriation in Nigeria. The Chapter presenteda legal analysis that compares Nigeria's LUA with the international standards established in Section 16 of the VGGTs. The Chapter also provided insight on whether the LSG followed international standards on expropriation, compensation, and resettlement when it expropriated land for the LFTZ.

The analysis reveals there are significant gaps between Nigeria's LUA and international standards on expropriation, compensation, and resettlement as established in the VGGTs. Section 51 of the LUA vaguely defines 'public purpose,' ostensibly granting State Governors broad discretion to interpret what constitutes a 'public purpose.' The LUA does not adequately limit the Governor's authority to expropriate land under the pretext of a public purpose and transfer such land to private companies that aim to use the land exclusively for profit-making activities that may not necessarily benefit the public. The LUA does not require State Governors to minimize the amount of land acquired to the amount necessary to achieve a public purpose.

Although Nigeria enacted an Environmental Impact Assessment Decree, which establishes limitations on the extent to which expropriation projects may harm the environment, Nigeria's laws do not require the government to be sensitive to areas of cultural, religious, or environmental significance or areas held by the poor and vulnerable groups, such as indigenous communities when deciding to expropriate.

The LUA does not require the government to survey affected landholders, provide information on the project, or consult landholders prior to expropriating land for development projects.

The LUA only grants compensation for statutory and customary rights of occupancy that are recognized by the State Governor. Compensation is limited to the improvements and crops on the land, but does not cover the value of the land itself. The LUA precludes holders of unfarmed, undeveloped land from obtaining any compensation when their land is expropriated. The LUA does not require compensation to be paid prior to the taking of possession of the acquired land. There is no established deadline for payment. The LUA does not grant affected landholders the right to negotiate compensation. The Lands Bureau is granted broad discretion to determine a rate of compensation. There is no guidance on valuing compensation to allow for judges to scrutinize compensation decisions.

On the other hand, Nigerian law complies with the VGGTs Section 16.1 calling for states to grant right to appeal because Section 44 of the Constitution of Nigeria provides the right to appeal compensation decisions in court. Additionally, I found that the LUA partially complies with VGGTs Section 16.9 because the LUA permits alternative land to be granted to affected landholders if their right of occupancy is revoked. However, the Governor has discretion to offer alternatives but is not legally obligated to do so: affected landholders can receive either monetary compensation or alternative land, but not both. The Nigeria government has not established resettlement procedures that ensure livelihood reconstruction for affected populations

7.2.5.1 Analysis of the Expropriation and Compensation Practices Followed in the LFTZ Expropriation Case

Chapter 6 also presented findings from a survey conducted in August 2017 of 140 households from 10 affected communities. The survey revealed that the LSG did not comply with international standards when expropriating land for the LFTZ. In particular the LSG failed to adequately survey, inform, and consult many of the affected communities living in the vicinity of the LFTZ. Only 34 of 140 household states that they were informed about the LFTZ project before the project began. Only five of 140 households said they were consulted about the implications of the project. Four of 140 households said there given an opportunity to give input in the expropriation plans.

In terms of whether affected landholders were provided compensation, Only 56 of 140 households (40%) surveyed were promised compensation, but only one household claimed they were given an opportunity to negotiate compensation. Only four of those 56 households (7%) were told how compensation was calculated. Only 38 respondents out of 140 (27%)

stated that they actually received any compensation and the vast majority of them (97%) felt that this compensation did not cover all of their losses.

7.2.5.2 Recommendations from Chapter 6

Based on the findings from the legal analysis, Chapter 6 submitted several recommendations for reforming Nigeria's LUA to ensure compliance with Section 16 of the VGGTs. Lawmakers in charge of reforming Nigeria's LUA should include a clear definition of public purpose to allow for judicial review of State Governor's expropriation decisions. State Governor's should thus be obliged to conduct a 'proportionality test,' which entails examining a proposed expropriation project to determine whether (a) the expropriation project is necessary to serve a public purpose (there are no less intrusive alternatives), (b) the project is suitable (reasonably likely to achieve the intended public benefit), and (c) the benefits deriving from the expropriation are proportionate to costs borne by affected populations and the environment.[686] The State Governor's decision on whether a project satisfies the proportionality test should be subject to oversight by the courts.

The LUA should require government and entities and/or project developers to conduct both an environmental impact assessment and social impact assessment prior to expropriating so that environmental and social issues associated with proposed development projects, including the project's impact on local land rights, will be thoroughly identified and managed. The LUA should establish a consultation and negotiation process whereby affected landholders must be surveyed, informed, and consulted about proposed development projects and the potential impact on their land rights and livelihoods. The LUA should stipulate that all members of communities, not just the chiefs, must be consulted about proposed projects and compensation entitlements. Such a requirement may reduce the risk of expropriation and compensation decisions being made behind closed doors as well as the risk of elite capture of compensation. The LUA should recognize the indigenous right to FPIC and require the government to be transparent and ensure meaningful community participation in expropriation, compensation, and resettlement decision-making.

The LUA should require that compensation must be granted directly to households and establish monitoring committees to ensure compliance with compensation plans and prevent elite capture by chiefs and other intermediaries. The LUA should require assessors of compensation to consider both the value of land as well as the value of improvements, crops, economic activities, disturbance to livelihood, and other incidental and collateral injuries suffered by landholders, even if the land in question is undeveloped. The LUA should base the calculation of compensation on the 'replacement cost' where land is

686 Hoops 2017.

expropriated in areas where land markets are weak or non-existent and thus 'market value' is difficult to ascertain. In cases where compensation is based on market value, the LUA should adopt the International Valuations Standards definition of 'market value.'

The LUA should require that compensation must be paid prior to the moment at which the government or private companies take possession of the land. In cases where possession is taken before compensation is paid, require the government to pay interest based on the delay. The LUA should require the government to provide affected communities with productive alternative land, where available. The LUA should require the government and project developers to provide investment and benefit-sharing arrangements whereby companies must allow affected landholders to own equity in development projects and invest in the education, healthcare facilities, and other basic amenities for affected landholders. The LUA should establish an independent valuation board with expert valuers charged with consulting and compensating affected landholders. The process for valuing land and crops should be well-documented and transparent, and valuers should reflect current market rates for the average amounts of crops, livestock, and other improvements found on the land.

7.3 Overall Findings from the Indicator Analysis

It is clear that Cambodia, India, Indonesia, Laos and Vietnam are leading the way in terms of compliance with expropriation, compensation, and resettlement standards established in VGGTs. These five Asian countries have relatively newer expropriation laws (all of which were passed in the last 8 years), which suggests there may be a growing trend among some countries to reform expropriation, compensation, and resettlement frameworks so they comply with international standards. On the other hand, Liberia, Namibia, Bangladesh and the Latin American countries assessed failed to achieve positive scores on the indicators due to their general lack of robust expropriation, compensation, and resettlement frameworks. At the time this study was conducted, Liberia was in the process of passing a Land Rights Bill, which, depending on the provisions included in the final version, may comply to some extent with international standards.

When looking at all of the findings from Chapters 2-5, there are no identifiable factors or characteristics that explain why some countries have enacted stronger laws related to expropriation, compensation, and resettlement than others. For example, I could not find evidence indicating that countries with higher income levels had relatively more 'yes' scores on the indicators (or evidence the lower income countries had relatively more 'no' scores on the indicators). Furthermore, I could not find evidence indicating common law countries scored better on the indicators than civil law countries (or vice versa). With the exception of India, Indonesia, Vietnam, there was no correlation found between countries that scored relatively well on the expropriation indicators and those that scored well on the compensation and resettlement indicators.

The drivers of legal reform vary depending on the country and context. In some of the countries, land reform projects funded by the World Bank and other donors contributed to the reformation of land expropriation laws by making such reforms a condition for funding.[687] For example, loans and investments by the World Bank and Asian Development Bank contributed significantly to the reform of Vietnam's resettlement policies and other laws passed in Asia.[688]

On the other hand, several governments have taken land law reform seriously because of internal pressure from citizens as opposed to external pressure from donors.[689] According to McAuslan, in South Africa, Tanzania, and Malawi, "the pressure to [reform laws was at least in part] the result of contested democratic politics and the perceived need to meet the concerns of rural voters."[690] McAuslan conducted a broad comparative study of the influences of land law reform in East Africa and found that,

> [...] there are both external and internal pressures operating on policy-makers in Africa to use the law to restructure land relations [...] The external, donor-driven pressures are aimed at facilitating the operation of a market for land, while some, at least, of the internal pressures pull in the direction of strengthening the security of tenure of those presently on the land. Facilitation a market in land widens the scope of the rights of landowners, while restricting their ability to dispose of land reduces their rights, whatever the merits of so doing; it is thus not always to easy to reconcile these pressures.[691]

India and Indonesia are two other countries in which the influence of massive populations of rural voters led to the passage of progressive land laws that provide relatively better

687 M. Adams, 'Breaking Good: Development Aid for Land Reform', *Overseas Development Institute*, London, 2002, pp. 33-40.

688 P.H. Ty, A.C.M. Van Westen, & A. Zoomers, 'Compensation and Resettlement Policies after Compulsory Land Acquisition for Hydropower Development in Vietnam: Policy and Practice', *Land*, Vol. 2, 2013, pp. 678-704.

689 P. McAuslan, 'Making Law Work: Restructuring Land Relations in Africa', 1998 *Development and Change*, Vol. 29, pp. 525-552. McAuslan 1998, pp. 526-527.

690 McAuslan 1998, p. 527.

691 P. McAuslan, 'Making Law Work: Restructuring Land Relations in Africa', *Development and Change*, Vol. 29, 1998, pp. 525-552, 529.

protection of rural land tenure.[692] In these countries widespread public support for changes to land governance processes, including expropriation processes, contributed to the passage of laws that complied with international standards.[693]

In Namibia and other countries, reforms to land laws were designed to further the status quo by bolstering existing arrangements, which have enabled land grabbing of fertile lands.[694] In some cases, government officials contested efforts to give legal effect to pro-rural poor policies, viewing such efforts as granting more rights to citizens and providing less rent-seeking opportunities for officials.[695] These officials feared legal reforms aimed at promoting transparent and participatory expropriation process, since the more transparency in decision-making around land, the more opportunities for the public to contest the government's exercise of power.[696]

In sum, there are a variety of factors that influence whether reforms to land expropriation laws become a priority for governments. An in-depth study of the root causes and drivers of legal reforms in the 50 countries would provide useful complimentary information, since this topic was not adequately covered in this book.

7.4 CONCLUDING REMARKS AND SUGGESTED AREAS OF FUTURE RESEARCH

If one adopts the assumption that the rule of law is essential for responsible land governance, then the passage of robust statutes and regulations is necessary to ensure that the VGGTs are adopted in the 50 countries assessed. While tracking the law on the books is necessary to measure progress, sufficiently measuring whether international standards are being adopted in the 50 countries requires a more in-depth understanding of how the rule of law differs from country to country. In many of the countries assessed, respect for the rule of law may be limited or even non-existent. In these countries, there are likely significant gaps between what is written in law and what is practiced on the ground. Nevertheless, the premise behind this study is that legal provisions in all 50 countries should be viewed as more than just words on a page: that they should carry weight and should be respected

---

692 D. Sathe, *The Political Economy of Land Acquisition in India*, Singapore, Springer Singapore, 2017; M.T. Sirait, B. White & U. Pradhan, 'Land Rights and Land Reform Issues for Effective Natural Resource Management in Indonesia', *in* G. Shivakoti, U. Pradhan & H. Helmi (Eds.), *Redefining Diversity & Dynamics of Natural Resources Management in Asia*, Vol. 1, Amsterdam, The Netherlands, Elsevier, 2017.

693 Mukerji, S., 'Land Acquisition in Contemporary India: The Growth Agenda, Legislation and Resistance', Indian Journal of Public Administration, Vol. 63, No. 1, 2017, pp. 98-99.

694 McAuslan 1998, p. 530.

695 McAuslan 1998, p. 530.

696 McAuslan 1998, p. 530.

by governments and private actors. My hope is that this study helps trigger a paradigmatic shift in countries where respect for the rule of law is still an aspiration and not yet a reality.

While this study argues that legal reform is a necessary precondition to responsible land governance, it is worth acknowledging that, in countries where the rule of law is weak or non-existent, and legal provisions are nothing more than words on a page, it may be equally if not more worthwhile to assess expropriation practices and monitor government actions related to expropriation on a case-by-case basis. An assessment of government capacity to enforce and implement expropriation legislation and regulations would serve as useful complimentary research, since, at the end of the day, laws are only as effective as implementing authorities enable them to be. Equally if not more important to the passage of reforms to expropriation, compensation, and resettlement procedures is the successful implementation and enforcement of these procedures.

A possible counterargument to the claim that legal reform is necessary to ensure expropriations comply with international standards is that courts, especially courts in common law countries, can be effective in filling gaps in the law. In these countries, strong legislative and regulatory provisions may not be necessary. In fact, in several countries, courts have stepped in and ruled against expropriation decisions that were found to serve private interests. In Sri Lanka, for example, the Supreme Court overruled a decision to expropriate land for a private golf resort in the Water's Edge case.[697] The Court made its decision despite the legislative provision stating that the Minister's declaration that land is needed for a public purpose "shall be conclusive evidence that such land…is needed for a public purpose."[698]

Nevertheless, this book contends that, even if courts are active and choose to thoroughly scrutinize expropriation decisions, there is still value in a study of constitutional, legislative, and regulatory frameworks applicable to expropriation. Lawmakers can use this study to strengthen legal frameworks so they comply law with and provide clear guidance on adopting international standards. Clearly prescribed guidance in the law can ensure that expropriations are executed in a fair, transparent, and participatory manner, and that sufficient compensation and resettlement assistance is provided to affected landholders. With more robust legislation and regulations, courts, affected landholders, and the general public will be better able to more effectively monitor whether expropriation decisions violate the law, and hold expropriating actors accountable of paying compensation and resettling affected landholders.

---

697 Government of Sri Lanka, *Water's Edge Judgement S.C.*, (F/R) No. 352/2007, 2007.

698 Government of Sri Lanka, *Land Acquisition Act CAP. 295*, 1950 (Amended 1994), Section 5(2).

Reforming expropriation laws in these 50 countries will require significant political momentum, public support, and a shift in thinking around expropriation. When determining whether legal reform is feasible, one must acknowledge various power dynamics as well as the political, social, and economic factors that influence decision-making around legal reform. For instance, in some case, donor agencies (e.g., World Bank) and private land investors may have a strong influence over whether a law gets passed. Investors may oppose the passage of legal reform that create hurdles, increase costs, or otherwise makes for a less attractive investment climate. Even in countries with large rural populations, the urgency of development projects and/or financial influences from investors may create incentives for the government and expropriating companies to oppose legal reforms or consider ways of circumventing costly legal obligations that entail fully compensating and resettling landholders. For this reason, investors may choose to invest in development projects in countries with weak legal frameworks (e.g., Nigeria as described in Chapter 6), so they can avoid robust compensation and resettlement requirements. Pro-poor land law reforms may be unappealing to government and private investors that currently benefit from the status quo because the establishment of more robust compensation packages and resettlement and rehabilitation procedures may slow down the land acquisition process and increase costs for project backers.

Once new laws are passed, there are a number of challenges associated with implementation. For new laws to be used effectively for the purpose of land tenure reform, expropriating entities will have to master new rules and navigate bureaucratic hurdles. Where laws have previously been used to influence land reforms, legal provisions often conferred authority on government officials, with few safeguards or external controls. These officials do not always use their expropriation authority for legitimate and justifiable purposes. In some cases, government officials may decide to turn a blind eye to violations or only selectively enforce the law in a way that advantages investors as opposed to landholders and the public.

Predatory governments may prefer laws that enable them to make false promises. Such government may convince the public that a proposed expropriation will create many jobs and 'economic development,' and use this justification as a pretext to disguise an expropriation that is actually intended solely to serve their own vested interests. Lawmakers must be mindful of these possibilities when drafting new legislation and regulations.

Following the conclusion of this study, there were a few remaining questions. First, can legal indicator research, which establishes a 'benchmark' measuring progress on legal reforms, be used to influence lawmakers in the countries assessed? Even if legislative provisions protect the land rights of the poor and vulnerable and require transparent and participatory land governance, is it possible to imagine a scenario in which all government and private sector actors comply with such provisions, especially when considering the weak rule of law in post-conflict countries included in this study (e.g. South Sudan and Myanmar)? The answers to these questions depend on the degree to which lawmakers, civil society, and other stakeholders are effective in influencing the enactment of laws that ensure expropriations equitably balance property rights with national needs. It remains to be seen whether this comparative legal analysis will move the needle forward and influence legal reforms on the ground.

If nothing else, the methodology and findings presented in this book provide a unique starting point for legal research to be conducted every few years to see if the adoption of international standards on expropriation, compensation, and resettlement is gaining traction at the national level. Such legal research can function as an effective awareness-raising mechanism by informing and influencing lawmakers to adopt international standards in domestic laws. Continuing to monitor progress on the implementation of the VGGTs will, without a doubt, be a difficult endeavor. However, my hope is that this study provides an entry point. By examining on the law on the books, the research presented in this study indicates whether countries have laid a solid foundation for realizing international standards.

Bibliography

Literature

Adams, M., 'Breaking Good: Development Aid for Land Reform', *Overseas Development Institute*, London, 2002, pp. 33-40

ADB, *Involuntary Resettlement Policy*. ADB, Bahasa, 1998.

ADB, *Compensation and Valuation in Resettlement: Cambodia, People's Republic of China, and India*, Rural Development Institute, Seattle, 2007.

ADB, 'Regional Technical Assistance (RETA)- 7433: Mainstreaming Land Acquisition and Resettlement Safeguards in Central and West Asia Region', *Country Assessment of Land Acquisition and Resettlement*, ADB, Bahasa, 2011.

ADB, *Land Acquisition and Resettlement Plan: Pakistan: Pehur High Level Canal Extension Project*, ADB, Bahasa, 2011.

ADB, *Papua New Guinea: Bridge Replacement for Improvement Rural Access Sector Project-Magi Highway*, ADB, Bahasa, 2014.

ADB, *Myanmar: Irrigated Agriculture Inclusive Development Project*, ADB, Bahasa, 2016.

ADB, *NEP: SASEC Roads Improvement Project*, ADB, Bahasa, 2016.

ADB, *Land Acquisition, Resettlement and Rehabilitation Policy for Infrastructure Development Projects*, ADB, Bahasa, 2014 (2071 BS).

African Development Bank Group, *Involuntary Resettlement Policy. African Development Bank*, Tunis, 2003.

Agbola T., & Jinadu, A.M., 'Forced eviction and forced relocation in Nigeria: The experience of those evicted from Maroko in 1990', *Environ. Urban.*, Vol. 9, 1997, pp. 271-288;

Akinwotu, E., 'The forced Evictions of Badia East, Lagos: 'This is not right", *The Guardian*. Available online: https://www.theguardian.com/cities/2015/oct/16/forced-evictions-badia-east-lagos-this-is-not-right (1 March 2018).

Alcorn, J., 'USAID Issue Brief: Tenure and Indigenous Peoples', USAID, Washington, DC, 2013.

Aldinger, P., 'Addressing environmental justice concerns in developing countries: Mining in Nigeria, Uganda and Ghana', *Georget. Int. Environ. Law Rev.*, No. 26, 2014, pp. 345.

Alemu, B., *Expropriation, Valuation, and Compensation in Ethiopia* (Academic Dissertation for the Degree of Doctor of Technology), Royal institute of Technology, Stockholm, Sweden, 2013.

Almeidam, F., *Legislative Pathways for Securing Community-Based Property Rights*, Rights and Resources Initiative (RRI), Washington, DC, 2017.

Al Jazeera, 'Report - 'Piracy in Nigeria- Power & People", November 2016. Available online: https://www.youtube.com/watch?v=866fXIAZsDk (accessed on 1 March 2018).

Aljazeera, *Police Displace Thousands in Nigeria's Otodo-Gbame Slum*, Aljazeera, Doha, 2017.

Amnesty International, 'At the Mercy of the Government: Violation of the Right to an Effective Remedy in Badia East, Lagos State, Nigeria', *Amnesty International*, London, 2013, p. 15.

Amnesty International, *Nigeria: World Bank 'dragging its feet' on resettlement package after forced eviction*, 2014.

Amnesty International, *Nigeria: Further Information: Forced Evictions in Lagos State Must Stop*, Amnesty International, London, 2017.

Anyuru, M.A., Rhoads, R., Mugyenyi, O., Ekwenyu, J. & Balemsa, T., *Balancing Development and Community Livelihoods: A Framework for Land Acquisition and Resettlement in Uganda*, ACODE Policy Research Series, No. 75, Advocates Coalition for Development and Environment, Kampala, Uganda, 2016.

Arezki, R., Deiniger, K. & Selod, H., *What Drives the Global "Land Rush"?*, Policy Research Working Paper 5864, The World Bank, Washington, DC, 2011.

Arid Environmental Consultancy (Pty) Ltd., *Resettlement policy framework*, World Bank Group, Washington, DC, 2008, p.12.

Atacama Consulting, *Resettlment and Compensation Action Plan for the Proposed Sindila Mini Hydropower Project in Sindila Sub-County*, Bundibugyo District, 2014.

Atahar, S., 'Development Project, Land Acquisition and Resettlement in Bangladesh: A Quest for Well Formulated National Resettlement and Rehabilitation Policy', *International Journal of Humanities and Social Science*, 3(7), 2013.

Australian Department of Foreign Affairs and Trade (DFAT), *Displacement and Resettlement of People in Development Activities*, DFAT, Canberra, 2015.

Bartolome, L. & Danklmaier, C. 'The Experience with Dams and Resettlement in Argentina', *Contributing Paper. World Commission on Dams*, Cape Town, 1999.

BBC, *Africa Business Report: Lekki Free Trade Zone*, 2010. Available online: https://www.youtube.com/watch?v=nk1bG57flNw (accessed on 8 February 2018).

BBC, 'Otodo-Gbame: Nigeria court rules eviction unconstitutional', *BBC News*, 2017. Available online: http://www.bbc.com/news/world-africa-40357103 (accessed on 15 October 2017).

Behrman, J., Meinzen-Dick, R. & Quisumbing, A., *The Gender Implications of Large-Scale Land Deals. Discussion Paper 01056*, International Food Policy Research Institute (IFPRI),Washington, DC, USA, 2011.

Bekkers V. & Edwards A., 'Legitimacy and Democracy: A Conceptual Framework for Assessing Governance Practices', *in* Bekkers, V., Dijkstra, G. & Edwards, A. (Eds.), *Governance and the Democratic Deficit: Assessing the Democratic Legitimacy of Governance Practices*, Oxford, Ashgate 2007.

Belize Social Investment Fund, *Land Acquisition and Involuntary Resettlement Policy Framework*, 2010.

Bell. A. & Parchomovsky, G., 'Takings Reassessed', *Va. Law Rev.* 2001, 87, 378.

Bell, A. & Parchomovsky, G., 'Taking Compensation Private', *Stanf. Law Rev.*, Vol. 59, 2007, pp. 871-906, 873-874.

Berg, L.A. & Desai, D., *Background Paper: Overview on the Rule of Law and Sustainable Development of the Global Dialogue on Rule of Law and the Post-2015 Development Agenda.* United Nations Development Program, New York, 2013.

Berliner, D., *Public Power, Private Gain: A Five-Year, State-By-State Report Examining the Abuse of Eminent Domain*, Institute for Justice, Arlington, Virginia, 2003.

Bingham, T., *The Rule of Law*, Penguin Books, London, England, 2011.

Botswana Department of Roads, *Resettlement Policy Framework WT/MTC/ROADS/SER/32/ 2007-2008*, World Bank, Washington, DC, 2008.

Bruce, J., & Boudreaux, K., *USAID Issue Brief: Land and Conflict: Land Disputes and Land Conflict Property Rights and Resource Governance Briefing Paper #12*, USAID, DC, 2013.

Business & Maritime West Africa, *Lekki Free Trade Zone: A Pathway to Economic Development in Nigeria*, Business & Maritime West Africa, 2012.

Byamugisha, F.F.K., *Securing Africa's land for shared prosperity : a program to scale up reforms and investments (English).* Africa development forum, World Bank Group, Washington, DC, 2013.

Cambodia Rehabilitation and Development Board, *Council for the Development Cambodia, Resettlement Rights or Project-Affected People.*

Cernea, M.M., 'The risks and construction model for resettling displaced populations', *World Development*, Vol. 25, 1997, pp. 1569-1587.

Cernea, M.M., *Impoverishment Risks, Risk Management, and Reconstruction: A Model of Population Displacement and Resettlement. In Proceedings of the UN Symposium on Hydropower and Sustainable Development*, Beijing, China, 27-29 October 2004.

Cernea, M.M., 'The 'Ripple Effect' in Social Policy and its Political Content: A Debate on Social Standards in Public and Private Development Projects', *in* Likosky, M. (Ed.), *Privatizing Development: Trans-National Law, Infrastructure and Human Rights*, Leiden-Boston, Martinus Nijhoff, 2005a, pp. 65-101.

Cernea, M.M., 'Compensation and benefit sharing: Why resettlement policies and practices must be reformed', *Water Science and Engineering*, Vol. 1, 2008, pp. 89-120.

Cernea, M.M., *Progress in India: New Legislation to Protect Persons Internally Displaced by Development Projects*, Brookings Institution, 2015.

Cernea, M.M., 'Foreword: State Legislation Facing Involuntary Resettlement: Comparing the Thinking in China and India on Development Displacement', *in* Padovani, F. (Ed.), *Development-Induced Displacement in India and China*, Lanham Maryland, Lexington Books, 2016.

Cernea, M.M., 'The State and Involuntary Resettlement: Reflections on Comparing Legislation on Displacement in China and India', *in* F. Padovani (ed.), *Development-Induced Displacement in India and China: A Comparative Look*, Lexington Book, Lanham, 2016.

Cernea, M.M. & Maldonado, J.K., *Challenging the prevailing paradigm of displacement and resettlement: Its evolution, and constructive ways of improving it, in* M. Cernea & J. Maldonado (eds.), *Challenging the Prevailing Paradigm of Displacement and Resettlement: Risks, Impoverishment, Legacies, Solutions*, Routledge, New York, 2018.

Cernea, M.M., Mathur, H.M., *Can Compensation Prevent Impoverishment? Reforming Resettlement through Investments and Benefit-Sharing*; Oxford University Press, New Delhi, India, 2008.

Chang, Y., 'Eminent Domain Law in Taiwan: New Law, Old Practice', *Kreisman Working Paper Series in Housing Law and Policy*, Paper 38, 2016.

Chavkin, S. & Hudson, M., 'New investigation reveals 3.4m displaced by World Bank', *International Consortium of Investigate Journalists*, 2015 (April).

Chu, J., Young, K. & Phiri, D., *Large-scale Land Acquisitions, Displacement and Resettlement in Zambia*, Institute for Poverty, Land and Agrarian Studies (PLAAS), 2015.

Cities Alliance, *Government of Brazil Passes Landmark Involuntary Resettlement Policy*, Cities Alliance, Brussels, 25 July 2013.

Cotula, L., *Legal Empowerment for Local Resource Control: Securing Local Rights Within Foreign Investment Projects*, International Institute for Environment and Development, London, UK, 2007.

Cotula, L., 'The new enclosures? Polanyi, international investment law and the global land rush', *Third World Q*, No. 34, 2013, pp. 1605-1629.

Cotula, L., Vermeulen, S., Leonard, R. & Keeley, J., *Land Grab or Development Opportunity? Agricultural Investments and International Land Deals in Africa*, Food and Agricultural Organizations of the United Nations (FAO).

Dagan, H., 'Expropriatory compensation, Distributive Justice, and the Rule of Law', *in* Hoops, B., Marais, E.J., Mostert H., Sluysman, J.A.M.A. & Verstappen, L.C.A. (Eds.), *Rethinking Expropriation Law I: Public Interest in Expropriation*, Den Haag, The Netherlands, Eleven International Publishing, 2015, pp. 349-365, 354.

Dam, K.W., *The law-growth nexus: The rule of law and economic development*. Brookings Institution Press, 2007.

Deininger, K., *Land policies for growth and poverty reduction*, The World Bank, Washington, DC; Oxford University Press, Oxford, 2003.

Deininger, K., Selod, H. & Burns, A., *The Land Governance Assessment Framework: Identifying and Monitoring Good Practice in the Land Sector*, the World Bank, Washington, DC, 2012, p. 85.

Dell'Angelo, J., D'Odorico, P., Rulli, M.C., Marchand, P., 'The tragedy of the grabbed commons: Coercion and disposession in the global land rush', *World Dev.*, No. 92, 2017, pp. 1-12.

Displacement Solutions, *Land Acquisition Law and Practice in Myanmar: Overview, Gap Analysis with IFC PS1 and PS5 and Scope of Due Diligence Recommendations*, Displacement Solutions, Geneva, 2015.

Downing, C., 'Eminent Domain in 21 st Century India: What New Delhi Can Learn From New London?', *Journal of International Law and Politics*, vol. 46, 2013, pp. 207-289, 245.

Downing, T., 'Mitigating social impoverishment when people are involuntarily displaced', *in* McDowell, C. (Ed.), *understanding impoverishment: the consequences of development-induced displacement*, Providence, RI and Oxfod, England, Berghahn, 1996, pp. 33-48.

Dubertret, F. & Wily, L.A., 'Percent of Indigenous and Community Lands', Data file from *LandMark: The Global Platform of Indigenous and Community Lands*, 2017.

Dunning, C., *a MCA Monitor Report from the Field: Honduras,* MCC, Washington, DC, 2011; MCC, *MCC Policy Reforms Show Why Resettlement Activities Matter*, MCC, Washington, DC, 2011.

Dyrkolbotn, S., 'On Benefit Sharing and the Compensatory Approach to Economic Development Takings', *in* Hoops, B., Marias, E.J., Mosters, H., Sluysman, J.A.M.A. & Verstappen, L.C.A. (Eds.), *Rethinking Expropriation Law II: Context, Criteria, and Consequences of Expropriation*, Den Haag, The Netherlands, Eleven International Publishing, 2015, pp. 319-355.

Egbula, M. & Zheng, Q., *West African Challenges No. 5: China and Nigeria: A Powerful South-South Alliance*, Sahel and West Africa Club Secretariat (SWAC/OECD), Paris, 2011.

European Parliament Research Service (EPRS), *Nicaragua: The Chinese Interocean Canal Project*, European Parliament, Brussels, 2015.

Ezeamalu, B. 'How Police bullet killed Lekki Free Trade Zone Boss', *Premium Times*, 2015.

FAO, '*Land Tenure Series 3: Land Tenure and Rural Development*', FAO, Rome, Italy, 2002.

FAO, *Voluntary Guidelines on the Responsible Governance of Tenure of Land, Fisheries and Forests in the Context of National Food Security*, FAO, Rome, Italy, 2012.

Flynn, S. & Vergara, L., *Land access and resettlement planning at La Granja. CSRM Occasional Papers: Mining-induced Displacement and Resettlement*, Centre for Social Responsibility in Mining, The University of Queensland, Brisbane, 2015.

Francis, P., 'For the use and common benefit of all Nigerians: Consequences of the 1978 land nationalization', *Afr. J. Int. Afr. Inst*, No. 54, 1984, pp. 5-28.

Freilich, R.H., 'Condemnation Blight: Analysis and Suggested Solutions', *in* A.T. Akerman & D.W. Dynkowski (Eds.), *Current Condemnation Law: Takings, Compensation and Benefits*, 2nd edn, Chicago, IL, USA, American Bar Association, 2006.

Garnett, N.S. 'The Public Use Question as a Takings Problem', *Geo Wash L. Rev.*, Vol. 71, 2003, pp. 934-982

Global Land Tool Network, *Forced Evictions-Towards Solutions?*, UN Habitat, Nairobi, 2007.

Goodland, R., 'Free, Prior, and Informed Consent and the World Bank Group', *Sustainable Development Law & Policy*, Vol. 4, Issue 2, Summer 2004, pp. 66-74.

Government of India, *The Right to Fair Compensation and Transparency in Land Acquisition, Rehabilitation, and Resettlement Act* (LARR Act), 2013.

Heinrich Bol Stiftung, *Urban Planning Processes in Lagos*, Heinrich Bol Stiftung, Lagos, 2016.

Hemadri, R., Mander, H. & Nagaraj, V., *Dams, Displacement, Policy and Law in India*, World Commission on Dams, 1999.

Hoecke, M.V., 'Methodology of Comparative Legal Research', *Law and Method*, 2015.

Hoops, B., *The Legitimate Justification of Expropriation: A Comparative Law and Governance Analysis*, Juta Law Publishers, Cape Town, 2017.

Hoops, B., 'The Public Purpose for the Expropriation of Land: A Framework for Assessing Its Democratic Legitimacy', *in* Hoops, B., Marais E.J., Mostert H., Sluysman J.A.M.A. & Verstappen L.C.A. (Eds.), *Rethinking Expropriation Law I: Public Interest in Expropriation*, Den Haag, The Netherlands, Eleven International Publishing, 2015, pp. 237-278.

Hoops, B., Saville, J. & Mostert, H., 'Expropriation and the Endurance of Public Purpose', *European Property Law Journal*, 4(2), 2015, pp. 115-151.

Horberry, J., 'International organization and EIA in developing countries', *Environ. Impact Assess. Rev*. Vol. 5, 1985, pp. 207-222.

IDE-Jetro, 'Land Acquisition Issues in Noida District: background to 'Land Wars' in India', *IDE-Jetro*, 2011.

Idhoko, K., 'The process of Land Acquisition in Nigeria: A case study of Oyo state', *Int. J. Innov. Res. Stud*, No. 5, 2016.

Ingalls, M.L., Diepart, J.-C., Truong, N., Hayward, D., Niel, T., Sem, T., Phomphakdy, M., Bernhard, R., Fogarizzu, S., Epprecht, M., Nanthavong, V., Vo, D.H., Nguyen, D., Nguyen,

P.A., Saphanthong, T., Inthavong, C., Hett, C. & Tagliarino, N., *The Mekong State of Land*, Centre for Development and Environment, University of Bern and Mekong Region Land Governance, Bern, Switzerland, Bern Open Publishing (BOP), 2018.

International Finance Corporation (IFC), *Performance Standards on Environmental and Social Sustainability, Performance Standard 5: Land Acquisition and Involuntary Resettlement*; IFC, Washington, DC, 2012.

IFC (International Finance Corporation) *Performance Standards on Environmental and Social Sustainability,* Performance Standard 7, IFC, 2012.

Inter-American Development Bank (IDAB), *Involuntary Resettlement. Inter-American Development Bank*, DC, 1998.

International Accountability Project (IAP), *Back to Development: A Call For What Development Could Be*, IAP, 2014.

International Institute for Environment and Development; International Fund for Agricultural Development, Rome, 2009.

ILO (International Labour Organization), *Convention No. 169, Indigenous and Tribal Peoples Convention, 1989*, ILO, Geneva, Switzerland, 1989.

Karmo, H., 'Land Rights Act Suffers Setback at Liberian Legislature', *Front Page Africa*, 2017.

Kashwan, P., 'Forest Policy, Institutions, and Redd+ in India, Tanzania, and Mexico', *Global. Environmental Politics*, Vol. 15, 2015, pp. 95-117.

Keatimilwe, K. & Mlangeni, J., 'Swaziland Country Report', *SAIEA*.

Keith, S., McAuslan, P., Knight, R., Lindsay, J., Munro-Faure, P. & Palmer, D., *Food and Agriculture Organization of the United Nations. Land Tenure Studies 10: Compulsory Acquisition of Land and Compensation*, Food and Agriculture Organization (FAO), Rome, Italy, 2008.

Keliang, Z., Prosterman, R., Jianping, Y., Ping, L., Riedinger, J., Yiwen, O, 'The Rural Land Question in China: Analysis and recommendations based on a seventeen-province survey', *JILP*, Vol. 38, 2006, pp. 761-839, 781.

Krier, J. & Serkin, C., 'Public Ruses', *Mich. St. Law Rev.* Vol. 2004, 2004, pp. 859-875.

Kropiwnicka, M., *A Brief Introduction to the Voluntary Guidelines on the Responsible Governance of Tenure of Land, Fisheries and Forests in the Context of National Food Security*; Actionaid, Johannesburg, South Africa, 2012.

LSG, *Memorandum of Understanding Between the Lagos State Government, the Ibeju-Lekki Local Government Council, Lekki Worldwide Investment Limited, and the Accredited Representatives of Villages and Communities (Idasho, Idotun, Ielge, Imobido, Itoke, Okunraiye, Ilekuru, Tiye, and Imagbon-Segun) Affected by the Lekki Free Trade Zone Project*, LSG, Lagos, 2007.

LSG, *Government Write Paper on the Report of the Tribunal of Inquiry into the Cause of Civil Disturbances at the Lekki Free Trade Zone on 12 October, 2015*, LSG, Lagos, 2016.

LANDac, *Afghanistan Food Security and Land Governance Factsheet*, LandAc, Utrecht, Netherlands, 2011.

Larbi, W.O., Antwi, A. & Olomolaiye, P., 'Compulsory land acquisition in Ghana: Policy and praxis', *Land Use Policy*, Vol. 21, 2004, pp. 115-127.

Larsen, G., *The World Bank Just Overhauled its Safeguards for the First in 30 Years*, World Resources Institute, Washington, DC, 2016.

Lazaro, V. *et al. Indigenous Peoples Rights Act: Legal and Institutional Frameworks, Implementation and Challenges in the Philippines. Discussion papers, East Asia and Pacific Region. Social Development, and Rural Development, Natural Resources and Environment Sectors*, World Bank, Washington, DC, 2008.

Lebrilla, L., 'The State of Compulsory Acquisition of Land and Compensation in the Philippines', *CPBDR Policy Brief No. 2014- 03*, 2014.

Lee, B., 'Just Undercompensation: The Idiosyncratic Premium in Eminent Domain', *Colum. L. Rev.*, Vol. 113, 2013, p. 613.

Lekki Free Zone Development Company, available online: http://lfzdc.org/about-us/ (accessed on 10 February 2018).

Lesotho Highlands Development Authority and Lesotho Highlands Water Commission, *Lesotho Highlands Water Project (LHWP) Phase II Compensation Policy 5th draft (v.50.08)*, 2014.

Lindsay, J., *PPP Insights: Compulsory Acquisition of Land and Compensation in Infrastructure Projects*, World Bank, Washington, DC, USA, 2012.

Lindsay, J., Deiniger, K. & Hilhorst, T., 'Compulsory land acquisition in developing countries: Shifting paradigm or entrenched legacy', *in* Kim, I., Lee, H. & Soming , I. (Eds.), *Eminent Domain: A Comparative Perspective,* Cambridge, Cambridge University Press, 2017.

Locke, J., *Second Treatise of Government,* 1960.

Lunney, G.S., 'Takings, Efficiency, and Distributive Justice: A Response to Professor Dagan', *Mich. Law Rev.,* Vol. 99, 2000, p.168.

Mahapatra R., *Acquisition Made Easy. Down To Earth,* 2011. Available online: http://www.downtoearth.org.in/blog/acquisition-made-easy-33633 (accessed on 1 March 2018).

Marais, E.J., 'When does state interference with property (now) amount to expropriation? An analysis of the Agri SA court's state acquisition requirement (part I)', *18 Potchefstroom Electronic Law Journal*, Vol. 18, 2015, pp. 2983-3031.

Marini, F., 'John Locke and the Revision of Classical Democratic Theory', *The Western Political Quarterly*, Vol. 22, No. 1, 1969.

Mathur, H.M., 'Resettling People Displaced by Development Projects: Some Critical Management Issues', *Social Change*, Vol. 36, No.1, 2006.

McAuslan, P., 'Making Law Work: Restructuring Land Relations in Africa', 1998 *Development and Change*, Vol. 29, pp. 525-552.

MCC, *Policy Reforms Matter: Promoting the Sustainability of MCC Programs in Honduras*, MCC, Washington, DC, 2010.

McDermott, M., Myers, M., Selabalo, C., Antonio, D., Potsiou, C. & Nystrom, S., *Introducing a guide to the valuation of unregistered land. In Proceedings of the Annual World Bank Conference on Land and Poverty*, Washington, DC, USA, 20-24 March 2017.

Merril, T., 'Incomplete Compensation for Takings', *N.Y.U. Envtl. L.J.*, Vol. *11*, 2002, 116.

Michaels, R., 'The Functional Method of Comparative Law' *in* M. Reimman & R. Zimmerman (Eds.), *Oxford Handbook on Comparative Law*, 2006, pp. 340-382.

Millennium Challenge Corporation (MCC), *Policy Reforms Matter: Promoting the Sustainability of MCC Programs in Honduras*, MCC, Washington, DC, 2010.

MC, *MCC Policy Reforms Show Why Resettlement Activities Matter*, MCC, Washington, DC, 2011.

Ministry of Cities, *Involuntary Resettlement Policy (No. 317)*, 2013. Available at: https://goo.gl/qbsMdA; World Bank, *Involuntary Resettlement in Brazil: A Review of Policies and Practices*, World Bank, Washington, DC, 2011.

Ministry of Lands of Kenya, Eviction and Resettlement Guidelines, 2009.

Mireille, I., Masengo, F. & Knox, A., *Implementation of Expropriation Law in Rwanda: Challenges and Ways Forward,* LAND, Project Policy Research Brief No.2, Kigali, July 2014.

Monteagudo, M., 'The Right to Property in Human Rights and Investment Law: A Latin American Perspective of an Unavoidable Connection', *SECO / WTI Academic Cooperation Project Working Paper Series 2013/06*, 2013.

Morka, F., *A Place to Live: A Case Study of the Ijora-Badia Community in Lagos, Nigeria*, United Nations Human Settlements Programme (UN Habitat), Nairobi, 2007.

Mostert, H., 'Trends in the South African Constitutional Court's jurisprudence on property protection and regulation', *Amicus Curia*, (72), 2007.

Mostert, H. 'The Poverty of Precedent on Public Purpose/Interest: An Analysis of Pre-Constitutional and Post-Apartheid Jurisprudence in South Africa', *in* B. Hoops, E.J. Marais, H. Mostert, J.A.M.A. Sluysmans & L.C.A Verstappen (eds) *Rethinking Expropriation Law*

I: Public Interest in Expropriation, Eleven International Publishing, Den Haag, The Netherlands, 2015, p. 77.

Mthembu-Salter, G., *Chinese Investment in African Free Trade Zones: Lessons from Nigeria's Experience*, South Africa Institute of International Affairs, Johannesburg, 2009.

Mukerji, S., 'Land Acquisition in Contemporary India: The Growth Agenda, Legislation and Resistance', *Indian Journal of Public Administration*, Vol. 63, No. 1, 2017, pp. 98-99.

Munro-Faure, P. & Palmer, D., 'An overview of the voluntary guidelines on the governance of tenure', *Land Tenure Journal*, Vol. 1, 2012, pp. 5-18.

Munub, S., K'akumu, O. & Mwangi, W., 'Involuntary Resettlement Policy and Praxis in Kenya: An Evaluation of Just Terms of Compensation', *International Journal of Environment, Ecology, Family and Urban Studies*, Vol. 6, No. 3, 2016, pp. 23-44

Nathaniel, V., 'The National Involuntary Resettlement Policy: A case for implementation', *Daily FT*, 2015.

Neate, L. 'Compulsory Acquisition of Land: The Need for Robust Governance to Deliver Public Interest Projects Through Land Assembly', *In Proceedings of World Bank Conference on Land and Poverty*, World Bank, Washington, DC, March 19-23, 2018.

Network of Indigenous People in Thailand, *The Rights of Indigenous Peoples in Thailand: 2nd Cycle Universal Periodic Review*, 2016.

Nolte, K., Chamberlain, W. & Giger, M., *International Land Deals for Agriculture: Fresh Insights form the Land Matrix: Analytical Report II*, Centre for Development and Environment, University of Bern, Bern, Switzerland, 2016.

Notess, L., Veit, P.G., Monterroso, I., Andiko, Sulle, E., Larson, A.M., Gindroz, A.S., Quaedvleig, J., Williams, A., *Scrambling for Land Rights: Reducing Inequity Between Communities and Companies*, World Resources Institute, Washington, DC, 2018.

Obi, C.I., 'Oil extraction, dispossession, resistance and conflict in Nigeria's oil-rich Niger Delta', *Can. J. Dev. Stud.*, No. 30, 2010, pp. 219-236.

Oliver-Smith, A., *Development and Dispossession: The Anthropology of Displacement and Resettlement*, School for Advanced Research Press, Santa Fe, NM, 2009.

Otubu, A.K., 'Land reforms and the future of land use act in Nigeria', *Niger. Curr. Law Rev*, No. 4, 2008, pp. 126-143.

Otubu, A.K., 'Private property rights and compulsory acquisition process in Nigeria: The past, present and future', *Acta Univ. Danub. Jurid*, No. 8, 2012, pp. 25-42.

Oxfam International, *Unearthed: Land, Power and Inequality in Latin America*, Oxfam, Oxford, UK, 2016.

Oxfam, International Land Coalition & Rights and Resources Initiative, *Common Ground: Securing land rights and safeguarding the earth*, Oxfam, Oxford, 2016.

Palmer, D., Fricska, S. & Wehrmann, B., 'Land Tenure Working Paper 11: Toward Improved Land Governance', *FAO*, Rome, Italy, 2009.

Peter, F., 'Political legitimacy', *in* E. N. Zalta (Ed.), *The Stanford Encyclopedia of philosophy (Summer 2016 Edition)*. Retrieved from: <https://plato.stanford.edu/archives/sum2016/entries/legitimacy/>.

Premium Times, *Investments in Lekki Free Trade Zone Hit 100 Billion*, Premium Times, Lagos, 2017.

Price, S., 'National Standards on Involuntary Resettlement: Are They Achievable?', Paper at XI International Congress of Anthropological and Ethnographical Sciences, Florence, 2003.

Price, S., 'Compensation, Restoration and Development Opportunities: National Standards on Involuntary Resettlement', *in* M.M. Cernea & H.M. Mathur, *The Resettlement Dilemma: Can Compensation Prevent Impoverishment?*, Oxford University Press, New Delhi, 2008, pp. 147-179.

Price, S., 'Is there a global safeguard for development displacement?', *in* Satiroglu, I. & Choi, N. (Eds.), *Development Induced Displacement and Resettlement: New Perspectives on Persisting Problems*, Routledge, Oxford, UK, 2015, pp. 127-141.

Quoqing, S., 'Comparing China's and the World Bank's displacement policies over time: the ascent of the "Resettlement with Development', *in* M. Cernea and J. Maldonado (Eds.), *Challenging the Prevailing Paradigm of Displacement and Resettlement*, Routledge, New York, NY, 2018.

Radin, J., *Reinterpreting Property*, University of Chicago Press, Chicago, IL, USA; London, UK, 1993, p. 154.

Rainforest Foundation US, 'Getting a Land Title in Peru is Almost Impossible for Indigenous Communities', UK. Available at: www.rainforestfoundation.org/landtitlesperu/.

Ramesh, J. & Khan, M., 'Land Acquisition Law: Winking at the States', *The Hindu*, 2 November 2016.

Raz, J., *The Rule of Law and Its Virtues in The Authority of Law: Essays on Law and Morality*, Clarendon Press, Oxford, UK, 1979, pp. 210, 213, 218.

Rew, A., Fisher, E. & Pandey, B., 'Policy Practices in Development-Induced Displacement and Resettlement', *Development-Induced Displacement: Problems, Policies and People*, Berghahn Books, Oxford, UK, 2006, pp. 38-69.

RRI, *Who Owns the World's Land? A Global Baseline of Formally Recognized Indigenous and Community Land Rights*, RRI, Washington, DC, 2015.

RRI *Potential for Recognition of Community Forest Resource Rights Under India's Forest Rights Act*, Washington, DC, RRI, 2015.

RRI and Bharti Institute of Public Policy, Indian School of Business, *Land Disputes and Stalled Investments in India*, RRI, Washington, DC, 2016.

RRI & TMP Systems, *Tenure and Investment in Africa: Comparative Analysis of Key Trends and Contextual Factors*, RRI, Washington, DC, USA, 2017.

RRI and TMP Systems, *Tenure and Investment in Asia*, RRI, Washinton, DC, 2017.

Robinson, B.E., Holland, M.B. & Naughton-Treves, L., 'Does secure land tenure save forests? A meta-analysis of the relationship between land tenure and tropical deforestation', *Global Environmental Change*, Vol. 29, 2014, pp. 281-293.

Robinson, P., 'Fair Notice and Fair Adjudication: Two Kinds of Legality', *Univ. Penn. Law Rev.*,Vol. 154, 2005, pp. 335-398.

Rose, H., Mugisha, F., Kananga, A. & Clay, D., *Implementation of Rwanda's Expropriation Law and Its Outcomes on the Population.* In Proceedings of the Annual World Bank Conference on Land and Poverty, Washington, DC, USA, 14-18 March 2016.

Rosenn, K., 'Expropriation in Argentina and Brazil: Theory and Practice', *Virginia Journal of International Law*, Vol. 15, No. 2, 1975.

Salcedo-La Viña, C. & Morarji, M., *Making Women's Voices Count in Community Decision-making on Land Investments* (Working Paper), World Resources Institute, Washington, DC, USA, 2016.

Sathe, D., *The Political Economy of Land Acquisition in India*, Springer Singapore, Singapore, 2017.

Satiroglu, I. & Choi, N. (Eds.), *Development Induced Displacement and Resettlement: New Perspectives on Persisting Problems*, Routledge, Oxford, UK, 2015, pp. 127-141.

Schlager, E. and Ostrom, E., 'Property-Rights Regimes and Natural Resources: A Conceptual Analysis', *Land Economics,* Vol. 68, No. 3, 1992, pp. 249-262.

Schoneveld, G.C., 'The geographic and sectoral patterns of large-scale farmland investments in sub-Saharan Africa', *Food Policy*, Vol. 48, 2014, pp. 34-50.

Scudder, T. & Colson E., 'From welfare to development: a conceptual framework for the analysis of dislocated people', *In* Hansen A. & Oliver-Smith, A., (Eds.), *Involuntary migration and resettlement: the problems and responses of dislocated people*, Westerview Press, Boulder, NV, 1982, pp. 267-287, 1982.

Shihata, I., 'Legal Aspects of Involuntary Population Resettlement', *in* M. Cernea & S. Guggenheim, *Anthropological Approaches to Resettlement Policy, Practice, and Theory*, Westview Press, Boulder, Colorado, 1993.

Sirait, M.T., White, B. & Pradhan, U., 'Land Rights and Land Reform Issues for Effective Natural Resourcse Management in Indonesia', *in* G. Shivakoti, U. Pradhan & H. Helmi (Eds.), *Redefining Diversity & Dynamics of Natural Resources Management in Asia*, Vol. 1, Elsevier, Amsterdam, The Netherlands, 2017.

Somin, I., 'Controlling the Grasping Hand: Economic Development Takings After Kelo' *George Mason Law & Economics Research Paper,* No. 06-01, 2007.

Somin, I., 'The story behind Kelo *v.* City of New London- how an obscure takings case got to the Supreme Court and shocked the nation', *Washington Post*, 29 May 2015.

Stern, S., 'Expropriation Effects on Residential Communities', *in* Hoops, B., Marais, E.J., Mostert, H., Sluysman, J.A.M.A. & Verstappen, L.C.A. (Eds.), *Rethinking Expropriation Law II: Context, Criteria, and Consequences of Expropriation*, , Eleven International Publishing, Den Haag, The Netherlands, 2015, pp. 359-391.

Stevens, C., Winterbottom, R., Springer, J. & Reytar, K., 'Securing Rights, Combating Climate Change', *World Resources Institute and Rights and Resources Initiative*, Washington, DC, 2014.

Stevens, C. & Dear, C., *Guidelines on Compulsory Displacement and Resettlement in USAID Programing*, United States Agency for International Development, Washington, DC, 2016.

Tagliarino, N.K., *Encroaching on Land and Livelihoods: How National Expropriation Laws Measure up against International Standards*, World Resources Institute, Washington, DC, 2016.

Tagliarino, N.K., 'The status of national legal frameworks for valuing compensation for expropriated land: An analysis of whether national laws in 50 countries/regions across Asia, Africa, and Latin America comply with international standards on compensation valuation', *Land*, No. 6, 2016.

Tagliarino, N.K., Bununu, Y.A., Michael, M.O., De Maria, M. & Olusanmi, A., 'Compensation for Expropriated Community Farmland in Nigeria: An In-Depth Analysis of the Laws and Practices Related to Land Expropriation for the Lekki Free Trade Zone in Lagos' *Land*, Vol. 7, 2018.

Tagliarino, N.K., 2018, 'Avoiding the Worst-Case Scenario: An Assessment of Compensation Eligibility Requirements Applicable to Indigenous Peoples and Local Communities in 30 Countries', *in* B. Hoops, E.J. Marais, L.V. Schalkwyk, N.K. Tagliarino *Rethinking Expropriation Law III: Fair Compensation*, Eleven International Publishing, Juta, Johannesburg, South Africa, 2018.

Tagliarino, N.K., 'The need for national-level legal protection of populations displaced by expropriation: land acquisition in 50 *countries*', *in* Cernea, M. and Maldonado, J. (Eds.) *Challenging the Prevailing Paradigm of Displacement and Resettlement: Risks, Impoverishment, Legacies and Solutions*. Routledge, New York, NY, 2018.

Tagliarino, N.K., 'Legal Limits on Government Authority to Expropriate Land: An Assessment of Expropriation Procedures in 50 Countries Across Asia, Africa, and Latin America', *In Proceedings of the Annual World Bank Conference on Land and Poverty*, Washington, DC, USA, 19-23 March 2018.

Tagliarino, N.K., 'Voluntary Guidelines Section 16 Indicators on Expropriation, Compensation, and Resettlement', University of Groningen, Groningen, Netherlands, 2018.

Tang, B., Wong, S. & Lau, M.C., 'Social impact assessment and public participation in China: A case study of land requisition in Guangzhou', *Environ. Impact Assess. Rev.* Vol. 28, 2008, pp. 57-72.

Tarabochia, M.L., 'Peru's Climate Commitment threatened by advancing oil palm', *Mongabay*. 2016. Available online: https://news.mongabay.com/2016/04/perus-climate-commitments-threatened-advancing-oil-palm (accessed on 1 March 2018).

Terminski, B., 'Development-Induced Displacement and Resettlement: Theoretical Frameworks and Current Challenges', *University of Geneva*, Research Paper 9/2013, Geneva, 2013, pp. 38, 86.

The Centre on Housing and Evictions (COHRE) & Social and Economic Rights Action Center (SERAC), *The Myth of the Abuja Master Plan: Forced Evictions as Urban Planning in Abuja*, COHRE, Geneva, SERAC, Lagos, Nigeria, 2008.

The Guardian (Nigeria), 'Ambode Approves N740M for Lekki Free Zone Communities', *The Guardian*, Lagos, Nigeria, 2016.

The Law of the Land: Women's Rights to Land. Available online: www.landesa.org/resources/property-not-poverty/ (accessed on 25 May 2017).

The Munden Project, 'The Financial Risks of Insecure Land Tenure: An Investment View', *RRI*, Washington, DC, 2012.

Times of India, 'Explaining delay in implementing forest rights in Mahan: Tribals', *Times of India*, New Delhi, 2013.

Totaro, P., *Nigerian Courts Rule Against Mass Eviction in Lagos: Activists*, Thomson Reuters, Toronto, Canada, 2017.

True Price & University of Groningen, *Towards a Protocol on Fair Compensation in Case of Land Tenure Changes. Input Document to a Participatory Process*; True Price, Amsterdam, The Netherlands; University of Groningen, Groningen, The Netherlands, 2016.

Tura, H.A., 'Land rights and land grabbing in Oromia, Ethiopia', *Land Use Policy*, Vol. 70, 2018, pp. 247-255.

United Nations Assistance Mission in Afghanistan (UNAMA), 'The Stolen lands of Afghanistan and Its People.' *UNAMA*, Kabul, Afghanistan, 2014.

United Nations, *Free Prior and Informed Consent of Indigenous Peoples*, United Nations Human Rights Office of the High Commissioner, Geneva, Switzerland, 2013.

United Nations. *Realizing Women's Rights to Land and Other Productive Resources*, HR/PUB/13/04, United Nations, New York, NY, USA, Geneva, Switzerland, 2013.

United Nations, 'Report of the Special Rapporteur on adequate housing as a component of the right to an adequate standard of living, and on the right to non-discrimination in this context', 2013 *United Nations*, A/HRC/25/54.

USAID, *Integrating Customary Land Tenure into Statutory Land Law*, USAID, Washington, DC, 2008.

USAID, *Strengthening Land Tenure and Property Rights in Angola*, 2008.

USAID, *Property Rights and Resource Governance Profile: Bangladesh*, 2010.

USAID, *Property Rights and Resource Governance Profile: Pakistan*, USAID, Washington, DC, 2010.

USAID, *Country Profile Property Rights and Resource Governance*, USAID, Mexico, 2011.

USAID, *LAND Project, Research Brief No.2*, Kigali, 2015.

Uygur, G., 'The Rule of Law: Is the Line Between the Formal and the Moral Blurred?', *in* B.I. Flores, K. Hiima & K.E. Eds, *Law, Liberty, and the Rule of Law*, New York, NY, USA, Springer, 2013.

Vanclay, F., 'Conceptualising social impact', *Environmental Impact Assessment Review*, Vol. 22, 2002, pp. 183-211.

Vanclay, F., 'Project induced displacement and resettlement: From impoverishment risks to an opportunity or development', *Impact Assessment and Project. Appraisal,* Vol. 35, 2017, pp. 3-21.

Vanclay, F., Esteves, A.M., Auchamp, I. & Franks, D., *Social Impact Assessment: Guidance for Assessing and Managing the Social Impacts of Projects*, International Association for Impact Assessment, Fargo, ND, USA, 2015.

van der Walt, A.J., *Constitutional Property Law,* 3rd edn, Juta, Cape Town, South Africa, 2011.

van der Walt, A.J. 'Constitutional Property Law', *ASSAL*, 2010.

van Eerd, M. & Banerjee, B., 'Working Paper I: Evictions, Acquisition, Expropriation and Compensation: Practices and selected case studies', *United Nations Human Settlements Programme,* Nairobi, 2013, pp. 12-13.

Veit, P.G., Nshala, R., Odhiambo, M.O. & Manyindo, J., *Protected Areas and Property Rights: Democratizing Eminent Domain in East Africa*, World Resources Institute, Washington, DC, 2008, p. 14.

Verstappen, L., 'Rethinking Public Interest in Expropriation Law: Introductory Observations' *in* Hoops, B., Marais, E.J., Mostert, H., Sluysman, J.A.M.A. & Verstappen, L.C.A. (Eds.), *Rethinking Expropriation Law I: Public Interest in Expropriation*, Eleven International Publishing, Den Haag, The Netherlands, 2015, pp. 15-25.

Verstappen, L., 'Multilevel governance of property titles in land: The voluntary guidelines on the responsible governance of tenure of land, fisheries, and forests in the context of national food security', *in* C. Godt Ed., *Regulatory Property Rights: The Transforming Notion of Property in Transnational Business Regulation*, Brill/Nijhoff, Leiden, Netherlands, 2016, pp. 98-118.

Vhughen, D. & Gebru, A., 'Large-Scale Acquisitions of Land in Ethiopia', 2013, *Focus on Land in Africa* (Brief).

Walicki, N. & Swain, M., *Pushed Aside: Displaced for 'Development' in India*. Norwegian Refugee Council (NRC) & Internal Displacement Monitoring Committee, Oslo, Norway, 2016.

Wickama, J., Ngailo, J., Masuki, K. & Mkalimoto, D., 'Eviction of Pastoralists from Mkomazi Game Reserve in North Eastern Tanzania: Analysis of new conflicts and impact on the affected communities', *ARI-Mlingano*, Tanga, Tanzania, 2005.

Wily, L.A., *Community-based land tenure management: Questions and answers about Tanzania's new Village Land Act, 1999*, International Institute for Environment and Development, 2003, Issue Paper no. 120. Available at: http://pubs.iied.org/pdfs/9295 IIED.pdf.

Wily, L.A., 'Custom and commonage in Africa. Rethinking the orthodoxies', *Land Use Policy Journal*, 2008, pp. 43-52.

Wily, L.A., *The tragedy of public lands: The fate of the commons under global commercial pressure*, International Land Coalition, Rome, 2011.

Wily, L.A., *Protecting Peoples' Interests? A Social Analysis of Land Expropriation Law of Afghanistan*, World Bank, Kabul, Afghanistan, 2013.

Wily, L.A., 'The law and land grabbing: Friend or foe?', *Law Dev. Rev.*, Vol. 7, 2014, pp. 207-242.

Wily, L.A., 2016, 'The road to land titling: Kenya finally enacts new laws', *Thompson Reuters Foundation News*, 2016. Available at: http://news.trust.org/item/20160902102932-xsime/.

Wily, L.A., 'Compulsory Acquisition as a Constitutional Matter: The Case in Africa', 2018, *Journal of African Law*, Vol. 62, 2018, pp. 77-103.

Wily, L.A., Tagliarino, N., Harvard Law and International Development Society (LIDS), Vidal, A., Salcedo-La Vina, C., Ibrahim, S., and Almeida, B. *Indicators of the Legal Security of Indigenous and Community Lands*. Data file from *The Global Platform of Indigenous and Community Lands, Landmark, 2017*. Available at: www.landmarkmap.org.

Wily, L.A., Veit, P., Smith, R., Dubertret, F., Reytar, K., and Tagliarino, N.,'Guidelines for Researching, Scoring and Documenting Findings on '*What National Laws Say About Indigenous & Community Land Rights*': Methodology document from *LandMark: The*

Global Platform of Indigenous and Community Lands, World Resources Institute, 2017. Available at: <www.landmarkmap.org>.

Wily, L.A., *Legal Indicator Scores on the Tenure Security of Indigenous and Community Land in Nigeria, on* LandMark Map, 2016. Available online: www.landmarkmap.org (accessed on 8 February 2018).

World Bank, *Bhutan - Rural Access Project: resettlement action plan: Policy framework for resettlement and rehabilitation of project affected persons*, World Bank, Washington, DC, 1990.

World Bank, *Operational Directives 4.30: Involuntary Resettlement*, World Bank, Washington, DC, 1990.

World Bank Environment Department, *Resettlement and development: the Bankwide review of projects involving involuntary resettlement 1986-1993*, World Bank, Washington, DC, 1994.

World Bank. *Resettlement and Development: The Bankwide Review of Projects Involving Resettlement 1986-1994 Paper 032*, World Bank, Washington, DC, USA, 1996.

World Bank, *Operational Policy 4.12: Involuntary Resettlement*, World Bank, Washington, DC, 2001 (revised 2013).

World Bank, *Community and Social Development Project Additional Finance (CSDP AF-2) Resettlement Policy Framework*, World Bank, Washington, DC, 2016.

World Bank, *Asmara Power Distribution and Rural Electrification Project*, World Bank, Washington, DC, 2004.

World Bank, *Indigenous Peoples Development Project*, World Bank, Washington, DC, 2006.

World Bank, *Ecuador- National System of Protected Areas: Resettlement Action Plan*, World Bank, Washington, DC, 2010.

World Bank, *Compulsory land acquisition and voluntary land conversion in Vietnam: the conceptual approach, land valuation and grievance redress mechanism*, World Bank, Washington, DC, 2011.

World Bank, *Land Acquisition and Resettlement Policy Framework: Proposed Geothermal Clean Energy Investment Project*, World Bank, Washington, DC, 2011.

World Bank, *Land Governance Assessment Framework Final Report: Nigeria*, World Bank, Washington, DC, USA, 2011.

World Bank, Land Governance Assessment Framework- Final Report (Tanzania), World Bank, Washington, DC, 2017.

World Bank, *Final Report: Improving Land Sector Governance in Ghana: Implementation of the Land Governance Assessment Framework*, World Bank, Washington, DC, 2012.

World Bank, *Honduras - Policy framework for involuntary resettlement within the implementation framework of the Disaster Risk Management Project: resettlement plan*, World Bank, Washington, DC, 2012.

World Bank, *Land Governance Assessment Framework Final Report for Peru,* World Bank, Washington, DC, USA, 2013.

World Bank, *Nicaragua Proyecto de Sostenibilidad del sector de agua y saneamiento rural: marco de Politica de Reasentamiento Involuntario*, World Bank, Washington, DC, 2013.

World Bank, *Agricultural Productivity and Food Security Project: additional financing - resettlement plan: Cadre de politique de reinstallation*, World Bank, Washington, DC, 2014.

World Bank, *Resettlement Action Plan- For the Sierra Leone Energy Access Project*, World Bank, Washington, DC, 2014.

World Bank, *Resettlement plan- Philippines: Water District Development Section Project*, World Bank, Washington, DC, 2014.

World Bank, *Burkina Faso - Sahel Growth Pole Project: resettlement plan (Vol. 2): Cadre politique de reinstallation des populations*, World Bank, Washington, DC, 2015.

World Bank, *Country and Lending Groups*. World Bank, Washington, DC, 2015. Available at: http://data.worldbank.org/about/country-and-lending-groups.

World Bank, *ESF: Bank on Human Rights Council. Key Human Rights Concerns and Recommendations Regarding the World Bank's Proposed Social and Environmental Safeguards*, World Bank, Washington, DC, 2015.

World Bank, *Land Governance Assessment Framework for Tanzania*, World Bank, Washington, DC, 2015.

World Bank, *Resettlement Liberia Accelerated Electricity Expansion Project, LACEEP*, World Bank, Washington, DC, 2015.

World Bank, *Cambodia- South East Asia Disaster Risk Management Project: resettlement plan: Resettlement policy framework*, World Bank, Washington, DC, 2016.

World Bank, *Land Governance Assessment Report: Kenya*, World Bank, Washington, DC, 2016.

World Bank, *Land Governance Assessment Framework Implementation in Ethiopia: Final Country Report*, World Bank, Washington, DC, 2016.

World Bank, *Land Governance Assessment Final Report: Brazil*, World Bank, Washington, DC, 2016.

World Bank, *Land Governance Assessment Framework Final Report: Ethiopia*, World Bank, Washington, DC, 2016.

World Bank, *Land Governance Assessment Framework Final Report: Kenya*, World Bank, Washington, DC, 2016.

World Bank, *Land Governance Assessment Framework: Country Reports*, World Bank, Washington, DC, 2016.

World Bank, *Land Governance Assessment Framework Synthesis Report (Afghanistan)*, World Bank, Washington, DC, 2016.

World Bank, *Land Governance Assessment Synthesis Report (Ethiopia)*, World Bank, Washington, DC, 2016.

World Bank, *Land Governance Assessment National Synthesis Report (Afghanistan)*, World Bank, Washington, DC, 2016.

World Bank, *Land Governance Assessment National Synthesis Report (India)*, World Bank, Washington, DC, 2016.

World Bank, *Land Governance Assessment Framework Final Report: Rwanda*, World Bank, Washington, DC, 2016.

World Bank, *Land Governance Assessment Framework: Zambia Country Report*, World Bank, Washington, DC, 2016.

World Bank, *Environmental and Social Standard 5 Land Acquisition, Restrictions on Land Use and Involuntary Resettlement*, World Bank, Washington, DC, 2017.

World Bank, *The World Bank Environmental and Social Framework*, World Bank, Washington, DC, 2017.

Wyman, K., 'The Measure of Just Compensation', *UC Davis Law Rev.* Vol. 41, 2007.

Yardley, J., 'Farmers Being Moved Aside by China's Real Estate Boom', *New York Times*, New York, NY, 2004.

Zeremariam, T.K. & Quinn, N., 'An evaluation of environmental impact assessment in Eritrea, Impact Assessment and Project Appraisal', Vol. 25, 1, 2007, 53-63.

CASES

Armstrong, *v.* United States, 364 U.S. 40, 49, 1960.

Housing Authority *v.* Midkiff 467 U.S. 229 (The Supreme Court of the United States 1984).

Kelo *et al. v.* City of New London *et al.*, 545 U.S. 469 (The Supreme Court of the United States 2005).

Radhey Shyam *v.* The State of Uttar Pradash, (2011) 5 SCC 553.

Savitri Dev *v.* State of Uttar Pradesh, Civil Appeal No. 4506 of 2015 (Supreme Court of India 2015).

Sooraram Pratap Reddy *v.* District Collector (2008) 9 S.C.C. 552.

South Africa Free State High Court, *Bartsch Consult (Pty) Limited v. Mayoral Committee of the Maluti-A-Phofung Municipality [2010] ZAFSHC 11*, 2010.

Supreme Court of the Philippines, *NIA v. Rural Bank, G. R. No. 185124*, 2012.

Supreme Court of the Philippines, *Supreme Court Decision G.R. No. 150640*, 2007.

Supreme Court of Uganda, *Pyrali Abdul Rasul Esmail v. Adrian Sibo (Constitutional Petition No. 9 of 1997).*

United States *v.* Commodities Tradition Corp, 339 U.S. 121, 123, 1950.

Treaties

International Covenant on Economic, Social and Cultural Rights, A/RES/2200: Art. 11, 1966. Available at: www.refworld.org/docid/3b00f47924.html.

UN, *Universal Declaration of Human Rights*, G.A. Res. 217 A (III): Art. 17, 1948. Available at: www.refworld.org/docid/3ae6b3712c.html.

UN, *International Covenant on Economic, Social and Cultural Rights*, A/ RES/2200, New York, 1966.

UN Committee on Economic, Social and Cultural Rights (CESCR), *General Comment No. 7: The right to adequate housing (Art. 11.1): forced evictions*, E/1998/22, 1997.

UN, *Basic Principles and Guidelines on Development-Based Evictions and Displacement*, A/HRC/4/18, 2007.

UN, *Declaration on the Rights of Indigenous Peoples*; G.A. Res. 61/295, U.N. Doc. A/RES/61/295, United Nations, New York, NY, USA, 2007.

UN, *Free Prior and Informed Consent of Indigenous Peoples*, United Nations Human Rights Office of the High Commissioner, Geneva, 2013.

UN. *Forced Evictions Fact Sheet No. 25/Rev.1*; United Nations: New York, NY, USA; Geneva, Switzerland, 2014.

Laws Reviewed

Afghanistan

Government of Afghanistan, *Law on Land Acquisition*, 2017.

Government of Afghanistan, *Law on Managing Land Affairs*, 2008.

Government of Afghanistan, *Presidential Decree of the Islamic Republic of Afghanistan Concerning Modification of a Series of Articles of the Land Expropriation Law Published in the Official Gazette #(794), 142, 14221. Decree of the President No. 83*, 2005.

Government of Afghanistan, *Constitution of Afghanistan*, 2004.

Government of Afghanistan, *Decree of the President No. 83*, 2003.

Government of Afghanistan, *Land Management Law*, 2000.

Government of Afghanistan, *Law and Pasture and Grazing Land*, 2000.

Government of Afghanistan, *Law on Land Expropriation*, 2000 (Amended 2005, 2010).

Government of Afghanistan, *Law of Land Survey, Verification and Registration*, 1976.

Afghanistan Ministry of Mineral and Water, *Irrigation Restoration and Development Project Resettlement Policy Framework*, 2010.

Angola

Government of Angola, *Constitution*, 2010.

Government of Angola, *Land Act No. 9/04*, 2004.

Government of Angola, *Decree No. 58/07 approving the Regulation for Land Concession*, 2007.

Government of Angola, *Decree Regarding Resettlement of Displacement People*, 2001.

National-Level Adoption of International Standards on Expropriation, Compensation and Resettlement

Argentina

Government of Argentina, *Ley No. 21.499 Nacional De Expropiaciones*, 1977.

Government of Argentina, *Constitution of Argentina*, 1853 (Revised 1994).

Bangladesh

Government of Bangladesh, *The Acquisition and Requisition of Immovable Property Ordinance*, 1982.

Government of Bangladesh, *Constitution of Bangladesh*, 1972, (Amended 2011).

Government of Bangladesh, *Acquisition of Waste Land Act*, 1950.

Belize

Belize Social Investment Fund, *Land Acquisition and Involuntary Resettlement Policy Framework*, 2010.

Government of Belize, *Housing and Town Planning Act*, 2000.

Government of Belize, *Land Acquisition (Public Purposes) Act*, 2000.

Government of Belize, *Constitution of Belize*. 1981.

Bhutan

Government of Bhutan, *Constitution of Bhutan*, 2008.

Government of Bhutan, *Land Act*, 2007.

Botswana

Government of Botswana, *Wildlife Conservation and National Parks Act (CAP 38:01)*, 1992.

Government of Botswana, *Chieftainship Act Chapter 41:01*, 1987.

Botswana Ministry of Lands and Housing, *Compensation Guidelines*, 1977 (Amended 2004).

Government of Botswana, *Tribal Land Regulations*, 1970.

Government of Botswana, *Tribal Land Act Chapter 32:02*, 1968 (Amended 2008).

Government of Botswana, *Constitution of Botswana*, 1966 (Amended 2006).

Government of Botswana, *Acquisition of Property Act Chapter 32:10*, 1955.

Brazil

Ministry of Cities, *Involuntary Resettlement Policy No. 317*, 2013.

Government of Brazil, *Land Law*, Law 4.504 of 1964.

Government of Brazil, *The Expropriation Law for Social Interest, Law 4.132 of Sept. 10*, 1962.

Government of Brazil, *The Law of Expropriation for Public Utility, Decree-Law No. 3.365 of June 21*, 1941.

Burkina Faso

Government of Burkina Faso, *Law 034-2012/AN Agrarian Reform Law*, 2012.

Government of Burkina Faso, *Law 034-2009/AN on Rural Land Tenure*, 2009.

Government of Burkina Faso, *National Rural Land Security Policy*, 2007.

Government of Burkina Faso, *Loi no. 006/97/ADP portant Code forestier au Burkina Faso*, 1997.

Government of Burkina Faso, *Constitution of Burkina Faso*, 1991 (Amended 2012),

National-Level Adoption of International Standards on Expropriation, Compensation and Resettlement

Cambodia

Government of Cambodia, *Law on Expropriation*, 2010.

Government of Cambodia, *Sub Decree on Procedures of Registration of Land of Indigenous Communities of 2009*, 2009.

Government of Cambodia, *Sub-Decree No. 146 on Economic Land Concessions*, 2005.

Government of Cambodia, *Law on Forestry*, 2002.

Government of Cambodia, *Law on Land*, 2001.

Government of Cambodia, *Constitution of Cambodia*, 1993.

China

Government of China, *Regulation on the Expropriation of Buildings on State-owned Land and Compensation*, 2011.

Government of China, *Property Rights Law*, 2007.

Government of China, *Regulation on Land Requisition Compensation and Resettlement of Migrants for Large and Medium Water Conservation and Hydropower Construction Projects*, 2006.

Government of China, *Constitution of China*, 2004.

Government of China, *Urban Housing Demolition and Relocation Management Regulations*, 2001.

Government of China, *The Law of Land Administration of the People's Republic of China*, 1998.

Government of China, *Regulations for the implementation of the Land Administration Law of the People's Republic of China*, 1991.

Government of China, *Law on Land Administration*, 1986 (amended 2004).

Ecuador

Government of Ecuador, *Resolución Nº 15 - Instructivo para sustanciar el proceso de expropiación en primera instancia*, 2013.

Government of Ecuador, *Constitution of Ecuador*, 2010.

Government of Ecuador, *Ley Nº 54 - Ley de Desarrollo Agrario*, 1997.

Eritrea

Government of Eritrea, *Constitution of Eritrea*, 1997.

Government of Eritrea, *Land Proclamation No. 58/1994*, 1994.

Ethiopia

Government of Ethiopia, *Federal Democratic Republic of Ethiopia Rural Land Administration and Land Use Proclamation No. 456/2005*, 2005.

Government of Ethiopia, *Proclamation No. 455/2005, Expropriation of Landholdings for Public Purposes and Payment of Compensation Proclamation*, 2005.

Government of Ethiopia, *Constitution of Ethiopia*, 1994.

Government of Ethiopia, *Public Ownership of Rural Lands Proclamation No. 31/1975*, 1975.

Government of Ethiopia, *Civil Code of Ethiopia*, 1960.

Ghana

Government of Ghana, *Constitution of Ghana*, 1992.

Government of Ghana, *Title Registration Act*, 1986.

Government of Ghana, *Administration of Lands Act*, 1962.

Government of Ghana, *State Lands Act, 1962.*

Government of Ghana, *State Lands Regulations*, 1962.

Government of Ghana, *Forestry Act*, 1927.

Honduras

Government of Honduras, *Decreto No 258/05 - Reforma la Ley de propiedad*, 2005.

Government of Honduras, *Decreto No. 191/05- Reforma la Ley de Propiedad*, 2005.

Government of Honduras, *Decreto No 12/00 - Ley para el dessarollo rural sostenible*, 2005.

Government of Honduras, *Decree 82/04 - Ley de propiedad*, 2004.

Government of Honduras, *Constitution of Honduras*, 1982.

Hong Kong

Government of Hong Kong, *Land Resumption Ordinance (CAP. 124)*, 1998.

Government of Hong Kong, *Basic Law of the Hong Kong Special Administrative Region of the People's Republic of China Government of Hong Kong*, 1990.

Government of Hong Kong, *Constitution of Hong Kong*, 1990.

India

Government of India, *The Right to Fair Compensation and Transparency in Land Acquisition, Rehabilitation (Amendment) Ordinance*, 2014.

Government of India. *The Right to Fair Compensation and Transparency in Land Acquisition, Rehabilitation and Resettlement (Social Impact Assessment and Consent) Rules*, 2014.

Government of India, *The Right to Fair Compensation and Transparency in Land Acquisition, Rehabilitation and Resettlement Act*, 2013.

Government of India, *Constitution of India*, 2007.

Government of India, *National Ministry of Environment and Forests, State of the Environment Report*, 2009.

Government of India, *The Scheduled Tribes and Other Traditional Forest Dwellers (Recognition of Forest Rights) Act*, 2006.

Indonesia

Government of Indonesia, *Acquisition of Land for Development in the Public Interest (Law No. 2 of 2012)*, 2012.

Government of Indonesia, *Constitutional Court Decision, PUTUSAN - Nomor 35/ PUU-X/2012*, Presidential Decree No. 71/2012, 2012.

Government of Indonesia, *Basic Agrarian Act*, 1960.

Government of Indonesia, *Act. 41 of 1999 on Forestry Affairs*, 1999.

Government of Indonesia, *Constitution of Indonesia*, 1945.

Kazakhstan

Government of Kazakhstan, *Law on State-Owned Property (No. 413-IV ZRK)*, 2011.

Government of Kazakhstan, *Land Code of the Republic of Kazakhstan*, 2003.

Government of Kazakhstan, *Constitution of Kazakhstan*, 1995.

Government of Kazakhstan, *Civil Code*, 1994.

Kenya

Government of Kenya, *Community Land Act*, 2016.

Government of Kenya, *Land Act*, 2012.

Government of Kenya, *Draft Evictions and Resettlement Bill*, 2012.

Government of Kenya, *National Land Commission Act (No. 5 of 2012)*, 2012.

Government of Kenya, *Land Acquisition Act (Repealed by Land Act 2012)*, 2010.

Government of Kenya, *Constitution of Kenya*, 2010.

Government of Kenya, *Forest Act*, 2005.

Laos

Government of Laos, *Decree on Compensation and Resettlement Management in Development Projects*, 2016.

Government of Laos, *Decree on the Implementation of the Land Law No. 88/PM*, 2008.

Government of Laos, *Decree on the Compensation and Resettlement of the Development Project*, 2005.

Government of Laos, *Decree on the Compensation and Resettlement of the Development Project No. 192/PM*, 2003.

Government of Laos, *Land Law No. 04 /NA*, 2003.

Lesotho

Government of Lesotho, *Land Act (Act No. 8 of 2010)*, 2010.

Government of Lesotho, *Constitution of Lesotho*, 1993.

Lesotho Highlands Development Authority and Lesotho Highlands Water Commission, *Lesotho Highlands Water Project (LHWP) Phase II Compensation Policy 5th draft (v.50.08)*, 2014.

Liberia

Government of Liberia, *Constitution of Liberia*, 1984.

Government of Liberia, *An Act to Establish Community Rights Law of 2008 with Respect to Forest Lands*, 2008, Sec. 1.3.

Government of Liberia, Draft Land Rights Act 2013 (pending).

Malaysia

Government of Malaysia, *Land Acquisition Rules*, 1998.

Government of Malaysia, *National Land Code*, 1965 (Amended 2008).

Government of Malaysia, *Federal Constitution*, 1974.

Government of Malaysia, *Land Acquisition Act*, 1960 (Amended 1992).

Government of Malaysia, *Land Development Act*, 1956.

Mexico

Government of Mexico, *Decree that Article 6 and the second paragraph of Article 20(a) of the Expropriation Act*, 2011.

Government of Mexico, *Regulations of the Agrarian Law on Matters of Organization of Rural Property*, 1996.

Government of Mexico, *Agrarian Law*, 1992.

Government of Mexico, *Regulations of the Institute for Administration of National Properties*, 1992.

Government of Mexico, *Expropriation Law*, 1936 (amended 2011).

Government of Mexico, *Constitution of Mexico*, 1917 (amended 2007).

Mongolia

Government of Mongolia, *Law on Allocation of Land to Mongolian Citizens for Ownership*, 2002.

Government of Mongolia, *Law on Land*, 2002.

Government of Mongolia, *Constitution of Mongolia*, 1992.

Myanmar

Government of Myanmar, *Constitution of Myanmar*, 2008.

Governments of Myanmar (and Pakistan). *Land Acquisition Act*, 1894.

Namibia

Government of Namibia, *Agricultural (Commercial) Land Reform Amendment Act*, 2014 (No. 1 of 2014).

Government of Namibia, *Communal Land Reform Act*, 2002 (Amended 2013).

Government of Namibia, *Constitution of the Republic of Namibia*, 1990.

Government of Namibia, *Agricultural (Commercial) Land Reform Act 6 of 1995*, 1995 (Amended 2013).

Nepal

Government of Nepal, *Guthi Corporation Act*, 1976.

Government of Nepal, *Constitution of Nepal*, 1977.

Government of Nepal, *Nepal: Preparation of National Resettlement Policy Framework*, ADB, Bahasa, 2006.

Government of Nepal, *New Policy Can Resolve Most of the Problems in Land Acquisition*, Undated.

Government of Nepal Office of the Investment Board, *Gov't introduces land acquisition policy*, Government of Nepal, Kathmandu, 2015.

Government of Nepal, *Land Acquisition Act 2034*, 1977.

Government of Nepal, *Forest Act 2049*, 1993.

Nicaragua

Government of Nicaragua, *Law of Communal Property Regime of the Indigenous Peoples and Ethnic Communities of the Autonomous Regions of the Atlantic Coast of Nicaragua and of the Rivers Bocay, Coco, Indio and Maiz*, 2003.

Government of Nicaragua, *Ley Nº 278 - Ley sobre propiedad reformada urbana y agrarian*, 1997.

Government of Nicaragua, *Civil Code*, 1904.

Nigeria

Government of Nigeria, *Constitution of Nigeria*, 1999.

Government of Nigeria, *Environmental Impact Assessment Decree*, 1992.

Government of Nigeria, *Land Use Act*, 1990.

Pakistan

Government of Pakistan, *Draft National Resettlement Policy*, 2002.

Government of Pakistan, *Constitution of Pakistan*, 1973.

Government of Pakistan, *Land Acquisition Act*, 1894.

Papua New Guinea

Government of Papua New Guinea, *Land Regulations*, 1999.

Government of Papua New Guinea. *Land Act*, 1996.

Government of Papua New Guinea, *Constitution of Papua New Guinea*, 1975.

Peru

Government of Peru, *Decree 1210 Decreto Legislativo Que Modifica La Decima Disposicion Complementaria Final Del Decreto Legislativo No. 1192, Que Aprueba La Ley Marco De Adquisicion y Expropriacion de Inmuebles, Transferencia De Inmuebles de Propriedad Del Estado, Liberacion de Interferencias y Dicta Otras Medidas Para La Ejecuion de Obras de Infrastructura*, 2016.

Government of Peru, *Constitution of Peru*, 1993. Available at: https://goo.gl/NRXIvr;

Government of Peru, *Decreto Legislativo Nº 1.192 - Ley Marco de Adquisición y Expropiación de inmuebles, transferencia de inmuebles de propiedad del Estado, liberación de Interferencias y dicta otras medidas para la ejecución de obras de infraestructura*, 2015.

Government of Peru, *Ley Nº 30.025 - Ley que facilita la adquisición, expropiación y posesión de bienes inmuebles para obras de infraestructura*, 2013.

Government of Peru, *Ley Nº 27.117 - Ley General de Expropiaciones (Repealed)*, 1999.

Philippines

Government of the Philippines, *Republic Act No. 9700 amending Republic Act No. 6657 on the Comprehensive Agrarian Reform Law 1988*, 2009.

Government of Philippines, *An Act to Facilitate The Acquisition of Right-of-Way, Site, or Location for National Government Infrastructure Projects and For other Purposes*, RA 8974, 2000.

Government of Philippines, *Indigenous People's Rights Act*, 1997.

Government of the Philippines, *Republic Act 7279 (Urban Development and Housing Act)*, 1992.

Government of the Philippines, *Comprehensive Agrarian Reform Law of 1988 (Republic Act No. 6577)*, 1988.

Government of Philippines, *Constitution of Philippines*, 1987.

Government of the Philippines. *Civil Procedure Rule 67*, 1997.

Rwanda

Government of Rwanda, *Law N.32/2015 of 11/06/2015 relating to expropriation in the public interest. Official Gazette N.35 of 31/08/2015*, 2015.

Government of Rwanda, *Law N.43/2013 of 16/06/2013 governing land in Rwanda*, 2013.

Government of Rwanda, *Law No. 18/2007 Relating to Expropriation in the Public*, 2007.

Government of Rwanda, *Organic Law No. 08/2005 Determining the Use and Management of Land in Rwanda*, 2005.

Government of Rwanda, *Constitution of Rwanda*, 2003.

Sierra Leone

Government of Sierra Leone, *Draft National Land Policy of Sierra Leone*, 2014.

Government of Sierra Leone, *Constitution of Sierra Leone*, 1991.

Government of Sierra Leone, *Public Lands Ordinance Cap. 116*, 1960.

Government of Sierra Leone, *Public Lands Ordinance*, 1960.

South Africa

Government of South Africa, *Communal Land Rights Act (No. 11 of 2004).*

Government of South Africa, *Property Valuation Act, 2014 (No. 17 of 2014)*, 2014.

Government of South Africa. *Promotion of Administrative Justice Act*, 2000.

Government of South Africa, *National Forest Act,* 1998.

Government of South Africa, *Prevention from and Illegal Eviction and Unlawful Occupation Act*, 1998.

Government of South Africa, *Interim Protection of Informal Land Rights Act 31 of 1996*, 1996 (Amended 2016).

Government of South Africa, *Communal Property Associations Act, No. 28 of 1997*, 1996.

Government of South Africa, *Constitution of South Africa*, 1996.

Government of South Africa, *Expropriation Act,* 1975.

South Sudan

Government of South Sudan, *Land Act*, 2009.

Government of South Sudan, *Transitional Constitution*, 2011.

Sri Lanka

Government of Sri Lanka, *Land Acquisition Regulations*, 2009.

Government of Sri Lanka, *Water's Edge Judgement S.C.*, (F/R) No. 352/2007, 2007.

Government of Sri Lanka, *National Involuntary Resettlement Policy*, 2001.

Government of Sri Lanka, *Constitution of Sri Lanka*, 1978.

Government of Sri Lanka, *Land Acquisition Act CAP. 295*, 1950 (Amended 1994).

Swaziland

Government of Swaziland, *Acquisition of Property*, Act No. 10 of 1961, 1961.

Government of the Kingdom of Swaziland, Support to NEPAD-CAADP Implementation, TCP/SWA/2910 (I).

Government of Swaziland, *Constitution of Swaziland, 2005.*

Taiwan

Government of Taiwan, Indigenous People's Basic Law, 2005.

Government of Taiwan, *Expropriation Act*, 2000.

Government of Taiwan, *Constitution of Taiwan (Amended 2000)*, 1947.

Government of Taiwan, *The Land Act*, 1930 (Amended 2006).

Tanzania

Government of Tanzania, *Village Land Regulations (L.N. No. 86 of 2001)*, 2002.

Government of Tanzania, *The Land (Assessment of the Value of Land for Compensation) Regulations*, 2001.

Government of Tanzania, *The Land Act*, 1999.

Government of Tanzania, *Village Land Act*, 1999.

Government of Tanzania, *Constitution of Tanzania*, 1977.

Government of Tanzania, *Land Acquisition Act (Act No. 47 of 1967)*, 1967.

Thailand

Government of Thailand, *Immovable Property Expropriation Act, B.E. 2530*, 1987.

Government of Thailand, *Regulation of the Prime Minister's Office on the Issuance of Community Land Title Deeds*, 2011.

Government of Thailand, *Act Promulgating the Land Code B.E. 2497*, 2008.

Government of Thailand, *Constitution of Thailand*, 2007.

Trinidad and Tobago

Government of Trinidad and Tobago, *Land Surveyors Act (33 of 1996)*, 1996.

Government of Trinidad and Tobago, *Land Acquisition Act Ch. 58:01*, 1994.

Government of Trinidad and Tobago, *Constitution of Trinidad and Tobago*, 1976 (amended 2000).

Government of Trinidad and Tobago, *Valuation of Land Act (Cap. 58:03)*, 1969 (amended 2009).

Government of Trinidad and Tobago, *Administration of Estates (Act 35 of 1913)*, 1913.

Uganda

Government of Uganda, *Land Act (No. 16 of 1998)*, 1998.

Government of Uganda, *Constitution of Uganda*, 1995.

Government of Uganda, *Land Acquisition* Act (Ch. 226), 1965.

Vietnam

Government of Vietnam, *Constitution of Vietnam*, 2014.

Government of Vietnam, *Regulations on Compensation, Support, and Resettlement Upon Land Expropriation by the State*, 2014.

Government of Vietnam, *Land Law No. 45/2013/QH13*, 2013.

Government of Vietnam, *Law on Forest Protection and Development*, 2004.

Zambia

Government of Zambia, *Constitution of Zambia*, 2016.

Government of Zambia, *Forest Act, No. 7*, 2015.

Government of Zambia. Land Acquisition (Prescribed Forms) Regulations (Cap. 189), 2006.

Government of Zambia, *Land Act No. 29 of 1995*, 1995.

Government of Zambia, *Land Acquisition Act*, 1970.

Zimbabwe

Government of Zimbabwe, *Constitution of Zimbabwe*, 2013.

Government of Zimbabwe, *Land Acquisition (Disposal of Rural Land) Regulations (S.I. No. 287 of 1999)*, 1999.

Government of Zimbabwe, *Land Acquisition Act, Ch. 20:10*, 1992.

Government of Zimbabwe, *Communal Land Act Ch. 20:04 (amended 2002)*, 1983.

Appendix

Table 19: Chapter 2- Expropriation Indicators

Y= Yes
P= Partial
N= No

	Do the national laws provide a clear definition of public purpose?	Does the national laws require the government to minimize the amount of land acquired?	Do the national laws require a social impact assessment?	Do the national laws require an environmental impact assessment?	Do the nation laws recognize FPIC?	Do the national laws require the government to weigh the costs and benefits of the expropriation?
Afghanistan[1]	Y	Y	Y	Y	N	N
Angola[2]	N	N	N	Y	N	N
Argentina[3]	N	N	N	Y	N	N
Bangladesh[4]	N	N	N	Y	N	N
Belize[5]	N	N	N	Y	N	N
Bhutan[6]	N	N	N	Y	N	N
Botswana[7]	N	N	N	Y	N	N
Brazil[8]	P	N	N	Y	P	N
Burkina Faso[9]	P	N	N	Y	N	Y
Cambodia[10]	P	N	N	Y	N	N
China[11]	P	N	N	Y	N	N
Ecuador[12]	P	N	N	Y	P	N
Eritrea[13]	N	N	N	N	N	N
Ethiopia[14]	N	N	N	Y	N	N
Ghana[15]	N	N	N	Y	N	N
Honduras[16]	N	N	N	Y	P	N
Hong Kong[17]	N	N	N	Y	N	N
India[18]	Y	Y	Y	Y	Y	Y
Indonesia[19]	Y	N	Y	Y	Y	Y
Kazakhstan[20]	P	N	N	Y	N	N
Kenya[21]	P	N	N	Y	N	N
Laos[22]	N	N	Y	Y	N	N
Lesotho[23]	P	Y	N	Y	N	N
Liberia[24]	N	N	N	Y	N	N
Malaysia[25]	N	Y	N	Y	N	N
Mexico[26]	P	N	N	Y	N	N
Mongolia[27]	Y	N	N	Y	N	N
Myanmar[28]	N	N	N	Y	N	N
Namibia[29]	N	N	N	Y	N	N
Nepal[30]	N	N	N	Y	N	N
Nicaragua[31]	N	N	N	Y	N	N
Nigeria[32]	P	N	N	Y	N	N

	Do the national laws require a feasibility study?	Do the national laws require the government to survey affected landholders?	Do the national laws require the government to inform affected landholders?	Do the national laws require the government to consult affected landholders?	Do the national laws grant reacquisition rights to affected landholders?
Afghanistan[1]	N	Y	Y	Y	N
Angola[2]	N	N	N	N	N
Argentina[3]	N	N	N	N	N
Bangladesh[4]	N	N	N	N	P
Belize[5]	N	N	Y	N	N
Bhutan[6]	N	N	N	N	N
Botswana[7]	N	N	N	N	N
Brazil[8]	N	N	N	P	N
Burkina Faso[9]	N	N	Y	Y	N
Cambodia[10]	N	P	Y	Y	Y
China[11]	Y	P	P	P	P
Ecuador[12]	N	N	P	P	N
Eritrea[13]	N	N	N	N	N
Ethiopia[14]	N	N	N	P	Y
Ghana[15]	N	N	N	N	Y
Honduras[16]	N	N	N	P	N
Hong Kong[17]	N	N	N	N	N
India[18]	Y	Y	Y	Y	P
Indonesia[19]	Y	Y	Y	Y	N
Kazakhstan[20]	N	N	N	N	N
Kenya[21]	N	N	N	N	Y
Laos[22]	N	Y	Y	Y	N
Lesotho[23]	N	N	N	Y	N
Liberia[24]	N	N	N	N	N
Malaysia[25]	Y	N	Y	N	N
Mexico[26]	N	N	N	N	N
Mongolia[27]	N	N	Y	N	N
Myanmar[28]	N	N	N	N	N
Namibia[29]	N	N	N	N	N
Nepal[30]	N	N	Y	N	Y
Nicaragua[31]	N	N	N	P	N
Nigeria[32]	N	N	N	N	N

	Do the national laws provide a clear definition of public purpose?	Does the national laws require the government to minimize the amount of land acquired?	Do the national laws require a social impact assessment?	Do the national laws require an environmental impact assessment?	Do the nation laws recognize FPIC?	Do the national laws require the government to weigh the costs and benefits of the expropriation?
Pakistan[33]	N	N	N	Y	N	N
Papua New Guinea[34]	P	N	N	Y	N	N
Peru[35]	N	N	N	Y	Y	N
Philippines[36]	N	N	N	Y	Y	N
Rwanda[37]	Y	N	N	Y	N	N
Sierra Leone[38]	N	N	N	Y	N	N
South Africa[39]	N	N	N	Y	N	N
South Sudan[40]	P	N	Y	Y	P	P
Sri Lanka[41]	N	N	N	Y	N	N
Swaziland[42]	P	N	N	Y	N	N
Taiwan[43]	P	Y	N	Y	Y	Y
Tanzania[44]	P	N	N	Y	P	N
Thailand[45]	P	N	N	Y	N	N
Trinidad and Tobago[46]	N	N	N	Y	N	N
Uganda[47]	N	N	N	Y	N	N
Vietnam[48]	P	N	N	Y	N	P
Zambia[49]	N	N	N	Y	N	N
Zimbabwe[50]	N	N	N	Y	N	N

	Do the national laws require a feasibility study?	Do the national laws require the government to survey affected landholders?	Do the national laws require the government to inform affected landholders?	Do the national laws require the government to consult affected landholders?	Do the national laws grant reacquisition rights to affected landholders?
Pakistan[33]	N	N	N	N	N
Papua New Guinea[34]	N	N	N	N	N
Peru[35]	N	P	P	P	N
Philippines[36]	N	P	N	P	P
Rwanda[37]	N	Y	Y	P	N
Sierra Leone[38]	N	N	N	N	Y
South Africa[39]	N	N	Y	N	N
South Sudan[40]		N	P	P	N
Sri Lanka[41]	N	N	N	N	N
Swaziland[42]	N	N	N	N	N
Taiwan[43]	Y	Y	Y	Y	Y
Tanzania[44]	N	N	Y	P	N
Thailand[45]	N	N	Y	P	N
Trinidad and Tobago[46]	N	N	Y	N	N
Uganda[47]	N	N	N	N	N
Vietnam[48]	N	Y	Y	N	N
Zambia[49]	N	N	N	P	N
Zimbabwe[50]	N	N	Y	N	P

Table 20: Chapter 3- Compensation Eligibility Indicators

	Is compensation provided for formally recognized IPLC tenure rights?	Is compensation provided for unregistered IPLC tenure rights?	Is compensation provided for formally recognized IPLC tenure rights regardless of whether the IPLCs developed or made improvements on the land?
Afghanistan[51] (all communities)	YES	PARTIAL	YES
Bangladesh[52] (all communities)	NO	NO	NO
Botswana[53] (all communities)	YES	NO	YES
Burkina Faso[54] (all communities)	YES	PARTIAL	YES
Cambodia[55] (indigenous communities)	PARTIAL	NO	NO
China[56] (all communities)	YES	NO	NO
Ethiopia[57] (all communities)	YES	NO	NO
Ghana[58] (all communities)	YES	NO	YES
Hong Kong[59] (all communities)	NO	NO	NO
India[60] (all communities)	YES	PARTIAL	YES
Indonesia[61] (all communities)	YES	NO	YES
Kazakhstan[62] (all communities)	NO	NO	NO
Kenya[63] (all communities)	YES	YES	YES
Liberia[64] (all communities)	YES	PARTIAL	YES
Malaysia[65] (all communities)	YES	NO	YES
Mongolia[66] (all communities)	NO	NO	NO
Namibia[67] (all communities)	YES	NO	NO
Nigeria[68] (all communities)	YES	NO	NO

	Is compensation provided for formally recognized IPLC tenure rights?	Is compensation provided for unregistered IPLC tenure rights?	Is compensation provided for formally recognized IPLC tenure rights regardless of whether the IPLCs developed or made improvements on the land?
Philippines[69] (indigenous communities)	YES	YES	YES
Rwanda[70] (all communities)	NO	NO	NO
South Africa[71] (all communities)	YES	YES	YES
South Sudan[72] (all communities)	YES	YES	YES
Sri Lanka[73] (all communities)	NO	NO	NO
Taiwan[74] (indigenous communities)	YES	NO	YES
Tanzania[75] (all communities)	YES	YES	PARTIAL
Thailand[76] (all communities)	NO	NO	NO
Uganda[77] (all communities)	YES	YES	YES
Vietnam[78] (all communities)	YES	PARTIAL	YES
Zambia[79] (all communities)	YES	YES	NO
Zimbabwe[80] (all communities)	YES	NO	PARTIAL

Table 21: Chapter 4- Compensation Valuation Indicators

	Does the law allow for assessors to follow an alternative approach instead of a "fair market value approach" to calculating compensation in cases where land markets are weak or non-existent?	Does the law require assessors to take into account the loss of business and other economic activities?	Does the law require assessors to take into account the improvements made on the land?	Does the law require assessors to take into account intangible land values (e.g. cultural, social, historical land values)?	A right to negotiate compensation prior to the moment at which the compensation decision is made?
Afghanistan[81]	NO	YES	YES	NO	NO
Angola[82]	NO	NO	YES	NO	NO
Argentina[83]	NO	NO	PARTIAL	NO	YES
Bangladesh[84]	NO	YES	YES	NO	NO
Belize[85]	YES	YES	YES	NO	YES
Bhutan[86]	PARTIAL	PARTIAL	NO	YES	PARTIAL
Botswana[87]	NO	YES	YES	NO	YES
Brazil[88]	NO	YES	YES	NO	NO
Burkina Faso[89]	NO	PARTIAL	YES	NO	YES
Cambodia[90]	YES	YES	PARTIAL	NO	YES
China[91]	NO	YES	YES	NO	YES
Ecuador[92]	NO	NO	NO	NO	NO
Eritrea[93]	NO	NO	NO	NO	YES
Ethiopia[94]	YES	PARTIAL	YES	NO	NO
Ghana[95]	YES	PARTIAL	PARTIAL	PARTIAL	YES
Honduras[96]	NO	NO	YES	NO	PARTIAL
Hong Kong[97]	NO	YES	PARTIAL	NO	YES
India[98]	PARTIAL	YES	YES	PARTIAL	YES
Indonesia[99]	NO	YES	YES	NO	YES
Kazakhstan[100]	NO	YES	PARTIAL	NO	YES
Kenya[101]	PARTIAL	YES	YES	NO	YES
Laos[102]	PARTIAL	YES	YES	PARTIAL	YES
Lesotho[103]	PARTIAL	YES	NO	NO	NO
Liberia[104]	NO	NO	NO	NO	NO
Mexico[105]	NO	NO	YES	NO	NO
Malaysia[106]	NO	YES	PARTIAL	NO	YES
Mongolia[107]	PARTIAL	PARTIAL	YES	NO	YES
Myanmar[108]	NO	YES	YES	NO	NO
Namibia[109]	NO	PARTIAL	PARTIAL	NO	PARTIAL
Nepal[110]	NO	YES	YES	PARTIAL	NO
Nicaragua[111]	NO	NO	NO	NO	PARTIAL
Nigeria[112]	NO	NO	YES	NO	NO

	Does the law provide affected populations with the right to opt for alternative land instead of compensation in cash?	Does the law establish special protections for women landholders regarding compensation entitlements?	Does the law require that compensation must be paid prior to the taking of possession of the land or within a specified timeframe thereafter?	Are affected populations granted the right to appeal decisions on the amount of compensation in court or before a tribunal?
Afghanistan[81]	YES	NO	NO	YES
Angola[82]	NO	NO	NO	NO
Argentina[83]	PARTIAL	NO	PARTIAL	YES
Bangladesh[84]	NO	NO	YES	YES
Belize[85]	NO	NO	NO	YES
Bhutan[86]	PARTIAL	NO	YES	NO
Botswana[87]	PARTIAL	NO	YES	PARTIAL
Brazil[88]	NO	NO	PARTIAL	YES
Burkina Faso[89]	PARTIAL	NO	NO	YES
Cambodia[90]	YES	NO	YES	YES
China[91]	NO	NO	PARTIAL	YES
Ecuador[92]	NO	NO	YES	YES
Eritrea[93]	YES	NO	YES	YES
Ethiopia[94]	PARTIAL	NO	YES	YES
Ghana[95]	YES	NO	NO	PARTIAL
Honduras[96]	NO	NO	NO	YES
Hong Kong[97]	NO	NO	NO	YES
India[98]	YES	PARTIAL	PARTIAL	YES
Indonesia[99]	YES	NO	YES	YES
Kazakhstan[100]	YES	NO	YES	YES
Kenya[101]	YES	NO	NO	YES
Laos[102]	YES	NO	YES	YES
Lesotho[103]	NO	NO	YES	PARTIAL
Liberia[104]	NO	NO	NO	YES
Mexico[105]	NO	NO	YES	NO
Malaysia[106]	NO	NO	PARTIAL	YES
Mongolia[107]	YES	NO	PARTIAL	YES
Myanmar[108]	NO	NO	NO	PARTIAL
Namibia[109]	NO	NO	PARTIAL	PARTIAL
Nepal[110]	YES	NO	PARTIAL	NO
Nicaragua[111]	NO	NO	NO	
Nigeria[112]	YES	NO	NO	YES

	Does the law allow for assessors to follow an alternative approach instead of a "fair market value approach" to calculating compensation in cases where land markets are weak or non-existent?	Does the law require assessors to take into account the loss of business and other economic activities?	Does the law require assessors to take into account the improvements made on the land?	Does the law require assessors to take into account intangible land values (e.g. cultural, social, historical land values)?	A right to negotiate compensation prior to the moment at which the compensation decision is made?
Pakistan[113]	NO	YES	YES	NO	NO
Papua New Guinea[114]	NO	NO	NO	NO	YES
Peru[115]	NO	YES	YES	NO	NO
Philippines[116]	NO	PARTIAL	YES	YES	YES
Rwanda[117]	NO	YES	YES	NO	PARTIAL
Sierra Leone[118]	YES	YES	YES	NO	YES
South Africa[119]	YES	YES	YES	NO	YES
South Sudan[120]	NO	PARTIAL	YES	NO	YES
Sri Lanka[121]	NO	YES	NO	PARTIAL	YES
Swaziland[122]	NO	YES	PARTIAL	NO	YES
Taiwan[123]	NO	YES	YES	NO	PARTIAL
Tanzania[124]	YES	YES	YES	PARTIAL	YES
Thailand[125]	NO	YES	PARTIAL	NO	NO
Trinidad and Tobago[126]	NO	NO	YES	NO	NO
Uganda[127]	NO	PARTIAL	PARTIAL	NO	YES
Vietnam[128]	NO	YES	YES	PARTIAL	YES
Zambia[129]	NO	NO	YES	NO	YES
Zimbabwe[130]	NO	PARTIAL	YES	NO	NO

	Does the law provide affected populations with the right to opt for alternative land instead of compensation in cash?	Does the law establish special protections for women landholders regarding compensation entitlements?	Does the law require that compensation must be paid prior to the taking of possession of the land or within a specified timeframe thereafter?	Are affected populations granted the right to appeal decisions on the amount of compensation in court or before a tribunal?
Pakistan[113]	NO	NO	NO	PARTIAL
Papua New Guinea[114]	NO	NO	PARTIAL	YES
Peru[115]	NO	NO	NO	YES
Philippines[116]	YES	NO	YES	YES
Rwanda[117]	PARTIAL	NO	YES	PARTIAL
Sierra Leone[118]	NO	NO	NO	YES
South Africa[119]	NO	NO	PARTIAL	YES
South Sudan[120]	YES	NO	PARTIAL	YES
Sri Lanka[121]	YES	NO	PARTIAL	YES
Swaziland[122]	NO	NO	YES	PARTIAL
Taiwan[123]	PARTIAL	NO	YES	YES
Tanzania[124]	YES	NO	NO	YES
Thailand[125]	NO	NO	YES	YES
Trinidad and Tobago[126]	NO	NO	PARTIAL	YES
Uganda[127]	NO	NO	YES	YES
Vietnam[128]	YES	NO	YES	NO
Zambia[129]	YES	NO	NO	YES
Zimbabwe[130]	PARTIAL	NO	YES	PARTIAL

Table 22: Chapter 5- Resettlement Indicators

	Is there a national-level, resettlement policy that is legally binding on all projects involving the expropriation of land?	Do the national laws provide displaced persons with relocation allowance?	Do the national laws provide displaced persons with alternative land, housing, or resettlement?	Do the national laws provide displaced persons with productive or suitable alternative land?
Afghanistan[131]	NO	NO	PARTIAL	NO
Angola[132]	NO	NO	NO	NO
Argentina[133]	NO	NO	PARTIAL	NO
Bangladesh[134]	NO	NO	NO	NO
Belize[135]	NO	NO	PARTIAL	NO
Bhutan[136]	NO	NO	PARTIAL	NO
Botswana[137]	NO	PARTIAL	PARTIAL	NO
Brazil[138]	NO	NO	NO	NO
Burkina Faso[139]	NO	NO	PARTIAL	NO
Cambodia[140]	NO	NO	NO	NO
China[141]	PARTIAL	YES	PARTIAL	NO
Ecuador[142]	NO	NO	NO	NO
Eritrea[143]	NO	NO	PARTIAL	NO
Ethiopia[144]	NO	PARTIAL	PARTIAL	NO
Ghana[145]	NO	NO	PARTIAL	PARTIAL
Honduras[146]	UNCLEAR	UNCLEAR	UNCLEAR	UNCLEAR
Hong Kong[147]	NO	PARTIAL	NO	NO
India[148]	YES	YES	YES	PARTIAL
Indonesia[149]	NO	PARTIAL	PARTIAL	NO
Kazakhstan[150]	NO	NO	PARTIAL	NO
Kenya[151]	NO	PARTIAL	PARTIAL	NO
Laos[152]	YES	YES	YES	YES
Lesotho[153]	NO	NO	NO	NO
Liberia[154]	NO	NO	NO	NO
Mexico[155]	NO	NO	NO	NO
Malaysia[156]	NO	PARTIAL	NO	NO
Mongolia[157]	NO	PARTIAL	PARTIAL	NO
Myanmar[158]	NO	PARTIAL	PARTIAL	NO
Nicaragua[159]	NO	NO	NO	NO
Namibia[160]	NO	NO	NO	NO
Nepal[161]	NO	PARTIAL	PARTIAL	NO
Nigeria[162]	NO	NO	PARTIAL	NO
Pakistan[163]	NO	PARTIAL	PARTIAL	NO
Papua New Guinea[164]	NO	NO	NO	NO
Peru[165]	NO	NO	NO	NO
Philippines[166]	PARTIAL	PARTIAL	YES	PARTIAL

	Do the national laws require the government to consult affected populations during the resettlement process?	Do the national laws require the government to minimize or avoid involuntary resettlement?	Do the national-level laws require the government or acquiring bodies to provide sufficient funding to implement resettlement programs?
Afghanistan[131]	NO	NO	NO
Angola[132]	NO	NO	NO
Argentina[133]	NO	NO	NO
Bangladesh[134]	NO	NO	NO
Belize[135]	NO	NO	NO
Bhutan[136]	NO	NO	NO
Botswana[137]	NO	NO	NO
Brazil[138]	NO	NO	NO
Burkina Faso[139]	NO	NO	NO
Cambodia[140]	NO	NO	NO
China[141]	YES	NO	NO
Ecuador[142]	NO	NO	NO
Eritrea[143]	NO	NO	NO
Ethiopia[144]	NO	NO	NO
Ghana[145]	NO	NO	NO
Honduras[146]	UNCLEAR	UNCLEAR	NO
Hong Kong[147]	NO	NO	NO
India[148]	YES	YES	YES
Indonesia[149]	NO	NO	NO
Kazakhstan[150]	NO	NO	NO
Kenya[151]	NO	NO	NO
Laos[152]	YES	YES	YES
Lesotho[153]	NO	NO	NO
Liberia[154]	NO	NO	NO
Mexico[155]	NO	NO	NO
Malaysia[156]	NO	NO	NO
Mongolia[157]	NO	NO	NO
Myanmar[158]	NO	NO	NO
Nicaragua[159]	NO	NO	NO
Namibia[160]	NO	NO	NO
Nepal[161]	NO	NO	NO
Nigeria[162]	NO	NO	NO
Pakistan[163]	NO	NO	NO
Papua New Guinea[164]	NO	NO	NO
Peru[165]	NO	NO	NO
Philippines[166]	PARTIAL	PARTIAL	NO

	Is there a national-level, resettlement policy that is legally binding on all projects involving the expropriation of land?	Do the national laws provide displaced persons with relocation allowance?	Do the national laws provide displaced persons with alternative land, housing, or resettlement?	Do the national laws provide displaced persons with productive or suitable alternative land?
Rwanda[167]	NO	NO	PARTIAL	NO
South Africa[168]	NO	PARTIAL	NO	NO
South Sudan[169]	NO	PARTIAL	PARTIAL	NO
Sierra Leone[170]	NO	PARTIAL	NO	NO
Sri Lanka[171]	NO	PARTIAL	PARTIAL	NO
Swaziland[172]	NO	NO	NO	NO
Taiwan[173]	NO	PARTIAL	PARTIAL	NO
Tanzania[174]	NO	PARTIAL	PARTIAL	NO
Thailand[175]	NO	NO	NO	NO
Trinidad and Tobago[176]	NO	NO	NO	NO
Uganda[177]	NO	NO	NO	NO
Vietnam[178]	YES	YES	YES	PARTIAL
Zambia[179]	NO	NO	PARTIAL	NO
Zimbabwe[180]	NO	NO	PARTIAL	NO

	Do the national laws require the government to consult affected populations during the resettlement process?	Do the national laws require the government to minimize or avoid involuntary resettlement?	Do the national-level laws require the government or acquiring bodies to provide sufficient funding to implement resettlement programs?
Rwanda[167]	NO	NO	NO
South Africa[168]	NO	NO	NO
South Sudan[169]	YES	NO	NO
Sierra Leone[170]	NO	NO	NO
Sri Lanka[171]	NO	NO	NO
Swaziland[172]	NO	NO	NO
Taiwan[173]	NO	PARTIAL	NO
Tanzania[174]	NO	NO	NO
Thailand[175]	NO	NO	NO
Trinidad and Tobago[176]	NO	NO	NO
Uganda[177]	NO	NO	NO
Vietnam[178]	YES	NO	YES
Zambia[179]	NO	NO	NO
Zimbabwe[180]	NO	NO	NO

Table 23: List of Country Peer Reviewers

Afghanistan	Dr. Michael McDermott International Land Policy, Legal, Institutional and Valuation Consultant
Argentina	Professor Keith Rosenn University of Miami Law School
Bangladesh	Mamun Ur Rashid Uttaran
Brazil	Professor Keith Rosenn University of Miami Law School
China	Dr. Linlin Li Land Academy for National Development
Cambodia	Sinù Fogarizzu International Land Coalition (ILC) Centre for Development and Environment (CDE) Country office in the Lao PDR
Indonesia	Susanna Price Australia National University
India	Pranab Choudhury, Researcher and Practitioner Centre for Land Governance, Natural Resources Management Council
Nigeria	Dr. Yakubu Bununu Ahmadu Bello University
Kenya	Dr. Liz Alden Wily Independent Land Tenure Specialist
Laos	Dr. Micah L. Ingalls Senior Scientist Mekong Region Land Governance, Center for Development and Environment (CDE)
Nepal	Nayna Jhaveri Independent Land Tenure Specialist
Rwanda	Mireil Biraro Assistant Lecturer in the Department of Land Administration and Management- iNES- Ruhengeri (Rwanda)
Sierra Leone	Michael Solis, Trocaire Sierra Leone Dr. Caitlyn Ryan, University of Groningen Faculty of Law
South Africa	Dr. Bjorn Hoops University of Groningen
Sri Lanka	Sam Pillai Independent Expert on Displacement and Resettlement Lalanath De Silva, Head of Independent Redress Mechanism at Global Climate Fund
Tanzania	Godfrey Massay Landesa Tanzania

Uganda	Onesmus Mugyenyi, Advocates Coalition for Development and Environment
	Russel Rhoades, Sun Valley State University
	Liz Neate, Chartered Surveyor (working pro bono), Land and Equity Movement in Uganda
Thailand	Mekong Region Land Governance, Center for Development and Environment (CDE)
Vietnam	Mekong Region Land Governance, Center for Development and Environment (CDE)

* 'Peer Reviewers' in this table mean scholars who either (1) were sent the legal indicator data and asked to verify the data's accuracy or (2) through personal communication were able to verify that I referred to the proper laws when conducting the indicator analysis.

I kindly request that others please email nicholas.tagliarino@gmail.com in case they see any errors or needed adjustments to the legal analysis. All of the data and information is available at https://landportal.org/book/dataset/nkt-vggt16.

Endnotes

1 Article 5 of the Law on Land Acquisition 2017 states that "An individual's property shall be expropriated only for the purpose of implementation of projects of public interest: (1) Creating military centers and defense and security establishments. (2) Implementing approved plans of competent authorities. (3) Extracting mines and underground reservoirs. (4) Constructing manufacturing factories. (5) Constructing highways, roads, railways and all transportation lines and related establishments included in governmental projects. (6) Constructing gas and petroleum pipeline. (7) Constructing governmental airports and relevant establishments. (8) Constructing communication and information technology establishments, optical fiber cable network, networks of state television and radio. (9) Constructing and installing networks of power transmission and its pillars, networks of warmth and steam-houses included in governmental projects. (10) Constructing electricity dams, dams for water reservoir, valleys, canals and streams included in governmental projects. (11) Constructing networks of water supply and canalization, centers of waste collection and landfills and sewage included in governmental projects. (12) Constructing health, educational, training, research, sport, entertainment centers and establishments, kindergartens, orphanages and all other social and cultural establishments included in governmental projects. (13) Building mosques and all other religious places included in governmental projects. (14) Constructing complexes and residential towns included in governmental projects. (15) Individuals' properties shall also be expropriated for the purpose of protection of frontage, extension and expansion of the cases stated in paragraph (1) of this article." Under article 8 of the Law on Land Acquisition 2017, the Expropriating Authority must determine whether the land expropriated is the exact minimum area needed for the project. Article 7 of the Land Acquisition Act, 2017 states "The Expropriating Authority shall provide reasons for necessity of expropriation along with its objectives, quantitative and qualitative specifications of land, type and location of project with different options of implementation area of project, social and economic impact and implementation timeframe of the project in details to the government." Article 8 of the Land Acquisition Act, 2017 also requires the Expropriating Authority to study and evaluate the environmental and social impacts of projects. Article 6 of the 2017 Law on Land Acquisition states "(1) Properties having historical and cultural monuments, and national protected areas shall not be expropriated. (2) Cultivatable lands and gardens, agricultural farms, forests, frontage of water resources and green areas which are important for environment protection shall be expropriated with the approval of the government." The Environment Law was enacted in 2005 and requires project developers to conduct an environmental impact assessment prior to initiating development projects. The laws assessed do not require the government to be sensitive to areas held by poor and vulnerable groups. The laws assessed do not recognize the indigenous right to Free Prior and Informed Consent (FPIC). According to Article 8 of the Law on Land Acquisition 2017, the Expropriating Authority must study and evaluate the environmental and social impacts resulting from the implementation of the project. According to Article 8 of the Law on Land Acquisition 2017, the Expropriating Authority must prepare a list of owners, possessors and affected persons in the area of expropriation. Article 8 of the Law on Land Acquisition 2017 states that the Expropriating Authority must provide reasons regarding public interests of the project. Article 9 of the Law on Land Acquisition 2017 states "The Expropriating Authority shall, after approval of the plan by the evaluation committee and approval of project by the government, inform the property owner and affected persons under expropriation, six months prior to its implementation through mass media and local competent administrative source regarding the following issues (1) Objective of expropriation; (2) Type and adequate size of property needed for expropriation (3) Detailed plan of the project (4) Estimation of value of property needed for expropriation on the basis of minimum and maximum value of the land (5) Ensuring allocation of prior and just payment of compensation (6) Starting date of project." According to Article 8 of the Law on Land Acquisition 2017, the Expropriating Authority must consult with the community in the area expropriated regarding the implementation of the project. The laws assessed do not grant affected persons the right to reacquire their land in the event that the project is abandoned or the land is no longer needed for a public purpose. Article 42 of the Law on Land Acquisition 2017, "Whenever the expropriated property, after implementation and conclusion of the project, is not used for the previously approved purpose by the Expropriating Authority; the Expropriating Authority shall hand over the expropriated property to the Municipality if located inside the scope of masterplan, and to the Arazi Office if located outside the scope of masterplan."

2 The laws assessed do not provide a clear definition of public purpose to allow for judicial review. Article 12(2) of the Land Law, 2004 provides that "the State and local authorities may expropriate lands if they are to be utilized for a specific purpose of public utility." Furthermore, article 21 of the Decree No. 58/07 (2007) approving the General Regulation for Land Concession provides that "Lands over which a private property right has been constituted may, in cases contemplated in law, be the object of expropriation for public use or for temporary requisition." However these laws do not define the terms public utility or public use. Article 132 of General Regulation for Land Concession, 2007 states "The state or local authorities may, at any moment, expropriate, all or in part, the conceded lands, when so determined by of public utility objectives." The laws assessed do not require the government to minimize the amount of land acquired to the amount necessary to achieve a public purpose. The laws assessed do not require the government or project developers to conduct a social impact assessment prior to expropriating land. Angola's Environmental Impact Assessment Law – Decree No. 51/04, of 23 July 2004, as amended by Executive Decree 241/16, of 25 May 2016, which lays down the rules and procedures related to the environmental impact assessment of public and private projects. The laws assessed do not require the government to be sensitive to areas held by poor and vulnerable groups. The laws assessed do not recognize the indigenous right to Free Prior and Informed Consent (FPIC). Article 9 of the Land Law, 2004 states that " Lands belonging to rural communities may be expropriated by public utility or be the object of requisition by way of just indemnification." The laws assessed do not require the government to weigh the costs and benefits of the project prior to expropriating land. The laws assessed do not require the government to identify all affected persons prior to expropriating land. The laws assessed do not require the government to provide affected landholders with the reasons for expropriation. The laws assessed do not require the government to consult the public or affected populations prior to expropriating land. The laws assessed do not grant affected persons the right to reacquire their land in the event that the project is abandoned or the land is no longer needed for a public purpose.

3 Ley No. 21.499,1977 does not provide a clear definition of public purpose to allow for judicial review. The laws assessed do not require the government to minimize the amount of land acquired to the amount necessary to achieve a public purpose. The laws assessed do not require the government or project developers to conduct a social impact assessment prior to expropriating land. The General Environmental Law NO. 25675, 2002 requires an environmental impact assessment to be conducted prior to the initiation of projects that may impact the environment. The laws assessed do not require the government to be sensitive to areas held by poor and vulnerable groups. The Constitution empowers Congress to guarantee respect for the community possession and ownership of lands [indigenous communities] traditionally occupy, but this is only a legislative directive (not a right) (Sec. 75(17), Constitution, 1994). Ley de Tierras Rurales is silent on whether indigenous/community lands are protected by law. NOTE: After ratifying the Convention 169, the Argentinian Government passed Law 26.160 to comply with Art. 14.2 of ILO Convention 169 to prevent forcible eviction of indigenous groups on ancestral lands, but this law was only temporarily in effect until 2013. In 2006, the government launched the Agenda of Indigenous Community Land Survey by the National Institute for Indigenous Affairs, but this program was weakly implemented in Argentina. Since 2012, legal reformers have proposed including indigenous land rights as form of property right granted protection by Argentina's Civil Code, but the Code has not yet been amended. The laws assessed do not require the government to weigh the costs and benefits of the project prior to expropriating land. The laws assessed do not require the government to identify all affected persons prior to expropriating land. The laws assessed do not require the government to provide affected landholders with the reasons for expropriation. The laws assessed do not require the government to consult the public or affected populations prior to expropriating land. The laws assessed do not grant affected persons the right to reacquire their land in the event that the project is abandoned or the land is no longer needed for a public purpose.

4 The Deputy Commissioner is granted broad direction to establish a public purpose justification ("whenever it appears to the deputy commissioner that any property in any locality is needed or is likely to be needed for any public purpose or in the public interest"). Interested persons can object to the decision, and the Divisional Commission rules on the Deputy Commissioner's decision. But the Deputy or Divisional Commissioner's decision is final and "shall be considered conclusive evidence that the land is needed for a public purpose." (Sec. 3-5 of 1982 Acquisition and Requisition of Immovable Property

Ordinance, 1982). The laws assessed do not require the government to minimize the amount of land acquired to the amount necessary to achieve a public purpose. The laws assessed do not require the government or project developers to conduct a social impact assessment prior to expropriating land. While the Acquisition of Immovable Property Ordinance 1982 does not require the government to be sensitive to areas of environmental, cultural, and religious significance, Bangladesh passed the Environmental Conservation Act (1995) and the Environmental Conservation Rules (1997) which established a mandatory requirement that all projects must undergo an environmental impact assessment before such projects can begin. The laws assessed do not require the government to be sensitive to areas held by poor and vulnerable groups. The laws assessed do not recognize the indigenous right to Free Prior and Informed Consent (FPIC). Bangladesh has not ratified ILO Convention 169, an international human rights treaty that recognizes the indigenous right to given consent prior to acquisition of their land by the government or outsiders. The laws assessed do not require the government to weigh the costs and benefits of the project prior to expropriating land. The laws assessed do not require the government to identify all affected persons prior to expropriating land. Section 6 of the 1982 Ordinance establishes a notice requirement, which must only describe the particulars of the property to be acquired but not the reasons for justifying the acquisition as a public purpose. (Sec. 6(2), 1982 Ordinance) The laws assessed do not require the government to consult the public or affected populations prior to expropriating land. Once an acquisition project ends, the land is transferred back to the Deputy Commissioner. The Deputy Commissioner "may restore it to the person from whom was requisitioned the property, or his successor-in-interest, or to such other person as may appear but is not to the Deputy Commissioner to be entitled" but the Deputy Commissioner is under no legal obligation to grant reacqusition rights to affected landholders. (Sec. 24, The Acquisition and Requisition of Immovable Property Ordinance, 1982).

5 Article 3 of the Land Acquisition (Public Purposes) Act 2004 states "Whenever the Minister considers that any land should be acquired for a public purpose, he may cause a declaration to that effect to be made in the manner provided by this Section and the declaration shall be prima facie evidence that the land to which it relates is required for a public purpose." The law does not provide a clear definition of public purpose to allow for judicial review. The laws assessed do not require the government to minimize the amount of land acquired to the amount necessary to achieve a public purpose. The laws assessed do not require the government or project developers to conduct a social impact assessment prior to expropriating land. Although the Land Acquisition (Public Purposes) Act does not require the government to be sensitive to areas of cultural, religious and environmental significance, Belize passed the Environmental Protection Act in 1992 and the Environmental Impact Assessment Regulations (1995), which makes it mandatory for all project developers to conduct an EIA if the project will significantly affect the environment. The laws assessed do not require the government to be sensitive to areas held by poor and vulnerable groups. The laws assessed do not recognize the indigenous right to Free Prior and Informed Consent (FPIC). Belize has not ratified ILO Convention 169, an international human rights treaty that recognizes the indigenous right to given consent prior to acquisition of their land by the government or outsiders. The laws assessed do not require the government to weigh the costs and benefits of the project prior to expropriating land. The laws assessed do not require the government to identify all affected persons prior to expropriating land. Article 3(3) of the Land Acquisition (Public Purposes) Act, 2000 states that expropriation declarations published in the Gazette must specify "(a) the district in which the land is situated; (b) a description of the land, giving the approximate area and such other particulars as are necessary to identify the land; (c) in cases where a plan has been prepared, the place where, and the time when a plan of the land can be inspected; (d) the public purpose for which the land is required." The laws assessed do not require the government to consult the public or affected populations prior to expropriating land. The laws assessed do not grant affected persons the right to reacquire their land in the event that the project is abandoned or the land is no longer needed for a public purpose.

6 Section 142 of the Land Act, 2007 states "the government may acquire a registered land for public interests." However, the Land Act does not provide a clear definition of public purpose to allow for judicial review. The laws assessed do not require the government to minimize the amount of land acquired to the amount necessary to achieve a public purpose. The laws assessed do not require the government or project developers to conduct a social impact assessment prior to expropriating land. Section 146 of the

Land Act, 2007 states "acquisition of the land occupied by religious monuments shall be avoided." The laws assessed do not require the government to be sensitive to areas held by poor and vulnerable groups. The laws assessed do not recognize the indigenous right to Free Prior and Informed Consent (FPIC). The laws assessed do not require the government to weigh the costs and benefits of the project prior to expropriating land. The laws assessed do not require the government to identify all affected persons prior to expropriating land. The laws assessed do not require the government to provide affected landholders with the reasons for expropriation. The laws assessed do not require the government to consult the public or affected populations prior to expropriating land. The laws assessed do not grant affected persons the right to reacquire their land in the event that the project is abandoned or the land is no longer needed for a public purpose.

7 Section 3 of the Acquisition of Property Act 1955 states "(1) the President may acquire any real property where the acquisition of such property is necessary or expedient- (a) in the interests of defence, public safety, public order, public morality, public health, town and country planning or land settlement; or (b) in order to secure the development or utilization of that or other property for a purpose beneficial to the community..." The laws assessed do not require the government to minimize the amount of land acquired to the amount necessary to achieve a public purpose. The laws assessed do not require the government or project developers to conduct a social impact assessment prior to expropriating land. While the Acquisition of Property Act, 1955 does not require the government to be sensitive to areas of cultural, environmental, and religious significance, Botswana enacted the Environmental Impact Assessment Act 2011 which requires project developers to conduct an EIA prior to initiating development projects. Presumably, this Act applies to expropriations and requires expropriating authorities to be sensitive to areas of environmental significance. The laws assessed do not require the government to be sensitive to areas held by poor and vulnerable groups. The laws assessed do not recognize the indigenous right to Free Prior and Informed Consent (FPIC). The laws assessed do not require the government to weigh the costs and benefits of the project prior to expropriating land. The laws assessed do not require the government to identify all affected persons prior to expropriating land. The laws assessed do not require the government to provide affected landholders with the reasons for expropriation. The laws assessed do not require the government to consult the public or affected populations prior to expropriating land. The laws assessed do not grant affected persons the right to reacquire their land in the event that the project is abandoned or the land is no longer needed for a public purpose.

8 Government authorities in Brazil can expropriate land in order to serve the public interest and social interest. The General Expropriations Law (Law no. 4132 of 1962) defines the circumstances in which expropriations for the social interest can be conducted. Article 2 defines the following as within the social interest: "I. the use of any unproductive or exploited property that does not correspond to the housing, work and consumption needs of the population centers in order to meet economic goals, II. the installation or intensification of crops in areas in which the farm is not subject to an agricultural zoning plan, III. the establishment and maintenance of colonies or cooperatives of settlement and agricultural work; IV. the maintenance of squatters in urban areas where, with the express or tacit tolerance of the owner, they have built their qualification, forming residential nuclei of more than 10 (ten) families; V. the construction of popular homes VI. the lands and waters susceptible of extraordinary valorization, by the conclusion of works and public services, especially of sanitation, ports, transportation, electrification storage of water and irrigation, in the case in which they are not said socially utilized areas; VII. the protection of the soil and the preservation of courses and sources of water and forest reserves; VIII. the use of areas, places or goods that, due to their characteristics, are appropriate to the development of tourist activities." Under the Constitution, land can be expropriated when it is not meeting its social function: The social function is met when the rural property complies simultaneously with, according to the criteria and standards prescribed by law, the following requirements: "(I) rational and adequate use; (II) adequate use of available natural resources and preservation of the environment; (III) compliance with the provisions that regulate labour relations; (IV) exploitation that favours the well-being of the owners and labourers (art. 186). Article 5 of the Expropriation Statute, 1941(Decreto-Lei No. 3.365/41) allows the government to expropriate land for" "public utility" "projects, which are defined as projects relating to " "a) national security; b) the defense of the State; c) public aid in case of disaster d) public health; e) the creation and improvement of population centers, their regular supply livelihoods; f) the industrial use of mines and mineral deposits, water and hydraulic

power; g) public assistance, works of hygiene and decoration, health houses, clinics, weather stations and medical supplies; h) the exploitation or conservation of public services; i) opening, maintenance and improvement of public roads or public parks; The execution of development plans; the parceling of land, with or without building to its best economic use, hygienic or aesthetic; The construction or expansion of industrial districts; j) the operation of public transport means; k) the preservation and conservation of historical and artistic monuments, isolated or integrated in urban or rural settings, as well as measures necessary to maintain them and enhance them the most valuable aspects or characteristic and also the local and landscape protection particularly endowed by nature; l) the preservation and proper maintenance of files, documents and other movable assets of historical or artistic value; m) the construction of public buildings, memorials and cemeteries; n) the creation of stadiums, airfields or airstrips for aircraft; o) the reissuing or disclosure of work or inventions of a scientific, artistic or literary nature; p) other cases provided by special law." Pursuant to Article 184 of the Constitution of Brazil, the government is also empowered to expropriate any rural property due to social interest for the purposes of agrarian reform (in case the property is not meeting its social function). The laws assessed do not require the government to minimize the amount of land acquired to the amount necessary to achieve a public purpose. The laws assessed do not require the government or project developers to conduct a social impact assessment prior to expropriating land. While there are no clear legal provisions which protect cultural or religious property from expropriation, the government and private developers must conduct an environmental impact assessment prior to initiating projects that have an impact on the environment pursuant to Environmental Protection Act, Chapter 328 (No. 22 of 1992), Amendment 2009 (No. 5); Environmental Impact Assessment Regulations 1995 (No. 107), Amendment 2007 (no. 24); Procedures Manual for the Preparation of an EIA, 2011. Article 231, Paragraph 3 of the Constitution states "Hydric resources, including energetic potentials, may only be exploited, and mineral riches in Indian land may only be prospected and mined with authorization of the National Congress, after hearing the communities involved, and the participation in the results of such mining shall be ensured to them, as set forth by law." Article 231, Paragraph 5 of the Constitution states "The removal of Indian groups from their lands is forbidden, except ad referendum of the National Congress, in case of a catastrophe or an epidemic which represents a risk to their population, or in the interest of the sovereignty of the country, after decision by the National Congress, it being guaranteed that, under any circumstances, the return shall be immediate as soon as the risk ceases." Brazil also ratified ILO Convention 169 (Indigenous and Tribal Peoples Convention), 1989 in 2002; this Convention establishes the right of indigenous populations to give FPIC to proposed develop projects that affect their land and natural resources. The laws assessed do not require the government to weigh the costs and benefits of the project prior to expropriating land. The laws assessed do not require the government to identify all affected persons prior to expropriating land. The laws assessed do not require the government to provide affected landholders with the reasons for expropriation. Article 231, Paragraph 3 of the Constitution of Brazil states "Hydric resources, including energetic potentials, may only be exploited, and mineral riches in Indian land may only be prospected and mined with authorization of the National Congress, after hearing the communities involved, and the participation in the results of such mining shall be ensured to them, as set forth by law." The laws assessed do not grant affected persons the right to reacquire their land in the event that the project is abandoned or the land is no longer needed for a public purpose.

9 Art. 297 of Law 034-2012/AN Agrarian Reform Law (2012) provides that "Involuntary transfer of real property rights for the public interest concerns carrying out operations such as: Transport infrastructure, including roads, railways, terminals; Construction and urban, agricultural, pastoral, land or mining; Military work; The conservation, protection of historical sites or monuments; Arrangements of hydraulic power and power distribution; Installation of utilities, the creation or maintenance of goods or works for public use; Remediation work; Any undertaking designed to meet or protect the public interest." The open-ended clause "any undertaking designed to meet or protect the public interest" suggests that the government's expropriation power is not limited to the given set of circumstances. The laws assessed do not require the government to minimize the amount of land acquired to the amount necessary to achieve a public purpose. The laws assessed do not require the government or project developers to conduct a social impact assessment prior to expropriating land. The Environmental Code of March 1997 requires project proponents to initiate a Notice d'Impact sur l'Environnement (NIE)

or initiate a full EIA. Presumably, this requirement applies when land is expropriated for projects that may impact the environment. The laws assessed do not require the government to be sensitive to areas held by poor and vulnerable groups. The laws assessed do not recognize the indigenous right to FPIC. Belize has not ratified ILO Convention 169, an international human rights treaty that recognizes the indigenous right to given consent prior to acquisition of their land by the government or outsiders. Article 302 of Law No. 34-2012 provides "the expropriating authority shall issue a statement of intent to conduct a public utility project with an indication of its purpose, its influence, its duration, its costs and advantages." The laws assessed do not require the government to identify all affected persons prior to expropriating land. Article 302 of Law No. 34-2012 provides "the expropriating authority shall issue a statement of intent to conduct a public utility project with an indication of its purpose, its purpose, its influence, its duration, its costs and advantages. This statement is broadcast for one month through the official channels of communication and by any appropriate means for populations affected by the project. In addition, the declaration mentions the upcoming opening of an investigation utility public; it should be displayed at City Hall and in any appropriate public place, as public notice, eight days before the start of the investigation and throughout its duration." Article 304 of Law No. 34-2012 provides that "During the period of investigation, the inhabitants of the locality concerned may consult the expropriation folder that enables them, if necessary, challenge, or the principle of operation, its financial importance or the place of performance. Comments may be entered on the register or be sent under investigation a note to the president of the commission ad hoc survey." Article 305 of Law No.34-2012 provides "the public inquiry is required prior to the declaration of public utility." The laws assessed do not grant affected persons the right to reacquire their land in the event that the project is abandoned or the land is no longer needed for a public purpose.

10 Article 7 of the Law on Expropriation 2010 provides that expropriation can only be carried out if it is implementing a project as set out in Article 5. Article 5 provides a list of public infrastructure projects for which land can be expropriated. Article 5 states "construction or expansion of railroads, roads, bridges, airports, ports and accompanying structures and equipment; b. construction or expansion of power stations, structures, equipment and lines for transmission and distribution of electrical energy; c. construction or expansion of buildings and equipment for postal, telecommunication and information technology systems; d. construction or expansion of roads, city space, vehicle parking lots, markets, parks, and public squares; e. construction or expansion of irrigation systems, clean water supply systems, sewage systems, and public interest spaces; f. construction or expansion of buildings for education, training, science, culture, health care, social security, and stadiums for performances to public audiences; g. construction or expansion of refineries, purification stations, buildings and equipment for protection of nature and the environment; h. construction or expansion of buildings and equipment for research and exploiting mines and other natural resources; i. construction or expansion of gas systems, fuel pipes, oil refineries, oil rigs, and other systems; j. construction or expansion of buildings/residences which are seriously destroyed by natural disasters such as earthquakes, floods, fires, and landslides etc., and for preparation for resettlement; k. construction or expansion of buildings for protecting and supporting residents; l. construction or expansion of border crossing posts; m. construction or expansion of or preparation for necessary construction for national defense or security; n. establishment of new sites for protection of natural resources, forests, cultural and archeological sites or protection of the environment; and o. the implementation as required by the nation in accordance with the determination made by the government"; The laws assessed do not require the government to minimize the amount of land acquired to the amount necessary to achieve a public purpose. The laws assessed do not require the government or project developers to conduct a social impact assessment prior to expropriating land. The Law on Expropriation 2010 does not require the government to be sensitive to areas of cultural, religious, and environmental significance when making expropriation decisions. However, under the Sub-Decree on Environmental and Social Impact Assessment (ESIA)s (1999), all projects in Cambodia must conduct an ESIA prior to initiating projects. The laws assessed do not require the government to be sensitive to areas held by poor and vulnerable groups. The laws assessed do not recognize the indigenous right to FPIC. The laws assessed do not require the government to weigh the costs and benefits of the project prior to expropriating land. Under the Law on Expropriation 2010, the Expropriation Committee must publicly conduct a survey by recording a detailed description of all rights of the owners and/or rightful owners (Art. 16, Law on Expropriation, 2010). However, the law does not

require the government to survey users, occupants and other tenure rights holders prior to expropriating land. Article 16 of the Law on Expropriation 2010 states "the Expropriation Committee shall arrange a public consultation with authorities at capital, provincial, municipal, district, khan levels, and with the commune and sangkat councils and village representatives or the communities affected by the expropriation in order to give them clear and specific information and to have opinions from all concerned parties about the proposal for a public physical infrastructure project." Article 9 of the Law on Expropriation 2010 states "The owner or rightful owner shall be given priority to buy the leftover of the required immovable property at the compensation rate. If the owner or rightful owner refuses to buy back the rest of the required immovable property, it shall be kept as state property."

11 'Public interest' is not defined by the Law on Land Administration, 1998. However, Section 8 of the Regulation on the Expropriation of Buildings on State-Owned Land and Compensation, 2011 provides that "Where, for public interests such as safeguarding the national security and promoting the national economic and social development, it is necessary to expropriate a building under any of the following circumstances, the people's government at the city or county level shall make a decision to expropriate the building: (1) necessary for national defense and foreign affairs; (2) necessary for the construction of energy, transportation, water and other infrastructures as organized and implemented by the government; (3) necessary for a public cause such as science and technology, education, culture, health, sports, environment and resource protection, disaster prevention and mitigation, protection of cultural relics, social welfare or municipal utilities as organized and implemented by the government; (4) necessary for the construction of a social security housing project as organized and implemented by the government; (5) necessary for the rebuilding of an old urban area where dilapidated buildings concentrate and infrastructure lags behind as organized and implemented by the government according to the relevant provisions of the Urban and Rural Planning Law; or (6) necessary for any other public interest as prescribed by a law or administrative regulation." The laws assessed do not require the government to minimize the amount of land acquired to the amount necessary to achieve a public purpose. The China National Development and Reform Commission (Guideline of 2002) requires social assessment in feasibility studies and development investments; however, this Guidelines is not legally binding. The Law of People Republic of China on Environmental Impact Assessment made environmental impact assessments legally binding and applicable to development projects that are likely to impact the environment. It was promulgated in 2002 and came into effect in September 2003. China's EIA regulations were updated in 2017. The laws assessed do not require the government to be sensitive to areas held by poor and vulnerable groups. The laws assessed do not recognize the indigenous right to FPIC. Article 52 of the Law on Land Administration, 1998 states that "in the process of the feasibility study for construction projects, land administrative departments may examine the related matters concerning the land for construction purposes and put forward their proposal according to the general plans for utilization of land, the annual plan for the use of land and standards for land used for construction purposes." Since this provision is limited to construction projects, the answer is partial yes. Article 12 provides "Article 12 of the 2011 Expropriation Regulations provides that." Before making a decision on building expropriation, the people's government at the city or county level shall make a social stability risk assessment according to the relevant provisions, and if the decision involves a large number of owners, it shall be made at the executive meeting of the government upon discussion. Before a decision on building expropriation is made, the compensation fees for expropriation shall be ready in full amount, deposited in a special purpose account and used for designated purpose only. Article 15 of the Regulation on the Expropriation of Buildings on State-Owned Land and Compensation, 2011 states "The building expropriation department shall organize surveys and registration of the ownership, location, use, construction area, etc. of buildings within the scope of expropriation, and the owners shall provide cooperation. The survey results shall be announced to the owners within the scope of expropriation." The law only applies to the expropriation of buildings on state owned land. See also Article 46 of Land Management Law. Article 10 of the Regulation on the Expropriation of Buildings on State-Owned Land and Compensation, 2011 provides that "the building expropriation department shall draft an expropriation and compensation plan and report it to the people's government at the city or county level. The people's government at the city or county level shall organize the relevant departments to demonstrate the expropriation and compensation plan and publish it for public opinions. The period for solicitation of public opinions shall be no less than 30 days." Article 48 of the Law on Land Administration, 1998

states "Once a plan for compensation and resettlement subsidies for requisitioned land is decided on, the local people's government concerned shall make it known to the general public and solicit comments and suggestions from the collective economic organizations, the land of which is requisitioned, and the peasants." Article 10 of the Regulation on the Expropriation of Buildings on State-Owned Land and Compensation, 2011 "The building expropriation department shall draft an expropriation and compensation plan and report it to the people's government at the city or county level. The people's government at the city or county level shall organize the relevant departments to demonstrate the expropriation and compensation plan and publish it for public opinions. The period for solicitation of public opinions shall be no less than 30 days." Article 11 of the 2011 Regulation states "The people's government at the city or county level shall publish in a timely manner the public opinions solicited and the amendments made according to the public opinions. Where buildings need to be expropriated due to the rebuilding of an old urban area, if the majority of the owners consider that the expropriation and compensation plan does not conform to the provisions of this Regulation, the people's government at the city or county level shall organize a hearing attended by the owners and the representatives of the public, and amend the plan according to the results of the hearing." Article 37 of the Law on Land Administration, 1998 states that "if the land [approved for non-agricultural construction projects] is not used for two years running, the people's government at or above the county level shall, with the approval of the original approving organ, take back the user's right to the use of the land without compensation. If the said land is originally owned by a peasant collectives, it shall be returned to the original collective economic organization of the village for resumption of cultivation."

12 Article 323 of the Constitution of Ecuador states "For the purposes of implementing plans for social development, sustainable management of the environment and public welfare, State institutions may, for reasons of public utility or social and national interest, declare the expropriation of goods, following fair appraisal, compensation and payment pursuant to the law." Art. 43 of Ley No. 54 of Ley de Desarrollo, 1997 states "the rustic lands of private domain can only be expropriated in the following cases: a) When they are exploited through precarious work systems or forms not contemplated in this Law as lawful; b) When practices are used for its exploitation, including the use of unfit technologies, which attempt seriously against the conservation of renewable natural resources. In this case, it must be the Director Executive of the INDA, who declares the expropriation, after the expiration of the term that must be granted so that these practices are rectified, which will be up to two calendar years and, in no case, less than one year; c) When lands suitable for agricultural exploitation have remained unexploited for more than two years consecutive and as long as they are not in protected areas, of ecological reserve, constitute forests protect or suffer from floods or other fortuitous events that make their cultivation impossible or exploitation; d) When the property is subject to great demographic pressure..." The laws assessed do not require the government to minimize the amount of land acquired to the amount necessary to achieve a public purpose. The laws assessed do not require the government or project developers to conduct a social impact assessment prior to expropriating land. Art. 43 of Ley No. 54 of Ley de Desarrollo, 1997 allows land to expropriated in cases "When lands suitable for agricultural exploitation have remained unexploited for more than two years consecutive and as long as they are not in protected areas, of ecological reserve, constitute forests protect or suffer from floods or other fortuitous events that make their cultivation impossible or exploitation..." Furthermore, the Environmental Law 1999 imposes an obligation on project developers to conduct an Environmental Impact Assessment prior to initiating development projects. EIA applies prior to the projects, activities or works that may cause significant adverse environmental impacts. Public, private and mixed investment projects are subject to the EIA. See Environmental Law, 1999; Consolidated Text of Environmental Management (TULA), 2003, mandated by Ministerial Agreement No. 006, 2014; Regulations for Mechanisms for Citizen Participation, Decree NO. 1040, 2008 and Agreement NO. 066, 2013. Article 57(7) of Constitution of Ecuador (2008) provides that Indigenous communes, communities, peoples and nations are recognized and guaranteed, in conformity with the Constitution and human rights agreements, conventions, declarations and other international instruments, the following collective rights...To free prior informed consultation, within a reasonable period of time, on the plans and programs for prospecting, producing and marketing nonrenewable resources located on their lands and which could have an environmental or cultural impact on them; to participate in the profits earned from these projects and to receive compensation for social, cultural and environmental damages caused to them. The consultation that

must be conducted by the competent authorities shall be mandatory and in due time. If consent of the consulted community is not obtained, steps provided for by the Constitution and the law shall be taken. The laws assessed do not require the government to weigh the costs and benefits of the project prior to expropriating land. The laws assessed do not require the government to identify all affected persons prior to expropriating land. Article 57(7) of the Constitution of Ecuador provides indigenous communities with the right "to free prior informed consultation, within a reasonable period of time, on the plans and programs for prospecting, producing and marketing nonrenewable resources located on their lands and which could have an environmental or cultural impact on them..." Presidential Decree 1247 (2012) establishes procedures for gathering the FPIC of communities prior to acquisition for hydrocarbon exploitation, but it is unclear whether this Decree applies when land is acquired for exploitation of other resources. Article 57(7) of the Constitution of Ecuador provides indigenous communities with the right "to free prior informed consultation, within a reasonable period of time, on the plans and programs for prospecting, producing and marketing nonrenewable resources located on their lands and which could have an environmental or cultural impact on them..." Presidential Decree 1247 (2012) establishes procedures for gathering the FPIC of communities prior to acquisition for hydrocarbon exploitation, but it is unclear whether this Decree applies when land is acquired for exploitation of other resources. The laws assessed do not grant affected persons the right to reacquire their land in the event that the project is abandoned or the land is no longer needed for a public purpose.

13 Article 50(1) of Eritrea's Land Proclamation, 1994 states that "the Government or appropriate government body shall have the right and power to expropriate land, where people have been settling on or land that has been used by others, for purposes of various developments and capital investment projects aimed at national reconstruction or other similar purposes. This right and power shall be enforced only upon the approval of the Office of the President or a body delegated by the President." The laws assessed do not require the government to minimize the amount of land acquired to the amount necessary to achieve a public purpose. The laws assessed do not require the government or project developers to conduct a social impact assessment prior to expropriating land. The 1994 Land Proclamation does not require the government to be sensitive to areas of cultural, environmental, and religious significance when expropriating land. Moreover, Eritrea has not enacted legally binding legislation that requires the government and project developers to conduct an environmental impact assessment prior to expropriating land. See: Zeremariam, T.K. & Quinn, N., 'An evaluation of environmental impact assessment in Eritrea, Impact Assessment and Project Appraisal', Vol. 25, 1, 2007, 53-63. The laws assessed do not require the government to be sensitive to areas held by poor and vulnerable groups. The laws assessed do not recognize the indigenous right to FPIC. Article 50(2) of the Land Proclamation, 1994 states "the government or appropriate government body, prior to expropriating such land, shall undertake the necessary study to ascertain that the land is fit for the purpose it is to be expropriated..." While this provision suggests that the government must determine whether the land is suitable to achieve the intended public purpose, it is unclear based on the wording of the provision whether the government is obliged to weigh the costs and benefits of the project prior to expropriating land. For this reason, the score for this indicator is 'partial', The laws assessed do not require the government to identify all affected persons prior to expropriating land. The laws assessed do not require the government to provide affected landholders with the reasons for expropriation. The laws assessed do not require the government to consult the public or affected populations prior to expropriating land. The laws assessed do not grant affected persons the right to reacquire their land in the event that the project is abandoned or the land is no longer needed for a public purpose.

14 Section 2(5) of the Expropriation of Landholdings for Public Purposes and Payment of Compensation Proclamation No. 455/2005 states 'public purpose' means "the use of land defined as such by decision of the appropriate body in conformity with urban structure plan or development plan in order to ensure the interest of the peoples to acquire direct or indirect benefits from the use of the land and to consolidate sustainable socio-economic development." Section 3 states "a woreda or an urban administration shall, upon payment in advance of compensation...have the power to expropriate rural or urban landholdings for public purpose where it believes that is should be used for a better development project to be carried out by public entitles, private investors, cooperative societies or other organs, or where such expropriation has been decided by the appropriate higher regional or federal government organ for the same purpose." Article 1464 of the Ethiopia Civil Code provides that "expropriation

proceedings may not be used for the purpose solely of obtaining financial benefits." The laws assessed do not require the government to minimize the amount of land acquired to the amount necessary to achieve a public purpose. The laws assessed do not require the government or project developers to conduct a social impact assessment prior to expropriating land. Environmental Impact Assessment Proclamation No. 299/2002 requires that an environmental impact assessment be conducted whenever a proposed development project is likely to impact the environment. The laws assessed do not require the government to be sensitive to areas held by poor and vulnerable groups. The laws assessed do not recognize the indigenous right to FPIC. The laws assessed do not require the government to weigh the costs and benefits of the project prior to expropriating land. The laws assessed do not require the government to identify all affected persons prior to expropriating land.The laws assessed do not require the government to provide affected landholders with the reasons for expropriation. Article 1465 of the Civil Code states that "where a public inquiry appears to be necessary, the declaration of public utility shall not be made until the public interest has been consulted...any interested party may, in the course of such inquiry, express his views or criticize the contemplated project." The answer for this indicator is 'partial' because the requirement only applies "where a public inquiry appears necessary", so there may be situations where land is acquired without public consultation. Article 1483 of the Ethiopian Civil Code states that "Where the project in view of which expropriation was ordered is abandoned, the former owners shall have a right of pre-emption on their former property."

15 Section 1 of the State Lands Act, 1962 states "(1) Whenever it appears to the President in the public interest so to do, he may, by executive instrument, declare any land specified in the instrument, other than land subject to the Administration of Lands Act, 1962 (Act 123), to be land required in the public interest; and accordingly on the making of the instrument it shall be lawful for any person, acting in that behalf and subject to a month's notice in writing to enter the land so declared for any purpose incidental to the declaration so made." The laws assessed do not require the government to minimize the amount of land acquired to the amount necessary to achieve a public purpose. The laws assessed do not require the government or project developers to conduct a social impact assessment prior to expropriating land. Ghana's Environmental Protection Council introduced the EIA process for industrial developments. A Government Administrative Directive made EIA a legal requirement in 1989. The government requires a "preliminary environmental Review" for all projects with potential environmental impacts. The laws assessed do not require the government to be sensitive to areas held by poor and vulnerable groups. The laws assessed do not recognize the indigenous right to FPIC. The laws assessed do not require the government to weigh the costs and benefits of the project prior to expropriating land. The laws assessed do not require the government to identify all affected persons prior to expropriating land. The laws assessed do not require the government to provide affected landholders with the reasons for expropriation. The laws assessed do not require the government to consult the public or affected populations prior to expropriating land. Article 20(6) of the Constitution of Ghana provides that "where the property is not used in the public interest or for the purpose for which it was acquired, the owner of the property immediately before the compulsory acquisition, shall be given the first option for acquiring the property and shall, on such reacquisition refund the whole or part of the compensation paid to him as provided for by law or such other amount as is commensurate with the value of the property at the time of the reacquisition." Since the law only grants reacquisition rights "immediately before the compulsory acquisition" and not subsequent to the compulsory acquisition, the answer for this indicator is partial.

16 The laws assessed do not provide a clear definition of public purpose to allow for judicial review. Article 106 of the Constitution of Honduras, 1986 states "No one may be deprived of his property except by reason of public need or interest defined by law or a decision based on law, and shall not take place without assessed prior compensation." Article 349 of the 1986 Constitution states "the expropriation of property for the purpose of agrarian reform or for developing and improving communities, or for any other purposes of national interest determined by the law, shall be carried out on the basis of just compensation by cash payments." Ley de Propiedad (aprobada por Decreto Nº 82-2004) does not contain a clear definition of public purpose to allow for judicial review. The laws assessed do not provide a clear definition of public purpose to allow for judicial review. Article 106 of the Constitution of Honduras states "No one may be deprived of his property except by reason of public need or interest defined by law or a decision based on law, and shall not take place without assessed prior compensation." Article

349 of the Constitution states "The expropriation of property for the purpose of agrarian reform or for developing and improving communities, or for any other purposes of national interest determined by the law, shall be carried out on the basis of just compensation by cash payments." Ley de Propiedad (aprobada por Decreto N° 82-2004) does not contain a clear definition of public purpose to allow for judicial review. The laws assessed do not require the government or project developers to conduct a social impact assessment prior to expropriating land. While there are no clear legal protections of areas of cultural and religious significance, the General Law of the Environment (Decree No. 104 of 1993) and the Regulation of the SINEIA issued under the Ministerial Agreement No. 189-2009 (December 31,2009) require an assessment of environmental impacts caused by all public or private projects. Article 95 of the 2004 Property Law provides that if the State intends the exploitation of natural resources in indigenous territories, it must inform and consult the affected indigenous populations before authorizing any inspection or exploitation. Honduras ratified ILO Convention 169 (the Indigenous and Tribal Peoples Convention) in 1995. The Inter-American Court of Human Rights recently held that the indigenous right to FPIC must be upheld and protected by the Honduran government (see Cultural Survival. 2016. "Indigenous Rights Win Major Steps Forward in Honduras"). The laws assessed do not require the government to weigh the costs and benefits of the project prior to expropriating land. The laws assessed do not require the government to identify all affected persons prior to expropriating land. The laws assessed do not require the government to provide affected landholders with the reasons for expropriation. Article 95 of the 2004 Property Law provides that if the State intends the exploitation of natural resources in indigenous territories, it must inform and consult the affected indigenous populations before authorizing any inspection or exploitation. The laws assessed do not grant affected persons the right to reacquire their land in the event that the project is abandoned or the land is no longer needed for a public purpose.

17 Section 3 of the Land Resumption Ordinance 1997 states that "whenever the Chief Executive in Council decides that the resumption of any land is required for a public purpose, the Chief Executive may order the resumption thereof under this Ordinance." The law does not provide a clear legal definition of public purpose to allow for judicial review. The laws assessed do not require the government to minimize the amount of land acquired to the amount necessary to achieve a public purpose. The laws assessed do not require the government or project developers to conduct a social impact assessment prior to expropriating land. The Lands Resumption Ordinance 1997 assessed does not require the government to be sensitive to areas of cultural, religious, and environmental significance when making expropriation decisions. However, Hong Kong also enacted an Environmental Impact Assessment Ordinance in 1998, which indicates that developers must conduct an EIA prior to initiating projects that impact the environment. The laws assessed do not require the government to be sensitive to areas held by poor and vulnerable groups. The laws assessed do not recognize the indigenous right to FPIC. The laws assessed do not require the government to weigh the costs and benefits of the project prior to expropriating land. The laws assessed do not require the government to identify all affected persons prior to expropriating land. The laws assessed do not require the government to provide affected landholders with the reasons for expropriation. The laws assessed do not require the government to consult the public or affected populations prior to expropriating land.

18 Section 2(1) of the LARR Act 2013 provides a clear list of public purposes and limits the government's authority to expropriate land to these purposes by stating "public purposes shall include…" According to the LARR Act, an Expert Group must appraise the Social Impact Assessment and report on whether "land proposed to be acquired is the absolute bare-minimum extent needed for the project and whether there are no other less displacing options available" (Sec. 7(5), LARR Act 2013). Section 8(1) of the LARR Act 2013 states that the government "shall ensure that only the minimum amount of land required for the project is proposed to be acquired." Even in cases of urgency, the law limits expropriation to the "minimum area required for the defence of India or nation security or for any emergencies arising out of natural calamities or any other emergency with approval of Parliament (Sec. 40(2), LARR Act 2013). Section 4 of the LARR Act 2013 requires a social impact assessment to be conducted prior to expropriating land. Section 4(4) states the Social Impact Assessment study shall, amongst other matters, include all the following, namely: (a) assessment as to whether the proposed acquisition serves public purpose; (b) estimation of affected families and the number of families among them likely to be displaced; (c) extent of lands, public and private, houses, settlements and other common properties

likely to be affected by the proposed acquisition; (d) whether the extent of land proposed for acquisition is the absolute bare-minimum extent needed for the project; (e) whether land acquisition at an alternate place has been considered and found not feasible; (f) study of social impacts of the project, and the nature and cost of addressing them and the impact of these costs on the overall costs of the project vis-a-vis the benefits of the project..." Section 4(5) of the LARR Act 2013 states "while undertaking a Social Impact Assessment study...the appropriate Government shall, amongst other things, take into consideration the impact that the project is likely to have on various components such as livelihood of affected families, public and community properties, assets and infrastructure particularly roads, public transport, drainage, sanitation, sources of drinking water, sources of water for cattle, community ponds, grazing land, plantations, public utilities such as post offices, fair price shops, food storage godowns, electricity supply, health care facilities, school and education or training facilities, anganwadis, children parks, places of worship, land for traditional tribal institutions and burial and cremation grounds." The government must also conduct an EIA before expropriating land (Section 4(4), LARR Act 2013; EIA Notification 2006). Section 41 of the LARR Act 2013 provides that "as far as possible, no acquisition of land shall be made in the Scheduled Areas. Where such acquisition does take place it shall be done as demonstrable last resort..." This provision provides some protection to lands held by Scheduled Tribes/Castes which are recognized by law as historically vulnerable groups in India. Article 4(4) of the LARR Act 2013 provides that 'the Social Impact Assessment shall, amongst other matters, include all the following, namely: (a) assessment as to whether the proposed acquisition serves public purpose; (b) estimation of affected families and the number of families among them likely to be displaced; (c) extent of lands, public and private, houses, settlement, and other common properties; (d) whether the extent of land proposed for acquisition is the absolute bare-minimum extent needed for the project; (e) whether land acquisition at an alternate place has been considered and found not feasible; (f) study of social impacts of the project, and the nature and cost of addressing them and the impact of these costs on the overall cost of the project vis-vis the benefits of the project. Section 16 of the LARR Act 2013 requires the Administrator for Rehabilitation and Resettlement to conduct a survey and undertake a census of affected families. The law also states that the Social Impact Assessment conducted must include an estimation of affected families and the number of families among them likely to be displaced (Sec. 4(4)(b), LARR Act, 2013). This survey must be conducted before the government can take possession of the land. Section 11 of the LARR Act 2013 requires the government to publish a notification in the Official Gazette, in newspapers, on the government website, and in the affected areas. The notification must "contain a statement on the nature of the public purpose involved, reasons necessitating the displacement of affected persons, summary of the Social Impact Assessment and particulars of the Administrator appointed for the purposes of rehabilitating and resettlement..." (sec. 11(3), LARR Act 2013). Section 18 of the LARR Act 2013 also provides that the Rehabilitation and Resettlement Scheme must be made available in local languages and published in affected areas. Section 5 of the LARR Act 2013 states that "whenever a Social Impact Assessment is required, the appropriate Government shall ensure that a public hearing is held at the affected area, after giving adequate publicity about the date, time and venue for the public hearing, to ascertain the views of the affected families to be recorded in the Social Impact Assessment Report." The Social Impact Assessment is then reviewed by and Expert Group, which takes a decision and submits to the Land Acquisition Authority; Land Acquisition Authority must then assess whether a proposed acquisition serves a bona fide public purpose (Secs. 4-5, 7(5), Sec. 8(1) LARR Act 2013. Section 101 of the LARR Act 2013 provides that "when any land acquired under this Act remains unutilised for a period of five years from the date of taking over the possession, the same shall be returned to the original owners or owners or their legal heirs, or, as the case may be, the Land Bank..." Since the LARR Act only provides acquisition rights after five years from the date of taking over possession and also suggests that the land may, in some cases, be submitted to the Land Bank instead of original owners, the score is 'partial' for this indicator.

19 Article 10 of the Law No. 2 of 2012 (Acquisition of Land for Development in the Public Interest) states that "Land in the Public Interest...shall be used for the development of: (a) the national defense and security; (b) public roads, toll roads, tunnels, rail lines, railway stations, and railway operating facilities; (c) reservoris, dams, dikes irrigation, drinking water mains, drainage and sanitation and other irrigation structures; (d) seaports, airports and terminals; (e) oil, gas and geothermal energy infrastructure; (f) power plaints, transmission, substations, grids, and distribution; (g) telecommunication

and informatics networks of the Government; (h) landfills and waste treatment sites; (i) hospitals of the Government/ the Regional Governments; (j) public safety facilities; (k) public cemeteries of the Government/ the Regional Governments; (l) social facilities; public facilities, and public green open space; (m) nature reserves and cultural sites; (n) offices of the Government/the Regional Governments/ the villages; (o) urban slum planning and/or land consolidation and rented low-income earner housing; (p) educational infrastructure or schools of the Government/the Regional Governments; (q) sport infrastructure of the Government/the Regional Governments; (r) and public marketplaces and public parking spaces." The laws assessed do not require the government to minimize the amount of land acquired to the amount necessary to achieve a public purpose. Section 15(2) of Law No. 2 of 2012 requires that a feasibility study must be prepared, and that the feasibility study must include an assessment of "environmental impacts and social impacts that may arise out of the Acquisition of Land and construction..." While the Law No. 2 of 2012 does not require the government to be sensitive to areas of cultural, religious, and environmental significance, Indonesia enacted the Basic Environmental Law No. 4 of 1982 and Government Regulations No. 29 (1986) which require the government and project developers to conduct an EIA prior to initiating development projects. The laws assessed do not require the government to be sensitive to areas held by poor and vulnerable groups. The laws assessed do not recognize the indigenous right to FPIC. Bangladesh has not ratified ILO Convention 169, an international human rights treaty that recognizes the indigenous right to given consent prior to acquisition of their land by the government or outsiders. Article 15(1) of Law. No. 2 of 2012 states that "the Land Acquisition planning documentation...shall be prepared under the feasibility study made in accordance with the laws and regulations." Article 15(2) states "the feasibility study shall include: (a) social-economic survey; (b) location feasibility; (c) analysis of cost and development benefits to the area and the community; (d) estimated land value; (e) environmental impacts and social impacts that may arise out of the Acquisition of Land and construction; and (f) other study as necessary." Article 27(2) of Law No. 2 of 2012 states "the Land Acquisition implementation as intended...shall include (a) inventory and identification of possession, ownership, use and utilizations of land..." Article 28 of the Law No. 2 of 2012 states "(1) inventory and identification of possession, ownership, use and utilization of land...shall include: (a) surveying and mapping on a parcel-by-parcel basis; and (b) gathering data on the Entitled Parties and the Objects of the Acquired Land." Article 55 of Law No. 2 of 2012 states "the Entitled Parties shall have the rights to have knowledge of the performance of the Acquisition of Land; and receive information about the Acquisition of Land." Article 15 of the 2012 Law states that "land acquisition plan in the public interest...shall be prepared in the form of Land Acquisition planning documentation that contains at least: (a) the objectives and purposes of the development plan; (b) consistency with the Regional Spatial Planning and the National/Regional Development plan; (c) land location; (d) land size needed; (e) general description of the land status; (f) estimated period of the implementation of Acquisition of Land; (g) estimated period of the implementation of construction; (h) estimated land value; and (i) budget plan." The Land Acquisition planning document shall be prepared under the feasibility study...the feasibility study shall include: "(a) socio-economic survey; (b) location feasibility; (c) analysis of cost and development benefit to the area and the community; (d) estimated land value; (e) environmental impacts and social impacts that may arise out of the Acquisition of Land and construction." Article 16 of Law No. 2 of 12 states "an Agency needing land together with the provincial government... (a) make notification of the development plan..." Article 17 of Law No. 2 of 2012 states "notification of the development plan...shall be directly or indirectly be provided to the community living at the planned locations of development in the Public Interest." Section 7(3) of Law No. 2 of 2012 states "(3) Acquisition of Land in the Public Interest shall be performed through planning with involving all the guardians and stakeholders." 'Guardians' means, inter alia, customary leaders and clerics. 'Stakeholders' means any person or party having interest in the objects of the disposed land, such as the Entitled Parties, the government, and the community. Article 18 of Law No. 2 of 2012 states that "the results of preliminary data collection [of the location of the development plan] shall be used as data to hold a Public Consultation on a development plan." Article 19 of Law No. 2 of 2012 states that "(1) a Public Consultation on a development plan... shall be held to achieve agreement on the location of the development plan with Entitled Parties... (2) a Public Consultation...shall be convened involving the Entitled Parties and the affected community and held at the place of the development plan in the Public Interest or at the agreed-upon place..." The laws assessed do not grant affected persons the right to reacquire their land in the event that the project is abandoned or the land is no longer needed for a public purpose.

20 Article 84 of the Land Code, 2003 states that "exception cases for the compulsory acquisition of land for public use are: 1) an international obligation; 2) provision of land for defense purposes, and specially protected natural areas, recreation, recreational, historical and cultural facilities, the establishment of functioning special economic zones; 3) the discovery and development of mineral deposits; 4) construction of roads, power lines, communication lines, pipelines, engineering and communication networks, public communities as well as objects of state significance; 5) demolition of dilapidated housing and emergency threatening collapse (caving); 6) execution of master plans for settlements in the construction of the facilities... as well as construction of facilities provided by state and regional programs and investment projects to ensure the public interest and achieving socially important goals. 3. The laws of the Republic of Kazakhstan may provide other exceptional cases of expropriation of land for public use..." The laws assessed do not require the government to minimize the amount of land acquired to the amount necessary to achieve a public purpose. The laws assessed do not require the government or project developers to conduct a social impact assessment prior to expropriating land. Article 90 of the Land Code 2003 states "Seizure of irrigated agricultural lands, practice grounds of agricultural, biological and irrigated- ameliorative, fish research and educational institutions, forest funs and inventory of water resources shall be allowed only in exceptional instances, linked with creation and development of specially protected natural areas, fulfillment of the international obligations, detection of mining fields under the land plot, construction of the roads, objects for use of renewable energy sources – solar and wind energy, power lines, communications lines and main pipelines, mechanical, electrical and plumbing systems in general use of the inhabited localities, as well as objects of national standing, in the absence of other choices of their probable placement." An EIA is also required under Law of the Republic of Kazakhstan of 21 October 2000, No. 86-II "On the Adhesion of the Republic of Kazakhstan to the Convention on Environmental Impact Assessment in a Transboundary Context"; Law of the Republic of Kazakhstan "On the Protection of the Environment"; Law of the Republic of Kazakhstan "On Environmental Expert Review"; Law of the Republic of Kazakhstan of 13 December 2005, No. 97 "On Ratification of the Framework Convention for the Protection of the Marine Environment of the Caspian Sea"; Instruction on Conducting Assessment of Environmental Impact of Planned Economic and Other Activities for Pre-feasibility, Pre-project and Project Documentation, given effect by Ministerial Order of 28 February 2004, No. 68-P; Guidelines on the Application in Practice of the Convention on Environmental Impact Assessment in a Transboundary Context; Guidelines on Public Participation in Environmental Impact Assessment in a Transboundary Context; Guidelines on the Carrying Out of Environmental Impact Assessment in a Transboundary Context for the Countries of Central Asia; Instruction on Conducting EIA of the planned economic and other activities for the pre-feasibility, pre-project and project documentation, approved by Ministerial Order no. 68- П, 28 February 2004; EIA Rules applied while developing state, sectoral, regional programs of economic development, industrial allocation schemes, Ministerial Order no. 129- П, 9 June 2003. The laws assessed do not require the government to be sensitive to areas held by poor and vulnerable groups. The laws assessed do not recognize the indigenous right to FPIC. The laws assessed do not require the government to weigh the costs and benefits of the project prior to expropriating land. The laws assessed do not require the government to identify all affected persons prior to expropriating land. The laws assessed do not require the government to provide affected landholders with the reasons for expropriation. The laws assessed do not require the government to consult the public or affected populations prior to expropriating land. The laws assessed do not grant affected persons the right to reacquire their land in the event that the project is abandoned or the land is no longer needed for a public purpose.

21 Sec. 110 of the Land Act, 2012 provides that "land may be acquired compulsorily...if the Commission certifies, in writing, that the land is required for public purposes or in the public interest as related to and necessary for fulfilling of the stated public purpose." Sec. 2 of the 2012 Land Act provides that 'public purposes' is defined as "(a) transportation including roads, canals, highways, railways, bridges, wharves and airports; (b) public buildings including schools, libraries, hospitals, factories, religious institutions and public housing; (c) public utilities for water, sewage, electricity, gas, communication, irrigation and drainage, dams and reservoirs; (d) public parks, playgrounds, gardens, sports facilities and cemeteries; (e) security and defense installations; (f) settlement of squatters, the poor and landless, and the internally displaced persons; and (g) any other analogous public purpose." The clause "any other analogous public purpose" suggests the government is not limited to enumerated list of pub-

lic purposes when deciding to expropriate land. The laws assessed do not require the government to minimize the amount of land acquired to the amount necessary to achieve a public purpose. The laws assessed do not require the government or project developers to conduct a social impact assessment prior to expropriating land. While the Land Act 2012 does not require the government to be sensitive to areas of cultural, religious and environmental significance, the Kenyan government passed the Environmental Management and Coordination Act 1999 which requires project developers to initiate an EIA prior to conducting a project that affects the environment. Presumably, this EIA requirement applies when land is expropriated for development projects. The laws assessed do not require the government to be sensitive to areas held by poor and vulnerable groups. The laws assessed do not recognize the indigenous right to FPIC. The laws assessed do not require the government to weigh the costs and benefits of the project prior to expropriating land. The laws assessed do not require the government to identify all affected persons prior to expropriating land. The laws assessed do not require the government to provide affected landholders with the reasons for expropriation. The laws assessed do not require the government to consult the public or affected populations prior to expropriating land. Sec. 110 of the Land Act, 2012 provides that "if, after land has been compulsorily acquired the public purpose or interest justifying the compulsory acquisition fails or ceases, the Commission may offer the original owners or their successors in title pre-emptive rights to re-acquire land, upon restitution to the acquiring authority the full amount paid as compensation."

22 Article 71 of Land Law 2003 states "when it is necessary to use the land for any individual or organization for public purposes, the State shall requisition the land and shall pay appropriate compensation to such individual or organisation." The law does not provide a clear legal definition of public purpose to allow for judicial review. The laws assessed do not require the government to minimize the amount of land acquired to the amount necessary to achieve a public purpose. Article 7 of Laos' Decree on Compensation and Resettlement Management in Development Projects (2016) states "Before project implementation or before the signing of a concession project, the project owner must collaborate with relevant organizations at all levels to collect information on people to be affected including a detail plan of compensation to contribute to the management and monitoring of social and environmental impacts in relation to project implementation." Furthermore, Article 17 obliges project owners to "make a report on environmental, social, and natural impact assessment, including the plan for the environmental, social and natural management..." While Laos' expropriation laws do not require the government to be sensitive to areas of cultural, religious, and environmental significance, the Lao government passed the Decree on Environmental Impact Assessment in 2010 which makes it mandatory for project developers to conduct an EIA prior to initiating projects that will significantly affect the environment. The EIA Decree 2010 applies to small and large investment projects conducted in Laos. The laws assessed do not require the government to be sensitive to areas held by poor and vulnerable groups. The laws assessed do not recognize the indigenous right to FPIC. The laws assessed do not require the government to weigh the costs and benefits of the project prior to expropriating land. Article 7 of the Decree on Compensation and Resettlement Management in Development Projects (2016) states that "before project implementation or before the signing of a concession project, the project owner must collaborate with relevant organizations at all levels to collect information on people to be affected including a detail plan of compensation to contribute to the management and monitoring of social and environmental impacts in relation to project implementation." Article 18 of Decree on Compensation and Resettlement Management in Development Projects (2016) states that affected landholders have the right to "receive the information on the development project, benefits and effects, the progress in the implementation of the plan of compensation, resettlement and rehabilitation of the livelihood of people throughout the implementation of the development project." Article 11(2) of the Decree on Compensation and Resettlement Management in Development Project (2016) states that affected populations have a right to "attend consultations at different levels [and] macaw comments to the plan of compensation, resettlement, and rehabilitation of their livelihood." The laws assessed do not grant affected persons the right to reacquire their land in the event that the project is abandoned or the land is no longer needed for a public purpose.

23 Section 48 of the Land Act, 2010 states "Whenever it appears to the Minister that land which is unallocated is required for public purpose or public interest, the Minister after consultation with the allocating authority having jurisdiction shall by notice in the Gazette declare the land to be so required."

Section 50 defines 'public purposes' as : "(a)providing roads, aerdromes, railways, canals, water supply, drainage, sewerage; (b) providing social services including but not limited to schools, hospitals, hostels, cemeteries, playing fields, parks, swimming baths, nature reserves, low income housing; (c) water conservation by means of watersheds, water catchment areas, reservoirs; (d) land conservation through afforestation, and erosion prevention; (e) providing Government housing for; residences, offices, storage; research and agricultural stations; and defense and security requirements; (f) furthering sport, culture, industry and tourism, including the provision of hotels; (g) providing any public utility service; (h) alleviation or eradication of consequences of natural disaster; and (i) providing any service which is in the public interest or would enhance or promote national resources and prosperity." Section 51(2) of the Land Act, 2010 states "the following shall constitute circumstances under which land may be expropriated in the public interest---(a) setting aside land for the development of agriculture by modern farming techniques; (b) construction or development of a new residential, commercial or industrial area; or (c) development or reconstruction of existing built-up area." Section 55(1) of the Land Act, 2010 states "Whenever it appears to the Minister that any land held by the Government or agency of the Government by operation of Part VIII and IX of this Act is surplus to the requirements for which it was acquired or allocated or permitted to be used, the Minister may, by notice published in the Gazette, revoke the expropriation declaration relating to the land, and such land shall revert to the State unless within 90 days from the date of revocation, the original title holder, having been given notice by the Commissioner, expresses interest to be allocated the land." The laws assessed do not require the government or project developers to conduct a social impact assessment prior to expropriating land. While the Land Act 2010 does not require the government to be sensitive to areas of cultural, religious and environmental significance, Lesotho passed the Environment Act 2008 which mandates that project developers conduct an EIA prior to initiating certain types of projects that may impact the environment. This EIA requirement applies when land is expropriated for development projects. The laws assessed do not require the government to be sensitive to areas held by poor and vulnerable groups. The laws assessed do not recognize the indigenous right to FPIC. The laws assessed do not require the government to weigh the costs and benefits of the project prior to expropriating land. The laws assessed do not require the government to identify all affected persons prior to expropriating land. The laws assessed do not require the government to provide affected landholders with the reasons for expropriation. Section 52(a) of the Land Act, 2010 states "the Government shall first negotiate with the holder of land rights which are the subject of potential expropriation and resort to expropriation only upon failure of the negotiations due to the unreasonableness of the holder of the rights to the land..." The laws assessed do not grant affected persons the right to reacquire their land in the event that the project is abandoned or the land is no longer needed for a public purpose.

24 Article 24 of the Constitution of Liberia, 1984 states "expropriation may be authorized for the security of the nation in the event of armed conflict or where the public health and safety are endangered or for any other public purposes..." The laws assessed do not require the government to minimize the amount of land acquired to the amount necessary to achieve a public purpose. The laws assessed do not require the government or project developers to conduct a social impact assessment prior to expropriating land. An EIA is required under Liberia's Environmental Protection and Management Law (EPML) of Liberia. See also Liberia's Environmental Impact Assessment Procedural Guideline 2006. According to Section 12 of the EPML, "The project proponent or applicant shall prepare an environmental review for project[s] or activities that may have a significant impact on the environment, and shall contain sufficient information to enable the Agency to determine whether a full environmental impact study should be required for the project." The laws assessed do not require the government to be sensitive to areas held by poor and vulnerable groups. The laws assessed do not recognize the indigenous right to FPIC. Belize has not ratified ILO Convention 169, an international human rights treaty that recognizes the indigenous right to given consent prior to acquisition of their land by the government or outsiders. The laws assessed do not require the government to weigh the costs and benefits of the project prior to expropriating land. The laws assessed do not require the government to identify all affected persons prior to expropriating land. While a national-level law, which establishes expropriation procedures relating to information, has not been enacted, the Constitution requires that "reasons for such expropriation are given" when land is acquired through expropriation (Art. 24). The laws assessed do not require the government to consult the public or affected populations prior to expropriating land. Arti-

cle 24 of the Constitution of Liberia, 1984 provides that "when property taken for public use ceases to be so used, the Republic shall accord the former owner or those entitled to the property through such owner, the right of first refusal to reacquire the property."

25 Sec. 3(1) of the Land Acquisition Act, 1960 states "the State Authority may acquire any land which is needed- (a) for any public purpose; (b) by any person or corporation for any purpose which in the opinion of the State Authority is beneficial to the economic development of Malaysia or any part thereof or to the public generally or any class of the public; or (c) for the purpose of mining or for residential, agricultural, commercial, industrial or recreational purposes or any combination of such purposes." S.Kulasingam & Anor v Commissioner of Lands, Federal Territory & Ors [1982] 1 MLJ 204 it was held: "The expression pubic purpose is incapable of a precise definition. It is still best to employ a simple common sense test, that is, to see whether the purpose serves the general interest of the community." Section 3E of the Land Acquisition Act (1960) provides that "the State Authority shall not approve the application for the acquisition of land for any purpose larger in are than that needed for that purpose." The laws assessed do not require the government or project developers to conduct a social impact assessment prior to expropriating land. While the Land Acquisition Act 1960 does not require the government to be sensitive to areas of cultural, religious, an environmental significance, Malaysia enacted the Environmental Impact Assessment Order in 1988 which requires the government and project developers to conduct an environmental impact assessment prior to initiating development projects. The laws assessed do not require the government to be sensitive to areas held by poor and vulnerable groups. The laws assessed do not recognize the indigenous right to FPIC. Belize has not ratified ILO Convention 169, an international human rights treaty that recognizes the indigenous right to given consent prior to acquisition of their land by the government or outsiders. Section 3A of the Land Acquisition Act (1960) provides that "the state Economic Planning Unit shall review the land acquisition plan on the aspects of 'public interest'", "the capacity and capability of the applicant to carry out the purpose for which the land is to be acquired", and "the feasibility of the project." The law also establishes as Committee to review land acquisition application; however, the State Authority has discretion under the Land Acquisition Act to make the final decision regarding whether to approve land acquisition for a proposed project. The laws assessed do not require the government to identify all affected persons prior to expropriating land. Section 4 (1) of the Land Acquisition Act, 1960 states "Whenever the State Authority is satisfied that any land in any locality in the State is likely to be needed for any of the purposes referred to in Section 3 a notification in Form A shall be published in the Gazette." The purpose of the proposed expropriation is required to be filled out in the form A. The laws assessed do not require the government to consult the public or affected populations prior to expropriating land. Section 68A of the Land Acquisition Act, 1960 states "Where any land has been acquired under this Act, whether before or after the commencement of this Section, no subsequent disposal or use of, or dealing with, the land, whether by the State Authority or by the Government, person or corporation on whose behalf the land was acquired, shall invalidate the acquisition of the land."

26 "Ley de Expropiacion 1936 allows the government to expropriate land for 'public utility'," 'Public utility' is defined by Article 1 of the Ley de Expropiacion, 1936 as "the establishment, operation, or consideration of a public service... the opening, expansion or alignment of streets, the constructions of roads, bridges and tunnels to facilitate urban and suburban expansion; the beautification expansion and rehabilitation of the towns and ports, the construction of hospitals, schools, parks, gardens, sports, land fields, office buildings for the Federal Government and for any work designed to provide services of collective benefit; the construction of public infrastructure works and the provision of public services, which require real estate and its improvements, derived from concession, contract or any act legally concluded in terms of the applicable legal provision...the conservation of places of panoramic beauty, of the object of art, of archaeological or historic buildings and monuments, and the things that are considered remarkable characteristics of our national culture... the satisfaction of collective needs in case of war or internal disorders; the supply of cities or centers of population, food or other consumer goods necessary, and the procedures used to combat or prevent the spread of epidemics, fires, plagues floods or other public calamites; the means used for national defense or for the maintenance of public peace... the defense, conservation, development or use of susceptible natural elements of exploitation... the equitable distribution of wealth...the creation, promotion or conservation of a company for the benefit of the community...necessary measures to prevent the destruction of the natural elements and

the damages that the property may be detrimental to the community...the creation of improvements to population centers...other cases provided by special law." (Unofficial English Translation). Article 93 of the Agrarian Law, 1992 states "The ejidal and communal assets may be expropriated by one or some of the following causes of utility publishes: I. The establishment, operation or conservation of a service or public function; II. The realization of actions for urban planning and ecological, as well as the creation and expansion of reserves territorial areas and areas for urban development, housing, industry and tourism; III. The carrying out of actions to promote and order the development and conservation of agricultural resources, forestry and fishing; IV. Exploitation of oil, its processing and conduction, the exploitation of other natural elements belonging to the Nation and the installation of benefit plants associated with said farms; V. Regularization of urban and rural land tenure; VI. Creation, promotion and conservation of production units of goods or services of undoubted benefit to the community; VII. The construction of bridges, roads, railways, landing fields and other works that facilitate transportation, as those subject to the Law of General Communications Routes and lines of energy conduction, hydraulic works, their steps of access and other related works; VIII. The rest provided for in the Expropriation Law and other laws." The laws assessed do not require the government to minimize the amount of land acquired to the amount necessary to achieve a public purpose. The laws assessed do not require the government or project developers to conduct a social impact assessment prior to expropriating land. An EIA is required by the General Law of Ecological Equilibrium and Environment Protection, 1998, amended by DOF 09-01-2015l Regulations of the General Law of Ecological Equilibrium, 2000, amended by DOF 31-10-2014. The laws assessed do not require the government to be sensitive to areas held by poor and vulnerable groups. The laws assessed do not recognize the indigenous right to FPIC. Belize has not ratified ILO Convention 169, an international human rights treaty that recognizes the indigenous right to given consent prior to acquisition of their land by the government or outsiders. The laws assessed do not require the government to weigh the costs and benefits of the project prior to expropriating land. The laws assessed do not require the government to identify all affected persons prior to expropriating land. The laws assessed do not require the government to provide affected landholders with the reasons for expropriation. The laws assessed do not require the government to consult the public or affected populations prior to expropriating land. The laws assessed do not grant affected persons the right to reacquire their land in the event that the project is abandoned or the land is no longer needed for a public purpose.

27 Article 35.1 of the Law on Allocation of Land to Mongolian Citizens for Ownership (2002) indicates that land may be expropriated "to ensure national defense and security...to create a permanent exploitation field for scientific and technological experiment and environmental or climatic observation...to build roads, lines and networks and other objects of national scale." Article 35.3 states "the decision to replace or take back Citizen' owned land for a fee shall clearly indicate the grounds of inevitable replacement or taking the land back." The laws assessed do not require the government to minimize the amount of land acquired to the amount necessary to achieve a public purpose. The laws assessed do not require the government or project developers to conduct a social impact assessment prior to expropriating land. While the Law on Allocation of Land to Mongolian Citizens for Ownership (2002) does not require the government to be sensitive to areas of cultural, religious and environmental significance, Mongolia passed the Law of Mongolia on Environmental Impact Assessments in 2012 whoich requiers project developers to conduct an EIA prior to initiating development projects in Mongolia. The laws assessed do not require the government to be sensitive to areas held by poor and vulnerable groups. The laws assessed do not recognize the indigenous right to FPIC. Belize has not ratified ILO Convention 169, an international human rights treaty that recognizes the indigenous right to given consent prior to acquisition of their land by the government or outsiders. The laws assessed do not require the government to weigh the costs and benefits of the project prior to expropriating land. The laws assessed do not require the government to identify all affected persons prior to expropriating land. Section 35.3 of the Law on Allocation of Land to Mongolian Citizens for Ownership (2002) provides that "the decision to replace or take back Citizen's owned land for a fee shall clearly indicate the grounds of inevitable replacement or taking the land back." The laws assessed do not require the government to consult the public or affected populations prior to expropriating land.

28 The law does not provide a clear definition of public purpose to allow for judicial review. Section 4 of the Land Acquisition Act 1894 states "Whenever it appears to the President of the Union that land

in any locality is need or is likely to be needed for any public purposes, a notification to that effect, shall be published in the Gazette, and the Collector shall cause public notice of the substance of such notification to be given at convenient places in the said locality." The laws assessed do not require the government to minimize the amount of land acquired to the amount necessary to achieve a public purpose. The laws assessed do not require the government or project developers to conduct a social impact assessment prior to expropriating land. While the Land Acquisition Act 1894 does not requirement the government to be sensitive to areas of cultural, environmental or religious significance, the Myanmar government passed the Environmental Impact Assessment Procedure in 2015 which makes it mandatory for the government and project developers to conduct an EIA prior to initiating projects in Myanmar. The laws assessed do not require the government to be sensitive to areas held by poor and vulnerable groups. The laws assessed do not recognize the indigenous right to FPIC. The laws assessed do not require the government to weigh the costs and benefits of the project prior to expropriating land. The laws assessed do not require the government to identify all affected persons prior to expropriating land. The laws assessed do not require the government to provide affected landholders with the reasons for expropriation. Section 9 of the Land Acquisition Act, 1894 states "the Collector shall then cause public notice to be given at convenient places on or near the land to be taken...Such notice shall state the particulars of the land so needed, and shall require all persons interested in the land to appear personally or by agent before the Collector at a time or place therein...to state the nature of their respective interests in the land." The laws assessed do not require the government to consult the public or affected populations prior to expropriating land. The laws assessed do not grant affected persons the right to reacquire their land in the event that the project is abandoned or the land is no longer needed for a public purpose.

29 The Constitution of Namibia, 1990 The Agricultural (Commercial) Land Reform Act, 1995, and the other laws assessed do not provide a clear definition of public purpose to allow for judicial review. The laws assessed do not require the government to minimize the amount of land acquired to the amount necessary to achieve a public purpose. The laws assessed do not require the government or project developers to conduct a social impact assessment prior to expropriating land. An EIA is required when proposed projects may impact the environment pursuant to Environmental Impact Assessment Regulations: Environmental Management Act, 2007. The laws assessed do not require the government to be sensitive to areas held by poor and vulnerable groups. The laws assessed do not recognize the indigenous right to FPIC. The laws assessed do not require the government to weigh the costs and benefits of the project prior to expropriating land. The laws assessed do not require the government to identify all affected persons prior to expropriating land. The laws assessed do not require the government to provide affected landholders with the reasons for expropriation. The laws assessed do not require the government to consult the public or affected populations prior to expropriating land. The laws assessed do not grant affected persons the right to reacquire their land in the event that the project is abandoned or the land is no longer needed for a public purpose.

30 Section 3 of the Land Acquisition Act, 1977 states "the Government of Nepal may, if it so deems necessary, acquire any land at any place for any public purpose." Section 2(b) of the Land Acquisition Act, 1977 states 'public purpose' means undertaken in the interest of or for the benefit or use of the general public, or functions to be undertaken by Government of Nepal, including the following: "(1) Project approved by Government of Nepal. (2) Project undertaken by local bodies in different levels." Section 4 of the Land Acquisition Act, 1977 states "(1) In case institution requests Government of Nepal for the acquisition of land for any of the following purposes, subject to payment of compensation and all other expenses under this Act, Government of Nepal may decide to have the land acquired for such institutions:- (a) To construct residential quarters for the staff, workers or laborers of the institution, or otherwise provide for their welfare, or undertake any function in the interest of the general public. (b) To operate a project connected with an institution fully owned by Government of Nepal, or to construct a go down for the storage of any commodes or material connected with or manufactured by any such institution." The laws assessed do not require the government to minimize the amount of land acquired to the amount necessary to achieve a public purpose. The laws assessed do not require the government or project developers to conduct a social impact assessment prior to expropriating land. The Nepal government has established EIA system for developmental projects with the formulation of Environmental Protection Rules 1997 as well as sectoral policy, laws and guidelines. In 2007, Nepal

ratified ILO Convention on Indigenous and Tribal Peoples (No. 169) adopted by the ILO in 1989. This legally binding international treaty guarantees the rights of indigenous people to consultation and participation in issues relating to their own development. However, there is no provision that establishes protection of indigenous land rights in the Land Acquisition Act, 1977, the score for this indicator is 'partial', The laws assessed do not require the government to weigh the costs and benefits of the project prior to expropriating land. The laws assessed do not require the government to identify all affected persons prior to expropriating land. Section 9 of the Land Acquisition Act, 1977 states, "the local officer shall issue a notification containing the following particulars in respect to the land...(a) the purpose for which the land is to be acquired..." The laws assessed do not require the government to consult the public or affected populations prior to expropriating land. Section 34 of the Land Acquisition Act, 1977 states "(1) If any land acquired pursuant to this Act is found unnecessary for the purpose for which it has been acquired, or there remains surplus land upon using for such purpose, it shall be returned to the expropriated land-owner...in case any land, acquired under this Act for any institution other than one fully owned by Government of Nepal is not utilized for the purpose...such land shall be returned to the expropriated landowner."

31 The laws assessed do not provide a clear definition of public purpose to allow for judicial review. Article 617 of the Civil Code (1904) states "Article 617 of the Nicaraguan Civil Code provides: No one can be deprived of property except by law or sentence based on this. Expropriation for reasons of public utility must be authorized by law or judgment based on it; and will not be checked without compensation. In case of war, it is not essential that compensation is prior. If these requirements are not fulfilled, the courts shall, and where appropriate, they restore possession to the expropriated." The laws assessed do not require the government to minimize the amount of land acquired to the amount necessary to achieve a public purpose. The laws assessed do not require the government or project developers to conduct a social impact assessment prior to expropriating land. While the laws assessed do not establish special protections for areas of cultural or religious significance, an environmental permit is required for all projects, works, industries or any other activity that for its characteristics can affect or deteriorate the environment or any of the natural resources according to the General Law for Natural Resources and the Environment, No. 217, 1996, and amended by Law No. 647, 2008; Regulations for Permits and Environmental Impact Evaluation, Decree NO. 45, 1994; System of Environmental Assessment Decree No. 76, 2006. Law 445, 2003 provides that "in cases regarding the granting of concessions and contracts for the rational exploitation of the resources found in the subsoil of the ethnic and indigenous communities' lands, by the State, the corresponding Regional Council shall issue the resolution upon consultation with indigenous communities on whose lands the natural resources are located. As a result of the consultation, the communities shall respond positively or negatively to the request of the Autonomous Regional Council." Article 17 of Law 445, 2003 provides that "in the cases where the community is opposed to the performance of the project, the granting of the concession, or the contract for exploitation, the Regional Council shall initiate a negotiate process with the community. In this negotiation process, the communities shall be represented by their traditional authorities, who shall be assisted by technical advisors of their choice. In all cases, the negotiation of the Regional Council shall foresee indemnification for eventual damages to the community, regardless of their participation in the project. Displacement or resettlement of the community will not be considered under any circumstances." Since these provision only apply to some (but not all) types of expropriation projects, the score for this indicator is 'partial', Nicaragua also ratified ILO Convention 169 (Indigenous and Tribal Peoples Convention), 1989 in 2010; this Convention establishes the right of indigenous populations to give FPIC to proposed develop projects that affect their land and natural resources. The laws assessed do not require the government to weigh the costs and benefits of the project prior to expropriating land. The laws assessed do not require the government to identify all affected persons prior to expropriating land. The laws assessed do not require the government to provide affected landholders with the reasons for expropriation. Nicaragua's score on this indicator is 'partial' because the consultation requirement only applies when land is expropriated in the Autonomous Regions of the Atlantic Coast and Rivers of Bocay, Coco, Indio, and Maiz. Law 445, 2003 provides that "in cases regarding the granting of concessions and contracts for the rational exploitation of the resources found in the subsoil of the ethnic and indigenous communities' lands, by the State, the corresponding Regional Council shall issue the resolution upon consultation with indigenous communities on whose lands the natural resources are

located. As a result of the consultation, the communities shall respond positively or negatively to the request of the Autonomous Regional Council." Article 17 of Law 445, 2003 provides that "in the cases where the community is opposed to the performance of the project, the granting of the concession, or the contract for exploitation, the Regional Council shall intitiate a negotiate process with the community. In this negotiation process, the communities shall be represented by their traditional authorities, who shall be assisted by technical advisors of their choice. In all cases, the negotiation of the Regional Council shall foresee indemnification for eventual damages to the community, regardless of their participation in the project. Displacement or resettlement of the community will not be considered under any circumstances." Since these provision only apply to indigenous populations but not all landholders affected by expropriations, the score for this indicator is 'partial', Nicaragua also ratified ILO Convention 169 (Indigenous and Tribal Peoples Convention), 1989 in 2010; this Convention establishes the right of indigenous populations to give FPIC to proposed develop projects that affect their land and natural resources. The laws assessed do not grant affected persons the right to reacquire their land in the event that the project is abandoned or the land is no longer needed for a public purpose.

32 Nigeria's Land Use Act, 1978 provides the government with broad discretion to determine what constitutes a public purpose for the compulsory acquisition of land. Sec. 51 of the Land Use Act 1978 states 'public purposes' includes- "(a) for exclusive Government use or for general public use; (b) for use by any body corporate directly established by law or by any body corporate registered under the Companies and Allied Matters Act as respects which the Government owns shares, stocks or debentures; (c) for or in connection with sanitary improvements of any kind; (d) for obtaining control over land contiguous to any part or over land the value of which will be enhanced by the construction of any railway, road or other public work or convenience about to be undertaken or provided by the Government; (e) for obtaining control over land required for or in connection with development of telecommunications or provision of electricity; (f) for obtaining control over land required for or in connection with mining purposes; (g) for obtaining control over land required for or in connection with planned urban or rural development or settlement; (h) for obtaining control over land required for or in connection with economic, industrial or agricultural development; (i) for educational and other social services..." The laws assessed do not require the government to minimize the amount of land acquired to the amount necessary to achieve a public purpose. The laws assessed do not require the government or project developers to conduct a social impact assessment prior to expropriating land. While the Land Use Act 1978 does not require State Governors to be sensitive to areas of cultural, environmental or religious significance, Section 2 of the Environmental Impact Assessment Decree requires the government or private sector bodies to conduct an Environmental Impact Assessment before initiating development projects in Nigeria. The EIA must include a description of the potential affected environment including specific information necessary to identify and assess the environmental impacts. The laws assessed do not require the government to be sensitive to areas held by poor and vulnerable groups. The laws assessed do not recognize the indigenous right to FPIC. The laws assessed do not require the government to weigh the costs and benefits of the project prior to expropriating land. The laws assessed do not require the government to identify all affected persons prior to expropriating land. The laws assessed do not require the government to provide affected landholders with the reasons for expropriation. The laws assessed do not require the government to consult the public or affected populations prior to expropriating land. The laws assessed do not grant affected persons the right to reacquire their land in the event that the project is abandoned or the land is no longer needed for a public purpose.

33 The law does not provide a clear definition of public purpose to allow for judicial review. Section 4 of the Land Acquisition Act 1894 states "Whenever it appears to the President of the Union that land in any locality is need or is likely to be needed for any public purposes, a notification to that effect, shall be published in the Gazette, and the Collector shall cause public notice of the substance of such notification to be given at convenient places in the said locality." The laws assessed do not require the government to minimize the amount of land acquired to the amount necessary to achieve a public purpose. The laws assessed do not require the government or project developers to conduct a social impact assessment prior to expropriating land. While the Land Acquisition Act 1894 does not requirement the government to be sensitive to areas of cultural, environmental or religious significance, Pakistan passed the Environmental Protection Act 1997 requires project developers to conduct an environmental impact assessment prior initiating projects. This requirement applies when land is expropriated for

development projects that impact the environment. The laws assessed do not require the government to be sensitive to areas held by poor and vulnerable groups. The laws assessed do not recognize the indigenous right to FPIC. The laws assessed do not require the government to weigh the costs and benefits of the project prior to expropriating land. The laws assessed do not require the government to identify all affected persons prior to expropriating land. The laws assessed do not require the government to provide affected landholders with the reasons for expropriation. Section 9 of the Land Acquisition Act, 1894 states "the Collector shall then cause public notice to be given at convenient places on or near the land to be taken...Such notice shall state the particulars of the land so needed, and shall require all persons interested in the land to appear personally or by agent before the Collector at a time or place therein...to state the nature of their respective interests in the land." The laws assessed do not require the government to consult the public or affected populations prior to expropriating land. The laws assessed do not grant affected persons the right to reacquire their land in the event that the project is abandoned or the land is no longer needed for a public purpose.

34 According to Section 2 of the Land Act, 1996 'public purpose' means "(a) the purpose of ensuring that land that is not being developed in a manner and to an extent conducive to the best interest, is properly developed; or (b) the purpose of making land available to citizens for- (i) subsistence farming where other land in the area for that purpose is sufficient; or (ii) for economic development so that they may share in the economic progress of the country; or (c) any educational, social welfare or community development purpose where other suitable land is either unavailable or insufficient; or (d) the purpose of preventing disruptive conduct on the part of a leaseholder in a declared land settlement scheme or development scheme from endangering the scheme; or (e) a purpose connected with the defense or public safety of Papua New Guinea; or (f) a purpose of public health, utility, necessity or convenience; or (g) the purposes of a hospital, school, training institution, public library or other similar institution; or (h) a purpose of or connected with navigation or the safety of navigation by land, air or water; or (i) the purposes of or connected with a quay, pier, wharf, jetty or landing place or port or harbour purposes or an aerodrome or landing pad; or (j) the purposes of or connected with a road, track, bridge, culvert, ferry or canal; or (k) a purpose of or connected with radio, telegraphic telephonic or other communication, and the purposes of the National Broadcasting Corporation or the Departments responsible for transport or civil aviation matters; or (l) the purposes of an oceanarium, or of an aquarium or of oceanographic research and education; or (m) the purposes of agricultural, horticultural, veterinary or forestry experimental treatment or demonstration institution, and the purpose of or a purpose connected with re-afforestation, water conservation, the prevention or control of soil erosion or the reclamation or rehabilitation of land; or (n) the purposes of a reservoir, aqueduct or water-course; (o) the purposes of or connected with the generation or supply of electricity; or (p) the purposes of a park or recreational area; or (q) a purpose of industrial development; or (r) the purpose of accomodation for employees of the State and any other prescribed authority, and the purpose of the settlement or resettlement of residents of urban areas; or (s) the purpose of ensuring that land designed under the Physical Planning Act 1989 for a particular use or uses is made available for that use or uses; (t) the purposes of a cemetery or other place for the interment of the dead; or (u) the purposes of a coronous pit or a quarry; or (v) the purposes of or a purpose connected with a welfare centre; or (w) a purpose declared by any law to be a public purpose for the purpose of this Act; or (x) a purpose ancilllary to or necessary or convenient for the carrying out of a purpose referred to in any of the preceding paragraphs of this definition." The laws assessed do not require the government to minimize the amount of land acquired to the amount necessary to achieve a public purpose. The laws assessed do not require the government or project developers to conduct a social impact assessment prior to expropriating land. An EIA is required under the Environment Act 2000 and the Environment (Permits) Regulation 2000 prior to initiating development projects that may impact the environment. The laws assessed do not require the government to be sensitive to areas held by poor and vulnerable groups. The laws assessed do not recognize the indigenous right to FPIC. The laws assessed do not require the government to weigh the costs and benefits of the project prior to expropriating land. The laws assessed do not require the government to identify all affected persons prior to expropriating land. The laws assessed do not require the government to provide affected landholders with the reasons for expropriation. Section 9 of the Land Acquisition Act, 1894 states "the Collector shall then cause public notice to be given at convenient places on or near the land to be taken...Such notice shall state the particulars of the land so needed, and

shall require all persons interested in the land to appear personally or by agent before the Collector at a time or place therein...to state the nature of their respective interests in the land." The laws assessed do not require the government to consult the public or affected populations prior to expropriating land. The laws assessed do not grant affected persons the right to reacquire their land in the event that the project is abandoned or the land is no longer needed for a public purpose.

35 The laws assessed do not provide a clear definition of public purpose to allow for judicial review. The laws assessed do not require the government to minimize the amount of land acquired to the amount necessary to achieve a public purpose. The laws assessed do not require the government or project developers to conduct a social impact assessment prior to expropriating land. Prior to initiating projects that will affect the environment, project developers must undergo an environmental impact assessment pursuant to the 2009 Law on the National System of Environmental Impact Assessment, SEIA (Law no. 27446) as amended by Decree No. 1078, 2007. See also Regulation of SEIA, Decree No. 019, 2009; Resolution NO. 157-2011-MINAM, LAW NO. 29968, 2012: Resolution No.016-2015 OEFA/ CD.
Peru ratified ILO Convention 169 (the Indigenous and Tribal Peoples Convention) in 1994. Since 1994, it has enacted a series of laws that require that the FPIC of indigenous populations must given to development projects affecting their land and resources. For example, article 2 of Law no. 29785 states "It is the right of Indigenous peoples or native to be consulted previously about the legislative or administrative measures that directly affect their collective rights, on their physical existence, cultural identity, quality of life or development." Furthermore, article 7 of Law No. 26505. The laws assessed do not require the government to weigh the costs and benefits of the project prior to expropriating land. Article 10 of Law No. 29785 (2011) states "The identification of Indigenous or native peoples to be consulted should be made by state agencies that promote the legislative or administrative measure on the base of the context of proposed measure, the level or direct relationship with the Indigenous peoples and the territorial scope of their reach." Since the law only requires that indigenous landholders be consulted (and not non-indigenous landholders), the score for this indicator is 'partial', Article 4(g) of Law No. 29785 states "Indigenous peoples or native have the right to receive from state agencies all the information necessary for them to express their point of view, adequately informed on the legislative or administrative measures to be consulted. The State has the obligation to give this information from the beginning of the consultation process and with due notice." Article 12 of Law No. 29875 requires state agencies to "provide information to Indigenous or native peoples and their representatives, from the beginning of the consultation process and with due notice, of the reasons, implications, impacts and consequences of legislative or administrative measure." Article 2 of Law No. 29785 states "It is the right of Indigenous peoples or native to be consulted previously about the legislative or administrative measures that directly affect their collective rights, on their physical existence, cultural identity, quality of life or development. Also appropriate is to make consultation on plans, programs and national and regional development projects that directly affect these rights." Article 3 of Law No. 29785 states "The purpose of consultation is to reach an agreement or consent among the State and Indigenous or native peoples according to the legislative or administrative measure that affects directly, through an intercultural dialogue that ensures their inclusion in decision-making process of the State and respectful measures of their collective rights." Since only indigenous landholders (and not non-indigenous landholders) have a right to be consulted prior to expropriating land, the score for this indicator is 'partial', The laws assessed do not grant affected persons the right to reacquire their land in the event that the project is abandoned or the land is no longer needed for a public purpose.

36 The laws assessed do not require the government or project developers to conduct a social impact assessment prior to expropriating land. Article III, Section 9 of the Constitution of the Philippines (1987) state "Private property shall not be taken for public use without just compensation" but does not define the term 'public use', Section 2 of Republic Act (RA) No. 8974, 2000 (An Act to Facilitate the Acquisition of Right-of-Way, Site, or Location for National Government Infrastructure Projects and For Other Purposes) allows the government to expropriate land for "national government projects" which are defined as "all national government infrastructure, engineering works and service contracts, including projects undertaken by government-owned and controlled corporations." Section 4 of RA 8974 states "whenever it is necessary to acquire real property for the right-of-way or location for any national government infrastructure project through expropriation, the appropriate implementing agency shall initiate the expropriation proceedings before the proper court..." The laws assessed do not require the government

to minimize the amount of land acquired to the amount necessary to achieve a public purpose. "The Indigenous People's Rights Act, 1997 establishes special legal protections for ancestral domains held by Indigenous Cultural Communities/Indigenous Peoples (ICCs/IPs)." Ancestral Domains are defined by Section 3(a) of the Act as "all areas generally belonging to ICCs/IPs comprising lands, inland waters, coastal areas and natural resources therein, held under a claim of ownership, occupied or possessed by ICCs/IPs, by themselves or through their ancestors, communally or individually since time immemorial, continuously to the present except when interrupted by war, force majeure or displacement by force, deceit, stealth, or as a consequence of government projects or any other voluntary dealings entered into by government and private individuals/corporations, and which are necessary to ensure their economic, social and cultural welfare. It shall include ancestral lands, forests, pasture, residential, agricultural, and other lands individually owned whether alienable and disposable or otherwise, hunting grounds, burial grounds, worship areas, bodies of water, mineral and other natural resources, and lands which may no longer be exclusively occupied by ICCs/IPs but from which they traditionally had access to for their subsistence and traditional activities, particularly the home ranges of ICCs/IPs who are still nomadic and/or shifting cultivators..." The Indigenous People's Act 1997 recognizes the indigenous right to FPIC. This right functions as a protection for indigenous lands. Section 3(g) of the Act states "Free Prior and Informed Consent... shall mean the consensus of all members of the ICCs/IPs to be determined in accordance with their respective customary laws and practices, free from any external manipulation, interference and coercion, and obtained after fully disclosing the intent and scope of the activity, in a language and process understandable to the community." Section 7(c) of the Act grants ICCs/IPs the right to "to stay in the territory and not to be removed therefrom." Section 7(c) also states "No ICCs/IPs will be relocated without their FPIC, nor through any means other than eminent domain. Where relocation is considered necessary as an exceptional measure, such relocation shall take place only with the free and prior informed consent of the ICCs/IPs concerned and whenever possible, they shall be guaranteed the right to return to their ancestral domains, as soon as the grounds for relocation cease to exist. When such return is not possible, as determined by agreement or through appropriate procedures, ICCs/IPs shall be provided in all possible cases with lands of quality and legal status at least equal to that of the land previously occupied by them, suitable to provide for their present needs and future development. Persons thus relocated shall likewise be fully compensated for any resulting loss or injury..." The laws assessed do not require the government to weigh the costs and benefits of the project prior to expropriating land. The laws assessed do not require the government to conduct a feasibility study prior to expropriation. Sec. 16(a) of of the Comprehensive Agrarian Reform Law, 1988 requires the Department of Agricultural to send notices of acquisition "after having identified the land, the landowners and the beneficiaries..." Sec. 4 states that "the comprehensive Agrarian Reform Law of 1988 shall cover, regardless of tenurial arrangement and commodity produced, all public and private agricultural lands..." So the score for this indicator is 'partial' since non-agricultural lands are not covered under the Act. The laws assessed do not require the government to provide affected landholders with the reasons for expropriation. Section 7(c) of the Indigenous People's Rights Act, 1997 establishes the right to Free Prior and Informed Consent, which is granted to indigenous populations. The Act indicates that indigenous communities must be consulted prior to the compulsory acquisition of their lands by the government and outsiders. However, the Act only applies to indigenous land and it is not clear that the government must consult non-indigenous communities when expropriating land. For this reason, the score for this indicator is 'partial', Only indigenous communities (ICCs/IPs) must be granted the right to return to their ancestral domains after an acquisition project ends (sec. 7(c), Indigenous People's Act 1997). Non-indigenous communities are not afforded reacquisition rights under the Philippines' national laws.

37 The laws assessed do not require the government or project developers to conduct a social impact assessment prior to expropriating land.Article 5 of Law No. 32/2015 Relating to Expropriation in the Public Interest contains a list of 'activities' in the public interest: "1) roads and railways lines; 2) water pipes and public reserves; 3) water sewage and treatment; 4) water dams; 5) rainwater pipes built alongside the roads; 6) waste treatment sites; 7) electric lines; 8) gas and oil pipelines and tanks; 9) communication lines; 10) airports and airfields, 11) motor car parks, train stations and ports; 12) biodiversity, cultural and historical reserved areas; 13) facilities meant for security and national sovereignty; 14) hospitals, health centers, dispensaries, and other public health related buildings; 15) schools and other related

buildings; government administrative buildings and those of public institutions; 17) public entertainment playgrounds, gardens and buildings; 18) markets, 19) cemeteries; 20) genocide memorial sites; 21) activities to land use and development master plans; minerals and other natural resources in the public domain." The laws assessed do not require the government to minimize the amount of land acquired to the amount necessary to achieve a public purpose. Article 10 of Law No. 32/2015 Relating to Expropriation in the Public Interest states that "the application for expropriation shall contain the following information:... (2) the document indicating that hte project does not degrade the environment." Furthermore, the Rwandan government passed the Organic Law n° 04/2005 of 08/04/2005 determining the modalities of protection, conservation and promotion of environment in Rwanda, which establishes a requirement that project developers must conduct an EIA prior to initiating projects that impact the environment. According to article 67, every project shall be subjected to environmental impact assessment, before obtaining authorization for its implementation. This applies to programmes and policies that may affect the environment. The laws assessed do not require the government to be sensitive to areas held by poor and vulnerable groups. The laws assessed do not recognize the indigenous right to FPIC. The laws assessed do not require the government to weigh the costs and benefits of the project prior to expropriating land. The laws assessed do not require the government to conduct a feasibility study prior to expropriation. Article 21 of Law No. 32/2015 Relating to Expropriation in the Public Interest states "Within seven (7) working days of taking the decision... the District or City of Kigali Mayor or the relevant Minister shall approve the list of the persons to be expropriated which serves as a basis for drawing up an inventory of the property to be expropriated." Article 10 of Law No. 32/2015 Relating to Expropriation in the Public Interest provides that the "application for expropriation shall contain the following information: (1) the description of the project proposal; (2) the indication that the project is aimed at the public interest; (3) the land master plan on which the project shall be carried out; (4) the document indicating that the project does not degrade the environment; (5) proof confirming the availability of the value of just compensation; (6) the explanatory note to verify that such a land or place suits the project; (7) the minutes indicating that the concerned population was sensitized about the importance of the project. The master plan mentioned in point 3° of this article shall indicate the following: (1) the plan or map indicating the land demarcations on which such activities shall be carried out; (2) the description of the items on that land; (3) the list indicating beneficiaries of that land; (4) the list of beneficiaries of activities on that land." Article 11 of Law No 32/2015 Relating to Expropriation in the Public Interest states "The relevant committee in charge of monitoring projects of expropriation in the public interest shall consider the relevance of the project within a period not exceeding thirty (30) days after receiving the request for expropriation and shall conduct a consultative meeting with the population living where the land is located concerning the relevance of the project of expropriation in the public interest. The committee shall inform them about the date, time, and venue of that meeting. The minutes of the meeting shall be signed by present members of the Committee." Article 11 of Law No 32/2015 Relating to Expropriation in the Public Interest states "The relevant committee in charge of monitoring projects of expropriation in the public interest shall consider the relevance of the project within a period not exceeding thirty (30) days after receiving the request for expropriation and shall conduct a consultative meeting with the population living where the land is located concerning the relevance of the project of expropriation in the public interest. The committee shall inform them about the date, time, and venue of that meeting. The minutes of the meeting shall be signed by present members of the Committee." The laws assessed do not grant affected persons the right to reacquire their land in the event that the project is abandoned or the land is no longer needed for a public purpose.

38 The laws assessed do not require the government or project developers to conduct a social impact assessment prior to expropriating land. Section 3(1) of the Public Lands Ordinance, 1960 states "Whenever the Governor in Council resolves that any land is required for any public work, the Governor may from time to time, by writing under his hand, authorise any person, together with his agents servants or workmen, to enter as often as may be necessary upon such land, and there to survey and take levels, to make borings or trial pits and to do such other acts as may be necessary with a view to the taking or appropriating of any such land." Section 3 enables the Governor to acquire land for public works. Section 2 defines 'public work' as "any work not coming within the provisions of the Railway Ordinance executed, maintained or repaired, and any measure or undertaking prosecuted, whether wholly or partly, at the public expense..." Section 21 of the Constitution of Sierra Leone states "No property of any

description shall be compulsorily, except where the following conditions are satisfied...(a) the taking of possession or acquisition is necessary in the interests of defence, public safety, public order, public morality, public health, town and country planning, the development or utilization of any property in such a manner as to promote the public benefic or the public welfare of citizens of Sierra Leone..." The laws assessed do not require the government to minimize the amount of land acquired to the amount necessary to achieve a public purpose. Sierra Leone's Environment Protection Agency Act, 2008 requires landholders to obtain an Environmental Impact Assessment License prior to engaging activities that may impact the environment. An EIA is required if the activity will cause environmental degradation or impact communities, ecosystem, or cause the diminution of the "aesthetic, recreational, scientific, historical, cultural or environmental quality." The laws assessed do not require the government to be sensitive to areas held by poor and vulnerable groups. The laws assessed do not recognize the indigenous right to FPIC. Belize has not ratified ILO Convention 169, an international human rights treaty that recognizes the indigenous right to given consent prior to acquisition of their land by the government or outsiders. The laws assessed do not require the government to weigh the costs and benefits of the project prior to expropriating land. The laws assessed do not require the government to conduct a feasibility study prior to expropriation. The laws assessed do not require the government to identify all affected persons prior to expropriating land. The laws assessed do not require the government to provide affected landholders with the reasons for expropriation. The laws assessed do not require the government to consult the public or affected populations prior to expropriating land.

39 The laws assessed do not require the government or project developers to conduct a social impact assessment prior to expropriating land. Section 2(1) of the Expropriation Act 1975 provides that "the Minister may, subject to an obligation to pay compensation, expropriate any property for public purposes or take the right to use temporarily any property for public purposes." The laws assessed do not require the government to minimize the amount of land acquired to the amount necessary to achieve a public purpose. The 2014 EIA Regulations were passed in South Africa and require that an EIA be conducted prior to initiating development projects that may impact the environment. The laws assessed do not require the government to be sensitive to areas held by poor and vulnerable groups. The laws assessed do not recognize the indigenous right to FPIC. The laws assessed do not require the government to weigh the costs and benefits of the project prior to expropriating land. The laws assessed do not require the government to conduct a feasibility study prior to expropriation. The laws assessed do not require the government to identify all affected persons prior to expropriating land. Section 33(2) of the Constitution of South Africa, 1996 provides that "everyone whose rights have been adversely affected by administrative action has the right to be given written reasons." See also Promotion of Administrative Justice Act 3 of 2000. The laws assessed do not require the government to consult the public or affected populations prior to expropriating land. The laws assessed do not grant affected persons the right to reacquire their land in the event that the project is abandoned or the land is no longer needed for a public purpose.

40 Article 70 of South Sudan's Land Act, 2009 states "(1) Any allocation of land for investment purposes shall be subject to a social, economic and environmental impact assessment to ensure that the social, economic and environmental implications of the activities on the land are taken into account before any decision is made thereon. (2) The process shall involve an analysis of the possible effects on the environment, biodiversities, people and assets. (3) A social, economic and environmental impact assessment shall be undertaken by both public and private sectors prior to any activities that may have impact on the environment and the people as determined by this Act or any other law or regulations." Sec. 73(5) of the Land Act (2009) provides that "(a) For the purpose of this Section, public interest includes but is not limited to – (a) exclusive for government or general public use; (b) planning of any new Government area or the extension or improvement of any existing Government premises; (c) sanitary improvements and urban development; (d) social housing, resettlement and reintegration; (e) control over land contiguous to any port, airstrip or airport; (f) control over land required for defense purposes; (g) control over land whose values enhanced by the construction of any railway, road, or public works about to be undertaken or provided by the Government; and (h) any other activity with a public purpose undertaken by the government as specified by any other law." Since the provision contains the clause "any other activity with a public purpose undertaken by the government..", the score for this indicator is partial. The laws assessed do not require the government to minimize the amount of land acquired

to the amount necessary to achieve a public purpose. Section 70 of the Land Act 2009 provides "any allocation of land for investment purposes shall be subject to a social, ecönomic and environmental impact assessment to ensure that social, economic and environmental implications of the activities on the land are taken into account before any decision is made thereon...a social, economic, environmental impact assessment shall be undertaken by both public and private sectors prior to any activities that may have impact on the environment and people." Section 66 and 67 of the Land Act 2009 provide special protections of pastoral lands and communal grazing land. Section 66 of the Land Act (2009) states "pastoral lands in Southern Sudan shall be delineated and protected by the appropriate level of land administration and management." Section 67 states that no person shall without permission "...carry out any activity on the communal grazing land which may prevent or restrict the residents of the traditional communities concerned from exercising their grazing rights..." The score for this indicator is 'partial' because these indicators suggest that the government and private entities must be sensitive to certain areas historically held and used by poor and vulnerable groups in South Sudan, such as communal grazers and pastoralists. The laws assessed do not require the government to weigh the costs and benefits of the project prior to expropriating land. The laws assessed do not require the government to conduct a feasibility study prior to expropriation. The laws assessed do not require the government to identify all affected persons prior to expropriating land. Section 74(4)-(5) of the Land Act (2009) requires the Minister to serve a notice to landowners and the public (through newspapers and other media), the plan must include "(a) a description of the land to be expropriated; (b) the nature of the interest intended to be expropriated and whether the interest is intended to be subject to any existing interest in the land; (c) an indication of the public purposes for which the interest is required; and (d) a statement of the reasons of expropriation by the public authority as provided for in this Section." Section 74 of the Land Act (2009) states that "the procedure for expropriation shall be based on a consultative process with the communities aor individuals concerned prior to conception of the plan of expropriation." Section 74(2) of the 2009 Land Act provides that "a public hearing may be carried out before expropriation for public purposes for large scale development." Since the provision contains the word 'may' and public hearings are only required for public purposes for large scale development, the score for this indicator is 'partial', The laws assessed do not grant affected persons the right to reacquire their land in the event that the project is abandoned or the land is no longer needed for a public purpose.

41 The laws assessed do not require the government or project developers to conduct a social impact assessment prior to expropriating land. Section 5(1) of the Land Acquisition Act 1950 provides that "where the Minister decides...that a particular land or servitude should be acquired...he shall make a written declaration that such land or servitude is needed for a public purpose..." Section 5(2) of the Land Acquisition Act, 1950 provides that "a declaration...in respect of any land or servitude shall be conclusive evidence that such land or servitude is needed for a public purpose." The law does not provide a clear legal definition of 'public purpose' to allow for judicial review. The laws assessed do not require the government to minimize the amount of land acquired to the amount necessary to achieve a public purpose. The Land Acquisition Act 1950 does not require the government to be sensitive to areas of cultural, religious, and environmental significance. However, the National Environmental (Amendment) Act, No. 56 of 1988 requires the government and project developers to submit an environmental impact assessment report (Sec. 23BB, National Environmental (Amendment) Act, No. 56 of 1988). The laws assessed do not require the government to be sensitive to areas held by poor and vulnerable groups. The laws assessed do not recognize the indigenous right to FPIC. The laws assessed do not require the government to weigh the costs and benefits of the project prior to expropriating land. The laws assessed do not require the government to conduct a feasibility study prior to expropriation. The laws assessed do not require the government to identify all affected persons prior to expropriating land. The laws assessed do not require the government to provide affected landholders with the reasons for expropriation. Section 9 of the Land Acquisition Act, 1894 states "the Collector shall then cause public notice to be given at convenient places on or near the land to be taken...Such notice shall state the particulars of the land so needed, and shall require all persons interested in the land to appear personally or by agent before the Collector at a time or place therein...to state the nature of their respective interests in the land." The laws assessed do not require the government to consult the public or affected populations prior to expropriating land. The laws assessed do not grant affected persons the right to reacquire their land in the event that the project is abandoned or the land is no longer needed for a public purpose.

42 The laws assessed do not require the government or project developers to conduct a social impact assessment prior to expropriating land. Section 3(1) of the Acquisition of Property Act, 1961 states the "The Minister may acquire any real property needed for public purpose, whether present or future, paying ushc consideration or compensation as may be agreed upon or determined under the provisions of the Act, and, in the case of immovable property, may acquire such property by freehold title or by leasehold for any term of years he may think proper." Section 2 of the Acquisition of Property Act defines 'public purposes' as "(a) for any Government or quasi-Government constructions or undertakings financed wholly or in part from public funds; (b) for or in connection with the construction or maintenance of Government hospitals or sanitary improvements of any kind, including reclamations; (c) for or in connection with the laying out of any new township, urban area, as provided for in any law, or village or the extension or improvement of any existing township, urban area or village; (c) for obtaining control over land contiguous to any railways or roads, or to other public works of convenience constructed or about to be undertaken by the Government; (e) for or in connection with the construction and maintenance of any aerdrome, landing group or airstrip and for providing access thereto; (f) for the construction of any railway authorised by legislation or for hte maintenance of working of any existing railway; (g) for any requirements of the Swaziland Electricity Board." The laws assessed do not require the government to minimize the amount of land acquired to the amount necessary to achieve a public purpose. Under the Environment Management Act, 2002 and the Environmental Audit, Assessment and Review Regulations, 2000 an EIA must be conducted prior to initiating projects that may impact the environment. The laws assessed do not require the government to be sensitive to areas held by poor and vulnerable groups. The laws assessed do not recognize the indigenous right to FPIC. The laws assessed do not require the government to weigh the costs and benefits of the project prior to expropriating land. The laws assessed do not require the government to conduct a feasibility study prior to expropriation. The laws assessed do not require the government to identify all affected persons prior to expropriating land. The laws assessed do not require the government to provide affected landholders with the reasons for expropriation. Section 9 of the Land Acquisition Act, 1894 states "the Collector shall then cause public notice to be given at convenient places on or near the land to be taken...Such notice shall state the particulars of the land so needed, and shall require all persons interested in the land to appear personally or by agent before the Collector at a time or place therein...to state the nature of their respective interests in the land." The laws assessed do not require the government to consult the public or affected populations prior to expropriating land. The laws assessed do not grant affected persons the right to reacquire their land in the event that the project is abandoned or the land is no longer needed for a public purpose.

43 Article 3 of the Expropriation Act, 2000 states "To establish any of the following undertakings for public interest purpose, the State may expropriate private land, to the extent strictly required by such undertaking: 1. National defense undertakings; 2. Communication or transportation undertakings; 3. Public utility enterprises; 4. Water conservancy undertakings; 5. Public health and environmental protection undertakings; 6. Government office buildings, office buildings of local self-governing bodies and other public buildings; 7. Educational, academic and cultural undertakings; 8. Social welfare undertakings; 9. State-owned enterprises; 10. Other undertakings for which land may be expropriated according to law. "According to Article 13 of the Expropriation Act, 2000 states "In applying for the expropriation of land or land improvements, a land use applicant shall prepare a detailed expropriation plan and submit it together with a map of the land or a list of the land improvements under expropriation and a map of proposed land use planning to the approving authority for approval, and notify the municipal or county (city) competent authority of the same. When reviewing the application referred to in the preceding paragraph, the Central Competent Authority shall review the following: 1. Is the expropriation for public interest purpose, necessary, appropriate and reasonable? 2. Does the land use applicant have the ability to carry out the undertaking? 3. Does the land expropriated for the proposed undertaking meet the current urban planning, regional planning or national land use planning? 4. Does the proposed undertaking facilitate the proper and reasonable use of land? 5. Is the financial assessment of the proposed undertaking reasonable and viable? 6. Is the resettlement plan proposed in accordance with Article 34-1 of this Act reasonable and viable? 7. Other matters that should be or may be reviewed according to law." Article 3-1 of the Expropriation Act, 2000 states that "Arable and pastoral lands in a special agricultural zone are not subject to expropriation unless it is an interspersed

odd piece of land that is difficult to circumvent. However the preceding provision does not apply to such land that is necessary for use by a national defense, communication or transportation, or water conservancy undertaking, or a public utility enterprise for erecting power transmission lines, or for use in an infrastructure project already approved by the Executive Yuan." Article 3-2 of the Expropriation Act, 2000 states "When considering expropriating land for establishing an undertaking, a land use applicant shall evaluate the public interest purpose and necessity of such undertaking and carry out overall evaluation and analysis of the following factors:... Cultural and ecological factors: Including changes in natural urban/rural sceneries, cultural relics, living conditions or life style caused by the expropriation plan, and its impacts on the ecological environment of the area, surrounding residents or the society as a whole." Article 7 of Expropriation Act, 2000 states "Land with historical relics or remains, or registered historical building thereon should be excluded from expropriation whenever possible. If it is impossible to exclude such land from expropriation, the land use applicant shall draft a preservation plan and seek the approval of the competent authority in charge of the relevant industry before proceeding with the expropriation." Article 3-1 of Expropriation Act, 2000 states "A land use applicant planning to establish an undertaking for public interest purpose should first survey and select the proper location of land and the area of land use based on the nature of the undertaking and actual needs, and should, whenever possible, avoid choosing farmland and give priority consideration to public land or land owned by state-owned enterprises without existing land use plan." Article 21 of the Indigenous People's Basic Law, 2005 states "When governments or private parties engage in land development, resource utilization, ecology conservation and academic research in indigenous land, tribe and their adjoin-land which owned by governments, they shall consult and obtain consent by indigenous peoples or tribes, even their participation, and share benefits with indigenous people. In the event that the governments, laws or regulations impose restrictions on indigenous peoples' utilization of the land in preceding paragraph and natural resources, the government shall consult with indigenous peoples, tribes or indigenous people and obtain their consent; the competent authority shall allocate ample funding in their budget to compensate their damage by restrictions. A fixed proportion of revenues generated in accordance with the preceding two paragraphs shall be allocated to the indigenous peoples' development fund to serve as returns or compensations. The central indigenous competent authority shall stipulate the regulations for delimiting the area of indigenous land, tribe and their adjoin-land which owned by governments, procedures to consult, to obtain consent by indigenous peoples or tribes and to participate and compensation to their damage by restrictions in preceding three paragraph." Article 10 of the Expropriation Act, 2000 states "Prior to submitting its plan for the proposed undertaking to the competent authority in charge of the relevant industry for approval, the land use applicant should hold a public hearing to hear the opinions of affected landowners and interested parties, unless the expropriation is for a national defense undertaking of secretive nature, or unless public hearings or explanatory meetings have been held earlier." Article 9 of the Expropriation Act, 2000 states "Unless the land has been taken by a zone expropriation project, or this Act or other laws provide otherwise, the original landowners of expropriated lands may apply to the municipal or county (city) competent authority for the redemption of their land ownerships within twenty (20) years from the date of public announcement of land expropriation at the price of the original amount of compensation without being subject to the provisions of Article 219 of the Land Act in case any of the following circumstances applies: 1. The land has not begun to be used according to the original expropriation plan three years after the payment of compensation is distributed. 2. The land has not been used for the originally approved undertaking. 3. The land is no longer used according to the original expropriation plan after it has been used accordingly for less than five (5) years." After receiving an application (from the original landowner) and verifying that the application complies with the preceding paragraph, the municipal or county (city) competent authority shall report to the original authority which approved the expropriation plan. After obtaining approval from the original approving authority, the municipal or county (city) competent authority shall notify the original landowners to repay the originally received compensation for land value as well as additional compensation for land value within six (6) months. The original landowners are deemed forfeiting their redemption right should they fail to repay the compensations within the prescribed time limit. Where the circumstance as described in Subparagraph 1 of Paragraph 1 hereof is not attributable to the fault of the land use applicant, the original landowners may not apply for the redemption of expropriated land. The term 'having begun to be used' as referred to in Subparagraph 1 of Paragraph 1 hereof shall mean that the construction of the main body of the undertaking has commenced, unless "the nature of the undertaking does not require any construction work."

44 The laws assessed do not require the government or project developers to conduct a social impact assessment prior to expropriating land. Section 3 of the Land Acquisition Act, 1967 states that "the President may...acquire any land for any estate or term where such land is required for any public purpose." Section 4(1) of the LAA, 1967 provides that "land shall be deemed to be required for a public purpose where it is required for any of the following purposes: (a) for exclusive government use, for general public use, for any Government scheme, for the development of agricultural land or for the provision of sites for industrial, agricultural or commercial development, social services or housing; (b) for or in connection with sanitary improvement of any kind, including reclamations; (c) for or in connection with the laying out of any new city, municipality, township or minor settlement or the extension or improvement of any existing city, municipality, township or minor settlement; (d) for or in connection with the development of any airfield, port or harbour; (E) for or in connection with mining for minerals or oil; (f) for use by the Community or a Corporation within the Community; (g) for use by any person or group of persons who, in the opinion of the President, should be granted such land for agricultural development." Section 4(2) of the LAA, 1967 states that "where the President is satisfied that a corporation requires any land for the purposes of construction of any work which in his opinion would be of public utility or in the public interest or in the interest of the national economy, he may, with the approval... of the National Assembly and by order published in the Gazette, declare the purpose for which such land is required to be a public purpose..." The laws assessed do not require the government to minimize the amount of land acquired to the amount necessary to achieve a public purpose. Under the Environment Management Act, 2004 and Environmental Impact Assessment and Audit Regulations, 2005, an EIA must be conducted prior to initiating projects that impact the environment. Section 4(6)(a) Village Land Act 1999 establishes a consent requirement that applies when the land acquired is less than 250 hectares. When Village land is transferred to General or Reserved land for a public purpose, communities must given consent. However, the answer for this indicator is 'partial' because, if more than 250 hectares of village land is acquired, the Minister must consider the views of villages but may approve such an acquisition without community consent. The laws assessed do not require the government to weigh the costs and benefits of the project prior to expropriating land. The laws assessed do not require the government to conduct a feasibility study prior to expropriation. The laws assessed do not require the government to identify all affected persons prior to expropriating land. Section 4(3) of the Village Land Act, 1999 provides that "the Minister shall cause to be published in the Gazette and sent to the village council having jurisdiction over the land which is subject of the proposed transfer, a notice specifying...brief statement of the reasons for the proposed transfer." See also Section 5 of the Land Act,1999. Section 4(6) of the Village Land Act, 1999 provides that while transfer for public purpose of Village to General or Reserved Land must have community consent if less than 250 hectares, Minister must only consider village views but may approve acquisition of village land when the acquired land is larger than 250 hectares. There is no explicit consultation requirement established by law that applies in cases where non-Village land is expropriated. The laws assessed do not grant affected persons the right to reacquire their land in the event that the project is abandoned or the land is no longer needed for a public purpose.

45 The laws assessed do not require the government or project developers to conduct a social impact assessment prior to expropriating land. Sec. 5 of the Immovable Property Expropriation Act, 1987 states "in the case where there is necessary for the State to acquire any immovable property for the provision of any necessary public utility or national defense, for the acquisition of natural resources, for town and city planning, for the development of agriculture, industry or land reform, or for other public purposes." Since the clause includes 'other public interests', the law only partially adopts VGGT principle 16.1. The laws assessed do not require the government to minimize the amount of land acquired to the amount necessary to achieve a public purpose. While the Immovable Property Expropriation Act 1987 does not require the government to be sensitive to areas of cultural, environmental and religious significance, Thailand passed the Regulation for the Preparation of Environmental Impact Assessment 1981 which makes it mandatory for project developers in Thailand to conduct an EIA prior to initiating projects in Thailand. The laws assessed do not require the government to be sensitive to areas held by poor and vulnerable groups. The laws assessed do not recognize the indigenous right to FPIC. Belize

has not ratified ILO Convention 169, an international human rights treaty that recognizes the indigenous right to given consent prior to acquisition of their land by the government or outsiders. The laws assessed do not require the government to weigh the costs and benefits of the project prior to expropriating land. The laws assessed do not require the government to conduct a feasibility study prior to expropriation. The laws assessed do not require the government to identify all affected persons prior to expropriating land. The Royal Decree (notification of expropriation) must include "(1) the purposes of the expropriation; (2) expropriation officer; (3) demarcated area to be expropriated as necessary..." (Sec. 6, Immovable Property Expropriation Act 1987). The Immovable Property Expropriation Act 1987 does not require the government to consult the public or affected populations prior to expropriating land. However, the Public Consultation Regulation of Government Project, B.E. 2548 (2005) requires all government project which may cause severe harm to people to arrange public consultation before starting the project. The laws assessed do not grant affected persons the right to reacquire their land in the event that the project is abandoned or the land is no longer needed for a public purpose.

46 The laws assessed do not require the government or project developers to conduct a social impact assessment prior to expropriating land. Section 3(1) of the Land Acquisition Act, 1994 (amended 2000) states "When it appears to the President that any land is likely to be required for any purposes which, in the opinion of the President, are public purposes, a Notice to that effect shall be published..." The laws assessed do not require the government to minimize the amount of land acquired to the amount necessary to achieve a public purpose. An EIA is required prior to initiating projects that impact the environment. See Environmental Management Act, 2000 and Certificate of Environmental Clearance Rules, 2001; Certificate of Environmental Clearance (Designated Activities) Order, 2001 & 2008 and amendments (2007 & 2008). The laws assessed do not require the government to be sensitive to areas held by poor and vulnerable groups. The laws assessed do not recognize the indigenous right to FPIC. The laws assessed do not require the government to weigh the costs and benefits of the project prior to expropriating land. The laws assessed do not require the government to conduct a feasibility study prior to expropriation. The laws assessed do not require the government to identify all affected persons prior to expropriating land. The notice requirement establishes that the proposed 'public purposes' must be included in the notice. Affected landholders must appear personally or through an agent claim their interest in land (See Land Acquisition Act, Form F). The laws assessed do not require the government to consult the public or affected populations prior to expropriating land. The laws assessed do not grant affected persons the right to reacquire their land in the event that the project is abandoned or the land is no longer needed for a public purpose.

47 The laws assessed do not require the government or project developers to conduct a social impact assessment prior to expropriating land. Section 3 of the Land Acquisition Act, 1965 states "'Whenever the Minister is satisfied that any land is required by the Government for a public purpose, he or she may, by statutory instrument, make a declaration to that effect." The laws assessed do not require the government to minimize the amount of land acquired to the amount necessary to achieve a public purpose. An EIA is require prior to initiating development projects that impact the environment. See National Environment Act, Cap 153 and the Environmental Impact Assessment Regulations, S.I. No. 13/1998. The laws assessed do not require the government to be sensitive to areas held by poor and vulnerable groups. The laws assessed do not recognize the indigenous right to FPIC. The laws assessed do not require the government to conduct a feasibility study prior to expropriation. The laws assessed do not require the government to identify all affected persons prior to expropriating land. The laws assessed do not require the government to provide affected landholders with the reasons for expropriation. The laws assessed do not require the government to consult the public or affected populations prior to expropriating land. The laws assessed do not grant affected persons the right to reacquire their land in the event that the project is abandoned or the land is no longer needed for a public purpose.

48 Article 61 of the 2013 Land Law 45/2013/QH13 provides a clear definition of the circumstances in which land may be recovered for national defense or security purposes. Article 62, however, contains the provision "implementation of projects which or decided by the Prime Minister, including...a) Projects on construction of industrial parks, export processing zones, hi-tech zones, economic zones, new urban centers; investment projects funded with official development assistance (ODA) capital; b) Projects on construction of offices of state agencies, central political and socio-political organiza-

tions, offices of foreign organizations with diplomatic functions; ranked historical-cultural relics and scenic spots, parks, squares, statutes, monuments and national public non-business facilities; c) Projects for construction of national technical infrastructure including transport, irrigation, water supply and drainage, electricity and communication facilities; oil and gasoline pipelines and depots; national reserve warehouses; facilities for waste collection and treatment." However, the clause is prefaced by the word 'including' which suggests that Prime Minister's discretion to expropriate land is not necessarily limited to the specified list. The Law on Land 2013 does not explicitly provide that the government must only acquire the minimum amount of land necessary to achieve a public purpose. While the Land Law 2013 does not establish specific obligations on the government to be sensitive to areas of environmental, cultural and religious significance, the Law on Environmental Protection (1993) sets a framework for EIA by which project developers must conduct an EIA prior to initiating projects in Vietnam. In December 2005, the Law on Environmental Protection was promulgated with a new scope of stipulation, structure and regulations for EIA. The laws assessed do not require the government to be sensitive to areas held by poor and vulnerable groups. The laws assessed do not recognize the indigenous right to FPIC. The laws assessed do not require the government to weigh the costs and benefits of the project prior to expropriating land. The laws assessed do not require the government to conduct a feasibility study prior to expropriation. Article 67 of the 2013 Law on Land indicates that when a decision to recover land is made, the competent state agencies must conduct a survey of the affected area. The law states that "land users whose land is recovered shall coordinate with agencies and organizations performing ground clearance in the process of the investigation, survey, measurement, inventory, and making of plans for compensation, support and resettlement. Article 67 of the 2013 Law on Land provide that state agencies must notify land users of land recovery. The contents to be notified must include land recovery, investigation, survey, measurement, and inventory plans. Article 69(1)(a) provides that notice (to affected persons) must be sent to every land user whose land is recovered, publicized in the meeting with people in the recovered area and through the mass media, posted up at offices of the commune-level People's Committee and at common public places of the residential areas of which land is recovered" Section 69(2)(a) of Land Law 2013 states "The organization in charge of compensation and ground clearance shall make the plan for compensation, support and resettlement and coordinate with the commune-level People's Committee in the locality to conduct consultations on the plans for compensation, support and resettlement in the forms of meetings with land users living in the recovered area, posting up the plan for compensation, support and resettlement at offices of the commune-level People's Committee and at common public places of the residential areas of which land is recovered." The laws assessed do not grant affected persons the right to reacquire their land in the event that the project is abandoned or the land is no longer needed for a public purpose.

49 The laws assessed do not require the government or project developers to conduct a social impact assessment prior to expropriating land. Sec. 3 of the Land Acquisition Act, 1970 states "the President may, whenever he is of the opinion that it is desirable or expedient in the interests of the Republic so to do, compulsorily acquire any property of any description." The Land Act, 1995 allows the President to alienate land for 'public purposes' which are defined by the Act as "(a) for the exclusive use of Government or for the general benefit of the people of Zambia; (b) for or in connection with sanitary improvements of any kind including reclamations; (c) for or in connection with the laying out of any new township or the extension or improvement of any existing township; (d) for or in connection with aviation; (e) for the construction of any railway authorised by legislation; (f) for obtaining control over land contiguous to any railway, road or other public works constructed or intended at any time to be constructed by Government; (g) for obtaining control over land required for or in connection with hydro-electric or other electricity generation and supply purposes; (h) for or in connection with the preservation, conservation, development or control of forest produce, fauna, flora, soil, water and other natural resources." The laws assessed do not require the government to minimize the amount of land acquired to the amount necessary to achieve a public purpose. An EIA is require prior to initiating development projects that impact the environment. See Environmental Management Act No. 12 of 2011 and Environmental Protection and Pollution Control (Environmental Impact Assessment) Regulations, 1997 The laws assessed do not require the government to be sensitive to areas held by poor and vulnerable groups. The laws assessed do not recognize the indigenous right to FPIC. The laws assessed do not require the government to weigh the costs and benefits of the project prior to expropriating land.

The laws assessed do not require the government to conduct a feasibility study prior to expropriation. The laws assessed do not require the government to identify all affected persons prior to expropriating land. The laws assessed do not require the government to provide affected landholders with the reasons for expropriation. Section 3(4) of the Land Act 1995 provides that "the President shall not alienate any land situated in a district or an area where land is held under customary tenure (a) without taking into consideration the local customary law on land tenure which is not in conflict with this Act; (b) without consulting the Chief and the local authority in the area in which the land to be alienated is situated, and in the case of a game management area, and the Director of National Parks and Wildlife Service, who shall identify the piece of land to be alienated; (c) without consulting any other person or body whose interest might be affected by the grant; and (d) if an applicant for a leasehold title has not obtained the prior approval of the chief and the local authority within whose area the land is situated." The laws assessed do not grant affected persons the right to reacquire their land in the event that the project is abandoned or the land is no longer needed for a public purpose.

50 The laws assessed do not require the government or project developers to conduct a social impact assessment prior to expropriating land. Section 3 of the Land Acquisition Act, 2004 states "the President, or any Minister duly authorised by the President for that purpose, may compulsorily acquire— [substituted by Act 14/2001 with effect from 12th June 2001.] (a) any land, where the acquisition is reasonably necessary in the interests of defence, public safety, public order, public morality, public health, town and country planning or the utilization of that or any other property for a purpose beneficial to the public generally or to any Section of the public; (b) any rural land, where the acquisition is reasonably necessary for the utilization of that or any other land— (i) for settlement for agricultural or other purposes; or (ii) for purposes of land reorganization, forestry, environmental conservation or the utilization of wild life or other natural resources; or (iii) for the relocation of persons dispossessed in consequence of the utilization of land for a purpose referred to in subparagraph (i) or (ii)." The laws assessed do not require the government to minimize the amount of land acquired to the amount necessary to achieve a public purpose. The Government of Zimbabwe gazetted the Environmental Management Act in 2002 and S.I 7 of 2007 (Environmental Impact Assessment and Ecosystems Protection) which compels prescribed projects listed under the first schedule of the EMA Act (Cap 20:27) to undergo an EIA process prior to implementation. The laws assessed do not require the government to be sensitive to areas held by poor and vulnerable groups. The laws assessed do not recognize the indigenous right to FPIC. The laws assessed do not require the government to weigh the costs and benefits of the project prior to expropriating land. The laws assessed do not require the government to conduct a feasibility study prior to expropriation. The laws assessed do not require the government to identify all affected persons prior to expropriating land. Section 5(1) of Land Acquisition Act, 2004 states "Where an acquiring authority intends to acquire any land otherwise than by agreement, he shall—(a) publish once in the Gazette and once a week for two consecutive weeks, commencing with the day on which the notice in the Gazette is published, in a newspaper circulating in the area in which the land to be acquired is situated and in such other manner as the acquiring authority thinks will best bring the notice to the attention of the owner, a preliminary notice— (i) describing the nature and extent of the land which he intends to acquire and stating that a plan or map of such land is available for inspection at a specified place and at specified times; and (ii) setting out the purposes for which the land is to be acquire..." The laws assessed do not require the government to consult the public or affected populations prior to expropriating land. Section 71(3)(d) of the Constitution of Zimbabwe, 2013 states "the law entitles any person whose property has been acquired to apply to a competent court for the prompt return of the property if the court does not confirm the acquisition."

51 The laws assessed suggest that customary tenure holders are legally entitled to compensation for expropriation in Afghanistan. Article 33(1) of the Law on Land Acquisition, 2017 states "A person who has in the implementation area of the project, procured a private property with informal (customary) deed and has built an arbitrary building on it, the building shall be valuated according to criteria set forth in article twenty-three of this law and the price of building shall be added to the original price of the land." According to Article 7 of Decree No. 83, 2003 "ownership of private property may be proved by [presentation of] valid legal and sharia based documents, provided that the invalidator document does not exist." The answer to the 'registration' indicator is partial because, according to Article 8 of the Land Management Law, 2000, "In the event that the landowner is not in possession of a legally valid

document while: (a) With the exception of the 2nd clause of this article, the property under his/her occupation is not registered in Principle Book of Government Lands; (b) Other people do not possess LVD over the same area of land; (c) Signs of construction and agricultural work have been observed on the land; (d) And where the neighbouring landowners have confirmed his occupation of the land for more than 15 years before 6th Jadi 1358* the abovementioned land, up to 10 jiribs of the grade one, shall be deemed to be his property." Furthermore, article 3 of the Law on Managing Land Affairs, 2008 defines 'owner' of land as "Owner: is the person that has manorial captured on his land, based on legal and religious documents." Article 5 of the Law on Managing Land Affairs, 2008 provides circumstances under which customary documents are considered 'trustworthy' and enforceable. Likewise, article 1 of the Law of Land survey, Verification and Registration provides that customary deeds are valid ownership documents. The law establishes a restriction on the types of land to which communities can claim rights; article 3(8)of the Law on Land Management Affairs, 2008 defines government lands as "Plat or plats of garden, watery, non-watery, hills, meadow, robe deplorable, forested, pasture, fitting deplorable, and many other lands that has registered in the properties' book." The Law on Land Acquisition, 2017 does not limit compensation to the value of developments or unexhausted improvements made on the land. Article 8 of the Land Management Law, 2000 establishes a 'time' restriction; landowners must prove they have lived on the land for more than 15 years before 6th Jadi 1358. Government of Afghanistan, *Law on Land,* 2000 Expropriation (Amended 2005); Government of Afghanistan, *Law on Managing Land Affairs*, 2008; Government of Afghanistan, *Land Management Law*, 2000; Government of Afghanistan, *Decree of the President*, No. 83, 2003; Government of Afghanistan, *Law and Pasture and Grazing Land*, 2000; Government of Afghanistan, *Constitution of Afghanistan*, 2004; LANDac, *Afghanistan Food Security and Land Governance Factsheet*, 2011; World Bank, *Land Governance Assessment National Synthesis Report (Afghanistan)*, 2016; Government of Afghanistan, *Law on Land Acquisition*, 2017; United Nations Assistance Mission in Afghanistan (UNAMA), 'The Stolen lands of Afghanistan and Its People.' *UNAMA*, Kabul, 2014; L.A. Wily, *Protecting Peoples' Interests? A Social Analysis of Land Expropriation Law of Afghanistan*, World Bank, Kabul, 2013.

52 The national-level statutory and regulatory frameworks assessed do not explicitly grant communities the right to receive compensation when their land is expropriated. According to the analysis of national laws conducted on LandMark, the national statutory and regulatory frameworks in Bangladesh do not recognize the tenure rights held by indigenous and local communities. Government of Bangladesh, *Constitution of Bangladesh*, 1972, (Amended 2011); Government of Bangladesh, *The Acquisition and Requisition of Immovable Property Ordinance*, 1982; U.S. Agency for International Development (USAID), *Property Rights and Resource Governance Profile*, Bangladesh.

53 Sec. 33(2) of the Chapter 32:02, Tribal Land Act, 1968 (amended 2008) recognizes community rights to receive compensation. Section 16 of the Tribal Land Act indicates that registration of community land in Botswana is compulsory. National Parks and most Wildlife reserves are state property under the Wildlife Conservation and National Parks Act (CAP 38:01), 1992. Section 16 of the Acquisition of Property Act CAP 32:10 indicates that compensation is not limited to developed land since affected persons can claim compensation for any damages sustained as a result of acquisitions. The laws assessed do not establish time requirements for receiving compensation. Government of Botswana, *Constitution of Botswana*, 1966 (Amended 2006); Government of Botswana, *Acquisition of Property Act Chapter 32:10*, 1955; Government of Botswana, *Tribal Land Act Chapter 32:02*, 1968 (Amended 2008); Government of Botswana, *Tribal Land Regulations*, 1970; Government of Botswana, *Chieftainship Act Chapter 41:01*, 1987; Government of Botswana, *Wildlife Conservation and National Parks Act (CAP 38:01)*, 1992.

54 Burkina Faso's laws recognize registered and unregistered customary rights as legitimate rights of possession, and these rights are granted the same level of legal protection as non-customary rights (secs. 2, 4, 6, 7, 13, Law No. 034-2009/AN On Rural Land Tenure). However, it is unclear whether unregistered community rights are granted the same level of compensation at compulsory acquisition (Arts. 30, 194, and 196, Law No. 034-2012). The laws assessed do not establish limits on the types of lands to which communities can obtain formally recognized rights. Communities may establish and manage own protected areas and access national forests under the Loi no. 006/97/ADP portant Code forestier au Burkina Faso. Compensation is not limited to developed land. Article 323 of Law No. 34/2012 (the Agrarian Reform law) provides "the compensation for expropriation should only cover the current

injury and some directly caused by the expropriation. It cannot extend to an uncertain damage, potential or indirect" (unofficial translation). Government of Burkina Faso, *Constitution of Burkina Faso (Amended 2012)*, 1991; Government of Burkina Faso, *Law 034-2012/AN Agrarian Reform Law*, 2012; *Government of Burkina Faso, Law 034-2009/AN on Rural Land Tenure*, 2009; Government of Burkina Faso, *Loi no. 006/97/ADP portant Code forestier au Burkina Faso*, 1997; Government of Burkina Faso, *National Rural Land Security Policy*, 2007.

55 When read together, articles 16 and 22 of the Law on Expropriation, 2010 indicate that compensation is limited to rightful "owners." Article 24-26 of the Land Law (2001) provide ownership rights to indigenous communities for cultivated and shifting cultivated lands, but not for other types of land held by communities (e.g. uncultivated areas). Furthermore, article 15 of the Land Law, 2001 classifies "any property that has a natural origin, such as forests, courses of navigable or floatable water, natural lakes, banks of navigable and floatable rivers and seashores" as "public property" of the state. The Sub Decree on Procedures of Registration of Land and Indigenous Communities (2009) requires communities to register their lands in order to receive recognition and compensation upon expropriation. It can be inferred that compensation is limited to cultivated community land (or areas of shifting cultivation) since Article 25 of Land Law (2001) provides that "the lands of indigenous communities include not only lands actually cultivated but also includes reserved areas necessary for the shifting of cultivation which is required by the agricultural methods they currently practice and which are recognized by administrative authorities." Since non-indigenous communities are only granted traditional user rights to forests, and the Law on Expropriation limits compensation to owners, non-indigenous communities are not granted the right to compensation for expropriation of their lands. Government of Cambodia, *Constitution of Cambodia*, 1993; Government of Cambodia, *Law on Expropriation*, 2010; Government of Cambodia, *Land Law of 2001*, 2001; Government of Cambodia, *Sub Decree on Procedures of Registration of Land of Indigenous Communities of 2009*, 2009; Government of Cambodia, *Law on Forestry*, 2003.

56 Article 42 of the Property Rights Law, 2007 provides the right to compensation for the expropriation of collectively-owned land. Article 9 of the 2007 Property Rights Law states that "unless otherwise provided by law, the establishment, modification, transfer and lapse of the right in real property shall only take effect upon registration pursuant to laws." Article 58 of the 2007 Property Rights Law broadly defines collectively owned property as "lands, forests, mountains, grasslands, unclaimed land and beaches owned collectively." Article 47 of the Law on Land Administration indicates that compensation may only be payable for cultivated land, suggesting that communities that hold and depend on uncultivated areas may not be granted compensation. Both Article 47 of the Law on Land Administration and Article 42 of the Property Rights Law indicate that compensation is only payable for crops and improvements (e.g. fixtures). Government of China, *Constitution of China*, 2004; Government of China, *The Law of Land Administration of the People's Republic of China*, 1998; Government of China, *Property Rights Law of the People's Republic of China*, 2007; Government of China, *Regulation on the Expropriation of Buildings on State-owned Land and Compensation*, 2011.

57 When read together, articles 1470 and 1489 of Ethiopia's Civil Code indicate that communities with customary tenure have a right to compensation when their lands are expropriated. In order to obtain compensation, communities must show a 'holding certificate' which is defined as a certificate of title issued by a competent authority as proof of rural land use right. (Section 2(14), Section 6(1)), Rural Land Administration and Land Use Proclamation (RLAALUP) (2005)). Under the RLAALUP, 'communal holding' is a defined as rural land which is given by the government to local residents for common grazing, forestry and other social services (Sec. 2(12), RLAALUP). However, it is unclear that compensation can be provided for land used for non-grazing and non- agricultural purposes. Section 7(3) of the RLAALUP provides that the "holder of rural land who is evicted for purpose of public use shall be given compensation proportional to the development he has made on the land and the property acquired, or shall be given substitute land thereon." The laws assessed do not establish time requirements for receiving compensation. Government of Ethiopia, *Constitution of Ethiopia*, 1994; Government of Ethiopia, *Expropriation of Landholdings for Public Purposes and Payment of Compensation Proclamation*, 2005; Government of Ethiopia, *Civil Code of Ethiopia*, 1960; Government of Ethiopia, *Public Ownership of*

Rural Lands Proclamation No. 31/1975, 1975; Government of Ethiopia, *Federal Democratic Republic of Ethiopia Rural Land Administration and Land Use Proclamation No. 456/2005*, 2005.

58 When read together, articles 20(2) and Article 267 of the Constitution of Ghana indicate that communities have a right to compensation for the expropriation of their lands. However, registration is compulsory under Section 110 of the Title Registration Act 1986. Section 4(1) of the State Lands Act, 1962 indicates that compensation is not limited to developed land. The laws assessed do not establish restrictions on the types of common properties communities for which communities can claim compensation: Article 257 of Constitution, which defines state lands, does not explicitly exclude certain types of ecosystems from customary ownership or management. Furthermore, Section 17 of the Forestry Act, 1927 provides that the ownership of land within a forest reserve shall not be altered by its constitution of a forest reserve, indicating that communities can own land in forest reserves. Government of Ghana, *Constitution of Ghana*, 1992; Government of Ghana, *State Lands Act, 1962; Government of Ghana. Administration of Lands Act*, 1962; Government of Ghana, *State Lands Regulations*, 1962; Government of Ghana, *Title Registration Act*, 1986; Government of Ghana, *Forestry Act*, 1927.

59 The Land Resumption Ordinance, 1998 provides compensation for registered property owners; however, Hong Kong's national laws do not provide a clear process by which Indigenous inhabitants can obtain formally recognized ownership rights to their land. Hong Kong's Basic Law, 1990 vaguely recognizes the 'traditional rights and interests' of Indigenous inhabitants in the Northern Territory, but there is no clear Indigenous ownership right to land recognized by law. Government of Hong Kong, *Basic Law of the Hong Kong Special Administrative Region of the People's Republic of China*, 1990; Government of Hong Kong, *Land Resumption Ordinance (CAP. 124)*, 1998, Section 2 and 8; Government of Hong Kong, *Constitution of Hong Kong*, 1990.

60 Section 3 of The Right to Fair Compensation and Transparency in Land Acquisition, Rehabilitation, and Resettlement Act (LARR Act) 2013 includes within the definitions of 'affected families', 'land owners', and 'persons interested' landholders granted forest rights under The Scheduled Tribes and Other Traditional Forest Dwellers (Recognition of Forest Rights) Act (FRA). The FRA 2006 defines 'forest rights' as "any other traditional right customarily enjoyed by the forest dwelling Scheduled Tribes or other traditional forest dwellers" (Sec. 3(1)(l), FRA, 2006). Customary forest rights must register to achieve legal recognition under the FRA 2006 (Sec. 6, Forest Rights Act, 2006). However, the score on the 'registration' indicator is partial because the LARR Act suggests that some 'affected families' may receive compensation even if their rights are not formally registered: Section 3(c)(iv) of the defines 'affected family' as "family whose source of livelihood for three years prior to the acquisition of the land is dependent on forests or water bodies and includes gatherers of forest produce, hunters, fisher folk and boatmen and such livelihood is affected due to the acquisition." The LARR Act 2013 and the FRA 2006 do not require that expropriated land must be developed in order for the forest communities to receive compensation (Secs. 25-30, LARR Act). The LARR Act 2013 and the FRA 2006 establish time requirements, which must be satisfied to obtain compensation. Sections 3(iii) and 3(iv) of the LARR Act 2013 define 'affected family' provide compensation for Scheduled Tribes and other traditional forest dwellers and families whose primary source of livelihood for three years prior to the acquisition of land is dependent on forests or water bodies. Additionally, Section 2(o) of the FRA 2006 provides that 'other traditional forest dweller' means "any member or community who has for at least three generations prior to the 13th day of December, 2005 primarily resided in and who depend on the forest or forest lands for bona fide livelihood needs." Government of India, *Constitution of India*, 2007; Government of India, *The Right to Fair Compensation and Transparency in Land Acquisition, Rehabilitation, and Resettlement Act*, 2013; Government of India, *The Scheduled Tribes and Other Traditional Forest Dwellers (Recognition of Forest Rights) Act*, 2006.

61 Article 40 of Law No. 2 of 2012 grants compensation to indigenous communities and other land tenure holders. Article 40 of Law No. 2 of 2012 defines "land tenure holders" as "parties holding means of proof issued by the competent official documenting the existence of the relevant land tenure, for example, the holders of deed of sale and purchase of unretitled land, the holders of deed of sale and purchase of uncertified customary titles/rights, and the holders of dwelling permits." In other words, the law implies that registration/formal documentation is required for communities to receiving com-

pensation when their lands are expropriated. The Constitutional Court held that, under the 1999 Forest Law, customary forests must be included as a category of 'titled forests' and thus granted the same level of protection as other titled forests. (Para. 3.13.3, 3.13. 6, Constitutional Court Decision "PUTUSAN - Nomor 35/PUU-X/2012"). The Constitutional Court's ruling suggests that compensation may be limited to community forest lands, and not granted for other types of common properties. Article 33 of Law No. 2/2012 does not establish a requirement that the land must be developed to receive compensation. Furthermore, the laws assessed do not establish time requirements for receiving compensation. Government of Indonesia, *Constitution of Indonesia*, 1945; Government of Indonesia, *Acquisition of Land for Development in the Public Interest (Law No. 2 of 2012)*, 2012; Government of Indonesia, *Act. 41 of 1999 on Forestry Affairs*, 1999; Government of Indonesia, *Basic Agrarian Act*, 1960; Government of Indonesia, *Constitutional Court Decision, PUTUSAN - Nomor 35/ PUU-X/2012*, Presidential Decree No. 71/2012, 2012.

62 The national-level statutory and regulatory frameworks assessed do not explicitly grant communities with customary tenure the right to receive compensation when their land is expropriated. In practice, community pastoralists sometimes manage municipal lands, but communities are not granted explicit legal rights to pasture lands. Government of Kazakhstan, *Constitution of Kazakhstan*, 1995; Government of Kazakhstan, *Land Code of the Republic of Kazakhstan*, 2003; Government of Kazakhstan, *Law on State-Owned Property (No. 413-IV ZRK)*, 2011; Government of Kazakhstan, *Civil Code*, 1994.

63 Section 5 of the 2012 Land Act recognizes interests in land held by customary landholders. Section 111 of said Land Act provides that just compensation shall be paid promptly in full to all persons with interests in land. Section 5(3) of the National Land Commission Act, 2012 states "...the Commission shall ensure that all unregistered land is registered within ten years from the commencement of this Act." Section 63(3) of the Constitution provides "any unregistered community land shall be held in trust by county governments on behalf of the communities." Section 6(2)-(3) of the Community Land Act, 2016 requires that communities register in order to obtain compensation, but states that "the respective county governments shall hold in trust for a community any monies payable as compensation for compulsory acquisition of any registered land..[And] upon registration of community land, the respective county governments shall promptly release the community all such monies payable for compulsory acquisition." In terms of whether there are restrictions on the types of lands for which communities can obtain formally recognized tenure, the definition of 'public land' under Article 62 of the Constitution indicates that certain land areas (e.g. forest reserves, national parks) are state property and therefore presumably may not be classified as community land. Article 63(2) of the Constitution of Kenya provides "(2) Community land consists of—(a) land lawfully registered in the name of group representatives under the provisions of any law; (b) land lawfully transferred to a specific community by any process of law; (c) any other land declared to be community land by an Act of Parliament; and (d) land that is— (i) lawfully held, managed or used by specific communities as community forests, grazing areas or shrines; (ii) ancestral lands and lands traditionally occupied by hunter-gatherer communities; or (iii) lawfully held as trust land by the county governments, but not including any public land held in trust by the county government under Article 62 (2). (3) Any unregistered community land shall be held in trust by county governments on behalf of the communities for which it is held." The 2005 Forest Act only recognizes customary use rights to forests, but does not provide compensation rights for communities. The Land Commission is charged with establishing rules for regulating the assessment of compensation (Sec. 111(2) and 113(1)(2), Land Act, 2012). The laws assessed do not establish time requirements for receiving compensation. Government of Kenya, Constitution of Kenya, 2010; Government of Kenya, Land Act, 2012; Government of Kenya, Land Acquisition Act (Repealed by Land Act 2012), 2010; Government of Kenya, *National Land Commission Act (No. 5 of 2012)*, 2012; Government of Kenya, *Forest Act*, 2005; Government of Kenya, *Community Land Act*, 2016.

64 Article 24 of the Constitution grants compensation to any affected landowner when their land is expropriated. Section 1.3 of the Community Rights Law 2009 defines 'customary land' as "land, including forest land, owned by the community individuals, groups, families or communities through longstanding rules recognized by the community. To be recognized as customary land, it is not necessary for the land to have been registered under statutory entitlements." Regarding whether registration is required for receiving compensation, the answer is 'partial' because it is not clear that communities have infor-

mal rights to non-forest land--the Community Rights Law 2009 only explicitly grants rights to forest land.(Sec. 2.3, Community Rights Law). The laws assessed do not establish development requirements or time requirements for receiving compensation. While 'Encroaching on Land and Livelihoods' did not account for rights to compensation, which are implicitly established under the Community Rights Law and Constitution of Liberia, Liberia's laws were reinterpreted to account for these rights in this paper. Government of Liberia, *Constitution of Liberia*, 1984; Government of Liberia, *An Act to Establish the Community Rights Law of 2009 with Respect to Forest Lands*, 2009; Government of Liberia, *Draft Land Rights Act*, 2014.

65 The Land Acquisition Act, 1960 defines 'land' as "means alienated land within the meaning of the State land law, land occupied under customary right and land occupied in expectation of title." The First Schedule of the Act provides that "in assessing the market value of any scheduled land which is Malay reservation land under any written law relating to Malay reservations, or a Malay holding under the Malay Reservations Enactment of Terengganu [Terengganu En. No. 17 of 1360 (A.H)], or customary land in the State of Negeri Sembilan or the State of Malacca, the fact that it is such Malay reservation land, a Malay holding, or customary land shall not be taken into account except where the scheduled land is to be devoted, after the acquisition, solely to a purpose for the benefit of persons who are eligible to hold the land under such written law." The Land Acquisition Act 1960 does not require customary tenure rights holders to develop or make improvements on their land in order to receive compensation. Government of Malaysia, *Federal Constitution*, 1974; Government of Malaysia, Land *Acquisition Act (Amended 1992)*, 1960; Government of Malaysia, National Land Code 1965 (Amended 2008), 2008; Government of Malaysia, *Land Development Act*, 1956.

66 The national-level statutory and regulatory frameworks assessed do not explicitly grant communities the right to receive compensation when their land is expropriated. According to Article 54 of the Law on Land, 2002, the government provides communities with collective use rights to summer and autumn settlements and rangelands; however, the state retains ownership of these areas. Article 30.1.8 of the Law on Allocation of Land, 2002 provides that 'owners' are entitled to compensation, but not other tenure rights holders. Government of Mongolia, *Constitution of Mongolia*, 1992; Government of Mongolia, *Law on Allocation of Land to Mongolian Citizens for Ownership*, 2002; Government of Mongolia, *Law on Land*, 2002.

67 Article 40 of the Communal Land Reform Act (CLRA) recognizes a right of customary tenure holders to obtain compensation for expropriation. Section 25(5)(c) of the Agricultural (Commercial) Land Reform Act 6 of 1995 provides that "no allowance shall be made for any unregistered right in respect of any other property or for any indirect damage or anything done with the object of obtaining compensation therefor...There are limitations on the types of lands to which communities can claim rights." The CLRA makes no provision for off-farm commonage as common property other than through leaseholds for commercial ranching & tourism enterprises. Section 15, 16, 21 and 23 of the CLRA sets limitations on the extent of communal land. Section 25 of the CLRA "if a board ratifies the allocation of customary land right...it must- (a) cause such right to be registered in the prescribed register in the name of the person to whom it was allocated; and (b) issue to that person a certificate of registration in the prescribed form and manner." Section 21 of the CLRA only provides the following types of rights to communal land "(a) a right to a farming unit; a right to a residential unit; (c) a right to any other form of customary tenure provides that may be recognized and described by the Minister..." Section 23 of said Act grants the Minister broad discretion to set limitations on the size of land that may be held under customary land rights. Section 40 and 42 of the CLRA indicate that compensation for extinguished rights may only be based on the improvements made on the land. The laws assessed do not establish 'time' restrictions on community tenure rights; Section 26 of the CLRA provides "a customary land right allocated under this Act endures for the natural life of the person to whom it is allocated" and then the right reverts to the Chief, surviving spouse, or children of the community member. Government of Namibia, *Constitution of the Republic of Namibia*, 1990; Government of Namibia, *Communal Land Reform Act*, 2002 (Amended 2013); Government of Namibia, *Agricultural (Commercial) Land Reform Act 6 of 1995*, 1995 (Amended 2013).

68 Compensation is payable to communities, but only to those communities that are residing in certain areas limited to certain areas, such as areas used for agriculture and grazing purpose (Sections 5 (1) (a), 5 (2), 6 (2), 51, Land Use Act (LUA), CAP 202, 1978). Section 6(5) of the LUA provides that "the holder and the occupier according to their respective interests of any customary right of occupancy revoked under sub-Section (2), shall be entitled to compensation for the value at the date of the revocation of their unexhausted improvements." Sub-Section 6(2) states "No single customary right of occupancy shall be granted in respect of an area of land in excess of 500 hectares if granted for agricultural purposes, or 5,000 hectares if granted for grazing purposes, except with the consent of the Governor." Customary rights are only recognized if granted by the Local Government under Section 6 of the LUA (see also Sec. 6 of the LUA). Compensation is payable only for unexhausted improvements (Secs. 6(5), 29(1), 29(4), LUA). The LUA does not establish any time requirements, which must be fulfilled by communities in order to receive compensation. Government of Nigeria, *Constitution of Nigeria*, 1999; Government of Nigeria, *Land Use Act CAP 202*, 1990.

69 Section 7(b) of Indigenous People's Rights Act 1997 (IPRA) provides Indigenous Peoples (IPs) with the right to receive just and fair compensation for any damages which they may sustain as a result of development projects. Section 71 of the IPRA establishes the Ancestral Domains Fund to cover compensation for expropriated lands. Sections 7 and 11 of the IPRA 1997 suggest that registering indigenous community land is voluntary but not necessarily required to receive compensation for expropriation. Section 11 of the IPRA provides "the rights of ICCs/IPs to their ancestral domains by virtue of Native Title shall be recognized and respected. Formal recognition, when solicited by ICCs/IPs concerned, shall be embodied in a Certificate of Ancestral Domain Title (CADT), which shall recognize the title of the concerned ICCs/IPs over the territories identified and delineated." The legal definition of 'Ancestral Domains' does not establish limits on the types of commons IPs can own. Section 3(a) of IPRA 1997 provides "Ancestral Domains ...refers to all areas generally belonging to ICCs/IPs comprising lands, inland waters, coastal areas, and natural resources therein, held under a claim of ownership, occupied or possessed by ICCs/IPs, by themselves or through their ancestors, communally or individually since time immemorial, continuously to the present...It shall include ancestral lands, forests, pasture, residential, agricultural, and other lands individually owned whether alienable and disposable or otherwise, hunting grounds, burial grounds, worship areas, bodies of water, mineral and other natural resources, and lands which may no longer be exclusively occupied by ICCs/IPs but from which they traditionally had access to for their subsistence and traditional activities, particularly the home ranges of ICCs/IPs who are still nomadic and/or shifting cultivators." The Comprehensive Agrarian Reform Law of 1988 provides that "ancestral lands of each indigenous cultural community shall include, but not be limited to, lands in the actual, continuous and open possession and occupation of the community." The laws assessed do not establish development (improvement) requirements or time requirements for receiving compensation. According to LandMark, national laws only apply to indigenous communities and not non-indigenous communities. Government of Philippines, *Constitution of Philippines*, 1987; Government of Philippines, *The Indigenous Peoples' Rights Act of 1997*, 1997; Government of the Philippines, *Comprehensive Agrarian Reform Law of 1988 (Republic Act No. 6577)*, 1988.

70 The 2013 Organic Law recognizes the following land tenure classifications: individual land, public land, and state land in the public domain. The Law does not recognize customary rights to communal land. According to the Liz Alden Wily's assessment of the LandMark legal indicators on the tenure security of IPLCs, "customary tenure and governance is extinguished on issue of formal title in favour of statutory terms and administration." Protected rights can only be acquired through registration/grant by the State. Article 20 of the Organic Law, 2013 indicates that registration is obligatory, but customary tenure is extinguished at registration. Government of Rwanda, *Constitution of Rwanda*, 2003; Government of Rwanda, *Law N.32/2015 of 11/06/2015 relating to expropriation in the public interest. Official Gazette N.35 of 31/08/2015*, 2015; Government of Rwanda, *Law N.43/2013 of 16/06/2013 governing land in Rwanda*, 2013.

71 When read together, Section 9 of the Expropriation Act, 1975 and Section 2 of the Communal Property Associations Act, 1996, and the Interim Protection Informal Land Rights Act (IPILRA) (1996) indicate that indigenous and local communities are entitled to compensation upon expropriation. Customary land is vested in the Sate or in the Ingonyama Trust in KanZulu-Natal.. Also, according to the World

Bank's Land Governance Assessment Framework (LGAF) Synthesis Report on South Arica found "a person (or community) who holds an informal right to land as defined in the Interim Protection of Informal Land Rights Act (IPILRA) (1996) may not be deprived of that right save with his or her consent or by expropriation if required in the public interest or for a public purpose (in which case compensation is payable)" (sec. 2, IPILRA). The IPLRA provides for tribal, customary, indigenous lands in rural areas and informal settlements to be protected as property (enforceable against the owners, the state) until registered but explicitly excludes tenants on registered properties (Sec. 1(1), IPLRA). However, tenants are granted legal protection under the Extension of Security Act 62 of 1997. The World Bank's LGAF study found that certain unregistered property rights, such as grazing rights, are not usually compensated. Sec. 2 of the IPILRA does not establish limitations on the types of community lands for which compensation may be paid or development (improvement) requirements. Furthermore, the National Forest Act 1998 allows for communities to claim ownership to forest land outside of protected areas and requires community consent if the government decides to create a protected area on any land held by State or Trusts on behalf of communities (Section 2(1), 8). The law establishes a time requirement: Section 1(1)(c) of the IPILRA indicates that one way to obtain a recognized right to land under the IPILRA is show "beneficial occupation of land for a continuous period of not less than five years prior to 31 December 1997." Since the Act provides (under Section 2) that compensation shall be paid when informal land rights are deprived, it can be implied that there are some time limits on who is eligible for compensation. Government of South Africa, *Constitution of South Africa*, 1996; Government of South Africa, *Expropriation Act (amended 2016)*, 1975; Government of South Africa, *Interim Protection of Informal Land Rights Act 31 of 1996*, 1996; Government of South Africa, *Communal Property Associations Act, No. 28 of 1997*, 1996; Government of South Africa, *National Forest Act*, 1998; World Bank, *Land Governance Assessment Framework Synthesis Report of South Africa*, 2016.

72 Section 75(3) of 2009 Land Act provides that "where any land is expropriated for public purpose and it is necessary to remove any person therefrom in customary occupation, compensation shall be paid as may be agreed upon." Section 64 of the Land Act states that "any community or persons affected by such activities in the area of investment shall be compensated..." Section 11(2) defines 'community land' as "(a) land lawfully registered in the name of group representatives under; (b) land lawfully held, managed or used by specific community as Section 57 of this Act or any other law for the time being in force; community forests, cultivation, grazing areas, shrines and any other (c) land lawfully transferred to a specific community by any process of law; (d) any other land declared to be community land by law." Section 39(3) of the 2009 Land Act provides "Right of ownership and derivative rights to land may be proven by any other practices recognized by communities in Southern Sudan in conformity to equity, ethics and public order." In terms of whether there is a restriction on the types of land, Section 10(2) of the Land Act indicates that communities within wetlands and forest areas designated as protected areas may not be entitled to compensation, since these areas are classified as 'public land.' Article 10(2)(c) of the Land Act defines 'public land' as land "in respect of which no private ownership including customary ownership may be established by any legal process." Since communities cannot obtain formal rights to public land, they may not be compensated in the case of expropriation. The laws assessed do not development (improvement) requirements or time requirements for receiving compensation. Government of South Sudan, *Transitional Constitution*, 2011; Government of South Sudan, *Land Act*, 2009.

73 The national-level statutory and regulatory frameworks assessed do not explicitly grant communities the right to receive compensation when their land is expropriated. According to the legal analysis conducted for LandMark, Sri Lanka's national and regulatory frameworks do not provide for recognition of community land rights. Government of Sri Lanka, *Constitution of Sri Lanka*, 1978; Government of Sri Lanka, *Land Acquisition Act CAP. 295*, 1950 (Amended 1994); Government of Sri Lanka, *Land Acquisition Regulations*, 2009.

74 Article 32 of the Indigenous Peoples Basic Law, 2005 provides "In cases of displacement or relocation of Indigenous Persons, the same shall be properly accommodated and compensated for the losses suffered as a result of forced displacement or relocation..." Article 2 of Indigenous Peoples Basic Law defines the 'Indigenous Persons' as "nationals who are registered either as Mountain Region Indigenous Peoples or as Plain Region Indigenous Peoples, and thereby obtain legal Indigenous status, being evidenced by the

household registration records of aforesaid Indigenous Persons." Article 2 defines 'Indigenous Peoples' Regions' as "areas recognized and approved by the Executive Yuan based on the official representation and application made by the Central Indigenous Authority who identifies 'Indigenous Peoples' Regions' as all areas within which Indigenous Peoples traditionally live and are duly recognized and officially defined by the Central Competent Authorities as Indigenous Peoples' geographically distinct Traditional Territories, Ancestral Domains, and/or Ancestral Lands which remain traditionally, culturally and historically distinct, hence, characteristically and intrinsically connected to the Indigenous ways of being, living, and relating." While the 1930 Land Act provides compensation for improvements (Article 242), but the broad definition of 'Indigenous Peoples' Regions' in the Indigenous Peoples Basic Law, 2005 indicates that compensation may be provided for undeveloped land. Furthermore, Article 246 indicates that compensation may be paid for graves and other commemorative objects. The laws assessed do not establish time requirements for receiving compensation. The national laws only apply to indigenous communities, but not non-indigenous communities. Government of Taiwan, *Constitution of Taiwan (Amended 2000)*, 1947; Government of Taiwan, *The Land Act (Amended 2006)*, 1930; Government of Taiwan, *Indigenous Peoples Basic Law*, 2005.

75 The Land Act, 1999 stipulates that one of its objectives is to ensure that all persons exercising powers under this Act will "pay full, fair and prompt compensation to any person whose right of occupancy or recognized long-standing occupation or customary use of land is revoked or otherwise interfered with to their detriment by the State under this Act or is acquired under the Land Acquisition Act" (Sec. 1(9), 22(1)), Land Act, 1999). Section 8 of the Village Land Regulations, 2001 provides "any villager occupying transferred land or hazard land under customary right of occupancy whether that customary right of occupancy is registered or not…" According to Alden Wily, another effect of the customary right of occupancy "is that if the Government wants to take land belonging to a villager or the village as a whole, it must pay the same levels of compensation for the land it would have to pay if the land were under a Granted Right of Occupancy or the person had a title deed. It is no longer legal for the Government to reimburse the farmer just for the value of the crops or buildings" (Village Land Regulations, Sec. 8-25). However, there is a partial restriction on the right to obtain compensation for undeveloped land: Section 12 of the Land Acquisition Act, 1967 states "no compensation shall be awarded in respect of any land which is vacant ground. (2) Where the development of any land acquired under this Act is inadequate whether such and is in an urban are or in a rural area, any compensation shall be limited to the value of the unexhausted improvements." Agricultural and pastoral lands are not considered vacant but must be in 'good estate management' to be eligible for compensation (Section 12(5)(b), Land Acquisition Act, 1967). The laws assessed do not establish restrictions on the types of land to which communities may be entitled to expropriation. Section 6 of the Land Act (1999) establishes that certain land areas are categorized as 'reserve land'; however, communities can claim compensation when their land is designated as reserve land. According to Liz Alden Wily's LandMark legal indicator assessment, "national parks, game reserves, wetland reserves involve extinction of customary rights with compensation." There is a 'partial' time requirement because "where land is used for cultivation or pasturage or mixed cultivation of pasturage, claimant must proved he or she was using the land for at least 12 months" (Section 12(4), Land Acquisition Act, 1967). Government of Tanzania, *Constitution of Tanzania*, 1977; Government of Tanzania, *Land Acquisition Act (Act No. 47 of 1967)*, 1967; Government of Tanzania, *The Land Act*, 1999; Government of Tanzania, *Village Land Act*, 1999; Government of Tanzania, *The Land (Assessment of the Value of Land for Compensation) Regulations*, 2001; Government of Tanzania, *Village Land Regulations (L.N. No. 86 of 2001)*, 2002; World Bank, *Land Governance Assessment Framework for Tanzania*, World Bank, DC, 2015.

76 The national-level statutory and regulatory frameworks assessed do not explicitly grant communities the right to receive compensation when their land is expropriated. Communities are granted temporary use rights under Regulation of the Prime Minister's Office on the Issuance of Community Land Title Deeds, 2010; however, compensation for expropriation is not provided by the regulation. According to the Network of Indigenous People in Thailand Fact Sheet "The Regulation of the Prime Minister's Office on the Issuance of Community Land Title Deeds 2010 does not provide legal recognition to traditional land tenure and resource management systems by indigenous peoples. It only allows communities to collectively manage and use State-owned land for their living while the State still retains its claim to ownership of these lands." Government of Thailand, *Constitution of Thailand*, 2007; Govern-

ment of Thailand, *Immovable Property Expropriation Act, B.E. 2530*, 1987; Government of Thailand, *Act Promulgating the Land Code B.E. 2497*, 2008; Government of Thailand, *Regulation of the Prime Minister's Office on the Issuance of Community Land Title Deeds*, 2011; Network of Indigenous People in Thailand, *The Rights of Indigenous Peoples in Thailand: 2nd Cycle Universal Periodic Review*, 2016.

77 When read together, Section 5 of the Land Acquisition Act, 1965 and Section 4 of the Land Act, 1998 indicate that communities are entitled to compensation when their land is expropriated. Section 4 of the 1998 Land Act states that "any person, family, or community holding land under customary tenure on former public land **may** acquire a certificate of customary ownership", however, certificates are not required for receiving compensation. Section 3(1) of the Land Act 1998 provides that "customary tenure is a form of tenure...providing for communal ownership and use of land"; customary landownership is also provided for by Article 237 of the Constitution. In terms of limits on the types of land, Section 44 of the Land Act excludes wetlands, forest reserves, national parks, and other protected areas from customary ownership, since the law states that these areas are held by the government in trust for the people. Section 77 of the 1998 Land Act provides that "the District Land Tribunal shall, in assessing compensation....take into account...(a) in the case of a customary owner, the value of land shall be the open market value of the unimproved land." The laws assessed do not establish time requirements for receiving compensation. Government of Uganda, *Constitution of Uganda*, 1995; Government of Uganda, *Land Acquisition Act*, 1965 (ch. 226); Government of Uganda, *Land Act (No. 16 of 1998)*, 1998.

78 Article 75(2) of the Law on Land 2013 provides the right to compensation for "communities and religious establishments using land which is not allocated or leased land by the State and having a certificate, or being eligible to be granted a certificate of land use rights and ownership of houses and other land-attached assets under this Law but not being granted that certificate yet." The law does not establish a restriction on the types of land to which communities can claim right. Article 29 of the 2004 Law on Forest Protection and Development provides that forests can be provided to village population communities. The 2013 Law on Land does not establish development (improvement) requirements, or time requirements for receiving compensation. Government of Vietnam, *Constitution of Vietnam*, 2014; Government of Vietnam, *Land Law No. 45/2013/QH13*, 2013; Government of Vietnam, *Regulations on Compensation, Support, and Resettlement Upon Land Expropriation by the State*, 2014; Government of Vietnam, *Law on Forest Protection and Development*, 2004.

79 When read together, Section 5 of the Land Acquisition Act, 1970 and Section 7(2) of the Land Act, 1995 indicate that communities have a right to receive compensation when their lands are expropriated. Section 7 of the 1995 Land Act provides that "every piece of land in a customary area which immediately before the commencement of this Act was vested in or held by any person under customary tenure shall continue to be so held and recognized." State land is broadly defined as 'land which is not situated in a customary area' (Section 2, Land Act, 1999). Furthermore, the Forest Act, 2015 indicates that communities can claim ownership to forest areas (Section 2, 49, 50). Section 15(1) of the Land Acquisition Act 1970 provides that "no compensation shall be payable in respect of undeveloped land or unutilized land. Save where the land acquisition is unutilized land to which an absentee owner is beneficially entitled, compensation shall be payable in respect of the unexhausted improvements on unutilized land." The law establishes a partial time requirement: Section 15(3) of the Land Acquisition Act, 1970 states that "in the case of land in a rural area which is used for agricultural, pastoral or mixed agricultural and pastoral purposes, the land shall not be deemed to be undeveloped unless such land has not been used for cultivation or pasturage or mixed cultivation and pasturage, as the case may be, at any time during the period of two years immediately preceding the publication of the notice to yield up possession." Government of Zambia, *Constitution of Zambia*, 2016; Government of Zambia, *Land Act No. 29 of 1995*; Government of Zambia, *Land Acquisition Act*, 1970; Government of Zambia, *Forest Act, No. 7*, 2015.

80 When read together, Section 3(4) of the Land Acquisition Act (LAA), 2002 and Sections 8(1)(a) and 12 of the Communal Land Act (CLA), 2004 (CLA) indicate that communities have a right to receive compensation for expropriated land. Under the CLA, 'communal land' is defined narrowly as land granted to communities under the Tribal Trust Land Act, 179, suggesting that registration is required and that there are restrictions on the types of common properties for which compensation claims may be made (Sec.3, CLA 2004). Furthermore, the Constitution suggests that compensation may only be provided

for agricultural land held by communities (Art. 295(1) of Zimbabwe's Constitution, 2013). Section 20 of the LAA 2002 provides compensation based on the value of the loss of land for land other than agricultural land required for resettlement purposes. When agricultural land is acquired for resettlement purposes, no compensation is payable in respect of its acquisition, except for improvements effected on it before its acquisition (Art. 72(3)(a); Art. 295(1) of Zimbabwe's Constitution, 2013). However, when non-agricultural land is acquired for non-resettlement purposes, compensation is for 'any loss reasonably incurred' (Sec. 20, LAA 2002)..." The laws assessed do not establish time requirements for receiving compensation. Government of Zimbabwe, *Constitution of Zimbabwe*, 2013; Government of Zimbabwe, *Land Acquisition Act, Ch. 20:10*, 1992; Government of Zimbabwe, *Communal Land Act Ch. 20:04 (amended 2002)*, 1983; Government of Zimbabwe, *Land Acquisition (Disposal of Rural Land) Regulations (S.I. No. 287 of 1999)*, 1999.

81 Article 27 of the Law on Land Acquisition, 2017 states "the Panel of Developing Bill of Valuation of Expropriated Properties shall, at the time of developing bill of valuation of expropriated properties and providing it to the government for approval, consider the following standards: 1- Estimated value of property in local market and neighboring areas during three months prior to preparation of the bill; 2- Observation of type, location, grade and core business value of expropriated properties." The laws assessed do not establish alternatives to the fair market value approach to calculating compensation in cases where land markets are weak or non-existent. Article 28 of the Law on Land Acquisition, 2017 states "Whenever the expropriated property is a commercial area, the price of it shall be confirmed in consideration of core business value of the adjacent commercial area and the compensation of it may be distributed in form of a business plot according to a specified price in the same project and in case of non-availability in a similar project." The Law on Land Acquisition 2017 also provides compensation for crops and trees (see articles 25, 26, and 27). Article 25 of the Law on Land Acquisition, 2017 states that "(1) Whenever there are buildings or establishments constructed on the expropriated property, the price of building and establishments shall be determined and appraised by relevant professional engineers in consideration of architectural and engineering standards, and added to the original price of the land." Furthermore, article 26 of the Law on Land Acquisition, 2017 states "(1) Whenever expropriated property is cultivated, apart from price of the property, price of seeds sowed, chemical fertilizers and costs of farming shall be figured out and if the crops are near to bloom and its grains are visible, the price of crops shall be added to the price of property, unless according to the provisions of this law, the owner or possessor is given his rights of production." The laws assessed do not provide compensation for intangible values (e.g. social, cultural, and spiritual values) associated with the land. The laws assessed do not provide affected populations with a right to negotiate compensation levels. Article 31 of the Law on Land Acquisition 2017 states "(1) Properties stated in articles twenty-five, twenty-six, twenty-seven, twenty-eight and twenty-nine of this law shall be compensated as following: 1- Equivalent land to the expropriated property in terms of type, location, grade and business value of related area according to the provisions of this law; 2- In case of unavailability of land equivalent to the expropriated property and extra land of government agencies, part of it in land, in consideration to the conditions set forth in Section (1) of this paragraph and the rest of it in cash; 3- In case of unavailability of land, total in cash. (2) All methods of payment of compensation shall be regulated through a separate regulation." The laws assessed do not require the government to follow a gender-sensitive approach to providing compensation. The laws assessed do not require that compensation must be paid prior to the taking of possession or within a fixed timeframe thereafter. Article 34 of the Law on Land Acquisition, 2017 states "(1) Whenever the owner or his/her legal representative is not satisfied regarding compensation of the expropriated property, he/she may present his/her objection statement with the reasons, within (60) days after the date of receiving information about compensation, to the Expropriating Authority. (2) The Expropriating Authority shall assess the objection stated in paragraph (1) of this article within 30 days and take appropriate decision. (3) Whenever the claimant is not satisfied with the decision of the Expropriating Authority, the issue shall be referred to jury. The Jury consists of: 1- Representative of relevant Union of Engineers. 2- Representative of Afghanistan Chamber of Commerce and Industries. 3- Representative of the people of the expropriated area. The decision of the jury is final if the parties agree; otherwise the issue shall be referred to a competent court." Government of Afghanistan, *Constitution of Afghanistan*, 2004; Government of Afghanistan, *Law on Land Acquisition*, 2017; Government of Afghanistan, *Law on Land Expropriation*, 2000 (Amended 2005, 2010); Government of Afghanistan,

Presidential Decree of the Islamic Republic of Afghanistan Concerning Modification of a Series of Articles of the Land Expropriation Law Published in the Official Gazette #(794), 142, 14221. Decree of the President No. 83, 2005; Government of Afghanistan, *Law on Managing Land Affairs*, 2008; Government of Afghanistan, *Land Management Law*, 2000; Government of Afghanistan, *Decree of the President No. 83*, 2003; Government of Afghanistan, *Law and Pasture and Grazing Land*, 2000; Government of Afghanistan, *Law of land survey, verification and registration*, 1976; L.A. Wily, *Protecting Peoples' Interests? A Social Analysis of Land Expropriation Law of Afghanistan*, Kabul, 2013; World Bank, *Land Governance Assessment Framework (final report)*, World Bank, Afghanistan, 2016.

82 The law does not provide alternatives to the fair market value approach in cases where land markets are weak or non-existent. Holders of land rights affected by expropriations for reserves may select compensation for rights lost or participation in the reserve as a stockholder in mixed economy associations established for the activities on the reserve land (Article 28, General Regulation on Land Concessions, 2007). The compensation paid for land expropriation for reserves shall be the fair value of the land as of the date of expropriation and cannot take into account the establishment of the reserve, and projects that were not completed on the land five years prior, and any improvements after notification of its status as a reserve (Article 30, General Regulation on Land Concessions, 2007). Article 30 of the General Regulation on Land Concession, 2007 provides compensation for 'private persons' and holders of property rights, suggesting that unregistered rights may not be compensated. Article 1 of the Land Law, 2004 defines 'land rights' as rights that apply to land integrated into the private domain of the State and that are of which the titleholders are individual persons or collective persons under public or private law. 'Title' is defined as 'Title (Foral)': a title approved by Government document, under which the State delimits the area of integrated lands in the public domain pertaining to the State And by it conceded to local authorities for autonomous administration. Furthermore, article 37 of the Land Law, 2004 suggests that rural communities with customary tenure must show titles to obtain compensation. The laws assessed do not require that compensation must reflect the economic activities associated with the land. The compensation paid for land expropriation for reserves shall be the fair value of the land as of the date of expropriation and cannot take into account the establishment of the reserve, and projects that were not completed on the land five years prior, and any improvements after notification of its status as a reserve. (Article 30, General Regulation on Land Concession, 2007). The law implies that any improvements made before the date of the notification of the land's status as a reserve must be accounted for in the assessment of compensation. The laws assessed do not provide compensation for intangible values (e.g. social, cultural, and spiritual values) associated with the land, alternative land as a compensation option. The laws assessed do not require the government to follow a gender-sensitive approach to providing compensation. The laws assessed do not require the government to pay compensation prior to taking possession of the land or within a specified timeframe thereafter. The laws assessed do not grant affected persons with the right to challenge compensation in courts. Government of Angola, *Constitution*, 2010; Government of Angola, *Land Act No. 9/04*, 2004; United States Agency for International Development (USAID), *Strengthening Land Tenure and Property Rights in Angola*, 2008.

83 Article 10 of Ley No. 21.499, 1977 states "The compensation shall only include the objective value of the good and the damages that arise directly as a consequence of the expropriation. For the compensation, the following shall not be taken into account: Circumstances of personal nature, affective values, hypothetical profits, or the greater value that the executed project could give to the good. Loss of profits shall not be paid. The value that corresponds to currency depreciation and the respective interests are part of the compensation" (Unofficial English translation). The law does not provide alternatives to the fair market value approach in cases where land markets are weak or non-existent. Ley No. 21.499, 1977 does not provide compensation for unrecorded rights held by Indigenous Peoples and local communities. Since the law states that compensation must not reflect loss of profits, it can be implied that compensation for the loss economic activities associated with the land is not provided by law. Article 11 of Ley No. 21.499, 1977 suggests that compensation for 'necessary' improvements may be paid, but the law does not provide compensation for all improvements. Thus the answer to the 'improvements' indicator is 'partial', The laws assessed do not provide compensation for intangible values (e.g. social, cultural, and spiritual values) associated with the land. The law provides affected persons with a right to negotiate compensation levels. Article 15 of Ley No. 21.499,1977 suggests that a compromise must be reached

between the affected person and the expropriating entity. If no compromise is reached the Tribunal de Tasaciones de la Nación must rule on the compensation amount. Article 12 of Ley No. 21.499,1977 establishes that compensation must be paid in cash, except when the payment for the expropriated property is made in another kind of value. This provision suggests that compensation may be payable in alternative land, although the provision is unclear. The laws assessed do not require the government to follow a gender-sensitive approach to providing compensation. Article 22 of Ley No. 21.499,1977 requires the expropriating body to pay the amount of compensation to a judge, but it is unclear whether the affected person must be paid this money prior to taking of possession of land. If the goods are immovable goods, the expropriator must deposit to the judge the amount of the value that the 'Tribunal de Tasaciones de la Nación' has determined. Once this value has been deposited, the judge will give to the expropriator the possession of the good. Article 15 of Ley No. 21.499 suggests that a compromise must be reached between the affected person and the expropriating entity. If no compromise is reached, the Tribunal de Tasaciones de la Nación must rule on the compensation amount. Government of Argentina, *Constitution of Argentina*, 1853 (Revised 1994); Government of Argentina, *Ley No. 21.499 Nacional De Expropiaciones*, 1977.

84 Section 8(1) of the Acquisition of Immovable Property Ordinance, 1982 provides that "In determining the amount of compensation to be awarded for any property to be acquired under this Part, the Deputy Commissioner shall take into consideration- (a) the market value of the property at the date of publication of the notice under Section 3: Provided that in determining such market value, the Deputy Commissioner shall take into account the average value, to be calculated in the prescribed manner, of the properties of similar description and with similar advantages in the vicinity during the twelve months preceding the date of publication of the notice under Section 3." The law does not provide alternatives to the fair market value approach in cases where land markets are weak or non-existent. The laws assessed do not provide compensation for unregistered customary tenure rights. The Acquisition and Requisition of Immovable Property Ordinance, 1982 states that compensation is limited to persons who are listed as owners in the land administration records. The Deputy Commissioner must take into account 'earnings' and "if in the consequence of the acquisition of the property, the person interested is likely to be compelled to change his residence or place of business, the reasonable expenses, incidental to such change" and "the damage that may be resulting from the diminution of profits" (Sec. 8(1)(d)-(f), Acquisition of Immovable Property Ordinance, 1982). According to Section 8 of the Acquisition of Immovable Property Ordinance, 1982, the Deputy Commissioner shall take into consideration: "(b) the damage that may be sustained by the person interested, by reason of the taking of any standing crops or trees which may be on the property at the time of taking possession thereof by the Deputy Commissioner; (c) the damage that may be sustained by the person interested, at the time of taking possession of the property by the Deputy Commissioner, by reason of severing such property from his other property; (d) the damage that may be sustained by the person interested, at the time of taking possession of the property by the Deputy Commissioner, by reason of the acquisition injuriously affecting his other properties, movable or immovable, in any other manner, or his earnings..." The laws assessed do not provide compensation for intangible values (e.g. social, cultural, and spiritual values) associated with the land. The laws assessed do not provide affected populations with a right to negotiate compensation levels. The laws assessed do not provide affected persons with alternative land as a compensation option. The laws assessed do not require the government to follow a gender-sensitive approach to providing compensation. The law provides that "the Deputy Commissioner shall, before taking possession of the property, tender payment of the compensation awarded by him to the person entitled thereto (unless the person protests the compensation amount) and shall paid it to them within 60 days of the deposit by the requiring persons" (Sec. 10, Acquisition of Immovable Property Ordinance, 1982). Compensation decisions can be appealed to an Arbitrator and then to the Arbitration Appellate Tribunal (Sec. 28, 34 1982 Ordinance). The Government appoints the Arbitrator. Government of Bangladesh, *Constitution of Bangladesh*, 1972 (Amended 2011); Government of Bangladesh, *The Acquisition and Requisition of Immovable Property Ordinance*, 1982; Government of Bangladesh, *Acquisition of Waste Land Act*, 1950; USAID, *Property Rights and Resource Governance*, Bangladesh, 2010.

85 According to Section 19 of the Land Acquisition (Public Purposes) Act Chapter 184, 2000, compensation must be based on "the value of the land shall, subject as hereinafter provided, be taken to be

the amount which the land, in its condition at the time of acquisition, if solid in the open market by a willing seller, might have been expected to have realized at the date of the second publication in the Gazette…" However, the Act provides an exception by stating "where land is, and but for the compulsory acquisition would continue to be, devoted to a purpose of such a nature that there is no general demand or market for land for that purpose, the compensation may, if the Board is satisfied that reinstatement in some other place is bona fide intended, be assessed on the basis of the reasonable cost of equivalent reinstatement." The laws assessed do not provide compensation for unregistered customary tenure rights. Section 36 of the Land Acquisition (Public Purposes) Act, 2000 provides that "Where land has been acquired by the Crown under this Act, the Registrar, notwithstanding anything to the contrary contained in the General Registry Act and rules made thereunder, shall- (a) in the case of unregistered land, receive and record as a deed a memorandum signed by the Minister signifying the acquisition or conveyance of the land without further proof and the memorandum shall be evidence of title in the Government to the land described therein, in fee simple absolute." Compensation is allowed "for any damage sustained by the person interested …by reason of the acquisition injuriously affecting his other property or his earnings" (Art. 19(a), Land Acquisition (Public Purposes) Act, 2000). The Land Acquisition (Public Purposes) Act, 2000 provides that "in assessing the compensation payable the Board shall assess separately the compensation payable in respect of…developed land and any buildings standing on the land." (Art. 20(b), Land Acquisition (Public Purposes) Act, 2000). The use of the terms 'buildings' and 'developed land' indicates that a wide range of improvements must be accounted for when assessing compensation levels. The laws assessed do not provide compensation for intangible values (e.g. social, cultural, and spiritual values) associated with the land. The law provides affected persons with a right to negotiate compensation levels. Section 14 of the Land Acquisition (Public Purposes) Act, 2000 provides that "the Board shall hold an inquiry at a place, date and time to be fixed by the Chairman, of which not less than fourteen clear days notice shall be given to the parties concerned, and every such inquiry shall be conducted in public." The Act further states "at the conclusion of the inquiry the Board shall decide upon claims for compensation and apportionments submitted to them…" The laws assessed do not provide affected persons with alternative land as a compensation option. The laws assessed do not require the government to follow a gender-sensitive approach to providing compensation. The Land Acquisition (Public Purposes) Act, 2000 does not require the government to pay compensation prior to the taking of possession or within a specified timeframe thereafter. Section 24 of the Land Acquisition (Public Purpose) Act provides that "an appeal shall lie to the Court of Appeal against the determination by the Board of any question of disputed compensation." Government of Belize, *Constitution of Belize*; Government of Belize, *Land Acquisition (Public Purposes) Act CAP 184*.

86 Section 151 of the Land Act, 2007 states "There shall be a Property Assessment and Valuation Agency established under the Ministry of Finance to valuate and fix the value of land and any other collateral property that may be acquired. The valuation of the land and property shall consider the total registered area, registered land category, its current use, location in relation to accessibility to vehicular road, immovable property, local market value, and other elements such as scenic beauty, cultural and historical factors, where applicable." Since the law mentions "other elements" which should be considered when calculating compensation, the answer is 'partial', The laws assessed do not provide compensation for unregistered customary tenure rights. Section 145 of the Land Act, 2007 states "Acquisition shall be in accordance to the procedure on acquisition of registered land." Section 151 of the Land Act, 2007 indicates that valuers must consider the land's 'current use', which presumably could include economic activities; however, the law is not entirely clear on whether compensation for economic activities must be provided in every case. For this answer, the score for this indicator is 'partial', Section 149 of the Land Act, 2007 states that "Compensation shall be provided for the immovable property on the acquired land." Section 151 of the Land Act, 2007 states "there shall be a Property Assessment and Valuation Agency established under the Ministry of Finance to valuate and fix the value of land and any other collateral property that may be acquired. The valuation of the land and property shall consider the total registered area, registered land category, its current use, location in relation to accessibility to vehicular road, immovable property, local market value, and other elements such as scenic beauty, cultural and historical factors, where applicable." Section 147 of the Land Act, 2007 provides rural landowners with a right opt for substitute land instead of cash compensation; however, it is unclear whether landowners can negotiate the amount of cash compensation. Section 141 of the Land Act, 2007 states

"The Government may provide substitute land or cash payment, or both, as compensation." Section 147 states "The landowner shall have the discretion to opt for substitute land or cash compensation offered by the Government in case of the land acquired from rural areas. Section 148 states "In case of the land acquired in Thromde, the landowner shall be provided cash compensation. If the land to be acquired is the only plot owned by the landowner in the Thromde, the Government shall consider a substitute land in the same Thromde. If the value of substitute land is inadequate additional cash compensation shall be provided subject to the value of land. Since there are limitations on the right to alternative land (e.g. limited to land in rural areas), the answer to the 'alternative land' indicator is 'partial', The laws assessed do not require the government to follow a gender-sensitive approach to providing compensation. Section 158 of the Land Act, 2007 provides that "the land under acquisition shall be taken over only after registering the substitute land in the name of the affected landowner or the cash compensation has been made to the landowner." The Land Act 2007 does not provide affected persons with the right to challenge compensation decisions in court. Government of Bhutan, *Constitution of Bhutan*, 2008; Government of Bhutan, *The Land Act of Bhutan*, 2007.

87 Section 16 of the Acquisition of Property Act, 1955 requires the Board of Assessment to consider the market value of the property acquired, but does not provide alternatives to the fair market value approach in cases where land markets are weak or non-existent. The laws assessed do not provide compensation for unregistered customary tenure rights. Section 16 of the Tribal Land Act, 1968 provides that "No person may occupy any other land granted under the provisions of Section 13 until there is issued to him by the land board a certificate of grant in the prescribed form...A duplicate copy of every certificate issued under the provisions of subSection (1) shall be retained by the secretary of the land board and kept in a register which shall be open to inspection on payment of such fees as may be prescribed." Section 33 of Tribal Land Act provides that "where land is granted [for public purposes] and there subsists over such land under customary form of tenure, the land board shall require the occupier to vacate the land...any person who is required to vacate land...may be granted the right to use other land, if available, and shall be entitled to adequate compensation from the State." Section 16(1)(e) of the Acquisition of Property Act, 1955 indicates that the Board must consider when assessing compensation "the reasonable expenses, if any, incidental to any change of residence or place of business of any person interested which is necessary in consequence of the acquisition." Section 16 of the Acquisition of Property Act, 1955 provides that the Board must disregard, when assessing compensation "any outlay on additions or improvements to the property to be acquired, which has been incurred after the date of service of the notice of acquisition under Section 5 unless such additions or improvements were in the opinion of the Board necessary." This provision indicates that the Board should consider, when assessing compensation, improvements made on the land prior to the date of notice of acquisition and 'necessary' improvements made after the date of notice of acquisition. The laws assessed do not provide compensation for intangible values (e.g. social, cultural, and spiritual values) associated with the land. The law provides affected persons with a right to negotiate compensation levels. Sections 10 and 11 of CAP 32-10 Acquisition of Property Act establish that an agreement must be reached on compensation levels and "the amount of such compensation, if not agreed upon, shall be determined by the Board." This implies that affected persons must be consulted about compensation levels in order to reach an agreement. Section 33 of Tribal Land Act, 1968 provides that "where land is granted [for public purposes] and there subsists over such land under customary form of tenure, the land board shall require the occupier to vacate the land...any person who is required to vacate land...may be granted the right to use other land, if available, and shall be entitled to adequate compensation from the State." However, the answer is 'partial' because the Acquisition of Property Act, 1955 does not provide alternative land as a compensation option. The laws assessed do not require the government to follow a gender-sensitive approach to providing compensation. Where compensation is payable, "the amount of such compensation shall be payable on registration of conveyance of title to the President by the Registrar of Deeds if such registration is necessary, or otherwise within two months of the receipt of the certified copy of the award by the Minister." (Section 21(b), Ch. 32:10 Acquisition of Property Act, 1955). Sections 10 and 11 of the Acquisition of Property Act, 1955 indicate that affected persons can challenge decisions on compensation, and that such disputes are settled by the Board of Assessment. The Board's decision on compensation is final (Section 20, Acquisition of Property Act). The answer to the "right to challenge compensation decisions" indicator is partial because the Board's decision is not appealable in court.

Section 26 of the Acquisition of Property Act, 1955 provides "Any person aggrieved by any delay in the payment of compensation due to him under this Act may apply to the High Court for the purpose of obtaining prompt payment thereof." Government of Botswana, *Constitution of Botswana*; Government of Botswana, *Acquisition of Property Act Chapter 32:10*, 1955; Government of Botswana, *Tribal Land Act Chapter 32:02*, 1968 (Amended 1994); Government of Botswana, *Tribal Land Regulations (Chapter 32:02)*, 1960, available at: http://faolex.fao.org/docs/pdf/bot26411.pdf.

88 Article 27 of Decree-Law No. 3.365 Regulating Land Expropriation for Public Use (1941) directs the court to pay special attention to the following factors in setting a value upon expropriated property. (1) Tax assessment value, (2) Acquisition cost, (3) Income derived from the property, (4) Location, (5) State of repair, (6) Valuation for insurance purposes, (7) Market value of comparable property during the past five years, (8) Enhance or depreciation of the expropriated party's remaining property. According to Rossen (1975), "Brazilian doctrine and case law has viewed the purpose of compensation as restoring the condemnee to his prior position, i.e., permitting purchase of a comparable asset." Additionally, Article 19 of the Land Statute, 1964 indicates that compensation must be based on the value of the property. The law does not provide alternatives to the fair market value approach in cases where land markets are weak or non-existent. The laws assessed do not provide compensation for unregistered customary tenure rights Decree-Law No. 3.365 regulating land expropriation for public use (1941), the Land Statute 1964, and the Expropriation Law for Social Interest, Law 4.132,1962 do not provide compensation for unrecorded or unregistered held by Indigenous Peoples and local communities. Article 15a of Decree-Law No. 3.365 regulating land expropriation for public use (1941) indicates that compensation may be based on the income deriving from the property. According to Rosenn (1975), Brazil courts have generally permitted claimants to recover lost profits during the period reasonably required to relocate or acquire a compare income-producing property. Article 19 of the Land Statute, 1964 indicates that compensation must reflect the value of the improvements. Additionally, article 1894 of the Constitution of Brazil provides "Useful and necessary improvements shall be compensated in cash." The laws assessed do not provide compensation for intangible values (e.g. social, cultural, and spiritual values) associated with the land. The laws assessed do not provide affected populations with a right to negotiate compensation levels. The laws assessed do not provide affected persons with alternative land as a compensation option. The laws assessed do not require the government to follow a gender-sensitive approach to providing compensation. Art. 184 of the Constitution states: The Union has the power to expropriate for social interest, for purposes of agrarian reform, rural property that is not fulfilling its social function, paying compensation in bonds redeemable in 20 years. Article 184 of the Constitution provides "The Union has the power to expropriate for social interest, for purposes of agrarian reform, rural property that is not fulfilling its social function, upon prior and just compensation in agrarian debt bonds, with a clause for preservation of real value, redeemable in up to twenty years, starting from the second year after issue, and whose utilization shall be defined in law." Article 28 of Decree-Law No. 3.365 regulating land expropriation for public use (1941) indicates that affected persons have a right to appeal the decision that fixes the prices of compensation. Government of Brazil, *Land Law, Law 4.504 of 1964*, 1964; Government of Brazil, *The Law of Expropriation for Public Utility, Decree-Law No. 3.365 of June 21*, 1941; Government of Brazil, *The Expropriation Law for Social Interest, Law 4.132 of Sept. 10*, 1962; Rosenn, Keith, *Expropriation in Argentina and Brazil: Theory and Practice. Virginia Journal of International Law. Vol. 15:2*, 1975; World Bank, *Land Governance Assessment Framework Synthesis Report*, 2016.

89 Article 323 of Law 034-2012/AN Agrarian Reform Law provides that "compensation for expropriation is determined taking into account in each case the damage material and moral [and] the state of the current value of the property." The law does not provide alternatives to FMV in cases where land markets are weak or non-existent. Burkina Faso's laws recognize unregistered customary rights as legitimate rights of possession with equity with non-customary rights but no statement as to whether requires formalization (certificate) for full equity. Articles 30, 194 and 196 of the Law 034-2012/AN Agrarian Reform Law imply equity of customary rights, including unregistered, as 'property assets' described as acquire either through assignment, certificate of evidence or 'acquisition by ordinary processes including inheritance, purchase, donations and legacies', Article 196 of Law No. 34/2012 provides that "Land and other properties of land assets of individuals are protected by the title, the land use rights and land use rights of rural people they are issued in accordance with the laws in force." Article 323

of Law 034-2012/AN Agrarian Reform Law provides that the compensation for expropriation shall relate only to the current injury and some directly caused by the expropriation. It cannot be extended to an uncertain damage, potential or indirect. Article 323 of Law 034-2012/AN Agrarian Reform Law indicates that compensation must reflect the improvements made on the land. The laws assessed do not provide compensation for intangible values (e.g. social, cultural, and spiritual values) associated with the land. The law provides affected persons with a right to negotiate compensation levels. Article 318 of Law No. 034-2012 states that "Interested parties are invited by the expropriating authority to appear in person or by proxy at a conciliation commission whose composition is determined by order of the minister concerned or the chairman of the local authority in order to agree to the amicably on the amount of compensation. The Committee notes or attempts to bring the parties agree on the amount of compensation to be calculated according to the bases specified in Article 324 below. A report stating the agreement or disagreement is drawn up and signed by the President and each member of the commission and the parties." Article 323 of Law No. 34/2012 provides "Expropriation may give rise to compensation in kind." The laws assessed do not require the government to follow a gender-sensitive approach to providing compensation. The laws assessed do not require that compensation must be paid prior to the taking of possession or within a fixed timeframe thereafter. Article 330 of Law No. 34/2012 states "In case of disagreement between the parties on the amount of compensation and in the absence conciliation, the administrative court is competent to hear the dispute." Government of Burkina Faso, *Constitution of Burkina Faso*, 1991 (Amended 2012); Government of Burkina Faso, *Law 034-2012/AN Agrarian Reform Law*, 1991; Government of Burkina Faso, *Law 034-2009/AN on Rural Land Tenure*, 2009.

90 Article 22 of the Expropriation Law, 2010 states that "financial compensation given to the property owner and/or rightful owner shall be based on a market price or replacement price on the date of declaration of expropriation." The laws assessed do not provide compensation for unregistered customary tenure rights. The Sub Decree on Procedures of Registration of Land and Indigenous Communities 2009 requires communities to register their lands in order to receive recognition and compensation. Article 29 of the Law on Expropriation, 2010 provides that "for the expropriation of a location where a business is in operation, the owner is entitled to support of additional compensation at a fair and just rate for the cost of the property that is actually affected..." Article 23 of the Law on Expropriation, 2010 requires that "the owner and/or the rightful owner has the right to compensation for actual damages commencing from the last date of declaration of expropriation for which they are entitled to fair and just compensation." The laws assessed do not provide compensation for intangible values (e.g. social, cultural, and spiritual values) associated with the land. The law provides affected persons with a right to negotiate compensation levels. Article 16 of the Law on Expropriation, 2010 states "Before proposing an expropriation project, the Expropriation Committee shall publicly conduct a survey by recording a detailed description of all rights of the owners and/or rightful owners to the immovable property and other properties which might be needed for compensation; all other related problems shall be recorded as well." According to Article 24 of Cambodia's Law on Expropriation, 2010, "compensation must be paid in cash, property or replacement rights, according to the actual situation and consent from the owner and/or the right owner and the Expropriation Committee." The laws assessed do not require the government to follow a gender-sensitive approach to providing compensation. Article 19 of the Law on Expropriation, 2010 provides "The expropriation of the ownership of immovable property and real right to immovable property can be exercised only if the Expropriation Committee has paid fair and just compensation to the property's owner and/or rightful owner in advance, in accordance with the compensation procedures and principles set out in Section 3 of Chapter 4 of this law." Article 34 of the Law on Expropriation, 2010 provides that "If there is a disagreement with the decision on the complaint by the Complaint Resolution Committee, the owner and/or the rightful owner may bring their complaint to the competent court, concerning expropriation procedures carried out improperly, the expropriation which is not for public and national interest, and the compensation which is not fair and just. The formalities and complaint procedures shall be determined by sub-decree." Government of Cambodia, *Constitution of Cambodia*, 1993. Available at: Government of Cambodia, *Law on Expropriation*, 2010 (Unofficial Translation); Government of Cambodia, *Land Law of 2001*, 2001, Chapter 3, Part 2, August 13; Government of Cambodia, *Sub Decree on Procedures of Registration of Land of Indigenous Communities of 2009*, June 9 2009.

91 Article 19 of the Regulation on the Expropriation of Buildings on State-owned Land and Compensation (2011) provides "the compensation for the value of the building expropriated shall not be less than the market price of real estate similar to the building expropriated on the date of announcement of the building expropriation decision. The value of the building expropriated shall be assessed by an eligible real estate price assessment institution according to the assessment measures for building expropriation." The law does not provide alternatives to the fair market value approach in cases where land markets are weak or non-existent. The laws assessed do not provide compensation for unregistered customary tenure rights Article 9 of the Property Law, 2007 provides that "unless otherwise provided by law, the establishment, modification, transfer and lapse of the right in real property shall only take effect upon registration pursuant to laws." Units and individuals that own or have the right to the use of the land under expropriation shall, within the time limit fixed in the announcement, register for compensation with the land administration department of the local people's government by presenting their certificates of land ownership or land-use right (Art. 46, Law on Land Administration, 1998). Article 19 of the Regulation on the Expropriation of Buildings on State-owned Land and Compensation (2011) provides that compensation must be provided "for the production or business interruption losses resulting form the building expropriation." Furthermore, Article 47 of Land on Land Administration, 1998 states that "compensation for expropriation of cultivated land shall be six to ten time the average annual output value of the expropriated land, calculated on the basis of three years preceding such requisition." Article 47 of the Law on Land Administration, 1998 provides that "expropriation compensation for cultivated land includes compensation for attachments on the land and young crops" but also states that these compensation procedures "shall be prescribed by provinces, autonomous regions and municipalities directly under the Central Government." The Regulation on the Expropriation of Buildings on State-owned Land and Compensation (2011) also indicates that compensation for improvements must be provided. Article 42 of the Property Rights Law, 2007 states "For expropriation of collectively-owned land, such fees shall be paid as compensations for the land expropriated, subsidies for resettlement, compensations for the fixtures and the young crops on land." The laws assessed do not provide compensation for intangible values (e.g. social, cultural, and spiritual values) associated with the land. The law provides affected persons with a right to negotiate compensation levels. Article 25 of the Regulation on the Expropriation of Buildings on State-owned Land and Compensation (2011) provides "the building expropriation department and an owner shall, according to this Regulation, enter into a compensation agreement on the method, amount and time of payment of compensation, location and area of the building provided for exchange of titles, relocation fees, temporary settlement fees or temporary dwelling, production or business interruption losses, time limit for relocation, transition manner, transition period and other matters. After a compensation agreement is signed, if one party fails to perform any obligation under the compensation agreement, the other party may file a lawsuit according to law." The laws assessed do not provide affected persons with alternative land as a compensation option. The laws assessed do not require the government to follow a gender-sensitive approach to providing compensation. Article 27 of he Regulation on Expropriation of Buildings on State-owned Land and Compensation, 2011 provides that "compensation shall be made before relocation in building expropriation." However, the other laws assessed do not require the government to pay compensation prior to the taking of possession or within a specified timeframe thereafter. Article 26 on the Regulation on Expropriation of Buildings on State-owned land (2011) provides that "An owner who disagrees on a compensation decision may apply for administrative reconsideration or file an administrative lawsuit according to law." Additionally, State Council's Document No. 28 of 2004, the Ministry of Land and Resources' Regulations on Public Hearings provides that a hearing must be held when there are disputes regarding compensation standards applied and the resettlement package. Under Article 16 of the Urban Structure Demolition Regulations, property owners may challenge decisions on compensation with the local court within three months of receiving an administrative decision. Government of the People's Republic of China, *Constitution of China*, 2004; Government of the People's Republic of China, *The Law of Land Administration of the People's Republic of China*, 1998; Government of China, *Property Law of the People's Republic of China*, 2007; Government of China, *Regulation on the Expropriation of Buildings on State-owned Land and Compensation*, 2011; Government of China, *Regulations for the implementation of the Land Administration Law of the People's Republic of China*, 1991; Government of China, *Regulations for the implementation of the Land Administration Law of the People's Republic of*

China (98), 1991; Goverment of China, *Regulation on Land Requisition Compensation and Resettlement of Migrants for Large and Medium Water Conservation and Hydropower Construction Projects*, 2006.

92 Article 44 of the Agrarian Development Law, 1997 provides that the price to be paid shall be the commercial appraisal updated practiced by INDA, unless there is agreement between the INDA and the parties concerned in accordance with the provisions of article 36 of the Public Procurement Act. If the affected were in disagreement over the price, the dispute will air before the competent ordinary courts in accordance with the rules set out in the Code of Civil Procedure. However, the law does not establish alternatives to FMV in cases where land markets are weak or non-existent. Article 4 of Resolución Nº 15 - Instructivo para sustanciar el proceso de expropiación en primera instancia indicates that compensation for unrecorded tenure rights may not provided under the Agrarian Development Law, 1997. The Agrarian Development Law, 1997 does not provide compensation for the economic activities associated with the land acquired. The Agrarian Development Law, 1997 does not provide compensation for improvements made on the land. The laws assessed do not provide compensation for intangible values (e.g. social, cultural, and spiritual values) associated with the land. Although the laws do not provide all affected populations with a right to negotiate compensation levels, article 57(7) of Constitution of Ecuador (2008) provides that Indigenous communes, communities, peoples and nations are recognized and guaranteed, in conformity with the Constitution and human rights agreements, conventions, declarations and other international instruments, the following collective rights:... To free prior informed consultation, within a reasonable period of time, on the plans and programs for prospecting, producing and marketing nonrenewable resources located on their lands and which could have an environmental or cultural impact on them; to participate in the profits earned from these projects and to receive compensation for social, cultural and environmental damages caused to them. The consultation that must be conducted by the competent authorities shall be mandatory and in due time. If consent of the consulted community is not obtained, steps provided for by the Constitution and the law shall be taken. Article 44 of the Agrarian Development Law, 1997 provides that "The aforementioned price must be paid in cash, without which payment INDA may not take possession of the land." The laws assessed do not require the government to follow a gender-sensitive approach to providing compensation. Article 44 of the Agrarian Development Law, 1997 provides that "The aforementioned price must be paid in cash, without which payment INDA may not take possession of the land." Article 44 of the Agrarian Development Law, 1997 provides that If the affected were in disagreement over the price, the dispute will air before the competent ordinary courts in accordance with the rules set out in the Code of Civil Procedure. Government, *Constitution of Ecuador*, 2010; Government of Ecuador, *Ley Nº 54 - Ley de Desarrollo Agrario*, 1997; Government, *Resolución Nº 15 - Instructivo para sustanciar el proceso de expropiación en primera instancia*, 2013.

93 Article 51 of the Land Proclamation No. 58/1994 provides that "Where the Government or appropriate government body expropriates land from holder(s) of right to land, the compensation, in cash or substitute land, shall be commensurate to the loss accruing to the holder of the right." The law does not provide alternatives to the fair market value approach in cases where land markets are weak or non-existent. The laws assessed do not provide compensation for unregistered customary tenure rights. Article 18 of the Land Proclamation, 1994 states "Rights of usufructuary 1) A person to whom a usufruct right over farming land has been granted, in accordance with this Proclamation, by the Land Administrative Body shall, by entering his name in the land register, have a private usufruct right over such land." Article 51 of the Land Proclamation No. 58/1994 provides that "Where the Government or appropriate government body expropriates land from holder(s) of right to land, the compensation, in cash or substitute land, shall be commensurate to the loss accruing to the holder of the right." The laws assessed do not provide compensation for intangible values (e.g. social, cultural, and spiritual values) associated with the land. The law provides affected persons with a right to negotiate compensation levels. Article 51(2) of the Land Proclamation, 1994 provides that "the extent or type of compensation shall be decided by agreement between the two parties." The laws assessed do not require the government to follow a gender-sensitive approach to providing compensation. Article 52 of the Land Proclamation, 1994 provides that "Compensation shall be paid to a holder of right whose land is expropriated in accordance with the above provisions before he leaves the land." Article 51(4) of the Land Proclamation provides that "where the parties disagree on the compensation, a petition or suit may be brought to the attention of the High Court in accordance with the relevant provisions of the Transitional Civil Code

of Eritrea." Government of Eritrea, *Constitution of Eritrea*, 1997; Government of Eritrea, *Land Proclamation No. 58/1994*, 1994.

94 Sec. 7(2) of Law No. 455/2005 provides that "the amount of compensation situated on the expropriated land shall be determined on the basis of the replacement cost of the property." According to Law NO. 455/2005, "'landholder[s]' entitled to compensation are individuals, private organizations or any other organ which has legal personality and has lawful possession over the land to be expropriated and owns property situated thereon." Rural landholders must show a 'holding certificate' which is defined as a certificate of title issued by a competent authority as proof of rural land use right. (Section 2(14), Rural Land Administration and Use Proclamation, 2005). Section 6(1) of the Proclamation on Rural Land Administration provides "the sizes of rural lands under the holdings of private persons, communities, governmental and non-governmental organizations shall be registered..." According to Ethiopia's World Bank LGAF Synthesis Report on Ethiopia, unrecorded rights to their land are not eligible for compensation of any kind (p. 86, synthesis report). Article 1474 of the Ethiopian Civil Code provides that "the amount of compensation or the value of the land that may be given to replace the expropriated land shall be equal to the amount of actual damage caused by expropriation." Although the Civil Code does not explicitly state that 'actual damage' includes 'loss of economic activity' the committee in charge of calculating compensation is required to "take into account any statement in which the parties concerned may have previously made regarding the value of the property or rights expropriated" (Ethiopia Civil Code, Art. 1475). This implies that economic activity may be accounted for in the calculation of compensation, but since indirect damage is not included (and economic activity could be interpreted as indirect damage) the answer is 'partial', The laws assessed do not provide compensation for intangible values (e.g. social, cultural, and spiritual values) associated with the land. Law No. 455/2005 does not establish a right to negotiate compensation levels. According to World Bank's Land Governance Assessment Framework Synthesis Report of Ethiopia, many scholars underscore the little participation of community in compensation decision-making and benefit packages, which implies government is the sole decision maker in compensation and benefit package computation. There is a big dissatisfaction on the less involvement of affected communities in the compensation computation process and on the level of compensation payment. Section 2 of Law No. 455/2005 provides that 'compensation' means payment to be made in cash or in kind or in both to a person for his property situated on his expropriated landholding. Furthermore, Section 8(4) of Law No. 455/2005 provides that "an urban landholder whose landholding has been expropriated under this Proclamation shall be provided with a plot of urban land, the size of which shall be determined by the urban administration to be used for the construction of a dwelling house." However, since rural landholders are not provided alternative land (but instead compensation for lost income), the answer is 'partial.' The laws assessed do not require the government to follow a gender-sensitive approach to providing compensation. "The competent authorities may not take possession of an expropriated immovable until they have paid the amount of compensation fixed" Ethiopian Civil Code, art. 1478(1). Where the sum is disputed, authorities must have paid disputed amount to the owner before taking possession. art. 1478(2). Article 1477 of the Ethiopian Civil Code states that "(1) an appeal shall lie to the court from the decisions of the [compensation appraisement] committee. (2) Such appeal shall be made within three months from the decision of the committee having been served on the interested." Government of Ethiopia, *Constitution of Ethiopia*, 1994; Government of Ethiopia, *Expropriation of Landholdings for Public Purposes and Payment of Compensation Proclamation*, 2005; Government of Ethiopia, *Civil Code of Ethiopia*, 1960; Government of Ethiopia, *Proclamation No. 456/2005 Rural Land Administration and Use Proclamation*, 2005.

95 Section 4 of the State Lands Act, 1962 provides that "the Minister may, having regard to the market value or the replacement value of the land or the cost of disturbance or any other damage suffered thereby, pay compensation in respect of that land or make an offer of land of equivalent value." Section 7 of the State Lands Act, 1962 provides that "'market value' means the sum of money which the land might have been expected to realise if sold in the open market by a willing seller at the time of the declaration." 'Replacement value' is defined by the State Lands Act as the value of the land where there is no demand or market for the land by reason of the situation or of the purpose for which the land was devoted at the time of the declaration...and shall be the amount required for reasonable re-instatement equivalent to the condition of the land at the date of the said declaration. The laws assessed do not provide compensation for unregistered customary tenure rights. Section 10 of the State Lands Regulations,

1962 provides that the "particulars of all land acquired under the Act and of all leases, licences, allocations and other grants of any right over or interest in any such land, shall be recorded and kept by the Chief Registrar of Lands." Article 267(1) of the Constitution provides "(1) All stool lands in Ghana shall vest in the appropriate stool on behalf of, and in trust for the subjects of the stool in accordance with customary law and usage..." However, Section 110 of the Title Registration Act 1986 provides "(a) where a land or an interest in land is vested in a stool or family, the stool or family shall be registered as proprietor of the land or the interest; (b) where a land or an interest in land vested in a skin is administered on behalf of the skin by any other person, the skin shall be registered as proprietor of the land or the interest and an entry shall be made in the land register showing the person who administers the land or the interest." Section 4 of the State Lands Act, 1962 provides that compensation must account for the 'cost of disturbance.' 'Cost of disturbance' is defined by Section 7 of the State Lands Act, 1962 as "the reasonable expenses incidental to any necessary change of residence or place of business by any person having a right or interest in the land." Section 4(5) of the State Lands Act, 1962 provides that "in assessing compensation under this Act account shall not be taken of the improvement on the land made within two years previous to the date of publication of [the acquisition notice]...unless the improvement was made in good faith and not made in contemplation of acquisition under this Act." The answer is partial because only good-faith improvements made within two-years prior the acquisition can be accounted for in the compensation level. Article 20(3) of the Ghana Constitution requires that "where compulsory acquisition or possession of any land effected by the State...involves displacement of any inhabitants, the State shall resettle the displaced inhabitants on suitable alternative land with due regard for their economic well-being and social and cultural values." However, the answer is 'partial' because Ghana has not passed legislation or regulations, which provide guidelines for implementing this provision. The law provides affected persons with a right to negotiate compensation levels. The law provides that "any person who claims a right or has an interest in any land...shall...submit in writing to the Lands Commission—the amount of compensation claimed and the basis for the calculation of the compensation" (Sec. 4, State Lands Act, 1962). Article 20(3) of the Constitution of Ghana provides that "where a compulsory acquisition or possession of land effected by the State... involves displacement of any inhabitants, the State shall resettle the displaced inhabitants on suitable alternative land with due regard for their economic well-being and social and cultural values." Furthermore, Section 4 of the State Lands Act, 1962 provides that the Minister may make an offer of land of equivalent value. The laws assessed do not require the government to follow a gender-sensitive approach to providing compensation. The State Lands Act, 1962 does not require that compensation must be paid prior to the taking of possession of land or within a specified timeframe thereafter. Section 10(4) of the Administration of Lands Act, 1962 provides that "a person dissatisfied with the failure of the Minister to grant compensation or with the amount of the compensation, may appeal to the appeal tribunal." Section 4(2) of the State Lands Act, 1962 provides that "where there is a dispute as to the right or interest claimed by reason of conflicting claims or interests, or any person is not satisfied with the compensation assessed by the Minister, the Minster may refer the matter to the Tribunal." Government of Ghana, *The Constitution of the Republic of Ghana 1992*, 1992; Government of Ghana, *State Lands Act*, 1962; Government of Ghana, *Administration of Lands Act*, 1962.

96 Article 82(2) of Decree No. 82-2004 (Property Law) provides that the expert valuers must make an appraisal made by experts based cadastral criteria, financial valuation, technical and market. However, the law does not provide alternatives to the fair market value approach in cases where land markets are weak or non-existent. The laws assessed do not provide compensation for unregistered customary tenure rights Article 81 of the Property Law, 2004 provides that "the owner of the expropriated property can not be deprived of it without having previously been made corresponding compensation." However, article 93 indicates that demarcation and titling of Indigenous and community lands may be a prerequisite to obtaining compensation. Article 87 also indicates that registration may be a prerequisite to obtaining compensation. Article 89 of the Property Law, 2004 provides "the real property held in community property...where there are transfers of rights registered in public records and in physical reality are bounded defined in such a way to identify the physical individuality of each of these rights or the co-assigns quotas, the Property Institute (IP) shall individualization." The Property Law, 2004 does not stipulate that compensation must include the economic activities associated with the land. Article 1 of Decreto N° 258/05 - Reforma la Ley de propiedad indicates that compensation must reflect

the improvements on the land. The laws assessed do not provide compensation for intangible values (e.g. social, cultural, and spiritual values) associated with the land. Under Article 82 of the Property Law, 2004, affected persons can appoint a person to the valuation committee, who presumably can negotiate compensation on their behalf. However, there is no clear right for affected persons to negotiate compensation directly with the valuers. The laws assessed do not provide affected persons with alternative land as a compensation option. The laws assessed do not require the government to follow a gender-sensitive approach to providing compensation. The Property Law 2004 does not require that compensation must be paid prior to the taking of possession or within a specified timeframe thereafter. Article 82(4) of Decree No. 82-2004 (Property Law) provides "If the owner or persons who dispute the ownership of the property to expropriate do not agree with the valuation established by resolution of the Institute of Property (IP), may appeal through the courts holding him the procedure in tax or tax matters says the Law of Contentious-administrative jurisdiction." Article 83 of the Property Law, 2004 also indicates that compensation allotments may be challenged in court.

97 Section 12 states that "the value of the land resumed shall be taken to be the amount which the land if sold by a willing seller in the open market might be expected to realize." Chapter 124, Land Resumption Ordinance, 1998. The law does not provide alternatives to the fair market value approach in cases where land markets are weak or non-existent. The laws assessed do not provide compensation for unregistered customary tenure rights The Land Resumption Ordinance, 1998 provides compensation for registered property owners; however, Hong Kong's national laws do not provide a clear process by which Indigenous inhabitants can obtain formally recognized ownership rights to their land. Hong Kong's Basic Law, 1990 vaguely recognizes the 'traditional rights and interests' of Indigenous inhabitants in the Northern Territory, but there is no clear Indigenous ownership right to land recognized by law. Sec. 10(d) of the Land Resumption Ordinance, 1998 provides that the Land Tribunal must account, in the determination of compensation, for "the amount of loss or damage to a business conducted by a claimant at the date of resumption on the land resumed or in any building erected thereon, due to the removal of the business from that land or building as a result of the resumption." Section 10(c) of the Land Resumption Ordinance, 1998 requires that the Land Tribunal, when assessing compensation, must account for "(c) the amount of loss or damage suffered by any claimant due to the severance of the land resumed or any building erected thereon from any other land of the claimant, or building erected thereon, contiguous or adjacent thereto." However, the law does not provide compensation for other improvements aside from buildings. The laws assessed do not provide compensation for intangible values (e.g. social, cultural, and spiritual values) associated with the land. The law provides affected persons with a right to negotiate compensation levels. Section 6 of the Land Resumption Ordinance, 1998 indicates that affected person have a right to file claims, including supporting documents, that specify how much compensation they should be entitled to. Affected persons can also accept or reject compensation awards, which demonstrates that there is, at least to some extent, a right to negotiate compensation levels. Section 8 states that "Any person claiming compensation by reason of the resumption of any land under this Ordinance, and being a person who has not been offered in writing compensation under Section 6(1)(a), or has not been served with a notice under Section 6(1)(b), may submit a claim in writing to Iity stating the nature of his estate or interest in the land and the amount which he seeks to recover." The laws assessed do not provide affected persons with alternative land as a compensation option. The Land Resumption Ordinance 1998 does not require that compensation is paid prior to the taking of possession of land or within a specified timeframe thereafter. Section 6 of the Land Resumption Ordinance, 1998 indicates that affected person have a right to file claims, including supporting documents, that specify how much compensation they should be entitled to. Affected persons can also accept or reject compensation awards, which demonstrates that there is, at least to some extent, a right to negotiate compensation levels. Government of Hong Kong, *Constitution of Hong Kong*, 1990; Government of Hong Kong, *Land Resumption Ordinance (CAP. 124)*, 1998; Government of Hong Kong, *Basic Law of the Hong Kong Special Administrative Region of the People's Republic of China*, 1990.

98 Section 26(3) of the LARR Act, 2013 provides that "where the market value...cannot be determined for the reason that - (a) the land is situated in such area where the transactions in land are restricted by or any other law for the time being in force in that area...the State Government...shall specify the floor price and minimum price per unit area of the said land based on the price calculated in the manner specified in sub-Section (1) in respect of similar types of land situated in the immediate adjoining

areas..." The answer is partial because it is unclear which approach the State Government is required to adopt when establishing a floor price/minimum price. Section 3(c)(iv) of the LARR Act 2013 defines 'affected family' as "family whose source of livelihood for three years prior to the acquisition of the land is dependent on forests or water bodies and includes gatherers of forest produce, hunters, fisher folk and boatmen and such livelihood is affected due to the acquisition." This provision suggests that compensation may be provided for some (but not all) unregistered tenure rights held by communities. The Collector shall take into account, "the damage (if any) sustained by the person interested at the time of the Collector's taking possession of the land by reason of the acquisition injuriously reflecting his other property, movable or immovable in any other manner, or his earnings" (Sec. 28, LARR Act, 2013). Section 28 further states that "compensation should take into account whether the person interested is compelled to change his residence of place of business and any bona fide damage resulting from diminution of profits." The Collector must take into account the value of attached to the land or buildings acquired, including the value of trees and plants attached to the land, the use of services by persons working in agriculture, forestry, and other fields (Sec. 29, LARR Act, 2013). The LARR Act, 2013 provides special requirements for Schedule Castes and Tribes in India (particularly vulnerable groups in India), which suggests that, in some cases, cultural, historical and other intangible value of land must be accounted for when assessing compensation. The law states "in case of land being acquired from members of the Scheduled Castes or the Scheduled Tribes, at least one-third of the compensation shall be paid to affected families initially as first installment and the rest shall be paid after taking over of the possession of the land...the affected families of the Scheduled Tribes shall be resettled preferable in the same Scheduled Area in a compact block so that they can retain their ethnic, linguistic and cultural identity" (Sec. 41(6)-(7), LARR Act). The law provides affected persons with a right to negotiate compensation levels. Section 26(1)(c) of the LARR Act, 2013 provides that the compensation amount must be consented to or agreed upon by affected families. Furthermore, Section 5 of the LARR Act, 2013 states "whenever a Social Impact Assessment is required...the appropriate Government shall ensure that a public hearing is held at the affected area...to ascertain the views of the affected families to be recorded in the Social Impact Assessment Report." The Second Schedule of the LARR Act, 2013 provides alternative forms of payment, such as alternative land. To some extent, the LARR Act, 2013 requires the government to follow a gender-sensitive approach to providing compensation. Section 3(m) of the LARR Act 2013 provides that "widows, divorcees, and women deserted by families shall be considered separate (affected) families...an adult of either gender with or without spouse children or dependents shall be considered as a separate family for purposes of this Act..." Section 38 of the LARR provides that compensation must be paid within three months of the Collector taking possession of the land. In cases of urgency, the Collector must tender payment of eighty percent of such compensation before taking possession, but in some cases is not required to pay the remaining amount of compensation. Section 40(5) of the LARR Act, 2013 provides that "no additional compensation will be required to be paid in case the project is one that affects the sovereignty and integrity of India, the security and strategic interests of the State or relations with foreign nations." Section 64 -74 of the LARR Act, 2013 provide that persons interested can object to decisions on the measurements of acquired land, the amount of compensation, the person to whom it is payable to first the Land Acquisition Authority and then the High Court. Government of India, *Constitution of India*, 2007; Government of India, *The Right to Fair Compensation and Transparency in Land Acquisition, Rehabilitation and Resettlement Act*, 2013; Government of India, *The Scheduled Tribes and Other Traditional Forest Dwellers (Recognition of Forest Rights) Act*, 2006; Government of India, *Right to Fair Compensation and Transparency in Land Acquisition, Rehabilitation and Resettlement (Social Impact Assessment and Consent) Rules*, 2014.

99 Although the law does not explicitly state that fair market value is used to assess compensation, Article 34 states "the Compensation value that is appraised by the Appraiser... shall be the value at the time of announcement of the location confirmation of development in the Public Interest" Acquisition of Land for Development in the Public Interest, Law No. 2 of 2012. The laws assessed do not provide alternatives to fair compensation in cases where land markets are weak or non-existent. The laws assessed do not provide compensation for unregistered customary tenure rights. Section 41(2) of Acquisition of Land for Development in the Public Interest, Law No. 2 of 2012 states "upon giving Compensation, the Entitled Parties to Compensation must deliver evidence of possession or ownership of Objects of the Acquired Land to the Agency needing land through the Land Administrator." Article 40 of Law No. 2.

of 2012 provides a list of persons entitled to compensation, and included on that list is 'land tenure holders', 'Land tenure holders' is defined as "parties holding means of proof issued by the competent official documenting the existence of the relevant land tenure, for example, the holders of deed of sale and purchase of unretitled land, the holders of deed of sale and purchase of uncertified customary titles/rights, and the holders of dwelling permits." 'Entitled Party' is defined in Section 2 of Law No. 2 of 2012 as "any party by whom objects of the acquired land are possessed or owned." Article 27(4) also indicates that Entitled Parties are those who hold titles to land. Article 33(f) of the Acquisition of Land for Development in the Public Interest, Law No. 2 of 2012 grants compensation for 'other appraisable loss.' 'Other appraisable loss' is defined by law as "nonphysical loss equivalent to money value, for example, loss due to loss of business or job, cost of change of location, cost of change of profession, and loss of value of the remaining property." Article 33 of Law No. 2 of 2012 grants compensation to buildings, plants and other objects related to the expropriated land. The laws assessed do not provide compensation for intangible values (e.g. social, cultural, and spiritual values) associated with the land. The law provides affected persons with a right to negotiate compensation levels. Article 37 of Law No. 2 of 12 provides "the Land Administrator shall conduct a negotiation with the Entitled Parties within thirty (30) working days of the submission of the results of appraisal of the Appraiser to the Land Administrator for determination of the form and/or the amount of Compensation under the results of appraisal of Compensation." Article 36 of Law No. 2 of 2012 states "the giving of Compensation may be made in the form of: (a) money; (b) substitute land; (c) resettlements; (d) shareholding"---'shareholding' means placement of shares in the relevant development activities in the public interest and/or the management thereof is made by agreement of the parties. Article 40 states "compensation for indigenous land shall be given in the form of substitute land, resettlements, or other forms as agreed upon by the relevant indigenous people." The laws assessed do not require the government to follow a gender-sensitive approach to providing compensation. Article 41of Law No. 2 of 2012 provides that "upon giving Compensation, the Entitled Parties to Compensation must (a) release titles..." Article 38 of Law No. 2 of 2012 states "(1) where there is agreement on the form and/or the amount of Compensation, the Entitled Parties may file an objection with the local district court within fourteen (14) working days of the negotiation on determination compensation...(2) the district court shall decide the form and/or the amount of compensation within thirty (30) working days of the receipt of the filing of objection." Government of Indonesia, *Constitution of Indonesia*, 1945; Government of Indonesia, *Acquisition of Land for Development in the Public Interest (Law No. 2 of 2012)*; Government of Indonesia, *Act. 41 of 1999 on Forestry Affairs*, 1999; Government of Indonesia, *Basic Agrarian Act*, 1960; Government of Indonesia, *Constitutional Court Decision, PUTUSAN - Nomor 35/ PUU-X/2012*, 2012.

100 Article 87(2) of the Land Code, 2003 provides that the price of land should include the market value of land and the rights there to, as well all losses in full borne by the landowner in connection with the compulsory acquisition of land. The law does not provide alternatives to the fair market value approach in cases where land markets are weak or non-existent. The laws assessed do not provide compensation for unrecorded rights held by communities. Compensation includes damages as a result of the expropriation, which include "the uncollected income which this person would receive in case of usual conditions of turnover if its right was not broken (lost profit) shall by the person which right is broken" Civil Code, 1994 (last amended 2014), Art. 9(4) (referred to by State-Owned property, Art. 67(4)). Article 67 of Law on State-Owned Property, 2011 provides that "the value of buildings and other real estate on the land is included in the compensation." However, since the law does not account for other types of improvements aside from buildings, the answer is 'partial.' The laws assessed do not provide compensation for intangible values (e.g. social, cultural, and spiritual values) associated with the land. The law provides affected persons with a right to negotiate compensation levels. Pursuant to Article 65(5) of the Law on State-owned Property, 2011 the standing committee of the local legislature is required to meet with those whose rights will be affected to discuss compensation, but not the public. Under Article 65(6) of the Law on State-Owned Property, the standing committee and affected persons must reach on agreement on the price of the withdrawn parcel of land, the payment due date, and other issues. Article 87(3) of the Land Code, 2003 indicates that alternative land may be provided as a compensation option. This provisions states "By agreement with the owner of the land or non-land user may be provided instead of land redeemed for expropriation for public needs, another plot of land provided by offsetting the cost of land or rights to it in the redeemed value of the land or rights to it in

the market value at the time of cessation of ownership or land use." The law assessed do not require the government to follow a gender-sensitive approach to providing compensation to affected populations. Payment must be made in a lump sum, no later than one month from the date of the agreement with the landowner, or, if expropriating through a court judgment, from the date on which the judgment takes effect. Compensation must be paid before the property right is transferred. Law on State-Owned Property, 2011, Art. 68(1), (4) Article 88 of the Land Code, 2003 states "If the owner or non-state land user disagrees with the decision to purchase his land for public needs, or with no agreement on the price of the redeemed land or other terms of redemption, the local executive authority which decided on redemption may bring a lawsuit on redemption of the land. Such action may be brought after one year but not later than two years from the date of the owner of the land user or non-site notification referred to in paragraph 2 of Article 85 of this Code, unless otherwise provided by legislative acts of the Republic of Kazakhstan. The land owner or land user has the right to non-state challenge in court the decision of the local executive body of the redemption of his land (land use rights)." Government of Kazakhstan, *Constitution of Kazakhstan*, 1995; Government of Kazakhstan, *Land Code of the Republic of Kazakhstan*, 2003; Government of Kazakhstan, *Law on State-Owned Property (No. 413-IV ZRK)*, 2011; Government of Kazakhstan, *Civil Code*, 1994.

101 The Land Act 2012 does not explicitly provide that the market value approach must be used when calculating compensation. Section 111 of the Land Act, 2012 states that "if land is acquired compulsorily under this Act, just compensation shall be paid promptly in full and to all persons whose interests in the land have been determined. (2) The Commission shall make rules to regulate the assessment of just compensation." Since it is unclear which approach must be used when calculating 'full' compensation, the answer is partial. Section 6(2)-(3) of the Community Land Act, 2016 requires that communities register in order to obtain compensation, but states that "the respective county governments shall hold in trust for a community any monies payable as compensation for compulsory acquisition of any registered land..[And] upon registration of community land, the respective county governments shall promptly release the community all such monies payable for compulsory acquisition." Since communities are entitled to compensation upon registration, but are guaranteed compensation before the registration process is complete, the answer for this indicator is 'partial', Section 126(b) of the Land Act, 2012 provides that "the compensation to be paid under Section 120 shall be limited to the damage done to trees, plants, growing crops and permanent improvements on the land, together with a periodical sum for diminution in the profits of the land and of adjoining land by reason of that use." The laws assessed do not provide compensation for intangible values (e.g. social, cultural, and spiritual values) associated with the land. Sec. 117 of Land Act 2012 states "where the land is acquired for the Government the Commissioner may agree with the person whom he has determined to be there proprietor of the land that that person, instead of receiving an award, shall receive a grant of land..." The laws assessed do not require the government to follow a gender-sensitive approach to providing compensation. Section 115 states that compensation must be paid 'promptly'; however, the law does not establish that compensation must be paid prior to the taking of possession or within a specified timeframe thereafter. Section 128 of the Land Act, 2012 provides that "any dispute arising out of any matter provided under this Act may be referred to the Land and Environment Court for determination." Section 115(1)(c) of the Land Act, 2012 also indicates that affected populations can dispute "the share in which compensation is to be paid." Government of Kenya, *Constitution of Kenya*, 2010; Government of Kenya, *Land Act*, 2012; Government of Kenya, *Community Land Act*, 2016; Government of Kenya, *Land Acquisition Act*, 2010 (Repealed by Land Act 2012).

102 Article 9 of the Decree on Compensation and Resettlement Management in Development Projects (2016) states that compensation must be based on "prices applied by the state, market prices or average prices applicable for a period of compensation and based on the types of properties and locations." However, there is no explicit indication that alternative approaches to FMV (e.g., replacement cost approach) may be used to calculate compensation in cases where land markets are weak or non-existent. Article 9 of the Decree on Compensation and Resettlement Management in Development Projects (2016) states that "project owners, in collaboration with the committee for compensation and resettlement at the local level, must estimate the value for compensation for land, constructed facilities, crop products, livestock, and potential incomes..." The inclusion of the term 'potential incomes' indicates that assessors must account for the economic activities associated with land when calculating compen-

sation. Article 4 of the Decree on Compensation and Resettlement Management in Development Projects (2016) states that "compensation value means the value calculated in the form of material, money or land to compensate the land, constructed facilities, agricultural products, livestock and incomes." Article 8(8) of the Decree on Compensation and Resettlement Management in Development Projects (2016) states that "the project owner has to pay more attention in the rehabilitation efforts if there are losses of cultures, religions and traditions of local people." The law provides affected persons with a right to negotiate compensation levels. Article 18 of the Decree on Compensation and Resettlement Management in Development Projects (2016) states that affected populations have a right to "make a written proposal to the related committee for compensation and resettlement to consider the issues related to compensation, resettlement and rehabilitation of their livelihood....[and] actively participate in the implementation of the plan of compensation..."Article 4 of the Decree on Compensation and Resettlement Management in Development Projects (2016) states that "compensation value means the value calculated in the form of material, money or land to compensate the land, constructed facilities, agricultural products, livestock and incomes which have been affected by development projects." The laws assessed do not require the government to follow a gender-sensitive approach to providing compensation. Article 8(11) of the Decree on Compensation and Resettlement Management in Development Projects (2016) states that "Project owners must complete the implementation of their compensation plans within twenty-four months as from the date the compensation plan is officially adopted. Failure by project owners to implement their compensation plans within the specified time frame, the project owners can submit applications to the compensation committees at the provincial or city levels for consideration to extend the implementation time frame. However, such time frame extension shall not exceed twelve months to complete the compensation plans. If the plans are still not completed there must be evaluations to identify the remaining parts of compensation for a new application for re-consideration." Article 24(3) of the Decree on Compensation and Resettlement Management in Development Projects (2016) indicates that, if an affected person is not satisfied with decisions of project owners on requests for compensation, the affected person can "make a request for justice to the National Assembly or to a court according to the judicial process." Government of Laos, *Decree on Compensation and Resettlement Management in Development Projects*, 2016; Government of Laos, *Decree on the Compensation and Resettlement of the Development Project*, 2005; Government of Laos, *Decree on the Implementation of the Land Law No. 88/PM*, 2008; Government of Laos, *Land Law No. 04 /NA*, 2003; Government of Laos, *Decree on the Compensation and Resettlement of the Development Project No. 192/PM*, 2003.

103 Article 56 of the Land Act 2010 states "In all cases in which the implementation of this Act results in compulsory acquisition of property, the person deprived of such property shall be entitled to compensation at market value." However, article 58(2) states that "in assessing compensation, regard shall be had-(a) to the value of the property as certified by an odd number of valuers one of whom shall be the Government valuer, having regard to the present and replacement value..." Since one of the valuers must 'have regard' to the replacement value, Lesotho received a 'partial' score for this indicator. The Land Act 2010 does not provide compensation for unrecorded tenure rights held by communities. Furthermore, the Act does not indicate that communities have a process for registering their land unless they form a corporation or association. A legal person is defined in Section 2 of Land Act 2010 as including any company or association or body or persons, corporate or incorporate, but there is no explicit provision for registration of collective property or even for council to hold in trust for community. Article 58(2)(b) of the Land Act, 2010 provides that compensation must reflect "(b) to the expenses incidental to any necessary change of residence or of place of business." The Land Act, 2010 does not explicitly require that compensation must reflect the improvements made on the land. The laws assessed do not provide compensation for intangible values (e.g. social, cultural, and spiritual values) associated with the land. The laws assessed do not provide affected populations with a right to negotiate compensation levels. The laws assessed do not provide affected persons with alternative land as a compensation option. The laws assessed do not require the government to follow a gender-sensitive approach to providing compensation. Article 60 of the Land Act, 2010 states that "compensation shall, in all cases of compulsory acquisition, be made before conclusion of expropriation." Article 59 of the Land Act, 2010 provides that "Where conflicting claims are submitted to the Minister pursuant to Section 58(1), the Minister shall, within one month from the last day of the period prescribed in Section

58(1), refer the case to a District Land Court having jurisdiction in the area where the land in question is situate." Government of Lesotho, *Constitution of Lesotho*, 1993; Government of Lesotho, *Land Act (Act No. 8 of 2010)*, 2010.

104 Article 24(ii) of the Constitution of Liberia, 1984 requires the 'prompt payment of just compensation'; however, does not specify that just compensation must be based on FMV. NOTE: The Land Rights Policy 2013 establish that "Just compensation for the land will be calculated based on fair market value assuming a willing buyer and a willing seller. Any change in fair market value as a result of the decision to expropriate will not be considered", but this is not binding law (Sec. 5.3.1.2). The law does not provide alternatives to the fair market value approach in cases where land markets are weak or non-existent. Section 1.3 of the Community Rights Law 2009 defines 'customary land' as " land, including forest land, owned by the community individuals, groups, families or communities through longstanding rules recognized by the community. To be recognized as customary land, it is not necessary for the land to have been registered under statutory entitlements." The answer is partial is it not clear that communities have informal rights to non-forest land--the Community Rights Law 2009 only explicitly grants rights to forest land. The Constitution of Liberia, 1984 does not require that compensation reflect the loss of economic activity. NOTE: According to the Land Rights Policy 2013, compensation should reflect economic loss: "compensation and projects to restore the natural resources and economic base of those relocated' is required" Sec. 5.3.1.8. The Constitution of Liberia, 1984 does not provide compensation for improvements. The laws assessed do not provide compensation for intangible values (e.g. social, cultural, and spiritual values) associated with the land. The laws assessed do not provide affected populations with a right to negotiate compensation levels. The laws assessed do not provide affected persons with alternative land as a compensation option. The laws assessed do not require the government to follow a gender-sensitive approach to providing compensation. Article 24 of the Constitution of Liberia requires the government to pay 'prompt' compensation, but does not require that compensation is paid prior to the taking of possession or within a specified timeframe thereafter. Article 24(iii) of the Constitution of Liberia, 1984 provides that "the compensation offered may be challenged freely by the owner of the property in a court of law with no penalty for having brought such action." Government of Liberia, *Constitution of Liberia*, 1984; Government of Liberia, *Draft Land Rights Act*, 2013 (pending).

105 Article 10 of the Expropriation Act 1936 (amended 1993) provides that "The price fixed at compensation for expropriated property, will be equivalent to commercial value to be fixed but may not be lower, in the case of real estate, the tax value contained in the Cadastral or collecting offices." Article 94 of the Agrarian Law, 1992 provides for expropriation of ejido or communidade land. The Commission of Appraisals of National Property, considering the market value of the expropriated assets, must determine the amount of compensation. The law does not provide alternatives to the fair market value approach in cases where land markets are weak or non-existent. The Expropriation Act 1936 (amended 2011), the Agrarian Law 1992, and the Regulations of the Agrarian Law on Matters of Organization of Rural Property, 1996 do not provide compensation for unrecorded tenure rights held by communities. Article 152 of the Basic Agrarian Law suggests that communities must obtain titles and certificates. The laws assessed do not provide compensation for unregistered customary tenure rights. The laws assessed do not provide compensation for the economic activities associated with the land. Article 16 of the Expropriation Act, 1936 (amended 1993) indicates that compensation must reflect the improvements made on the land. The laws assessed do not provide compensation for intangible values (e.g. social, cultural, and spiritual values) associated with the land. The laws assessed do not provide affected populations with a right to negotiate compensation levels. The laws assessed do not provide affected persons with alternative land as a compensation option. The laws assessed do not require the government to follow a gender-sensitive approach to providing compensation. Article 94 of the 1992 Agrarian Law provides that "The land subject to expropriation may be occupied only by payment or deposit the amount of the compensation, which shall preferably be chosen in the National Trust Fund for Ejido Development or, failing that, by sufficient collateral." The Expropriation Act, 1936 (amended 2011) and the Agrarian Law (1992) does not provide affected persons a right to appeal compensation decisions. Government of Mexico, Constitution of Mexico, 1917 (amended 2007); Government of Mexico, *Expropriation Law*, 1936 (amended 2011); Government of Mexico, *Decree that Article 6 and the second paragraph of Article 20(a) of the Expropriation Act are amended*, 2011; Government of Mexico, *Agrarian Law*, 1992; Government of Mexico, *Regulations of the Agrarian Law on Matters of Organi-*

zation of Rural Property, 1996; Government of Mexico, *Regulations of the Institute for Administration of National Properties*, 1992; United States Agency for International Development (USAID), *Country Profile Property Rights and Resource Governance*, USAID, Mexico, 2011.

106 The Land Acquisition Act, 1960 states that "in determining the amount of compensation to be awarded for any scheduled land acquired under this Act there shall be taken into consideration the following matters and no others: (a) the market value as determined in accordance with Section 1 of this Schedule. . ." First Schedule, sec. 2. "In assessing the market value of any scheduled land, the valuer may use any suitable method of valuation to arrive at the market value provided that regard may be had to the prices paid for the recent sales of lands with similar characteristics as the scheduled land which are situated within the vicinity of the scheduled land and with particular consideration being given to the last transaction on the scheduled land within two years from the date with reference to which the scheduled land is to be assessed under subparagraph (1)." First Schedule, sec. (1)(1A). The laws assessed do not provide compensation for unrecorded rights held by communities. Section 2 of the Land Acquisition Act, 1960 defines 'land' as alienated land within the meaning of the State land law, land occupied under customary right and land occupied in expectation of title. Furthermore, Section 1(2A) of the First Schedule indicates that only communities living in formally recognized regions are entitled to compensation. In assessing the market value of any scheduled land which is Malay reservation land under any written law relating to Malay reservations, or a Malay holding under the Malay Reservations Enactment of Terengganu [Terengganu En. No. 17 of 1360 (A.H)], or customary land in the State of Negeri Sembilan or the State of Malacca, the fact that it is such Malay reservation land, a Malay holding, or customary land shall not be taken into account except where the scheduled land is to be devoted, after the acquisition, solely to a purpose for the benefit of persons who are eligible to hold the land under such written law." The law provides that "if, in consequence of the acquisition, he is or will be compelled to change his residence of place of business, the reasonable expenses, if any, incidental to such change" Land Acquisition Act, 1960, First Schedule, Section 2(e). The law provides that market value should reflect improvements; however, compensation is limited to improvements made within the two years prior to the acquisition, and such improvements must be "bona fide and not made in contemplation" of the acquisition. The law states the compensation should not account for "an increase by means of any improvement made by the owner or his predecessor in interest within two years before the declaration...was published in the Gazette, unless it be proved that such improvement was made bona fide and not in contemplation of proceedings for the acquisition of the land;" Land Acquisition Act, 1960, First Schedule 1(3)(a). The laws assessed do not provide compensation for intangible values (e.g. social, cultural, and spiritual values) associated with the land. The law provides affected persons with a right to negotiate compensation levels. The law provides that "the Land Administrator shall also enquire into the respective interests of all persons claiming compensation or who in his opinion are entitled to compensation in respect of the scheduled land, and into the objections, if any, made by any interested person to the area of any scheduled land" Land Acquisition Act, 1960, Sec. 12(2). Section 21 of the Land Acquisition Act, 1960 also establishes a procedure by which affected persons can accept or reject compensation offers. The laws assessed do not provide affected persons with alternative land as a compensation option. The laws assessed do not require the government to follow a gender-sensitive approach to providing compensation. Section 18 states that "the Land Administrator may take possession- (a) of any land in respect of which an award has been made under Section 14, such possession being taken at the time of the service upon the occupier of such land of a notice....(b) of any land specified in a Certificate of Urgency issued...whether or not any award has been made in respect of such land..." Thus, the answer to the 'prompt payment' indicator is partial since, when a Certificate of Urgency is issued, acquired land can be possessed without payment of compensation awards. Land Acquisition Act, 1960. Section 37(1) states "any person interested...may...make objection to- (a) the measurement of the land; (b) the amount of compensation; (c) the persons to whom it is payable; (d) the apportionment of the compensation." Land Acquisition Act 1960. Section 40(c) of the Act provides "the opinion of each assessor on the various heads of compensation claimed by all persons interested shall be given in writing and shall be recorded by the Judge." 40D. (1) "In a case before the Court as to the amount of compensation or as to the amount of any of its items the amount of compensation to be awarded shall be the amount decided upon by the two assessors. (2) Where the assessors have each arrived at a decision which differs from each other then the Judge, having regard to the opinion of each assessor, shall elect to concur with the

decision of one of the assessors and the amount of compensation to be awarded shall be the amount decided upon by that assessor." Government of Mongolia, *Constitution of Mongolia*, 1992; Government of Mongolia, *Law on Allocation of Land to Mongolian Citizens for Ownership*, 2002; Government of Mongolia, *Law on Land*, 2002.

107 The answer is 'partial' because the fair market value method is used during emergency situations, but this method is not used as the standard method for assessing compensation. Pursuant to Article 37.2 of the Law on Allocation of Land to Mongolian Citizens for Ownership, when expropriating land in emergency situations, the government is required to pay "the value of the land and the damages according to the market rate at that time or . . . allocate other land not worse than the expropriated land [in] status and quality." (Art. 37.2). According to Article 35.5, under the standard method for land expropriation, the government and the expropriated party are supposed to negotiate the amount of compensation. The Law on Allocation of Land to Mongolian Citizens for Ownership, 2002 citizens for ownership does not grant compensation to communities with unrecognized tenure rights. While 'economic activity' or business damages are not explicitly mentioned in the law, the requires that the assessment of compensation accounts for "damages to be caused to the owner due to replacement of taking back of the land based on the special needs of he state..." (Art. 40.1.5, Law on the Allocation of Land for Mongolian Citizens, 2002). Article 40.1.3 of the The Law on Allocation of Land to Mongolian Citizens for Ownership, 2002 requires the state should account for "the value of immovable property attached to the land previously owned" when calculating compensation amounts, and 40.1.4 state that compensation includes "investment made by the owner to the land shall be paid." The laws assessed do not provide compensation for intangible values (e.g. social, cultural, and spiritual values) associated with the land. The law provides affected persons with a right to negotiate compensation levels. Under the standard (non-emergency) expropriation process, the government must negotiate with individual landowners to set compensation levels. (Art. 35.5, Law on Allocation of Land to Mongolian Citizens for Ownership). Section 35.5.5 of the Law on Allocation of Land to Mongolian Citizens for Ownership, 2002 location, size, status and quality of the land to be allocated in replacement of the land taken back for the special needs of the state. Section 36.4 of the If Citizen's owned land becomes unusable due to establishment of the public servitude on the land, the Citizen shall have the right to demand from the entity that has established the public servitude to purchase the land and to compensate damages caused to the land. Section 37.2 states that "if it becomes impossible to return the expropriated land, the owner shall be compensated for the value of the land and the damages according to the market rate of that time or the damages shall be compensated by allocating other land not worse than the expropriated land by its status and quality." The laws assessed do not require the government to follow a gender-sensitive approach to providing compensation. When expropriating land under the standard method, the government must not undertake any "[a]ctivities directed at" expropriation until it has paid compensation and/or provided replacement land "not worse than the previously owned land [in] status and quality." (Article. 40.1, Law on Allocation of Land to Mongolia Citizens for Ownership). When expropriating land for emergency uses, there is no such requirement, which indicates that the answer is partial. Art. 37.1-2 of this Law states "during occurrence of environmental or public disasters . . . land owned by Citizens may be expropriated . . . if it becomes impossible to return the expropriated land, the owner shall be compensated." However, there is no deadline for payment that applies when land is expropriated for emergency purposes. Section 37.3 of the Law on Allocation of Land to Mongolian Citizens for Ownership, 2002 provides that "if there is a dispute regarding the determination of the rate of the expropriated land and damages caused to the land owner, it shall be resolved by Court."

108 Section 23 of Land Acquisition Act (LAA) 1894 provides that the Court must take into consideration the value of land. However, laws assessed do not establish alternatives to FMV in cases where land markets are weak or non-existent. The laws assessed do not provide compensation for unrecorded rights held by communities. The LAA,1894 does not provide compensation for unrecorded rights held by Indigenous People and local communities. Under Section 23 of LAA, 1894, the Collector must consider damages resulting from loss of business or profits when assessing compensation. Under Section 23 of LAA, 1894, the Court, when assessing compensation claims, must consider crops, trees, and improvements on the land when assessing compensation. The laws assessed do not provide compensation for intangible values (e.g. social, cultural, and spiritual values) associated with the land. The laws assessed do not provide affected populations with a right to negotiate compensation levels. The laws assessed do

not provide affected persons with alternative land as a compensation option. The laws assessed do not require the government to follow a gender-sensitive approach to providing compensation. The LAA 1894 does not require that compensation is paid prior to the taking of possession of land or within a specified timeframe thereafter. The Collector has initial authority to determine compensation amounts (Section 11(ii) of LAA 1894). If an affected person disagrees with the compensation amount, they may "require that the matter be referred by the Collector for determination of the Court" (Section 18, LAA 1894). However, the answer is partial because Article 30 states "When the amount of compensation has been settled under Section 11, if any dispute arises as to the apportionment of the same or any part thereof, or as to the persons to whom the same or any part thereof is payable, the Collector may refer such dispute to the decision of the Court." Government of Myanmar, *Constitution of Myanmar*; Government of Myanmar, *Land Acquisition Act*, 1894.

109 Section 25 states that "the amount of compensation to be paid to an owner in respect of property...shall be determined with due regard to...the amount which the land would have realized if sold on the date of notice on the open market by a willing seller to a willing buyer; and (ii) an amount to compensate any actual financial loss caused by the expropriation.." Agricultural (Commercial) Land Reform Act 6 of 1995. The law does not provide alternatives to the fair market value approach in cases where land markets are weak or non-existent. The laws assessed do not provide compensation for unregistered customary tenure rights. Section 25(5)(c) of the Agricultural (Commercial) Land Reform Act 6 of 1995 provides that "no allowance shall be made for any unregistered right in respect of any other property or for any indirect damage or anything done with the object of obtaining compensation therefor... There are limitations on the types of lands to which communities can claim rights." Section 25 of the Agricultural (Commercial) Land Reform Act 6 of 1995 provides that "the amount of compensation to be paid to an owner in respect of property expropriated...shall be determined with due regard to... (ii) an amount to compensate any actual financial loss caused by the expropriation." Although the law does not explicitly state that compensation must reflect the loss of economic activity connected with land, it can be implied that economic activity is included in the clause "any actual financial loss." Since this provision only applies when agricultural land is expropriated for land reform purposes, the answer is 'partial', Section 25(5)(b) of the Agricultural (Commercial) Land Reform Act 6 of 1995 provides that "improvements made after the date of [the acquisition] notice on or to the property in question, except where they were necessary for the property maintenance of existing improvements or where they were undertaken in pursuance of obligations entered into before that date, shall not be taken into account." The answer is partial because compensation levels can reflect improvements so long as they are "necessary for the property maintenance or were undertaken in pursuance of obligations before the on which the acquisition was publicly announced." Section 40 of the Communal Land Reform Act of 2002 provides compensation for necessary improvements when customary rights are extinguished. The laws assessed do not provide compensation for intangible values (e.g. social, cultural, and spiritual values) associated with the land. When agricultural land is expropriated for land reform purposes, the law provides that "an owner whose property has been expropriated...shall...deliver....to the Minister a written statement indicating...the amount claimed by the owner as compensation and how much of that amount represents each of the respective amounts" (Sec. 22(1)(b)). Section 27 provides that compensation shall "in the absence of agreement, on the application of any party concerned be determined by the Lands Tribunal." Agricultural (Commercial) Land Reform Act 6 of 1995. The laws assessed do not provide affected persons with alternative land as a compensation option. The laws assessed do not require the government to follow a gender-sensitive approach to providing compensation. Section 24 states that "Minister may, prior to the determination of the compensation...but not before the date on which the State takes possession, pay such portion of the amount offered as compensation...but not more than 80 per cent of that amount..." Since the Minister has discretion, but is not required, to make an advanced payment of compensation, the answer is partial. Agricultural (Commercial) Land Reform Act 6 of 1995. For expropriation of agricultural land, Compensation decisions can be disputed through arbitration. Sec. 27(3) provides "the Minister and an owner, or a lessee under an unregistered lease, [are not prevented from] submitting by agreement any dispute concerning the amount of compensation to be paid in terms of this Act in respect of the expropriation of property, to arbitration in terms of the Arbitration Act, 1965 Agricultural (Commercial) Land Reform Act 6 of 1995." Government of Namibia, *Constitution of the Republic of Namibia*, 1990; Government of Namibia, *Communal Land*

Reform Act, 2002 (Amended 2013); Government of Namibia, *Agricultural (Commercial) Land Reform Act 6 of 1995*; Government of Namibia, *Agricultural (Commercial) Land Reform Amendment Act*, 2014 (No. 1 of 2014).

110 Section 16(2) of the Land Acquisition Act, 1977 provides that compensation should reflect "the price of the land at the time of the publication of a notice of land acquisition under Section 9." The law does not provide alternatives to the fair market value approach in cases where land markets are weak or non-existent. Under the Forest Act, 2049 (1993) and the Forest Regulation, 2051 (1995), communities are granted the right for a Community Forest User Groups for the development, conservation, and utilization of collectively-managed forests. However, the government can extinguish these Group's rights without compensation. The Land Acquisition Act 1977 does not indicate that compensation may be provided for unrecorded rights held by communities. Section 16(1)(b) of the Land Acquisition Act, 1977 provides that compensation should cover "the losses suffered by the affected person as a result of his having been required to shift the resident or the place of his/her business by reason of the acquisition of the land." Section 16(2)(b) the Land Acquisition Act, 1977 provides that compensation should reflect "the value of the crops, houses, wall, shed, etc, if any, acquired along with the land." Section 15 of the Expropriation Act, 1975 provides that "in the case of Guthi (religious) lands acquired under this Act, compensation shall be paid in accordance with the provisions of the Guthi Corporation Act, 1976." This provision indicates that in some cases, compensation may reflect the spiritual value associated with the land. The laws assessed do not provide affected populations with a right to negotiate compensation levels. The Land Acquisition Act, 1977 provides "14. Allotment of Other Lands in Exchange: In case any person whose land is wholly acquired under this Act wants to obtain compensation in the form of land elsewhere, Government of Nepal may, in exchange for such land, allot him/her any waste land, or land belonging to itself, or any other land which it is going to allot or sell in accordance with prevailing Nepal law, if available." The laws assessed do not require the government to follow a gender-sensitive approach to providing compensation. Section 37 of the Land Acquisition Act, 1977 provides that "In case the concerned person fails to receive compensation within the time limit prescribed for the purpose under the different provisions of this Act, or refuses to accept it, the local officer shall issue a notice prescribing a final time-limit of three months for receiving such compensation. In case the concerned person fails to receive compensation even with in such time-limit, he/she shall not be entitled to any compensation." The answer is partial because the Act, after the three month time limit expires, affected persons no longer have a right to receive just compensation. Section 7.3 of the Land Acquisition Act, 1977 provides that "in case the concerned person is not satisfied with the amount of compensation...he/she may file a complaint with the chief District Officer on which he/she receives information thereof, and in such cases the decision of the Chief District Officer shall be final." In other words, affected persons are not permitted to challenge compensation decisions in court. Government of Nepal, *Constitution of Nepal*, 1977; Government of Nepal, *Land Acquisition Act*, 2034; Government of Nepal, *Guthi Corporation Act*, 1976.Government of Nepal, *Forest Act*, 2049 (1993).

111 The Civil Code (1904), Constitution of Nicaragua, Ley sobre propiedad reformada urbana y agraria (1997), and other laws assessed do not establish guidelines for assessing compensation. Article 617 of the Nicaraguan Civil Code provides "No one can be deprived of property except by law or sentence based on this. Expropriation for reasons of public utility must be authorized by law or judgment based on it; and will not be checked without compensation. In case of war, it is not essential that compensation is prior. If these requirements are not fulfilled, the courts shall, and where appropriate, they restore possession to the expropriated." Article 44 of the Constitution provides "By virtue of the social function of property, for reason of public utility or social interest, this right is subject to the limits and obligations imposed by the laws regarding its exercise. Immovable property mentioned in the first paragraph may be the subject of expropriation in accordance with the law following the cash payment of fair compensation." The law does not provide alternatives to the fair market value approach in cases where land markets are weak or non-existent. The laws assessed do not provide compensation for unregistered customary tenure rights held by communities. The laws assessed do not provide compensation for the economic activities associated with the land. The laws assessed do not provide compensation for improvements made on the land. The laws assessed do not provide compensation for intangible values (e.g. social, cultural, and spiritual values) associated with the land. Although the laws do not provide all affected populations with a right to negotiate compensation levels, Law 445 (Law of Communal

Property Regime of the Indigenous Peoples and Ethnic Communities of the Autonomous Regions of the Atlantic Coast of Nicaragua and of the Rivers Bocay, Coco, Indio and Maiz), requires consultation and negotiation with communities whenever the government grants a concession to a third party for the purpose of natural resource extraction. Article 16 of Law 445 provides that "in cases regarding the granting of concessions and contracts for the rational exploitation of the resources found in the subsoil of the ethnic and indigenous communities lands, by the State, the corresponding Regional Council shall issue the resolution upon consultation with the indigenous communities on whose lands the natural resources are located. As a result of the consultation, the communities shall respond positively or negatively to the request of the Autonomous Regional Council." Article 17 further states "In the cases where the community is opposed to the performance of the project, the granting of the concession, or the contract for exploitation, the Regional Council shall initiate a negotiation process within the community." Article 18 states "when the consultation process is completed for the execution of the project or the granting of the concession or contract, the community, the respective Autonomous Regional Council and the interested entity or company shall sign an agreement specifying the technical terms and the participation in the economic benefits of the community." Article 2 of Law 445 defines 'consultation' as "the expression and delivery of the technical information regarding the operation or project, followed by a process of discussion and decision making. The communities shall have interpreters to translate everything that is said during said process into their own languages and shall be assisted by technicians, experts on the subject matter. Both the interpreter as well as the technician, shall be chosen by communities." The laws assessed do not provide affected persons with alternative land as a compensation option. The laws assessed do not require the government to follow a gender-sensitive approach to providing compensation. The laws assessed do not require the government to pay compensation prior to acquisition or within a specified timeframe thereafter. The laws assessed do not provide affected persons with a right to challenge compensation decisions in court. Government of Nicaragua, *Ley Nº 278 - Ley sobre propiedad reformada urbana y agraria*; Government of Nicaragua, *Civil Code*; Government of Nicaragua, *Ley Nº 445 - Ley de régimen de propiedad comunal de los pueblos indígenas y comunidades étnicas*, 2003.

112 Section 29(1) of the Land Use Act, 1978 (amended 1990) states "the holder and the occupier shall be entitled to compensation for the value at the date of revocation of their unexhausted improvements." There is no indication from the Land Use Act that there are alternatives to FMV in cases where land markets are weak or non-existent. Customary rights are only recognized if granted by the Local Government under Section 6 of the Land Use Act, 1978. Section 6 (1) states that "it shall be lawful for a Local Government in respect of land not in an urban area. (a) to grant customary rights of occupancy to any person or organisation for the use of land in the Local Government areas for agricultural residential and other purposes. (b) to grant customary right of occupancy to any person or organisation for the use of land for grazing purposes and such other purposes ancillary to agricultural purposes as may be customary in the Local Government area concerned." Section 36(3) states "On the production to the Local Government by the occupier of such land, at his discretion, of a sketch or diagram or other sufficient description of the land in question and on application therefore in the prescribed form the Local Government shall if satisfied that the occupier or holder was entitled to the possession of such land whether under customary rights or otherwise howsoever, and that the land was being used for agricultural purposes at the commencement of this Act register the holder or occupier as one to whom a customary right of occupancy had been issued in respect of the land in question." The Land Use Act, 1978 does not provide compensation for economic activities associated with the land. Section 29(4) (b)-(c) of the Land Use Act, 1978 provides that "compensation under Subsection (1) of this Section shall be, as respects....(b) building, installation or improvements thereon, for the amount of the replacement cost of the building, installation or improvement, that is to say, such cost as may be assessed on the basis of the prescribed method of assessment as determined by the appropriate officer less any depreciation, together with interest at the bank rate for delayed payment of compensation and in respect of any improvement in the nature of reclamation works, being such cost thereof as may be substantiated by documentary evidence and proof to the satisfaction of the appropriate officer; (c) crops on land apart from any building, installation or improvement thereon, for an amount equal to the value a prescribed and determined by the appropriate officer." The laws assessed do not provide compensation for intangible values (e.g. social, cultural, and spiritual values) associated with the land. The laws assessed do not

provide affected populations with a right to negotiate compensation levels. Section 33 of the Land Use Act, 1978 stipulates that "(1) where a right of occupancy in respect of any developed land on which a residential building has been erected is revoked under this Act, the Governor or the local government, as the case may be, may in his or its discretion offer in lieu of compensation payable in accordance with the provisions of this Act, resettlement in any other place or area by way of a reasonable alternative accommodation (if appropriate in the circumstances)." The laws assessed do not require the government to follow a gender-sensitive approach to providing compensation. Section 29(7) of the Land Use Act, 1978 states that "the title of the holder of a right of occupancy shall be extinguished on receipt by him of a notice given under Subsection (6) of this Section or on such later date as may be stated in the notice". Sec. 30(1) of the Constitution of Nigeria, 1999 provides "(b) any person claiming such compensation [shall be given] a right of access, for determination of his interest in the property and the amount of compensation, to the High Court having jurisdiction in that part of Nigeria." Government of Nigeria, *Constitution of Nigeria*, 1999; Government of Nigeria, *Land Use Act*, 1978.

113 Section 23 of Land Acquisition Act (LAA) 1894 provides that the Court must take into consideration the value of land. The law does not provide alternatives to the fair market value approach in cases where land markets are weak or non-existent. The Land Acquisition Act 1894 does not provide compensation for unrecorded rights held by Indigenous People and local communities. Under Section 23 of LAA 1894, the Collector must consider damages resulting from loss of business or profits when assessing compensation. Under Section 23 of LAA 1894, the Court, when assessing compensation claims, must consider crops, trees, and improvements on the land when assessing compensation. The laws assessed do not provide compensation for intangible values (e.g. social, cultural, and spiritual values) associated with the land. The laws assessed do not provide affected populations with a right to negotiate compensation levels. The laws assessed do not provide affected persons with alternative land as a compensation option. The laws assessed do not require the government to follow a gender-sensitive approach to providing compensation. The LAA 1894 does not require that compensation is paid prior to the taking of possession of land or within a specified timeframe thereafter. The Collector has initial authority to determine compensation amounts (Section 11(ii) of LAA 1894). If an affected persons disagrees with the compensation amount, they may "require that the matter be referred by the Collector for determination of the Court (Section 18, LAA 1894). However, the answer is partial because Article 30 states "When the amount of compensation has been settled under Section 11, if any dispute arises as to the apportionment of the same or any part thereof, or as to the persons to whom the same or any part thereof is payable, the Collector may refer such dispute to the decision of the Court. Government of Pakistan, *Constitution of Pakistan*; Government of Pakistan, *Land Acquisition Act*, 1984.

114 Section 23 of the Land Act, 1996 provides that "(1) In the determination of the amount of compensation payable in respect of land acquired by compulsory process under this Act, regard shall be had to–(a) the value of the land at the date of acquisition; and (b) the damage (if any) caused by the severance of the land from other land in which the claimant had an interest at the date of acquisition; and (c) the enhancement or depreciation in value of the interest of the claimant, at the date of acquisition, in other land adjoining or severed from the acquired land by reason of the carrying out of, or the proposal to carry out, the public purpose for which the land was acquired." The law does not provide alternatives to the fair market value approach in cases where land markets are weak or non-existent. Under the Voluntary Customary Land Registration Act, 2009, registration of customary land is voluntary. Therefore, customary landowners are recognized regardless of registration. Section 13(5) of the Land Act, 1996 provides "Where the owner of an interest in land, who has provided the particulars referred to in Subsection (2), suffers loss by reason of the notice to treat having been given and withdrawn, the State is liable to pay to him such compensation as is determined by agreement between the owner and the Minister or, in the absence of agreement, by action as determined by a court of competent jurisdiction." Furthermore, Section 14 of the Land Act, 1996 provides "the interest of every person in land or a chattel to which a notice of acquisition applies is, on the date of acquisition, converted into a right to compensation under this Act. (2) Where an easement, right, power, privilege or other interest in, over or in connection with land that did not previously exist as such is acquired, the interest of every person in the land is, on the date of acquisition, and to the extent to which the interest is affected by the acquisition, converted into a right to compensation under this Act." The Land Act, 1996 does not establish a requirement that compensation must be paid for the economic activities associated with

land. The particulars of the compensation may be established through claims or through agreement, but the law itself does not guarantee a right to compensation for economic activities. The Land Act, 1996 does not establish a requirement that compensation must be paid for the improvements on the land. The particulars of the compensation may be established through claims or through agreement, but the law itself does not guarantee a right to compensation for improvements. The laws assessed do not provide compensation for intangible values (e.g. social, cultural, and spiritual values) associated with the land. The laws assessed do not provide affected populations with a right to negotiate compensation levels. The laws assessed do not provide affected persons with alternative land as a compensation option. The laws assessed do not require the government to follow a gender-sensitive approach to providing compensation. Section 25 of the Land Act, 1996 provides "The Minister may, on behalf of the State, enter into an agreement with the owner of land as to the amount of compensation to which the owner will be entitled if the land is acquired by compulsory process under this Act within a time specified in the agreement. (2) If the land is acquired by compulsory process under this Act– (a) within the time specified in the agreement; and (b) while the owner who made the agreement is still the owner of the land, the compensation payable to him in respect of the acquisition shall be deemed to have been determined by agreement at the amount specified in the agreement." In other words, the deadline for paying compensation must be established in the agreement, but the law itself does not explicitly state that compensation must be paid prior to the taking of possession or within a specified time. However, the answer is partial because Section 47 of the Land Act indicates that the Minister must pay interest on compensation at the rate of 3% per annum from the date of acquisition of the land. Section 22 of the 1996 Land Act provides that "(1) Where a claim for compensation has been rejected by the Minister, the claimant may bring an action against the State in the National Court claiming a declaration that he was, immediately before the date of acquisition of the land, entitled to the interest specified in the claim." Section 27 also permits claimants to appeal compensation decisions through arbitration. Government of Papua New Guinea, *Constitution of Papua New Guinea*; Government of Papua New Guinea, *Land Act*, 1996; Government of Papua New Guinea, *Land Regulations*, 1999.

115 Article 13.1 of Legislative Decree No. 1192 (2015) establishes market value as the criteria for assessing compensation. Article 4.12 defines valuation as including the commercial value, the value of the financial loss meaning compensation for any damage including, if applicable, consequential damages and lost profits. Additionally article 4.12 provides that compensation must reflect the value of commercial property, compensation for any damage, including consequential damages or lost profits. The laws assessed do not provide compensation for unregistered customary tenure rights. Articles 6.2-6.3 of Legislative Decree No. 1192 (2015) indicate that the right to property is evidenced by a document, and that registered owners may certify their rights by a certain data and by providing documentary evidence. Article 4.3 indicates that a certificate of ownership may need to be shown in order to qualify for compensation. Article 70 of the Constitution provides that "No one shall be de deprived of his property, except, exclusively, on grounds of national security or public need determined by law, and upon cash payment of the appraised value, which must include compensation for potential damages." Since the law states that compensation must include an assessment of potential damages, it implies that the economic activities associated with the land must be accounted for in compensation allotments. Additionally, article 13.2 provides that "the value of economic damage includes compensation for any damage, comprising only to lost profits and damages...the amount of compensation includes compensation for tax expenses." Article 15.3 provides compensation for economic damages. Additionally article 4.12 provides that compensation must reflect the value of commercial property, compensation for any damage, including consequential damages or lost profits. Article 13.1 of Legislative Decree No. 1192 (2015) provides that market value of property must include value of buildings, improvements, and crops. The laws assessed do not provide compensation for intangible values (e.g. social, cultural, and spiritual values) associated with the land. Under article 20.3 of legislative Decree No. 1192 (2015), affected persons (referred to by law as the 'taxpayer') must submit a response indicating whether they accept the offer for compensation. However, there is no clear right to negotiate the compensation; the law only provides affected persons with the right give "acceptance or rejection." The laws assessed do not provide affected persons with alternative land as a compensation option. The laws assessed do not require the government to follow a gender-sensitive approach to providing compensation. Decree No. 1192 (2015) does require that compensation must be paid prior to taking or within specified timeline thereafter. Article

34-35 indicates that affected persons can challenge expropriation and compensation decisions through arbitration. Article 34.1 provides that a review of the appraised value of the expropriated property is permissible grounds for arbitration.

116 Section 6 of RA 8974 provides "Guidelines for Negotiated Sale. - Should the implementing agency and the owner of the property agree on a negotiated sale for the acquisition of right-of-way, site or location for any national government infrastructure project, the standards prescribed under Section 5 hereof shall be used to determine the fair market value of the property, subject to review and approval by the head of the agency or department concerned." The law does not provide alternatives to the fair market value approach in cases where land markets are weak or non-existent. Sections 7 and 11 of the Indigenous People's Rights Act (IPRA), 1997 suggest that registering indigenous community land is voluntary but not necessarily required to receive compensation for expropriation. Section 11 of the IPRA provides "the rights of ICCs/IPs to their ancestral domains by virtue of Native Title shall be recognized and respected. Formal recognition, when solicited by ICCs/IPs concerned, shall be embodied in a Certificate of Ancestral Domain Title (CADT), which shall recognize the title of the concerned ICCs/IPs over the territories identified and delineated." Economic activity of farmers must be accounted for; however, it is unclear whether other types of economic activity (aside from farming) must be reflected in the compensation amount. Section 17 of the Comprehensive Agrarian Reform Law of 1988 (Republic Act No. 6657) provides that the "economic benefits contributed by farmers and farmworkers and by the Government to the property...shall be considered as additional factors to determine" value of compensation. Sec. 5 of R.A. No. 8974 provides that "in order to facilitate the determination of just compensation, the court may consider, among other well-established factors, the following relevant standards...(e) the reasonable disturbance compensation for the removal and/or demolition of certain improvements on the land and for the value of the improvements thereon." Section 7 states "Valuation of Improvements and/or Structures. - The Department of Public Works and Highways and other implementing agencies concerned, in coordination with the local government units concerned in the acquisition of right-of-way, site or location for any national government infrastructure project, are hereby mandated to adopt within sixty (60) days upon approval of this Act, the necessary implementing rules and regulations for the equitable valuation of the improvements and/or structures on the land to be expropriated." Section 71 of the Indigenous People's Act No. 8371. Ancestral Domains Fund. - There is hereby created a special fund, to be known as the ancestral domain fund, an initial amount of One hundred thirty million pesos (P130,000,000) to cover compensation for expropriated lands, delineation and development of ancestral domains. Section 3 of Act. No. 8371 provides that 'Ancestral Domains' "refers to all areas generally belonging to ICCs/IPs comprising lands, inland waters, coastal areas and natural resources therein, held under a claim of ownership, occupied or possessed by ICCs/IPs, by themselves or through their ancestors." Section 32 of the Indigenous People's Act states that "the State shall preserve, protect and develop the past, present and future manifestations of their cultures as well as the right to restitution of cultural, intellectual, religious, and spiritual property taken without their free and prior informed consent or in violation of their laws, traditions, and customs." The law provides affected persons with a right to negotiate compensation levels. Section 6 of RA 8974 provides "Guidelines for Negotiated Sale. - Should the implementing agency and the owner of the property agree on a negotiated sale for the acquisition of right-of-way, site or location for any national government infrastructure project, the standards prescribed under Section 5 hereof shall be used to determine the fair market value of the property, subject to review and approval by the head of the agency or department concerned." Furthermore, Section 7 of the Indigenous People's Rights Act, 1997 establishes the Indigenous populations have a right to FPIC before their land is taken. Section 5(h) of the RA 8974 provides that compensation should account for "such facts and events as to enable the affected property owners to have sufficient funds to acquire similarly-situated lands of approximate areas as those required from them by the government, and thereby rehabilitate themselves as early as possible." For indigenous peoples, there is a provision which provides affected persons "in all possible cases with lands of quality and legal status at least equal to that of the land previously occupied by them, suitable to provide for their present needs and future development ..." RA 8371 (1997), Section 7(c). For agrarian reform takings, the compensation can be paid in a combination of cash, government securities, tax credit, etc. RA 6657, Section 18." The laws assessed do not require the government to follow a gender-sensitive approach to providing compensation. The law provides that "upon the filing of the complaint or at any time there-

after and after due notice to the defendant, the plaintiff shall have the right to take or enter upon the possession of the real property involved if he deposits with lized government depositary an amount equivalent to the assessed value of the property for purposes of taxation to be held by such bank subject to the orders of the court" (Civil Procedure, Rule 67, Section 2). "Upon payment by the plaintiff to the defendant of the compensation fixed by the judgment, with legal interest thereon from the taking of the possession of the property, or after tender to him of the amount so fixed and payment of the costs, the plaintiff shall have the right to enter upon the property expropriated and to appropriate it for the public use or purpose defined in the judgment, or to retain it should he have taken immediate possession thereof under the provisions of Section 2 hereof" (Section 10). See Section 4 of R.A. 8974 The court appoints commissioners to determine the appropriate compensation and has the power to adopt, set aside or amend the determination, to "make such order or render such judgment as shall secure to the plaintiff the property essential to the exercise of his right of expropriation, and to the defendant just compensation for the property so taken." Civil Procedure, Rule 67, Section 8. Government of the Philippines, *Constitution of the Philippines*, 1987; Government of the Philippines, *The Indigenous Peoples' Rights Act of 1997*, 1997; Government of the Philippines, *Supreme Court Decision G.R. No. 150640*, 2007; Government of the Philippines, *Republic Act, No. 8974, An Act to Facilitate the Acquisition of Right-of-Way, Site or Location for National Government Infrastructure Projects and For Other Purpose*; Government of the Philippines, *Comprehensive Agrarian Reform Law of 1988*, 1988 (Amended 2009); Government of the Philippines, *Republic Act No. 9700 amending Republic Act No. 6657 on the Comprehensive Agrarian Reform Law 1988*, 2009; Supreme Court of the Philippines, *NIA v. Rural Bank, G. R. No. 185124*, 2012; Government of the Philippines, *Civil Procedure Rule 67.*

117 Article 22 of Law No. 32/2015 Relating to Expropriation in the Public Interest states "Land values and prices for property incorporated on land consistent with the prevailing market rates provided under this Law shall be established by the Institute of Real Property Valuers in Rwanda. The list of land values and prices for property incorporated on land shall be reviewed every year and approved by the regulatory Council for the real property valuation in Rwanda before it becomes effective. The unit prices for land and property incorporated thereon shall be published every year in the Official Gazette of the Republic of Rwanda." "The laws assessed do not establish alternatives to the fair market value approach to calculating compensation in cases where land markets are weak or non-existent." Article 27 of Law No. 32/2015 Relating to Expropriation in the Public Interest states "The properties subject to valuation for the payment of fair compensation due to expropriation in the public interest are: 1° land; 2° activities carried out on land for its efficient management or rational use; 3° compensation for disruption caused by expropriation." "The Law suggests that economic activities may be compensated in the event of expropriation." Article 27 of Law No. 32/2015 Relating to Expropriation in the Public Interest states "the properties subject to valuation for the payment of fair compensation due to expropriation in the public interest are: 1° land; 2° activities carried out on land for its efficient management or rational use; 3° compensation for disruption caused by expropriation." The laws assessed do not provide compensation for intangible values (e.g. social, cultural, and spiritual values) associated with the land. The right to negotiate compensation amounts is not explicitly provided by Law No. 32/2015 Relating to Expropriation in the Public Interest. However, Article 25 of Law No. 32/2015 states "the valuation of land and property incorporated thereon shall be conducted in the presence of land owner and that of the owner of property incorporated on land or their lawful representatives and in the presence of representatives of local administrative entities." Law No. 32/2015 Relating to Expropriation in the Public Interest does not explicitly provide alternative land as a form of compensation to affected landholders. However, article 39 of Law No. 32/2015 Relating to Expropriation in the Public Interest states "In case of payment of fair compensation in kind, the type of fair compensation agreed upon shall be paid in accordance with the agreed upon fair compensation." The laws assessed do not require the government to follow a gender-sensitive approach to providing compensation. Article 36 of Law No. 32/2015 Relating to Expropriation in the Public Interest states "The approved fair compensation shall be paid within a period not exceeding one hundred and twenty (120) days from the day of its approval by the District or City of Kigali Council or the relevant Ministry. If fair compensation is not paid within the period provided under Paragraph One of this Article, expropriation shall become null and void unless otherwise agreed upon between the expropriator and the person to be expropriated. Subsequent to receiving fair compensation, the expropriated person shall have a period not exceeding one hundred

and twenty (120) days to relocate." While the right to challenge compensation decisions in court is not explicitly provided by law, Article 33 of Law No. 32/2015 Relating to Expropriation in the Public Interest states "Within seven (7) days after the approval of the valuation report by the expropriator, any person to be expropriated who is not satisfied with the assessed value of his/her land and property incorporated thereon shall indicate in writing grounds for his/her dissatisfaction with the valuation report. Any person contesting the assessed value shall, at his/her own expense, engage the services of a valuer or a valuation firm recognized by the Institute of Real Property Valuers in Rwanda to carry out a counter-assessment of the value. The counter-assessment report must be available within ten (10) days from the application for counter valuation by the person to be expropriated." Government of Rwanda, *Constitution of Rwanda*, 2003; Government of Rwanda, *Law No. 32/2015 Relating to Expropriation in the Public Interest*, 2015; Government of Rwanda, *Law No. 18/2007 Relating to Expropriation in the Public Interest*, 2007; Government of Rwanda, *Organic Law No. 08/2005 Determining the Use and Management of Land in Rwanda*, 2005; I. Mireille, F. Masengo & A. Knox, *Implementation of Expropriation Law in Rwanda: Challenges and Ways Forward*, LAND, Project Policy Research Brief No.2, Kigali, July 2014; USAID LAND Project, *Research Brief No.2*, Kigali; USAID LAND Project.

118 Section 18(1)(g) of the Public Lands Ordinance, Ch. 116 (1960) provides "where land is, and but for the compulsory acquisition would continue to be, devoted to a purpose of such a nature that there is no general demand or market for land for that purpose, the compensation may, if the Court is satisfied that reinstatement in some other place is bona fide intended, be assessed on the basis of the reasonable cost of equivalent reinstatement." The laws assessed do not provide compensation for unregistered customary tenure rights. Sections 8 and 9 of the Public Lands Ordinance, Chapter 116 (1960) provides that "within eight days after any such appropriation, the Director of Surveys and Lands shall cause a plan of the land so set out, appropriated and taken as aforesaid, together with a certificate, under his hand, to the effect that the same has been taken and appropriated for the service of the Colony, to be registered in the Office of the Registrar General. 9. When any land has been taken and appropriated for the service of the of the Colony, whether under the provisions of this or any other Ordinance, the registration of a plan of such Land, together with the certificate in the Office of the Registrar General, as in the last Section mentioned, shall conclusive evidence that such land has been set out, appropriated and taken for the service of the Colony under the Provisions of this Ordinance." Section 18 of the Public Land Ordinance (1960) states that "the Court shall take into consideration the following matters and no others, namely...(e) if, in consequence of the acquisition, he is compelled to change his residence or place of business, the reasonable expenses, if any, incidental to such change." Section 18 of the Public Lands Ordinance, Ch. 116 (1960) the Court shall take into consideration "(d) the damage, if any, sustained by the person interested at the time of the taking and appropriation of the land by reason of the acquisition injuriously affecting his other property whether movable or immovable in any other manner or his actual earnings." The laws assessed do not provide compensation for intangible values (e.g. social, cultural, and spiritual values) associated with the land. The law provides affected persons with a right to negotiate compensation levels. Section 16 of Public Lands Ordinance Ch. 116 (1960) provides affected persons with a right negotiate. Section 16 provides "it shall be lawful for the Governor, for and on behalf of Her Majesty, to contract and agree with the owner or occupier or any other person interested in any land which may be appropriated and taken for the service of the Colony, or be affected by the exercise Colony, or be affected by the exercise of any of the powers as regards such land Granted by this Ordinance, for the compensation to be allowed, either in respect of the actual value of the land, or in respect of damages incurred by reason of the exercise of any of the said powers, and any sum or sums so agreed on as last aforesaid, or which shall be awarded under the provisions of this Ordinance, shall be paid by the Accountant General." The laws assessed do not provide affected persons with alternative land as a compensation option. The laws assessed do not require the government to follow a gender-sensitive approach to providing compensation. Section 20(4) of the Public Lands Ordinance, Ch. 116(1960) provides "(4) In all cases where any compensation has been awarded, except where a valid written title to the land shall be delivered, payment thereof shall be postponed until the period of one year shall have elapsed from the date of the judgment, or judgment on appeal, whereupon it may be paid over to the person who shall then appear by the judgment of the Court to have the best right thereto, and such payment shall, as concerns the Colonial Government, operate as a complete discharge and acquaintance of such compensation and of all claims in respect of such lands or any interest therein: Provided that such payment shall not hinder any subsequent proceedings at the instance of any persons having or alleging

better right thereof as against the person to whom such payment may have been made." This provision does not indicate that compensation must be paid prior to taking of possession or within a specified timeframe thereafter. Article 21 of the Constitution establishes a right to access courts and obtain an impartial and independent authority for the determination of "the amount of any compensation to which he is entitled and for the purpose of obtaining prompt payment of that compensation." Sections 17 and 20 of the Public Lands Ordinance Chapter 116 (1960) also indicates that affected persons appeal compensation. Government of Sierra Leone, *Constitution of Sierra Leone*, 1991; Government of Sierra Leone, *Draft National Land Policy of Sierra Leone*, 2014; Government of Sierra Leone, *Public Lands Ordinance Cap. 116*, 1960.

119 Section 12(1)(a) of the Expropriation Act 1975 provides that compensation should be based on "the amount which the property would have realized if sold on the date of notice in the open market by a willing seller to a willing buyer, and an amount to make good any actual financial loss caused by the expropriation...Provided that where the property expropriated is of such nature that there is no open market therefore, compensation therefore may be determined on the basis of the amount it would cost to replace the improvements on the property expropriated, having regard to the depreciation thereof for any reason..." Section 2 of the Property Valuation Act, 2014 defines 'value; as' "value (a), means the value of property identified for purposes of land reform, which must reflect an equitable balance between the public interest and the interests of those affected by the acquisition, having regard to all the relevant circumstances, including the—(a) current use of the property; (b) history of the acquisition and the use of the property; (c) market value of the property; (d) extent of direct state investment and subsidy in the acquisition and beneficial capital improvement of the property; and (e) purpose of the acquisition." Section 2(3) of the Interim Protection of the Informal Land Rights Act (IPILRA), 1996 (amended 2015) grants informal tenure rights holders the right to compensation when they are deprived of their land rights. Article 25(6) of the Constitution of South Africa, 1996 provides "A person or community whose tenure of land is legally insecure as a result of past racially discriminatory laws or practices is entitled, to the extent provided by an Act of Parliament, either to tenure which is legally secure or to comparable redress." However the IPILRA excludes tenants from protection. Section 12(1)(a) of the Expropriation Act 1975 provides that compensation should be based on the amount which the property would have realized if sold on the date of notice in the open market by a willing seller to a willing buyer, and an amount to make good any actual financial loss caused by the expropriation. Pursuant to the Expropriation Act 1975, owners must submit a written statement indicating "full particulars of all improvements thereon which, in the opinion of the owner, affect the value of such land." Expropriation Act, 1975, sec. 9 (c). See also Section 12(1)(a) of the Expropriation Act, 1975. The laws assessed do not provide compensation for intangible values (e.g. social, cultural, and spiritual values) associated with the land. The law provides affected persons with a right to negotiate compensation levels. Section 9 of the Expropriation Act 1975 provides that "an owner whose property has been expropriated in terms of this Act, shall...deliver...to the Minister a written statement indicating—if any compensation was in the notice of expropriation offered for such property, whether or not he accepts that compensation..." Section 14 of the Expropriation Act 1975 indicates that an agreement between affected persons and the Minister must be reached and that, in the absence of an agreement, compensation must be determined by the Supreme Court or by arbitration. The laws assessed do not provide affected persons with alternative land as a compensation option. The laws assessed do not require the government to follow a gender-sensitive approach to providing compensation. The law provides that "on the date of taking possession, the state must have paid 'not less than eighty per cent of such amount to the owner... Interest is payable from the date on which the State takes possession of the property in question...of any outstanding portion of the amount of compensation payable..." (The Expropriation Act, 1975 sec. 11(1),12(3)(a)). Section 14 of the Expropriation Act, 1975 establishes that, in the absence of agreement, the amount of compensation must be determined by a provincial or local division of the Supreme Court. Government of South Africa, *Constitution of South Africa*, 1996; Government of South Africa, *Expropriation Act*, 1975; Government of South Africa, *Communal Land Rights Act (No. 11 of 2004)*; Promotion of Administrative Justice Act 3 of 2000; Government of South Africa, *Constitutional Court Decision. Agri South Africa v. Minister of Minerals and Energy (CCT 51/12) [2013]*; Government of South Africa, *Property Valuation Act, 2014 (No. 17 of 2014)*, 2014; South Africa Free State High Court, *Bartsch Consult (Pty) Limited v Mayoral Committee of the Maluti-A-Phofung Municipality [2010] ZAFSHC 11*, 2010.

120 Section 4 of the Land Act 2009 provides 'compensation' means remuneration in consideration for a wrong done or right removed, according to the market value of the property when this remuneration is recognized and done in accordance with the law. Section 75(1) of the Land Act provides that "The compensation shall be just, equitable, and shall take into account the following factors –(a) the purpose for which the land is being utilized; (b) the land market value; and (c) the value of the investment in it by those affected and their interest." The law does not provide alternatives to the fair market value approach in cases where land markets are weak or non-existent. Section 75(3) states "Where any land is expropriated for public purpose and it is necessary to remove any person therefrom in customary occupation, compensation shall be paid as may be agreed upon." Section 39(3) of the Land Act, 2009 provides that "right of ownership and derivative rights to land may be proven by any other practices recognized by communities in Southern Sudan in conformity to equity, ethics and public order." While the law does not explicitly require that compensation reflect the economic activity attached to the land, Section 75 of the 2009 Land Act requires that compensation levels reflect "the purpose for which the land is being utilized." Section 75 of the Land Act states "(c) the value of the investment in [the land] by those affected and their interest." The laws assessed do not provide compensation for intangible values (e.g. social, cultural, and spiritual values) associated with the land. The law provides affected persons with a right to negotiate compensation levels. Section 75 of the 2009 Land Act requires that an agreement on compensation must be reached, but the law also provides that the Compensation Committee is charged with determining compensation levels. It can be implied that, in order to reach an agreement on level of compensation, a consultation proceeding with affected persons may be required. Section 75(2) of the 2009 Land Act provides that "the compensation shall be in cash or in kind or both according to the agreement." The laws assessed do not require the government to follow a gender-sensitive approach to providing compensation. Section 75(7) provides "Where payment of compensation is not made within sixty days of transfer of the property, the affected persons shall, in addition, receive interest on the sum due at commercial rates, recoverable until such compensation is fully paid." Section 75(5) of the 2009 Land Act states "No transfer of ownership or rights over land shall be made until the type, amount, method and timing of the payment of compensation has been agreed upon with this affected." Thus there is no guarantee compensation will be paid promptly. Section 77 of the 2009 Land Act provides that "any person affected by the plan of expropriation, without consequent compensation, may resort to court proceedings for compensation and any other consequence deriving from the expropriation." Government of South Sudan, *Transitional Constitution*, 2011; Government of South Sudan, *Land Act*, 2009.

121 Section 45(1) of the Land Acquisition Act, 1950 provides that "the market value of a land in respect of which a notice under Section 7 has been published shall, subject as hereinafter provided, be the amount which the land might be expected to have realized if sold by a willing seller in the open market as a separate entity on the date of publication of that notice in the Gazette:" According to the Land Acquisition Regulations, 2008, "To fulfill the requirement of the definition of compensation, in addition to the compensation under Section 1 and 2 above, which are based on the 'market value',.." In other words, the law does not provide alternatives to the fair market value approach in cases where land markets are weak or non-existent. The laws assessed do not require the government to provide compensation for unrecorded rights held by Indigenous Peoples and local communities. Sec. 46 of the Land Acquisition Act, 1950 provides that "compensation should account for any loss of earnings from any business carried on the land and any reasonable expenses effecting any change of residence..." The Land Acquisition Regulations, 2008 states that "when the [acquired' building is used for occupation and or business purposes or is intended to be used for occupations and or business purposes, the difference between the cost of re-construction and the value of building [...]should be paid as an additional compensation." Section 46A stipulates that "in determining...the compensation to be paid to any person for the acquisition of any land, no account shall be taken of any improvements made on the land by the State whether before or after the date of commencement of this Act" CAP. 295, Land Acquisition Act, 1950. The Temple Lands (Compensation) Ordinance Cap. 296 provides some additional protections when temple lands are acquired under the CAP. 295, Land Acquisition Act, 1950. The law provides affected persons with a right to negotiate compensation levels. Section 9(1) establishes that the acquiring officer must hold an inquiry to hear "(b) such claims for compensation as may have been notified to him within the time allowed thereof by the notice or...the respective interests of persons claiming compensation." . CAP. 295, Land Acquisition Act, 1950. Section 36 provides that "(1) any person to whom com-

pensation for the acquisition of any land is payable under this Act may enter into a written agreement with the acquiring officer of the district in which that land is situated to accept, in lieu of the whole or any part of such compensation, a transfer of any other land which is the property of the Crown. Such agreement shall be signed by that person and by that acquiring officer. The amount of compensation in lieu of which the transfer is accepted shall be specified in such agreement." Ch. 295 Land Acquisition Act, 1950. The laws assessed do not require the government to follow a gender-sensitive approach to providing compensation. Section 38 of the Land Acquisition Act (CAP. 295), 1950 provides that "at any time after an [compensation] award is made, the Minister may by Order published in the Gazette- (a) where the award relates to the acquisition of land, direct the acquiring officer of the district in which that land is situated, or any other officer authorized in that behalf by such acquiring officer, to take possession of that land for and on behalf of the State..." However, the answer is partial because Section 38(A) provides that "where any land is being acquired for the purposes of a local authority and the preliminary valuation of that land made by the Chief Valuer of the Government does not exceed the specified sum, the immediate possession of such land on the group of urgency, within the meaning of the proviso to Section 38 shall be deemed to have become necessary, and accordingly the Minister may make an Order of possession under Section 38 of this Act." Sections 4, 9-11, 22, 28 establish procedures by which affected persons can challenge compensation decisions in court. In particular, Section 10(2) provides that "a claimant whose claim is wholly or partly disallowed, or a party to a dispute which is determined, by the decisions of an acquiring officer under subSection (1) may, within fourteen days of the service on him of notice of the decision, make application to that acquiring officer for the reference of the claim or dispute...Every reference...shall be made to the District Court or the Primary Court having jurisdiction..." Claimants may file appeals to the board if they are dissatisfied with their compensation allotment. Land Acquisition Act (CAP. 295), 1950. Government of Sri Lanka, *Constitution of Sri Lanka*; Government of Sri Lanka, *Land Acquisition Act CAP. 295*, 1950 (Amended 1994); Government of Sri Lanka, *Land Acquisition (Amendment) Act (No. 13 of 1986)*, 1986; Government of Sri Lanka, *Land Acquisition Regulations*, 2009; Government of Sri Lanka, *Water's Edge Judgment S.C. (F/R) No. 352/2007*, 2007; Government of Sri Lanka, *National Involuntary Resettlement Policy*, 2001.

122 Section 15(1) of the Acquisition of Property Act 1961 (No. 10 of 1961) provides that the Board shall take into consideration the market value of the property at the date of the service of the notice of the acquisition. However, the laws assessed do not provide alternatives to market value in cases where land markets are weak or non-existent. The Acquisition of Property Act, 1961 (No. 10 of 19610 does not provide compensation for unrecorded tenure rights held by communities. The law grants the Minister power to acquire 'real property' which is defined by the Act as "any real right in immovable property in Swaziland other than a mortgage bond over immovable property, and include any lease of immovable property, any rights to the use of public water whether derived from the common law or from statute, any servitude, or the creation of any servitude, and any land granted or ceded to any corporation, company or person." Section 15(1) of the Acquisition of Property Act 1961 (No. 10 of 1961) states that "the Board...shall take into consideration...(e) any reasonable expenses incidental to a change of residence or place of business of a person interested which is necessary in consequence of the acquisition." Section 16 provides "If the Minister has in pursuance of a notice under Section 7 entered into possession of any property, the Board may award compensation to the owner of such property and to all persons entitled to any title or interest therein for loss of rents and profits for the period between the time the Minister so entered into possession and the time when the consideration-due under an agreement has been paid to the persons entitled thereto or compensation has been paid under this Act." Section 15(2) of the Acquisition of Property Act 1961 (No. 10 of 1961) provides that the Board shall not take into consideration "(f) any outlay on additions or improvements to the property incurred after the date of publication... unless such additions or improvements were, in the opinion of the Board necessary." The laws assessed do not provide compensation for intangible values (e.g. social, cultural, and spiritual values) associated with the land. The law provides affected persons with a right to negotiate compensation levels. Section 9 of the Acquisition of Property Act 1961 (No. 10 of 1961) provides that "if for three months after the service and publication... or if the persons who may have lodged any claim and the Minister do not agree as to the amount of the compensation to be paid for the estate or interest in the property belonging to such person, or which he is by this Act enabled to sell and conveyor lease, or if such person has not given satisfactory evidence in support of his claim or if separate and conflicting claims are made in respect of the same property, the amount of compensation due, if any, and every such case of disputed interest or

title shall be settled as provided for in this Act." Government of Swaziland, *Constitution of Swaziland*; Government of Swaziland, *Acquisition of Property Act*, 1961 (No. 10 of 1961).

123 Article 30 of the Land Expropriation Act, 2000 provides "the value of expropriated land shall be compensated based on its current market value. The value of land reserved for public facilities in the urban planning area shall be compensated based on the average market value of its adjoining lands not reserved for public facilities. The market value referred to in the preceding paragraph shall be forwarded by the municipal or county (city) competent authority to the Land Value Evaluation Committee for determination. Municipal or county (city) competent authorities should constantly survey the market values within their jurisdiction and ask its Land Value Evaluation Committee to determine the extent of change in the market values of expropriated lands once every six months as basis for adjusting the compensation for expropriation. The market value survey and assessment procedure, method and matters of compliance therefor with respect to the determination of market values mentioned in the preceding three paragraphs shall be prescribed by the Central Competent Authority." Article 33 of the Land Expropriation Act, 2000 provides "If the expropriated land or land improvement was originally provided for legal business operations, the loss sustained due to the cessation of business or shrinkage of business scale as a result of land or land improvement expropriation shall be compensated." Article 31 of the Land Expropriation Act, 2000 states "The compensation for expropriated constructional improvements shall be determined based on their replacement cost at the time of expropriation. The compensation for agricultural improvements shall be determined based on the value of the ripened crops thereof, provided the crops are due to ripen in less than one year from the date of expropriation, or based on the cost incurred in their planting and cultivation with reference to their current value, provided the crops are due to ripen in more than one year from the date of expropriation. The compensation for constructional and agricultural improvements shall be jointly determined by the municipal or county (city) competent authority and the relevant authorities. The criteria for the assessment of compensation for constructional and agricultural improvements shall be prescribed by the Central Competent Authority." The laws assessed do not provide compensation for intangible values (e.g. social, cultural, and spiritual values) associated with the land. Article 11 of the Land Expropriation Act, 2000 provides "Prior to applying for the expropriation of lands or land improvements, a land use applicant should negotiate with the owners or by other means to reach an agreement on the price of acquisition, unless there is an urgent need due to public security to use land for an undertaking of national defense, communication or transportation or water conservancy where no such agreement could be reached with land or land improvement owners due to time constraint. If the owners refuse to participate in the negotiation or the land use applicant and owners fail to reach an agreement after negotiation and the applicant is unable to acquire the lands or land improvements by other means, the applicant may apply for expropriation according to this Act." Article 21 of the Indigenous Peoples Basic Law, 2005 establishes "In consultation with Indigenous Peoples, the Government or any private entity shall obtain their free and prior informed consent (FPIC) and/or maximum participation, as well as share with the concerned Indigenous Peoples benefits generated from exploration, development, exploitation and utilization of natural resources and lands within Indigenous people's Regions, as well as ecological and academic researches thereon. In the event that any government and/or any enactments and rules of law may impose such restrictions on Indigenous Peoples as to limit their utilization of their lands and natural resources, the Government shall first consult with Indigenous Peoples concerned or Indigenous Persons concerned and obtain their free and prior informed consent (FPIC). A fixed proportion of revenues generated under specified circumstances described in the preceding two paragraphs shall be duly allocated to Indigenous Peoples under the Indigenous Peoples' Development Funds as returns on investment and/or compensations." Article 22 states "the Government shall obtain free and prior informed consent (FPIC) from the affected Indigenous Peoples on the site and formulate a common management mechanism prior to establishing national parks, national scenery, forest district, ecological protection zone, recreation zone and other resource management institutions. Rules and regulations governing aforesaid policies, projects, and activities shall be duly prescribed by the concerned Central Competent Authorities in collaboration with the Central Competent Indigenous Affairs Authority." Indigenous populations have right to seek alternative land in the event of relocation, but the Land Act 1930 (amended 2005) does not grant this right. Article 32 of Indigenous People's Basic Law, 2005 provides "The Government shall not displace or relocate any Indigenous Person from his or her

land, except in cases of imminent and obvious danger. In cases of displacement or relocation of Indigenous Persons, the same shall be properly accommodated and compensated for the losses suffered as a result of forced displacement or relocation as is referred to in the preceding paragraph." Furthermore, Article 34 of the Land Expropriation Act, 2000 provides "If there are low-income households or medium-low income households with facts of inhabitation one year before the public announcement of expropriation, such household members become homeless or are in similar situation due to the expropriation of the constructional improvements they live in, and their situations are found true by the social workers of the municipal or county (city) government, the land use applicant shall draft a resettlement plan and include it in the expropriation plan. The resettlement plan referred to in the preceding paragraph include housing placement." The laws assessed do not require the government to follow a gender-sensitive approach to providing compensation. Article 20 of the Land Expropriation Act, 2000 provides that "Compensation for the expropriated land or land improvements shall be paid within fifteen (15) days after the expiration of the public announcement period. The preceding provision does not apply to additional compensation under Paragraph 5 of Article 22 herein." Article 22 of the Land Expropriation Act, 2000 provides "If any person with an interest in the expropriated land or land improvement objects to the matters being publicly announced... he shall raise the objection by submitting a written statement to the municipal or county (city) competent authority within the announcement period. Upon receiving such an objection, the municipal or county (city) competent authority shall forthwith investigate the matter and notify the interested person of the findings and actions taken in writing...In case the interested person disagrees with the decision referred to in the preceding paragraph, the municipal or county (city) competent authority may refer the matter to the Land Value Evaluation Committee for re-consideration. If the interested person still disagrees with the result of reconsideration, he may file for administrative remedy according to law." Article 46 of the Land Expropriation Act, 2000 provides that "any failure to effect payment for the difference in land value referred to in Subparagraph 1 of the preceding paragraph after the expiration of the prescribed time limit shall be brought to the court for compulsory enforcement." Government of Taiwan, *Constitution of Taiwan*, 1947 (Amended 2000); Government of Taiwan, *Land Expropriation Act*, 2000; Government of Taiwan, *The Land Act*, 1930 (Amended 2006); Government of Taiwan, *Indigenous People's Basic Law*, 2005.

124 Section 10 of the Village Land Regulations, 2001 states that "the market value of any land unexhausted improvement shall be arrived at by use of comparative method evidenced by actual recent, sales of similar properties or by the use of income approach or replacement cost method where the property is of a special nature and not saleable. " Section 8 of the Village Land Regulations, 2001 provides "the following may claim compensation in respect of village land which is transferred to general or reserved land...(b) any villager occupying transferred land or hazard land under customary right of occupancy whether that customary right of occupancy is registered or not..." Compensation shall include loss of profit. "The net monthly profit of the business carried out on the land shall be assessed, evidenced by audited accounts where necessary and applicable, and multiplied by thirty six months in order to arrive at the loss of profits payable" (Sec. 9, The Land (Assessment of the Value of Land for Compensation) Regulations, 2001). Also, Section 15 of the Village Land Regulations, 2001 provides "The net monthly profit of the business carried out on the land shall be assessed and multiplied by thirty six (36) months in order to arrive at the loss of profits payable." Section 13 of the Village Land Regulations states that "compensation for loss of any interest in land shall include value of unexhausted improvement disturbance allowance, transport allowance, accommodation allowance and loss of profits." The Land (Assessment of the Value of Land for Compensation) Regulations, 2001 also indicates that compensation for improvements is provided by law. Sec. 25 of the Village Land Act Regulations, 2001 provides that compensation may take the form of 'access to communal assets', Although this term is not defined by law, it can be implied that this potentially may include intangible assets (historical/cultural values) of the community. The law provides affected persons with a right to negotiate compensation levels. Section 11(2) of the Land Acquisition Act, 1967 provides compensation levels must be agreed upon and that persons entitled to compensation must consent to the type of compensation they receive, which implies that affected person have a right to negotiate compensation levels. Section 11(2) of the Land Acquisition Act, 1967 provides "The President may, with the consent of the person entitled to compensation...make to the person entitled to compensation a grant of public land not exceeding in value the value of the land acquired, for an estate not exceeding the estate acquired and upon the same terms and

conditions as the land acquired was held...in lieu of or in addition to any compensation payable." The laws assessed do not require the government to follow a gender-sensitive approach to providing compensation. Section 15 permits the President to enter into possession of any land before compensation is paid; however, the Minister must pay interest at a rate of six percent per annum from the date when possession is taken. The Minister can pay compensation 'at any time' after the publication of the acquisition notice in the Gazette. Land Acquisition Act, 1967 (Sec. 14(2)). Section 13 of the Land Acquisition Act 1967 provides that affected populations can challenge compensation decisions in the High Court. Government of Tanzania, *Constitution of Tanzania*, 1977; Government of Tanzania, *Land Acquisition Act (Act No. 47 of 1967)*, 1967; Government of Tanzania, *The Land Act*, 1999; Government of Tanzania, *Village Land Act*, 1999; Government of Tanzani, *The Land (Assessment of the Value of Land for Compensation) Regulations*, 2001; Government of Tanzania, *Village Land Regulations*, 2002.

125 Section 21 of the Immovable Property Expropriation Act, 1987 states "Unless otherwise prescribed by any Act on immovable property expropriation, the followings shall be taken into the consideration in determining the amount of compensation to be paid to the entitled person under Section 18: (1) commercial price of immovable property to be expropriated on the date the Royal Decree enacted under Section 6 comes into force; (2) price of immovable property appraised for collection of local tax; (3) price of immovable property appraised for collection of tax on registration of right and juristic act; (4) conditions and location of that immovable property." The law does not provide alternatives to the fair market value approach in cases where land markets are weak or non-existent. The laws assessed do not provide compensation for unrecorded rights held by communities. The law states "If the owner of, or the person who legally takes possession of, immovable property to be expropriated, lives or runs business or other legally works on the immovable property to be expropriated and such person may be susceptible to damage on the ground that he has to leave that immovable property, compensation for such damage shall also be determined." (Section 21(5), Immovable Property Expropriation Act, 1987). Section 24 of the Immovable Property Expropriation Act, 1987 provides that compensation for a higher price of land shall not be calculated as a result "(1) tenement or construction built or constructed on, or agricultural cultivation, development or lease on, that land after the date the Royal Decree...comes into force without permission of the officer, except planting of rice, farming or gardening done in regular manner" Thus, the answer is partial because only improvements related to planting of rice, farming or gardening and other types of improvements permitted by the 'officer' can be included in the assessment of compensation. The laws assessed do not provide compensation for intangible values (e.g. social, cultural, and spiritual values) associated with the land. The laws assessed do not grant affected populations a right to negotiate compensation amounts. The laws assessed do not provide affected persons with alternative land as a compensation option. The laws assessed do not require the government to follow a gender-sensitive approach to providing compensation. Section 11 of the Immovable Property Expropriation Act, 1987 provides that "If the deal to buy immovable property under Section 10 is success, the officer or his entrusted person shall, within one hundred and twenty days as from the date of sale contract has been made, pay the total amount of the price specified in the contract to the owner of, or the person who legally takes possession of, that immovable property." Section 26 of the Immovable Property Expropriation Act, 1987 provides that persons entitled to compensation may challenge compensation decisions in court. Government of Thailand. 2007, *Constitution of Thailand*; Government of Thailand, *Immovable Property Expropriation Act, B.E. 2530*, 1987; Government of Thailand, *Act promulgating the Land Code B.E. 2497*, 2008.

126 Section 12(1)(d) of the Land Acquisition Act, 1994 provides that "where land is, and but for the compulsory acquisition would continue to be, devoted to a purpose of such a nature that there is no general demand or market for land for that purpose, the compensation may, if a Judge is satisfied that reinstatement in some other place is bona fide intended, be assessed on the basis of the reasonable cost of equivalent reinstatement." The law does not provide alternatives to the fair market value approach in cases where land markets are weak or non-existent. The laws assessed do not provide compensation for unregistered customary tenure rights. The Land Acquisition Act, 1994 does not explicitly provide compensation for unrecorded rights held by communities. The Land Acquisition Act, 1994 does not explicitly provide compensation for the economic activities associated with the expropriated land. Section 12(1)(e)(iv) states that no allowance should be made on account of "any outlay or improvement on such land which has been made, commenced or effected before the date of the taking of possession of the

land under Section 4(1) or the date of publication in the Gazette of the declaration made under Section 5(3), whichever is the earlier, with the intention of enhancing the compensation to be awarded therefor in the event or with a view of such land being required, for public purposes." This provision implies that improvements made without the intention of enhancing compensation can be accounted for in the assessment of compensation. Sections 12(5)-(6) state "For the purposes of this Section there shall be a presumption that an improvement to land was made at the time reflected for that improvement in the assessment rolls maintained in accordance with the Lands and Buildings Taxes Act. (6) In a dispute as to the amount of compensation payable, the burden of proving that an improvement was not made at the time referred to in subSection (5) is on the person interested." The laws assessed do not provide compensation for intangible values (e.g. social, cultural, and spiritual values) associated with the land. The laws assessed do not provide affected populations with a right to negotiate compensation levels. The laws assessed do not provide affected persons with alternative land as a compensation option. The laws assessed do not require the government to follow a gender-sensitive approach to providing compensation. The answer is 'partial' because claimants can petition for advance payment of compensation, made before possession of their land is taken; however, without a petition, advance payment is not required by law (sec. 22). The law further states that "the amount of any advance payment...shall not exceed eighty percent of an amount equal to the compensation as estimated to be payable..." (sec. 22(3), Land Acquisition Act Ch. 58:01, 1994). Interest accrues as of the date the possession of land is taken (sec 20). Section 11 of the Land Acquisition Act Ch. 58:01, 1994 provides that "any dispute as to compensation payable under this Act shall be determined by a Judge in accordance with the provisions of this Part." Government of Trinidad and Tobago, *Constitution of Trinidad and Tobago*, 1976 (amended 2000); Government of Trinidad and Tobago, *Valuation of Land Act (Cap. 58:03)*, 1969 (amended 2009); Government of Trinidad and Tobago, *Land Acquisition Act (Cap. 58:01)*, 1994 (amended 2000).

127 Section 41(6) of the Land Act, 1998 (amended 2010) states that "any compulsory acquisition for land... shall be at a fair market valuation assessed on a willing seller willing buyer basis..." Section 77 of the Land Act, 1998 states "1) The district land tribunal shall, in assessing compensation referred to in Section 76(1)(b) take into account the following—in the case of a customary owner, the value of land shall be the open market value of the unimproved land; the value of the buildings on the land, which shall be taken at open market value for urban areas and depreciated replacement cost for the rural areas; the value of standing crops on the land, excluding annual crops which could be harvested during the period of notice given to the tenant. In addition to compensation assessed under this Section, there shall be paid as a disturbance allowance 15 percent or, if less than six months' notice to give up vacant possession is given, 30 percent of any sum assessed under Subsection (1). The rates set out in the list of rates of compensation referred to in Section 59(1)(e) shall be used in determining the amount of compensation payable." The laws assessed provide compensation for unregistered customary tenure rights. Section 4 of the Land Act, 1998 provides that "any person, family or community holding land under customary tenure on former public land may acquire a certificate of customary ownership in respect of that land in accordance with this Act. A certificate for customary ownership shall be in the prescribed form and shall be issued by the board. An application for a certificate of customary ownership shall be in the prescribed form and shall be submitted, together with the prescribed fee, to the committee of the parish in which the land the subject of the application is situated." Since Section 4 of the Land Act provides that a person 'may' acquire a certificate, but is not legally obligated to do so, the law suggests that recognition and compensation may be provided regardless of registration. Section 77 of the Land Act, 1998 provides "Computation of compensation. (1) The district land tribunal shall, in assessing compensation referred to in Section 76(1)(b) take into account the following... the value of standing crops on the land, excluding annual crops which could be harvested during the period of notice given to the tenant." Since compensation is only based on standing crops (not other forms of economic activity), the answer is partial. Improvement-based compensation is limited to "the value of the buildings on the land" and "the value of the standing crops, excluding annual crops", which indicates the appropriate indicator score is 'partial' (Sec. 77, Land Act 1998). The laws assessed do not provide compensation for intangible values (e.g. social, cultural, and spiritual values) associated with the land. The law provides affected persons with a right to negotiate compensation levels. Section 5 of the Land Acquisition Act, 1965 requires that "all persons having an interest in the [acquired] land to appear personally or by the agent before the assessment officer on a day and at a time and place specified in the notice in order to

state- the amount and particulars of their claims to compensation for those interests." Section 41(6) of the 1998 Land Act states that "no person from whom land is to be acquired under this Section shall be required to vacate that land until he or she has received the compensation awarded to, or agreed to, by him or her." The laws assessed do not provide affected persons with alternative land as a compensation option. The laws assessed do not require the government to follow a gender-sensitive approach to providing compensation. Section 41(6) of the Land Act, 1998 states that "no person from whom land is to be acquired under this Section shall be required to vacate that land until he or she has received the compensation awarded to, or agreed to, by him or her." Sec. 13 of the Land Acquisition Act, 1965 states "Where an award is made under Section 6, any person awarded or claiming that he or she should have been awarded compensation may within sixty days of the date of the award appeal to the High Court by way of objection to any or all of the following—the total amount of the compensation awarded"; the apportionment of the compensation; any failure or refusal of the assessment officer to include him or her in the apportionment. Government of Uganda, *Constitution of Uganda*, 1995; Government of Uganda, *Land Acquisition Act 1965 (ch. 226)*, 1965; Government of Uganda, *Land Act (No. 16 of 1998)*, 1998 (amended 2010); Government of Uganda, *Supreme Court Decision Pyrali Abdul Rasul Esmail v. Adrian Sibo (Constitutional Petition No. 9 of 1997)*.

128 Article 74(3) of the Land Law, 2013 provide that the compensation upon land recovery by the State must be made in a democratic, impartial, equal, public, timely and lawful manner. But the law does not provide alternatives to FMV in cases where land markets are weak or non-existent. Article 75(2) of the Law on Land 2013 provides that "Communities and religious establishments using land which is not allocated or leased land by the State and having a certificate, or being eligible to be granted a certificate of land use rights and ownership of houses and other land-attached assets under this Law but not being granted that certificate. Article 88 of the Land Law, 2013 provides "upon the land recovery of the State, if organizations, households, individuals, overseas Vietnamese or foreign-invested enterprises have to stop production and business which causes them damage, they are entitled to compensation for the damage..."Article 90 provides compensation for agriculture output. Article 88 of the Law on Land 2013 provides that "if land-attached assets are damaged upon land recovery by the State, lawful owners of those assets are entitled to compensation." Article 89 compensation for damage to houses and construction facilities on land which is recovered by the state. Article 87 of the Land Law 2013 provides that "for investment projects that are decided by the National Assembly or approved in principle by the Prime Minister and require relocation of all population, affecting all the livelihood, socio-economic activities, and cultural traditions of the community...the Prime Minister shall decide on the policy framework for compensation, support and resettlement." However, the answer is 'partial' because Vietnam has not passed legislation or regulations which provides guidelines for implementing this provision. The law provides affected persons with a right to negotiate compensation levels. Article 69(2)(a) of the Land Law 2013 provides "The organization in charge of compensation and ground clearance shall make the plan for compensation, support and resettlement and coordinate with the commune-level People's Committee in the locality to conduct consultations on the plans for compensation, support and resettlement in the forms of meetings with land users living in the recovered area, posting up the plan for compensation, support and resettlement at offices of the commune-level People's Committee and at common public places of the residential areas of which land is recovered." The laws assessed do not require the government to follow a gender-sensitive approach to providing compensation. Article 93 provides that "within 30 days after decision on the land recovery by the competent state agency takes effect, agencies and organizations in charge of compensation shall pay compensation and support to people whose land is recovered." Article 69(d) provides that "in case the land users in the recovered area do not cooperate with the organization in charge of compensation and ground clearance for investigation, survey, measurement and inventory, the commune-level People's Committee and Vietnam Fatherland Front in the locality and the organization in charge of compensation and ground clearance shall mobilize and persuade the land users to cooperate..." Article 69(d) further provides that "if the land users still do not cooperate with the organization in charge of compensation and ground clearance within 10 days...the chairperson...shall issue a decision on compulsory inventory. Land users whose land is to be recovered shall comply with that decision. In case the land users do not comply with the decision, the chairperson of the district-level People's Committee shall issue a decision on enforcement

of the decision on compulsory inventory and organize the enforcement..." Government of Vietnam, *Constitution of Vietnam*, 2014; Government of Vietnam, *Land Law No. 45/2013/QH13*, 2013.

129 Section 12 of the Land Acquisition Act, 1970 states that "in assessing adequate compensation...the Minister and the Court shall act in accordance with the following principles...(b)the value of property....be the amount which the property might be expected to realize if solid in the open market by a willing seller at the time of [the notice] publication..." The law does not provide alternatives to the fair market value approach in cases where land markets are weak or non-existent. The Land Act 1995 indicates that customary rights exist without registration. Sec. 7 of the 1995 Land Act provides that "every piece of land in a customary area which immediately before the commencement of this Act was vested in or held by any person under customary tenure shall continue to be so held and recognized and any provision of this Act or any other law shall not be so construed as to infringe any customary right enjoyed by that person before the commencement of this Act." The laws assessed do not require the government or acquiring bodies to pay compensation for the economic activities associated with the land. Section 15(2) of the Land Acquisition Act, 1970 provides that "save where the land acquired is unutilized land to which an absentee owner is beneficially entitled, compensation shall be payable in respect of unexhausted improvements on unutilized land...provided that such compensation shall be limited to the value, for which the purpose the land is acquired, of such unexhausted improvements." According to Section 15(6), 'Unexhausted improvements' are defined as "any quality permanently attached to the land directly resulting from the expenditure of capital or labour and increasing the productive capacity, utility or amenity thereof, but does not include the results of ordinary cultivation other than standing crops and growing produce." The laws assessed do not provide compensation for intangible values (e.g. social, cultural, and spiritual values) associated with the land. The law provides affected persons with a right to negotiate compensation levels. A consultation proceeding with affected persons, by which affected person and the Minister can agree on compensation levels, is implicitly established by Sec. 10 of the Land Acquisition Act, 1970. Section 10 of the Land Acquisition Act, 1970 states that "where any property is acquired by the President...shall on behalf of the Government pay in respect thereof...such compensation in money as may be agreed...provided that where the property acquired is land the President may, with the consent of the person entitled to compensation, make such person...a grant of other land..." Section 10 of the Land Acquisition Act, 1970 requires that "where any property is acquired by the President under this Act the Minister shall on behalf of the Government pay in respect thereof, out of moneys provided for the purpose by Parliament, such compensation in money as may be agreed or, in default of agreement, determined in accordance with the provisions of this Act: Provided that where the property acquired is land the President may, with the consent of the person entitled to compensation, make to such person, in lieu of or in addition to any compensation payable under this Section, a grant of other land not exceeding in value the value of the land acquired, for an estate not exceeding the estate acquired and upon the same terms and conditions, as far as may be practicable, as those under which the land acquired was held." The laws assessed do not require the government to follow a gender-sensitive approach to providing compensation. Section 17 of the Land Acquisition Act, 1970 provides that "where a notice to acquire any land under this Act has been published in terms of Section seven, the persons entitled to transfer the land shall, notwithstanding anything to the contrary contained in any other law or in any order of any court otherwise than under this Act, within two months of the publication of such notice transfer the same to the President." Section 11(1) provides that, if there is a dispute over compensation outstanding within six weeks of the acquisition notice, then any person claiming an interest can file a claim in the High Court; however, the law does not explicitly require compensation to be paid before possession is taken or within a fixed timeframe thereafter. "Where any dispute arises as to the amount of compensation, the Minister or any person claiming to be entitled to compensation may, and shall if such dispute is not settled within the aforementioned period of six weeks, refer such dispute to the Court which shall determine the amount of compensation to be paid." Section 11(2), the Land Acquisition Act, 1970. Government of Zambia, *Constitution of Zambia*, 2016; Government of Zambia, *Land Act No. 29 of 1995*, 1995; Government of Zambia, *Land Acquisition Act*, 1970; *Land Acquisition (Prescribed Forms) Regulations (Cap. 189)*, 1970.

130 The laws assessed do not establish alternatives to fair market value in cases where land markets are weak or non-existent. Section 20(2)(b) of the Land Acquisition Act, 2002 provides "in assessing such compensation the value of the land shall be taken into account regard being had to its nature, location

and quality and any other factor bearing on its value." The law does not provide alternatives to the fair market value approach in cases where land markets are weak or non-existent. The laws assessed do not provide compensation for unregistered customary tenure rights. Articles 23-28 of the Traditional Leaders Act 1998 provide that "The Minister shall cause all Communal Land to be surveyed for the purpose of showing, by way of maps, the boundaries demarcating each village and such maps shall be filed of record at the offices of the Ministry for which the Minister is responsible with copies for the areas for which each rural district council is responsible, to be held at the offices of the rural district council and the district administrator concerned." Compensation for non-agricultural land should reflect "any actual expense or loss which has been or may reasonably be incurred or suffered directly as a result of the action taken by the acquiring authority and which has not already been taken into account, directly or indirectly, in assessing compensation" for the loss of land. By implication this should include the loss of economic activity (Land Acquisition Act, 2002, sec. 20(1)(b)). However, compensation for agricultural land can only reflect improvements on the land (not the economic activity associated with the land). The law provides that "as soon as possible after a preliminary notice has been published in respect of any agricultural land required for resettlement purposes, a designated valuation officer shall prepare a preliminary estimate of the compensation payable for improvements or the land, as the case may be, in terms of this Part in respect of the acquisition, and shall transmit his preliminary assessment to the Compensation Committee." (Land Acquisition Act, 2002, 29(B)(1)). When calculating compensation for agricultural land required for resettlement purposes, consideration must be given to "the age, nature and condition of the buildings and improvements on it" (Part II, p. 18, Land Acquisition Act, 2002). The laws assessed do not provide compensation for intangible values (e.g. social, cultural, and spiritual values) associated with the land. The laws assessed do not grant affected populations a right to negotiate compensation amounts. The answer is partial because, under Section 12 of the Communal Land Act, 1983 provides alternative land as a compensation option. However, it is not clear that alterative land may be provided as a compensation option when land other than communal land is expropriated. The laws assessed do not require the government to follow a gender-sensitive approach to providing compensation. Whether or not the compensation relates to the acquisition of land other than agricultural land required for resettlement purposes, Iity must pay to the claimant the full amount offered within 3 months of the date on which the opening day of the hearing is finally fixed (Land Acquisition Act, 2002, Sec. 25(1)(b)). Article 71(3)(e) of the Zimbabwe Constitution, 2013 states "the law entitles any claimant for compensation to apply to a competent court for the determination of-- i. the existence, nature and value of their interest in the property concerned; ii. the legality of the deprivation; and iii. the amount of compensation to which they are entitled; and to apply to the court for an order directing the prompt payment of any compensation." However, when agricultural land is acquired, claimants can only file claims for a determination of compensation for improvements on the land (Article 72(3), 2013 Zimbabwe Constitution). Affected populations cannot appeal compensation decisions (other than those relating to improvements) in Court. Government of Zimbabwe, *Constitution of Zimbabwe*, 2013; Government of Zimbabwe, *Land Acquisition Act (CAP 20:10)*, 1992; Government of Zimbabwe, *Land Acquisition (Disposal of Rural Land) Regulations (S.I. No. 287 of 1999)*, 1999; Government of Zimbabwe, *Communal Land Act, No. 2 of 1982 (2002)*.

131 Afghanistan has not enacted a national-level resettlement law or policy that is legally binding on all development projects. The Law on Land Expropriation, 2000 (amended 2005) does not establish procedures for rehabilitation and resettlement. The Ministry of Energy and Water developed a draft Resettlement Policy Framework in 2010. However, this framework is not legally binding to all development projects in Afghanistan. The Law on Land Expropriation does not require the government or acquiring bodies to develop a resettlement plan to accommodate displaced persons. The laws assessed do not provide displaced persons with relocation allowance. Article 13 of the Law on Land Expropriation, 2000 provides "A land plot of the same value shall be distributed to those whose house- land has been expropriated, or if requested so by the owner, another residential house owned by Emirates shall be put at his disposal, in accordance with the specified criteria." Article 14 of the Law states "Instead of paying the price for an expropriated land to the owner of such land, another piece of land, equivalent to such land, may be distributed to the owner upon his agreement. If such new land has a grade higher than that expropriated, the owner shall pay the difference to the Emirates and vice versa." The laws assessed do not provide displaced persons with productive alternative land. The laws assessed do not require

the government to consult displaced persons during the resettlement process. The laws assessed do not require the government to minimize or avoid involuntary resettlement. The laws assessed do not require the government or project developers to provide sufficient funding to implement resettlement programs. According to the World Bank LGAF Final Report for Afghanistan "an adequate resettlement policy has not been incorporated into the applicable law and it does not have any provisions for providing clear and fair resettlement options for people whose land has been appropriated..*[the Land Expropriation Law]* does any not have any provisions for providing fair resettlement options for people whose land has been appropriated" (pp. 98, 173). Government of Afghanistan. 2017. Law on Land Acquisition; Government of Afghanistan. 2004. Constitution of Afghanistan; Government of Afghanistan. 2000 (Amended 2005, 2010). *Law on Land Expropriation*; Government of Afghanistan. 2005. Presidential *Decree of the Islamic Republic of Afghanistan Concerning Modification of a Series of Articles of the Land Expropriation Law* Published in the Official Gazette #(794), 142, 14221. *Decree of the President No. 83. Government of Afghanistan, Law on Managing Land Affairs*, 2008; Government of Afghanistan, *Land Management Law*, 2000; Government of Afghanistan, *Decree of the President No. 83*, 2003; Government of Afghanistan, *Law and Pasture and Grazing Land*, 2000; Government of Afghanistan, *Law of land survey, verification and registration*, 1976; L.A. Wily, *Protecting Peoples' Interests? A Social Analysis of Land Expropriation Law of Afghanistan*, World Bank, Kabul, 2013; World Bank, *Land Governance Assessment Framework (final report) Afghanistan*. World Bank, DC, 2016.

132 Angola has not enacted a national-level resettlement law or policy that is legally binding on all development projects. Angola enacted a Decree Regarding Resettlement of Displaced People (2001) which addresses resettlement of persons displaced by the conflict, acknowledges a right to housing, and provides for new government allocations of land (Article 14) (USAID 2007). However, this Decree does not provide explicit rights to displaced persons who were forcibly evicted as a result of expropriations. Furthermore, a study conducted by USAID "found no reliable studies on the implementation of this law with regard to allocations of land to displaced persons" (USAID 2008). The laws assessed do not provide displaced persons with relocation allowance. The laws assessed do not provide displaced persons with alternative land, housing, or resettlement. The laws assessed do not provide displaced persons with productive alternative land. The laws assessed do not require the government to consult displaced persons during the resettlement process. The laws assessed do not require the government to minimize or avoid involuntary resettlement. The laws assessed do not require the government or project developers to provide sufficient funding to implement resettlement programs. Government of Angola, *Constitution*, 2010. Available at: https://goo.gl/w27hcN; Government of Angola, *Land Act No. 9/04*, 2004; Government of Angola, *Decree No. 58/07 approving the General Regulation for Land Concession*; United States Agency for International Development (USAID), *Strengthening Land Tenure and Property Rights in Angola, Land Law and Policy: Overview of Legal Framework*, USAID, DC, 2007.

133 Ley No. 21.499, 1977 Nacional de Expropiaciones does not establish procedures for rehabilitating and resettling displaced persons affected by land expropriations. The other national-level laws assessed do not establish rehabilitation and resettlement procedures. The laws assessed do not provide displaced persons with relocation allowance. Article 12 of Ley No. 21.499,1977 establishes that compensation must be paid in cash, except when the payment for the expropriated property is made in another kind of value. This provision suggests that compensation may be payable in alternative land, although the provision is unclear. The laws assessed do not provide displaced persons with productive alternative land. The laws assessed do not require the government to consult displaced persons during the resettlement process. The laws assessed do not require the government to minimize or avoid involuntary resettlement. The laws assessed do not require the government or project developers to provide sufficient funding to implement resettlement programs. According to Bartolome and Danklmaier (1999) in Argentina, "there is no general policy framework concerning displacement and resettlement of populations affected by large-scale development projects. Each project develops its own policy according to the circumstances, the private or public nature of the endeavor and – this is very influential – the origin of the funds. Until the seventies it was only the so-called Public Interest Appropriation Law the one applied to such cases. This law considered monetary compensations for proprietors of the land and goods affected, with no provisions for resettlement or other kinds of compensations or mitigation measures." L. Bartolome & C. Danklmaier , 'The Experience with Dams and Resettlement in Argentina', *Contributing Paper. World Commission on Dams*, Cape Town, 1999; Government of Argentina,

Constitution of Argentina, 1853 (Revised 1994); Government of Argentina, *Ley No. 21.499 Nacional De Expropiaciones*, 1977.

134 Bangladesh has not enacted a national-level resettlement law or policy that is legally binding on project involving the expropriation of land. The Acquisition and Requisition of Immovable Property Ordinance, 1982 provides compensation for expropriation. However, the Ordinance does not establish resettlement and rehabilitation procedures for accommodating displaced persons. The laws assessed do not provide displaced persons with alternative land, housing, or resettlement. The laws assessed do not provide displaced persons with productive alternative land. The laws assessed do not require the government to consult displaced persons during the resettlement process. The laws assessed do not require the government to minimize or avoid involuntary resettlement. The laws assessed do not require the government or project developers to provide sufficient funding to implement resettlement programs. According to Atahar (2013) "Under the law, there is no obligation to relocate or provide assistance for relocation, especially for those who lose a homestead... Therefore, various forms of support during relocation are essential, but no help is provided under the law... Existing law does not establish any provisions to alleviate the long-term impact on people's livelihood that is caused by forced displacement. The country's legal system blatantly ignores the socioeconomic rehabilitation of the involuntarily displaced." The laws assessed do not provide displaced persons with relocation allowance. Government of Bangladesh, *Constitution of Bangladesh*, 1972 (Amended 2011). Available at: https://goo.gl/CrxLAJ; Government of Bangladesh, *The Acquisition and Requisition of Immovable Property Ordinance*, 1982; Government of Bangladesh, *Acquisition of Waste Land Act*, 1950; USAID, *Property Rights and Resource Governance*, Bangladesh, 2010; S. Atahar, 'Development Project, Land Acquisition and Resettlement in Bangladesh: A Quest for Well Formulated National Resettlement and Rehabilitation Policy', *International Journal of Humanities and Social Science* , 3(7), 2013.

135 Belize has not enacted a national-level resettlement law or policy that is legally binding on all development projects. The Land Acquisition (Public Purposes) Act, 2000, provides for compensation in the event of land expropriation, but does not provide resettlement or rehabilitation procedures for accommodating displaced persons. The Housing and Town Planning Act, 2000, requires accommodation to be secured for persons displaced by housing and town-planning development projects, but the legal norms in question only apply to housing schemes, and not to all development projects. The laws assessed do not provide displaced persons with relocation allowance. The laws assessed, in some situations, provide displaced persons with alternative land, housing, or resettlement. Article 11(1) (a) and article 19 of the 2000 Housing and Town Planning Act (Chapter 182 of the Laws of Belize) provide that the Housing Minister may "provide housing accommodation for persons displaced", but this only triggers a partial score because it does not necessarily oblige the Housing Minister to provide such accommodation; it only provides Minister discretion to do so. The laws assessed do not provide displaced persons with productive alternative land. The laws assessed do not require the government to consult displaced persons during the resettlement process. The laws assessed do not require the government to minimize or avoid involuntary resettlement. The laws assessed do not require the government or project developers to provide sufficient funding to implement resettlement programs. The Belize Social Investment Fund wrote a draft Land Acquisition and Involuntary Resettlement Policy Framework in 2010, but this not legally binding when land is expropriated. Government of Belize, *Constitution of Belize*; Government of Belize, *Land Acquisition (Public Purposes) Act CAP 184*; Government of Belize, *Housing and Town Planning Act*, 2000; Belize Social Investment Fund, *Land Acquisition and Involuntary Resettlement Policy Framework*, 2010.

136 Bhutan has not enacted a national-level resettlement law or policy which is legally binding on all development projects. The Land Act 2007 provides landowners with compensation for expropriated land in the form of cash or alternative land (if the land acquired is in rural area (Art. 147)). However, the Land Act 2007 does not establish rehabilitation and resettlement procedures for accommodating displaced persons affected by development projects. The laws assessed do not provide displaced persons with relocation allowance. Section 141 of the Land Act, 2007 states "The Government may provide substitute land or cash payment, or both, as compensation." Section 147 states "The landowner shall have the discretion to opt for substitute land or cash compensation offered by the Government in case of the land acquired from rural areas." Section 148 states "In case of the land acquired in Thromde, the

landowner shall be provided cash compensation. If the land to be acquired is the only plot owned by the landowner in the Thromde, the Government shall consider a substitute land in the same Thromde. If the value of substitute land is inadequate additional cash compensation shall be provided subject to the value of land." Since there are limitations on the right to alternative land (e.g. limited to land in rural areas), the answer is 'partial.' The laws assessed do not provide displaced persons with productive alternative land. The laws assessed do not require the government to consult displaced persons during the resettlement process. The laws assessed do not require the government to minimize or avoid involuntary resettlement. The laws assessed do not require the government or project developers to provide sufficient funding to implement resettlement programs. A resettlement action plan was developed by borrowers of World Bank funds for the 'Rural Access Project' in Bhutan, but this plan is project-specific and thus not legally binding on all development projects involving the expropriation of land. Government of Bhutan, *Constitution of Bhutan*, 2008; Government of Bhutan, *The Land Act of Bhutan*, 2007; World Bank, *Bhutan - Rural Access Project: resettlement action plan: Policy framework for resettlement and rehabilitation of project affected persons*, World Bank, DC.

137 Botswana has not enacted a national-level resettlement law or policy that is legally binding on all development projects. Botswana's Acquisition of Property Act CAP 32-10 t, 1955 (Amended 2008) provides compensation to landholders affected by expropriation. Furthermore, the Tribal Land Act, 1968 grants compensation for improvements made on tribal land. However, these laws do not establish rehabilitation and resettlement procedures for accommodating displaced persons. Section 16(1)(e) of the Acquisition of Property Act CAP 32-10 provides that compensation should include "the reasonable expenses, if any, incidental to any change of residence or place of business of any person interested which is necessary in consequence of the acquisition." Furthermore, Section 33(2) of the Tribal Land Act provides that "any person who is required to vacate land under the provisions of subSection...and shall be entitled to adequate compensation from the State for the following, if applicable... (c) The costs of resettlement..." Section 33 of Tribal Land Act, 1968 provides that "where land is granted [for public purposes] and there subsists over such land under customary form of tenure, the land board shall require the occupier to vacate the land... any person who is required to vacate land...may be granted the right to use other land, if available, and shall be entitled to adequate compensation from the State." However, the answer is 'partial' because the Acquisition of Property Act, 1955 does not provide alternative land as a compensation option. Thus, it is unclear whether non-Tribal landholders are granted to the right to alternative land as a compensation option. The laws assessed do not provide displaced persons with productive alternative land. The laws assessed do not require the government to consult displaced persons during the resettlement process. The laws assessed do not require the government to minimize or avoid forced evictions. The laws assessed do not require the government or project developers to provide sufficient funding to implement resettlement programs. As a requirement for World Bank funding, Botswana developed a Resettlement Policy Framework (RPF) to be used as a guiding instrument to the implementation of Output Based Long Term Road Contracts (OPRC) in Botswana. However, this Policy Framework is project-specific and thus not legally binding on all projects. Government of Botswana, *Constitution of Botswana*; Government of Botswana, *Acquisition of Property Act Chapter 32:10*, 1955; Government of Botswana, *Tribal Land Act Chapter 32:02*, 1968 (Amended 1994); Government of Botswana, *Tribal Land Regulations (Chapter 32:02)*, 1960;Botswana Department of Roads, *Resettlement Policy Framework WT/MTC/ROADS/SER/32/2007-2008*, World Bank, DC, 2008.

138 Brazil has not enacted a national legislation on involuntary resettlement that is legally binding on all development projects. However, in 2013, the Brazil Ministry of Cities passed a resettlement policy to safeguard the rights of urban residents who are involuntarily resettled from their homes. But this resettlement policy is not legally binding and only applies to projects implemented by the Ministry of Cities, including the Program of Growth Acceleration. Brazil has not enacted national legislation on involuntary resettlement that is legally binding on all development projects. There are legally binding provisions that provide the right to compensation for expropriation in the Brazilian Federal Constitution on land expropriation, a decree-law on expropriation for public purposes (Decree-law Nº 3,365, 1941), and a federal law that defines the cases of expropriation in the social interest (Federal Law Nº 4,132, of September 10, 1962). However, these laws do not establish procedures for accommodating and resettling displaced persons. According to World Bank (2011), as is common in many countries, land acquisition and involuntary resettlement in Brazil is governed mostly by federal and state legislation on land expro-

priation. There is no specific national policy or guideline to address physical displacement (relocation) or economic displacement (loss of income sources or livelihoods) of those affected by development projects." The Ministry of Cities Involuntary Resettlement Policy (2013) indicates that Resettlement and Compensatory Measures Plan produced by developers and submitted to the Ministry of Cities for approval must accommodate displaced persons by financial support to relocate (See Annex of Involuntary Resettlement Policy (2013)). The Ministry of Cities Involuntary Resettlement Policy (2013) indicates that Resettlement and Compensatory Measures Plan produced by developers and submitted to the Ministry of Cities for approval must accommodate displaced persons by providing alternative housing. The laws assessed do not provide displaced persons with productive alternative land. Article 4 of the Ministry of Cities Involuntary Resettlement Policy (2013) provides "the Resettlement and Compensatory Measures Plan shall be prepared with the participation of families affected by the work, before being sent to the Ministry of Cities. The Ministry of Cities Involuntary Resettlement Policy (2013) indicates that Resettlement and Compensatory Measures Plan produced by developers and submitted to the Ministry of Cities for approval must show evidence that alternatives to implementing the project were studied "with the view of avoiding involuntary resettlement." The laws assessed do not require the government or project developers to provide sufficient funding to implement resettlement programs. Government of Brazil, *Land Law, Law 4.504 of 1964*, 1964; Government of Brazil, *The Law of Expropriation for Public Utility, Decree-Law No. 3.365 of June 21, 1941*, 1941; Government of Brazil, *The Expropriation Law for Social Interest, Law 4.132 of Sept. 10, 1962*; K. Rosenn, 'Expropriation in Argentina and Brazil: Theory and Practice', *Virginia Journal of International Law*, Vol. 15:2, 1975. Available at: https://goo.gl/R34Gl9; World Bank, *Land Governance Assessment Framework Synthesis Report*, World Bank, DC, 2016; Ministry of Cities, *Involuntary Resettlement Policy (No. 317)*, 2013. Available at: https://goo.gl/qbsMdA; World Bank, *Involuntary Resettlement in Brazil: A Review of Policies and Practices*, World Bank, DC, 2011.

139 Burkina Faso has not enacted a national-level resettlement law or policy which is legally binding on all development projects. The RAF (La loi portant Réorganisation Agraire et Foncière) (Law 034-2012) establishes expropriation and compensation procedures. However, the Law does not establish other resettlement and rehabilitation procedures. The laws assessed do not provide displaced persons with relocation allowance. Article 329 provides that under some projects, compensation may be in the form of resettlement of the beneficiaries (of compensation for expropriation). However, the law does not necessarily provide alternative land in every case. The laws assessed do not provide displaced persons with productive alternative land. The laws assessed do not require the government to consult displaced persons during the resettlement process. The laws assessed do not require the government to minimize or avoid forced evictions. The laws assessed do not require the government or project developers to provide sufficient funding to implement resettlement programs. Several World Bank project resettlement action plans have been published in Burkina Faso. Government of Burkina Faso, *Constitution of Burkina Faso*, 1991 (Amended 2012); Government of Burkina Faso, *Law 034-2012/AN Agrarian Reform Law*; Government of Burkina Faso, *Law 034-2009/AN on Rural Land Tenure*, 2009; World Bank, *Bagre Growth Pole Project: resettlement plan (Vol. 3): Plan d'actions de reinstallation des populations affectees par l'amenagement de 1130 HA a Bagre*, World Bank, DC, 2014;World Bank, *Burkina Faso - Sahel Growth Pole Project: resettlement plan (Vol. 2): Cadre politique de reinstallation des populations*, World Bank, DC, 2015; World Bank, *Agricultural Productivity and Food Security Project: additional financing - resettlement plan: Cadre de politique de reinstallation*, World Bank, DC, 2014.

140 Cambodia has not enacted a national-level resettlement policy that is legally binding on all development projects involving the expropriation of land. According to the Cambodian Rehabilitation and Development Board, a national resettlement policy has been drafted but this document has not yet been adopted as a sub-decree. Article 4 of the Law on Economic Land Concessions, 2o05 establishes criteria that economic land concessions must provide solutions for resettlement issues, in accordance with the existing legal framework and procedures. The Contracting Authority shall ensure that there will not be involuntary resettlement by lawful landholders and that access to private land shall be respected. The Law Land 2001 does not establish rehabilitation and resettlement provisions. In 2014, an Asian Development Bank funded project drafted an updated resettlement framework applicable to flood damage emergency reconstruction projects in Cambodia. However, this resettlement framework is not legally binding on all development projects in Cambodia. The laws assessed do not provide

displaced persons with relocation allowance. The laws assessed do not provide displaced persons with alternative land, housing, or resettlement. The laws assessed do not provide displaced persons with productive alternative land. The laws assessed do not require the government to consult displaced persons during the resettlement process. The laws assessed do not require the government to minimize or avoid involuntary resettlement. The laws assessed do not require the government or project developers to provide sufficient funding to implement resettlement programs. According to Price (2008), "A Cambodia National Resettlement Action plan (NRAP) was prepared, discussed at an national workshop and a draft National Resettlement Policy was prepared that requires [rehabilitation and resettlement procedures]...The NRAP gives a number of recommendations for a concomitant legal instrument, a regulatory framework, an requisite capacity-building measures." I found no evidence that this Resettlement Action plan was signed into law. Government of Cambodia, *Constitution of Cambodia*, 1993; Government of Cambodia, *Law on Expropriation (Unofficial Translation)*, 2010; Government of Cambodia, *Land Law of 2001, Chapter 3, Part 2. August 13*, 2001; Government of Cambodia, *Sub Decree on Procedures of Registration of Land of Indigenous Communities of 2009*, June 9, 2009; Cambodia Rehabilitation and Development Board, *Council for the Development Cambodia, Resettlement Rights or Project-Affected People*; World Bank, *Cambodia- South East Asia Disaster Risk Management Project: resettlement plan: Resettlement policy framework*, World Bank, DC, 2016; S. Price, 'Compensation, Restoration and Development Opportunities: National Standards on Involuntary Resettlement', in M.M. Cernea & H.M. Mathur (Eds), *The Resettlement Dilemma: Can Compensation Prevent Impoverishment?*, Oxford University Press, New Delhi, 2008, pp. 147–179.

141 Article 51 of the Law on Land Administration, 1998 provides "The rate of compensation for expropriation of land to build large or medium-sized water conservancy or hydroelectric projects and the measures for resettling relocated people shall be prescribed separately by the State Council." The State Council has established rules for reservoir-related resettlement to assist displaced populations to reach or exceed their original living standard (Article 4, Regulations on Compensation and Resettlement for Medium and Large Water Facilities and Hydropower Construction. 1991). The State Council also passed the Regulation on Land Requisition Compensation and Resettlement of Migrants for Large and Medium Water Conservation and Hydropower Construction Projects (2006). The Urban Housing Demolition and Relocation Management Regulation provides for alternative housing temporary resettlement (Art. 31). In 2001, China passed Regulation on Resident-Resettlement for the Yangtze River Three Gorges Project Construction. However, the score on this indicator is 'partial' because there are no comprehensive resettlement regulations which apply to all development projects (in addition to hydroelectric projects). The Law on Land Administration 1998 provides resettlement subsidies for displaced persons (referred to by law as "agricultural populations needing resettlement"). Article 47 of the Law on Land Administration states "resettlement subsidies for expropriated cultivated land shall be calculated according to the agricultural population needing to be resettled. The agricultural population needing to be resettled shall be calculated by dividing the area of expropriated cultivated land by the average area of the original cultivated land per person of the unit the land of which is expropriated. The standard resettlement subsidies to be divided among members of the agricultural population needing resettlement shall be four to six times the average annual output value of the expropriated cultivated land calculated on the basis of three years preceding such expropriation. However, the maximum resettlement subsidies for each hectare of the expropriated cultivated land shall not exceed fifteen times its average annual output value calculated on the basis of three years preceding such expropriation." Article 31 of the Urban Housing Demolition and Relocation Management Regulations, 2001 also provides for relocation allowance. Article 17 of the Regulation on the Expropriation of Buildings on State-owned Land and Compensation, 2011 provides compensation "for the relocation or temporary settlement resulting from the building expropriation" See also Article 22 of Regulation on the Expropriation of Buildings on State-owned Land and Compensation. Articles 31 of the Urban Housing Demolition and Relocation Management Regulations, the property owner is entitled to moving expenses and transitional resettlement subsidy and that resettlement subsidies can be in the form of either cash subsidy or provision of a transitional home. However, aside from urban property owners wishing to obtain a 'transitional home', the laws assessed do not ensure that displaced persons are granted alternative land. The laws assessed do not provide displaced persons with productive alternative land. Article 48 of the Law on Land Administration states "Once a plan for compensation and resettlement subsidies

for requisitioned land is decided on, the local people's government concerned shall make it known to the general public and solicit comments and suggestions from the collective economic organizations, the land of which is requisitioned, and the peasants." The laws assessed do not require the government to minimize or avoid involuntary resettlement. Government of the People's Republic of China, *Constitution of China*, 2004; Government of the People's Republic of China, *The Law of Land Administration of the People's Republic of China*, 1998; Government of China, *Property Law of the People's Republic of China*, 2007. Available at: https://goo.gl/FYWy2N; Government of China, *Regulation on the Expropriation of Buildings on State-owned Land and Compensation*, 2011; Government of China, *Regulations for the implementation of the Land Administration Law of the People's Republic of China*, 1991; Government of China, *Regulations for the implementation of the Land Administration Law of the People's Republic of China (98)*, 1991; Government of China, *Regulation on Land Requisition Compensation and Resettlement of Migrants for Large and Medium Water Conservation and Hydropower Construction Projects*, 2006; Government of China, *Urban Housing Demolition and Relocation Management Regulations*, 2001.

142 Ecuador has not enacted a national-level legally binding resettlement and rehabilitation policy that is applicable to all development projects. Article 323 of Ecuador's Constitution (last updated in 2015 with implementation of changes made based on a 2011 referendum) mentions that expropriation with respect to the execution of social development projects will include compensation, and that "confiscation is prohibited", but the Constitution makes no mention of resettlement policy. The laws assessed do not provide displaced persons with relocation allowance. The laws assessed do not provide displaced persons with alternative land, housing, or resettlement. The laws assessed do not provide displaced persons with productive alternative land. The laws assessed do not require the government to consult displaced persons during the resettlement process. The laws assessed do not require the government to minimize or avoid involuntary resettlement. Ecuador developed a resettlement action plan for a World Bank project on the national system of protected areas, but this plan is project-specific and thus not legally binding on all development projects involving the expropriation of land. Government, *Constitution of Ecuador*, 2010; Government of Ecuador, *Ley N° 54 - Ley de Desarrollo Agrario*, 1997; Government, *Resolución N° 15 - Instructivo para sustanciar el proceso de expropiación en primera instancia*, 2013; World Bank, *Ecuador- National System of Protected Areas: Resettlement Action Plan*, World Bank, DC, 2010.

143 Eritrea has not enacted a national-level resettlement policy which is legally binding on all development projects. The Land Proclamation No. 58/1994 provides compensation for expropriation but does not establish procedures for rehabilitating displaced persons after their land is acquired in a compulsory manner. The laws assessed do not provide displaced persons with relocation allowance. Article 51 of the Land Proclamation No. 58/1994 provides that "Where the Government or appropriate government body expropriates land from holder(s) of right to land, the compensation, in cash or substitute land, shall be commensurate to the loss accruing to the holder of the right." The laws assessed do not provide displaced persons with productive alternative land. The laws assessed do not require the government to consult displaced persons during the resettlement process. The laws assessed do not require the government to minimize or avoid involuntary resettlement. Eritrea developed a resettlement action plan for a World Bank project called the "Asmara Power Distribution and Rural Electrification Project." According to the resettlement action plan developed for that project, "Whereas the law relating to Land administration and tenure in Eritrea is wide and varied, entitlements for payment of compensation are essentially based on right of ownership (i.e. allocation and land titles and and/or customary ownership)", meaning that displaced populations are not entitled to resettlement and rehabilitation assistance under Eritrean law. Government of Eritrea, *Constitution of Eritrea*, 1997; Government of Eritrea, *Land Proclamation (No. 58/1994)*, 1994; World Bank, *Asmara Power Distribution and Rural Electrification Project*, World Bank, DC, 2004.

144 Ethiopia has not enacted a national-level resettlement policy which is legally binding on all development projects. The Expropriation of Landholdings for Public Purposes and Payment of Compensation Proclamation No. 455/2000 provides relocation allowance and displacement compensation to affected 'landholders.' These landholders are defined as "an individual, government or private organization or any other organ which has legal personality and has lawful possession over the land to be expropri-

ated and own property situated thereon." However, Ethiopia has not established rehabilitation and resettlement procedures for accommodating all displaced persons, regardless of their tenure rights. Section 7.5 of the Expropriation of Landholdings for Public Purposes and Payment of Compensation Proclamation No. 455/2005 provides "The cost of removal, transportation and erection shall be paid as compensation for a property that could be relocated and continue its service as before." However, the answer is 'partial' because the law does not provide relocation allowance to non-landholders (i.e. displaced persons with no legal rights to land). Section 8 of Proclamation No. 455/2005 provides alternative land to displaced urban landholders; however, the Proclamation does not provide displaced rural landholders with alternative land. The laws assessed do not provide displaced persons with productive alternative land. The laws assessed do not require the government to consult displaced persons during the resettlement process. The laws assessed do not require the government to minimize or avoid involuntary resettlement. According to the World Bank LGAF study of Ethiopia, "[a] Resettlement policy does not exist [in Ethiopia]; if resettlement takes place than it is in an ad-hoc manner... Where foreign and local investors have acquired extensive land in Benishangul Gumuz and Gambella regions, resettlement program has been launched to relocate communities away from their previous home areas. Both the Regions and the federal government justify the relocation on the grounds that this will enable local authorities to provide essential services such as education, health, clean water, etc. Conversely, interviews held with local farmers in Gambella shows that the relocation is done for investors to provide them access to land and other resources" (World Bank, 2016, pp. 88, 93). Government of Ethiopia, *Constitution of Ethiopia*, 1994; Government of Ethiopia, *Proclamation No. 455/2005 Expropriation of Landholdings for Public Purposes and Payment of Compensation Proclamation*, 2005; Government of Ethiopia, *Civil Code of Ethiopia*, 1960; Government of Ethiopia, *Proclamation No. 456/2005 Rural Land Administration and Use Proclamation*, 2005; World Bank, *Land Governance Assessment Framework Implementation in Ethiopia- Final Country Report*, World Bank, DC, 2016.

145 Although Ghana grants displaced persons a constitutional right to suitable alternative land, Ghana has not enacted a national-level resettlement policy that is legally binding on all development projects. The State Lands Act, 1962 provides compensation, in cash or alternative land, to affected populations. However, Ghana has not enacted rehabilitation and resettlement procedures for accommodating all displaced persons affected by expropriation. Article 20(3) of the Constitution of Ghana, 1993 provides the right of displaced persons to resettle on "suitable alternative land with due regard for their economic well-being and social and cultural values." Ghana has not enacted legislation or regulation for implementing this constitutional provision. The laws assessed do not provide displaced persons with relocation allowance. The laws assessed do not require the government to consult displaced persons during the resettlement process. The laws assessed do not require the government to minimize or avoid involuntary resettlement. According to the World Bank LGAF report for Ghana, "the State Lands Act, Act 125 of 1962.... has been widely used for compulsory land acquisitions in the country did not impose a duty on the state to resettle them Only monetary compensation or land of equivalent value could be the duty of the state to do. However, since 1993, the constitution has made resettlement mandatory by stating that where the compulsory acquisition of land involves the displacement of any inhabitants, the state shall resettle them on suitable alternative land having regard to their economic well-being and socio-cultural values. While such cases are infrequent, a most recent example was the Bui Dam Project in the Brong-Ahafo Region of Ghana. This involved the displacement of smallholder farmers for a hydro-electric project and while attempts at resettling these farmers have been on-going, it was all clear to panel members that comparable assets and maintenance of social and economic status of these affected populations was not achievable." Government of Ghana, *The Constitution of the Republic of Ghana*, 1992; Government of Ghana, *State Lands Act*, 1962; Government of Ghana, *Administration of Lands Act*, 1962; World Bank, *Final Report: Improving Land Sector Governance in Ghana: Implementation of the Land Governance Assessment Framework*, World Bank, DC, 2012.

146 According to a Millennium Challenge Corporation report (Dunning 2011) "Honduras passed a law, which made MCC's complete resettlement process as the process that must be used for resettlement in all transportation infrastructure projects... The government of Honduras was so impressed with the MCC resettlement process that it adopted a new Fast Track Law that replicated the MCC resettlement scheme." According to a separate MCC report (MCC 2011), "The Honduran Congress passed a decree allowing MCA-Honduras to go beyond what the present but outdated national resettlement

law requires and to implement a resettlement program that meets international standards." However, I could not find a copy of this law online, which is why the indicator answer is 'unclear', In 2012, as part of a World Bank-funded project, Honduras formulated a policy framework for involuntary resettlement within the implementation framework of a disaster risk management project, but this policy is project-specific and relating to disaster risk management (not expropriation), and thus is outside the scope of this legal analysis. Government of Honduras, *Constitution of Honduras*, 1982; Government of Honduras, *Decree 82/04 - Ley de propiedad*, 2004; Government of Honduras, *Decreto No 191/05 - Reforma la Ley de Propiedad*; Government of Honduras, *Decreto No 258/05 - Reforma la Ley de propiedad*. Available at: https://goo.gl/Q9ofCG; Government of Honduras, *Decreto No 12/00 – Ley para el dessarollo rural sostenible*. Available at: https://goo.gl/I4J72v; Millennium Challenge Corporation (MCC), *Policy Reforms Matter: Promoting the Sustainability of MCC Programs in Honduras*, MCC, DC, 2010; World Bank, *Honduras - Policy framework for involuntary resettlement within the implementation framework of the Disaster Risk Management Project: resettlement plan*, World Bank, DC, 2012; C. Dunning, *a MCA Monitor Report from the Field: Honduras*, MCC, DC, 2011; MCC, *MCC Policy Reforms Show Why Resettlement Activities Matter*, MCC, DC, 2011; MCC, *Policy Reforms Matter: Promoting the Sustainability of MCC Programs in Honduras*, MCC, DC, 2010.

147 Hong Kong has not enacted a regional-level resettlement policy which is legally binding on all development projects. The Lands Resumption Ordinance, 1997 requires the government to compensate people for expropriation of their land, or cancellation of their lease (known as resumption, since almost all land is owned by the government in Hong Kong). Section 10 (2) of the Land Resumption Ordinance, 1998 provides that Tribunal shall determine the compensation (if any) payable , which includes the amount of any expenses reasonably incurred by him in moving from any premises owned or occupied by him on the land resumed to, or in connection with the acquisition of, alternative land or land and buildings. The laws assessed do not provide displaced persons with alternative land, housing, or resettlement. The laws assessed do not provide displaced persons with productive alternative land. The laws assessed do not require the government to consult affected populations during the resettlement process. The laws assessed do not indicate that the government is to minimize or avoid involuntary resettlement. *Constitution of Hong Kong*, 1990; Government of Hong Kong, *Land Resumption Ordinance (CAP. 124)*, 1998; Government of Hong Kong, *Basic Law of the Hong Kong Special Administrative Region of the People's Republic of China*, 1990.

148 The Right to Fair Compensation and Transparency in Land Acquisition, Rehabilitation and Resettlement Act, 2013 (LARR Act) provides robust rehabilitation and resettlement procedures for accommodating persons displaced by expropriations. The LARR Act, 2013 provides that "each affected family which is displaced shall get a one-time financial assistance of fifty thousand rupees as transportation cost for shifting of the family, building materials, belongings and cattle." (LARR Act, 2013 Second Schedule, Provision 6). The Second and Third Schedule of the LARR Act, 2013 provides for alternative land, housing, and resettlement. Provision 2 of the Second Schedule provides that, for irrigation projects, "far as possible in lieu of compensation" affected families owning agricultural land in the affected area who loses land or has become a marginal farmer or landless, shall be allotted a minimum of one acre of land in the command area of the acquisition projects. Scheduled Castes and Tribes must be provided equivalent land or two and a half acres, whichever is lower. Since this right is limited to irrigation projects and there is a limit on the number of productive acres granted, the answer for this indicator is 'partial', Section 16(5) of the LARR Act, 2013 provides that, when preparing a rehabilitation and resettlement scheme, the Administrator of Rehabilitation and Resettlement must conduct a public hearing after giving adequate publicity about the date, time and venue. After the hearing occurs, the Administrator must complete a specific report on the claims and objections raised in the public hearing (Section 16(6), LARR Act). Section 16 also provides that the Administration must conduct a survey and undertake a census of the affected families, which shall include "(a) particulars of lands and immovable properties being acquired of each family; (b) livelihoods lost in respect of land losers and landless whose livelihoods are primarily dependent on the lands being acquired; (c) a list of public utilities and Government buildings which are affected or likely to be affected, where resettlement of affected families is involved; and (e) details of any common property resources being acquired." According to the LARR Act, 2013 an Expert Group must appraise the Social Impact Assessment and report on whether "land proposed to be acquired is the absolute bare-minimum extent needed for the project and whether

there are no other less displacing options available." (Sec. 7(5), LARR Act). Section 8(2) requires the appropriate Government to examine the report of the Collector on Expert Group on Social Impact Assessment and, after consider the reports, recommend such area for acquisition which would ensure minimum displace of people, minimum disturbance and minimum adverse impact on the individuals affected (Sec. 8(2), LARR Act). Section 39 provides that the Collector must "as far, as possible, not displace any family which has already been displaced by the appropriated Government, and, if so, shall pay additional compensation..." Government of India, *Constitution of India*, 2007. Available at: https://goo.gl/i2FQla; Government of India, *The Right to Fair Compensation and Transparency in Land Acquisition, Rehabilitation and Resettlement Act*, 2013; Government of India, *The Scheduled Tribes and Other Traditional Forest Dwellers (Recognition of Forest Rights) Act*, 2006; Government of India, *Right to Fair Compensation and Transparency in Land Acquisition, Rehabilitation and Resettlement (Social Impact Assessment and Consent) Rules*, 2014.

149 The Acquisition of Land for Development in the Public Interest (Law No. 2 of 2012) provides the right to resettlements for affected populations, including Indigenous populations, who are displaced as a result of expropriation. However, there is no comprehensive rehabilitation and resettlement policy enacted at the national-level that is legally binding on all development projects. Article 33(f) grants compensation for 'other appraisable loss', 'Other appraisable loss' means "nonphysical loss equivalent to money value, for example, loss due to loss of business or job, cost of change of location, cost of change of profession, and loss of value of the remaining property." Article 36 of Law No. 2 of 2012 provides that "the giving of compensation may be in the form of....resettlements..." 'Resettlements' is defined by the law as "a process of replacing the Entitled Party's land with the land of different location as agreed upon during the process of Acquisition of Land." Article 40 of Law No. 2 of 2013 states "compensation for indigenous land shall be given in the form of substitute land, resettlements, or other forms as agreed upon by the relevant indigenous people." The laws assessed do not provide displaced persons with productive alternative land. The laws assessed do not require the government to consult displaced persons during the resettlement process. The laws assessed do not require the government to minimize or avoid involuntary resettlement. In 2011, as part of a World Bank-funded project, Indonesia developed a land acquisition and resettlement policy framework for a Geothermal Clean Energy Investment Project, but this framework is project-specific and thus not legally binding on all projects involving the expropriation of land. Government of Indonesia, *Constitution of Indonesia*, 1945. Available at: https://goo.gl/h6HCp7; Government of Indonesia, *Acquisition of Land for Development in the Public Interest (Law No. 2 of 2012)*; Government of Indonesia, *Act. 41 of 1999 on Forestry Affairs, 1999; Government of Indonesia, Basic Agrarian Act*, 1960; World Bank, *Land Acquisition and Resettlement Policy Framework: Proposed Geothermal Clean Energy Investment Project*, World Bank, DC, 2011.

150 Kazakhstan has not enacted a national-level resettlement policy which is binding on all development projects involving the expropriation of land. The laws assessed do not provide for a relocation allowance for displaced persons. Article 87(3) of the Land Code, 2003 indicates that alternative land may be provided as a compensation option; however alternative land is not necessarily provided in every case. This provisions states "By agreement with the owner of the land or non-land user may be provided instead of land redeemed for expropriation for public needs, another plot of land provided by offsetting the cost of land or rights to it in the redeemed value of the land or rights to it in the market value at the time of cessation of ownership or land use." Additionally, Article 15 of the Housing Relations Act provides that "hen a residential house is demolished due to compulsory alienation of land plots for state requirements, the owner shall be provided with a suitable dwelling place owned by him/her or the total market value of a dwelling place of his/her choice before demolition of his/her dwelling place." The laws assessed do not provide displaced persons with productive alternative land. The laws assessed do not require the government to consult displaced persons during the resettlement process. Under the laws assessed, the government is not legally obligated to avoid or minimize involuntary resettlement. The laws assessed Government of Kazakhstan, *Constitution of Kazakhstan*, 1995; Government of Kazakhstan, *Land Code of the Republic of Kazakhstan*, 2003; Government of Kazakhstan, *Law on State-Owned Property (No. 413-IV ZRK)*, 2011; Government of Kazakhstan, *Civil Code*, 1994.

151 Kenya has not enacted a national-level resettlement policy that is applicable when land is expropriated. An Evictions and Resettlement Bill was submitted to Parliament in 2012 and 2014; however, this

Bill has not passed into law. The Ministry of Lands also published Eviction and Resettlement Guidelines in 2009. According to Munub *et al.* (2016), "...mixed data analyses...concluded that policy and legal frameworks fell short in just compensation for involuntary resettlement in Kenya... statutory frameworks and compensation values fell short of the socio-cultural and economic expectations of project displaced persons." Section 123 of the Land Act, 2012 provides "Acquisition of other land on account of severance (1) At any time before possession is taken of any land acquired under this Act, the Commission may, revoke a direction to acquire the land, and, shall determine and pay compensation for all damage suffered and all costs and expenses reasonably incurred by persons interested in the land by reason of or in consequence of the proceedings for acquiring the land." This provision implies that relocation allowance may be provided as part of compensation in some cases. According to both the 2012 Land Act (114(2)), the government 'may agree' to grant land in lieu of monetary payment of compensation in situations where land is expropriated, but the government is not legally obligated to do so. The laws assessed do not provide displaced persons with alternative productive land. The laws assessed do not require the government to consult displaced persons during the resettlement process. The laws assessed do not require the government to minimize or avoid forced evictions. According to the World Bank's LGAF study of Kenya, there is no resettlement law enacted in Kenya. Government of Kenya, *Constitution of Kenya*, 2010. Available at: https://goo.gl/HiKrqK; Government of Kenya, *Land Act*, 2012; Government of Kenya, *Community Land Act*, 2016; Government of Kenya, *Land Acquisition Act (Repealed by Land Act 2012)*, 2010; Government of Kenya, *Draft Evictions and Resettlement Bill*, 2012; Ministry of Lands of Kenya, *Eviction and Resettlement Guidelines*, 2009; S. Munub, O. K'akumu & W. Mwangi, 'Involuntary Resettlement Policy and Praxis in Kenya: An Evaluation of Just Terms of Compensation', *International Journal of Environment, Ecology, Family and Urban Studies*, Vol. 6, No. 3, 2016, pp. 23-44; World Bank, *Kenya Land Governance Assessment Report*, World Bank, DC, 2016.

152 The Decree on Compensation and Resettlement Management in Development Projects (2016) establishes robust resettlement and rehabilitation procedures for accommodating displaced populations. The decree applies to "development projects of the state and private sectors including foreign and domestic project, affected people and all relevant stakeholders who are subject to compensation and resettlement." Article 16 of the Decree on Compensation and Resettlement Management in Development Projects (2016) states "The project owner must provide additional assistance for the relocated affected throughout the transitional period for at least three years or over according to the consideration of the provincial, city Committee for Compensation and resettlement since the relocation of the affected from their original living areas with the following additional assistance: 1. The project owner must provide food, consumer goods for each of the relocated affected in accordance with the household registration books on the day of registration of rights of the affected throughout the transitional period; 2. Compensation for the revenue losses during the relocation period for the affected present on the relocation day." Article 10 of the Decree on Compensation and Resettlement Management in Development Projects (2016) states that "project owners must work in coordination with the committee for compensation and resettlement at the local levels concerned to....identify new resettlement areas... [and] prepare resettlement plans." Article 12 of the 2016 Decree states that "1. the resettlement area must be ensured with stability and safety in terms of prevention of natural disasters and infrastructures and facilities must be established in compliance with standards." Article 12 of the Decree on Compensation and Resettlement Management Projects (2016) states that "the new houses to be build for the affected people must be at least equivalent to the forms and sizes of the original houses of the affected people." Article 15 of the 2016 Decree states that project owners must provide "agricultural land in appropriate ways including the creation of new livelihood options and stable income generation activities...in addition to agriculture production activities...the level of livelihood conditions of the affected hoouseholds must be upgraded or at least be at the same original level." Article 18 of the Decree on Compensation and Resettlement Management in Development Projects (2016) provides that affected populations have a right to "receive the information on the development projects...attend consultations at different levels, make comments to the plan of compensation, resettlement and rehabilitation...[and] make a written proposal to the relocated committee for compensation and resettlement." The laws assessed do not require the government to minimize or avoid involuntary resettlement. Article 17(3) of the Decree on Compensation and Resettlement Management in Development Projects (2016) obliges project owners to "make plans of compensation, resettlement and rehabilitation of livelihood of people

in Lao language in combination with the plan for the environmental, social and natural management, follow-up and examination of his development project which must ensure to incorporate sufficient costs to be included in the project cost. If the budget is not enough during the implementation, the project owner is obliged to take responsibility." Government of Laos, *Decree on Compensation and Resettlement Management in Development Projects*, 2016; Government of Laos, *Decree on the Compensation and Resettlement of the Development Project*, 2005; Government of Laos, *Decree on the Implementation of the Land Law No. 88/PM*, 2008; Government of Laos, *Land Law No. 04 /NA*, 2003; Government of Laos, *Decree on the Compensation and Resettlement of the Development Project No. 192/PM*, 2003.

153 Lesotho has not enacted a national-level resettlement law or policy that is legally binding on all development projects. In 2014, the Lesotho Highlands Development Authority and the Lesotho Highlands Water Commission developed a draft compensation policy for the Lesotho Highlands Water Project. The Compensation Policy for the Lesotho Highlands Water Project was finally approved in 2016. However, it is unclear whether this Compensation Policy is being implemented yet in practice. This Compensation Policy provides some procedures for resettling and rehabilitating displaced persons; however, this Policy is project-specific and thus not legally binding on all development projects involving the expropriation of land. The laws assessed do not provide displaced persons with relocation allowance. The laws assessed do not provide displaced persons with alternative land, housing, or resettlement. The laws assessed do not provide displaced persons with alternative land, housing, or resettlement. The laws assessed do not require the government to consult displaced persons during the resettlement process. The laws assessed do not require the government to minimize or avoid forced evictions. Government of Lesotho, *Constitution of Lesotho*, 1993; Government of Lesotho, *Land Act (Act No. 8 of 2010)*, 2010. Available at: http://faolex.fao.org/docs/pdf/les119080.pdf; Lesotho Highlands Development Authority and Lesotho Highlands Water Commission, *Lesotho Highlands Water Project (LHWP) Phase II Compensation Policy 5th draft (v.50.08)*, 2014.

154 Liberia has not enacted a national-level resettlement law or policy that is legally binding on all development projects involving the expropriation of land. The laws assessed do not provide displaced persons with relocation allowance. The laws assessed do not provide displaced persons with alternative land, housing, or resettlement. The laws assessed do not provide displaced persons with alternative land, housing, or resettlement. The laws assessed do not require the government to consult displaced persons during the resettlement process. The laws assessed do not require the government to minimize or avoid forced evictions. For a World Bank-funded project conducted in Liberia, a resettlement policy framework was developed for the Liberia Accelerated Electricity Expansion Project LACEEP. The framework states that "[in Liberia] there is no statute that clearly defines the manner by which said individual or group can be compensated or resettled. Further, most of the statutes concerning the subject matter were enacted many years ago and some issues therein do not meet present day reality..." Government of Liberia, *Constitution of Liberia*, 1984; Government of Liberia, *Draft Land Rights Act, 2013 (pending)*; World Bank, *Resettlement Liberia Accelerated Electricity Expansion Project LACEEP*, 2015.

155 Mexico has not enacted a national-level resettlement procedure that is legally binding on all development projects. The Agrarian Law (1992) provides compensation for the expropriation of land, but the Agrarian Law does not establish procedures for resettling and rehabilitating displaced persons affected by expropriations. The laws assessed do not provide displaced persons with relocation allowance. The laws assessed do not provide displaced persons with alternative land, housing, or resettlement. The laws assessed do not provide displaced persons with alternative land, housing, or resettlement. The laws assessed do not require the government to consult displaced persons during the resettlement process. The laws assessed do not require the government to minimize or avoid involuntary resettlement. In 2006 and 2010, resettlement policy frameworks were developed for the following World Bank-funded projects: "Indigenous Peoples Development Project" and "Decentralized Infrastructure reform and Development Project", but these frameworks are project-specific and thus not legally binding on all projects involving the expropriation of land. Government of Mexico, *Constitution of Mexico*, 1917 (amended 2007); Government of Mexico, *Expropriation Law*, 1936 (amended 2011); Government of Mexico, *Decree that Article 6 and the second paragraph of Article 20(a) of the Expropriation Act are amended*, 2011; Government of Mexico, *Agrarian Law*, 1992; Government of Mexico, *Regulations of the Agrarian Law on Matters of Organization of Rural Property*, 1996; Government of Mexico, *Regulations*

of the Institute for Administration of National Properties, 1992; United States Agency for International Development (USAID), *USAID Country Profile Property Rights and Resource Governance: Mexico*, 2011; World Bank, *Mexico- Decentralized Infrastructure reform and development project: resettlement action plan*, World Bank, DC, 2010; World Bank, *Indigenous Peoples Development Project*, World Bank, DC, 2006.

156 Malaysia has not enacted a national-level legally binding rehabilitation and resettlement procedures applicable to all development projects involving the expropriation of land. The Land Acquisition Act (1960) provides for compensation for land expropriation but does not establish any rehabilitation and resettlement procedures for accommodating populations displaced by expropriations. Section 2(e) of the Land Acquisition Act (1960) First Schedule provides that the amount of the compensation should take into account "if, in consequence of the acquisition, he is or will be compelled to change his residence or place of business, the reasonable expenses, if any, incidental to such change." The laws assessed do not provide displaced persons with alternative land, housing, or resettlement. The laws assessed do not provide displaced persons with productive alternative land. The laws assessed do not require the government to consult displaced persons during the resettlement process. The laws assessed do not require the government to minimize or avoid involuntary resettlement. Government of Malaysia, *Federal Constitution*, 1974; Government of Malaysia, *Land Acquisition Act No. 486*, 1960 (Amended 1992); Government of Malaysia, *Land Acquisition Rules*, 1998; Government of Malaysia, *National Land Code*, 1965 (Amended 2008); Government of Malaysia, *Land Development Act*, 1956.

157 Mongolia has not enacted comprehensive national law that establishes rehabilitation and resettlement procedures. The Constitution of Mongolia, Law on Land, and Law on Allocation of Land to Mongolian Citizens contain provisions indicating the compensation may be provided for expropriated land. However, the government is not legally obligated to resettle or rehabilitate displaced persons. Article 43.2 on the Law on Land (2002) provides that "the decision of removal of land in possession with or without replacement and with compensation shall take into account the prior agreement with the land possessor, the value of immovable constructions, other properties and the costs to vacate the land estimated at current prices." In other words, the cost of relocation might potentially be included in the agreement between parties but the government is not necessarily legally obligated to provide relocation allowance. The Law on Allocation of Land to Mongolian Citizens for Ownership, 2002 provides 'replacement' of land as an option for compensation. Section 35.5 states that the state shall make preliminary agreement with the land owner regarding location, size, status and quality of the land to be allocated in replacement of the land taken back for the special needs of the state. Section 36.4 provides that if Citizen's owned land becomes unusable due to establishment of the public servitude on the land, the Citizen shall have the right to demand from the entity that has established the public servitude to purchase the land and to compensate damages caused to the land. Section 37.2 states that "if it becomes impossible to return the expropriated land, the owner shall be compensated for the value of the land and the damages according to the market rate of that time or the damages shall be compensated by allocating other land not worse than the expropriated land by its status and quality." The laws assessed do not provide displaced persons with productive alternative land. The laws assessed do not require the government to consult displaced persons during the resettlement process. The laws assessed do not require the government to minimize or avoid involuntary resettlement. Government of Mongolia, *Constitution of Mongolia*, 1992; Government of Mongolia, *Law on Allocation of Land to Mongolian Citizens for Ownership*, 2002; Government of Mongolia, *Law on Land*, 2002.

158 Myanmar has not enacted a national level resettlement procedure that is legally binding on all development projects. The Land Acquisition Act (LAA), 1894 does not include procedures for resettling and rehabilitating persons displaced by acquisition of the land by the state. Section 80 of Myanmar's National Land Use Policy, adopted in 2016, establishes as a priority "Determine the best methods for the construction of housing estates, and related infrastructure, for resettlement of existing residents and land users in urban areas, including their livelihood development, with the involvement of financial support from the private sector." The laws assessed do not guarantee relocation allowance to all displaced persons. However, Section 15 of the Land Acquisition Act, 1894 provides that in determining the compensation to be awarded, the Collector shall take into consideration, "fifthly, if, in consequence of the acquisition of the land by the Collector, the person interested is compelled to change his residence

or place of business, the reasonable expenses (if any) incidental to such change." Section 31 (3) of Land Acquisition Act, 1894 provides that the Collector may with the sanction of the President make any arrangements with persons having limited interest for grant of other land instead of awarding money compensation. However, the law does not guarantee alternative land, housing or resettlement to the displaced persons. The laws assessed do not provide displaced persons with productive alternative land. The laws assessed do not require the government to consult displaced persons during the resettlement process. The laws assessed do not require the government to minimize or avoid involuntary resettlement. In 2016, Myanmar's Ministry of Agriculture, Livestock and Irrigation developed a resettlement policy framework for an Irrigated Agricultural Inclusive Development Project, but this framework is project specific and thus not legally binding on all development projects involving the expropriation of land. According to a report by Displacement Solutions (2015), there is an "absence of any policy on resettlement following land acquisition and [a] general lack of attention on this issue... Neither resettlement action plans nor livelihood restoration plans are recognized in law or policy in contemporary Myanmar." Government of Myanmar, *Constitution of Myanmar*; Government of Myanmar, *Land Acquisition Act*, 1894; Asian Development Bank, *Myanmar: Irrigated Agriculture Inclusive Development Project*, Asian Development Bank, Bahasa, 2016; Displacement Solutions, *Land Acquisition Law and Practice in Myanmar: Overview, Gap Analysis with IFC PS1 and PS5 and Scope of Due Diligence Recommendations*, Displacement Solutions, Geneva, 2015.

159 Nicaragua has not enacted a national-level resettlement policy that is binding on all development projects involving the expropriation of land. The laws assessed do not provide displaced persons with relocation allowance. The laws assessed do not provide displaced persons with alternative land, housing, or resettlement. The laws assessed do not provide displaced persons with productive alternative land. The laws assessed do not require the government to consult displaced persons during the resettlement process. The laws assessed do not require the government to minimize or avoid involuntary resettlement. According to USAID's Land Tenure profile of Nicaragua, "the extent of the [Government of Nicaragua's] use of its power of expropriation in recent years is not reported." In 2014, Nicaragua launched a project to build a canal that connects the Pacific and Atlantic Ocean. But according to one study, "roughly 300 communities, including indigenous communal land [holders], are affected by the canal route and up to 30 000 people face resettlement. There is concern about HKND's (the project developers discretion to handle expropriation of land, since Law 840, which the National Assembly passed in 2013 that grants a 50-year concession and implementation agreement to HKD, severely limits compensation for expropriation and the right to appeal" (EPRS 2015). In 2013, as part of the a World Bank funded projects called Sustainable Rural Water Supply and Sanitation Sector Project, a resettlement policy framework was adopted, but this framework is project-specific and thus not binding on all development projects involving the expropriation of land. *Government of Nicaragua, Ley Nº 278 - Ley sobre propiedad reformada urbana y agraria*; Government of Nicaragua, *Civil Code*; Government of Nicaragua, *Ley Nº 445 - Ley de régimen de propiedad comunal de los pueblos indígenas y comunidades étnicas*, 2003; European Parliament Research Service (EPRS), *Nicaragua: The Chinese interOocean canal project*, European Parliament, Brussels, 2015; World Bank, *Nicaragua Proyecto de Sostenibilidad del sector de agua y saneamiento rural: marco de Politica de Reasentamiento Involuntario*, 2013.

160 Namibia enacted a National Resettlement Policy in 2001 to address to "eradicate inequitable access to land resources through an efficient and participatory land reform process." However, this policy does not establish procedures for accommodating persons displaced who must involuntarily resettle as a consequence of expropriation. The National Resettlement Policy is meant to support the land reform effort by aiding people who wish to voluntarily resettle due to genocide, war, Apartheid, and historic injustices. The Policy applies to certain target groups, such as the San Community, Ex-soldiers, Returnees, refugees, landless and destitute people, and people from overcrowded communal areas. The answer is 'partial' because it is not clear this Policy would apply to populations involuntarily resettled as a result of expropriation except for in the context of land reform. The Agricultural (Commercial) Land Reform Act 6 of 1995 provides compensation to affected landholders when land is expropriated; however, this law and other laws assessed do not establish resettlement and rehabilitation procedures for accommodating displaced persons. The laws assessed do not provide displaced persons with relocation allowance. The laws assessed do not provide displaced persons with alternative land, housing, or resettlement. The laws assessed do not provide displaced persons with alternative land, housing,

or resettlement. The laws assessed do not require the government to consult displaced persons during the resettlement process. The laws assessed do not require the government to minimize or avoid involuntary resettlement. Government of Namibia, *National Resettlement Policy*, 2001; Government of Namibia, *Constitution of the Republic of Namibia*, 1990; Government of Namibia, *Communal Land Reform Act*, 2002 (Amended 2013); Government of Namibia, *Agricultural (Commercial) Land Reform Act 6 of 1995*; Government of Namibia, *Agricultural (Commercial) Land Reform Amendment Act*, 2014 (No. 1 of 2014).

161 Nepal has not enacted a national resettlement and rehabilitation procedure applicable to all development projects. The Land Acquisition Act (LAA) (1977) does not include any procedures for resettlement and rehabilitating populations displaced as a result of expropriation. Section 16.2 of the LAA, 1977 provides that while determining the amount of compensation for land to be acquired for institutions other than local bodies, and institutions fully owned by government of Nepal, the compensation fixation committee shall take the following criteria to consideration "The losses which the concerned person will suffer as a result of shifting his/her residence, or the place of his/her business, by reason of the acquisition of his/her land." Section 14 of the LAA, 1977 provides "Allotment of Other Lands in Exchange: In case any person whose land is wholly acquired under this Act wants to obtain compensation in the form of land elsewhere, Government of Nepal may, in exchange for such land, allot him/her any waste land, or land belonging to itself, or any other land which it is going to allot or sell in accordance with prevailing Nepal law, if available." Furthermore, Section 42 of the Guthi Corporation Act, 1976, alternative land may be provided as compensation option when Gothic land is acquired in a compulsory manner. The laws assessed do not provide displaced persons with alternative land, housing, or resettlement. The laws assessed do not require the government to consult displaced persons during the resettlement process. The laws assessed do not require the government to minimize or avoid involuntary resettlement. The Asian Development Bank helped draft a Resettlement Policy Framework in 2006, but there was no evidence found by I that this 2006 Policy Framework was ever enacted as binding law (ADB 2006). According to a study conducted by the Asian Development Bank, "the LAA 1977 is inadequate to effectively deal with the problem of involuntary resettlement. Besides the LAA 1977, there are other related Acts. However, they do not address issues of resettlement of people affected by development projects. In Nepal, most development projects are donor funded. A lack of adequate resettlement policies and the necessity for a comprehensive national policy for resettlement has caused donor run projects to formulate and implement their own project specific resettlement policies." In 2014, the Asian Development Bank helped draft the Land Acquisition, Resettlement and Rehabilitation Policy for Infrastructure Projects, 2014 (2071 BS), and apparently this project was approved by the Nepal government. According to one source, "the Ministry of Land Reform and Management has initiated the process of formulating a new Land Acquisition Act in line with the policy." In 2016, an Asian Development Bank resettlement plan was formulated for the NEP: SASEC Roads Improvement Project, but this resettlement plan is project specific and thus not legally binding on all development projects involving the expropriation of land. Government of Nepal, *Constitution of Nepal*, 1977; *Land Acquisition Act*, 2034; Government of Nepal, *Guthi Corporation Act*, 1976; Government of Nepal, *Forest Act*, 2049 (1993); Government of Nepal, *Nepal: Preparation of National Resettlement Policy Framework*, ADB, Bahasa, 2006; Government of Nepal, *New Policy Can Resolve Most of the Problems in Land Acquisition*, Government of Nepal, Kathmandu; ADB, *Land Acquisition, Resettlement and Rehabilitation Policy for Infrastructure Development Projects*, ADB, Bahasa, 2014 (2071 BS); Government of Nepal Office of the Investment Board, *Govt introduces land acquisition policy*, Government of Nepal: Kathmandu, 2015; Asian Development Bank, *NEP: SASEC Roads Improvement Project*, Asian Development Bank , Bahasa, 2016.

162 Nigeria has not enacted a national-level resettlement policy which is legally binding on all development projects involving the expropriation of land. Furthermore, the Land Use Act, 1978 does not provide adequate procedures for resettling displaced persons affected by expropriations. Section 2(2)of the Land Use Act establishes the "Land Use and Allocation Committee" which is charged with "advising the Governor on any matter connected with the resettlement of persons affected by the revocation of rights of occupancy on the ground of overriding public interest under this Act." The Land Use Act 1978 provides alternative land as a compensation option for holders of rights of occupancy. But there is no clear right to resettlement granted to displaced persons (Sec. 33, Land Use Act 1978). The laws assessed

do not provide displaced persons with relocation allowance. Section 33 of the Land Use Act, 1978 stipulates that "(1) where a right of occupancy in respect of any developed land on which a residential building has been erected is revoked under this Act, the Governor or the local government, as the case may be, may in his or its discretion offer in lieu of compensation payable in accordance with the provisions of this Act, resettlement in any other place or area by way of a reasonable alternative accommodation (if appropriate in the circumstances)." The laws assessed do not provide displaced persons with alternative land, housing, or resettlement. The laws assessed do not require the government to consult displaced persons during the resettlement process. The laws assessed do not require the government to minimize or avoid involuntary resettlement. According to Amnesty International (2014), "Following the forced eviction and pressure from the community and human rights organizations, the Lagos state government, in collaboration with the World Bank, agreed to develop and implement a Resettlement Action Plan (RAP) for the Badia East residents in line with the World Bank's Resettlement Policy Framework. However, the World Bank has failed to publicly disclose the draft RAP to the residents of Badia East making it impossible for them to have a say on its contents." In 2016, a resettlement policy framework was developed for the World Bank-funded project "Nigeria- Community and Social Development Project", but this framework is project specific and thus not legally binding on all projects involving the expropriation of land. Amnesty International, *Nigeria: World Bank 'dragging its feet' on resettlement package after forced eviction*, 2014; World Bank, *Community and Social Development Project Additional Finance (CSDP AF-2) Resettlement Policy Framework*, World Bank, DC; Government of Nigeria, *Constitution of Nigeria*, 1999; Government of Nigeria, *Land Use Act*, 1978.

163 Pakistan has not enacted a legally binding rehabilitation and resettlement procedure applicable to all development projects involving the expropriation of land. According to Price (2008), Pakistan drafted a National Resettlement Policy and Resettlement Ordinance in 2001 but this policy is neither adopted nor legally binding on all development projects involving the expropriation of land. According to USAID (2010), "The draft policy and ordinance legislation expanded the categories of people entitled to compensation to include unregistered tenants, occupants and users of land, employees, and businesses. The drafts also allowed for compensation in the form of land. The government has not adopted the draft policy and ordinance, but their terms guide some resettlement projects." The Land Acquisition Act 1894 does not establish procedures for resettling and rehabilitating displaced person (ADB, 2011). The laws assessed do not expressly grant relocation allowance to all displaced persons. However, Section 15 an 23 of the Land Acquisition Act, 1894 provides that in determining the compensation to be awarded to entitled landholders, the Collector shall take into consideration, "fifthly, if, in consequence of the acquisition of the land by the Collector, the person interested is compelled to change his residence or place of business, the reasonable expenses (if any) incidental to such change." The laws assessed do not guarantee alternative land, housing or resettlement to the displaced persons. But Section 31(3) of the Land Acquisition Act, 1894 provides "the Collector may… instead of awarding a money compensation in respect of any land, make any arrangement with a person having a limited interest in such land, either by the grant of other lands in exchange, the remission of land-revenue on other lands held under the same title, or in such other way as may be equitable having regard to the interests of the parties concerned." However, the Collector is not legally obligated to provide alternative land. The laws assessed do not provide displaced persons with productive alternative land. The laws assessed do not require the government to consult displaced persons during the resettlement process. The laws assessed do not require the government to minimize or avoid involuntary resettlement. 1973. A Land Acquisition and Resettlement Plan was developed for the Pakistan: Pehur High Level Canal Extension Project, but this resettlement plan is project-specific and thus not legally binding on all development projects involving the expropriation of land. Government of Pakistan, *Constitution of Pakistan*; Government of Pakistan, *Land Acquisition Act*, 1984; Asian Development Bank, 'Regional Technical Assistance (RETA)- 7433: Mainstreaming Land Acquisition and Resettlement Safeguards in Central and West Asia Region', *Country Assessment of Land Acquisition and Resettlement*, ADB, Bahasa, 2011; Government of Pakistan, *Draft National Resettlement Policy*, 2002; United States Agency for International Development, *Property Rights and Resource Governance Profile: Pakistan*, USAID, DC, 2010; Asian Development Bank (ADB), *Land Acquisition and Resettlement Plan: Pakistan: Pehur High Level Canal Extension Project*, ADB, Bahasa, 2011; S. Price, 'Compensation, Restoration and Development Opportunities: National Standards on Involuntary Resettlement', in M.M. Cernea & H.M. Mathur (Eds), *The*

Resettlement Dilemma: Can Compensation Prevent Impoverishment?, Oxford University Press, New Delhi, 2008, pp. 147–179.

164 Papua New Guinea has not enacted a legally binding rehabilitation and resettlement procedure for all development projects. The laws assessed do not provide displaced persons with relocation allowance. The laws assessed do not provide displaced persons with alternative land, housing, or resettlement. The laws assessed do not provide displaced persons with productive alternative land. The laws assessed do not require the government to consult displaced persons during the resettlement process. The laws assessed do not require the government to minimize or avoid involuntary resettlement. According to a report published by the Asian Development Bank, "[Papua New Guinea] does not have any specific resettlement policies at the National, Provincial or local level for relocating and resettling people which would apply to the APs being relocated. PNG however does have relating to acquisition of land and assets by the state for public purposes (eminent domain), and related legal procedures, compensation payable, and the legally defined procedures for receiving and facilitating the resolution of affected persons' concerns and grievances are all incorporated in the Land Act of 1996." In 2014, a resettlement policy framework was formulated for an Asian Development Bank- funded project called "Bridge Replacement for Improvement Rural Access Sector Project", but this framework is project-specific and thus not legally binding on all projects in PNG involving the expropriation of land. ; Government of Papua New Guinea, *Land Act*, 1996; Government of Papua New Guinea, *Land Regulations*, 1999; Asian Development Bank, *Papua New Guinea: Bridge Replacement for Improvement Rural Access Sector Project- Magi Highway*, Bahasa, 2014; Government of Papua New Guinea, *Constitution of Papua New Guinea*.

165 Peru has not enacted a legally binding rehabilitation and resettlement procedure for all development projects involving the expropriation of land. The laws assessed do not provide displaced persons with relocation allowance. The laws assessed do not provide displaced persons with alternative land, housing, or resettlement. The laws assessed do not provide displaced persons with productive alternative land. The laws assessed do not require the government to consult displaced persons during the resettlement process. The laws assessed do not require the government to minimize or avoid involuntary resettlement. Government of Peru, *Constitution of Peru*, 1993. Available at: https://goo.gl/NRXIvr; Government of Peru, *Decreto Legislativo Nº 1.192 - Ley Marco de Adquisición y Expropiación de inmuebles, transferencia de inmuebles de propiedad del Estado, liberación de Interferencias y dicta otras medidas para la ejecución de obras de infraestructura*, 2015; Government of Peru, *Ley Nº 27.117 - Ley General de Expropiaciones (Repealed)*, 1999; Government of Peru, *Ley Nº 30.025 - Ley que facilita la adquisición, expropiación y posesión de bienes inmuebles para obras de infraestructura*, 2013; Government of Peru, *Decree 1210 Decreto Legislativo Que Modifica La Decima Disposicion Complementaria Final Del Decreto Legislativo No. 1192, Que Aprueba La Ley Marco De Adquisicion y Expropriacion de Inmuebles, Transferencia De Inmuebles de Propriedad Del Estado, Liberacion de Interferencias y Dicta Otras Medidas Para La Ejecuion de Obras de Infraestructura*, 2016.

166 Philippines has not enacted national level legally binding rehabilitation and resettlement procedure applicable to all development projects involving the expropriation of land. According to Price (2008), Philippines drafted National Resettlement Policy but this policy has not yet adopted and is thus not legally binding on all development projects involving the expropriation of land. Section 17 and 18 of Executive Order 1035, 1985, however, provides for relocation/resettlement of tenants affected by land acquisitions. Section 18 of Executive Order 1035 of 1988 provides "The government implementing agencies/instrumentalities concerned shall extend financial assistance to the displaced tenants of agricultural lands, cultural minorities and settlers who are duly accredited by the Ministry of Agrarian Reform/Bureau of Forest Development/Office of Muslim Affairs and Cultural Communities. In the case of cultural minorities payment of such financial assistance shall be based on land occupancy certificates pursuant to the provision of P.D. 419." The answer is partial because it is not clear that relocation allowance must be provided to all displaced persons. Section 9 of RA8974, 2000 provides "Squatter Relocation. - The government through the National Housing Authority, in coordination with the local government units and implementing agencies concerned, shall establish and develop squatter relocation sites, including the provision of adequate utilities and services, in anticipation of squatters that have to be removed from the right-of-way or site of future infrastructure projects. Whenever applica-

ble, the concerned local government units shall provide and administer the relocation sites." Republic Act 7279 or the Urban Development and Housing Act mandates the provision of a resettlement site, the provision of basic services, and to the government's best ability, the provision of safeguards for the homeless and underprivileged citizens, including those who lack security of tenure. This applies to those informal settlers affected by development projects (Lazaro 2008). Section 7(c) of the RA 8974 (Indigenous People's Rights Act, 1997) establishes that Indigenous Peoples must be provided "in all possible cases with lands of quality and legal status at least equal to that of the land previously occupied by them, suitable to provide for their present needs and future development..." (Section 7(c), RA 8371 (1997)). For agrarian reform takings, the compensation can be paid in a combination of cash, government securities, tax credit, etc. (RA 6657, Section 18). According to Section 7 of Indigenous People's Rights Act, when the return of expropriated ancestral land is not possible, ICCs/IPs shall be provided in all possible cases with lands of quality and legal status at least equal to that of the land previously occupied by them, suitable to provide for their present needs and future development. Section 7(c) of the Indigenous People's Rights Act, 1997 provides "Where relocation is considered necessary as an exceptional measure, such relocation shall take place only with the free and prior informed consent of the ICCs/IPs concerned and whenever possible..." The answer is 'partial' because this law only applies when indigenous land is expropriated. The government is not obligated to consult non-indigenous affected populations during the resettlement process. The government can only require indigenous communities to relocate from their lands where relocation "is considered necessary as an exceptional measure" (Sec. 7(c), Indigenous Peoples Rights Act, 1997). (Section 7 (c) Indigenous People's Right Act). The answer is 'partial' because the government is only obliged to minimize or avoid forced evictions in cases involving indigenous land. In 2014, a resettlement plan was developed for the Philippines: Water District Development Sector Project, but since this plan is project-specific it is not legally binding on all projects involving the expropriation of land. According to Price (2008), "significant progress was made in...the Philippines. Output included a draft National resettlement policy, a draft Executive Order on Resettlement, resettlement guidelines, and a capacity building proposal." Government of the Philippines. 1985. Executive Order No. 1035 Providing the procedures and guidelines for expeditious acquisition by the government or private real properties or rights thereon for infrastructure and other government development projects; Government of the Philippines, *Constitution of the Philippines*, 1987; Government of the Philippines, *The Indigenous Peoples' Rights Act of 1997*, 1997; Government of the Philippines, *Supreme Court Decision G.R. No. 150640*, 2007. Available at: https://goo.gl/PC2fwj; Government of the Philippines, *Republic Act, No. 8974, An Act to Facilitate the Acquisition of Right-of-Way, Site or Location for National Government Infrastructure Projects and For Other Purpose*; Government of the Philippines, *Comprehensive Agrarian Reform Law of 1988*, 1988 (Amended 2009); Government of the Philippines, *Republic Act No. 9700 amending Republic Act No. 6657 on the Comprehensive Agrarian Reform Law*, 1988 (2009); Supreme Court of the Philippines, *NIA v. Rural Bank, G. R. No. 185124*, 2012. Available at: https://goo.gl/W9jeC3; Government of the Philippines, *Republic Act 7279 (Urban Development and Housing Act)*, 1992; Government of the Philippines, *Civil Procedure Rule 67*; World Bank, *Resettlement plan- Philippines: Water District Development Section Project*, World Bank, DC, 2014; L. Lebrilla, 'The State of Compulsory Acquisition of Land and Compensation in the Philippines', *CPBDR Policy Brief No. 2014- 03*, 2014; Lazaro *et al*, *Indigenous Peoples Rights Act: Legal and Institutional Frameworks, Implementation and Challenges in the Philippines. Discussion papers, East Asia and Pacific Region. Social Development, and Rural Development, Natural Resources and Environment Sectors*, World Bank, DC, 2008.

167 Rwanda has not enacted a national-level resettlement policy which is legally binding on all development projects. The 2007 Expropriation Law establishes provisions for compensating landholders affected by expropriations, but does not establish procedures for resettling and rehabilitating displaced persons. In 2011, the Rwanda Environmental Management Authority did publish a draft "Resettlement Policy Framework and Process Framework for Lake Victoria Environmental Management Project Phase II." However, this policy framework is not binding on all development projects involving the expropriation of land. The extent to which this resettlement policy has been implemented is unclear. The laws assessed do not provide displaced persons with relocation allowance. The law provides that "through agreement between the person to expropriate and the one to be expropriated, the just compensation may be monetary or an alternative land and a building equivalent to the determination of just monetary compensa-

tion." (Art. 23, Law No. 18/2007 Relating to Expropriation in the Public Interest). The laws assessed do not provide displaced persons with alternative land, housing, or resettlement. The laws assessed do not require the government to consult displaced persons during the resettlement process. The laws assessed do not require the government to minimize or avoid involuntary resettlement. According to the World Bank LGAF study of Rwanda, "Resettlement policy does not exist; if resettlement takes place then it is in an ad-hoc manner" (World Bank 2016, p. 75). According to Rose *et al.* (2016) "Although the option of facilitated resettlement through compensation in the form of replacement land is provided for in the law, it is rarely used by expropriating entities and almost never preferred by expropriated households." World Bank, *Land Governance Assessment Framework- Final Report- Rwanda*, World Bank, DC, 2016; Government of Rwanda, *Constitution of Rwanda*, 2003; Government of Rwanda, *Law No. 18/2007 Relating to Expropriation in the Public Interest*, 2007 (Amended 2015); Government of Rwanda, *Organic Law No. 08/2005 Determining the Use and Management of Land in Rwanda*, 2005; I. Mireille, F. Masengo & A. Knox, 'Implementation of Expropriation Law in Rwanda: Challenges and Ways Forward', *Policy Research Brief No.2*, LAND Project, Kigali, 2014; USAID LAND Project, *Research Brief No.2*, USAID LAND Project, Kigali; Rose *et al*, 'Implementation of Rwanda's Expropriation Law and Its Outcomes on the Population', *Paper prepared for the Annual World Bank Conference on Land and Poverty*, DC, March 2016, pp. 14-18.

168 South Africa has not enacted a national-level rehabilitation and resettlement policy for land that has been expropriated. The Expropriation Act 1975 establishes procedures for compensating landholders affected by expropriation, but this Act does not establish procedures resettling and rehabilitating displaced persons. The laws assessed do not provide displaced persons with alternative land. The laws assessed do not provide displaced persons with alternative productive land. The laws assessed do not require the government to consult displaced persons during the resettlement process. The laws assessed do not require the government to minimize or avoid involuntary resettlement. Government of South Africa. 1996. Constitution of South Africa; Government of South Africa. Expropriation Act 1975; Government of South Africa. Communal Land Rights Act (No. 11 of 2004). Available at: https://goo.gl/xcpD2X; Promotion of Administrative Justice Act 3 of 2000; Government of South Africa. Constitutional Court Decision. Agri South Africa v. Minister of Minerals and Energy (CCT 51/12) [2013]; Government of South Africa. 2014. Property Valuation Act, 2014 (No. 17 of 2014); South Africa Free State High Court. 2010. Bartsch Consult (Pty) Limited v Mayoral Committee of the Maluti-A-Phofung Municipality [2010] ZAFSHC 11.

169 The Land Act 2009 provides in Article 72 that "The Government of Southern Sudan, State Government or private company shall proceed with a resettlement plan for the communities affected by an expropriation plan described in Chapter XII of this Act or by any investment activity." While relocation allowance is not explicitly provided by law, In addition to the provisions of Section 75 of the Land Act 2009, Section 72(3) provides that "the Government of Southern Sudan, State Government and private companies shall assist internally displaced persons and returnees in their efforts to improve their livelihood." Section 75(2) of the 2009 Land Act provides that "the compensation shall be in cash or in kind or both according to the agreement." The laws assessed do not provide displaced persons with alternative productive land. Article 72(3) The Land Act, 2009 provides that internally displaced persons shall be consulted and shall have opportunities to participate in planning and implementing resettlement programs. The laws assessed do not require the government to minimize or avoid involuntary resettlement. Government of South Sudan, *Transitional Constitution*, 2011; Government of South Sudan, *Land Act*, 2009.

170 Sierra Leone has not enacted a national-level rehabilitation and resettlement policy for land that has been expropriated. Section 18.1(e) of the Public Land Ordinance, CAP 116 provides "In determining the amount of compensation to be awarded for land acquired under this Ordinance, the Court shall take into consideration…if, in consequence of the acquisition, he is compelled to change his residence or place of business, the reasonable expenses, if any, incidental to such change." The laws assessed do not guarantee displaced persons the right to alternative land, housing, or resettlement. The laws assessed do not grant displaced persons productive alternative land. The laws assessed do not require the government to consult displaced persons during the resettlement process. The laws assessed do not require the government to minimize or avoid involuntary resettlement. In 2012, a resettlement plan

was formulated as part of a World Bank-funded Sierra Leone Energy Access project; however, since this resettlement plan is project specific, it is not legally binding on all development projects involving the expropriation of land. Government of Sierra Leone, *Constitution of Sierra Leone*, 1991; Government of Sierra Leone, *Draft National Land Policy of Sierra Leone*, 2014; Government of Sierra Leone, *Public Lands Ordinance Cap. 116*, 1960; World Bank, *Resettlement Action Plan- For the Sierra Leone Energy Access Project*, World Bank, DC, 2014.

171 In 2001, Sri Lanka's Cabinet approved the National Involuntary Resettlement Policy. However, Policy did not officially pass into law and is thus not legally binding on all development projects in Sri Lanka. According to Nathaniel (2015), "although the NIRP has been officially recognized by Cabinet, and has been successfully applied in the past, the policy has not been adopted consistently in all cases of development-induced land acquisitions. Since its official recognition, the Government has embarked on various development projects in which it has failed to comply with the NIRP...Since the policy has not been passed into law, implementing agencies are not obliged to actually apply the policy. Full compliance with NIRP requires the government to amend existing laws in order to bring them in line with NIRP principles." The Land Acquisition Act, 1950 and Land Acquisition Regulations provide compensation to landholders affected by expropriation; however, these laws do not establish procedures for rehabilitating and resettling persons displaced by expropriations. According to the Land Acquisition Regulations, 2008, "To fulfill the requirement of the definition of compensation, in addition to the compensation under Section 1 and 2 above, which are based on the 'market value', compensation for Disturbance based on the 'value to owner' basis should be paid under following Sub-headings, after taking into consideration the written claims...expenses for finding alternative accommodation... Cost incurred in change of residence... cost of advertising... refixing cost of fixtures and fittings... expenses incurred for transport..." Section 36 of the Land Acquisition Act (Ch. 295), 1950 provides that "(1) any person to whom compensation for the acquisition of any land is payable under this Act may enter into a written agreement with the acquiring officer of the district in which that land is situated to accept, in lieu of the whole or any part of such compensation, a transfer of any other land which is the property of the Crown. Such agreement shall be signed by that person and by that acquiring officer. The amount of compensation in lieu of which the transfer is accepted shall be specified in such agreement." The laws assessed do not provide displaced persons with alternative land, housing, or resettlement. The laws assessed do not require the government to consult displaced persons during the resettlement process. The laws assessed do not require the government to minimize or avoid involuntary resettlement. Government of Sri Lanka, *Constitution of Sri Lanka*; Government of Sri Lanka, *Land Acquisition Act CAP. 295*, 1950 (Amended 1994); Government of Sri Lanka, *Land Acquisition (Amendment) Act*, 1986 (No. 13 of 1986); Government of Sri Lanka, *Land Acquisition Regulations*, 2009. Available at: https://goo.gl/dg58cf; Government of Sri Lanka, *Water's Edge Judgement S.C. (F/R) No. 352/2007*, 2007; Government of Sri Lanka, *National Involuntary Resettlement Policy*, 2001; V. Nathaniel, 'The National Involuntary Resettlement Policy: A case for implementation', *Daily FT*, 2015.

172 A Rural Resettlement Task Force under the Ministry of Agriculture and Co-operatives drafted the National Rural Resettlement Policy in 2003. The purpose of this policy is to guide the planning, implementation and monitoring of rural resettlement. According to a Commission of the European Communities 2006 draft report, the Rural Resettlement Policy was officially adopted, but I could not access this law online, which is why the score is "unclear." The Acquisition of Property Act, 1961 (No. 10 of 1961) does not establish procedure for resettling and rehabilitating persons displaced by expropriations. Government of Swaziland, *Constitution of Swaziland*; Government of Swaziland, *Acquisition of Property Act*, 1961; European Commission (EC), *Swaziland Country Environment Profile (Draft Report)*, EC, Brussels, 2006; K. Keatimilwe & J. Mlangeni, 'Swaziland Country Report', *SAIEA*; New Partnership for Africa's Development (NEPAD) and FAO, Government of the Kingdom of Swaziland, Support to NEPAD-CAADP Implementation, TCP/SWA/2910 (I).

173 Taiwan has not enacted a national-level rehabilitation and resettlement policy that is binding on all projects involving the expropriation of land. Article 31 of the Indigenous Basic Law, 2005 provides "The Government shall not displace or relocate any Indigenous Person from his or her land, except in cases of imminent and obvious danger. In cases of displacement or relocation of Indigenous Persons, the same shall be properly accommodated and compensated for the losses suffered as a result of forced

displacement or relocation as is referred to in the preceding paragraph." According to article 34 of the Land Expropriation Act, 2000, relocation fees may be provided under certain circumstances for certain land holders that meet a specific criteria. Since there are certain restrictions imposed on the right to receive relocation allowance, the answer is 'partial', Indigenous populations have right to seek alternative land in the event of relocation, but non- Indigenous landholders are not always granted this right in every expropriation case. Article 32 of Indigenous People's Basic Law, 2005 provides "The Government shall not displace or relocate any Indigenous Person from his or her land, except in cases of imminent and obvious danger. In cases of displacement or relocation of Indigenous Persons, the same shall be properly accommodated and compensated for the losses suffered as a result of forced displacement or relocation as is referred to in the preceding paragraph." Furthermore, Article 34 of the Land Expropriation Act, 2000 provides "If there are low-income households or medium-low income households with facts of inhabitation one year before the public announcement of expropriation, such household members become homeless or are in similar situation due to the expropriation of the constructional improvements they live in, and their situations are found true by the social workers of the municipal or county (city) government, the land use applicant shall draft a resettlement plan and include it in the expropriation plan. The resettlement plan referred to in the preceding paragraph includè housing placement." The laws assessed do not grant displaced persons productive alternative land. Article 208 of the Land Act, 1930 states that "the area of land to be compulsorily purchased shall be limited to what is strictly required for [public] undertakings." Furthermore, article 3 of the Land Expropriation Act, 2000 provides "whenever possible, avoid choosing farmland and give priority consideration to public land or land owned by state-owned enterprises without existing land use plan…Arable and pastoral lands in a special agricultural zone are not subject to expropriation unless it is an interspersed odd piece of land that is difficult to circumvent." Article 7 of the Land Expropriation Act, 2000 limits the power to expropriation land with a historical relics or remains. The answer for the "minimize or avoid involuntary resettlement" indicator is 'partial' because, while there are certain limitations on the types of land that can be expropriated, it is unclear whether 208 of the Land Act necessarily requires the government to minimize resettlement in every case. Government of Taiwan, *Constitution of Taiwan*, (Amended 2000); Government of Taiwan, *The Land Act*, 1930 (Amended 2006); Government of Taiwan, *Indigenous People's Basic Law*, 2005; Government of Tawain, *Land Expropriation Act*, 2000 (amended 2012); Y. Chang, 'Eminent Domain Law in Taiwan: New Law, Old Practice', *Kreisman Working Paper Series in Housing Law and Policy*, Paper 38, 2016.

174 Tanzania has not enacted a national-level resettlement policy that is legally binding when land is expropriated. According to the LGAF report for Tanzania "Since there is no comprehensive resettlement policy but fragmentary resettlement policies for different development schemes... the policies lack legal underpinnings thus save only hortatory aims. A comprehensive national resettlement policy should be developed, approved and operationalized." Compensation must include a 'transport allowance' (sec. 3, Land Act 1999 no. 4). "Transport Allowance shall be the actual costs of transporting twelve tons at luggage by rail or road (whichever is cheaper) within twenty kilometers from the point of displacement." sec. 11, The Land (Assessment of the Value of Land for Compensation) Regulations, 2001. Section 13 of the Village Land Regulations states that "compensation for loss of any interest in land shall include… transportation allowance." Section 11(2) of the Land Acquisition At, 1967 provides "The President may, with the consent of the person entitled to compensation...make to the person entitled to compensation a grant of public land not exceeding in value the value of the land acquired, for an estate not exceeding the estate acquired and upon the same terms and conditions as the land acquired was held...in lieu of or in addition to any compensation payable." The laws assessed do not grant displaced persons productive alternative land. The laws assessed do not require the government to consult displaced persons during the resettlement process. The laws assessed do not require the government to minimize or avoid involuntary resettlement. World Bank, Land Governance Assessment Framework- Final Report (Tanzania), World Bank, DC; Government of Tanzania, *Constitution of Tanzania*, 1977; Government of Tanzania, *Land Acquisition Act (Act No. 47 of 1967)*, 1967; Government of Tanzania, *The Land Act*, 1999; Government of Tanzania, *Village Land Act*, 1999; Government of Tanzania, *The Land (Assessment of the Value of Land for Compensation) Regulations*, 2001; Government of Tanzania, *Village Land Regulations*, 2002.

175 Thailand has not enacted a national-level legally binding rehabilitation and resettlement procedure. The Constitution guarantees fair compensation paid in 'due course' (Section 42). The Immovable Property Expropriation Act (1987) does not contain any rehabilitation and resettlement procedures.
The laws assessed do not provide displaced persons with relocation allowance. The laws assessed do not provide displaced persons with alternative land, housing, or resettlement. The laws assessed do not grant displaced persons productive alternative land. The laws assessed do not require the government to consult displaced persons during the resettlement process. The laws assessed do not require the government to minimize or avoid involuntary resettlement. Government of Thailand, *Constitution of Thailand*, 2007; Government of Thailand, *Immovable Property Expropriation Act, B.E. 2530*, 1987; Government of Thailand, *Act promulgating the Land Code B.E. 2497*, 2008.

176 Trinidad and Tobago has not enacted a national-level resettlement policy that is binding in all situations where land is expropriated for public purposes. The laws assessed do not provide displaced persons with relocation allowance. The laws assessed do not provide displaced persons with alternative land, housing, or resettlement. The laws assessed do not grant displaced persons productive alternative land. The laws assessed do not require the government to consult displaced persons during the resettlement process. The laws assessed do not require the government to minimize or avoid involuntary resettlement. Government of Trinidad and Tobago, *Constitution of Trinidad and Tobago*, 1976 (amended 2000); Government of Trinidad and Tobago, *Valuation of Land Act (Cap. 58:03)*, 1969 (amended 2009); Government of Trinidad and Tobago, *Land Acquisition Act (Cap. 58:01)*, 1994; Trinidad and Tobago, *Land Surveyors Act (33 of 1996)*; Government of Trinidad, *Administration of Estates (Act 35 of 1913)*, 1913.

177 Section 75 of the Uganda Land Policy 2014 provides "to protect the land rights of internally-displaced persons, Government will take special measures to: (i) Consider restitution of land, housing and property or adequate compensation or resettlement; and (ii) put in place mechanisms and structures for claiming restitution, compensation or resettlement." However, a national-level resettlement policy that is legally binding and applicable when land is expropriated has not been adopted. The laws assessed do not grant a relocation allowance to displaced persons. The laws assessed do not provide displaced persons with alternative land, housing, or resettlement. The laws assessed do not grant displaced persons productive alternative land. The laws assessed do not require the government to consult displaced persons during the resettlement process. The laws assessed do not require the government to minimize or avoid involuntary resettlement. In 2014, a resettlement and compensation plan was created for the IFC-funded "Proposed Sindila Mini Hydropower Project in Sindila Sub-County, Bundibugyo District, Uganda", but this plan is project-specific and thus not legally binding on all development projects in Uganda involving the expropriation of land. Government of Uganda, *Constitution of Uganda*, 1995; Government of Uganda, *Land Acquisition Act 1965 (ch. 226)*, 1965; Government of Uganda, *Land Act (No. 16 of 1998)*, 1998 (amended 2010); Government of Uganda, *Supreme Court Decision Pyrali Abdul Rasul Esmail v. Adrian Sibo (Constitutional Petition No. 9 of 1997)*; Anyuru *et al*, 'Balancing Development and Community Livelihoods: A Framework for Land Acquisition and Resettlement in Uganda', *ACODE Policy Research Series*, No. 75, 2016; Atacama Consulting, *Resettlement and Compensation Action Plan for the Proposed Sindila Mini Hydropower Project in Sindila Sub-County*, Bundibugyo District, 2014.

178 While there is no national-level resettlement policy enacted in Vietnam that is legally binding on all projects involving the expropriation of land, the Land Law 2013 contains several resettlement and rehabilitation requirements. Article 85 of the Land Law 2013 requires that a resettlement project must be conducted before any land recovery by the government can take place. Article 85 states "Provincial- and district-level People's Committees shall develop and implement the resettlement projects before conducting the land recovery. 3. Land recovery can only be conducted after the construction of houses and infrastructure in the resettlement area is completed." Article 91 of Land Act 2013 provides compensation for transportation costs upon land recovery by the State. Article 91 states "Upon land recovery by the State, people whose assets need to be moved shall be compensated for the cost of dismantlement, transportation and installation. In case of moving machinery or production lines, the damage caused during the process of dismantlement, transportation and installation must also be compensated." However, compensation is limited to assets, and thus the answer is 'partial', Article 74

of Land Act states in Paragraph 2 that the compensation must be made in the form of allocating a new land with the same land use purpose as the recovered land. Only if such land is not available, compensation must be made in money. Article 86(2) of the Land Law, 2013 provides "People whose land is recovered shall be resettled in the same place if the resettlement projects are developed or conditions for resettlement arrangement exist in the recovered area. Convenient locations are prioritized for those who hand over the recovered land early or people with meritorious services to the revolution." The answer is 'yes' because article 86 appears to apply to all 'people' whose land is recovered. Alternative land is not limited to titleholders or others with legally recognized rights to land. The laws assessed do not grant the displaced person any productive alternative land. Article 69 (2)(a) of the Land Law, 2013 provides "The organization in charge of compensation and ground clearance shall make the plan for compensation, support and resettlement and coordinate with the commune-level People's Committee in the locality to conduct consultations on the plans for compensation, support and resettlement in the forms of meetings with land users living in the recovered area..." The procedures for compensating and resettling displaced persons are laid out in Decree- Regulations on Compensation, Support and Resettlement Upon Land Expropriation by the State (2014). The laws assessed do not require the government to minimize or avoid involuntary resettlement. Government of Vietnam, *Constitution of Vietnam*, 2013. Available at: https://goo.gl/m3odvI; Government of Vietnam, *Land Law No. 45/2013/QH13*, 2013; Government of Vietnam, *Decree- Regulations on Compensation, Support and Resettlement Upon Land Expropriation by the State*, 2014; World Bank, *Compulsory land acquisition and voluntary land conversion in Vietnam: the conceptual approach, land valuation and grievance redress mechanism*, World Bank, DC, 2011.

179 Zambia has not enacted a national-level resettlement procedure that is binding whenever land is expropriated for public purposes. According to an article published by Chu *et al.* (2015), "Currently, Zambia does not have a finalized National Resettlement Policy in place to guide processes of resettlement and compensation. In an effort to address this gap, the government drafted a National Resettlement Policy (NRP) in 2013, a process spearheaded by the OVP. It has also published 'Guidelines for the Compensation and Resettlement of Internally Displaced Persons' in an attempt to domesticate the African Union's Convention of 2012 for the Protection and Assistance of Internally Displaced Persons (IDP) in Africa (the Kampala Convention)." According Zambia Daily Mail article published in January 2016, "the Government has come up with a national resettlement policy to help provide a mechanism for dealing with both voluntary and involuntary resettlement." However, there is no evidence from my review that this resettlement policy is currently legally binding in Zambia. The Land Acquisition Act, 1970 provides compensation to affected landholders when their land is expropriated. The laws assessed do not provide displaced persons with relocation allowance. Section 10 of the Land Acquisition Act, 1970 requires that "where any property is acquired by the President under this Act the Minister shall on behalf of the Government pay in respect thereof, out of moneys provided for the purpose by Parliament, such compensation in money as may be agreed or, in default of agreement, determined in accordance with the provisions of this Act: Provided that where the property acquired is land the President may, with the consent of the person entitled to compensation, make to such person, in lieu of or in addition to any compensation payable under this Section, a grant of other land not exceeding in value the value of the land acquired, for an estate not exceeding the estate acquired and upon the same terms and conditions, as far as may be practicable, as those under which the land acquired was held." The laws assessed do not grant displaced persons productive alternative land. The laws assessed do not require the government to consult displaced persons during the resettlement process. The laws assessed do not require the government to minimize or avoid involuntary resettlement. According to the World Bank LGAF study of Zambia, "Resettlement policy exists (Zambia Daily Mail, 2016), but is only in part of the cases applied. The Department of Resettlements under the Vice President's Office is mandated to carry out resettlement activities. However, inadequate capacity in public institutions, functional centralisation and inadequate coordination makes the land transfer processes slow and costly." Government of Zambia, *Constitution of Zambia*, 2016; Government of Zambia, *Land Act No. 29 of 1995*, 1995; *Land Acquisition Act*, 1970; *Land Acquisition (Prescribed Forms) Regulations (Cap. 189)*; J. Chu, K. Young & D. Phiri, *Large-scale Land Acquisitions, Displacement and Resettlement in Zambia*, Institute for Poverty, Land and Agrarian Studies (PLAAS), 2015; Zambia Daily Mail, *Resettlement policy vital for development*, 2016; World Bank, *Land Governance Assessment Framework: Zambia Country Report*, World Bank, DC, 2016.

180 Zimbabwe has not enacted a national-level resettlement policy that is binding in all situations where land is expropriated for public purposes. The laws assessed do not provide displaced persons with relocation allowance. The answer is partial because, under Section 12 of the Communal Land Act, 1983 provides alternative land as a compensation option. However, it is not clear that alternative land may be provided as a compensation option when land other than communal land is expropriated. The laws assessed do not grant displaced persons productive alternative land. The laws assessed do not require the government to consult displaced persons during the resettlement process. The laws assessed do not require the government to minimize or avoid involuntary resettlement. Government of Zimbabwe, *Constitution of Zimbabwe*, 2013; Government of Zimbabwe, *Land Acquisition Act (CAP 20:10)*, 1992. Available at: https://goo.gl/CaOYCT; Government of Zimbabwe, *Land Acquisition (Disposal of Rural Land) Regulations (S.I. No. 287 of 1999)*, 1999; Government of Zimbabwe, *Communal Land Act, No. 2 of 1982*, 2002.

Previously Published in the Vastgoed, Omgeving & Recht Series

Volume 1 W.D. Kolkman, R.J.L. Timmer, L.C.A. Verstappen en F.J. Vonck, *Verbetering betrouwbaarheid basisregistratie Kadaster*, 2012

Volume 2 N. Vegter, De vereniging van eigenaars, 2012

Volume 3 I. Visser, *De executoriale verkoop van onroerende zaken door de hypotheekhouder*, 2013

Volume 4 F.J. Vonck, *De flexibiliteit van het recht van erfpacht*, 2013

Volume 5 L.C.A. Verstappen & F.J. Vonck (red.), *Naar een verbeterde vastgoedketen*, 2015

Volume 6 B. Hoops, E.J. Marais, H. Mostert, J.A.M.A. Sluysman & L.C.A. Verstappen (red.), *Rethinking Expropriation Law I. Public Interest in Expropriation*, 2015

Volume 7 B. Hoops, E.J. Marais, H. Mostert, J.A.M.A. Sluysman & L.C.A. Verstappen (red.), *Rethinking Expropriation Law II. Context, Criteria, and Consequences of Expropriation*, 2015

Volume 8 B. Hoops, L. Rostill & R. Koolhoven (red.), *Property Law Perspectives V*, 2017

Volume 9 B. Hoops, E.J. Marais, L. van Schalwyk & N.K. Tagliarino (red.), *Rethinking Expropriation Law III. Fair Compensation*, 2018

Volume 10 B. Hoops, *Landjepik in Nederland / Illegal Land Use in the Netherlands. Een verkennend empirisch onderzoek naar het gebruik zonder recht van gemeentegrond / An explorative empirical study on the use of municipal land without any right*, 2018

Volume 11 N. K. Tagliarino, *National Level Adoption of International Standards on Expropriation, Compensation and Resettlement*, 2019

9 789462 36940

Printed by Libri Plureos GmbH in Hamburg,
Germany